REPORTS OF THE TRIALS OF COLONEL AARON BURR

VOLUME I

REPORTS OF THE TRIALS OF COLONEL AARON BURR

*In the Circuit Court of the United States,
Summer Term, 1807*

VOLUME I

DA CAPO PRESS • NEW YORK • 1969

A Da Capo Press Reprint Edition

This Da Capo Press edition of
Reports of the Trials of Colonel Aaron Burr
is an unabridged republication of the
first edition published in Philadelphia
in 1808.

Library of Congress Catalog Card Number 69-11321

Published by Da Capo Press
A Division of Plenum Publishing Corporation
227 West 17th Street
New York, N.Y. 10011

REPORTS

OF THE TRIALS OF

COLONEL AARON BURR,

LATE VICE PRESIDENT OF THE UNITED STATES,)

FOR

TREASON,

AND FOR

A MISDEMEANOR,

In preparing the means of a Military Expedition against Mexico, a territory of the King of Spain, with whom the United States were at peace,

IN THE

CIRCUIT COURT OF THE UNITED STATES,

Held at the city of Richmond, in the district of Virginia, in the Summer Term of the year 1807.

TO WHICH IS ADDED,

AN APPENDIX,

CONTAINING

THE ARGUMENTS AND EVIDENCE

IN SUPPORT AND DEFENCE OF THE MOTION AFTERWARDS MADE BY THE COUNSEL FOR THE UNITED STATES,

TO COMMIT

A. Burr, H. Blannerhassett and I. Smith,

TO BE SENT FOR TRIAL TO THE STATE OF KENTUCKY,

FOR

TREASON OR MISDEMEANOR,

ALLEGED TO BE COMMITTED THERE.

TAKEN IN SHORT HAND

BY DAVID ROBERTSON,

COUNSELLOR AT LAW.

IN TWO VOLUMES....VOL. I.

PHILADELPHIA:

PUBLISHED BY HOPKINS AND EARLE.

FRY AND KAMMERER, PRINTERS.

1808.

PREFACE.

THIS publication contains a full and correct statement of all the testimony and documents adduced on the two trials of Col. BURR, for treason and misdemeanor, and on the motion made by the counsel for the United States, to commit the accused, for the purpose of sending them to Kentucky, to be tried for similar offences committed there; also the arguments of the counsel and the opinions of the judges on all the points discussed. The proceedings previous to the trials, before and while the grand jury were in deliberation, are also detailed, but the first part of them not so *fully* as the rest of the report; because it was the middle of June, before the reporter was prevailed on to undertake the publication. He has however consulted the best sources of information, in order to enable him to present to the public a correct statement of those preliminary proceedings which occurred from the commencement of the term till he began the report. He was present in court, during a considerable part of that interval, and has therefore been aided by his recollection.

The report of the trials might be perfect, and would be long, even if all those proceedings were omitted. But they are inserted, because it was deemed more satisfactory to the public to give a connected historical detail of all the proceedins against colonel Burr from his first arrest, till the decision of the final motion against himself, I. Smith and H. Blannerhassett, than to limit the publication to a statement, however full, of the trials only. For such a detail would most probably enable the reader to judge most correctly of the views of the accused, and of the nature and tendency of the great scheme or plot which has thrown the country into such a state of agitation and alarm, and of the measures adopted to counteract and defeat it. For the same purpose, and to elucidate the subject, there are prefixed a concise account of his first examination before the Chief Justice, the opinion pronounced thereon, and the opinion of the supreme court of the United States, in the case of Bollman and Swartwout.

The arguments of the counsel on all points of importance are detailed *verbatim* as uttered: and those of a subordinate nature are considerably condensed, as the report would otherwise have been too voluminous and expensive. As much of the authorities referred to are inserted, as will enable *any* reader to comprehend their application. The opinions of the court, on most of the points, are published as written and delivered by the Chief Justice, and in the few other cases as uttered.

In whatever view these trials are to be regarded, they must be deemed very interesting. But when we consider the celebrity of the party accused, the stations and characters of some of those implicated with him, the magnitude and extent of their supposed designs, the danger to the union of the states apprehended therefrom, the learned and profound doctrines which were so ably and elaborately discussed by such eminent counsel, and the great talents of the court, this report .cannot but be highly important and valuable. Perhaps no trial for treason has taken place in any country, in which more ability, learning, ingenuity and eloquence have been displayed. All the important decisions on treason, in England and this country, were acutely and thoroughly examined, and considered; and their application to the questions before the court discussed with great ingenuity and skill: nor was less industry or judgment shown in arguing the application and effect of the constitution of the United States, and of the common law, if it existed at all as a law of the union. On the motion to commit, the effect of the plea of " *autrefois acquit*" or the doctrine of a former acquittal, was also ably investigated.

It is believed that this report will be amusing and interesting to all persons capable of reading and understanding; and that to the lawyer, politician and man of general information, it will be particularly gratifying and useful, as it will comprehend a valuable treatise on criminal law, and especially high treason. The reporter has used his best exertions to make the accuracy of the publication correspond with the importance of the work. How far he has succeeded, he now submits to the judgment and candour of the court, the counsel engaged in the cause, and the public.

CONTENTS

OF THE

FIRST VOLUME.

CONTENTS.

CONTENTS.

Alterations, Additions and Corrections.

Page 5, Line 39, for ' who' read ' which'
7,   16, for ' that' read ' the'
25,   1, dele ' so'
25,   17, for ' moved' read ' proved'
33,   20, dele ' of fieri facias'
33,   25, for ' that' read ' they'
34,   37, for ' deny him' read ' be denied'
38,   42, for ' in' read ' on'
40,   43, for ' it' read ' they'
54,   47, for ' argument' read ' agreement'
55,   6, for ' of' read ' and'
70,   1, after the comma the sentence ought to read thus: ' I trust that unless some hard-mouthed precedents, from old black letter books, be found to justify this procedure, it will be disregarded'
Page 72, Line 33, for ' prejudicate' read ' prejudice'
75,   46, for ' with' read ' to'
100,   4, after ' things' add ' to'
121,   31, for ' 27th' read ' 22d'
124,   11, for ' 27th' read 22d'
127,   34, after ' that' add ' it'
136,   34, for ' hæc' read ' hac'
173,   20, for ' 15th' read ' 5th'
222,   9, for ' person' read ' prisoner'
237,   41, for ' motion' read ' instance'
241,   30, after ' this' read ' because it is'
257,   23, for ' attach' read ' attack'
274,   30, after ' relevancy' add ' of his evidence'
283,   16, for ' that' read ' lest'
292,   13, for ' 3d' read ' 2d'
302,   44, for ' cares' read ' ears'
310,   33, for ' would' read ' could'
315,   40, after ' refers' dele ' to'
315,   41, after ' question' dele ' ;'
328,   15, for ' impel' read ' compel'
337,   6, before ' command' read ' a'
343,   19, after ' facilitating' dele ' to'
349,   15, for ' gentlemen' read ' gentleman'
381,   2, for ' returned' read ' retained'
387,   20, for ' juryman' read ' witness'
387,   21, for ' witness' read ' juryman'
398,   23, for ' severally' read ' several'
401,   47, after ' kingdom' add ' that'
413,   35, for ' has' read ' is'
421,   41, for ' Pegrom' read ' Pegram'
438,   12, after ' and' dele ' we'
440,   41, for ' and' read ' but'
444,   20, for ' influence' read ' inference'
444,   38, for ' assemblage' read ' assembly'
483,   19, for ' those' read ' that'
516,   33, for ' him' read ' them'
534,   36, for ' note a' read ' note B'
538,   5, for ' Teurnley' read ' Fernley'
542,   16, for ' note a' read ' note B'
543,   22, after ' Fries' insert ' †'
552,   13, for ' the present' read ' this'
562,   2, dele ' this'
562,   26, before ' 33 Hen. 8' read ' By'
562,   26, after ' 281' dele ' By'
562,   43, after ' be' add ' so'
564,   2, for ' be' read ' were'
565,   17, for ' and' read ' when'

THE EXAMINATION

OF

COLONEL AARON BURR.

RICHMOND, Monday, March 30th, 1807.

COLONEL AARON BURR, who had been arrested
on the Tombigbee river, in the Mississippi Territory, on the
19th day of February last, and brought to this city under a
military escort on Thursday evening the 26th instant, remained under guard until this day, when he was delivered over to
the civil authority, by virtue of a warrant issued by the chief
justice of the United States, grounded on the charges of a
high misdemeanor, in setting on foot and preparing, within
the territories of the United States, a military expedition, to
be carried on from thence against the dominions of the king of
Spain, with whom the United States then were and still are at
peace; and also of treason against the United States.

Between the hours of twelve and one o'clock, major Scott,
the marshal of the district of Virginia, attended by two of his
deputies, waited on colonel Burr, at his lodgings at the Eagle
Tavern, and, after informing him in the most respectful manner, of the nature and object of his visit, conducted him through
an awfully silent and attentive assemblage of citizens to a retired room in the house, where he was brought before chief
justice Marshall for examination. The counsel and a witness
for the United States, the counsel for the prisoner, the marshal and his deputies, and a few friends invited by the counsel
of colonel Burr, were alone admitted.

This mode of proceeding occasioned some degree of dissatisfaction among the citizens; but the following statement of facts,
which we are authorised to say is correct, will readily account
for it. When the attorney for the district applied to the chief
justice for a warrant, some conversation ensued on the manner
of examination. Mr. Marshall observed that it was indifferent
to him whether it was held at the capitol or at the Eagle
Tavern. Mr. Hay objected to the latter, that no room was sufficiently large to receive the crowd that would attend, which

would be a source of considerable inconvenience. Mr. Marshall observed, that this difficulty could be obviated by having the examination in private. To which Mr. Hay assented, on the condition, that if there were a discussion by counsel, they should adjourn to the capitol.

The evidence introduced on this occasion consisted of a copy of the record in the case of Bollman and Swartwout in the supreme court of the United States, (containing the affidavits of general Eaton, general Wilkinson, and others) ; and also of the verbal testimony of major Perkins, the gentleman by whom colonel Burr was apprehended; the substance of which we are authorised to assert, is correctly as follows: On the night of the 18th or 19th of February last, he was at Washington court-house. At about 11 o'clock, as he was standing at the door of the house occupied by the sheriff, he observed two men coming down the road. The moon afforded him light enough to enable him to see objects at some distance. The foremost man, who was thirty or forty yards before his companion, and who turned out to be colonel Burr, passed near the door without stopping or speaking. Burr's companion stopped and inquired the way to major Hinson's: the way was pointed out, but Perkins informed him that the major was from home, and that, in consequence of a late rise in the waters, he would experience some difficulty in getting there that night; the stranger, however, went on. Perkins, struck with this midnight journey, the silence of the person who had first passed, the unwillingness of the travellers to stop at a public place, where they and their horses might have been accommodated, and their determination to continue their route to Hinson's, after information was given that he was from home, communicated to the sheriff his suspicion, that these men must be under the influence of some extraordinary motive. Possibly they might be robbers, or perhaps one of them was Burr endeavouring to effect his escape. He had been informed that Burr had left Natchez. Impressed by these suspicions, he urged the sheriff, who had gone to bed, to rise and go with him to Hinson's. After some time the sheriff agreed to accompany him, and they went to Hinson's, where they found both the travellers. Burr, who had been in the kitchen to warm himself, soon came into the room where his companion and Perkins were. He spoke very little, and did not seem willing to be observed. Perkins eyed him attentively, but never got a full view of his face. He discerned that Burr once glanced his eye at him, apparently with a view to ascertain whether Perkins was observing him; but withdrew it immediately. The latter had heard Mr. Burr's eyes mentioned as being remarkably keen, and this glance from him strengthened his suspi-

cions. He determined immediately to take measures for apprehending him. He accordingly left the place, after men
tioning in a careless manner the way he meant to take. The
way he indicated was opposite to the course he thought Burr
would pursue. After getting beyond the reach of observation,
he took the road to Fort Stoddart, and obtained the aid of the
commandant and four soldiers. The circumstances of the arrest have been already stated to the public.

Perkins further said, that, while they were on their way to
Washington, at Chester Town or courthouse, in the back part
of South-Carolina, Mr. Burr, observing a small collection of
people, got off his horse, went into the company, asked for a
magistrate, and complained of being under an illegal arrest
and military guard. Perkins, however, soon reinstated him on
his horse, and directed the guard to proceed. The people
manifested no disposition to interfere.

After the evidence was gone through, Mr. Hay submitted
to the chief justice a motion in writing for the commitment
of the prisoner on the two charges above mentioned. A discussion was then agreed, on both sides, to be necessary; and,
in pursuance of the arrangement previously made, Mr. Hay
moved for an adjournment to the capitol, to which the counsel
of colonel Burr readily assented. Colonel Burr was then admitted to bail in the sum of five thousand dollars for his appearance on the following day at ten o'clock.

TUESDAY, 31st March, 1807.—Present, John Marshall, chief
justice of the United States. Counsel for the prosecution, Cæsar
A. Rodney, attorney general for the United States; George
Hay, attorney of the United States for the district of Virginia.
Counsel for colonel Burr, Edmund Randolph, esquire, John
Wickham, esquire.

At ten o'clock, the chief justice was seated on the bench,
and the court room crowded with citizens. Colonel Burr arrived at half past ten o'clock, and apologised for the delay, declaring that he had misapprehended the hour at which he was
bound to appear.

On the suggestion of the counsel, that it would be impossible
to accommodate the spectators in the court room, the chief justice adjourned to the hall of the house of delegates.

Mr. HAY, the attorney for the United States, for the district of Virginia, moved, that the prisoner should be committed
in order to take his trial upon two charges, exhibited against
him on the part of the United States: 1st, For a high misdemeanor, in setting on foot, within the United States, a military

expedition against the dominions of the king of Spain, a foreign prince, with whom the United States, at the time of the offence, were, and still are, at peace. 2d, For treason in assembling an armed force, with a design to seize the city of New-Orleans, to revolutionize the territory attached to it, and to separate the western from the Atlantic states.

He stated the first offence to be a violation of the fifth section of an act of congress, passed on the 5th of June, 1794, intitled, " an act in addition to the act for the punishment of certain crimes against the United States," continued for limited periods by several succeeding laws, and continued without limitation by an act passed in 1799. The said section provides, " that if any person shall, within the territory or juris-
" diction of the United States, begin or set on foot, or provide
" or prepare the means for any military expedition or enter-
" prize, to be carried on from thence against the territories or
" dominions of any foreign prince or state, with whom the
" United States are at peace, every person so offending shall,
" upon conviction, be adjudged guilty of a high misdemeanor,
" and shall suffer fine and imprisonment, at the discretion of
" the court in which the conviction shall be had, so as that
" such fine shall not exceed three thousand dollars, nor the
" term of imprisonment be more than three years." He supported this charge by the letter of the prisoner addressed to general Wilkinson, and insisted that it showed probable cause to suspect him of having committed this offence; nay, that he had actually committed it, and that this construction of the letter was deliberately adopted by the supreme court of the United States; that the intention of the prisoner to commit these offences was perfectly clear from the evidence.

But, secondly, he insisted, that there was probable cause to suspect, that the prisoner had committed an act of treason; that he intended to take possession of New-Orleans, make it the seat of his dominion, and the capital of his empire; and that this charge was proved by the affidavits exhibited in the cases of Bollman and Swartwout, and he referred to the opinion of the supreme court in those cases, as supporting the doctrine for which he contended, that there was just ground of suspicion against him. He went minutely into an examination of the evidence, to show that he was correct, and among other circumstances mentioned his flight from justice.

Mr. WICKHAM, in behalf of the prisoner, contended, that there was no evidence of treason committed by colonel Burr; that there was nothing like an overt act, or probable ground to believe him guilty of such an offence; that the letter in cypher to general Wilkinson was not delivered by Mr. Burr, nor

proved to be written by him ; that a comparison of the hand-
writing was inadmissible evidence ; that if it were written by
him, the contents of it might be mistaken, and general Wilkinson acknowledged that it could not be fully interpreted; that
the definition of treason was clearly marked out by the constitution itself, and could not be mistaken. He contested the propriety and effect of the evidence relied on by the attorney for
the United States, and insisted, that if any thing could be inferred from it, an invasion of the territories of the king of
Spain, a power with which we were in an intermediate state
between war and peace, was by far the most probable ; that if
his intention were to attack the Spanish settlements, it was
not only innocent, but meritorious ; that there were strong circumstances at that time to justify the expectation of a war with
Spain; and he appealed to the message of the president of the
United States, at the opening of the session of congress, to
prove the provocations on the part of Spain, and the probability
of such an event; that if we remained at peace with that power,
still colonel Burr might very innocently contemplate some individual enterprize, and the president recommended strong
settlements beyond the Mississippi; that as to what was deemed a flight, he only exercised a right in endeavouring to escape
from military despotism. He concluded, that there was not a
shadow of evidence to support the charge of treason ; and as
to the other, the evidence was trivial; but if deemed sufficient
to put him on his trial, it was a bailable offence; and as, unfortunately for colonel Burr, he was brought to the place where
he had fewer friends or acquaintances, than in almost any other
part of the United States, it would be cruelty in counsel to
insist on his giving bail in a considerable sum.

Mr. Randolph enforced the same principles in behalf of the
accused. He denied that there was any evidence to support
either of the charges; that, though long conversant with criminal jurisprudence, he never before heard of a conjecture of
an overt act of treason attempted to be proved from a supposed
intention! which was as inconsistent with law and justice as
with charity. But whatever the intention might have been, the
law required, that a criminal act must be proved, to support
a prosecution; that the government, who had caused him to
be brought such a great distance from his friends and the scene
of intelligence, ought not to avail itself thereof to oppress him;
that as treason was of all crimes the most heinous, it required
the strongest evidence to support it; whereas here there was
no proof except what was vague, weak, and unsatisfactory; that
he had not fled from justice, but from military oppression,
(which he had a right to resist) after he had been acquitted in

Kentucky, and a grand jury in the Mississippi Territory had found him not guilty. Notwithstanding the alarm excited, nothing like an overt act of treason in levying war was proved. No military preparations existed, not a single soldier was enlisted; nay, not even a servant extraordinary has been shown to have attended him; that there was no evidence that Swartwout's communication with Wilkinson was authorised by Burr, or that he faithfully delivered the message, if entrusted with one; that therefore the affidavit of Wilkinson proved nothing: that his being in the western country, and engaged in collecting persons to settle some valuable lands, were the only circumstances which remained to subject him to the slightest shade of suspicion; and these were strangely converted into acts of " levying war;" that the terrible alarm at New-Orleans was imputable to the conduct of general Wilkinson, whose arbitrary and violent proceedings, and magnifying accounts of danger, were calculated to make the people tremble for their personal safety. As to his attempt to escape in South Carolina, Mr. Randolph concluded that any other man would in the same circumstances have endeavoured to escape from military persecution and tyranny; and that the manner in which he was treated, was barbarous, inhuman and oppressive, to the last degree. That, according to the doctrine contended for by the counsel for the United States, a man might be apprehended in the district of Maine, and carried as far as the Tombigbee, illegally, without redress any where between those places, for want of evidence; and when brought to the place appointed for his trial, the court would not try him, but wait for further evidence, if the commitment appeared to be right on the face of it, which would annihilate, altogether, the benefit of the writ of habeas corpus. He concluded, that there was no evidence of an overt act to support the charge of treason, and that it ought to be renounced. As to the other point, the fitting out an expedition against the dominions of the king of Spain, he asked, where it was prepared? in what state? Virginia, Ohio, Kentucky, or the Mississippi Territory? That they had no arms, no ammunition; that they had some boats calculated only to accommodate families removing to form new settlements. He hoped, that if the judge should think that a recognisance ought to be required, it should be in as small a sum as possible.

Colonel BURR rose, he said, not to remedy any omission of his counsel, who had done great justice to the subject. He wished only to state a few facts, and to repel some observations of a personal nature. The present inquiry involved a simple question of treason or misdemeanor. According to the constitution, treason consisted in acts; that an arrest could only be justified by the suspicions of acts, whereas, in this case, his honour was invited to issue a warrant upon mere conjecture; that alarms existed without cause; that Mr. Wilkinson alarmed the president, and the president alarmed the people of Ohio. He appealed to historical facts. No sooner did he understand that suspicions were entertained in Kentucky of the nature and design of his movements, than he hastened to meet an investigation. The prosecution not being prepared, he was discharged. That he then went to Tennessee. While there he heard that the attorney for the district of Kentucky was preparing another prosecution against him; that he immediately returned to Frankfort, presented himself before the court, and again was honourably discharged; that what happened in the Mississippi Territory was equally well known; that there he was not only acquitted by the grand jury, but they went farther, and censured the conduct of that government; and if there had been really any cause of alarm, it must have been felt by the people of that part of the country; that the manner of his descent down the river, was a fact which put at defiance all rumours about treason or misdemeanor; that the nature of his equipments clearly evinced that his object was purely peaceable and agricultural; that this fact alone ought to overthrow the testimony against him; that his designs were honourable, and would have been useful to the United States. His flight, as it was termed, had been mentioned as evidence of guilt. He asked, at what time did he fly? In Kentucky he invited inquiry, and that inquiry terminated in a firm conviction of his innocence; that the alarms were at first great in the Mississippi Territory, and orders had been issued to seize and destroy the persons and property of himself and party; that he endeavoured to undeceive the people, and convince them that he had no designs hostile to the United States, but that twelve hundred men were in arms for a purpose not yet developed; the people could not be deceived; and he was acquitted, and promised the protection of the government; but the promise could not be performed; the arm of military power could not be resisted; that he knew there were military orders to seize his person and property, and transport him to a distance from that place; that he was assured by the officer of an armed boat, that it was lying in the river ready to receive him on board. Was it his duty to remain there thus situated? That he took the advice of his best friends, pursued the dictates of his own judgment, and abandoned a country where the laws ceased to be the sovereign power; that the charge stated in a hand-bill, that he had forfeited his recognisance, was false; that he had forfeited no recognisance; if he had forfeited any recognisance, he asked, why no proceedings had taken place for the breach of it? If he was to be prosecuted for such breach, he wished to know why he was brought to this place? Why not carry him to the place where the breach happened? That more than three months had elapsed since the order of government had issued to seize and bring him to that place; yet it was pretended, that sufficient time had not been allowed to adduce testimony in support of the prosecution. He asked, why the guard who conducted him to that place, avoided every magistrate on the way, unless from a conviction that they were acting without lawful authority? Why had he been debarred the use of pen, ink, and paper, and not even permitted to write to his daughter? That in the state of South Carolina, where he happened to see three men together, he demanded the interposition of the civil authority; that it was from military despotism, from the tyranny of a military escort, that he wished to be delivered, not from an investigation into his conduct, or from the operation of the laws of his country. He concluded, that there were three courses that might be pursued,—an acquittal, or a commitment for treason, or for a misdemeanor; that no proof existed in support of either, but what was contained in the affidavits of Eaton and Wilkinson, abounding in crudities and absurdities.

Mr. RODNEY, the attorney general of the United States, then addressed the judge. He observed, that when he considered the numerous and attentive audience, the public anxiety so strongly excited, the character charged, and the crime of which he was accused, he was more than usually embarrassed; that he had never felt more for any person than for the prisoner, who was no less than the late vice president of the United States, esteemed for his transcendent talents, and whom he once considered as his friend, and treated as such in his own house; that he now stood charged with the most heinous crime; that it was incumbent on those who prosecuted, to prove probable cause to believe his guilt, and that the chain of circumstances showed, without doubt, that he was guilty: that, however, he would endeavour to convince him, by his manner of conducting the prosecution, that the government was not influenced by malicious or vindictive passions, to persecute him.

That the gentlemen on the other side had argued as if they were then before a jury upon the principal trial, and demanded such legal evidence as would be sufficient to convict him on such trial: that the law however, required no such plenary testimony in this incipient stage of the proceedings; that to show probable cause to authorise a commitment, ex parte testimony was admissible; and unless it manifestly appeared that he was innocent, he ought to be committed; whereas before a jury, such testimony would be excluded, and his innocence would be presumed till his guilt appeared ; that on the trial the law required two witnesses to an overt act of treason; and that his confession would be unavailing unless made in open court; that on the present inquiry, two witnesses were not requisite to prove an overt act, and that ex parte evidence of his confession must be admitted; that it was true, that the constitution required two witnesses of an overt act to convict the prisoner; but that the sixth article of the amendments to the constitution, rendered probable cause only necessary to justify the issuing a warrant to take a man into custody, and of course to commit him for trial. That there were two charges against him : one for a crime against the constitution ; the other for a violation of the act of congress passed in 1794, to prevent the safety and peace of the United States from being put in jeopardy, by the daring enterprises of unauthorised individuals; on both of which he would make a few remarks. In the first place he contended, that the mystery in which this business was enveloped, afforded just grounds of suspicion. If the settlement of lands merely was intended, why were dark and corruptive messages sent to military commanders? why was a letter in cypher sent to the commander in chief, when he was supposed to be at St. Louis? why, when it was found he was not there, was another sent to Natchitoches, and from thence to New-Orleans? That it was an important fact, that colonel Burr in the preceding year had been throughout that whole country; that it was the practice every day to take the confession of accomplices as evidence against their principals, though made to escape punishment themselves ; that here the case was much stronger, for the confessions of Bollman and Swartwout to general Wilkinson were perfectly voluntary—with the design of engaging him in the criminal projects of colonel Burr: Their disclosure ought to have the more weight, because they knew the contents of the letters which they delivered, which stated them to be in his confidence; and they declared themselves his partizans; that the affidavit of general Wilkinson, by which these facts are proved, was certainly good as a piece of ex parte testimony in this stage of the business, though inadmissible on the trial; that the declaration of Swartwout, as stated in that affidavit, proves the intention of the prisoner to have been to seize on New-Orleans, and plunder it, as preparatory to his expedition against Mexico; that the supreme court, in the case of Bollman and Swartwout, had adjudged, that if an end cannot be accomplished without treasonable means, the end itself was treasonable; and of course the project of the prisoner must have been to perpetrate treason. Mr. Rodney further contended, that the treasonable intention thus proved by Wilkinson was strongly fortified by the deposition of general Eaton, which was unquestionable evidence in this stage of the prosecution; that there could be no doubt of the truth of the statements of this gallant soldier; this man of true honour and most respectable character, who had rendered such memorable services to his country by traversing the deserts of Lybia, and by the conquest of Derne; that his communications to him were begun in the same cautious manner with those to general Wilkinson; that in both instances, he pretended at first to be in the confidence of the government, but afterwards proceeded by degrees to develop his treasonable plans; that the territory of Orleans, or some other territory belonging to the United States, was to be revolutionized; that there was to be some seizure at New-Orleans; that no doubt remained of the treasonable intention; that the only doubt was, whether there was sufficient proof of force having been actually embodied, and that all the circumstances rendered that fact very probable. Mr. Rodney here expatiated on the evidence : the letter of colonel Burr written in July; his intention to wait till he heard from the military commander at New-Orleans ; Swartwout's statement; Eaton's deposition; the activity of colonel Burr in Ohio, Kentucky, Tennessee, and the Mississippi Territory, and his cautious mysterious conduct; and that in this incipient stage of the proceedings, stronger testimony could not be reasonably expected ; that the government, however vigilant it had been, had not had sufficient time to obtain it; and that he ought to be put on his trial; that if he should be acquitted by a jury of his country, it would give no man more heartfelt pleasure than himself.

When Mr. Rodney concluded, Mr. HAY observed, that if the judge should be of opinion, that the prisoner ought to be put on his trial, and that he might be admitted to bail, he wished to make some observations on the amount of the sum in which the recognisance should be taken. He cited the 1st vol. of the laws of the United States, p. 144, and 2d vol. p. 275, to show, that it was discretionary with the judge to admit to bail, whether he should be of opinion that he ought to be tried for treason or misdemeanor. The chief justice answered, that he would certainly give him an opportunity to make the observations he desired ; and that he intended himself, to deliver his opinion in writing, to prevent any misrepresentations of expressions which might fall from him. As it could not be prepared till the next day, colonel Burr's recognisance was renewed for his appearance at the capitol on the following day at ten o'clock.

WEDNESDAY, 1st April, 1807.—The chief justice delivered the following opinion in the presence of a numerous audience:

I am required on the part of the attorney for the United States to commit the accused on two charges:

1st. For setting on foot and providing the means for an expedition against the territories of a nation at peace with the United States.

2d. For committing high treason against the United States.

On an application of this kind I certainly should not require that proof which would be necessary to convict the person to be committed, on a trial in chief; nor should I even require that which should absolutely convince my own mind of the guilt of the accused: but I ought to require, and I should require, that probable cause be shown; and I understand probable cause to be a case made out by proof furnishing good reason to believe that the crime alleged has been committed by the person charged with having committed it.

I think this opinion entirely reconcileable with that quoted from judge Blackstone. When that learned and accurate commentator says, that "if upon an inquiry it manifestly appears that no such crime has been committed, or that the suspicion entertained of the prisoner was wholly groundless, in such cases only it is lawful totally to discharge him, otherwise he must be committed to prison or give bail," I do not understand him as meaning to say that the hand of malignity may grasp any individual against whom its hate may be directed, or whom it may capriciously seize, charge him with some secret crime, and put him on the proof of his innocence.* But I understand that the foundation of the proceeding must be a probable cause to believe there is guilt; which probable cause is only to be done away in the manner stated by Blackstone. The total failure of proof on the part of the accuser would be considered by that writer as being in itself a legal manifestation of the innocence of the accused.

In inquiring therefore into the charges exhibited against Aaron Burr, I hold myself bound to consider how far those charges are supported by probable cause.

The first charge stands upon the testimony of general Eaton and general Wilkinson.

The witness first named proves that among other projects

* The chief justice explicitly stated to the reporters, that, in making the above observations, he had no allusion to the conduct of the government in the case before him, but only meant an elucidation of the general doctrine laid down by Blackstone. He was induced, he said, to make these remarks, because it had been suggested to him by a friend, after he had delivered his opinion, that his meaning in the above expressions might possibly be misapprehended.

which were more criminal, colonel Burr meditated an expedition against the Mexican dominions of Spain. This deposition may be considered as introductory to the affidavit of genera Wilkinson, and as explanatory of the objects of any military preparations which may have been made.

I proceed then to that affidavit.

To make the testimony of general Wilkinson bear on colonel Burr, it is necessary to consider as genuine the letter stated by the former to be, as nearly as he can make it, an interpretation of one received in cypher from the latter. Exclude this letter, and nothing remains in the testimony, which can in the most remote degree affect colonel Burr. That there are to the admissibility of this part of the affidavit great and obvious objections, need not be stated to those who know with how much caution proceedings in criminal cases ought to be instituted, and who know that the highest tribunal of the United States has been divided on them. When this question came before the supreme court, I felt the full force of these objections, although I did not yield to them. On weighing in my own mind the reason for and against acting, in this stage of the business, on that part of the affidavit, those in favour of doing so appeared to me to preponderate, and, as this opinion was not overruled, I hold myself still at liberty to conform to it.

That the original letter, or a true copy of it accompanied by the cypher, would have been much more satisfactory, is not to be denied: but I thought, and I still think, that, upon a mere question whether the accused shall be brought to trial or not, upon an inquiry not into guilt but into the probable cause, the omission of a circumstance which is indeed important, but which does not disprove the positive allegations of an affidavit, ought not to induce its rejection or its absolute disbelief, when the maker of the affidavit is at too great a distance to repair the fault. I could not in this stage of the prosecution absolutely discredit the affidavit, because the material facts alleged may very well be within the knowledge of the witness, although he has failed to state explicitly all the means by which this knowledge is obtained.

Thus, general Wilkinson states that this letter was received from colonel Burr, but does not say that it was in his hand writing, nor does he state the evidence which supports this affirmation. But, in addition to the circumstance that the positive assertion of the fact ought not perhaps, in this stage of the inquiry, to be disregarded, the nature of the case furnishes that evidence.

The letter was in cypher. General Wilkinson it is true, does not say that a cypher had been previously settled between colonel Burr and himself, in which they might correspond on subjects which, though innocent, neither of them might wish to subject to the casualties of a transportation from the Atlantic to the Mississippi; but when we perceive that colonel Burr has written in cypher, and that general Wilkinson is able to decypher the letter, we must either presume, that the bearer of the letter was also the bearer of its key, or that the key was previously in possession of the person to whom the letter was addressed. In stating particularly the circumstances attending the delivery of this letter, general Wilkinson does not say that it was accompanied by the key, or that he felt any surprise at its being in cypher. For this reason, as well as because there is not much more security in sending a letter in cypher accompanied by its key, than there is in sending a letter not in cypher; I think it more reasonable to suppose that the key was previously in possession of Wilkinson. If this was the fact, the letter being written in a cypher previously settled between himself and colonel Burr, is, in this stage of the inquiry at least, a circumstance which sufficiently supports the assertion, that the letter was written by colonel Burr.

The enterprize described in this letter is obviously a military enterprize, and must have been intended either against the United States, or against the territories of some other power on the continent, with all of whom the United States were at peace.

The expressions of this letter must be admitted to furnish at least probable cause for believing, that the means for the expedition were provided. In every part of it, we find declarations indicating that he was providing the means for the expedition; and as these means might be provided in secret, I do not think that further testimony ought to be required to satisfy me, that there is probable cause for committing the prisoner on this charge.

Since it will be entirely in the power of the attorney general to prefer an indictment against the prisoner, for any other offence which he shall think himself possessed of testimony to support, it is in fact, immaterial whether the second charge be expressed in the warrant of commitment or not; but as I hold it to be my duty to insert every charge alleged on the part of the United States, in support of which probable cause is shown, and to insert none in support of which probable cause is not shown, I am bound to proceed in the inquiry.

The second charge exhibited against the prisoner, is high treason against the United States in levying war against them.

As this is the most atrocious offence which can be committed against the political body, so is it the charge which is most capable of being employed as the instrument of those malignant and vindictive passions which may rage in the bosoms of contending parties struggling for power. It is that, of which the people of America have been most jealous, and therefore, while other crimes are unnoticed, they have refused to trust the national legislature with the definition of this, but have themselves declared in their constitution that "it shall consist only in levying war against the United States, or in adhering to their enemies giving them aid and comfort." This high crime consists of overt acts which must be proved by two witnesses or by the confession of the party in open court.

Under the control of this constitutional regulation, I am to inquire whether the testimony laid before me furnishes probable cause in support of this charge. The charge is, that the fact itself has been committed, and the testimony to support it must furnish probable cause for believing that it has been actually committed, or it is insufficient for the purpose for which it is adduced.

Upon this point too, the testimony of general Eaton is first to be considered. That part of his deposition which bears upon this charge is the plan disclosed by the prisoner for seizing upon New-Orleans, and revolutionizing the western states.

That this plan, if consummated by overt acts, would amount to treason, no man will controvert. But it is equally clear, that an intention to commit treason is an offence entirely distinct from the actual commission of that crime. War can only be levied by the employment of actual force. Troops must be embodied, men must be assembled in order to levy war. If colonel Burr had been apprehended on making these communications to general Eaton, could it have been alleged that he had gone further than to meditate the crime? Could it have been said that he had actually collected forces and had actually levied war? Most certainly it could not. The crime really completed was a conspiracy to commit treason, not an actual commission of treason.

If these communications were not treason at the instant they were made, no lapse of time can make them so. They are not in themselves acts. They may serve to explain the intention with which acts were committed, but they cannot supply those acts if they be not proved.

The next testimony is the deposition of general Wilkinson, which consists of the letter already noticed, and of the communications made by the bearer of that letter.

This letter has already been considered by the supreme court of the United States, and has been declared to import, taken by itself or in connexion with Eaton's deposition, rather an expedition against the territories of the United States. By that decision I am bound, whether I concurred in it or not. But I did concur in it. On this point the court was unanimous.

It is, however, urged that the declarations of Swartwout may be connected with the letter and used against colonel Burr. Although the confession of one man cannot criminate another, yet I am inclined to think that, on a mere inquiry into probable cause, the declaration of Swartwout made on this particular occasion, may be used against colonel Burr. My reason for thinking so is, that colonel Burr's letter authorizes Mr. Swartwout to speak in his name. He empowers Mr. Swartwout to make to general Wilkinson verbal communications explanatory of the plans and designs of Burr, which Burr adopts as his own explanations. However inadmissible therefore, this testimony may be on a trial in chief, I am inclined to admit it on this inquiry.

If it be admitted, what is its amount? Upon this point too, it appears that the supreme court was divided. I therefore hold myself at liberty to pursue my own opinion, which was, that the words "this territory must be revolutionized," did not so clearly apply to a foreign territory as to reject that sense which would make them applicable to a territory of the United States, at least so far as to admit of further inquiry into their meaning. And if a territory of the United States was to be revolutionized, though only as a mean for an expedition against a foreign power, the act would be treason.

This reasoning leads to the conclusion that there is probable cause for the allegation that treasonable designs were entertained by the prisoner so late as July last, when this letter was written.

It remains to inquire whether there is also probable cause to believe, that these designs have been ripened into the crime itself by actually levying war against the United States.

It has been already observed, that to constitute this crime, troops must be embodied, men must be actually assembled; and these are facts which cannot remain invisible. Treason may be machinated in secret, but it can be perpetrated only in open day and in the eye of the world. Testimony of a fact which in its own nature is so notorious ought to be unequivocal. The testimony now offered has been laid before the supreme court of the United States, and has been determined in the cases of Bollman and Swartwout, not to furnish probable cause for the opinion that war had been actually levied. Whatever might have been the inclination of my own mind in that case, I should feel much difficulty in departing from the decision then made, unless this case could be clearly distinguished from it. I will, however, briefly review the arguments which have been urged, and the facts now before me, in order to show more clearly the particular operation they have on my own judgment.

The fact to be established is, that in pursuance of these designs previously entertained, men have been actually assembled for the purpose of making war against the United States; and on the showing of probable cause that this fact has been committed, depends the issue of the present inquiry.

The first piece of testimony relied on to render this fact probable, is the declaration of Mr. Swartwout, that "colonel Burr was *levying* an armed body of 7,000 men from the state of New-York and the western states and territories, with a view to carry an expedition against the Mexican provinces." The term "*levying*" has been said, according to the explanation of the lexicons, to mean the embodying of troops, and therefore to prove what is required. Although I do not suppose that Mr. Swartwout had consulted a dictionary, I have looked into Johnson for the term, and find its first signification to be "to raise," its second "to bring together." In common parlance, it may signify the one or the other. But its sense is certainly decided by the fact. If when Mr. Swartwout left colonel Burr, which must be supposed to have been in July, he was actually embodying men from New-York to the western states, what could veil his troops from human sight? An invisible army is not the instrument of war, and had these troops been visible, some testimony relative to them could have been adduced. I take the real sense then in which this term was used to be, that colonel Burr was raising, or in other words engaging or enlisting men through the country described, for the enterprize he meditated. The utmost point to which this testimony can be extended is, that it denotes a future embodying of men, which is more particularly mentioned in the letter itself, and that it affords probable cause to believe that the troops did actually embody at the period designated for their assembling, which is sufficient to induce the justice to whom the application is made to commit for trial.

I shall readily avow my opinion, that the strength of the presumption arising from this testimony ought to depend greatly on the time at which the application is made. If soon after the period at which the troops were to assemble, when full time had not elapsed to ascertain the fact, these circumstances had been urged as the ground for a commitment on the charge of treason, I should have thought them intitled to great consideration. I will not deny, that in the cases of Bollman and Swartwout, I was not perfectly satisfied that they did not warrant an inquiry into the fact. But I think every person must admit that the weight of these circumstances daily diminishes. Suspicion may deserve great attention, when the means of ascertaining its real grounds are not yet possessed; but when those means are or may have been acquired, if facts to support suspicion be not shown, every person, I think, must admit, that the ministers of justice at least ought not officially to entertain it. This, I think, must be conceded by all; but whether it be conceded by others or not, it is the dictate of my own judgment, and in the performance of my duty I can know no other guide.

The fact to be proved in this case is an act of public notoriety. It must exist in the view of the world, or it cannot exist at all. The assembling of forces to levy war is a visible transaction, and numbers must witness it. It is therefore capable of proof; and when time to collect this proof has been given, it ought to be adduced, or suspicion becomes ground too weak to stand upon.

Several months have elapsed, since this fact did occur, if it ever occurred. More than five weeks have elapsed, since the opinion of the supreme court has declared the necessity of proving the fact, if it exists. Why is it not proved?

To the executive government is intrusted the important power of prosecuting those, whose crimes may disturb the public repose, or endanger its safety. It would be easy, in much less time than has intervened since colonel Burr has been alleged to have assembled his troops, to procure affidavits establishing the fact. If, in November or December last, a body of troops had been assembled on the Ohio, it is impossible to suppose that affidavits establishing the fact could not have been obtained by the last of March. I ought not to believe that there has been any remissness on the part of those who prosecute, on this important and interesting subject; and consequently, when at this late period no evidence, that troops have been actually embodied, is given, I must say, that the suspicion, which in the first instance might have been created, ought not to be continued, unless this want of proof can be in some manner accounted for.

It is stated by the attorney for the United States, that, as affidavits can only be voluntary, the difficulty of obtaining them accounts for the absence of proof.

I cannot admit this position. On the evidence furnished by this very transaction of the attachment felt by our western for their eastern brethren, we justly felicitate ourselves. How inconsistent with this fact is the idea, that no man could be found who would voluntarily depose, that a body of troops had actually assembled, whose object must be understood to be hostile to the union, and whose object was detested and defeated by the very people who could give the requisite information!

I cannot doubt that means to obtain information have been taken on the part of the prosecution; if it existed, I cannot doubt the practicability of obtaining it; and its nonproduction, at this late hour, does not, in my opinion, leave me at liberty to give to those suspicions which grow out of other circumstances, that weight to which at an earlier day they might have been entitled.

I shall not therefore insert in the commitment the charge of high treason. I repeat, that this is the less important, because it detracts nothing from the right of the attorney to prefer an indictment for high treason, should he be furnished with the necessary testimony.

The chief justice having delivered his opinion, observed, that, as colonel Burr would be put on his trial for carrying on a military expedition against a nation with whom the United States were at peace, his case was of course bailable.

Mr. Wickham wished to say something as to the sum in which colonel Burr should be recognised to appear.

Chief Justice.—I have thought a good deal on the subject, but have formed no very deliberate opinion. Bail ought certainly to be required in a sum sufficiently serious to insure the appearance of the party, but not so large as to amount to oppression. It has occurred to me, that, under all the circumstances of the case, ten thousand dollars would be about right, and would avoid the two extremes.

Mr. Hay.—I have no doubt of Mr. Burr's ability to procure bail for any sum which might be exacted, even without asking for it. I do not think ten thousand dollars adequate; nor would I ask a larger sum if I did not think it could be obtained without subjecting colonel Burr to any kind of inconvenience. From the facility with which bail was offered a few days ago, I have discovered a disposition in certain gentlemen of this place to relieve colonel Burr from the humiliation of an imprisonment.

Mr. Wickham.—I should suppose, sir, that five or six thousand dollars would be sufficient. It should be recollected, that colonel Burr is to give bail to answer the charge of a misdemeanor only. He is here among strangers. Perhaps, in no part of the United States, has colonel Burr fewer acquaintances than in Richmond. And however easy it might be for him to procure bail among his friends or connexions, I am very apprehensive he will not be able to obtain it here for so large a sum as ten thousand dollars. With respect to his ability to procure bail for any amount, as stated by Mr. Hay, I do expect that that observation, like some others of that gentleman, is not well warranted. Upon this point I am unable to express any decided opinion, as it is a subject with which I am personally unacquainted. But as to the *spirit*, which, it is insinuated by Mr. Hay, has been shown by certain gentlemen to relieve colonel Burr, I am enabled explicitly to state the opinions of others, of a very different nature. It is true that two gentlemen stepped forward a few days ago, and relieved colonel Burr from the horrors of a dungeon. Their sole object was to assist a gentleman in distress, who had been dragged here by a military force more than a thousand miles. Gentlemen might be willing to be bound for two days, who would reluctantly engage for a longer time. Besides, I have heard several gentleman of great respectability, who did not doubt but colonel Burr would keep his recognisance, express an unwillingness to appear as bail for him, lest it might be supposed they were enemies to their country. I hope this sentiment is incorrect; but it certainly will have its influence. I doubt very much whether he can procure bail, considering his remote situation from his friends, and the apprehensions just mentioned.

Mr. HAY.—I did state, sir, my belief to be, that colonel Burr could find bail for any sum which might be demanded. Mr. Wickham has been pleased to say, that this observation, like some others of mine, is not well warranted. I therefore consider it my duty to state candidly and correctly the reasons which have induced me to form that opinion. In the first place; two gentlemen, having no acquaintance with colonel Burr, on the first day of the examination voluntarily stepped forward, and offered themselves as his bail. This proves the prevailing sentiment among certain gentlemen. This sentiment, we may fairly presume, is not confined to those two gentlemen alone. Secondly; I have been well informed, that colonel Burr could give bail in one hundred thousand dollars. Mr. Wickham has not mentioned names, nor shall I state the source of my information. I do not pretend to say, that this large sum should be required. But when it is considered, that, at the next court, evidence of assembling troops may be adduced, which will constitute the crime of treason, and prevent the appearance of colonel Burr, I do think that a sum sufficiently large should be fixed on to insure that object.

Colonel BURR.—I had no expectation, sir, that any thing would be taken into consideration but the subject immediately

vernment of our country, such conspiracy is not treason. To conspire to levy war, and actually to levy war, are distinct offences. The first must be brought into operation by the assemblage of men for a purpose treasonable in itself, or the fact of levying war cannot have been committed. So far has this principle been carried, that in a case reported by Ventris, and that mentioned in some modern treatise on criminal law, it has been determined, that the actual enlistment of men to serve against the government does not amount to levying war. It is true, that in that case the soldiers enlisted were to serve without the realm, but they were enlisted within it, and if the enlistment for a treasonable purpose could amount to levying war, then war had been actually levied.

It is not the intention of the court to say, that no individual can be guilty of this crime who has not appeared in arms against his country. On the contrary, if war be actually levied, that is, if a body of men be actually assembled for the purpose of effecting by force, a treasonable purpose, all those who perform any part, however minute or however remote from the scene of action, and who are actually leagued in the general conspiracy, are to be considered as traitors. But there must be an actual assembling of men for the treasonable purpose, to constitute a levying of war.

Crimes so atrocious as those which have for their object the subversion, by violence, of those laws and those institutions which have been ordained, in order to secure the peace and happiness of society, are not to escape punishment because they are not ripened into treason. The wisdom of the legislature is competent to provide for the case; and the framers of our constitution, who not only defined and limited the crime, but with jealous circumspection attempted to protect their limitation, by providing, that no person should be convicted of it, unless on the testimony of two witnesses to the same overt act, or on confession in open court, must have conceived it more safe that punishment in such cases should be ordained by general laws, formed upon deliberation, under the influence of no resentments, and without knowing on whom they were to operate, than that it should be inflicted under the influence of those passions which the occasion seldom fails to excite, and which a flexible definition of the crime, or a construction which would render it flexible, might bring into operation. It is therefore more safe, as well as more consonant to the principles of our constitution, that the crime of treason should not be extended by construction to doubtful cases; and that crimes not clearly within the constitutional definition should receive such punishment as the legislature in its wisdom may provide.

To complete the crime of levying war against the United States, there must be an actual assemblage of men for the purpose of executing a treasonable design. In the case now before the court, a design to overturn the government of the United States in New-Orleans by force, would have been unquestionably a design which, if carried into execution, would have been treason; and the assemblage of a body of men for the purpose of carrying it into execution, would amount to levying of war against the United States; but no conspiracy for this object, no enlisting of men to effect it, would be an actual levying of war.

In conformity with the principles now laid down have been the decisions heretofore made by the judges of the United States.

The opinions given by judge Patterson and judge Iredell, in cases before them, imply an actual assembling of men, though they rather designed to remark on the purpose to which the force was to be applied, than on the nature of the force itself. Their opinions, however, contemplate the actual employment of force.

Judge Chase, in the trial of Fries, was more explicit.

He stated the opinion of the court to be, " that if a body of people conspire and meditate an insurrection to resist or oppose the execution of any statute of the United States by force, they are only guilty of a high misdemeanor; but if they proceed to carry such intention into execution by force, that they are guilty of the treason of levying war; and the *quantum* of the force employed, neither lessens nor increases the crime; whether by one hundred, or one thousand persons, is wholly immaterial. "The court are of opinion," continued judge Chase, on that occasion, " that a combination or conspiracy to levy war against the United States is not treason, unless combined with an attempt to carry such combination or conspiracy into execution; some actual force or violence must be used in pursuance of such design to levy war, but it is altogether immaterial whether the force used is sufficient to effectuate the object; any force connected with the intention, will constitute the crime of levying war."

The application of these general principles to the particular case before the court will depend on the testimony which has been exhibited against the accused.

The first deposition to be considered is that of general Eaton. This gentleman connects in one statement the purport of numerous conversations held with colonel Burr throughout the last winter. In the course of these conversations were communicated various criminal projects which seem to have been revolving in the mind of the projector. An expedition against

Mexico seems to have been the first and most matured part of his plan, if indeed it did not constitute a distinct and separate plan, upon the success of which other schemes still more culpable, but not yet well digested, might depend. Maps and other information preparatory to its execution, and which would rather indicate that it was the immediate object, had been procured; and for a considerable time, in repeated conversations, the whole efforts of colonel Burr were directed to prove to the witness, who was to have held a high command under him, the practicability of the enterprize, and in explaining to him the means by which it was to be effected.

This deposition exhibits the various schemes of colonel Burr, and its materiality depends on connecting the prisoners at the bar in such of those schemes as were treasonable. For this purpose the affidavit of general Wilkinson, comprehending in its body the substance of a letter from colonel Burr, has been offered and was received by the circuit court. To the admission of this testimony great and serious objections have been made. It has been urged, that it is a voluntary, or rather an extrajudicial affidavit made before a person not appearing to be a magistrate, and contains the substance only of a letter, of which the original is retained by the person who made the affidavit.

The objection that the affidavit is extrajudicial, resolves itself into the question, whether one magistrate may commit on an affidavit taken before another magistrate: For if he may, an affidavit made as the foundation of a commitment, ceases to be extrajudicial, and the person who makes it would be as liable to a prosecution for perjury as if the warrant of commitment had been issued by the magistrate before whom the affidavit was made.

To decide that an affidavit made before one magistrate would not justify a commitment by another, might in many cases be productive of great inconvenience, and does not appear susceptible of abuse if the verity of the certificate be established. Such an affidavit seems admissible on the principle that before the accused is put upon his trial, all the proceedings are ex parte. The court therefore overrule this objection.

That which questions the character of the person who has on this occasion administered the oath is next to be considered.

The certificate from the office of the department of state has been deemed insufficient by the counsel for the prisoners; because the law does not require the appointment of magistrates for the territory of New-Orleans to be certified to that office; because the certificate is in itself informal, and because it does not appear that the magistrate had taken the oath required by the act of congress.

The first of these objections is not supported by the law of the case, and the second may be so easily corrected, retaining however any final decision, if against the prisoners, until the correction shall be made. With regard to the third, the magistrate must be presumed to have taken the requisite oaths, since he is found acting as a magistrate.

On the admissibility of that part of the affidavit which purports to be as near the substance of the letter from colonel Burr to general Wilkinson as the latter could interpret it, a division of opinion has taken place, in the court. Two judges are of opinion that as such testimony delivered in the presence of the prisoner on his trial would be totally inadmissible, neither can it be considered as a foundation for a commitment. Although in making a commitment the magistrate does not decide on the guilt of the prisoner, yet he does decide on the probable cause, and a long and painful imprisonment may be the consequence of his decision. This probable cause therefore ought to be moved by testimony in itself legal, and which, though from the nature of the case it must be ex parte, ought, in most other respects to be such as a court and jury might hear.

Two judges are of opinion that in this incipient stage of the prosecution an affidavit stating the general purport of a letter may be read, particularly where the person in possession of it is at too great a distance to admit of his being obtained, and that a commitment may be founded on it.

Under this embarrassment it was deemed necessary to look into the affidavit for the purpose of discovering whether if admitted, it contains matter which would justify the commitment of the prisoners at the bar on the charge of treason.

That the letter from colonel Burr to general Wilkinson relates to a military enterprize meditated by the former has not been questioned. If this enterprize was against Mexico, it would amount to a high misdemeanor; if against any of the territories of the United States, or if in its progress the subversion of the government of the United States, in any of their territories was a mean clearly and necessarily to be employed, if such mean formed a substantive part of the plan, the assemblage of a body of men to effect it would be levying war against the United States.

The letter is in language which furnishes no distinct view of the design of the writer. The cooperation, however, which is stated to have been secured, points strongly to some expedition against the territories of Spain. After making these general statements the writer becomes rather more explicit and says, "Burr's plan of operations is to move down rapidly from the falls on the 15th of November with the first 500 or 1000 men in light boats now constructing for that purpose, to be at Natchez between the 5th and 15th of December, there to meet

Wilkinson : then to determine whether it will be expedient in the first instance to seize on or to pass by Baton Rouge. The people of the country to which we are going are prepared to receive us. Their agents now with Burr say that if we will protect their religion and will not subject them to a foreign power, in three weeks all will be settled."

There is no expression in these sentences which would justify a suspicion that any territory of the United States was the object of the expedition.

For what purpose seize on Baton Rouge? why engage Spain against this enterprize, if it was designed against the United States?

"The people of the country to which we are going are prepared to receive us." This language is peculiarly appropriate to a foreign country. It will not be contended that the terms would be inapplicable to a territory of the United States, but other terms would more aptly convey the idea, and Burr seems to consider himself as giving information of which Wilkinson was not possessed. When it is recollected that he was the governor of a territory adjoining that which must have been threatened, if a territory of the United States was threatened, and that he commanded the army, a part of which was stationed in that territory, the probability that the information communicated related to a foreign country, it must be admitted, gains strength.

"Their agents now with Burr say that if we will protect their religion and will not subject them to a foreign power, in three weeks all will be settled."

This is apparently the language of a people who, from the contemplated change of their political situation, feared for their religion, and feared that they would be made the subjects of a foreign power. That the Mexicans should entertain these apprehensions was natural, and would readily be believed. They were, if the representation made of their dispositions be correct, about to place themselves much in the power of men who professed a faith different from theirs, and who by making them dependent on England, or the United States, would subject them to a foreign power.

That the people of New-Orleans, as a people, if really engaged in the conspiracy, should feel the same apprehensions, and require assurances on the same points, is by no means so obvious.

There certainly is not in the letter delivered to general Wilkinson, so far as that letter is laid before the court, one syllable which has a necessary or a natural reference to an enterprize against any territory of the United States.

That the bearer of this letter must be considered as acquainted with its contents, is not to be controverted. The letter and his own declarations evince the fact.

After stating himself to have passed through New-York and the western states and territories, without insinuating that he had performed on his route any act whatever, which was connected with the enterprize, he states their object to be "to carry an expedition to the Mexican provinces."

This statement may be considered as explanatory of the letter of colonel Burr, if the expressions of that letter could be thought ambiguous.

But there are two other declarations made by Mr. Swartwout, which constitute the difficulty of this case. On an inquiry from general Wilkinson, he said, "this territory would be revolutionized, where the people were ready to join, and that there would be some seizing, he supposed, at New-Orleans.

If these words import that the government, established by the United States in any of its territories, was to be revolutionized by force, although merely as a step to, or a mean of executing some greater projects, the design was unquestionably treasonable, and any assemblage of men for that purpose would amount to a levying of war. But on the import of the words a difference of opinion exists.

Some of the judges suppose they refer to the territory against which the expedition was intended, others to that in which the conversation was held. Some consider the words, if even applicable to the territory of the United States, as alluding to a revolution to be effected by the people, rather than by the party conducted by colonel Burr.

But whether this treasonable intention be really imputable to the plan or not, it is admitted that it must have been carried into execution by an open assemblage of men for that purpose, previous to the arrest of the prisoner, in order to consummate the crime as to him; and a majority of the court is of opinion, that the conversation of Mr. Swartwout affords no sufficient proof of such assembling.

The prisoner stated, that " colonel Burr, with the support of a powerful association, extending from New-York to New-Orleans, was levying an armed body of 7,000 men, from the state of New-York and the western states and territories, with a view to carry an expedition to the Mexican territories."

That the association, whatever may be its purpose, is not treason, has been already stated. That levying an army may or may not be treason, and that this depends on the intention with which it is levied, and on the point to which the parties have advanced, has been also stated. The mere enlisting of men without assembling them, is not levying war. The question then is, whether this evidence proves colonel Burr to have advanced so far in levying an army, as actually to have assembled them.

It is argued, that since it cannot be necessary that the whole 7,000 men should have assembled, their commencing their march by detachments to the place of rendezvous, must be sufficient to constitute the crime.

This position is correct, with some qualification. It cannot be necessary that the whole army should assemble, and that the various parts which are to compose it should have combined. But it is necessary there should be an actual assemblage, and therefore this evidence should make the fact unequivocal.

The travelling of individuals to the place of rendezvous would perhaps not be sufficient. This would be an equivocal act, and has no warlike appearance. The meeting of particular bodies of men, and their marching from places of partial to a place of general rendezvous, would be such an assemblage.

The particular words used by Mr. Swartwout are, that colonel Burr was levying an armed body of 7,000 men. If the term levying, in this place, imports that they were assembled, then such fact would amount, if the intention be against the United States, to levying war. If it barely imports that he was enlisting or engaging them in his service, the fact would not amount to levying war.

It is thought sufficiently apparent, that the latter is the sense in which the term was used. The fact alluded to, if taken in the former sense, is of a nature to force itself upon the public view, that, if the army had been actually assembled, either together, or in detachments, some evidence of such assembling would have been laid before the court.

The words used by the prisoner in reference to seizing at New-Orleans, and borrowing perhaps by force from the bank, though indicating a design to rob, and consequently importing a high offence, do not designate the specific crime of levying war against the United States.

It is, therefore, the opinion of a majority of the court, that, in the case of Samuel Swartwout, there is not sufficient evidence of his levying war against the United States to justify his commitment on the charge of treason.

That both the prisoners were engaged in a most culpable enterprize against the dominions of a power at peace with the United States, those who admit the affidavit of general Wilkinson cannot doubt. But that no part of this crime was committed in the district of Columbia, is apparent. It is therefore the unanimous opinion of the court, that they cannot be tried in this district.

The law read on the part of the prosecution is understood

to apply only to offences committed on the high seas, or in any river, haven, bason, or bay, not within the jurisdiction of any particular state. In these cases there is no court which has particular cognizance of the crime, and therefore the place in which the criminal shall be apprehended, or, if he be apprehended where no court has exclusive jurisdiction, that to which he shall be first brought, is substituted for the place in which the offence was committed.

But in this case, a tribunal for the trial of the offence, wherever it may have been committed, had been provided by congress; and at the place where the prisoners were seized by the authority of the commander in chief, there existed such a tribunal. It would too be extremely dangerous to say, that because the prisoners were apprehended, not by a civil magistrate, but by the military power, there could be given by law a right to try the persons so seized in any place which the general might select, and to which he might direct them to be carried.

The acts of congress, which the prisoners are supposed to have violated, describe as offenders those who begin or set on foot, or provide or prepare the means for any military expedition or enterprize to be carried on from thence against the dominions of a foreign prince or state, with whom the United States are at peace.

There is a want of precision in the description of the offence, which might produce some difficulty in deciding what cases would come within it. But several other questions arise, which a court, consisting of four judges, finds itself unable to decide; and therefore, as the crime with which the prisoners stand charged has not been committed, the court can only direct them to be discharged. This is done with the less reluctance, because the discharge does not acquit them from the offence, which there is probable cause for supposing they have committed; and if those whose duty it is to protect the nation by prosecuting offenders against the laws shall suppose those who have been charged with treason to be proper objects for punishment, they will, when possessed of less exceptionable testimony, and when able to say at what place the offence has been committed, institute fresh proceedings against them.

The order of the court was as follows:

The United States $\left.\begin{array}{c} \\ vs. \\ \textit{Swartwout.} \end{array}\right\}$ On a writ of *habeas corpus.*

The arguments of the attorney general, and of the attorney of the United States for the district of Columbia, and the arguments of the counsel for the prisoner having been heard; and the record of the circuit court for the county of Washington, containing the order by which the said Samuel Swartwout was committed on the charge of treason in levying war against the United States, and the testimony on which the said commitment was made, having been inspected and attentively considered, the court is of opinion that that testimony does not furnish probable cause for supposing that the said Samuel Swartwout levied war against the United States, and doth therefore direct, that he be forthwith discharged from the custody of the marshal.

The same order with regard to Bollman.

THE TRIAL

OF

COLONEL AARON BURR.

CITY OF RICHMOND, FRIDAY, 22d May, 1807.

Court of the United States for the fifth circuit and district of Virginia.

PRESENT—JOHN MARSHALL, chief justice of the United States; and CYRUS GRIFFIN, judge of the district of Virginia.

The court was opened at half past twelve o'clock; when colonel Aaron Burr appeared, with his counsel, Messrs. Edmund Randolph, John Wickham, Benjamin Botts, and John Baker.

Counsel for the prosecution; Messrs. George Hay, district attorney, William Wirt, and Alexander Mac Rae.

The clerk having called the names of the gentlemen who had been summoned on the grand jury, Mr. Burr's counsel demanded a sight of the panel; which was shown to them: when Mr. Burr addressed the court to the following effect:

May it please the court,

BEFORE any further proceeding with regard to swearing the jury, I beg leave to remark some irregularity that has taken place in summoning part of the panel. This is the proper time to make the exception. I understand that the marshal acts not under an act of congress, but a law of the state of Virginia, by which he is required to summon twenty-four freeholders of the state to compose the grand jury. When he has summoned that number, his function is completed. He cannot on any account summon a twenty-fifth. If, therefore, it can be made to appear, that the marshal has struck off any part of the original panel, and substituted other persons in their stead, the summons is illegal. Such is the law and the dictate of true policy; for in important cases, like the present, a different course would produce the most injurious consequences. I consider it proper to ask the marshal and his deputies, what persons they have summoned, and at what periods: whence it may be known, whether some have not been substituted in place of others struck off the panel. When we have settled this objection, I shall proceed to exceptions of a different nature.

Mr. Botts observed, that it was the 29th section of the judicial act, which refers to the state law, besides a distinct act, which enumerates other duties; that neither of these laws specified any particular mode by which marshals were to summon juries in different districts. By the first section of the Virginia act, the sheriff is to summon twenty-four freeholders, any sixteen of whom appearing are to constitute a grand jury. The first section does not state that he is to make a return, but a distinct section inflicts a penalty, if he violate the duties prescribed by the first section; that is, if he fail " to summon a grand jury, and return a panel of their names." Colonel Burr is anxious to have nothing more than a fair trial. The reports circulated, and prejudices excited against him, justify a strict attention to his rights. He therefore asks the strictest scrutiny into past and subsequent measures. An important interest is involved in the authority of the grand jury. And if there be any irregularity in the marshal's summons, it ought now to be rectified. By the act of Virginia, a sheriff, and by the act of congress a marshal, are mere ministerial officers bound to discharge certain duties. He is to summon twenty-four jurors. When that act is done, it is irrevocable, and his duty at an end. This court only possesses the authority to excuse any of those who have been summoned, and to direct the marshal to substitute others, till the necessary quorum be completed.

Mr. Botts further observed, that he had no intention of casting the slightest imputation on the marshal for his conduct in this transaction; that his honourable character placed him above suspicion, and the fault, if any, must have arisen from official misconceptions; that he did not propose to interrogate major Scott in any manner that might possibly criminate him; but that the court had a right to inquire, and, if any error was committed, to correct it. That if he was overruled in this motion, he would then crave leave of the court to produce testimony as to the facts: that he took it for granted, that if a single moment intervened between the summoning of a juror and the meeting of a court, the court alone had the power to discharge him; that with regard to the present panel it would appear, that the marshal, after summoning one individual, had notified another to attend; in other words, he had summoned him according to the legal definition of the term " summons." That this was not the duty of the marshal; that when the original panel was complete, his duty was at an end, and he must return that very panel precisely, without any addition. What mischiefs might not result from a different practice, particularly in cases of extreme importance, where the government was concerned, since the marshal himself depended on the government for the duration of his commission?

Mr. Botts therefore contended, that the ministerial duties of a marshal ceased with the summons which he gave; and that, if the jurors did not appear, it was the privilege of the court to supply any deficiency. He cited the decision of the supreme court of the United States in the case of Marbury v. Madison, to show, that when the ministerial duties of an officer were discharged, his power necessarily ceased, and his act was irrevocable. This doctrine was of universal application in law, both in America and England. It was applicable to a sheriff, after he had served a common writ of *fieri facias*. If he summon a petit juryman, who fails to appear before the court, it is the right of the court alone to fine or to excuse him. Mr. Botts then concluded, that he would ask the marshal, who were the twenty-four whom he had first summoned; for that may constitute the grand jury. Every one beyond that number was illegally summoned. It was the right of colonel Burr to demand such a purgation of the panel.

Mr. HAY, the district attorney, observed, that he was not prepared to make any observations upon this question, as it was a point which he had never before had any occasion to consider; that the proposition was, however, of no great importance, since, if any of them were set aside, there would still be a sufficient number to constitute a grand jury; or the deficiency might be supplied by a new summons among the bystanders. If there were, in reality, any objection to the regularity of the summons, he was willing to accommodate the opposite counsel; that he was not certain how far it was strictly proper to interrogate, or examine into the time of summoning the different members of the panel, as he had not been very conversant with business of this kind. He was, however, content that the court should decide; and if it should be their opinion that the marshal should be interrogated, how many jurymen he had summoned, and when he had discharged them, he should feel perfectly satisfied.

Mr. WICKHAM.—Before we go into this inquiry, we declare, that we mean no personal imputation upon the respectable gentleman who is the marshal. His intentions were certainly pure. It is an error of judgment alone to which we object. But in the present case, where such important interests are at stake, and where such unjustifiable means have been used to prejudice the public mind against colonel Burr, it is his right to take every advantage which the law gives him. We are prepared to show, that when a person is bound in a recognisance, he has a right, at this period of the business, to come before the court with his exceptions to the grand jury; and if in any other case, why not in one of such deep importance as the present? In support of this position, Mr. Wickham cited 2 Hawkins's Pleas of the Crown, page 307, sect. 16, and 3 Bacon's Abridgment, page 725. Whether we might afterwards file a plea in abatement for the error committed, is not now to be discussed. It is colonel Burr's anxious desire, that this whole affair should terminate here, and that this grand jury may determine his case.

The chief justice called for the law of Virginia.

Mr. HAY read it.—Revised Code, page 100, sect. 2.—The construction put upon this part of the law seems to me far more rigid than sound sense warrants. By this law, the marshal is empowered to select twenty-four freeholders, legally qualified to serve on the grand jury. The officer, in many cases necessarily ignorant of the situation of an individual, summons him to attend. The person informs him, that, from some personal misfortune, some domestic calamity, or some indispensable business, it is impossible for him to attend. We ask, whether the accurate construction of this law forbids him to summon another in his place? Where is the legal authority to prove, that when he has once summoned twenty-four jurymen, his ministerial function is at an end? The moment it appears in court, that the legal number of jurors is not present, he is to fill up his panel from the bystanders. We appeal to the candour of the opposite counsel, to point out the real distinction between the two cases. Why should the marshal have the right to fill up his panel, when it is once ascertained before the court, that some of the jurymen have not actually attended, and yet deny him the right of substituting others in the place of those he has summoned, but who, he is satisfied, before the meeting of the court, cannot attend? Instead of a difference, the two cases are strikingly parallel. What the fact was, Mr. Hay said he knew not, but he believed that some of those who were said to be substituted had not been positively summoned by the marshal, but had been merely applied to, to know whether they could attend.

Mr. WICKHAM contended, that the counsel for the United States had not fairly met the question. There is a doubt whether colonel Burr has not a right to come forward with his exceptions *now* to the grand jury. As the authorities on this subject are short, he would take the liberty of reading them to the court. (He read those he before cited.) From these authorities it manifestly appears, that a person bound in a recognisance, had a right, before the grand jury were sworn, to state his exceptions to the mode of impaneling them. It is for this reason that colonel Burr has, in this stage of the business, come forward with his objections. Mr. Hay contends, that our construction of the law is more rigid than sound policy demands. But when the words of the law are obvious, why should we resort to a dubious construction? " *Ita lex scripta est.*" But if we are to wander into the wide field of policy, how completely would it bear against the gentleman's cause! God forbid, sir, that I should utter the slightest imputation upon the character and official conduct of major Scott; they soar above suspicion. But if once the marshal, who holds his commission at the will of the government, were permitted to alter the panel as he pleased, the life of every citizen in this state would be held at his pleasure. It is therefore essentially important, that the ministerial officer should rigidly pursue the statute from which he derives his authority. And what is his duty in the present instance? He is to summon twenty-four freeholders to serve on the grand jury, any sixteen of whom may constitute a quorum. Mr. Hay had declared, that this provision was mere matter of form; for if there be not a sufficient number present to constitute a quorum, the marshal may make up to the full number twenty-four. But that is not the fact. If sixteen jurymen attend, the marshal cannot add one more. Let us then apply a suppositious case. The marshal, if notified that one of the jury whom he has summoned cannot attend, is authorised, according to Mr. Hay's doctrine, to summon a substitute. It is no impediment to the exercise of this authority, that there be the legal quorum of sixteen remaining upon the panel; he may proceed to summon substitutes till he completes the whole number twenty-four. And yet, if the case were to happen in court, the marshal would certainly have no authority to complete the whole number. Why then suppose such a difference of authority in and out of court? Why not rather suppose, that the marshal has no authority to do *that* out of court, which he cannot do before the court. Let us suppose another case. A grand juror has been summoned for several weeks before the meeting of the court. The bare authority of the marshal is sufficient, according to this doctrine, to excuse him from serving, and to substitute another in his

place, only one hour before the meeting of the court. Mr.
Wickham declared he could mention the case of a man who
had been excused from this very panel.

Major Scott (the marshal.)—Name him, sir: I demand his
name.

Mr. Wickham declared, that he meant no imputation upon
major Scott, but he would not submit to such interruptions.
If no sufficient excuse is given by the absent juror, he is subject to a fine. Is it then contended, that the marshal is to
judge in the place of the court? not only to relieve the person
of the juror, but his property also from the fine? The words
of this law are too plain to be mistaken. It admits of no latitude of construction. But if the marshal has really transcended his authority, yet I do not hesitate to declare my opinion,
that he intended to discharge his duty with fidelity. It was
only an error in judgment, to which all men, however well
versed in the law, are liable.

Mr. Hay.—Will the court indulge me with a single additional remark? I stated before, that when the marshal found,
that one of the jury whom he had before summoned could not
attend, he was authorised to summon a substitute. Mr. Wickham, however, contends, that the marshal cannot summon
others, after sixteen have appeared. But for what reason? Because there is, in reality, no occasion for it. The object of the
law is already attained. The grand jury is complete, and it is
unnecessary to take up further time, when the grand jury is
legally full. But before the court convenes, how is it possible
for the marshal to know how many of those summoned will
attend? According to the doctrine of the opposite counsel,
there may be no grand jury.

The chief justice inquired, whether the question had ever
come before the state courts?

Mr. Randolph.—Not, sir, to my knowledge. In nearly
thirty years practice, (and a considerable part of that time I
was attorney general for the commonwealth) no occasion has
occurred for such an objection. I have never seen a case
where it was so absolutely necessary to assert every privilege
belonging to the accused, as in this. But as to the *right* itself,
abstractedly considered, I have never hesitated a moment
about its existence. It is written in broad intelligible characters.
Sir, if we ever submit to these relaxations of the rights of the
accused, a time may possibly come, when we may lament the
precedent we have established; when men less virtuous than the
present respectable marshal, shall succeed to his functions. But
the question in the present case is, not what has been the prac-

tice in the state courts, but what is the right? If this right has never been before asserted, it is because there never was an occasion which so imperiously demanded it as the present; because there never was such a torrent of prejudice excited against any man, before a court of justice, as against colonel Burr, and by means which we shall presently unfold.

CHIEF JUSTICE.—As this question has never been decided before the state courts, we must refer to the words of the act of assembly. There can be no doubt that this is the time when the accused has a right to take exceptions to the jury; and the only doubt can be, is this a proper exception? The marshal is authorised by law to summon twenty-four jurymen; but he is not to summon a twenty-fifth. Of course, the twenty-fifth is not legally summoned, unless he has the power to discharge a person already summoned. He has no such power, unless the jury be composed of bystanders. The twenty-four first summoned must compose the jury, sixteen of whom constitute a quorum. It follows, therefore, that no one can be on the grand jury, unless he be one of the twenty-four first summoned, or one who has been selected from the bystanders by the direction of the court. When the panel has been once completed by the marshal, its deficiencies can be supplied only from the bystanders.

The chief justice further observed, that he was not well acquainted with the practice in the state courts; but he believed the practice of sheriffs to be, to excuse a man summoned on the jury, if they are satisfied that his excuse is reasonable. So it may have been with the officer of this court, who acted, he had no doubt, with the most scrupulous regard to what he believed to be the law. That the court, however, thought the marshal had no such dispensing power. One very obvious reason against the marshal's possessing this power of substitution, is, that if a person summoned should come into court, and prove that he had been actually summoned, he certainly would be on the grand jury, if one of the twenty-four first summoned. The general principle is, that when a person is put in the panel he stands upon it, and cannot be displaced by the marshal. There is an evident distinction between actually summoning a grand juryman, and merely talking to a person about summoning him. The court is therefore of opinion, that a person substituted in the place of one actually summoned, cannot be considered as being on the panel.

Mr. BURR.—The court having established the principle, we must ask their aid to come at the facts. We wish to know, when certain persons were summoned, when discharged, and whether other persons were substituted in their stead.

The marshal said, that he had not the least objection to state all the facts necessary to be known on this occasion. A few days ago he had received a letter from colonel John Taylor, of Caroline, one of those whom he had summoned on the jury, in which he states, that a hurricane of wind had destroyed his carriage-house, and with it his carriages, so that he could not use them; and that his indisposition prevented his riding to Richmond on horseback. This letter he had laid before both their honours, and the chief justice had deemed his excuse reasonable. He had then summoned Mr. Barbour to serve in colonel Taylor's place. He had also received a letter from Mr. John Macrae, informing that he was going to leave the state for his health. He had in consequence summoned doctor Foushee in his place. The marshal added, that he felt it to be his duty to bring twenty-four jurymen into court, and acted upon this principle.

The court decided, that Mr. Barbour and Dr. Foushee, the substituted persons, were not on the grand jury.

Mr. BURR.—I understand that the panel is now reduced to sixteen, and that this is the proper time to make any other exceptions to the panel. It is with regret, that I shall now proceed to exercise the privilege of challenging for favour. In exercising this right, I shall perhaps appeal to the authority of the court to try these jurors. Lest it may be contested, it is better to settle the principle first.

Mr. HAY, without directly contesting, called for the law to justify the application.

Mr. BURR.—Let it be distinctly understood, that I claim the same right of challenging " for *favour*" the grand jury, that I have of challenging the petit jury. I admit, that it is not a peremptory challenge, but that I must show good cause to support the challenge. It will be of course necessary to appoint triers to decide, and before whom the party and the witnesses to prove or disprove the favour, must appear.

Mr. BOTTS.—There can be no question, that a person standing in the situation of colonel Burr, may challenge the jury for favour. In civil cases, any individual may challenge a jury for favour or partiality to his antagonist; a fortiori, it must exist in criminal cases. Mr. Botts here cited authority in support of his principle, and admitted, that the cause of challenge must be proved by testimony; that it was necessary to prevent such impurity from creeping into the commencement of this trial, as must contaminate all its subsequent stages; that no reflection against the integrity of the present jurors was intended; but in principles of plain common sense it was proper to remove every cause that might defeat the purposes of justice.

Mr. HAY disavowed the intention of opposing substantial

exceptions, and admitted the law to be as stated by the opposite counsel.

Mr. BURR.—I shall, then, proceed to name the persons and causes of challenge. The first I shall mention is William B. Giles, against whom there are two causes of challenge. The first is a matter of some notoriety, because dependent on certain documents or records: the second is a matter of fact, which must be substantiated by witnesses. As to the first, Mr. Giles, when in the senate of the United States, had occasion to pronounce his opinion on certain documents by which I was considered to be particularly implicated. Upon those documents he advocated the propriety of suspending the writ of habeas corpus. The constitution however forbids such suspension, except in cases of invasion or insurrection, when the public safety requires it. It was therefore to be inferred, that Mr. Giles did suppose, that there was a rebellion or insurrection, and a public danger, of no common kind. It is hardly necessary to observe, that with this rebellion, and this supposed danger, I myself had been supposed to be connected. Perhaps this may be a sufficient reason to set aside Mr. Giles. But if not, I shall endeavour to establish by evidence, that he has confirmed these opinions by public declarations; that he has declared that these documents, involving me, contained guilt of the highest grade.

Mr. BOTTS.—There is no necessity of adding any thing to the observations of colonel Burr. If the right of challenge exists, the right to try the challenge exists also. But while I am up, I will declare, that no reflection is intended to be made on the character or conduct of Mr. Giles. That gentleman will be candid enough to admit, that there is not the least design to wound his feelings. It is with the utmost reluctance that colonel Burr has prevailed upon himself to advance this exception. I have authorities, however, to prove, that these two causes are sufficient to disqualify Mr. Giles. The first relates to his public, the second to his individual conduct.

Mr. HAY.—How many of the panel does the counsel mean to object to?

Mr. BOTTS.—Only two.

Mr. GILES.—As to exceptions to myself personally, I can have no objection to have them tried. The court will, however, perceive the delicate situation in which I shall be placed. The triers will have to interrogate witnesses, and the result either way is ineligible. I have no objection to state to the court every impression I have ever had upon this subject. But to culling witnesses to detail loose conversations, so liable to be misunderstood, forgotten, or misrepresented, I am certainly opposed.

Mr. HAY.—I was about to make a proposition which might relieve us from all this useless embarrassment, and which might gratify the views of the accused. If the gentlemen who are challenged on the jury will consent to withdraw themselves, I can have no objection. I am content that every one who has made declarations expressive of decisive opinion, should be withdrawn from the jury. I am not disposed to spend time on such points as these.

Mr. BURR.—It will certainly save time, and I assent to the proposition.

Mr. GILES.—The circumstances which have just occurred place me in an unpleasant situation. I have no objection to disclose, in the usual way, with candour, the real state of my mind in relation to the accused. But I have an objection to the introduction of witnesses to prove casual expressions, which are so liable to be misconceived. In the *present* state of things, expressions might be imputed to me which I never used, or expressions which I really used might be mistaken or misrepresented by the witness; or the witness might deduce inferences from my expressions which they did not justify. It was by no means agreeable to me to have been summoned on this grand jury. But for some time past I have invariably pursued this maxim : " *neither to avoid nor to solicit any public appointment; but when called to the discharge of any public duty by the proper authority, conscientiously to attempt its execution.*" In undertaking to serve on the present grand jury, I was influenced by the same consideration. With respect to my public conduct, I presume it is of public notoriety, and will speak for itself. I not only voted for the suspension of the privilege of the writ of *habeas corpus*, in certain cases, but *I* proposed that measure. I then thought, and I still think, that the emergency demanded it ; that it was fully justified by the evidence before the senate ; and I now regret that the nation had not energy enough to support the senate in that measure. This opinion was formed upon the state of the evidence before the senate, which, in all questions of a general nature, is of a very different character from the legal evidence necessary in a judicial investigation. My mind is, however, free to receive impressions from judicial evidence. In relation to the accused, I feel very desirous, and have often so expressed myself, that the various transactions imputed to him should undergo a full and fair judicial investigation ; and that, through that *medium*, they should receive their just and true *character*, whatever in point of fact it might be, and that he should be presented in that character to the world. I have no personal resentments against the accused ; and if he has received any information inconsistent with this statement, it is not true. However, as it is left to me to elect, whether to serve on the grand jury or not, I will certainly withdraw.

CHIEF-JUSTICE.—The court thinks, that if any gentleman has made up and declared his mind, it would be best for him to withdraw.

Mr. BURR.—A gentleman who has prejudged this cause, is certainly unfit to be a juryman. It would be an effort above human nature for this gentleman to divest himself of all prepossessions. I believe his mind to be as pure and unbiassed as that of any gentleman under such circumstances. But the decisive opinion he has formed upon this subject, though in his public character, disqualifies him for a juryman. But he is one of the last men on whom I would wish to cast any reflections. So far from having any animosity against him, he would have been one of those whom I should have ranked among my personal friends.

The other gentleman whom I shall challenge is Wilson Cary Nicholas.

Mr. Nicholas desired that the objections against him should be stated.

Mr. BURR.—The objection is, that he has entertained a bitter personal animosity against me ; and therefore I cannot expect from him that pure impartiality of mind which is necessary to a correct decision. I feel the delicacy of my situation ; but if the gentleman will consent to withdraw, I will waive any further inquiry.

Colonel WILSON C. NICHOLAS rose, and addressed the court as follows :

My being in this situation certainly was not a thing of choice. When I was summoned by the marshal, I urged him in the strongest manner to excuse me. I mentioned to him, that it would be extremely inconvenient to me to attend the court, and that it would be very unpleasant to serve on the jury, on account of the various relations in which I had stood to colonel Burr. I had been in congress at the time when the attempt was made to elect colonel Burr president of the United States. My feelings and opinions on that occasion are well known. I had served three years in the senate while colonel Burr was president of that body, and was one of those who, previous to the last election, had taken a very decided part in favour of the nomination of the present vice president, for the office at that time filled by colonel Burr. Moreover, from the time that colonel Burr first went to the western country, my suspicions were very much excited as to his probable objects, in that part of the United States; in consequence of which I gave early and perhaps too great credit to the charges which were brought against him. Such was my opinion of the importance of New-Orleans, not only to the prosperity, but to the union of the states, that I felt uncommon anxiety at what I believed to be the state of our affairs in the west, and had expressed my impressions very freely in conversation, and in letters to my friends during the last winter. Under these circumstances, I doubted the propriety of my being put on the jury; *but I felt no distrust of myself*, as I was confident that I could discharge the duty under a just impression of what I owe to my country, to the accused, and to my own character. The marshal assured me, that he felt the strongest disposition to oblige me, but that he thought he could not do it, consistently with his duty. He supposed there was scarcely a man to be found, who had not formed and expressed opinions about colonel Burr. That he too was in a situation of great delicacy and responsibility, and that, without the utmost circumspection on his part, he would be exposed to censure. I renewed my application to the marshal several times, and always received the same answer. Thus situated, I determined to attend the court, both from a sense of duty, and because I would not put it in the power of the malicious, and those disposed to slander me, to assign motives for absenting myself, which had no kind of influence on me. Another reason for pursuing this course presented itself some time after I had formed this determination. I conceived that an attempt had been made to deter me from attending this court. I was informed by a friend in the city, that he had heard, that one of the most severe pieces which had ever been seen, was preparing for publication, if I did attend, and serve on the grand jury. From what quarter this attack was to come, I do not know. The only influence which that circumstance had, was to confirm me in the determination I had made; as I was much more inclined to defy my enemies, than to ask their mercy or forbearance. From the first I hesitated, whether I ought not to make the same representation to the court, that I had made to the marshal. As I was in doubt on the subject before I came from home, I committed to paper the substance of what I have now said, and consulted three gentlemen who were lawyers, men of honour, and my personal friends. Their advice to me was not to mention it, for they did not believe that the court would or ought to discharge me for the reasons I had mentioned. As I was in doubt myself, I determined to follow their advice, and the more readily as they seemed confident that I would not be discharged, and I was not scrupulous of acquiring, in this way, a reputation for scrupulous delicacy. I was perfectly willing, that my reputation should rest on the general tenor of my life, and did not believe that my character required such a prop. At present I feel myself embarrassed how to act. I certainly was, and am, anxious not to serve on the jury, but am unwilling to

withdraw, lest it should be thought that I shrink from the discharge of public duty of great responsibility, and I am not willing to be driven from the discharge of that duty in a way which
should lead to a belief, that the objection to me is either acknowledged to be well founded, or has been sustained by the court.
Upon this subject, the example of Mr. Giles has great weight
with me. That consideration, and a hope that my motives cannot now be misunderstood or misrepresented, will induce me to
do as he has done.

Colonel Burr.—The circumstance mentioned by the gentleman, that an attempt has been made to intimidate him, must
have been a contrivance of some of my enemies, for the purpose
of irritating him, and increasing the public prejudice against
me ; since it was calculated to throw a suspicion on my cause.
Such an act was never sanctioned by me, nor by any of my
friends. I view it with indignation, and disclaim any knowledge
of the fact in question.

The court established the following, as being the proper questions to be put to the jurors : First, Have you made up your
mind on the case, or on the guilt or innocence of colonel Burr,
from the statements you have seen in the papers or otherwise ?
and finally, Have you formed and expressed (or delivered) an
opinion on the guilt or innocence of colonel Burr (or the accused ?)

Major Joseph Eggleston now addressed the court to this
effect:

I understood the court to say, that this was the proper time to
apply to be excused from serving on the grand jury. Having
been summoned by the marshal to serve as a grand juror, I
wrote a letter to that officer, desiring him to excuse me ; but he
refused. In addition to some private reasons, there is one of a
public nature, which I hope will exempt me from being retained
on the jury. As soon as I read the deposition of general Eaton
in the newspapers, I felt and expressed considerable warmth and
indignation on the subject likely to come before the grand jury;
and on that account it might be both indelicate and improper in
me to serve on the grand jury, however correct the decision of
that body might be.

The chief justice having asked whether he had formed and
expressed an opinion on this subject, major Eggleston repeated
what he had said as to his warmth after reading general Eaton's
deposition, and said, that he had expressed his opinion in public
company ; yet he declared his belief, that he could so far divest
himself of his previous opinions and feelings, as to be able to
decide according to the testimony and the law. It had been

said, that a bias might imperceptibly remain upon the minds of men of the purest intentions, and as it might possibly be the case with him, he again desired to be excused.

Mr. Burr.—Under different circumstances, I might think and act differently; but the industry which has been used through this country to prejudice my cause, leaves me very little chance, indeed, of an impartial jury. There is very little chance that I can expect a better man to try my cause. His desire to be excused, and his opinion that his mind is not entirely free upon the case, are good reasons why he should be excused; but the candour of the gentleman, in excepting to himself, leaves me ground to hope, that he will endeavour to be impartial. I pray the court to notice, from the scene before us, how many attempts have been made to prejudge my cause. On this occasion I am perfectly passive.

Chief-Justice.—What are your impressions now? Have you formed a decisive opinion on this case?

Mr. Eggleston.—I have formed some opinion on the statement and evidence I have seen; and if no other evidence were to be produced, I should probably retain it. I am willing to hear other testimony, but I wish to be excused.

The court did not excuse him.

The panel was here called over, and fourteen only appeared: upon which the marshal requested the clerk to add thereto the names of John Randolph and William Foushee. The court then instructed the clerk to place Mr. Randolph as foreman, who being called on to take the foreman's oath, addressed the court thus:

May it please the court,

I wish to be excused from serving. I will state the reasons of that wish. I have formed an opinion, not on the case now before the court, because I know not what that case is; but concerning the nature and tendency of certain transactions imputed to the gentleman now before you. I do trust, that without arrogating to myself any thing more than becomes a man, I would divest myself of this prepossession upon evidence. But I should be wanting in candour to the court and the party accused, if I did not say, that I had a strong prepossession.

Mr. Burr.—Really I am afraid, that we shall not be able to find any man without this prepossession.

Chief Justice.—The rule is, that a man must not only have formed, but declared an opinion, in order to exclude him from serving on the jury.

Mr. Randolph.—I do not recollect to have declared one.

Upon which Mr. Randolph was sworn as foreman, and the rest of the panel called to the book, until it was Dr. Foushee's turn. He stated to the court, that he felt some difficulty about the propriety of serving on the jury; that, after hearing the number of excuses which were made and overruled by the court, he was unwilling to bring himself before the court, to claim an exemption from serving. But having the same feelings with other gentlemen, he must move the court to excuse him.

After a few desultory remarks by Mr. Burr and Mr. Wickham, doctor Foushee stated, that after having read the president's message, general Eaton's deposition, and the publications in the newspapers respecting colonel Burr, and having heard little but from those publications, he had formed an opinion of colonel Burr's guilt; and unless other testimony were adduced, his impression would probably be retained. That his present opinion might, however, be said to be merely hypothetical, and predicated on the supposition of the truth of general Eaton's testimony, and those other publications: but that he would as easily divest his mind of prejudice as any other man; and that, on the exhibition of other testimony, he might change his opinion.

Mr. WICKHAM and Mr. RANDOLPH delivered their opinions as to the impropriety of the doctor serving as a grand juror. And

Mr. HAY insisted, that he was a proper juror; that there was not a man in the United States, who probably had not formed an opinion on the subject: and if such objections as these were to prevail, Mr. Burr might as well be acquitted at once.

Mr. BURR.—This gentleman has said, that from the evidence he has already seen, he has made up his mind; but that, on hearing other testimony, he may change it. But as a grand juror, he will only hear testimony on one side. The evidence which will be laid before the grand jury, will be altogether on the part of the United States, and ex parte; and no testimony to remove the impressions, which he has already imbibed, will be offered. There will be an accumulation of evidence on the same side to increase the bias already on his mind, and nothing on the other to counteract it. I hope therefore the court will suffer him to withdraw.

Dr. FOUSHEE.—I have stated what other gentlemen have done: that if the testimony I have seen be true, and nothing brought to counteract it, my impression will of course remain unchanged. I ask, if others are not excused, why this discrimination against me? However indisposed I may be to serve, I shall not withdraw but by the direction of the court.

After some observations by Messrs Wickham, Randolph and Hay, the chief justice observed, that the difference seemed to be, that Dr. Foushee had made up an opinion both as to law and fact; whereas other gentlemen had formed an opinion only as to certain facts. Consequently Dr. Foushee was permitted to withdraw.

Colonel JAMES BARBOUR being next called, excepted to himself on a principle in some degree similar to that on which Dr. Foushee claimed to be excused: that of being impressed with sentiments unfavourable to colonel Burr. But his excuse was deemed insufficient by the court.

The grand jury were then sworn, and were as follows:

John Randolph, junior, foreman.

Joseph Eggleston,	John Mercer,
Joseph C. Cabell,	Edward Pegram,
Littleton W. Tazewell,	Munford Beverly,
Robert Taylor,	John Ambler,
James Pleasants,	Thomas Harrison,
John Brockenbrough,	Alexander Shephard,
William Daniel,	and
James M. Garnett,	James Barbour.

The CHIEF JUSTICE then delivered an appropriate charge to the grand jury, in which he particularly dwelt upon the definition and nature of treason, and the testimony requisite to prove it. After which they retired.

Colonel BURR then addressed the court, and stated his wish, that the court should instruct the grand jury on certain leading points, as to the admissibility of certain evidence which he supposed would be laid before the grand jury by the attorney for the United States.

Mr. HAY hoped, that the court would proceed as they had always done before, and that they would not grant particular indulgences to colonel Burr, who stood on the same footing with every other man charged with a crime. That they had already charged the jury on certain material principles, and he trusted that the court would not depart from established rules, or adopt a new precedent, to oblige the accused.

Mr. BURR.—Would to God that I did stand on the same ground with every other man. This is the first time I have ever been permitted to enjoy the rights of a citizen. How have I been brought hither?

The CHIEF JUSTICE said it was improper to go into these digressions.

Mr. BURR said, that the attorney for the United States had mistaken his meaning, if he supposed that he wished to be considered as standing there on a different footing from other citizens; that he viewed himself as only entitled to the same privileges and rights which belonged to every other citizen; that how much soever he may have disapproved of certain principles laid down by the supreme court in their late decisions, he should not at present insist on his objections to them; that there were many points on which the best informed jurymen might be ignorant, or entertain doubts. All he wished the court to do now was, to instruct the jury on certain points relating to the testimony; for instance, as to the article of papers.

Mr. HAY pledged himself that no attempt should be made to send up any testimony to the jury without the knowledge of the court.

Mr. RANDOLPH observed, that it was not on particular parts, but on certain principles of testimony, that he wished instructions from the court to the jury: for instance, to instruct them how many witnesses were necessary to satisfy them that an overt act was committed; how far facts committed in different districts, should be suffered to bear upon a single act committed in one district; how far facts done in one district, ought to be admitted as evidence to confirm the commission of other facts in another district; and what in short was proper evidence to be laid before them.

Mr. HAY objected to this proceeding as extraordinary; that the opposite counsel would require from the court a dissertation on the whole criminal law, upon every point which might possibly occur; that the jury were the proper judges, and if they had doubts let them apply to the court for instructions.

Mr. WICKHAM observed, that this was not an ordinary case as had been said; that the man who thought so must have shut his eyes against the host of prejudices raised against his client; that the attorney for the United States had said, that there was no man who had not formed an opinion on it; that he did not require a dissertation on criminal law in general, but merely that the court would instruct the jury on certain points of law and evidence; that the necessity of instructing arose from the peculiarity of this case; that there might be witnesses from different parts of the United States, who would state facts not connected with colonel Burr; that there were witnesses to show what was done in the western country when he was hundreds of miles distant; that the jury ought to know from the court how much of this vast mass of testimony ought to have a legal application.

Mr. HAY inforced his former objection, that if the law was to be laid down by the court, they would certainly wish to have it explained by both sides; that the gentlemen on the other side wished the court to decide without argument, on matters the most important; that as the jury were very intelligent, and the court had already given a general definition of principles, the correct course was to proceed in the usual way, without wasting time in unnecessary argument.

Mr. BOTTS said, that in a case of such unexampled importance, which was sufficiently attested by the busy crowd around them, the noise in the country, the curiosity of the people, and the activity of the government, no reasonable objection could be made to even wasting a few minutes; that it was a case where the prisoner required, and ought to receive, the benefit of every legal right which the court could furnish.

CHIEF JUSTICE observed, that there would certainly be a difficulty in the court's giving dissertations on criminal or penal laws; that he was not prepared at present to say, whether the same evidence was necessary before the grand jury as before the petit jury; whether two witnesses to an overt act were required to satisfy a grand jury: this was a point which he would have to consider. That he had not made up his mind on the evidence of facts said to be done in different districts, how far the one could be adduced as evidence in proof or confirmation of the other; but his present impression was, that facts done *without* the district, may be brought in to prove the material fact said to be done *within* the district, when that fact was charged.

The question was postponed for further discussion, on Mr. Hay pledging himself, that no evidence should be laid before the grand jury, without notice being first given to colonel Burr and his counsel.

Several witnesses on behalf of the United States were called and recognised to appear to-morrow, at eleven o'clock A. M.

The court adjourned till then.

SATURDAY, 23d May, 1807.

Present the same Judges as on yesterday.

The proceedings of yesterday being read, and the names of the jury called over, several witnesses on the part of the United States appeared and were recognised to attend on the court.

The counsel for colonel Burr observed, that if it met the approbation of the court, the discussion on the propriety of giving special instructions to the grand jury would take place on Monday next.

This proposition was assented to, and it was understood that Mr. Burr's counsel were to give due notice of the propositions they intended to submit.

The grand jury appearing pursuant to adjournment, the chief justice informed them, that the absence of general Wilkinson, a witness deemed important by the counsel for the United States, and the uncertainty of his arrival at any particular period, made it necessary that they should be adjourned.

Some conversation ensued between the court and bar, with respect to the propriety of adjourning the grand jury to some future day in the term.

The CHIEF JUSTICE stated it as his opinion, that as there was no necessity for calling over the names of the grand jury every day, they might be considered in contemplation of law, still in their chambers till they were called into court, and it might be understood that they would not be called till some particular day. This he said was the practice in some of the states, nor did he know any sound objection to it: but unless it was considered by counsel on both sides, that this course was free from *all exception*, he should be unwilling on any account to adopt it.

The counsel for colonel Burr stated that they knew no objection to the measure, but were unwilling to express any decided opinion, especially as colonel Burr was not then in court.

The chief justice said, that he felt much inclined to accommodate the grand jury; but until further consideration of the subject, they would stand adjourned till Monday following.

The court adjourned till then accordingly.

MONDAY, 25th May, 1807.

The court met according to adjournment: present the same judges as on Saturday.

The grand jury appeared in court, and on its being stated by their foreman, that they had been two days confined to their chambers, and had no presentment to make or bill before them, Mr. Hay observed, that he had two bills prepared, but wished to postpone the delivery of them till the witnesses were present, and it was ascertained that all the evidence relied on by the counsel for the prosecution could be had. He thought it probable, that in the course of a week, he should hear of general

Wilkinson, who was still absent, and whose testimony was deemed very important.

A further conversation took place, as to the propriety of adjourning the grand jury to a distant day of the term, and Monday next was mentioned, as the time when they would probably be required to attend.

The CHIEF JUSTICE observed, that from the researches which he had been able to make, he was still inclined to favour the opinion which he had expressed on Saturday, that there was no necessity for *calling* the grand jury *every day*. This opinion was the result of his reflection upon principle, not formed from any positive authority on the subject.

Mr. WICKHAM having stated, that as a number of witnesses were attending at a considerable distance, on the part of colonel Burr, it might be important to know when the grand jury would be again called.

Mr. HAY observed, that a motion might be made, which would render their presence necessary, even on that day.

Mr. WICKHAM then requested, that before any order should be taken in relation to the adjournment of the grand jury, the counsel for the United States might state the nature and object of his motion.

Mr. HAY.—The object of my motion is to commit Mr. Burr on a charge of high treason against the United States. On his examination there was no evidence of an overt act, and he was committed for a misdemeanor only. The evidence is different now.

Mr. WICKHAM hoped, that the application might be made and counsel heard.

Mr. HAY.—Gentlemen may be assured that they will be apprised of the application; but is it their wish that it should be made, and the subject discussed in presence of the grand jury?

Colonel BURR.—The gentleman has mistaken the object of my counsel as far as it is comprehended in my motion. The design was not that the grand jury might hear, but that the impropriety of mentioning the subject in the presence of the grand jury, might be made more manifest. I think it may be demonstrated, that while there is a grand jury attending, before whom a question may be determined, there is an obvious impropriety in submitting it to any other tribunal for any other purpose.

The grand jury were requested to withdraw.

Mr. HAY renewed his application, stating more at large the grounds on which it was made; and moved the court to commit Mr. Burr on a charge of high treason against the United States, on the evidence formerly introduced, and on additional testimony to be now brought forward.

Mr. WICKHAM inquired what sort of evidence was intended to be introduced: whether that of witnesses to be examined *viva voce*, or affidavits in writing? Mr. Hay answered, that where the witnesses were present he intended to examine them *viva voce;* but where they were absent to make use of their affidavits regularly taken and certified.

Mr. BOTTS.—We may have cause of much regret, that the attorney of the United States, has not given us some previous notice of this application. From the engagements between the prosecuting and defending counsel, to interchange information of the points intended to be discussed, we had a right to expect, that upon a subject like this, involving questions new and important, we should not have been taken by surprize. Indeed, from the common courtesy and candour of the attorney of the United States, we might have reasonably calculated on a previous communication. This interchange of civility and information, usual even in cases of inferior importance, was more necessary in this case, because the application is as unfortified by precedent as it is unexpected; and because it involves questions of deep consideration and weighty importance.

Mr. HAY interrupted Mr. Botts.—Since the gentleman complains of being taken by surprize, I am willing to postpone the motion till to-morrow.

Mr. BOTTS.—Not a moment's postponement. Although we sustain considerable inconvenience by being thus suddenly and unexpectedly called upon without reflection, or authorities, yet we should experience greater by a day's delay. I shall therefore beg leave to make a few remarks on this extraordinary application, and the pernicious effects such an extraordinary measure, if generally practised, would inevitably produce. The organ particularly appropriated for the consideration of the evidence which this motion calls for, is the grand jury; and the motion is to divest the grand jury of the office, which the constitution and laws have appropriated to them, and to devolve it upon the court. The grand juror's oath is to inquire into all crimes and misdemeanors committed within the district of the state of which they are freeholders. Their office is to perform that which the court is now called upon to perform. To them belongs the exclusive duty of inquiring and examining into all species of evidence, which may lead to a conviction of the crime of which colonel Burr is now charged; but there is a great objection to the exercise of this examining and committing power by a high law officer, who is to preside upon the trial, when the grand jury, the appropriate tribunal, is in session. He is obliged, previously, without a full hearing of both sides of the case, to commit himself, upon the case of the accused. Every one will agree, that a judge, should, if possible, come to the office of trial as free from prepossession, as if he never heard of the case before. It is true, that when a grand jury is not embodied, in order to avoid a failure of justice, and to prevent the guilty from escaping, the measure which the gentleman now proposes, would not only be proper but necessary. The examining and committing office of the judge is, in such cases, justified by the necessity of the case; but then it is because the appropriate body of inquest is not impaneled to perform the office. The necessity does not exist here. This novel mode of proceeding would give the attorney for the United States the chance of procuring an opinion from the court, unfavourable to the accused. Failing in that chance, he would then resort to his only legal one—before the grand jury. Why should this court step out of its ordinary course to forestal or influence the deliberations of the grand jury and the public? The motion is without precedent, or reason to warrant such a precedent; it is oppressive and against all principle; it is unreasonable and oppressive that the functions of the grand jury should be suspended, in order that the court should assume them. Although in the absence of the grand jury, it would be proper in the court to determine a question of commitment, yet the history of our criminal jurisprudence yields no instance of such a motion during the session of the grand jury. I did expect, that some solitary reason would have been given, by the gentleman for the prosecution, in support of his motion; I did expect, sir, that all the books of England would have been ransacked; I did suppose, sir, that the musty pages of folios and quartos would have been opened to support his argument; I did expect, at least, sir, that one case of state practice would have been produced. In this expectation I am disappointed. I say then, sir, that the motion before the court is without precedent, unreasonable in its nature, inconvenient in its effects, and oppressive in its end; of a piece with the long course of oppression which has been practised against colonel Burr, but has been hitherto unknown in this country; unheard of in any country which enjoys the blessings of freedom, and which, I trust, will never again be repeated in these states.

Colonel Burr appears in this court ready to go on with his trial; he wishes no delay; he is opposed to every measure which may occasion delay, or procrastinate the business. His great object is to satisfy his country, the minds of his fellow citizens, and even his prosecutors, that he is innocent. We have suffered already two or three days to pass away in idle discussion, or without doing any thing: and yet we are told, at last, after the lapse of several months; after a grand jury have been convened and gone into their room; after attending with great inconvenience to themselves and expense to the state; after *all this*, we are told, that the business of commitment is again to be gone over; that the evidence which ought to be given to the grand jury, the only proper tribunal at this time for its consideration, is to be submitted to the court. We have, sir, made enough of sacrifices; we have been deprived of our legal rights; our person and papers have been seized; we have been subjected to a military persecution unparalleled in this country; given into the custody of the satellites of military despotism, and guarded by the rigid forms of military law: surely our wrongs ought now to end. It was rumoured that he would not appear; but he has appeared. We come to ask a legal trial: an examination into the charges which have been preferred against us. The government has had the time and necessary means of preparation, and they ought to be prepared. Our pleasure was, to await the pleasure of the prosecution, unless that pleasure should be found to be oppressive. But we are told now, that the indictment cannot go up; but in the mean time an inquisition must be held. Permit me to advert, for a solitary moment, to one circumstance: If we had sought every legal advantage, our motion would have preceded theirs; our motion would have been, that, if they were not ready to present their evidence before the grand jury, colonel Burr should be discharged from the recognisance already given.

The laws of congress have adopted our rules and practice in the states, in proceedings upon indictments for misdemeanors. You were of opinion, you well remember, sir, that nothing more than probable cause of suspecting a misdemeanor appeared against colonel Burr. Even after an indictment in Virginia for a misdemeanor, nothing more than a summons can go against the person indicted. No court, in the commonwealth, ever permitted a capias to go in the first instance, unless the case passed *sub silentio.* Now arrest and bail are utterly incompatible with a summons; and surely, if an *indictee* cannot be arrested, one merely suspected, cannot be held to bail. The conduct of judge Chase, in awarding a *capias* against Callender, was the subject of one of the charges in his impeachment. Mr. Hay, vehemently and ably contended, that a summons only ought to have issued against him.

I know that the court may have an impression that I am wandering from the subject. I will soon show what application the recognisance already taken has to the motion to examine witnesses, in order to commit for treason.

Notwithstanding colonel Burr was committed upon a charge of misdemeanor, when according to the state laws he would not have been committed, a public prejudice has been excited against the lenity of the measure; and attempts have been made, through newspapers and a popular clamour, to intimidate every officer who might have any concern in the trial. This public prejudice would be increased by the present motion rather than allayed, if the necessary explanation should not be made. The multitude around us must hear what is passing, and we cannot submit to a course which would further invest the public mind with the poison already too plentifully infused. I do not charge the attorney of the United States with a design to excite or increase this public prejudice; but I know it will be increased, unless care be taken to show, that the public clamour has been groundless. I take it for granted, that after this view of the subject, whatever motive dictated the application, it will now be abandoned, and that the gentleman will withdraw his motion. I will not weary out the patience of the court, but conclude by saying, that I sit down in anxious hope, that the success of this motion may not add to the catalogue of colonel Burr's grievances.

The chief justice inquired whether the counsel for the prosecution intended to open the case more fully?

Mr. HAY had not intended to open it more fully; he did not himself entertain the least doubt, that if there was sufficient proof produced to justify the commitment of colonel Burr, the court had completely the right to commit him. That the general power of the court to commit, could not be questioned; and if gentlemen contended, that it ought not to be exercised in the present case, it was incumbent on them to show it. That Mr. Botts himself had not denied it. That his whole argument turned on the question, not whether the court had the right, but whether it was expedient now to exercise it. Its expediency depended on the evidence; if that was sufficient, there could be no doubt of the power. That if the court once admitted, as an exception to this principle, that the grand jury was in session, they would establish a precedent fraught with the most injurious consequences.

Mr. WICKHAM.—It certainly would have been an accommodation to us, if the gentlemen had given us notice of their intended motion. We come into this discussion completely off our guard, completely unprepared; and it may be presumed, that it was merely an omission in the opposite counsel, not to have given us notice of the motion which they intended to bring forward. Because it was distinctly understood between us, (by an argument made, I believe, in the hearing of the court), that if any specific motion was to be made on either side, timely notice of its nature and object was to be given. I am sorry that they have departed from their agreement in the present instance; but if I have not forgotten every principle of law which I ever learnt, of every principle of common justice, this motion cannot be supported.

Mr. HAY.—The gentleman will permit me to set him right. He might have relied on my candour, that when I was about to lay my indictments before the grand jury, I would have given him timely notice of my intention. They might then have moved for the instruction to the jury, which they are so anxious to obtain. This was the only understanding between us on the subject; our agreement extended no further; much less to the particular case before the court. On the other hand, there was a very strong reason against our making this communication. I feel no hesitation, sir, in assigning this reason: and I hope that it will wound neither the feelings of the prisoner, nor of his counsel. I did not intend to have laid it before the court, but I now conceive myself called upon to be thus explicit. The fact is this. Mr. Wilkinson is known to be a material witness in this prosecution; his arrival in Virginia, might be announced in this city, before he himself reached it. I do not pretend to say what effect it might produce upon colonel Burr's mind; but certainly colonel Burr would be able to effect his escape, merely upon paying the recognisance of his present bail. My only object then was to keep his person safe, until we could have investigated the charge of treason; and I really did not know, but that if colonel Burr had been previously apprised of my motion, he might have attempted to avoid it. But I did not promise to make this communication to the opposite counsel, because it might have defeated the very end for which it was intended. I have said, that the only pledge I gave, merely related to the indictments to be sent up to the grand jury.

Mr. WICKHAM observed, that after this explanation, he must suppose, that he had misapprehended the extent of their agreement. He knew the gentleman too well to think that he had intentionally misled him; but what could he think of the motion he had made? It was a strange episode which he weaved into his tale; it may be good poetry indeed, but it was not certainly proper matter of argument. Every man who hears me, every man who has ever read on the subject, must know, what are the feelings which dictate these suspicions of colonel Burr. Some mortification was felt by his enemies, (not that the attorney for the United States himself ever felt it), that he returned here for trial. But here colonel Burr *is*, and always will be ready to meet every charge they may think proper to bring against him; and to face every man who dares to say any thing against him. The gentleman will not open his case, and why? Because when he has heard our arguments against his motion, he may come out with the adverse arguments against us. If they do not choose to open their case, we hope the court will grant us the right of concluding the argument.

Here a desultory conversation ensued upon the order of proceeding.

Mr. EDMUND RANDOLPH observed, that the power of the court to commit, was not denied; but that the expediency of committing, while a grand jury was in session, was denied; that it was improper that an inquiry which belonged exclusively to that body, should be transferred to the court.

Mr. HAY said, that it made no difference in law, whether the grand jury were in session or not; that the grand jury being in session could not deprive the court of the power with which they were vested. Let me state a case, said Mr. Hay. Suppose colonel Burr had only arrived at Richmond this morning, instead of having been brought at the period of his first examination, would his counsel contend, that the court would not think it proper to commit him, instead of bringing the question immediately before the grand jury, when the prosecutor was not furnished with the necessary evidence? This is precisely the case at present. From additional evidence, which has come into my possession since his examination, it appears to me, that upon a disclosure of it to the court, they will see proper that he should be committed on the charge of treason; but to complete this evidence still more, the testimony of general Wilkinson is essential; and until his arrival, it would be improper to submit it to the grand jury; although it is necessary, for the reasons I have stated, that it should be submitted at present to the court.

Mr. WICKHAM meant to support his arguments on the grounds of law and precedent: he read the revised code of Virginia, page 103, sect. 10. which he contended were plainly in his favour. He observed, that the present motion was unprecedented in a system of criminal jurisprudence, which was upwards of one hundred years old. If this motion be a proper one, there must be some precedents in this country or in England. If there be none such their motion cannot be supported; and as the gentlemen have not produced them, it is fair to infer, that there are none such. It is therefore obvious that the present motion is contrary to the acts of Virginia, as well as to the common law. The attorney for the United States says, that he can take no final measures, till general Wilkinson is present. His deposition is greatly relied upon. Now, sir, I refer to you as well as to the supreme court of the United States, where you presided, that the facts contained in that deposition did not amount to treason, but to a probable proof of a misdemeanor only. As to general Eaton's, it is not relied on; the sole reliance of the prosecution is on Wilkinson's: of course, if Wilkinson himself were present, he would prove nothing new. But if general Wilkinson be so material a witness, why are they not prepared to go with him before the grand jury? Why is he not here? He is a military officer, bound implicitly to obey the head of the government. In the war of Europe, a general has been known to march the same distance at the head of his army, in a shorter time than general Wilkinson has had to pass from New-Orleans to this place. He is bound to go wherever the government directs him: to march to Mexico; to invade the Floridas; or to come to this city. Perhaps there are other reasons for his not coming: but let us not press this subject.

What, sir, is the tendency of this application? What is the motive? I have no doubt, the gentlemen mean to act correctly. I wish to cast no imputation; but the counsel and the court well know, that there are a set of busy people, (not I hope employed by the government) who, thinking to do right, are labouring to ruin the reputation of my client. I do not charge the government with this attempt; but the thing is actually done. Attempts have been made. The press, from one end of the continent to the other, has been enlisted on their side to excite prejudices against colonel Burr. Prejudices? Yes, they have influenced the public opinion by such representations, and by persons not passing between the prisoner and his country, but by ex parte evidence and mutilated statements. Ought not this court to bar the door, as much as possible, against such misrepresentations? to shut out every effort to excite further prejudices, until the case is decided by a sworn jury? not by the floating rumours of the day, but by the evidence of sworn witnesses? The attorney for the United States offers to produce his testimony: no doubt, the most violent; no doubt, the least impartial which he can select: testimony, which is, perhaps, to be met and overthrown by superior evidence. Do they, besides, wish that the multitude around us should be prejudiced by garbled evidences? Do precedents justify such a course as this? Produce your witnesses, they may say. No, sir, colonel Burr is ready for a trial; but he wishes that trial to come before a jury. I do not pretend to understand the motives which led to those things: it is enough, that they produce these mischievous effects upon ourselves. Should government, hereafter, wish to oppress any individual; to drag him from one end of the country to the other by a military force; to enlist the prejudices of the country against him;

they will pursue the very same course which has now been taken against colonel Burr. He is here, ready for trial. They
admit that their testimony is not sufficient to bring him before
a grand jury, and of course, to find an indictment against him.
Why then is this partial evidence to be exhibited on a motion
for commitment? It is to nourish and keep alive the prejudices
already circulated against him. Will they then, press a motion
like this? Be it so. I hope the motion will be rejected, and that
the court will stand between the innocent and his pursuers: for
every man is presumed to be innocent, before he is found
guilty.

Mr. WIRT.—May it please your honours,

The attorney for the United States, believing himself possessed of sufficient testimony to justify the commitment of Aaron
Burr for high treason, has moved the court to that effect. In
making this motion, he has merely done his duty. It would
have been unpardonable in him to omit it; yet the counsel for
the defence complain of the motion and the want of notice.
As to the latter objection, it must be palpable, that the nature
and object of the motion rendered notice improper. The gentlemen would have the attorney to announce to the party accused, that he was, at length, in possession of sufficient evidence
to justify his commitment for high treason ; and, that being apprehensive he might not be disposed to stand this charge, he intended, as soon as the accused came into court next morning,
to move his commitment! This would really be carrying po-
liteness beyond its ordinary pitch. It would not have deserved
the name of candour, sir; it would, in fact, have been an invitation to the accused to make his escape. But, as gentlemen
seem to doubt, at least with an air of some earnestness, the propriety of this motion at this time, and express their regret that
they have not had time to examine its legality, the attorney
has offered to waive the motion until tomorrow, to give gentlemen the opportunity which they profess to desire; but no, sir,
they will not even have what they say they want, when offered
by the attorney. Another gentleman, after having demanded
why this motion was made, and by that demand drawn from the
attorney an explanation of his motives, has been pleased to
speak of the attorney's statement, of his apprehensions, as an
episode, which "though good poetry," he says, "had better
have been let alone, when such serious matters of fact were in
discussion." It may be an episode, sir: if the gentleman pleases, he is at liberty to consider the whole trial as a peice of
epic action, and to look forward to the appropriate catastrophe.
But it does not appear to me to be very fair, sir, after having
drawn from the attorney an explanation of his motives, to com-

plain of that explanation: if a wound has been inflicted by the explanation, the gentlemen who produced it, should blame only themselves. But, sir, where is the crime of considering Aaron Burr as subject to the ordinary operation of the human passions? Towards any other man, it seems, the attorney would have been justifiable in using precautions against alarms and escapes: it is only improper when applied to this man. Really, sir, I recollect nothing in the history of his deportment, which renders it so very incredible, that Aaron Burr would fly from a prosecution. But at all events, the attorney is bound to act on general principles, and to take care that justice be had against every person accused, by whatever name he may be called, or by whatever previous reputation he may be distinguished. This motion, however, it seems, is not legal, at this time, because there is a grand jury in session. The amount of the position is, that though it may be generally true, that the court possesses the power to hear and commit, yet, if there be a grand jury, this power of the court is suspended; and the commitment cannot be had unless in consequence of a presentment or bill of indictment found by that body. The general power of the court being admitted, those who rely on this exception, should support it by authority; and therefore, the *loud call* for precedents, which we have heard from the other side, comes improperly from that quarter. We ground this motion in the general power of the court to commit: let those who say that this general power is destroyed by the presence of a grand jury, show one precedent to countenance this original and extraordinary motion. I believe, sir, I may safely affirm, that not a single reported case or dictum can be found, which has the most distant bearing towards such an idea. Sir, no such dictum or case ought to exist. It would be unreasonable and destructive of the principles of justice: for if the doctrine be true at all, that the presence of a grand jury suspends the power to hear and commit by any other authority, it must be uniformly and universally true in every other case as well as this, and in every case which can be proposed while a grand jury is sitting. Now, sir, let us suppose, that immediately on the swearing of this grand jury, and their retiring to their chamber, Aaron Burr had for the first time been brought to this town; the members of the evidence scattered over the continent; the attorney, however, in possession of enough to justify the arrest and commitment of the accused for high treason, but not enough to authorise a grand jury to find a true bill. What is to be done? The court disclaims any power to hear and commit, because there is a grand jury; the grand jury cannot find a true bill, because the evidence is not sufficient to warrant such a finding: the natural and unavoidable consequence would be, that the man must be discharged: and then, according to Mr. Wickham's principles of ethics, that every man must be supposed to intend the natural consequences of his own acts, the gentlemen who advocate this doctrine intend, that Aaron Burr shall be discharged without a trial.

I beg you, sir, to recollect what was said by gentlemen the other day, when you were called upon to give an additional charge to the grand jury. You were told that a grand jury should require the same evidence to find a true bill, which a petty jury would require to convict the prisoner. Connect this principle with the doctrine in question: the sitting of the grand jury suspends all power to commit by any other body, and the grand jury cannot find a true bill, unless on evidence on which they would convict as a petit jury: connect these two principles, and consider the immaturity of evidence, which always exists at the period of arrest and commitment: and the sitting of the grand jury, instead of being a season of admonition and alarm, becomes a perfect jubilee to the guilty. But it is said, that this is " an attempt to divest the constitutional organ of its just and proper power." I believe, sir, it was never before heard, that an application to commit for safe keeping, was an encroachment on the power of the grand jury. Would the gentlemen have us to address this motion to the grand jury? they might as well propose, that we should submit the bill of indictment to the court, and desire them to say, whether it is a true bill or not? This would be indeed, the "shifting of powers," of which the gentleman complains. As it is, sir, there is no manner of collision between the power, which we call upon the court to exercise, and the proper power of the grand jury. The justices arrest and commit, for safe keeping; then comes the function of the grand jury, to decide on the truth of the indictment exhibited against the prisoner. The two offices are distinct in point of time, and totally different in their nature and objects. But it is said, that "there is a great inconvenience in submitting a great law officer to the necessity of expressing an opinion on the crime, on a motion like this—that the judge like the juror, should come to the trial with his mind pure and unbiassed." This argument does not apply to the *legality* of the power, which we call upon the court to exercise; it goes merely to the expediency of exercising it: and if the argument be true, the court ought never to commit, whether the grand jury be sitting or not. This, however, sir, is a matter for *legislative*, not for *judicial* consideration. Whenever the legislature shall decide, by the force of this argument, that the court which commits shall not sit on the trial in chief, a motion like this will become improper. At present, however, the legislature has left this power with the court, and we claim its exercise for considerations of the most serious importance to truth and justice.

But, sir, we are told, that this investigation is calculated to keep alive the public prejudices; and we hear great complaints about these public prejudices. The country is represented as being filled with misrepresentations and calumnies against Aaron Burr; the public indignation it is said, is already sufficiently excited. This argument is also inapplicable to our right to make this motion; it does not affect the *legality* of our procedure. But if the motion is likely to have this effect, we cannot help it. No human institution is free from inconveniences; the course we hold is a legal one, a necessary one : we think it a duty. It is no answer to us to say, that it may produce inconveniences to the prisoner. But let us consider this mournful tale of prejudices, and the likelihood of their being excited by this motion. Sir, if Aaron Burr be innocent, instead of resisting this motion, he ought to hail it with triumph and exultation. What is it that we propose to introduce? not the rumours that are floating through the world, nor the *bulk* of the multitude, nor the speculations of newspapers; but the *evidence of facts.* We propose, that the whole evidence exculpatory as well as accusative, shall come before you; instead of exciting, this is the true mode of correcting prejudices. The world, which it is said has been misled and inflamed by falsehood, will now hear the truth. Let the truth come out, let us know how much of what we have heard is false, how much of it is true; how much of what we feel is prejudice, how much of it is justified by fact. Whoever before heard of such an apprehension as that which is professed on the other side? *prejudice excited by evidence!* Evidence, sir, is the great corrector of prejudice. Why then does Aaron Burr shrink from it? It is strange to me that a man, who complains so much of being, without cause, illegally seized and transported by a military officer, should be afraid to confront this evidence: evidence can be promotive only of truth. I repeat it then sir, why does he shrink from the evidence? The gentlemen on the other side can give the answer. On our part, we are ready to produce that evidence. Permit me now, sir, to turn to the act of assembly which has been read by Mr. Wickham. Into what embarrassment must the ingenious and vigorous mind of that gentleman have been driven, before he would have taken refuge under this act of assembly? It is but to read it to see that it has no manner of application whatever to this motion; that it applies to the case of a person *already committed;* declaring that such person shall be bailed, if not indicted at the first term after his commitment, and discharged if not indicted at the second term. Revised code, page 103. sec. 10. It begins thus,

" When any person committed for treason."—Now, sir, is Aaron Burr committed for treason? If not, it is obvious that the clause has no manner of application to him. Why, sir, the object of this motion is to commit him; gentlemen must have been in strange confusion when they resorted to this law. Mr. Wickham asks, if general Wilkinson be a material witness, why he is not here? Who is general Wilkinson? says that gentleman. Is he not the instrument of the government, bound to a blind obedience? I am sorry for this and many other declamatory remarks which have been unnecessarily and improperly introduced; but the gentleman assures us, that no imputation is meant against the government. Oh no, sir; colonel Burr indeed has been oppressed, has been persecuted; but far be it from the gentleman to charge the government with it. Colonel Burr indeed has been harassed by a military tyrant, who is " the instrument of the government bound to a blind obedience;" but the gentleman could not by any means be understood as intending to insinuate aught to the prejudice of the government. The gentleman is understood, sir; his object is correctly understood. He would divert the public attention from Aaron Burr, and point it to another quarter. He would, too, if he could, shift the popular displeasure which he has spoken of, from Aaron Burr to another quarter. These remarks were not intended for your ear, sir; they were intended for the people who surround us; they can have no effect upon the mind of the court. I am too well acquainted with the dignity, the firmness, the illumination of this bench, to apprehend any such consequence. But the gentlemen would balance the account of popular prejudices; they would convert this judicial inquiry into a political question; they would make it a question between Thomas Jefferson and Aaron Burr. The purpose is well understood, sir; but it shall not be served. I will not degrade the administration of this country by entering on their defence. Besides, sir, this is not our business; at present we have an account to settle, not between Aaron Burr and Thomas Jefferson, but between Aaron Burr and the laws of his country. Let us finish his trial first. The administration too will be tried before their country; before the world. They, sir, I believe, will never shrink, either from the evidence or the verdict. Let us return to Aaron Burr. " Why is not general Wilkinson here?" Because it was impossible in the nature of things for him to be here by this time. It was on the first of April that you decided on the commitment of Aaron Burr for the misdemeanor; until that decision was known, the necessity of summoning witnesses could not be ascertained. General Wilkinson is the commander in chief of the American troops, in a quarter where his presence is rendered important by the temper of the neighbourhood: to summon him on the mere possibility of commitment would have afforded a ground of clamour, perhaps a just one, against the administration. The *certainty* that Aaron Burr would be put upon his trial, could not have been known at Washington till the 5th or 6th of April. Now, sir, let the gentlemen on the other side make a slight calculation. Orleans is said to be 1500 or 1600 miles from this place. Suppose the United States mail travelling by a frequent change of horses and riders, a hundred miles per day, should reach Orleans in 17 days from the federal city, it would be the 24th or 25th of April (putting all accidents out of the question,) before general Wilkinson could have received his orders to come on. Since that time until this, he has had thirty days to reach Richmond. Could a journey of 1500 or 1600 miles be reasonably performed in thirty days? Who can bear a journey of 50 miles per day for thirty days together? But sir, general Wilkinson is not here; due means have been used to bring him hither; his materiality is ascertained by his affidavit, and the attorney does not choose to send up the indictment in his absence. But we admit, it seems, that we are not ready to make good our charge. In my opinion there is evidence enough to prove the treason independently of general Wilkinson. But it is important in every point of view, that that gentleman should be here. It is important to his own reputation: it is important to the people of the United States that he should be here; and on the part of the grand jury, sir, there is no calculating what inferences unfavourable to the prosecution might be drawn from the mere circumstance of his absence. The attorney is therefore, in my opinion, very right not to hazard the justice and the fair trial of this case, by sending up the indictment in general Wilkinson's absence.

But it seems that Wilkinson's affidavit has been already decided to have no relation to the charge of treason. To what general Wilkinson's affidavit tended while it was inomalated, insulated, or connected only with that of general Eaton, is no proof of what its tendency may be now, in connection with the great mass of additional testimony which we have collected. Sir, we say that it is the key-stone which binds the great arch of evidence now in our possession. As to sending up the indictment, it is out of the question; truth and justice require that it should not now be sent up. But we hope, sir, that the motion to commit Aaron Burr will be received, because we think it not only a legal, but also a just and necessary measure of precaution.

Mr. HAY.—On this occasion, I beg leave to make one or two preliminary remarks. I stand here engaged in the performance of a very serious duty. The duty I have to perform is, indeed, most serious and important. The subject now before us is one which deeply affects the character of the government; and the charge is the most solemn and interesting that can be exhibited against any individual. The motion I have to make is, that Aaron Burr may be committed on a charge of treason against the United States!

Sir, it was natural to suppose, that such a serious charge would have made a most serious impression upon Aaron Burr's mind; that he would have roused all the energies of his understanding in his service, in vindicating himself, and not in casting imputations upon the government. Why then does he turn from defending himself to attack the administration? Why these complaints of persecution which have fatigued our ears? I most solemnly deny the charge. I most confidently avow, that there is not a tittle of evidence to support it. None can be produced, unless it be a persecution, that the government brings him before a legal tribunal, where his guilt or innocence will be impartially established. Aaron Burr stands accused of the highest crimes and misdemeanors; he stands charged with a deliberate design of involving his country in all the horrors of a civil insurrection, or of entangling her in a war with a foreign nation. This is the true question before the court; and instead of meeting this charge with the energy and firmness which became him; instead of confronting it with his evidence, he complains forsooth of persecution! And where, sir, is this tremendous persecution? " Because he was sent here by a military authority?" But Aaron Burr has been tried in the country where he was arrested? Was Blannerhasset's island in the Mississippi territory? Or ought he not to have been conveyed to that judicial district, which possessed a competent jurisdiction? But if Aaron Burr ought to have been sent hither, by what number of men should he have been escorted? Was it by one man only; from whom he could have been so easily rescued, and whose vigilance he could most probably have eluded? Or ought he to have been conveyed, as he really was, by the energy of men, like Perkins, whose unshrinking firmness, and whose humanity (in the presence of Aaron Burr himself I avow it, let him deny it if he can), had completely qualified him for the safe transportation of his prisoner? But, sir, when this cry and yell of persecution is once excited, it is not easy to set bounds to its fury. Not contented with inveighing against the pretended persecution of the government; a government which never did persecute; a government which cannot persecute, and which will for ever stand firm in the affections of the people, from the integrity and intelligence which mark its measures. Not contented with lavishing their complaints against that government, the counsel for the prisoner have even turned against the humble instruments, who conduct the prosecution. They seriously complain, that we have given them no previous notice of this motion; and these are the very men, who have so often offered motions to this court, without the slightest intimation to ourselves. Sir, I most positively assert, that no notice in the present case ought to have been given. I shall not pretend to assert, that Aaron Burr was disposed, under the present state of things, to effect his escape. But, I say, that supposing such to have been the fact, and supposing that, availing himself of the information which we had imparted, he should have taken to flight; I appeal to the candour of every impartial man; I appeal to the candour of the opposite counsel themselves, whether I should not have been guilty of a most gross violation of my duties?

But they say, he ought not to be committed, because the presence of the grand jury suspends the authority of this court. But where are the precedents which justify this position? I have not made many researches into this case; because I did not suppose that there was a single sceptic at this bar who would deny the universality of the proposition that we have laid down; that it was the right of the court to commit in every case where they deemed it proper. They say, that in this case, the power of the grand jury and the court are concurrent. Strange that they should forget the immense difference between their powers! the evidence which is sufficient before the latter, is widely different from that which is necessary to be produced to the former. The testimony requisite to induce the court to commit the person accused is less than we are bound to submit to the grand jury, and much less than that which alone is admissible before the petit jury. I will quote the authority of the gentlemen against themselves. They say, that stronger evidence is necessary before the grand jury than before a court for the examination of a prisoner. I think differently myself; but certain it is, that affidavits are not admissible to be sent to the grand jury; although they may be used to convince the court that it is proper to commit. For my part, I think we are already in possession of *viva voce* evidence not only sufficient to commit colonel Burr, but to induce the grand jury to find in favour of both the indictments: but I will boldly inquire, whether I should discharge my honest duty, were I to submit my indictments before the grand jury at this moment, when I have not all the material evidence which we may possess? Sir, these gentlemen may cast their groundless censures upon me; but in vain: all their clamours will never move me from my purpose. The course which I am pursuing is sufficient to satisfy my own conscience; and it is indifferent to me whether ten or ten thousand men should join in my condemnation.

Mr. Botts asserts, that we have produced no authorities to prove our position; and that we have none to produce. But is it right to be continually recurring to precedents? Is there no allowance to be made for the operations of common sense, in any case? Where cases of doubt and difficulty occur, a reference of this kind is certainly proper to enlighten and fortify our own judgments. But even admitting the propriety of introducing precedents in the whole extent for which gentlemen contend, it is their business and not ours to comply with the requisition for precedents. We stand upon the broad, general principle, that courts have the power to commit. If gentlemen contest this principle in the present case, why do they not introduce their countervailing authorities?

I regret that my duty did not permit me to give my friend Mr. Wickham notice of this motion, that he might have more seriously meditated upon the subject before he urged his objections. If he had understood it with his usual correctness, he never would have troubled the court with the law of Virginia: for this law has not the slightest bearing upon the specific proposition before you.

Mr. Wickham inquires why we do not at once send up our indictments before the grand jury? Suppose, sir, we should pursue the course which he recommends; suppose we should send up our indictments on the evidence which is now in our possession; several days might elapse before they would be able to investigate this body of evidence. In the mean time, some of those numerous persons, who are prying into every hole and corner of this city, might probably catch some distant hint of the probable decision of the jury. They have certainly too much discretion not to keep their own counsel: but it is absolutely impossible to exclude completely the busy eye of curiosity. Some vague insinuations may probably escape; something which might justify a suspicion of their determination. Suppose, then, that Aaron Burr was to be actuated by these considerations; suppose that his fears, (if fears he can feel) should prompt him to escape; what, sir, would become of our indictment? Mr. Burr may quit the United States; he may flee for ever beyond the jurisdiction of this country; and in that case, the whole world would ridicule us for the course we had pursued. Or let us even suppose that we were to withdraw this motion, where would be our security? Must we trust to the indulgence of Mr. Burr himself for remaining in this city and standing his trial?

We expect general Wilkinson here in a few days. We have an affidavit which positively states, that an express to New-Orleans, to command his presence on this trial, was met on the frontiers of the Mississippi Territory; we have also letters from the attorney general of the United States, explicitly stating, that general Wilkinson has been officially authorised to leave the army of the United States, and select whatever mode of transportation he might think proper. [Here Mr. Hay read the affidavit, showing that the express to general Wilkinson, had been seen in Athens, in the state of Georgia.] In the mean time.

what is colonel Burr's situation? It is completely optional with him, whether to stay here and face his accusers, or to avail himself of his liberty and leave the United States. We call upon this court to exercise the authority with which they are invested; and by binding over colonel Burr, as well on the charge of high treason, as of a misdemeanor, to detain him here for a satisfactory trial.

We scarcely expected to have been asked, why general Wilkinson was not here? The gentleman himself has said, that he is a general. Can he then leave his army at any time, and without the permission of the government? Make, however, a computation of time. The attorney general left this city on the 4th or 5th of April. He reached Washington on the 7th or 8th. Allow then a reasonable time for an express from Washington to New-Orleans; and for a man of general Wilkinson's age and bulk to travel to this city; and is it probable that he could have arrived here before this period? If he availed himself of the liberty and means to come by water; the gales have been lately very severe. And even two of the grand jury have assured me, that if general Wilkinson was exposed to the late tempestuous weather, he will probably never see the United States. Mr. Wickham has expatiated upon the attempts made to prejudice the public opinion through the medium of the press. Sir, a great deal has been said in the newspapers upon this transaction; and a great deal will yet be said. But are the presses shut against colonel Burr, when even in this very city certain presses have been found to vindicate his motive and designs? But what of all this? The public mind is hostile to any encroachment upon the liberty of the press; and it ought to be so. Where a crime of such gigantic enormity, as that attributed to Aaron Burr, arises in this country, the printers will speak, and they ought to speak; the purest motives will command them to speak. If there have been publications against colonel Burr, innumerable communications have also appeared in his favour; and if the publications against him have contained the severest strictures, they have resulted from his own character and conduct; and he has no right to complain.

He stands on the fairest ground which his conduct and character can reach. But if in truth prejudices have been improperly excited against him, why does he wish to close the only door to his own vindication, by excluding the evidence. His counsel exclaim, " Send the evidence to the grand jury." Surely if colonel Burr wishes to have the evidence before the jury, he should be much more anxious to have it before the court. The jury will have one side of the evidence only before them; and that will be completely against himself. Both, however, will go before the court. Why, then, does he shrink from the evidence? If an unjust prejudice assails him, the light of truth and evidence will dissipate it. Why does he shrink?

The gentlemen on the other side, continued Mr. Hay, do not do us justice. They charge us with persecution and oppression. Sir, I never contemplated or wished to hurt Aaron Burr. I scorn it. I look not to him. I look only to the duties which I am solemnly bound to perform. One remark more, sir, and I have done : Gentlemen on the other side, insist upon the insufficiency of our evidence; because we have withheld our indictments from the grand jury, they have hastily inferred, that we feel our evidence to be too feeble to satisfy the jury. They are mistaken, sir. I assure them that they are mistaken. I conscientiously believe, that we have evidence enough, even throwing out the depositions themselves, to satisfy the grand jury of the guilt of Aaron Burr. But, sir, puerile indeed would it be for us, under the present state of things, to submit our case before the grand jury, on the evidence before us, when we are every moment expecting better.

Mr. EDMUND RANDOLPH addressed the court to the following effect :

Sir, it would have been impossible for us, even had we received due notice of this motion, to have availed ourselves of the time that was allowed to us. That would have been impossible, because the enormity of the proposition itself, would have baffled all our consideration, and all our researches. Mark the course, sir, which has been pursued towards my unfortunate client. First he was brought here under a military escort. Then that little folio of depositions and affidavits, was laid before your honour : then the charge of treason : and then that little cock-boat which was destined to attend this great ship, on a foreign expedition. You heard it all, sir, and what did you say? You bound colonel Burr to bail, simply on the charge of a misdemeanor, to appear here at the opening of court; but not contented with this security, you superadded, that he was not to leave the court until it had discharged him. You opened the door, too, for an ulterior prosecution; you declared, that if the attorney for the United States should obtain any additional evidence, the judgment which you then rendered, would not prevent his indicting colonel Burr on the charge of treason.

Sir, thus stands the case, as it was understood by the whole universe. On Friday, we came here to meet the whole world; Friday, however, passes away, and nothing is done. On Saturday, we came here again; Saturday, also, passes away, and nothing is done. But on Sunday, sir, (for it seems that day, which, to the generality of mankind, is a day of rest, is a day of activity to some,) is broached this new fangled doctrine, which now excites our astonishment. They demand precedents, sir, for our conduct; and who are they that require it? Why, sir, they that take things out of the ordinary course of the law. For thirty years, I never saw such a proceeding: I have never read of such a one in the English books ; and yet, these gentlemen call upon us for precedents. If we were asked for our reasons sir, we should have enough to offer : and first, a judge in the federal court, sitting in the capacity which your honour now fulfils, is in the same relation to the accused, as an examining judge is in the state courts. But, sir, who ever invited a single magistrate, or a state court to augment the bail of any individual in the situation of colonel Burr? If a man was bound, in a distant county, to answer to a misdemeanor, and another crime was to be brought against him, to be predicated on the very same evidence, have you, sir, ever known the trying court to increase his bail? There never was such an example, sir.

Mr. Botts' remark, sir, is not to be answered. You are changing the constitutional organ of justice. You are completely blotting out the functions of a grand jury. The witnesses will be all produced before you : but no, improper as this proceeding will be, it is still less so, than that which they will actually pursue. None of the United States' witnesses will be brought before you, but those whom they may think it politic to introduce; and depend upon it, that such testimony will be garbled for the ears of this court, as may be expected to bias their judgment. Well, sir, and what will be the consequence? When the grand jury are about to retire to their own chamber, they will be told that you have demanded additional bail. Are you then, sir, to be a pioneer of blood for the grand jury? Is not this precedent outrageous, sir? The boasted principle, that no man is to be condemned but upon the verdict of twenty-four of his peers, is gone. Throughout this town, it will be universally reported, that you have solemnly declared Aaron Burr to be guilty of high treason against the United States; and some of those, to whom the rumour may extend, may hereafter be impaneled on the petit jury. And will they feel themselves altogether unbiassed by your judgment? Why, sir, let it be declared at once, that the grand jury is to be struck out as an intermediate organ of justice.

Do not, I pray you, sir, let us suffer for the delays and negligence of other people. I cannot blame the United States' attorney. It is his business to obey the instructions of the government ; and if the witnesses are not here, it is certainly no fault of his : but surely there is time enough to travel from New-Orleans to this city in seventeen days; even with the gigantic " bulk" of general Wilkinson himself.

Mr. Hay says, our tone is changed. And how, sir? We demand a trial now. We demand a fair trial. But must we not, therefore protest against a measure, which is calculated to defeat this object? Certainly, sir. You are called upon to prejudice the minds of the grand jury. But, sir, in this interesting case, where liberty and life themselves are endangered, I trust that some hard-mouthed precedents, from old black letter books, will be found in opposition to this procedure. We have come here to answer to every charge, which may be urged against us: we come here to answer in a precedented and constitutional manner; but little did we expect that the court would decide in the first instance, instead of the grand jury; that the sentiments of the grand jury were to be prejudicated by an unconstitutional decision; and that the court itself was to commit its opinion on certain points, which would be regularly brought before them for argument and for decision at some of the ulterior stages of the prosecution. " Why," said Mr. Wirt, " do you shrink?" Sir, trace the course of the prosecution, and see who it is that retires from the contest. On Friday the United States' attorney was not ready; on Saturday he was not ready; and now indeed he will not probably be ready before Monday next. Sir, who is it that shrinks? and yet does the attorney positively aver, that he has evidence enough!

We are charged, sir, with addressing the multitude. Mr. Wirt says that he could, but would not imitate the example; but neither he nor Mr. Hay hath spared the theme. Sir, I will not deny the justness of his eulogiums upon the administration; but permit me only to remark, that there has been a certain conduct observed towards colonel Burr which excites my deepest astonishment. When I look at the first man in the government, I behold an individual whom I have long known, and whose public services have commanded my admiration. When I look at the second, sir, he has my whole heart. But, sir, the inquiry which is now before us relates not so much to the intention as to the effect. An order has been given to treat colonel Burr as an outlaw, and to burn and destroy him and his property. And sir, again; when the house of representatives demanded certain information, as it was their right and their duty to do, the president granted it: and would to God, sir! that he had stopped here, as an executive officer ought to have done. He proceeded, however, to say that colonel Burr was guilty of a crime; and consequently to express an opinion, which was calculated to operate judicially upon the judges and the juries. Such was the substratum of all the censures, which have been heaped upon colonel Burr.

Mr. Randolph proceeded to touch upon a subject to which Mr. Hay had referred. Colonel Burr was arrested in the Mississippi Territory. Was there no court there? was there no judge of integrity to try him? arrested too after he had been acquitted by a grand jury! Well! he was transported thence (with humanity it has been said), dragged on by eight musqueteers, who were ready to shoot him at a moment's warning; refused any appeal to the judicial authority; denied even the melancholy satisfaction of writing to his only child. Was all this humanity? Dragged before this court, which derives its only jurisdiction from a little speck of land on the Ohio. Yes! sir; but for that little spot of an island, Virginia never would have enjoyed this honour! What is all this, sir, but oppressive and bitter inhumanity? I trust, sir, from what I have said, that no one will think with Mr. Wirt, that I am shifting the question from colonel Burr to Mr. Jefferson. I should not have made the observations which have escaped me, but to show that my client is justified by his situation in stating every objection that he can to the present measure.

Mr. Randolph observed, that at least one disadvantage would result from this inquiry; that it was not clear, as Mr. Hay had asserted, that the affidavits would be laid before the court only, and not before the grand and petit juries, for the grand jury would soon be possessed of the substance of them; and that it was next to impossible for them to separate the impressions thus illegally to be produced on their minds, from the weight of the legal *viva voce* testimony.

Mr. Randolph said, that he did not understand Mr. Hay's expressions about certain persons in holes and corners; that if however he meant spies, there were none such employed by colonel Burr; but, although the government certainly had employed no spies, yet it has excited so much prejudice against colonel Burr, that it was sufficient to make every man in the country desirous of contributing his full quota of information against him. Mr. Randolph concluded with remarking, that the present argument had perhaps been permitted to embrace too wide a field of discussion; and that there were two great questions which he should submit to the consideration of the court: 1st, Whether there were any precedents in favour of the present motion? and 2d, If a proposition like this, and of such great importance, was adopted without any precedent to support it, whether it would not expose every man in the country to the danger of oppression?

Mr. Randolph contended, that this was a charge which the judge had already decided, on a former examination; that it was not a supplemental crime, but the old one; that perhaps there might be some little affidavit to splice out some defect in the former evidence; but what would be the consequence of this proceeding? Day after day, another and another affidavit would be brought forth. Facts like polypi, are easily cut into two or three pieces; each of which may be made to form a new and entire body; and each of those atoms is to require a new recognisance. For one affidavit there must be a bail of 1000 dollars: another affidavit, another 1000 dollars; until the burden of bail is so oppressive as to leave no other resource, but in the four walls of a prison.

Mr. HAY observed, that he should simply notice one remark of Mr. Randolph's. That gentleman had used the expression of " pioneer of blood;" but surely it would not have escaped him, had he but for one moment seriously reflected upon the court whom he addressed, upon the counsel he opposed, or the government. Satisfied of this, Mr. Hay said he should pass the observation by, without further notice.

Mr. Randolph had stated, that no similar case had occurred in his thirty years practice. It was not wonderful that such a case had not occurred in the time when that gentleman was attorney for the commonwealth. A great change has taken place in the system of our government. At that time no federal court existed. The mode of proceeding in the state courts is different from that here. In the system of penal law established in the commonwealth of Virginia, there is an examining court intervening between the arrest and commitment of a prisoner, and his being charged before the grand jury; but this court has the power to examine as well as to commit. Moreover, the United States are a most extensive country, compared to that of Virginia; a most material witness may now be 1500 miles from the court, before which he is to appear; and may be at the same time at the head of an army; in all which circumstances, the federal and the state sovereignties are different. So that this difference altogether defeats the application of Mr. Randolph's experience to this subject, even if that experience had been admitted as a good authority in the state courts. But even that gentleman would admit, that had a similar case occurred before the state courts, the accused would have been committed. Mr. Randolph asserts, that this motion is made to draw forth the opinion of the court, and thus to prejudicate the minds of the grand jury. But Mr. Randolph has certainly forgotten, that this intelligent and impartial jury are on their oaths and their consciences; and surely this court will not pay so little compliment to their independence, as to admit, that its own opinion will be sufficient to bias their judgment; more particularly too, when the point before the court is so different from that before the jury. It is the business of the court to commit; and of the jury to indict: and it is certainly the privilege of the court to decide upon written testimony, although that point may not be perfectly established and settled as it relates to the grand jury. How the court would decide upon this point, Mr. Hay said, he could not pretend to know. There is another consideration, which should be weighed by the opposite counsel. The grand jury is now already embodied. They are ready to proceed with any business which may be brought before them; but my great object, said Mr. Hay, is to prosecute colonel Burr on the charge of treason. I make this declaration, because I believe him to have been guilty of it. Let us suppose, however, that the grand jury was to discharge colonel Burr, from the misdemeanor; and then that I was to bring the present motion before the court; what resource then would Mr. Randolph have? From the present proceeding, however, Mr. Burr would derive the advantage of an immediate trial; whereas, according to the other mode of proceeding, weeks and months might escape, before he would be brought to trial; and certainly it is, in every point of view, more desirable, both for the government and himself, to terminate this business at once, than to impose upon us the necessity of moving for an adjourned trial.

Mr. Randolph says, "We are ready; we were ready on Friday; we were ready on Saturday, &c." Sir, there are two sorts of readiness: one in point of fact, and one under certain circumstances. Now these gentlemen will scarcely persuade me, that they could be ready to resist the weight of evidence, if it were ready to be laid before them ; but there is certainly no difficulty in believing, that they are now ready to proceed to trial, when the whole evidence, and particularly general Wilkinson's, is not present. One more remark: Mr. Randolph has expressed a reverence for Mr. Jefferson, which is not certainly derived from trifling considerations. I will make but one remark, and that gentleman will agree with me in the opinion: Survey the many peopled globe, through all ages and nations, and you will not find a man more anxiously bent upon promoting the liberty of the people. This was certainly the idea which Mr. Randolph intended to convey. Mr. Randolph next proceeded to Mr. Madison, upon whom he has not hesitated to lavish the most unreserved encomiums. Surely then, after this solemn declaration of the oldest counsel for the prisoner, we shall hear no more about persecution. Sir, it is a state of things, which it is impossible to reconcile with the amiable character ascribed to the two first officers in the government.

Mr. WICKHAM observed, that he should offer a few remarks on the supplementary arguments of Mr. Hay. That in this case colonel Burr's counsel had called, they had a right to call, for precedents; that Mr. Randolph, who had so ably represented this commonwealth, as a criminal prosecutor for many years, had never known a single one to justify this motion; that however true it might be, that the state of Virginia was now of smaller extent than the whole of the United States, yet it was then cut up into as small judicial districts, as the United States at present are, and that the witnesses in a criminal prosecution might have been scattered over those districts, as they are said to be in the present circumstances; that Mr. Randolph had represented not one of those districts, but the whole; not only on this side of the mountains, but beyond them; and even the uncultivated region of Kentucky, where travelling was at that time liable to so many difficulties, and from which it was so extremely laborious to transport the witnesses to this side of the mountains; that it was not until Kentucky had been more thickly populated, that a particular court had been established there. And what is the case in England and her dependencies? Certainly that island is not equally extensive with the United States; but her subjects may, at all events, be scattered over the world. Why then, is there no precedent in that country? Is it not probable, that a man might happen to be as far from the court of king's bench, as general Wilkinson is from this court? and yet there is no precedent to justify this motion. What is the crime? Is it of so little importance that this court, upon the production of every little affidavit, should consent to hear new motions for a commitment? This crime is treason! it is "a levying of war" against the United States! and where is the proof of it? where were colonel Burr's forces? was his army like that of Bayes, kept in disguise? Wilkinson's testimony cannot establish this fact; for it is the opinion of the chief justice, that his affidavit does not at all bear upon this subject; and yet two months have since elapsed, and no testimony has been collected. Wilkinson's deposition contains an improbable, mysterious tale, about a key and cypher. Mr. Wickham said, that he would not, at present, expose this transaction; but does this mysterious tale constitute treason? "You, sir, have already decided, that there is no treason in Wilkinson's deposition; but were the man himself in court, what could he establish further, than his deposition can do?" Mr. Hay is satisfied, that he has sufficient evidence to convict colonel Burr. No man doubts his ability, or his inclination to discharge his duty. Why, then, does he not lay his indictments before the jury? Because, there happens to be a man in New-Orleans, and one, perhaps, in the East Indies; and, therefore, "to make assurance doubly sure," he must wait for their appearance: and all this too, whilst the gentleman most seriously protests against oppression and delay. Though the gentleman may not be conscious of such a sentiment, as that of wishing to oppress colonel Burr, there must still be something like it in his heart: but whatever the motive may be, the result to ourselves is the same. It produces delay, and all its consequent oppressions. No court should sanction this proceeding. This case is like that of a man, whose cause stands for trial. When subpœnas after subpœnas have been issued; when sums after sums have been expended; he moves for a continuance of his suit, and at the very same time, he insists upon the sufficiency of his evidence. Surely the court would rule him to trial. Why is not the attorney for the United States ready for trial? He has, indeed, made a computation of time, to show, that Wilkinson could not have been here before this period; and he has besides, introduced an affidavit to show, that an express was on his way to Orleans, to give him an early summons. There is however, nothing in proof, that the drawer of this affidavit was not imposed on, by this express; or that the express himself was not mistaken, as to the contents of his dispatches. And how stands the computation as to time? The post goes from Washington to New-Orleans, in seventeen days. Mr. Rodney left this city, in the last of March. The express must, therefore, have reached New-Orleans, about the 20th of April; and yet, where is Wilkinson? Though the Mississippi runs down to New-Orleans, and opposes a strong current to those who ascend it, yet it is surely a reasonable proposition, that on land it requires no longer time to come than to go, and yet general Wilkinson is not here!

Mr. Hay says, it is of no consequence, whether the grand jury is present or not. But is this consonant with the sound principles of law? Is it constitutional, sir, where there is a particular body, set apart for the investigation of facts, for the court to step in, and rudely take this power from them? He says, that, perhaps, he shall not send up his bills before the present grand jury. But I trust in God, sir, that this determination will be overruled by the court; and that if this prosecution is ever to be closed, we may see the curtain dropt upon it now and for ever! If, sir, the counsel for the prosecution obtain a postponement of this trial, and for want of evidence on their part, we might probably contend, that colonel Burr, if bound to bail at all, should be held in a smaller recognisance than at present. But we shall waive this right. It is not our wish to discharge the grand jury, but to set this question at rest forever.

We have said, that we were ready for trial. We are so, sir, in fact, as well as in the abstract. The prosecutors say, that we do not believe them to be ready: but how can the gentleman suppose, that we mean to pay so poor a compliment to his veracity, as to believe, that he acts upon his own facts, as if he, himself, did not believe them to be true?

The gentleman, sir, has warmly eulogized the present administration. As a private citizen, sir, no man has less to say with the politics of this country than myself. That gentleman has drawn a picture of our national prosperity; and I am happy to hope, that it is true to the life, in every thing, one feature only excepted. What, however, will he say of the persecution of my client? Sir, let that gentleman draw the most animated picture of our happiness, which his imagination can supply; let it be howsoever cheering, or howsoever just, it will be but little alleviation to the wounds of my persecuted client, that he is the only man in the nation whose rights are not secure from violation.

Mr. BURR then rose and addressed the court to the following effect:

I am not, I hope, sir, wasting the time of the court upon the present occasion. The motion proposed, is admitted on all hands, to be important; and it is certainly a new one. Perhaps it was to have been expected, that on a point so novel, some precedents would have been produced; but, in this expectation we have been disappointed. Its novelty will, however, be productive of another effect. It will still better qualify it for making another small feature in a picture of oppressions and grievances, which have never been paralleled in the records of criminal law.

The case is this; no man denies the authority of the court, to commit for a crime; but no commitment ought to be made, except on probable cause. This authority is necessary; because policy requires, that there should be some power to bind an accused individual for his personal appearance, until there shall have been sufficient time to obtain witnesses, for his trial; but this power ought to be controlled as much as possible.

The question in the present case, is, whether there is probable cause of guilt; and, whether time ought to be allowed to collect testimony against me? This time ought generally to be limited; but there is no precise standard on the subject; and much is of course left to the sound discretion of the court. Two months ago, however, you declared, that there had been time enough to collect the evidence, necessary to commit, on probable cause; and surely, if this argument was good then, it is still better now.

As soon as a prosecutor has notice of a crime, he generally looks out for witnesses. It is his object to obtain probable cause for committing the accused. Five months ago, a high authority declared, that there was a crime; that I was at the head of it; and it mentioned the very place, too, where the crime was in a state of preparation. The principal witness against me, is said to be Mr. Wilkinson. Now, from what period is the time to be computed? If, from the time I was suspected, five months; if, from the time when I was seized, three months; or is it to be only computed from the time when I was committed? So that it is near forty days since the notice must have arrived at New-Orleans. But a vessel navigates the coast, from New-Orleans to Norfolk, in three weeks. I contend, however, that witnesses ought to be procured, from the very time when the crimes are said to be committed. There is, then, no apology for the delay of the prosecution, as far as it respects the only person for whom an apology is attempted to be made.

There are other serious objections to my situation. Must I be ready to proceed to trial? True, sir, but then it must be in their own way. Are we then on equal terms here? Certainly not. And again, as to affidavits. The United States can have compulsory process to obtain them; but I have no such advantage. An ex parte evidence, then, is brought before this court, on a motion for commitment. The evidence on one side only is exhibited; but if I had mine also to adduce, it would probably contradict and counteract the evidence of the United States. Well, sir, and these affidavits are put into the newspapers, and they fall into the hands of the grand jury. I have no such means as these, sir; and where then is the equality between the government and myself.

The opinion of the court, too, is to be committed against me. Is this no evil?

A sufficient answer, sir, has been given to the argument about my delay; and its disadvantages to myself have been ably developed. But my counsel have been charged with declamation against the government of the United States. I certainly, sir, shall not be charged with declamation; but surely it is an established principle, sir, that no government is so high as to be beyond the reach of criticism; and it is more particularly laid down, that this vigilance is more peculiarly necessary, when any government institutes a prosecution : and one reason is, on account of the vast disproportion of means which exists between it and the accused. But, if ever there was a case which justified this vigilance, it is certainly the present one, when the government has displayed such uncommon activity. If, then, this government has been so peculiarly active against me, it is not improper to make the assertion here, for the purpose of increasing the circumspection of the court.

Mr. Burr observed, that he meant by persecution, the harassing of any individual, contrary to the forms of law; and that his case, unfortunately, presented too many instances of this description. He would merely state a few of them. He said, that his friends had been every where seized by the military authority; a practice truly consonant with European despotisms. He said, that persons had been dragged by compulsory process before particular tribunals, and compelled to give testimony against him. His papers, too, had been seized. And yet, in England, where we say they know nothing of liberty, a gentleman, who had been seized and detained two hours, in a back parlour, had obtained damages to the amount of one thousand guineas. He said, that an order had been issued to kill him, as he was descending the Mississippi, and seize his property. And yet, they could only have killed his person, if he had been formally condemned for treason. He said, that even post-offices had been broken open, and robbed of his papers; that, in the Mississippi Territory, even an indictment was about to be laid against the postmaster; that he had always taken this for a felony; but that nothing seemed too extravagant to be forgiven by the amiable morality of this government. All this, said Mr. Burr, may only prove that my case is a solitary exception from the general rule. The government may be tender, mild and humane to every one but me. If so, to be sure it is of little consequence to any body but myself. But surely I may be excused if I complain a little of such proceedings. Mr. Burr said, there seemed to be something mingled in those proceedings, which manifested a more than usual inclination to attain the ends of justice : as far as it related to himself, perhaps, these things were of no account; but what was then to be said of those and other measures, such as the suspension of the *habeas corpus* act, which concerned the whole nation? If in the island of Great Britain such a measure was calculated to produce so much disturbance, what kind of sensation ought it to produce in this country.

Our president, said Mr. Burr, is a lawyer, and a great one too. He certainly ought to know what it is, that constitutes a war. Six months ago, he proclaimed that there was a civil war. And yet, for six months have they been hunting for it, and still cannot find one spot where it existed. There was, to be sure, a most terrible war in the newspapers; but no where else. When I appeared before the grand jury, in Kentucky, they had no charge to bring against me, and I was consequently dismissed. When I appeared for a second time, before a grand jury, in the Mississippi Territory, there was nothing to appear against me; and the judge even told the United States attorney, that if he did not send up his bill before the grand jury, he himself would proceed to name as many of the witnesses as he could, and bring it before the court. Still there was no proof of war. At length, however, the Spaniards invaded our territory, and yet, there was no war. But, sir, if there was a war, certainly no man can pretend to say, that the government is able to find it out. The scene to which they have now hunted it, is only 300 miles distant, and still there is no evidence to prove this war.

Mr. Burr requested the court to consider the consequence which would now result from a commitment for treason; that if he were bound now, the law of Virginia declared, that he should so remain until the next term; that this delay was the very inconvenience he would wish to avoid; and that he presumed he was to remain in prison six months, until they could find out this war.

Here the arguments closed, and the court then adjourned till to-morrow morning at ten o'clock.

TUESDAY, MAY 26th, 1807.

The following Opinion was delivered by the Chief Justice of the United States, on Mr. Hay's motion to commit colonel Burr.

IN considering the question which was argued yesterday, it appears to be necessary to decide:

1st, Whether the court, sitting as a court, possesses the power to commit any person charged with an offence against the United States.

2dly, If this power be possessed, whether circumstances exist in this case which ought to restrain its exercise.

The first point was not made in the argument, and would, if decided against the attorney for the United States, only change the mode of proceeding. If a doubt can exist respecting it, that doubt arises from the omission in the laws of the United States to invest their courts, sitting as courts, with the power in question. It is expressly given to every justice and judge, but not to a court.

This objection was not made on the part of colonel Burr, and is now mentioned, not because it is believed to present any intrinsic difficulty, but to show that it has been considered.

This power is necessarily exercised by courts in discharge of their functions, and seems not to have been expressly given; because it is implied in the duties which a court must perform, and the judicial act contemplates it in this light. They have cognisance of all crimes against the United States; they are composed of the persons who can commit for those crimes; and it is obviously understood, by the legislature, that the judges may exercise collectively the power which they possess individually, so far as is necessary to enable them to retain a person charged with an offence in order to receive the judgment which may finally be rendered in his case. The court say, this is obviously understood by the legislature; because there is no clause expressly giving to the court the power to bail or to commit a person, who appears in discharge of his recognisance, and against whom the attorney for the United States does not choose to proceed; and yet the thirty-third section of the judicial act evinces a clear understanding in the legislature, that the power to take bail is in possession of the court.

If a person shall appear in conformity with his recognisance, and the court passes away without taking any order respecting him, he is discharged. A new recognisance, therefore, or a commitment on the failure to enter into one, is in the nature of an original commitment, and this power has been uniformly exercised.

It is believed to be a correct position, that the power to commit for offences of which it has cognisance, is exercised by every court of criminal jurisdiction, and that courts as well as individual magistrates are conservators of the peace.

Were it otherwise, the consequence would only be, that it would become the duty of the judge to descend from the bench, and, in his character as an individual magistrate, to do that which the court is asked to do.

If the court possesses the power, it is certainly its duty to hear the motion which has been made on the part of the United States; for, in cases of the character of that under consideration, its duty and its power are coextensive with each other. It was observed when the motion was made, and the observation may now be repeated, that the arguments urged on the part of the accused rather prove the motion on the part of the United States unnecessary, or that inconveniences may result from it, than the want of a legal right to make it.

The first is, that the grand jury being now in session ready to receive an indictment, the attorney for the United States ought to proceed by bill instead of applying to the court, since the only purpose of a commitment is to bring the accused before a grand jury. This statement contains an intrinsic error which destroys its operation. The commitment is not made for the sole purpose of bringing the accused before a grand jury; it is made for the purpose of subjecting him personally to the judgment of the law, and the grand jury is only the first step towards that judgment. If, as has been argued, the commitment was simply to detain the person until a grand jury could be obtained; then its operation would cease on the assembling of a grand jury; but such is not the fact. The order of commitment retains its force while the jury is in session, and if the prosecutor does not proceed, the court is accustomed to retain a prisoner in confinement, or to renew his recognisance to a subsequent term.

The arguments drawn from the general policy of our laws; from the attention which should be bestowed on prosecutions, instituted by special order of the executive; from the peculiar inconveniences and hardships of this particular case; from the improper effects which inevitably result from this examination, are some of them subjects for the consideration of those who make the motion, rather than of the court; and others go to the circumspection with which the testimony in support of the motion ought to be weighed, rather than to the duty of hearing it.

It has been said that colonel Burr already stands charged with treason, and that, therefore, a motion to commit him for the same offence is improper. But the fact is not so understood by the court. The application to charge him with treason was rejected by the judge to whom it was made, because the testimony offered in support of the charge did not furnish probable cause for the opinion, that the crime had been committed. After this rejection, colonel Burr stood, so far as respected his legal liability to have the charge repeated, in precisely the same situation as if it had never been made. He appears in court now as if the crime of treason had never before been alleged against him. That it has been alleged, that the government had had time to collect testimony for the establishment of the fact, that an immense crowd of witnesses are attending for the purpose, that the prosecutor in his own judgment has testimony to support the indictment, are circumstances which may have their influence on the motion for a commitment, or on a continuance, but which cannot deprive the attorney for the United States of the right to make his motion. If he was about to send up a bill to the grand jury, he might move that the person he designed to accuse, should be ordered into custody, and it would be in the discretion of the court to grant or to reject the motion.

The court perceives and regrets that the result of this motion may be publications unfavourable to the justice, and to the right decision of the case; but if this consequence is to be prevented, it must be by other means than by refusing to hear the motion. No man, feeling a correct sense of the importance which ought to be attached by all to a fair and impartial administration of justice, especially in criminal prosecutions, can view, without extreme solicitude, any attempt which may be made to prejudice the public judgment, and to try any person, not by the laws of his country and the testimony exhibited against him, but by public feelings, which may be and often are artificially excited against the innocent, as well as the guilty. But the remedy, for a practice not less dangerous than it is criminal, is not to be obtained by suppressing motions, which either party may have a legal right to make.

If it is the choice of the prosecutor on the part of the United States to proceed with this motion, it is the opinion of the court that he may open his testimony.

Mr. HAY then rose, and observed, that he was struck with the observations of the court relative to " publications," and he would attempt if possible to make some arrangement with the counsel on the other side to obviate that inconvenience; and he understood they were disposed to do the same.

The counsel on both sides then retired by permission of the court for this purpose. They returned in a short time; and Mr. Hay informed the court that the counsel for the United States, and for colonel Burr, not having yet been able to agree upon any arrangement which would attain his object, namely, that of having colonel Burr recognised in a sum sufficiently large to insure his appearance to answer the charge of high treason against the United States, without incurring the inconvenience resulting from a public disclosure of the evidence at this early stage of the proceeding, wished to have further time for that desirable purpose. This was granted by the court, and it then adjourned till next day.

WEDNESDAY, MAY 27th, 1807.

Mr. HAY informed the court, that all hopes of the arrangement which he had mentioned yesterday were at an end: for he had received a letter from colonel Burr's counsel, positively refusing to give additional bail. He therefore deemed it his duty to go on with the examination of the witnesses in support of his motion to commit Mr. Burr. He observed, that he regretted extremely that it became necessary in his judgment to pursue this course. He felt the full force of the objections to a disclosure of the evidence, and to the necessity of the court's declaring its opinion, before the case was laid before a jury; but those considerations must yield to a sense of what his engagements to the United States imperiously demanded of him: that in adducing the evidence, he should observe something like chronological order. He should first read the depositions of the witnesses who were absent, and afterwards bring forward those who were present, so as to disclose all the events, as they successively happened.

Mr. WICKHAM stated that there were two distinct charges against colonel Burr. The first was for a misdemeanor, for which he had already entered into recognisance; the second was a charge of high treason against the United States, which was once proposed without success, and is now again repeated. On this charge the United States must substantiate two essential points: 1st, That there was an overt act committed; and 2dly, That colonel Burr was concerned in it. Every thing that does not bear upon these points is of course inadmissible; the course therefore laid down by the attorney for the United States is obviously improper. He proposes to examine his witnesses in a kind of chronological order.

Colonel Burr requires that the evidence should be taken in strict legal order. The court and even the opposite counsel will see the propriety of observing this order. If the attorney for the United States has affidavits to produce, let him first demonstrate that they have a right to produce them. We first call upon him to prove, by strict legal evidence, that an overt act of treason has been committed. If he cannot establish that one point, all the evidence which he can produce, is nugatory and unavailing.

Mr. HAY had no doubt, that the gentleman would, if he could, suppress all the evidence; that although that gentleman had been so good as to prescribe for him the course he ought to pursue, he should still pursue his own course; and he would assure that gentleman, that he was almost the last person in the world, whose advice on the present occasion he would pursue. Mr. Hay observed, that he could not consent to such a separation of the evidence, as that gentleman required; that he should lay all his evidence before the court, and that the court must separate for themselves.

The two charges which are brought against Aaron Burr are naturally and intimately blended. They form distinct parts of one great design. What that great design was, in all its bearings and ramifications, I am not absolutely certain; but I have always conceived, that before Mexico was invaded, New-Orleans was to be taken. How then is it possible to separate these two great allegations? This monstrous design consists of two great plots; both going on together; and both so strongly connected, that accomplishing the one is preparatory to accomplishing the other. If Aaron Burr's object was to plant his standard in Mexico, he was first to have seized the shipping and banks of New-Orleans. We ask then, how can we separate line by line, and word by word, the evidence produced to prove these two distinct allegations? The designs are connected: and the evidence is connected.

Mr. Burr rose to speak, when Mr. Hay proceeded to the following effect: I have a little more yet to say. If, sir, exceptions are thus to be continually taken to the most common measures; if in this way every inch of ground is to be disputed, contrary to every practice that has prevailed in our country; instead of ten hours, or ten days, this trial will take up ten years. What an extraordinary proceeding is this, sir! Why, sir, we are not to steer our course even five inches without encountering some unusual difficulty or other! and yet these gentlemen talk of precedents. And where, sir, are the precedents for this, that the counsel before an examining court is to be instructed how to bring out his evidence? I never saw such a thing done before; such a thing ought not to be done. It is novel in itself, it is impossible to be supported. Gentlemen may make motions as they please: but they will not drive me from my purpose. I will or I will not produce my evidence, whether it pleases them or not. And sir, it is a poor compliment indeed that these gentlemen offer to the bench whom they address! If a deposition states any thing or a witness says any thing which is irrelevant to the case, cannot the court be trusted with these distinctions? Cannot they decide, whether this evidence is to be weighed, or that to be rejected? Do they distrust the judgment of the court? No, sir, they do not; but they wish to hamper us with every trifling difficulty, which they can throw into our path. The present, sir, is a most serious allegation. It affects the life and character of the accused. He has come forward with assertions of his own innocence; and he charges us with persecution. But, sir, does it evince any consciousness of innocence, thus to be going against every precedent established in this or any other country? Sir, I trust, that the court will go on in spite of all opposition.

Mr. WICKHAM stated, that having taken the liberty of suggesting this course of proceeding, he should advance a few observations on it; and he did this the more readily, because it had been insinuated that no man, standing like himself as a professional man, would have made a motion of this sort. [Mr. Hay declared he had said no such thing.] Mr. Wickham said he had rights as counsel for his client, and he had rights belonging to himself. No man is heard for himself; but so long as they employed professional men to defend them, these had a right to pursue the best course they could devise for the benefit of their client. He would therefore go on.

Mr. Hay speaks of two distinct charges; the invasion of Mexico, and the seizing of New-Orleans: but he declares them to be necessarily blended. How so? Could not a man "levy war" against the United States without an invasion of Mexico? In Pennsylvania we have seen an insurrection against the United States, but no invasion of Mexico. Much is said of the loss of time, and of certain difficulties thrown in the way of the prosecution.

As to the first, sir, let the world decide whether he or we have most pleaded for delay; at all events, we cannot entertain any fear that this court will be impatient. As to the difficulties in their way, we will say this: let the gentlemen pursue a regular course; let them bring this business before the grand jury, and we shall make no objections. But, sir, if they pursue this course over and over again; if they are continually throwing difficulties in our way; we shall mete out to them the same measure which they mete to us. Who has ever known a proceeding like the present? Who has ever heard of the practice of coming out at such a stage as this with a distinct substantive charge, not growing out of the evidence before the court, but from other sources? Surely these gentlemen do not cry out for mercy: they stand upon the law; and law they shall have. Gentlemen say, that no such exception as this was ever taken before an examining magistrate. But, sir, where are the reporters that attend private magistrates, to record their precedents? Magistrates are to go by law; and what law? They must observe the rules of evidence. Would gentlemen introduce their witnesses without swearing them? But the court must have all the evidence before them; and " they must separate" the good from the bad: but is this consistent with common sense; is it consistent with the books? The practice has always been, when an attorney introduces a writing into court, for the court to ask what he is to prove by it; when he introduces a paper, to show the general contents of that paper. This was the practice on the memorable trials of Hardy and Tooke in England. In chancery business, indeed, a practice has crept in for the judge himself to read papers without knowing any thing of their general contents; but this is done merely for the sake of convenience, and will not certainly apply to criminal prosecutions.

It is asked, " Are we afraid to trust the court" with this evidence ? No, sir, we are afraid to trust the court with nothing : but we do fear to prejudicate the mind of the grand jury, by this premature and illegal exhibition of evidence. Let the time come, when colonel Burr is to come regularly before the jury, and we shall then see who shrinks from the testimony. A number of other remarks have been made, sir, about colonel Burr's apprehensions. All propriety and decorum have been set at nought: every idle tale which is set afloat has been eagerly caught at. The people here are interested by them; and they circulate all over the country. Sir, if the attorney for the United States shall choose to send up his bills before the grand jury, then I hope the whole evidence will be laid before the world, and we shall hear no more of rumours and prejudices.

These gentlemen say, " Shall you pretend to order us; shall you dictate ?" No, sir, the law must dictate. The gentlemen, indeed, have produced a series of irrelevant writings and papers; and they must, forsooth, pursue a chronological order. No, sir, away with such informalities. Let gentlemen prove an assemblage of men for war. Let them prove the overt act. If they do not, I confidently hope, that colonel Burr will be discharged. Mr. Wickham here read a quotation from Foster's Discourses on High Treason.

Mr. Burr did not expect an opinion of the court, since no motion had been made. Mr. Wickham had only given notice to the opposite side, that they should follow the strictest rules of law. If it was for a suit of 10*l.* only, he should ask for the laws of evidence.

The Chief Justice said, it would certainly be better, if evidence was produced to prove the facts first, and the evidence to show their colouring : for no evidence certainly has any bearing upon the present case, unless the overt act be proved. However, if the attorney for the United States thinks the chronological order the best, he may pursue his own course; but the court trusts to him, that he will produce nothing which does not bear upon the case.

Mr. Wirt.—We coincide with the opinion of the court, that an overt act ought to be proved, and that we ought to produce no evidence at all, unless we believed we had enough to prove the overt act. We do believe that we have sufficient evidence for this purpose; but we think it best to pursue something like a chronological order: to take this conspiracy in its germ, to go on step by step, and to trace out every event as it subsequently arose.

Mr. HAY observed that it would be necessary to give evidence to show the temper of mind of the accused : as for instance, Mr. Stoddert would show his hostility to the administration, and even to the government. To show this disposition of mind might lead to treasonable designs, to plans, and thence to overt acts. This was the natural order of things, and of the evidence. He hoped, that in drawing out this evidence, the court would rely upon his candour and humanity, that he would produce none which he did not believe to bear upon the fact.

Mr. RANDOLPH said, that however he might respect that gentleman's humanity, he knew too well the temper of any prosecution to expect much from it. They are for strict law, said Mr. Randolph, and so are we. In England, before a witness is heard, it must be stated in general terms what he intends to prove. The same practice ought to prevail here. Let the attorney for the United States state the substance of each part of the testimony he is to produce, and the court will then perceive, whether it is calculated to bear upon the case itself, or whether it is only intended to inflame the public prejudices against colonel Burr. We demand, that the overt act be first proved : without that, the accessorial evidence is of no kind of use. Let that be established, and the accessory facts will then have their weight. I hope, sir, if the attorney for the United States does not introduce his evidence on that point, we shall be at liberty to suppress all the irrelevant testimony.

Mr. BOTTS said he should leave it to the court.

Mr. HAY.—Agreed.

The CHIEF JUSTICE decided, that the attorney for the United States might pursue whatever course he thought best.

Mr. BOTTS.—Send us the written testimony before you submit it to the court.

Mr. HAY.—As I said before, I shall take up the depositions first, and then the *viva voce* testimony in a chronological order. I shall first introduce general Wilkinson's deposition.

Some desultory conversation then ensued, between Mr. Hay and Mr. Botts, on the latter demanding the liberty of examining the deposition. At length, Mr. Hay handed the paper to him. Mr. Botts then addressed the court.

Mr. BOTTS.—In my objections to general Wilkinson's affidavit, I may be compelled to question the correctness of principles, in favour of which the court has expressed an impression. It has been our misfortune, to have been drawn out into a desultory discussion of some of the propositions, fixing limits to the examination; when these propositions had such relation to each other, and among themselves, as to render it difficult to fortify one effectually against assault, without the support of the others. And although the subject was not wanting in novelty or importance, to fit it for solemn argument, yet the complaints of the prosecutor, so often, so loudly, and so causelessly repeated, have forced from the court a premature intimation of judgment. I feel the perplexity of my situation most sensibly, and shall hope for the indulgence of the court, if I should unwarily stray into the seeming indecorum of resisting, now and then, an inclination of the mind of the bench. Whenever I venture into a scene so delicate, I shall present to the court authorities not to be resisted.

The opinion of the supreme court overruling the objection, that the oath administered to general Wilkinson was extrajudicial, fixes the law for this court. The best evidence that the nature of the case will admit of, should be produced. This rule applies to every stage of every case in every court. The failure to produce the best evidence that the nature of the case admits of, furnishes a presumption, that the higher evidence left behind, would, if produced, make against the party offering the weaker. All this is familiar in civil cases, where 40s. may be the quantum of interest in litigation. The benefit of this common law, and common sense, ought not to be lost, when the liberty of a citizen is concerned; when a six months' imprisonment in a dungeon may be the object of the motion. The supreme court considered an affidavit as the best evidence the case then admitted of. The accusation was fresh, and neither time nor means had been allowed for procuring a personal attendance. Now, the accusation is old, and the government has had all the necessary means of bringing the witness here. The circumstances do, therefore, now admit of higher evidence than an ex parte affidavit.

The *viva voce* testimony of general Wilkinson is the right of my client. No man should be deprived of the benefit of a cross examination, without necessity. You have in another place said, sir, that it was to be made out only by inference from general Wilkinson's affidavit, that colonel Burr was the writer of the letter in cypher. If the witness was here, he would impugn that inference, by swearing that it was not in colonel Burr's hand writing. If general Wilkinson was present, would you admit his affidavit? If he ought to have been present, and the government would not get him, shall the prosecution be favoured for its negligence?

But the present charge is confined to high treason, in levying war against the United States; and the great question is, whether Wilkinson's evidence is in any form pertinent to the charge? I do not mean to urge the objection, that if it develops any criminal purpose, it is not a treasonable purpose; for this construction has been settled by the supreme court. Admitting for the time, that it contained evidence of a treasonable purpose, and that the opinion of the supreme court is to be overruled, still the evidence would be most impertinent upon the present charge of *actual* treason.

I have alluded to legal propositions, intended to be pressed, as forming legal restrictions upon the task in which we are engaged. I will first combine them, that their fitness to each other, and their collective effects, may be seen. My second process will be to disunite them, and by an analytical comparison of them with the known principles of our treason laws, to ascertain their legality.

No evidence of any matter ought to be given, until proof shall be adduced, that there was an actual war levied in the district of Virginia; and, until it is proved that an overt act of treason, in that war, was done by colonel Burr, which proofs shall be by two witnesses at least. First, It must be proved that there was an actual war. A war consists wholly in acts, and not in intentions. The acts must be in themselves acts of war; and if they be not so intrinsically, words or intentions cannot make them so. In England, when conspiring the death of the king was treason, the *quo animo* formed the essence of the offence; but in America, the national convention has confined treason to the act. We cannot have a constructive war within the meaning of the constitution. An intention to levy war, is not evidence that a war was levied. Intentions are always mutable and variable; the continuance of guilty intentions is not to be presumed. If this were not the case, the avowal of a purpose to levy war would fix the crime. For a proved intention might be attached to the next innocent act of the person who formed it; and so, preparations of emigration be turned into a levying of war. It has been eloquently declared, that war cannot exist in a closet, or a corner; but when levied, it must be in the face of the world. This cannot be true, if the recesses of the bosom are to be explored for any of the ingredients in the composition of the crime of levying war. The guilty intention must be made manifest from the act alone. General Wilkinson professes to know nothing but of intentions, which are not evidence of acts.

Secondly, The war must not only have been levied, but colonel Burr must be proved to have committed an overt act of treason in that war. A treasonable intention to cooperate is no evidence of an actual cooperation. The acts of others, even if in pursuance of his plan, would be no evidence against him. It might not be necessary that he should be present, perhaps; but he must be, at the time of levying the war, cooperating by acts, or, in the language of the constitution, be committing overt acts. The acts of associates, in a treasonable plan, in countries where the doctrine of constructive war prevails, can never be given in evidence, against the accused, until after the plan has been proved on the latter, and until such acts shall appear to have been within the limits of that plan. 1 East's Crown Law, 96, 97. Part of the proof in this affidavit is of the declarations of a supposed associate, as to what the plan itself was. But in this country, as there cannot be a constructive treasonable war, plans, and acts of associates, can only come in when the former have been executed, and the latter have been visibly and publicly assisted. Tucker's Black. vol. 4. Appendix B.

Thirdly, The overt act by the accused, in an actual war, must not only be proved, but it must be proved to have been committed within this district. The fifth article of the constitution of the United States, and the eighth article of the amendments to the constitution, require, that the trial shall be by a jury of the district where the offence was committed. The oath of the grand jury is, accordingly, to inquire of offences within the district. The jurisdiction of this court is also limited, by express law, to offences within the district; and it is obviously true, that the court's jurisdiction cannot be broader in an incipient inquiry than it would be in its connexion with a jury on a final trial. Doctor Blackstone, in the fourth volume of his Commentaries, 303, refers to the oath of the grand jury, " to inquire" into offences committed within the body of the county, and denies the right of the grand jury to inquire into facts out of the county. In preparing a work for the grand jury the court cannot disregard the limits of their power. The crime to be committed in the district must be wholly committed there. At the common law, if the stroke was given in one county, and the person striken died in another, the murderer could not be prosecuted in either. To remedy this defect, and to provide for others similar to it, many provisions have been made by the English parliament. 4 Black. 303, 4, 5. But the English parliament never did alter the common law, as it respected the crime of levying an actual treasonable war. Kelyng, 15. The constitution and act of congress have both adopted the rule of location. Tucker's Blackstone, vol. 4. Appendix B. 49, 50, 51. Granting then, that intention may make that war, which would not otherwise be so, still, as a formed intention is no proof of its own continuance or execution, the intention must be proved to have been cotemporaneous and homogeneous with the act in the district. In this view, the intention forms a constituent part of the offence. If one constituent part of the offence can be brought from without the district, and coupled with others in the district, any one constituent part, or number of constituent parts, of the crime, may be brought from without the district. Then one component part only happening in Virginia, out of one hundred necessary to its completion, would give this court jurisdiction; and thence one, out of one hundred parts of a crime, would be a crime within the meaning of the constitution. Let us view the consequences of this logic.

Upon proof against colonel Burr touching a crime, part of which was committed in this district, he may be tried and ac quitted. In Ohio he may be indicted, and evidence may be prepared touching the same crime. Can he plead autrefois acquit in bar, by averring, that the crimes charged in the two states was one and the same? His averment would be against the record of the indictment charging a complete separate crime in each district. Will you, sir, put upon the constitution such a construction as will subject a citizen to be hunted down, by trial after trial, in state after state, as long as the persecuting spirit of a wicked executive may last? Do not understand me to allude, in this, to the present administration, the characters of which I have been in the habit of admiring; but the construction now to be fixed must go down to posterity, and may be made instrumental in effecting the worst of state oppressions.

Remember that colonel Burr has forborn to avail himself of this legal principle in Kentucky and in the Mississippi Territory, in order that the merits of his case might come before the inquests; but it ought now to be agreed that he should protect himself from being harassed further, by calling into exercise the great principles of the constitution, declaring that no man shall be twice put in jeopardy of his life for the same offence. See amendments to constitution. Now, what part of the affidavit speaks of a fact within the district?

Fourthly, The overt act of treason by colonel Burr within the district must be proved by two witnesses. The constitution and act of congress require two witnesses, not only to the act, but to the treasonable quality of the act. After full time has been afforded to collect all the witnesses in the power of the government, the accused ought not to be deprived of his liberty, unless it was believed that the evidence collected would convict him: imprisonment is only intended for trial and not for punishment. By what does general Wilkinson's affidavit make out intentions? The answer is, by the confessions of the accused or of his supposed associates. The confessions of the accused, by the express words of the constitution, are not evidence, unless made in open court. Confessions are often admitted, from necessity, to get at crimes that deal in secrecy; as larceny, forgery and robbery: but the safety of the people requires that crimes, which deal in publicity, as does the crime of a treasonable war, should not be proved by evidence so incapable of exculpatory proof. When an honourable gentleman (Mr. Giles) was challenged the other day upon a suggestion of his having expressed himself upon the case of the accused, he said he was indisposed to hear evidence of unguarded expressions, in which the witness might have mistaken his meaning; have misunderstood what he said, or not have heard all that he said; or have substituted his own inferences for the words of the speaker. Blackstone and Foster have characterised it to be the most dangerous species of evidence, ever liable to misconstruction and abuse. But if the constitution has proscribed it, why now question its exclusion? If the confessions of the accused, out of court, could not be evidence, against him, could the confessions of real accomplices be evidences against him? Yet the evidence of Wilkinson relates, in part, to the confession of pretended accomplices, no way proved to have been authorised by colonel Burr to say or to do any thing.

But why, it may be asked, is colonel Burr afraid to hear illegal evidence, if he is consciously innocent?

We see witnesses from different and distant parts of the United States, whose names, faces and characters, are alike unknown to colonel Burr. He cannot ascertain upon what parts of his life or conduct they are expected to speak, or upon what information their evidence may rest. His character has long been on public torture; and wherever that happens, with either a good or a bad man, the impulses to false testimony are numerous. Sometimes men emerge from the sinks of vice and obscurity into patronage and distinction by circulating interesting tales, as all those of the marvelous kind are. Others, from expectations of office and reward, volunteer; while timidity, in a third class, seeks to guard against the apprehended danger, by magnifying trifling stories of alarm. These works of exaggeration and propagation are frequently the subjects of idle amusement. The authors, until they commit themselves, have no just conception of the mischiefs they are hatching; but when they are afterwards called to give testimony, perjury will not appal them, if it be necessary to save their reputations for consistency or veracity. If the evidence be restricted within the legal limits, the purest of characters, under accusation of treason, will have hazard enough to run. A judge, whose experience of these dangers was great, thus speaks on the subject: " The rule of rejecting all manner of evidence in criminal prosecutions, that is foreign to the point in issue, is founded on sound sense and common justice. For no man is bound, at the peril of life or liberty, fortune or reputation, to answer, at once, and unprepared, for every action of his life." Few, even of the best of men, would choose to be put to it. And had not those concerned in the state prosecutions, out of their zeal for the public service, sometimes stepped over this rule in the case of treason, it would, perhaps, have been needless to have made an express provision against it in that case. Foster's C. L. 246.

Mr. WICKHAM regretted that so much time had been consumed; but hoped the court would acquit them of any intention to waste it. When any illegal motion was introduced by
the opposite counsel, he felt it as a serious duty due to his
client to resist it with firmness. That for his own part he should
not forget that he was before the circuit court of the United
States, nor should he so far lose his respect for their discernment as to bring forward motions, which he believed to be illegal, only to waste the time of the court; that he hoped none
but legal evidence would be suffered to be introduced; none
but competent witnesses to be heard; and if this rule was not
rigidly adhered to, what was to prevent the counsel on the other
side from producing any and every kind of evidence that they
pleased?

It cannot be supposed, said Mr. Wickham, that we are afraid
of this affidavit. What is in it, which has not been already
known and scattered in every loose sheet of a newspaper
throughout the United States? It is not that we resist it in
point of fact; but on the ground of principle. We wish two
points to be settled: are affidavits to be read at all on such a
motion, and at such a crisis of the prosecution as this? and if
so, ought they to be read if the witnesses themselves were
present? Would it be right, if they were in the next street or
the next county? Would it in fact be right if there was time
enough to produce the ' viva voce' testimony itself? Mr. Burr
had a right to be confronted with general Wilkinson. He had
a right to crossquestion and examine him on all the statements which he has made. The government had power to
bring him here. Why is he not here? Ought not some satisfactory excuse to be made for him? He is an officer of this government; and the government might have procured his attendance, as well by a special order as by a civil process. Has any
subpœna been taken out, inquired Mr. Wickham, addressing
himself to the clerk?

The clerk replied, that no subpœna filled up with general
Wilkinson's name had issued from his office; but that blank
subpœnas had been taken out.

Mr. Wickham.—No one knows, sir. There was time enough
to have him here. The mail travels from Washington to New-
Orleans in seventeen days. He might have come; but if he has
not, why is not some satisfactory excuse brought forward? We
want, sir, to see this gentleman crossexamined. We want to
see him confronted with other witnesses. This is one ground
on which we object to the production of this affidavit.

Another ground is, that according to the decision of the supreme court of the United States, this affidavit does not bear

upon the present motion. Mr. Swartwout, who was said to be connected with colonel Burr, was discharged by them, because this affidavit did not apply to the charge of treason. Are counsel then to be suffered to produce testimony on any subject that they please? A third objection is, that general Wilkinson does not relate a single act, committed in the district of Virginia. In Virginia? no, nor any where else. The attorney for the United States says, that he will prove the overt act hereafter. But, sir, I repeat it, that the rules of evidence apply not only to the admissibility of evidence, but to the order in which it is to be produced. Let them first prove an overt act, if they can; and then they are at full liberty to prove the colour of it.

Again, sir, this deposition is not the best evidence which could be produced, and which the laws require. General Wilkinson speaks of a cyphered letter, and of its contents, as well as he can make them out. Now, sir, where is this letter; and where is the key to it? Why are they not here? Why are they not produced before you? For these reasons, Mr. Wickham hoped, that the court would not suffer the affidavit to be read in evidence.

Mr. HAY.—We shall not, sir, be carried from our course by speeches, however long or animated they may be. But, sir, permit me to give those gentlemen a little information. Why talk of the affidavit before you? Do these gentlemen know, that we can positively prove the astonishment, the regret, and the denunciation which escaped from Mr. Burr, when he first heard of the publication of his cyphered letter! Let them first know what we can prove, before they abandon themselves to their triumph. General Wilkinson's affidavit is the first in the series of our proofs, and it is for this reason that we wish to commence with it.

Mr. EDMUND RANDOLPH.—Sir, we do not know what those gentlemen expect to prove; but we do object to the production of general Wilkinson's affidavit from what is already known: we know it to be perfectly inapplicable to the present question. Sir, this species of evidence is directly in the face of our bill of rights, and of the constitution of the United States. " In all cri-
" minal prosecutions, the accused shall enjoy the right to a speedy
" and public trial, by an impartial jury of the state and district
" wherein the crime shall have been committed; which district
" shall have been previously ascertained by law; and to be in-
" formed of the nature and cause of the accusation; to be con-
" fronted with the witnesses against him, &c." Colonel Burr,
then, sir, has a general constitutional right to be confronted with the witnesses against him. Let gentlemen show any exception to it, if they can. And what have they done? Why, they have shown here an obsolete, an evaporated affidavit, for which there

is no necessity and no law. The law positively declares, that the best evidence is always to be had; that when a witness is attainable, his affidavit is not to be admitted as testimony. We stand, therefore, sir, upon the bill of rights. Gentlemen may, indeed, attempt to evade its provisions by saying, that they can hereafter prove the material act; but I hope that this court will never countenance such illegal proceedings.

The CHIEF JUSTICE stated, that the supreme court of the United States had already decided, that an affidavit might be admitted under certain circumstances; but they had also determined, that general Wilkinson's affidavit did not contain any proof of an overt act; that he was certainly extremely willing to permit the attorney for the United States to pursue his own course in the order of drawing out his evidence, under a full confidence that he would not waste the time of the court by producing any extraneous matter; but where was the necessity of producing general Wilkinson's affidavit first? If there was no other evidence to prove the overt act, Wilkinson's affidavit goes for nothing; for so the supreme court of the United States have already decided; and by that decision he should have conceived himself bound, even if he had dissented from it. Why then produce this affidavit?

Mr. HAY observed, that there was a great difference between the course prescribed by the court, and the one which he would himself have pursued; and that he seriously believed, if he had been left to himself, he would at least have satisfied the court itself that his own course was the best. That as to general Wilkinson's affidavit, it might even now be confronted with witnesses; as Messrs. Bollman and Swartwout were present, and would say whether such and such conversations were ever held, as are detailed in this affidavit. That he was now before an examining court, and not before the petit jury: why then the same strictness of evidence now as would be required on the trial in chief? That he really believed it was the intention of the opposite counsel, by dint of long speeches, to attempt to drive him into their course: but that they ought to know he never consulted the counsel opposed to him; and that they would be the last persons in the world, whose opinions he would consult on the present occasion. That he seriously believed, that the evidence which he possessed, would, beyond the possibility of a doubt, convince the mind of the court, not only of the existence of a traitorous design, but of an overt act; and that all that he asked, was the liberty of producing this evidence in the order which he thought best. Is no part of this deposition, then, admissible? Not a word?

The CHIEF JUSTICE observed, that he thought no part of it admissible at this time; that general Wilkinson's affidavit either contained proof of the treasonable design, which was no proof of the overt act, or it related to conversations, which, however strongly they might bear upon those who held them, did not bear upon colonel Burr.*

Mr. HAY asked, how the court was to be satisfied of the contents of any paper, before it was read to them. An affidavit might contain both the proof of the overt act, and a traitorous design. Was such a paper as this to be read under the decision of the court? or how was the court to know, whether a paper might not contain some proof of the overt act satisfactory to them, unless they had an opportunity of inspecting that paper?

Mr. WICKHAM.—These gentlemen talk of delay; and yet they would produce to this court whole masses of evidence that are perfectly irrelevant to the present question. They declare that they will not pursue our advice; and that we are the last persons whom they would take for counsellors. Sir, we do not ask them; all that we want is, that they would pursue the strict principles of law and legal evidence. One of the best rules of evidence is the order of evidence. If a man is charged with a crime, must not the deed itself exist before any testimony is produced as to the intention with which it is done? I hope that no testimony will be suffered to be introduced before the act itself shall be produced; and I call upon this court to inforce the strict order of evidence.

Mr. BURR observed, that in point of fact, it was very immaterial to him, whether this affidavit was read or not; that what he particularly wanted, was, that the great principles of evidence should be laid down, which would be equally applicable to this, and to all other affidavits. He consented that the court might have this deposition read, if they thought proper.

Mr. HAY.—This deposition will prove that it was one of Aaron Burr's objects to seize upon Mexico. Then, if we can prove by some other evidence, that this object was connected with an attack upon the United States, is not this deposition of material importance in that point of view? If both must be proved, does it make any difference which we begin with? If a conspiracy has been planned of a misdemeanor and of treason so strongly combined that they are made to go on together, and the accomplishment of the one facilitates the accomplishment of the other, is it not of material consequence to prove the misde-

* The chief justice observed, in a subsequent stage of this business, that an idea had since struck his mind, which he thought it material to state; that he had not recollected that these conversations were said to be held by persons who were said to be authorised by colonel Burr; and of course that their conversations would bear upon him.

meanor? I have not myself seen Mr. Taylor, or Mr. Allbright; but I am credibly informed, that they will prove an armed assemblage of men on Blannerhasset's island.

The CHIEF JUSTICE observed, that if there was no fact, or no overt act of treason before the court, the court could have nothing to say to the present motion; that if therefore, no fact was proved, the court could not grant the motion for the prosecution; that he should be extremely sorry to waste the time of the court, and to launch into a variety of irrelevant subjects, when there was actually no testimony to prove the overt act itself, and thus to give the court a competent jurisdiction over the case.

Mr. HAY.—I am bound, sir, to obey the decision of the court. However much I may lament that decision, I shall certainly acquiesce in their order. If I understand the court —

The CHIEF JUSTICE said, that he was of opinion, that unless there be a fact to be proved, no testimony ought to be produced. The question before the court was not whether there had been a treasonable intent, but an overt act. That fact itself must be proved, before there can be any treason, or any commitment for treason. General Wilkinson's affidavit was, accordingly, put aside.

Mr. HAY then called Peter Taylor, who was Mr. Blannerhasset's gardener, and Jacob Allbright, a labourer, who had worked on his island, who gave their testimony. [It is omitted here, because it will be fully detailed in a subsequent and more important part of the report.] After these witnesses had been examined, the affidavit of Jacob Dunbaugh was offered, which was "taken on the fifteenth of April, 1807, before B. Cenas, a justice of the peace," to which was subjoined a certificate of governor William C. C. Claiborne, dated " at New-Orleans, the sixteenth of April, 1807," stating "that B. Cenas was a justice of the peace for the county of New-Orleans."

To the reading of this affidavit several objections were taken by the counsel for colonel Burr, but those most relied on were the following: 1st, That an affidavit could, under no circumstances, be read, unless it were shown, that the witness could not be produced, and that the government had not had sufficient time to procure the attendance of Jacob Dunbaugh. 2dly, That though the governor of New-Orleans had certified that B. Cenas was a justice of the peace, yet he had not said, that it was the same B. Cenas before whom that affidavit was taken. 3dly, That B. Cenas had not stated in the caption of his certificate, or elsewhere, that the affidavit was taken " at New-Orleans," so as to show, that he was acting within his jurisdiction.

The argument on these points was continued to the adjourn-ment of the court, who took time to consider the subject till the next day.

THURSDAY, MAY 28th, 1807.

The court met according to adjournment.

LUTHER MARTIN, Esq. appeared as the counsel of colonel Burr.

On the motion made yesterday, to exclude the evidence of Jacob Dunbaugh, the CHIEF JUSTICE delivered the opinion of the court as follows:

On the part of the United States, a paper, purporting to be an affidavit, has been offered in evidence, to the reading of which two exceptions are taken:

1st, That an affidavit ought not to be admitted, where the personal attendance of the witness could have been obtained.

2dly, That this paper is not so authenticated as to entitle itself to be considered as an affidavit.

That a magistrate may commit upon affidavits has been de-cided in the supreme court of the United States, though not without hesitation. The presence of the witness, to be examin-ed by the committing justice, confronted with the accused, is certainly to be desired; and ought to be obtained, unless consi-derable inconvenience and difficulty exist in procuring his at-tendance. An ex parte affidavit, shaped, perhaps, by the per-son pressing the prosecution, will always be viewed with some suspicion, and acted upon with some caution; but the court thought, it would be going too far to reject it altogether. If it was obvious, that the attendance of the witness was easily at-tainable, but, that he was intentionally kept out of the way, the question might be otherwise decided.

But the particular case before the court does not appear to be of this description. The witness resides at a great distance; and there is no evidence, that the materiality of his testimony was known to the prosecutors or to the executive in time to have directed his attendance. It is true, that general instruc-tions, which would apply to any individual, might have been sent, and the attendance of this, or any other material witness, obtained under those instructions; but it would be requiring too much, to say, that the omission to do this ought to exclude an affidavit. This exception, therefore, will not prevail.

The second is, that the paper is not so authenticated as to be introduced as testimony on a question, which concerns the li-berty of a citizen. This objection is founded on two omissions in the certificate.

The first is, that the place at which the affidavit was taken does not appear,

The second, that the certificate of the governor does not state the person who administered the oath to be a magistrate ; but goes no farther than to say, that a person of that name was a magistrate.

That, for aught appearing to the court, this oath may, or may not, in point of fact, have been legally administered must be conceded. The place, where the oath was administered, not having been stated, it may have been administered where the magistrate had no jurisdiction, and yet the certificate be perfectly true. Of consequence, there is no evidence before the court, that the magistrate had power to administer the oath, and was acting in his judicial capacity.

The effect of testimony may often be doubtful, and courts must exercise their best judgment in the case; but of the verity of the paper there ought never to be a doubt. No paper writing ought to gain admittance into a court of justice as testimony, unless it possesses those solemnities which the law requires. Its authentication must not rest upon probability, but must be as complete as the nature of the case admits of: this is believed to be a clear legal principle. In conformity with it is, as the court conceives, the practice of England and of this country, as is attested by the books of forms ; and no case is recollected, in which a contrary principle has been recognised. This principle is, in some degree, illustrated by the doctrine with respect to all courts of limited jurisdiction. Their proceedings are erroneous, if their jurisdiction be not conclusively shown. They derive no validity from the strongest probability that they had jurisdiction in the case: none, certainly, from the presumption, that being a court, an usurpation of jurisdiction will not be presumed. The reasoning applies in full force, to the actings of a magistrate, whose jurisdiction is local. Thus, in the case of a warrant, it is expressly declared, that the place where it was made ought to appear.

The attempt to remedy this defect, by comparing the date of the certificate given by the magistrate with that given by the governor cannot succeed. The answer given at bar to this argument, is conclusive: the certificate wants those circumstances, which would make it testimony; and without them no part of it can be regarded.

The second objection is equally fatal. The governor has certified, that a man of the same name with the person who has administered the oath is a magistrate; but not, that the person, who has administered it, is a magistrate.

It is too obvious to be controverted that there may be two, or more persons of the same name, and, consequently, to produce that certainty, which the case readily admits of, the certificate of the governor ought to have applied to the individual, who administered the oath. The propriety of this certainty and precision in a certificate, which is to authenticate any affidavit to be introduced into a court of justice, is so generally admitted, that I do not recollect a single instance in which the principle has been departed from. It has been said, that it ought to appear that there are two persons of the same name, or the court will not presume such to be the fact. The court presumes nothing. It may or may not be the fact, and the court cannot presume that it is not. The argument proceeds upon the idea, that an instrument is to be disproved by him who objects to it, and not that it is to be proved by him who offers it. Nothing can be more repugnant to the established usage of courts. How is it to be proved, that there are two persons of the name of Cenas in the territory of Orleans? If, with a knowledge of several weeks, perhaps months, that this prosecution was to be carried on, the executive ought not to be required to produce this witness, ought the prisoner to be required, with the notice of a few hours, to prove that two persons of the same name reside in New-Orleans?

It has been repeatedly urged, that a difference exists between the strictness of law, which would be applicable to a trial in chief, and that which is applicable to a motion to commit for trial. Of the reality of this distinction, the present controversy affords conclusive proof. At a trial in chief, the accused possesses the valuable privilege of being confronted with his accuser. But there must be some limit to this relaxation, and it appears not to have extended so far as to the admission of a paper not purporting to be an affidavit, and not shown to be one.

When it is asked, whether every man does not believe that this affidavit was really taken before a magistrate? it is at once answered, that this cannot affect the case. Should a man of probity declare a certain fact within his own knowledge, he would be credited by all who knew him; but his declaration could not be received as testimony by the judge who firmly believed him. So a man might be believed to be guilty of a crime, but a jury could not convict him, unless the testimony proved him to be guilty of it. This judicial disbelief of a probable circumstance does not establish a wide interval between common law and common sense. It is believed in this respect to show their intimate union.

The argument goes to this, that the paper shall be received and acted upon as an affidavit, not because the oath appears to have been administered according to law, but because it is probable that it was so administered.

This point seems to have been decided by the constitution: " The right of the people" says that instrument, " to be secure in their persons, houses, papers, and effects, against unreasonable searches and seizures, shall not be violated; and no warrants shall issue but upon probable cause, supported by oath or affirmation, and particularly describing the places to be searched, and the persons or things be seized." The cause of seizure is not to be supported by a probable oath, or an oath that was probably taken, but by oath absolutely taken. This oath must be a legal oath; and if it must be a legal oath, it must legally appear to the court to be so. This provision is not made for a final trial; it is made for the very case now under consideration. In the cool and temperate moments of reflection, undisturbed by that whirlwind of passion with which in those party conflicts which most generally produce acts or accusations of treason the human judgment is sometimes overthrown, the people of America have believed the power even of commitment to be capable of too much oppression in its execution, to be placed, without restriction, even in the hands of the national legislature. Shall a judge disregard those barriers which the nation has deemed it proper to erect?

The interest which the people have in this prosecution, has been stated; but it is firmly believed, that the best and true interest of the people is to be found in a rigid adherence to those rules, which preserve the fairness of criminal prosecutions in every stage.

If this was a case to be decided by principle alone, the court would certainly not receive this paper; but if the point is settled by decision, it must be conformed to.

It has been said to be settled in the supreme court of the United States by admitting the affidavit of Wilkinson, to which an exception was taken, because it did not appear that the magistrate had taken the oaths prescribed by law. It was said, that as by law he could not act, until he had taken the oaths, and he was found acting, it must be presumed that this prerequisite was complied with; that is, that his acting as a magistrate under his commission was evidence that he was authorised so to act. It will not be denied that there is much strength in the argument; but the cases do not appear to be precisely parallel.

The certificate that he is a magistrate, and that full faith is due to his acts, implies, that he has qualified, if his qualification is necessary to his being a complete magistrate, whose acts are entitled to full faith and credit.

It is not usual for a particular certificate, that a magistrate has qualified, to accompany his official acts.

There is no record of his qualification, and no particular testimonial of it could be obtained.

These observations do not apply to the objections which

exist. But it is said that the certificate is the same with that in Wilkinson's affidavit.

If this objection had been taken and overruled, it would have ended the question; but it was not taken, so far as is now recollected, and does not appear to have been noticed by the court. It is not recollected by the judge who sat on that occasion to have been noticed. A defect, if it be one, which was not observed, cannot be cured by being passed over in silence.

The case in Washington was a civil case, and turned upon the point, that no form of the commission was prescribed, and consequently, that it was not necessary to appear on the face of it that it was directed to magistrates.

That it was the duty of the clerk to direct it to magistrates, and he should not be presumed to have neglected his duty, in a case in which his performance of it need not appear on the face of the instrument.

That the person, intending to take this exception, ought to have taken it sooner, and not surprise the opposite party when it was too late to correct it.

But the great difference is, that the privy examination was a mere ministerial act: the administering an oath is a judicial act. The court is of opinion that the paper, purporting to be an affidavit made by Dunbaugh, cannot be read, because it does not appear to be an oath.

Mr. Hay observed, that as the examination of colonel Burr for treason had already taken up much time without any progress in the business, and, from the disposition manifested by his counsel, it might last not only ten days, but even ten years longer, he considered it his duty, from information which he had received that morning, to suggest to the court the propriety of binding colonel Burr in a further recognisance from day to day, till the examination could be ended. He stated, on the authority of a letter just come to hand from the secretary at war, that general Wilkinson, with several other witnesses, might be expected here between the 28th and 30th of this month. This circumstance, said he, renders it essential that he should be considered in custody, until he gives security that his person shall be forthcoming to answer the charge of treason against the United States. The gentlemen, who appear as counsel for colonel Burr, may be, and no doubt are, sincere in the opinion they have expressed, that he will not shrink from the charges exhibited against him, and will not, in any conjuncture of circumstances which may occur, fly from a trial; but those gentlemen must pardon me for saying, that I entertain a very different opinion. I must believe, that his regard for the safety of his own life, would, if he perceived it in danger, prevail over his regard for the interest of his securities. I give notice therefore, that I consider him as being already in custody to answer the motion I have made for his commitment, and that he cannot be permitted to go at large without giving security for his appearance from day to day. His situation now is the same as that when he was first apprehended and brought before a single judge for the purpose of examination. Your honour at that time considered him as in custody, and bound him over from day to day; and I only contend, that the same course should be pursued at this time.

Mr. WICKHAM.—The gentleman thinks he has obtained the effect of his motion, merely by having made it. I cannot perceive the propriety of a motion to compel colonel Burr to give bail in any sum, before the probable cause to believe him guilty of treason has been shown. When he was brought before your honour for examination, you conceived the sum of 5000 dollars sufficient security for his daily appearance. But a recognisance has already been given in double that sum, binding him not to depart without the leave of this court. Yet now, although no probable proof of treason has been exhibited, Mr. Hay requires the court to demand of colonel Burr additional security! I trust that such a motion will not prevail.

Mr. MARTIN.—It has been already decided, by the supreme court of the United States, that not a single expression in Wilkinson's affidavit amounts to any proof of the charge of treason. The motion of the gentleman amounts to this: " We have no evidence of treason, and are not ready to go to trial for the purpose of proving it; we therefore move the court to increase the bail."

Mr. RANDOLPH.—The first motion of the counsel for the United States was to commit colonel Burr on the ground of probable cause only. This goes a step farther, and wishes the same thing to be done on the ground of a probable cause of a probable cause; but we trust that we shall not be deprived of our liberty, or held to bail on a mere uncertain expectation of evidence.

Mr. MAC RAE.—The gentlemen seem to consider the recognisance already taken as sufficient for all circumstances, and that colonel Burr will comply with it at any rate; but we have not the same expectation that he will appear, in case he discovers that sufficient evidence for his conviction has been obtained. When they speak of the sum in which he was bound on a former occasion, they do not recollect the circumstances which induced the judge to take bail in so small a sum; it was expressly mentioned by your honour, that his having been brought to a place at a distance from the circle of his friends, and the nature of the offence, (a misdemeanor only) induced you to hold him to bail in that sum; and the charge of treason was altogether excluded from view in taking the recognisance.

Mr. WIRT.—Mr. Wickham, in saying that my friend Mr. Hay thought he had obtained the object of his motion merely by having made it, clearly misconceived the object of the motion now before the court. The motion we made yesterday was to commit colonel Burr on a charge of treason: our motion to day is to hold him in custody to abide the opinion which the court may pronounce upon the question of commitment. The gentlemen say, that we have secured the object we have in view by the recognisance already taken. The court expressly excluded the charge of treason from that recognisance, which applies only to the misdemeanor. Let us suppose that the motion to commit colonel Burr was made out of court before a single magistrate: if the examination of witnessess in support of the motion occupied more than one day, would the magistrate let him go at large, while it was depending? Would he not rather, either have him retained in custody, or take security for his appearance, and renew it every evening until the motion should be determined? This is all that we ask of the court to do. The recognisance which has been given applies to the misdemeanor only. If therefore it should be forfeited by his going away, we should have had no security for his answering the charge of treason; a much more enormous offence, and attended with a very different punishment. We contend therefore that additional security ought to be taken.

Mr. BOTTS.—I shall endeavour to place this subject in some measure in a new light. It has been said, that the former examination of colonel Burr did not preclude this motion; if so, every new edition of the volume of evidence would justify a renewal of the motion to demand additional bail. Thus motions might be heaped upon motions, and bail upon bail, until the perpetual imprisonment of the accused might be the consequence.

It was a practice, in former times, to drown a person accused of being a witch, in order to try her. I think that practice is renewed on the present occasion, in another shape; a motion is made to commit colonel Burr for treason, before the evidence can be gone through by which alone it can be ascertained that he ought to be committed. The court are requested to predetermine the effect of the evidence, and commit, before they have decided whether they ought to commit: besides, no warrant has been issued against colonel Burr on the present occasion:

he has not been arrested for treason, and therefore cannot be considered as in custody for that offence.

Mr. HAY then made some farther observations on the importance of the charge of treason (which is of the highest nature, involving the reputation and life of the prisoner,) and the great necessity therefore of the most ample security to compel his appearance to answer it. He stated that this examination might last many days; that after the court had made up an opinion that colonel Burr ought to be committed, he might march off and leave the court to pronounce it; so that an order to commit might be made by the court, and no person found on whom it could be executed. Such an event, he said, would excite the laughter and scorn of all the people of the United States. He mentioned that an immense expense had been incurred by the government in collecting witnesses, and preparing for this trial; that therefore he did not wish the whole of that expense to be thrown away. General Wilkinson is expected to arrive between the 28th and 30th of this month: if he arrives, both the bills of indictment will be immediately sent to the grand jury. This is the first instance in which the ministers of the law have been requested to say to the accused, " You may do as you please, and go at large until we pronounce sentence." The gentlemen contend for new principles in favour of colonel Burr; but, I trust that greater privileges will not be granted to him than to the humblest deluded victim of his ambition. The circumstance that he has already entered into a recognisance to answer for a misdemeanor, is no argument to exempt him from entering into another on a charge of treason. Shall the accused clear himself of a responsibility for one crime by his having committed or being charged with another? This would indeed be to violate that maxim of law, that no man shall be benefited by his own wrong. Mr. Botts has contended that there is a difference between the case on the examination and that now before the court; that in the first instance a warrant had been issued, but none in the present; but a warrant is certainly unnecessary, now that the prisoner is before the court. The object of a warrant is to bring him before you. When this has been done, it is *functus officio;* here is colonel Burr, before the court. It is therefore immaterial how he came before it; but he ought to be considered in custody, until discharged by the due course of law.

The CHIEF JUSTICE delivered the opinion of the court, the substance of which was as follows: It is certainly necessary that a person accused should be retained in custody, or required to give security for his appearance while his examination is depending. The amount of the security to be required, must depend, however, upon the weight of the testimony against him. On a former occasion, colonel Burr was held to bail for his daily appearance in the sum of five thousand dollars only, because there was no evidence before the judge to prove the probability of his having been guilty of treason. When the examination was completed, the sum of ten thousand dollars was considered sufficient to bind him to answer the charge of a misdemeanor only, because the constitution requires that excessive bail should not be taken; but that recognisance had no application to the charge of treason. Yet, whether additional security ought to be required in the present stage of this business, before any evidence has appeared to make the charge of treason probable, is a question of some difficulty. It would seem, that evidence sufficient to furnish probable cause must first be examined, before the accused can be deprived of his liberty, or any security can be required of him. Yet, before this could be done, he might escape and defeat the very end of the examination. In common cases, where a person charged with a crime is arrested and brought before a magistrate, the arrest itself is preceded by an affidavit, which furnishes grounds of probable cause. The prisoner therefore is continued in custody, or bailed until the examination is finished: but here there has been no arrest for treason, and colonel Burr is not in custody for that offence. The evidence then must be heard to determine whether he ought to be taken into custody; but as the present public and solemn examination is very different from that before a single magistrate; as very improper effects on the public mind may be produced by it; I wish, that the court could be relieved from the embarrassing situation in which it is placed, and exempted from the necessity of giving any opinion upon the case, previously to its being acted upon by the grand jury. It is the wish of the court, that the personal appearance of colonel Burr could be secured without the necessity of proceeding in this inquiry.

Colonel BURR rose, and observed, that he denied the right of the court to hold him to bail in this stage of the proceedings; that the constitution of the United States was against it; declaring that no person shall be arrested without probable cause made out by oath or affirmation. But if the court were embarrassed, he would relieve them by consenting to give bail; provided it should be understood, that no opinion on the question even of probable cause was pronounced by the court, by the circumtance of his giving bail.

The CHIEF JUSTICE said, that such was the meaning of the court.

Mr. MARTIN said, for his part, he should prefer that all the evidence should be fully gone into. Instead of fearing that public prejudice would thereby be excited against colonel Burr, he believed it would remove all the prejudices of that sort which now prevailed.

The Chief Justice.—As a bill will probably be sent up to the grand jury, the court wishes to declare no opinion either way.

Some conversation then occurred relative to the quantum of bail; and colonel Burr mentioned, that he would propose that the sum should be ten thousand dollars, if he should be able to find security to that amount, of which he expressed himself to be doubtful. Mr. Hay contended, that fifty thousand dollars would not be too much. But the court finally accepted of the offer made by colonel Burr; who after a short interval, entered into a recognisance with four securities, to wit, Messrs. Wm. Langburn, Thomas Taylor, John G. Gamble, and Luther Martin; himself in the sum of ten thousand dollars, and each security in the sum of two thousand five hundred dollars, conditioned, that he would not depart without leave of the court.

Mr. Martin, when offered as security for colonel Burr, said, that he had lands in the district of Virginia, the value of which was more than double the sum; and that he was happy to have this opportunity to give a public proof of his confidence in the honour of colonel Burr, and of his conviction that he was innocent.

All further proceedings in the case were thereupon postponed, until the next day.

Friday, May 29th, 1807.

The court met, but as the witnesses had not arrived, it was adjourned till Monday next, at 10 o'clock.

Monday, June 1st, 1807.

The court met according to adjournment. Present, the Chief Justice and judge Griffin.

The grand jury having been called over, Mr. Hay observed, that he felt great embarrassment and difficulty as to the course which ought to be pursued; he had confidently expected the arrival of general Wilkinson, and was disappointed. He was, therefore, unwilling to subject the grand jury to the inconvenience of farther attendance: but he thought it proper to inform the court, that he had this morning received a number of affidavits of witnesses, residing in the neighbourhood of Chillicothe, and of Blannerhasset's island, which bore directly upon the charge of treason against colonel Burr. Those affidavits, however, had been taken in such a manner, that, according to the opinion lately given by the court, concerning the affidavit of Jacob Dunbaugh, they were not admissible as evidence, and would not be permitted to be read. He expected to hear from general Wilkinson, (if he should not appear in person) by the Lynchburgh mail, which he understood would arrive on Wednesday morning. He, therefore, hoped, that the grand jury would not be unwilling to make a farther sacrifice of a portion of their time for the public good, and would consent to wait with patience.

The grand jury were adjourned until Tuesday, ten o'clock.

TUESDAY, June 2d, 1807.

General Wilkinson not having arrived, no business was done to-day, but the court adjourned till to-morrow morning, ten o'clock.

WEDNESDAY, June 3d, 1807.

The court met according to adjournment.

The same judges present as yesterday.

The names of the grand jury being called over, they retired to their chamber. A few minutes after, the attorney for the United States entered, and observed, that he had a proposition to submit to the court, which he wished the grand jury to hear. He requested, therefore, that they might be called in.

Counsel for Mr. Burr. We have no objection.

The chief justice directed the marshal to call the jury into court.

Some minutes intervened before they appeared. In the mean time, Mr. HAY informed the court, that he only wished to know from the grand jury, at what time it would be most convenient for them to attend the court, if they were adjourned to some distant day, should such an adjournment equally suit the arrangements of the opposite counsel; that he had just made a calculation with his friend the marshal, which satisfied him that general Wilkinson had not, perhaps, sufficient time to reach this city. The distance from New-Orleans, on the map, was about 1370 miles; if he came by land, he must travel on horseback; but judging him by himself, he could not probably ride more than thirty miles per day: by these data he would require about forty-five days (besides a fragment of a few miles) to travel from New-Orleans to this city. This calculation would bring him to the 14th or 15th of this month. He was, therefore, willing, if it suited the wishes of the opposite counsel, to have the grand jury adjourned for about ten days; that general Wilkinson's situation called upon the court to make this arrangement; he need not expatiate upon the importance of his official duties, nor the perilous condition of that part of the country, where the head of the army ought always to be present; that general Wilkinson should be detained here as short a time as possible; and, that it would be particularly inconvenient for him to stay here until the meeting of an intermediate court for the present trial; that it was, therefore, the interest of the United States to have the trial concluded during the present term ; and, that he had no doubt the very same considerations would lead every member of the grand jury, cheerfully to submit to any private inconvenience which they might sustain, but punctually to return at the time appointed by the court.

The CHIEF JUSTICE observed, that there could be no difficulty on the part of the court.

Mr. HAY.—General Wilkinson's situation, as commander in chief of the forces of the United States, is a very delicate one. His official duties may require him to return immediately after his arrival at this place. Our affairs in that part of the union are also in a very unsettled state. If he should be compelled to return after the adjournment of the court, it may not be in his power to be here either at a special court, or at the next term. He hoped that the proposition to adjourn the grand jury to a distant day would meet with the approbation of colonel Burr and his counsel.

Mr. WICKHAM owned, that this communication somewhat surprised him, as Mr. Hay had, but a few days before, announced to the court, from a letter of the secretary of war, that general Wilkinson would be here between the 28th or 30th of of May.

Mr. HAY observed, that the letter from general Dearborn admitted of an easy explanation: that according to Mr. Minnikin's affidavit, the express could not have reached New-Orleans before the 3d or 4th of May, and that this exceeded the time which general Dearborn had allowed. His opinion was founded on the circumstance of the messenger leaving Washington on a certain day, and of course his reaching New-Orleans on a certain day. That Mr. Minnikin's affidavit had shown the calculation to be not altogether correct; that Mr. Minnikin had, therefore, given him some information, which general Dearborn could not have possessed. Mr. Hay was sorry he could not inform the court how general Wilkinson travelled, and of course how to make any calculation about the time of his arrival.

The CHIEF JUSTICE said, that before the grand jury came in, he could not but express his regret at the great inconvenience which they were likely to sustain; but he believed, that less of it would arise from the course pointed out by the United States' attorney than from any other. The court would continue to sit as usual ; its ordinary business would go on; and no further steps would be taken in the prosecution, until the return of the grand jury. The court would observe, that it seemed desirable, in every point of view, that this business should be closed during the present term; that a number of witnesses were now present, all of whom would not probably attend at any other term, and that it would be more convenient for the court itself to wait a fortnight longer after its usual period of adjournment, than to hold an intermediate court for this purpose.

Mr. WICKHAM had no doubt himself, that if general Wilkinson had intended to have come at all, he would have been here before this time; certainly the government had not failed in its duty in taking every necessary measure to have him here. If the grand jury was adjourned to some distant day, the great difficulty would be to collect them all again at the end of the time appointed; and that if general Wilkinson was to come at all, he may be expected here every day; and that of course, it was better to adjourn the grand jury only from day to day.

Mr. HAY stated, that a large allowance ought to be made for the distance and uncertainty of the journey; and that he should remind the court of a corresponding fact. Mr. Perkins, who escorted colonel Burr, left Fort Stoddert about the 23d or 24th of March; but he himself did not reach this city before the thirty-third or thirty-sixth day. Now, Mr. Perkins certainly travelled with greater advantages than general Wilkinson would; as he pressed or purchased horses to expedite his journey. Admit, then, Mr. Perkins used due diligence, (and he has been even charged with too much) how can general Wilkinson be certainly expected? Gentlemen ought not to be so confident in their hopes. General Wilkinson will be here, as sure as he is a living man. Nothing but death will prevent him.

The CHIEF JUSTICE observed, that a large calculation ought certainly to be made; as the distance was very considerable, and it was very uncertain when general Wilkinson set out, or how he travelled.

At this moment, the grand jury returned into court.

Mr. HAY addressed them in the following terms:

Gentlemen of the Grand Jury,—I have already stated to the court and the opposite counsel, that this business should be concluded, if possible, during your present session. I have moved the court, that you be called again at the end of ten days, or a fortnight. My calculation is, that general Wilkinson cannot be here before the 14th or 15th of this month. I am sorry to detain you here a single moment; but I flatter myself, that you will still continue to display the same praise-worthy patience which has hitherto marked your conduct. I am, therefore, anxious to consult your own convenience as much as possible; and I wish to know, at what time it will be most convenient for you to return to this place, if you are adjourned to a distant day.

Mr. JOHN RANDOLPH, (the foreman). Any time, may it please the court, shall be most convenient to ourselves, that is most convenient to the court and the parties. We should, however, prefer a distant day.

Mr. BURR observed, that there were manifest inconveniences in the measure proposed. He had, for instance, a number of witnesses here, from a distance; would it not be inconvenient for them to be kept here? Certainly, however, they may be detained; but why an adjournment to a distant day? Mr. Wilkinson may be expected here every day. The attorney's estimate of the time is not perhaps correct. Perkins came about the same distance as Mr. Wilkinson is to come; but he performed his journey in thirty-one days. What we want, however, is some data from the government on this subject; such, for instance, as the time when the express left Washington. As to Minnikin's affidavit, what great reliance can be placed in it? Did he certainly identify the express? But suppose that the express reached New-Orleans about the time mentioned; Mr. Wilkinson may come by water, and is to be expected here every day. Mr. Burr hoped that this measure would not be adopted; particularly as it was uncertain, whether eight or ten days hence all of the grand jury would meet here again. Mr. Wilkinson may be near to this place at this moment; and he may arrive almost immediately after the jury is adjourned. Adjourn them from day to day. According to Mr. Dearborn's letter, Mr. Wilkinson ought to have been here between the 28th and 30th of May; allowing, however, six days more than he said, Mr. Wilkinson may be expected here to-morrow.

Mr. HAY observed, that it was of no sort of importance to him, personally, or officially, to what time the grand jury was adjourned; all that he wished was, that the public business should go on, and this prosecution closed during the present court. Whether general Wilkinson would be here to-morrow, or a fortnight hence, he knew not; he merely made the present proposition for the accommodation of the grand jury. If gentlemen, on the other side, choose to object to it, and the court would adjourn the jury from day to day, he was satisfied. He had, in the early part of April, received a letter from Mr. Rodney, stating, that every exertion would be made to have him here: it was not probable that the messenger could have arrived in New-Orleans, before the 3d or 4th of May. If general Wilkinson travelled by land, he would not come so expeditiously as Mr. Perkins, because Mr. Perkins had exhausted the frontier parts of Georgia of its horses. Such, at least, was Mr. Minnikin's representation.

Mr. MARTIN submitted to the court, whether it was not better to adjourn the jury from day to day. Any calculation on such a subject was uncertain; it was uncertain whether general Wilkinson would travel by land or by water: but if he came by land, he might certainly travel further than the gentleman had allowed—thirty miles a day; nor would he be obliged to use the same horse, as that gentleman had also supposed. As general Wilkinson was a military gentleman, he would not be confined to thirty miles a day; nor might he deny himself the convenience of frequent relays of horses. And suppose that he should arrive here to-morrow, all the other important witnesses are present, and the business might be concluded before the time should come to which the grand jury may be adjourned. He hoped, therefore, that the court would not adjourn them to a distant day. As to himself, he said, he did not wish his own situation to enter into the consideration of the grand jury, or the court; that certainly he ought to be on the Eastern Shore, on ————, to attend the court; but that notwithstanding this circumstance, he was determined to stay here, so long as he could expect to do any service to the gentleman whom he had come to defend.

Mr. WICKHAM stated, that if general Wilkinson did not even arrive here in two or three days, intelligence at least might be obtained within that time, of the period of his arrival. Every post from the north or south might bring the information; every person that came by land or water might do so: under such circumstances, ought they to be adjourned for ten days, or a fortnight?

Mr. RANDOLPH, (the foreman).—It is, sir, almost indifferent to the jury, what steps may be taken; they have made no motion for their prorogation or their discharge. Their great anxiety is, to fulfil their duty.

The CHIEF JUSTICE said, that he was fully impressed with the patience which the grand jury had manifested; perhaps Monday next would be as convenient for them as any other day, to reassemble.

Mr. HAY hoped, that the grand jury would be punctual in their attendance, as he sincerely wished to have the business closed during this term; and a number of witnesses were present, who cannot all be expected here again.

Mr. WICKHAM expressed his opposition to their adjournment; for although the jury had hitherto exhibited so much patience, yet if they retired home, some one might find his domestic affairs in such a situation as to think himself excused from further attendance.

CHIEF JUSTICE. Let it then be understood, that not before Monday next, three o'clock, will the jury be called again.

A desultory conversation here ensued between the jury and the chief justice, some of the former wishing as distant a time as possible. Tuesday was then named; when Mr. Wickham observed, that if the grand jury preferred Tuesday, he should have no objection; although he himself should prefer an earlier day.

CHIEF JUSTICE.—Gentlemen of the grand jury, you will attend here on Tuesday next, at two o'clock.

TUESDAY, June 9th, 1807.

The court met according to adjournment. Present, the CHIEF JUSTICE of the United States, and CYRUS GRIFFIN, the district judge.

It will be recollected, that on Wednesday last, (the 3d inst.) the grand jury were adjourned till this day, at two o'clock. At the hour of three, all the members appeared; their names having been called,

Mr. HAY observed, that it was proper for him to inform the court, that he had received no further information respecting general Wilkinson, except what was contained in a Norfolk paper, (the Public Ledger) received by the mail of this morning; a paragraph of which stated, that a vessel had arrived there in twenty-seven days from New-Orleans, and that, at the departure of the vessel from the latter place, which must have been about the 11th of last month, general Wilkinson was still in New-Orleans; and nothing was said as to his intention of leaving it. There were gentlemen on the grand jury just from Norfolk, who would be able to state whether the information might be relied on or not. He said that he had confidently expected general Wilkinson here before this time; but that he might have been led into the mistake by the information of Mr. Minnikin, as to the progress which the express had made, when he saw the messenger on his way to New-Orleans. It was possible that in the latter part of his journey, he might not have been able to move with as much rapidity as upon his first setting out; but from a knowledge of the fact that general Wilkinson was at New-Orleans at that time, his hopes were much stronger that he would certainly be here. The express would go directly to him, and he would have nothing to do but to prepare for his journey to this place: he wished the subject might be postponed for a few days. For the sake of economy, for the sake of that justice which is due to the public and to the accused, he hoped that no objection would be made to this course. Almost all the witnesses were here; that he was sorry to be forced to make so many apologies to the grand jury, who had already manifested so much patience; but he begged them to recollect the extreme importance of the present trial, and that it would, perhaps, be the last time that they were to be placed in this situation.

The CHIEF JUSTICE presumed, that the mail from Norfolk would not arrive here until the day after to-morrow.

Mr. HAY said that it had arrived the day before.

Mr. MARTIN.—I have an extract from another Norfolk paper, one day later than the one quoted by the attorney, which conveys in substance, the same information. The ship news, in the same paper state, that the Hannah had left New-Orleans twenty-seven days before.

Mr. HAY.—These may be different vessels.

Mr. MARTIN.—The same vessel, sir.

Mr. HAY.—These vessels may convey some intelligence to Washington respecting general Wilkinson, which may consequently reach ourselves.

Mr. BURR.—I hope, sir, it will not be understood, from the observations of my friend, Mr. Martin, that I mean to take any part in this business. I shall certainly not interfere with the grand jury in this stage of the affair. The proposition of the gentleman has my cordial concurrence.

The CHIEF JUSTICE observed, that if the jury were adjourned till Thursday, some passenger might, perhaps, arrive in the next Norfolk mail, with some intelligence about general Wilkinson.

Mr. HAY presumed, that the jury would not probably be wanting before Saturday.

Mr. BURR hoped the jury would be adjourned for as short a time as possible; at all events, not longer than Thursday.

CHIEF JUSTICE.—This is Tuesday; the attorney for the United States cannot probably expect general Wilkinson before Thursday, if he comes by water.

Mr. HAY knew not how he was to come; if by water, he certainly could not be expected before that time; and if by land, he would certainly require one day to recover from the fatigue of travelling.

The CHIEF JUSTICE then observed to the grand jury, that they were adjourned till Thursday, ten o'clock.

Mr. BURR then addressed the court. There was a proposition which he wished to submit to them. In the president's communication to congress, he speaks of a letter and other papers which he had received from Mr. Wilkinson, under date of 21st of October. Circumstances had now rendered it material, that the whole of this letter should be produced in court; and further, it has already appeared to the court, in the course of different examinations, that the government have attempted to infer certain intentions on my part, from certain transactions. It becomes necessary, therefore, that these transactions should be accurately stated. It was, therefore, material to show, in what circumstances I was placed in the Mississippi Territory; and of course, to obtain certain orders of the army and the navy which were issued respecting me. I have seen the order of the navy in print; and one of the officers of the navy had assured me, that this transcript was correct. The instructions in this order were, to destroy my person and my property in descending the Mississippi. Now I wish, if possible, to authenticate this statement; and it was for this purpose, when I passed through Washington lately, that I addressed myself to Mr. Robert Smith. That gentleman seemed to admit the propriety of my application, but objected to my course. He informed me, that if I would apply to him through one of my counsel, there could be no difficulty in granting the object of my application. I have since applied in this manner to Mr. Smith, but without success. Hence I feel it necessary to resort to the authority of this court, to call upon them to issue a subpœna to the president of the United States, with a clause, requiring him to produce certain papers; or in other words, to issue the subpœna *duces tecum*. The attorney for the United States will, however, save the time of this court, if he will consent to produce the letter of the 21st October, with the accompanying papers, and also authentic orders of the navy and war departments.

Mr. RANDOLPH observed, that he knew not whether it was necessary for him to support colonel Burr's motion: that he had been informed by him of his application, through a friend, to Mr. Smith, and of Mr. Smith's refusing to grant the application, unless it were made through one of his counsel: that he had himself, therefore, addressed a letter to Mr. Smith informing him of colonel Burr's statement. In answer to this he had received a letter, which seemed like a personal communication to himself; but as he had not requested him to withhold it from colonel Burr, and as it contained information material to him, he had shown it to colonel Burr.

Mr. Randolph regretted that he had not the letter then about him; but the substance of it was, that the order which had been alluded to was only for the officer to whom it had been addressed, and was to be seen only by him. He added, that he had written in reply to Mr. Smith, that he never would have applied to him for it, but for the two reasons, that it had already appeared in a Natchez Gazette, and that Mr. Van Ness, the friend of colonel Burr, had informed him of Mr. Smith's unconditional promise to furnish the order, if he was properly applied to for it.

Mr. Burr observed, that to avoid all possible misconception, he thought it proper to state, that Mr. Van Ness had assured him of Mr. Smith's positive and unqualified promise to furnish the answer, if applied for through counsel.

Mr. Hay declared that he knew not for what this information could be wanted; to what purpose such evidence could relate, and whether it was to be used on a motion for commitment, or on the trial in chief.

Mr. Burr, Mr. Wickham, and Mr. Martin observed, that perhaps on both: according as circumstances might require.

Mr. Hay.—I suppose this court will not proceed but upon facts. Now, a letter of the 21st of October is spoken of; but has this letter been yet identified? He hoped that the court would not issue the subpœna *duces tecum*, until they were satisfied that they had the authority to issue it, and that the information required was material in the present case.

Mr. Wickham observed, that the present was simply intended as a notice of a motion to be brought before the court; which motion might be discussed either to day or to-morrow.

Mr. Hay declared, that all delay was unnecessary; but he pledged himself, if possible, to obtain the papers which were wanted; and not only those, but every paper which might be necessary to the elucidation of the case.

Chief Justice observed, that all delay was obviously improper; that if the papers were wanted, they ought to be obtained as soon as possible, and not, perhaps, delay the ulterior stages of the prosecution.

Mr. Hay stated, that he had already received a communication from Mr. Wickham on this subject, and intended to have informed him that he would write for all the papers which were wanted, (and he had no doubt he should obtain them) if the court judged them material. The fact was, that he had already in his possession Mr. Randolph's correspondence with Mr. Smith, and the order from the navy department; but in his own opinion, they no more related to the present prosecution than the first paragraph of the first page of the acts of congress.

Chief Justice inquired whether the Natchez Gazette was not in court.

Mr. Burr.—No, sir, but I have already seen the same order in other papers; and have no doubt that almost every person has. At Natchez it was a subject of surprise, that such an order had ever found its way into a public print.

Mr. HAY repeated, that if the gentleman would furnish him with a list of such papers as they wanted, he would attempt to obtain them, if the court thought them material. Of what use were they? Were they too to be laid before the grand jury, to distract their attention, and to present, under another point of view, another subject for their consideration? He had supposed, that the mass of matter to be laid before them was large enough already.

CHIEF JUSTICE observed, that it was impossible to determine their use, without hearing them. He would much rather that the counsel on both sides should make an arrangement with each other suitable to them both; and that the court itself was not now disposed to make any arrangement; but if the parties could not come to any agreement, he should then wish to hear some argument on the subject to satisfy him, whether the court had the right to issue a subpœna *duces tecum.*

Mr. BURR observed, that he had been told it was the constant practice in this state to issue such subpœnas upon the application of a party.

CHIEF JUSTICE had no doubt it was the custom to do it, where there was no great inconvenience to the party summoned; that it seldom occurred; but that he was inclined to think, where great inconveniences would result to the party summoned, that the materiality of his testimony should be fully shown. If papers are to be obtained from a clerk's office, such a subpœna may be issued, and though not upon affidavit, yet where there has been good cause shown.

Mr. MARTIN said, that there would be no inconvenience, as the president might just transmit the papers wanted by mail.

Mr. HAY observed, that Mr. Martin's remark superseded any further proceeding. Why apply to the court to issue a subpœna to the president, unless perhaps it was the necessary form for obtaining the papers.

CHIEF JUSTICE.—The reason is, that in case of a refusal to send the papers, the officer himself may be present to show cause. This subpœna is issued only where fears of this sort are entertained.

Mr. HAY said, that no application had yet been made to the secretary of state, for general Wilkinson's letter; nor to the department of war, for its order.

Mr. MARTIN.—If one department refuses, we may presume that the others will.

Mr. BURR.—If the gentleman grants our demand, he may propose any alteration in its form that he pleases.

Mr. RANDOLPH.—If any arrangement can be made to obtain these papers, we would rather that it should be a voluntary act on the part of the government.

Mr. HAY.—I will attempt to obtain these papers; any, in fact, that gentlemen may want, if the court will but say they are material.

Mr. WICKHAM.—Colonel Burr's counsel know little of the importance of these papers, but from himself; and from that, they are fully persuaded of their great importance. The attorney for the United States says, that so far as his personal exertions will go, he will attempt to obtain them, and firmly believes that his application will be successful. But, sir, at Washington they may entertain very different views from himself. Under such circumstances, it is better to encounter the delay of three or four days, to obtain the authority of this court, than trust to an expedient, which may be unavailing. But I see no necessity for any such delay, as the order may at once issue, by consent of parties. As to the order from the navy department, a copy may be sufficient; the original is already gone out. As to Wilkinson's letter, we wish to see itself here; and surely it may be trusted in the hands of the attorney for the United States.

Mr. HAY.—It seems then, that the copies of papers from the government of the United States will not be received. They are not to be trusted. After such an observation, sir, I retract every thing that I have promised: let gentlemen, sir, take their own course.

Here some warm desultory conversation took place at the bar, when,

Mr. WICKHAM observed, that as the unfortunate expression fell from him, he thought it proper to explain. He had intended no insinuation against the fairness of the conduct of the government: that the distinction he had drawn between an original and a copy, simply resulted from his anxiety to obtain the highest possible degree of evidence; hence he preferred the original to the copy: that if Wilkinson was here it would be necessary to meet him with his own letter; perhaps in no other way.

Mr. HAY.—That explanation removes the difficulty.

Mr. WICKHAM.—We wish to confront him with his own letter.

Mr. HAY.—Perhaps they may not be able to remove the original, as it is already filed in the department of state.

Mr. MARTIN.—We are ready to go on with the discussion.

Mr. WICKHAM.—The president's message mentioned, that this was a letter to himself.

Mr. HAY.—I hope the court will remember that remark. The letter these gentlemen then want is addressed to Thomas Jefferson. Have they a right to demand any but public letters

Mr. MARTIN.—The president's message said, it was addressed to him as president of the United States.

Mr. HAY.—If it be a public letter, it is of course deposited in the department of state. I have no objection, since this insinuation has been removed, to repeat my promise to apply for these papers, if the court thinks them material; and when the business arrives at the proper stage, they may then be produced. I hope that no more time will be wasted in these preliminary stages; and that such arrangements may be adopted as will prevent this useless consumption of time.

Mr. RANDOLPH had no reason to believe, that there had been more delay on his side, than on the other; that if time was to be consumed at all, more would be employed in removing greater difficulties than had already been done; that he, however, only hinted at this now. He declared with Mr. Wickham his perfect concurrence in this measure.

Mr. BOTTS.—We are unanimous on this point, I am sure. Sir, I cannot sit down, and hear complaints so unnecessarily repeated, about the waste of time. It is time, sir, to be done with them. It is time that we should enjoy something like the liberty of speech. Mr. Hay makes, I think, about a dozen times as many speeches as any other gentleman; and each speech longer than those of other persons; and yet we cannot open our mouths, without his sounding loudly his complaints to the ears of this hall. On this case of unequal magnitude, shall we not be suffered to declare our opinions, without this unnecessary complaint about the consumption of the court's time? We feel the magnitude of our duties, and we shall firmly discharge them in spite of Mr. Hay. It is obvious to you, sir, and to every body, that the delay is not with us. If, sir, you call for an argument, we are ready to proceed : but if you are satisfied, we shall be silent.

CHIEF JUSTICE.—If the attorney for the United States is satisfied that this court has a right to issue the subpœna *duces tecum*, I will grant the motion.

Mr. HAY.—I am not, sir.

CHIEF JUSTICE.—I am not prepared to give an opinion on this point; and, therefore, I must call for an argument.

Mr. HAY.—When I said that there had been a great consumption of time, I certainly did not mean to insinuate that *they* only consumed it. I have certainly had my full proportion. I thought, however, that my proposition would have saved some time; and I am still willing to repeat my promise.

Mr. RANDOLPH.—That the court may understand us, I will read to them the form of the subpœna which we wish to obtain. [Here Mr. Randolph read the sketch before him.]

Mr. Botts.—We will be under the direction of the court, whether we shall proceed in the argument to day or to-morrow.

Chief Justice.—Unquestionably there must be an argument, if the attorney for the United States disputes the authority of the court to grant the motion.

Mr. Hay.—Whatever other gentlemen may think on this subject, I have not the least doubt that these papers will be produced, because Mr. Robert Smith has voluntarily furnished me with the order of the navy department. But although I may procure these papers, let it be distinctly understood, that I shall object to their being unnecessarily produced.

Mr. Botts.—It will take four days at least to interchange letters between this city and Washington, and two or three days to copy the papers, so that six days will be totally lost to us. In the mean time, thirty or forty witnesses, and sixteen grand jurymen (they might, perhaps, require them) would be detained here; and after all, the attorney's application to the government might be unavailing.

Mr. Hay.—Since then gentlemen, sir, will press this subject, I ask no more than that they will waive this discussion till to-morrow.

The court was then adjourned till to-morrow, eleven o'clock.

WEDNESDAY, JUNE 10th, 1807.

The court met according to adjournment.

The subject of the subpœna *duces tecum* was resumed.

The following affidavit, drawn up and sworn to by Mr. Burr, was read, in support of the motion for the subpœna.

" AARON BURR, maketh oath, that he hath great reason to believe, that a letter from general Wilkinson to the president of the United States, dated 21st October, 1806, as mentioned in the president's message of the 22d January, 1807, to both houses of congress, together with the documents accompanying the said letter, and copy of the answer of said Thomas Jefferson, or of any one by his authority, to the said letter, *may* be material in his defence, in the prosecution against him. And further, that he hath reason to believe, the military and naval orders given by the president of the United States, through the departments of war and of the navy, to the officers of the army and navy, at or near the New-Orleans stations, touching or concerning the said Burr, or his property, will also be material in his defence.

" AARON BURR.

" Sworn to in open court, 10th June, 1807."

Mr. HAY begged leave to give notice to the court and the opposite counsel, that in conformity to the information which he had yesterday given, he had addressed a letter to the president, stating the motion that was to be made this day, and suggesting the propriety of sending on the papers required; but reserving to himself the right of retaining them, till the court saw them, and determined their materiality. He hoped to have them in his possession in five days. He should however object to the affidavit produced, and to the right of colonel Burr to make the motion at the present time. It was a preliminary question, which he wished first to be determined, whether any man, standing in colonel Burr's situation, had a right to make such a motion. He believed the fact to be, that if these papers should ever come to hand, they would not go out of the hands of the court; for he was satisfied, that they could not be material in this case, from the substance of one of those very papers, which was already in his possession. He wished not to waste the time of the court; but there were several preliminary points, which he should be obliged to submit to their consideration; and before the discussion could be ended, the papers would be here. He confessed himself extremely unwilling to enter into any discussion on these papers. Gentlemen might take it for granted if they pleased, that he felt a disinclination to furnish them with these papers; but the fact was not so. Gentlemen ought themselves to have applied for them; for he was satisfied, from the character of the government, that every necessary paper would have been cheerfully supplied. He had no doubt the court, and even the opposing counsel, would acquiesce in the same opinion. He trusted that the present motion was not made to show the talents of gentlemen; he assured them that if general Wilkinson should come, they would have a splendid opportunity of displaying them, to their hearts' content. He requested them once more to deliberate on his propositions.

Mr. MARTIN assured the gentleman, that there was no need for further deliberation; that it was strange, that the gentleman should complain so much of the consumption of time, at the very moment when he spoke of the long period he should require for this discussion, and the many preliminary points which he had to submit. The gentleman too had spoken warmly of certain impressions and opinions, and even of our own; but he trusted, that the gentleman would leave it to themselves to declare their own impressions: that it was impossible for him to search their hearts, and that he was sure, that nothing, that had yet fallen from them, justified the eulogies upon the government, which he had been kind enough to attribute to them.

Mr. WICKHAM observed, that Mr. Hay had promised the appearance of these papers; and that was all they wanted. The object was not to bring the president here, but to obtain certain papers which he had in his possession. That the effect of the process required, was the result promised by Mr. Hay. As to the objection, that part of the papers was confidential; would it not be easy to make an indorsement on such as the president would not wish to go out of the court? That, however, Mr. Hay's promises might be unavailing: at Washington they might entertain very different views from him. As to the opportunity of displaying talents, nothing would be better calculated to defeat that object than for the attorney for the United States to give his consent that process should issue.

Mr. HAY had not heard the gentleman distinctly. He thought he heard the word ' consent;' but he assured him, he had not consented, and never would *consent* to such a proposition.

Mr. MARTIN then rose to open the motion; when some desultory discussion ensued as to the order of proceeding.

Mr. HAY contended, that this question was premature; that the preliminary question, whether colonel Burr was entitled to make this motion, ought first to be settled. If the court pleased, he would state the ground on which he denied the existence of this right.

The chief justice having decided, that Mr. Hay might state his objections, the latter proceeded to this effect:

The motion now made by Mr. Burr, as far as he could understand it, was to obtain from the court a subpœna to the president of the United States, to attend this court with an original letter written to him by general Wilkinson, and referred to in his communication to congress, of the 27th January, 1807. He contended that it was premature; that colonel Burr was not authorised to make it by any legal precedents that could be shown, or by any statute in force in this country, while he remained in his present situation. What was that situation? He had been committed for a misdemeanor and recognised to appear before this court; in consequence of which he was now present. No bills had yet been sent to the grand jury. In this situation, colonel Burr applies to this court for a compulsory process, or a subpœna *duces tecum*, to the president of the United States, commanding him to attend with certain papers, and if he does not attend, or the papers are not produced, the court may then be applied to, to issue an attachment against him.

Now I contend, said Mr. Hay, that no individual, charged with a crime, has any right to legal process, until the grand jury have found a true bill, and the prosecutor has announced his intention to proceed thereupon. Gentlemen will please to point out in the constitution of the United States, in the laws of congress, or in the common law, the smallest right to make this motion. They will search in vain, in the various materials and reports of the common law, for a precedent to justify this attempt. The acts of congress supply them with no authority; and there is nothing in the constitution which relates to the subject, except the eighth amendment, which most obviously refers to a different stage of the prosecution from this. " In all criminal prosecutions, the accused shall enjoy the right to a speedy and public trial, &c.—to have compulsory process for obtaining witnesses in his favour, and to have the assistance of counsel for his defence." Will gentlemen contend that this clause relates to any of the preliminary steps of the prosecution, before the prosecution itself is commenced by the finding of the bill? This clause was never intended for any of the preliminary steps: the arrest, transportation, or examination, of the accused. Its object was to secure to every man the benefit of ' *a fair and impartial trial,*' not on the examination before the examining magistrate, but on the trial before the petit jury. When the trial commences, it is *then* that the accused is to be confronted with the witnesses against him; it is *then* that he is entitled to compulsory process for obtaining witnesses in his favour; it is *then* that he is to have counsel for his defence. It is true, sir, that in this first stage, (*incipient* stage as it is called in fashionable phrase) Aaron Burr has already not one counsel, but *four;* and not only counsel in this district, but celebrated counsel from other states. It is true also, that the clerk of this court has already issued subpœnas; but these subpœnas were gratuitous, and had they been refused, there was no law to compel him to grant them. But do all these circumstances prove, that Aaron Burr has authority at this stage of the business to make the present application to the court? But let us suppose that they have obtained what they require; that this subpœna has issued, and that the president is here; that he has been called to this court from Washington, where national concerns of such deep weight and importance are entrusted to his guidance; what then?

Mr. Wickham begged leave to interrupt Mr. Hay. It was not in fact a subpœna for the president, but only for certain papers, which they required.

Mr. Hay.—Even that supposition does not remove the prematurity of the present motion. I ask what is to be done with these papers, if brought hither by this subpœna? If the president were to come here with them in his pocket, I will say nothing of the manifest and many inconveniences which his absence from the seat of government might occasion, but I ask, what would be done with these papers? The gentlemen cannot answer this question. *I* only am competent to answer. And why? Because no kind of use can be made of this evidence until I have laid my bills before the grand jury, and until they have found them to be true. Will gentlemen proceed on such calculations; that the bills *will be sent up*, and that they will certainly be found to be true bills? If general Wilkinson comes, (and that he will I can entertain no doubt, from the intelligence I have heard this morning) the prosecution will certainly progress; and in that case only can these papers be wanted.

There is another little difficulty in this case. *When* is this process to be made returnable? Some day must be named; but can the court possibly name any day, when the witnesses or the papers shall be wanted? Do the records of this court indicate any particular day when the trial is to commence? Sir, such a nomination would be completely arbitrary. Let an indictment be first found, and a day set for the trial; and on that day this process may be made returnable. But, sir, if a day could be fixed, it does not appear that this testimony will be wanted during this term. It depends on the arrival of general Wilkinson. It literally depends on the *winds* and the *waves*. The very language of the process confirms this argument. How could the evidence be heard before the accused is put upon his trial? Perhaps it may be said, that this evidence will be wanted in case we repeat our motion to commit Aaron Burr for high treason, and which we certainly shall attempt, if general Wilkinson does not make his appearance. On this point, two remarks only are necessary to be made. The first is, that no such motion is actually before the court. And the second is, that if such motion were made, the court would have no right to issue process before the trial. The court has no more rights for this purpose than an individual magistrate would have; and in fact it was only a very few days ago, that the court did actually consider themselves placed in this very situation. Now if such an application had been made to your honour out of doors, is there any law in America, (or in any part of the civilized world) to justify a postponement of the examination until a subpœna has been granted? It is true, that evidence on both sides has been sometimes produced; but this took place when the evidence happened to be present: but there does not exist a single precedent, in all the annals of jurisprudence, where the course of an examination has been suspended by an application for subpœnas, and the writing for the witnesses. The present motion, therefore, is manifestly premature. Mr. Hay confessed, that his object was to save time: he was confident that the documents would be forwarded in a much shorter time than they could possibly obtain them by this process. Why were they not sooner applied for? Though there had been some correspondence between Mr. Randolph and Mr. Smith, about an order from the navy department, yet never before yesterday was the materiality of general Wilkinson's letter suggested; although it had been publicly known to exist as long ago as the 27th of January. The accused and his counsel knew this, yet they never made any attempts to obtain it, or ever stated its materiality.

Mr. WICKHAM would not inquire, whether it was the object of the gentleman to save or to obtain time; though probably the last, as gentlemen seemed very solicitous to send on a messenger to Washington, to obtain instructions directing them *how* to act; but if the saving of time was an object with the court, the course which he recommended was the best calculated to obtain it. It was the shortest way to resort at once to that expedient, which must be at last employed, if the expectations of the attorney for the United States should turn out to be fallacious, and his application at Washington should prove to be unavailing. The clerk himself, if called upon for subpœnas, must issue them absolutely. It was the practice, and it was the law; but instead of applying to the clerk, they deemed it necessary, in a case of such importance, to make their application directly to the court. They were more willing too to prefer this course, as they did not wish the presence of the president, but only of certain papers; and it was not therefore their wish to obtain a common subpœna for his person, but a subpœna *duces tecum* for those papers.

This is the first time I have heard, since the declaration of American Independence, that an accused man is not to obtain witnesses in his behalf. What has the gentleman himself done? Are there not witnesses present whom he has summoned, under the authority of this court, and at his own special instance? And will he at last admit, that there is to be no kind of equality between the accused and the prosecution; and that we are to remain here perfectly mute, and bound hand and foot, to wait the decision of his own witnesses?

But at what time are we to be entitled to these privileges? At the period of colonel Burr's transportation? That is a most unwarrantable proceeding; there is no such case recognised by the constitution; and therefore there could be nothing in that constitution to give us the right of founding any judicial proceeding on such a step. But, sir, such an illegal transaction entitles us to still more; it entitles us to the protection of every citizen in the country, as well as of this court. Suppose that colonel Burr were now put on his examination; would he not have a right to examine any witnesses who were beyond the bar; and of course to subpœna every man who would be brought before you during the term of examination? This practice is every day pursued by judges and magistrates in superior and inferior courts. Why not in the present case?

It has been said, that there is nothing in this country to justify such an application; that there are no precedents. But I will quote, sir, another trial, which was similar in its proceedings, and similar, I trust, in its results. I refer to the cases of Smith and Ogden, before the circuit court of New-York. Subpœnas were actually taken out, before the trial, for Messrs. Madison and Dearborn; and even the expenses of their travelling were tendered to them: but the proceedings did not even stop here. For a motion for an attachment was made before the court, founded upon the proof of serving these subpœnas, and the proof of offered compensation. The argument at length closed on this motion for attachment; but no man doubted the right of the court to issue subpœnas. The only question was, whether at that time, an attachment ought to issue. The court was unanimous about the right of subpœnas; but on the attachment, they were divided: judge Patterson being for it, and judge Talmadge against it.

We are however, asked, sir, for what purpose do we wish to procure this evidence? It is at their option to say, whether bills shall be laid before the grand jury or not. Granted, sir; it *is* in the power of the attorney for the United States to send up his bills or not. But should these bills be found true, and the trial come on, may we not be ruled to trial *instanter*, and without the aid of our witnesses? But what was done the other day, may hereafter be repeated. Witnesses are introduced on behalf of the United States, and others perhaps would have been on the motion for commitment. This motion is for the present only suspended; but if that be the case, may not the testimony now required, be relevant to our defence? The attorney for the United States triumphantly declares, that we must do as he pleases; and that we know not what he intends to do. That is true, sir; but may not we too, do something? May not colonel Burr move for his discharge? As he is to remain here until the court pleases to discharge him, may he not move for his recognisance to be discharged? Have we no right also to all the means which are necessary for the fair administration of justice?

" No time is stipulated for the return of the subpœna." This is a great difficulty indeed! It will be admitted, then, that the court has a right to issue a subpœna; and yet, because there happens to be no particular provision about the day, this right must be necessarily null. But, sir, is this objection really justified by practice? Has not the court a right to fix a day for the return of the processes of this sort, according to their own convenience, or the convenience of parties?

But why have we not applied for these documents sooner? Yes, sir, it is asked of us, why we have not made this application sooner; and yet even now does the gentleman wish to delay it. He declared that we have made it too soon; and yet now he declares that we have made it too late. Now, it cannot be both: if it be too late, it certainly cannot be too soon.

We have heard some remarks upon colonel Burr's privileges: and among others, upon the four counsellors who are to defend him. But what kind of an argument is this? If we turn to the laws of congress, we shall find, there is one attorney for the United States appropriated to each district; and yet there are no less than three counsellors employed on the present occasion. No doubt there is a law providing for the payment of the two others out of the treasury; but with what propriety can these gentlemen complain of my client making such arrangements as may suit his convenience or his interest? But what are all these remarks to the subpoena *duces tecum?* Sir, it is useless to multiply arguments on this subject. It is a settled rule, since the ancient times of King John; since the formation of magna charta itself, that the accused has a right to subpoena witnesses; and not only to any other form, but subpoena *duces tecum,* under such modifications as the court may please to prescribe.

Mr. MARTIN read an extract from the case of Smith and Ogden, in New-York, about issuing an attachment.

Mr. HAY asserted, that this extract did not prove the position contended for; that there was no case of a subpoena having issued before the finding of an indictment; that if the clerk ever had issued them, it was a mere voluntary unauthorised act. He challenged the experienced gentleman from Maryland to cite a single instance of an application to a court for subpoenas, before the finding of a bill of indictment.

Mr. MARTIN replied, that if there were no precedents on this very point, it was because this objection never was made before, and he hoped never would be made again.

Here a desultory conversation ensued; when,

Mr. HAY observed, that gentlemen affected to believe, that the present course pursued by the prosecution was dictated by a wish to suppress the evidence; that he conjured the gentlemen to remember that he had voluntarily applied for the papers which they wanted, and had no doubt of obtaining them; and that he made these remarks to guard any human being from the suspicion, that there was a disposition to refuse the papers; that he should exert himself with no less zeal to obtain the evidence that was wanted for colonel Burr, than that which might be produced against him.

The CHIEF JUSTICE observed, that he would not at present deliver any decided opinion upon the point, though he was disposed to believe, that the accused had a right to apply for subpœnas. He cited the case of a man, who had been some time before brought before him and condemned for counterfeiting bank notes. In that case the prisoner had attempted to delay the trial by pretending that he had witnesses in Baltimore; which plea had been rejected by the court, principally on the ground that he had not before summoned those witnesses. The chief justice, however, observed, that he should not decide this question at present, but reserve it for future decision; in the mean time, the counsel might proceed with the other part of the argument.

Some conversation here ensued, between Mr. BOTTS and Mr. HAY, on the interpretation of an act of congress, in which the term "accused" was employed.

Mr. MARTIN then rose to support the propriety of granting this particular subpœna. He laid down as a general principle, in all civil or criminal cases, that every man had a right to process to establish his rights or his innocence. Mac Nally's Evidence, vol. i. p. 255. Does there exist a single case in the British authorities in opposition to this doctrine? Surely these gentlemen do not intend to represent the president as a kind of sovereign, or as a king of Great Britain. He is no more than a servant of the people. But even the British king may be called upon to give testimony to his people. It is true, he is not obliged to be subpœnaed, and to appear in a court of justice; but his testimony under his sign manual is received as authentic evidence.

CHIEF JUSTICE.—The counsel on the opposite side admit, that the president may be summoned.

Mr. MARTIN.—They have surely never admitted it before. However, I am happy that is now admitted; as it will spare me a part of my argument. I will proceed then to the others. The next question is, whether the president can be summoned to attend with certain papers. One of them we want is an original letter from general Wilkinson, of the 21st October, and received by the president on the 27th of November. This letter, as appears by colonel Burr's affidavit, is considered by him as necessary to his defence; and his counsel, so far as they understand the subject, are of the same opinion. The other papers are copies of official orders by the navy and war departments. It may be said, sir, that if application were made to those departments, colonel Burr had a right to the papers: for we had supposed, that every citizen was entitled to such copies of official papers as are material to him. And I have never heard of but one instance where they were refused; and this was most certainly under presidential influence.

Mr. RANDOLPH here enumerated the particulars of his own correspondence with Mr. Robert Smith, secretary of the navy.

Mr. MARTIN proceeded to the following effect: I have asserted, that colonel Burr was entitled to a copy of these orders. We intended to show, that these orders were contrary to the constitution and the laws, and that they entitled colonel Burr to the right of resistance. We intended to show, that by this particular order his property and his person were to be destroyed; yes, by these tyrannical orders the life and property of an innocent man were to be exposed to destruction. We did not expect these originals themselves. But we did apply for copies; and were refused under presidential influence. In New-York, on the farcical trials of Ogden and Smith, the officers of the government screened themselves from attending, under the sanction of the president's name. Perhaps the same farce may be repeated here: and it is for this reason that we apply directly to the president of the United States. Whether it would have been best to have applied to the secretaries of state, of the navy and war, I cannot say. All that we want is, the copies of some papers, and the original of another. This is a peculiar case, sir. The president has undertaken to prejudge my client by declaring, that " Of his guilt there can be no doubt." He has assumed to himself the knowledge of the Supreme Being himself, and pretended to search the heart of my highly respected friend. He has proclaimed him a traitor in the face of that country, which has rewarded him. He has let slip the dogs of war, the hell-hounds of persecution, to hunt down my friend. And would this president of the United States, who has raised all this absurd clamour, pretend to keep back the papers which are wanted for this trial, where life itself is at stake? It is a sacred principle, that in all such cases, the accused has a right to all the evidence which is necessary for his defence. And whoever withholds, wilfully, information that would save the life of a person, charged with a capital offence, is substantially a murderer, and so recorded in the register of heaven. Can it then be presumed that the president would be sorry to have colonel Burr's innocence proved? No, it is impossible. Would the president of the United States give his enemies (for enemies he has, like other great and good men) would he give them the proud opportunity of saying that colonel Burr is the victim of anger, jealousy, and hatred? Will he not act with all possible candour? When told that certain papers are material to our defence, will he not be proud to say to us, " Sirs, you may have them; I will grant you every possible advantage." Had this been done, the attorney for the United States (and perhaps the executive) never would have said that these papers are no more material to us than the first paragraph of the laws of congress. These gentlemen forget, that it is not their province to decide, whether the evidence is material to us or not. It is for the court to say, whether it bears upon the case; and whether it is to go before the petit jury, or to come before themselves, if the motion to commit for treason be continued.

They seem to think, that we are not even to be trusted with these papers. But why do they attribute motives to colonel Burr's counsel, which they would themselves disdain? Why not do as much honour to ourselves, as to the president of the United States himself?

It may be suggested, that this is a private and confidential letter from general Wilkinson to the president. It was so said, indeed, yesterday. But if the president were here himself, the court would have a right to demand, whether in confidential conversations general Wilkinson had not given very different statements from those which he might here produce? What, sir, if general Wilkinson had reposed as much confidence, if he had instilled as much poison into the ear of the president, as Satan himself breathed into the ear of Eve; the president would have been still responsible to a court of justice, and bound to disclose his communications. The law recognises none of this kind of confidence. I refer your honours to 2 Atkins, 524, from which it appears that no man is privileged to withhold secrets: And to 11 State Trials, Dutchess of Kingston's case: There a physician entreated of the court to excuse him; but even his professional confidence (though of the most delicate nature) would not screen him. Lord Barrington in that case conjured them to excuse his giving in testimony what had been disclosed to him in all the confidence of private friendship. All his solicitations were disregarded. In MacNally, page 250, it is declared, that there can be no secrets, but those which are confided to counsellors and attorneys. Now let us suppose, that this information was conveyed to him by a letter; nay, by a private and confidential letter: Could we not have the president produced here; could we not examine him, whether he had ever received such a letter?

But perhaps we shall be told, that this would be making too free with high characters; that we call the honour of general Wilkinson into question; and that it is not less than treason to suppose it possible, that general Wilkinson is not as pure as an angel. But, sir, will it be forgotten, that this man has already broken the constitution to support his violent measures; that he has already ground down the civil authorities into dust; and subjected all around him to a military despotism? Is it possible to believe, that such a man may not swerve from the strict line of rectitude and decorum? To show the ease with which one man may be destroyed by another man or by a faction, and with the same unfeeling indifference as a philosopher sees rats struggling in an air pump, I will read a quotation from Tucker's Blackstone. [Here he read it.] Mr. Martin produced several instances, where the originals of recorded papers were brought before a court of justice.

Respecting copies of the navy orders for destroying the property and person of colonel Burr, it is very material to possess them. It may be necessary to show, that these acts, which the prosecutors are pleased to deem treasonable, were in fact nothing but justifiable means for defending his own rights.

Mr. MAC RAE.—May it please the court: I regret extremely, that on a question so simple, and so eminently divested of all personal feelings, as the present, the counsel for the prisoner should have considered it as their duty to wander so widely from the subject before us. I could have wished, sir, that instead of talking about shadows; instead of complaining against certain pretended persecutions attributed to the government of the United States; instead of indulging in defamation and abuse against the officers of government, which can neither be justified nor excused, they had confined their observations to the single and simple question now presented to your consideration: Whether this court had the right to issue a subpœna *duces tecum*, addressed to the president of the United States? I will not, sir, imitate the example which has been thus bountifully set me, however ample may be the materials, or however rich the harvest which is now spread before me. Whatever I may think of the guilt of Aaron Burr; by whatever emotions of disgust and indignation my bosom may be agitated by a contemplation of his conduct, I will attempt to suppress my opinions and feelings for the present. The time may come, sir, when I shall be at full liberty to give them loose. When Aaron Burr shall be put upon his trial; when he shall attend at your bar as a dangerous and indicted criminal, I shall not hesitate, sir, in the presence of the petit jury, in the presence of this court, and in the presence of the whole world, to express all my opinions and feelings. But, sir, I shall waive this privilege for the present. I cannot but consider it as highly indecorous, when contemplating this single question, to embrace all the merits of the case. Mr. Martin need not have talked so much of the president's elevation. He need not have taken such uncommon pains to expatiate upon the high office which he fills, nor so invidiously compare it with the irresponsible monarchy of England; as if the present president considered himself superior to the laws. Although, in this country, the decisions of our courts may be considered as doubtful, it is perhaps certain, that a subpœna ought not to go against him; yet, sir, anxious to show to the world that we feel nothing of that spirit of persecution, which has been so industriously and idly attributed to our government; solicitous to give an unerring proof of the principles on which we act, we shall not shelter ourselves under these precedents established by the courts of the United States. Elevated as our illustrious president is, yet our principles are, that when life is in jeopardy, he may be summoned like any individual, where he is able to disclose important facts, and when the national interests will admit of his attendance. As, then, we admit that a subpœna may issue against him as well as against any other man, where was the necessity of expatiating so widely upon his elevated station? When all the facts which relate to this transaction come to be fully developed ; when truth, and not passion, shall guide our understanding, I do not hesitate to affirm my belief, that the bolt, which has been levelled against his reputation, will vanish into air. I am sorry, sir, to be under the necessity of making such remarks as these, but let the blame fall where it is due, upon the gentleman from Maryland, who has extorted them, and not upon myself. And here, sir, permit me to read the affidavit on which this motion is grounded. I do not understand from this affidavit, that any other order is required from the navy department, than the one which was addressed to commodore Shaw, and is said to have been published in the Natchez Gazette. That order is already in court; and the attorney for the United States has pledged himself to produce it, if the court will but decide on the propriety of its exhibition. The only new paper, therefore, which is required by this affidavit, is the original letter of general Wilkinson to the president of the United States.

Mr. WICKHAM here observed, that the gentleman had mistaken the object of the application. We not only (said he) want this letter, but the order of the navy department. They tell us they have the order, and are ready to produce it ; but we doubt the identity of this copy. Without meaning any imputation upon Mr. Smith, we say, that they have several orders from his department. Let us see this order then, and we may ascertain whether it be the identical one, which we want. Let us but inspect the order which these gentlemen have in their possession, and if it be the one which we require, the process to be issued may be made more limited in its operation.

Mr. HAY.—The secretary of the navy inclosed this order to me; for what purpose I know not, unless it was for the sake of showing it. But as I am not particularly intsructed on this point, I do not conceive myself authorised to produce it at present. I will exhibit this paper, if the court thinks it material.

Mr. WICKHAM.—We have a right to apply to the president of the United States for the copy of any order; but if it is alleged to be a state paper, it must not be refused on the allegations of counsel, but on the oath of the officer.

Mr. MAC RAE.—Is your subpœna then to be addressed to these other officers?

Mr. WICKHAM.—No, sir, to the president alone, who has all these offices under his control.

Mr. MAC RAE.—I will attempt to satisfy the court, that the counsel have not grounded their motion upon this affidavit. [Here Mr. Mac Rae read the affidavit.] "MAY be material to his defence." Now, sir, how is this? I had always understood before, that all applications of this kind must be founded upon *positive averment;* that the party was not at liberty to state vague and loose conjectures, but that he must give *undoubting* assertions; and what was still further, that he should swear that these documents were material to his defence. The oath is not, that they *may* possibly be of use; that they *may* or *may not* be material. On this subject it is not merely sufficient to advance some precarious conjectures; but the party must *explicitly* state his belief, not that they *may* be, but that they *are* material. Nay, still further; in criminal cases, the party is not merely required by the court to say, that they are material, but to say in what respect they are so. In these points then, this affidavit is essentially defective. It certainly does not state how these documents are material; it does not even assert that they are material, but only advances a conjecture that they may be so.

I believe, sir, on the authority of a decision of the court of the United States, in the case of Cooper, of Northumberland, (p. 13 of the report of the trial) it may be shown, that the present party has no authority to demand these papers.

And, sir, the case of Cooper was materially distinguished from the one before the court in this important feature; that the public officers were in the very city, and on the very spot, where the the trial was conducted. The seat of government was then at Philadelphia, and not at Washington. This case, sir, was well known to every individual, who was interested in the politics of those times. It is sufficient merely to repeat, that Cooper was sued for a libel; that he put in two pleas: first, not guilty : secondly, justification; and that in order to support his plea of justification, he applied to the court for a subpœna to the president of the United States to obtain certain public documents. And what did the judge decide? He decided that the subpœna ought not to issue, and declared in strong terms against the principle now contended for.

But, sir, strong as that opinion is in our favour, and though it completely goes to deprive the prisoner of the privilege which he claims; and though it is to be considered as law in the courts of the United States; yet, sir, abhorring any thing that looks like persecution, we should have disdained to shelter ourselves under this abominable precedent. We desire that the prisoner may possess all the information which is necessary to his defence. It is my sincere wish, in this as well as in every other point, to give him all the assistance, which evidence can afford. From our souls, do we abhor every, the slightest thing which wears the appearance of persecution. Sir, I have only read this authority, to show, that we might easily have refused this demand under one of the precedents established by a court of the United States.

Mr. Martin has said, that no secrets ought to be withheld from a court of justice, except those which have been confidentially entrusted to legal counsel; that this is the only exception to the general doctrine of evidence; and that in all other cases, the witnesses may be compelled to give information. The exception recognised by Mr. Martin, certainly does exist; but Mr. Martin has taken ground too narrow, nor is that the only case where the witness is permitted to keep his information to himself. Sir, if a confidential communication has been made to Thomas Jefferson, he is not responsible to a court of justice for its contents. I speak, sir, with due submission to the court; but I ground my opinion principally on a decision of the supreme court of the United States. My position is, that if a communication is confidentially made to Thomas Jefferson, he is not bound to appear before this or any other court, to disclose it. It is unnecessary to collect arguments to demonstrate the soundness of the policy on which this principle is founded: that would be an easy task. But, sir, instead of wasting my time and that of the court upon the policy of the measure, I will refer you at once to a precedent. In the case of Marbury v. Madison, in the supreme court of the United States, Cranch's Reports, pages 143, 144, 145, Mr. Lincoln, the attorney general, was called into court, and it was vehemently contended, that he might be compelled to give information like any other citizen. Mr. Lincoln stated his objections in the following terms: First, " That he did not think himself bound to disclose his official transactions, while acting as secretary of state." Second, "That he ought not to be compelled to answer any thing which might tend to criminate himself." The court supported him in these objections. It follows from these opinions, that the court should always receive special information about the papers, which a party wishes to obtain, before they authorise him to demand them. They ought to ascertain whether these papers contain confidential communications to the head of the government. But, sir, if the papers which are called for by the affidavit of Aaron Burr be of a public nature, why should the court issue a subpœna *duces tecum* to demand them? The opposite counsel may rest assured, and the attorney for the United States has actually pledged himself solemnly to this court, that he would spare no exertions to obtain a copy of them, if the copy would be sufficient; or the originals, if copies will not avail.

But, sir, if this letter be of a confidential nature, it is not the duty of the president of the United States to produce it in this court or any where else.

And where is the propriety of directing this subpœna in any event to the president? If it be a public letter, it is undoubtedly deposited with every other paper of the same complexion in the archives of state. Why then is not this subpœna addressed to the secretary of state, instead of the president of the United States? There is no specific reason why this informality is adopted; for gentleman do not even pretend that they want the president's person. All that they pretend to require are certain papers in his possession; and these are evidently to be obtained, without the necessity of dragging him from Washington to this city. But, sir, if these papers are not of a public nature, but confidential communications, then it is not necessary or proper to subpœna Thomas Jefferson.

One remark more and I have done. The gentlemen insist upon the necessity of producing in this court the original letter from general Wilkinson to the president of the United States. I will suggest an expedient, which may obviate every possible inconvenience. If your honours say, that a copy of this letter may be read in evidence, like copies of all other documents in the departments of government, then also will the attorney for the United States consent, that this copy may be read and have the very same effect as the original. But gentlemen may contend that general Wilkinson would object to this copy. Sir, general Wilkinson would have no right to urge such an objection; and much less, when he should understand that this very copy is expressly introduced into the court, on the principle of possessing the same validity as the original itself. But, sir, if general Wilkinson should dare to raise this objection; if he should pretend to declare that this was not his letter, or that it was not an authenticated and correct copy, a few days only would elapse when the original would certainly be produced.

Mr. Mac Rae concluded with repeating his sincere wish, that every proper testimony necessary to the prisoner's defence should be produced; but with expressing his hopes, that no such step as at that time recommended by the opposite counsel, would be sanctioned by the court.

Mr. BOTTS.—In a government of laws, where majesty and prerogative are proscribed, and where the authorities of all the public functionaries are to be exercised for the benefit of the people, there are but few instances in which the policy of state secrecy can prevail. In the national intercourse with foreign states, where the relations present subjects fit for privacy, the rare duty of concealment may occur. Some time ago, when the hue and cry of treason was rung through the country, there might have been

an excuse for the claim of securing from the eye of the suspected, particular acts of the cabinet. At this moment it
will not be pretended, that the public good can require, that
colonel Burr should not have the means from the departments
required for his justification.

Can any innocent purpose, said Mr. Botts, be subserved by
the president's withholding the documents demanded? and will
the counsel malign him by imputing to him a guilty one? The act
of congress provides fees for copies from the ministerial offices
under the control of the president, and every individual has a
right to demand them on paying the statuary charges. If individuals in common have this right, why has it been denied to colonel
Burr, whose fate may depend in some degree on them? One of
the copies was promised, but the promise was forgotten. State
policy in England has done a great deal of mischief; it has
often sheltered wicked and corrupt ministers from the punishment due to their crimes: yet even there (where the principles
of liberty are not understood so well as in this country) in Sir
Home Popham's trial, Lord Melville, president of the board
of admiralty, was compelled, a few months ago, to appear and
give evidence concerning the instructions he had given to that
admiral. I do not now complain of the illiberal caution of the
gentlemen in keeping hidden their written evidence, which, if
known in time, we might refute; but such testimony as we think
material in our defence, we are at any rate entitled to without
favour from them. But the gentlemen have made a concession
of great liberality! They say they are willing that the president
may be summoned to attend, but not to give evidence when he
does attend: not to disclose any thing but what he may himself
condescend to make known. The president may be, and no
doubt is, a very great and good man; but while his policy in relation to the accused is so completely enveloped in mystery, the
counsel for the prosecution must pardon us, if we cannot consent
to pin our faith on his sleeve, and if we choose rather to betake
ourselves to our legal rights.

The opinion given by judge Chase on the trial of Cooper,
was reprobated by the politics of those gentlemen who prosecute for the United States; and yet they now wish to avail
themselves of that authority. I congratulate them upon their dereliction of the old democratic opinions which prevailed at the
time of Cooper's trial, and which I thought would have gone
with my friends to their graves.

Mr. MAC RAE observed, that Mr. Botts had misrepresented
the object for which he had introduced the opinion of judge
Chase; that he had not pretended to use it as authority; but,
on the contrary, had expressly declared that he scorned to avail
himself of it.

Mr. Wickham said, that judge Chase's opinion pronounced in the case of Cooper was not correctly understood. It was not that the president could not be summoned as a witness, but that he ought not to be summoned to give evidence against himself.

Mr. Botts proceeded to say, that even that qualified opinion of judge Chase had been reprobated by the gentlemen; but now they shelter themselves under it in effect, because they use it as authority against the success of the present motion.

The gentlemen contend that the executive must judge whether the documents require secrecy or not. But how can this judgment be exercised until they are called upon? And how can the government be legally called on but by process of subpœna *duces tecum?* When this is served the president may make out his return.

As to the argument that a copy of general Wilkinson's letter will be sufficient: Suppose, said Mr. Botts, general Wilkinson should swear to one thing, and the copy of his letter should say another; would you condemn him upon the president's certificate merely that the paper produced contained a true copy of a letter from him?

He concluded with observing, that, if a time shall ever arrive when a person shall stand accused of a crime of the highest nature; of a crime by which his life is endangered, if a part of the testimony shall be concealed by those who administer the government, and no policy of state requires it; and yet the court does not compel it to be produced to screen the devoted victim; it will be a disastrous time for our country!

Mr. Wirt.—The counsel for the prosecution do not deny that the general subpœna *ad testificandum*, may be issued to summon the president of the United States, and that he is as amenable to that process as any other citizen. If his public functions disable him from obeying the process, that would be a satisfactory excuse for his non-attendance *pro hæc vice;* but does not go to prove his total exemption from the process. We think farther, sir, that a man, standing in the situation of the prisoner, has also the right to demand all papers material for his defence, wheresoever they may be, the disclosure of which will not compromit the national safety; but then the papers required must be shown to be material for his defence. The subpœna *ad testificandum*, is a matter of right, and the prisoner might have demanded it from the clerk without the intervention of the court; but here is a motion for a subpœna *duces tecum*, to compel the president to produce certain papers of state, the materiality of which is not shown.

I shall contend first, sir, that the subpœna *duces tecum* is not a process of right; that the motion for it, is a motion addressed to the discretion of the court; and that the court may award or withhold it as they see fit.

In the next place, I shall contend, that this discretion of the court should be controlled and determined only by the relevancy and materiality of the papers required.

And, thirdly, that in the present instance, the relevancy and materiality of the papers required are so far from being shown, that, from every thing which appears, they are both immaterial and entirely irrelevant.

I shall proceed to show, in the first place, that the subpœna *duces tecum* is not a process of right, but that the application for it is addressed merely to the discretion of the court.

Mr. Wickham.—That is admitted, sir; we admit that it is an application to the sound discretion of the court.

Mr. Wirt.—I thank you for the admission, sir. You have relieved me from the unnecessary trouble of so much of my argument. It being conceded then, that this is an application to the discretion of the court, the question naturally presents itself, by what circumstances should that discretion be controlled and determined? Should it be by the mere wish of the prisoner? If so, it is in vain that the court possesses any discretion on the subject; the only discretion exercised about it, is the discretion of the prisoner. He has but to ask and have; and by his mere wish, he changes this from a process flowing from the discretion of the court, into a process of absolute right. Consider this wide and bold doctrine on the ground of expediency. Would you summon any private individual from the remotest part of the United States, to produce a paper on the mere wish of the prisoner, without his defining the paper and showing how it bore upon his defence? If you would, you put the pursuits and the peace of every individual in the United States at the mercy of the prisoner's caprice and resentments. This argument, from inconvenience, assumes an attitude of the most awful and alarming importance, when you extend it to a case like this before the court. A prisoner seldom has any cordial amity for the government by which he is prosecuted for a crime. The truth is, that he feels himself in a state of war with that government; and the more desperate his case, the more ardent will be his spirit of revenge. Would you expose the offices of state to be ravaged at the mere pleasure of a prisoner, who, if he feels that he must fall, would pant for nothing more anxiously than " to *grace* his fall and make his ruin glorious," by dragging down with him the bright and splendid edifice of the government? Sir, if Aaron Burr has the right, at his mere wish, to call one paper from the government, he has the same right to call any other; and so, one after another, might divulge and proclaim to the world, every document and secret of state, however delicate our foreign relations might be, and however ruinous the disclosure to the honour and prosperity of the country. These, sir, are topics offered to the discretion of the court.

It is certainly much to be wished, that a rule could be devised, which, while it should protect the rights of the prisoner, should also protect the public offices from being wantonly and unnecessarily violated. I think there is such a rule. It is this: it is by requiring that the prisoner who calls for a paper, should show that the paper applies to his case, and is requisite for his defence. When he shall have done this, I hold that he will be entitled to call for any paper. It will then rest with the president of the United States, the officer appointed by the people to watch over the national safety, to say whether that safety will be endangered by divulging the paper. Surely, sir, justice to the prisoner requires no more than that he should possess such papers as are material for his defence; and will not the court require that he should show that materiality, before they give way to his call? If they do it, if they say that it is enough for the prisoner to wish a paper, to have it; they put themselves, as well as the chief magistrate of the Union, in danger of becoming the mere ministers of the prisoner's whim, or malice and resentment; but by adopting the rule which I have proposed, they would avoid these consequences and do all that justice requires for the prisoner.

When the subject was first mentioned, it was said, by one of your honours, that it is usual to award the subpœna *duces tecum* on the mere motion of the party, unsupported by any affidavit as to the purpose for which the paper was required. This is true, sir; such an affidavit is not generally required; but why is it not? Because the relevancy and materiality of the paper are admitted by the adverse counsel, or are palpable from the nature of the issue and of the paper required. The docket, for example, presents the case of a writ of right, or an action of ejectment; the name of the action, shows that the title of land is in question. One of the parties moves for a subpœna *duces tecum* directed to the clerk of another court, and requiring him to bring up a deed or a will which forms a link in the claim of his title. The adverse counsel, if he be present, admits by his silence the propriety of the motion; or if his silence has not that effect, the nature of the issue and of the paper required, show at once the relevancy and materiality of the latter. Hence it has happened, that these motions are usually unsupported by affidavit. But is this the case here? The relevancy and materiality of the papers called for are not admitted by us: are that relevancy and materiality palpable from the nature of the points in issue and the papers required? Let us see if they be. The two charges against the prisoner are, first of high treason; and secondly, misdemeanor, in setting on foot an expedition against the territories of a nation with whom we are at peace. For the purpose of his defence, he says he wants a letter from general Wilkinson to the president; which letter contains a declaration of his guilt; and also certain orders from the department of war, which he says directed the burning and destruction of himself, his people, and his property. Now, sir, what possible tendency can either of these papers have to acquit the prisoner of the treason or the misdemeanor? As to the orders, which have been depicted as being so sanguinary and despotic, I affirm, with the power of proof to support me, that such orders never were given; though if it be true, that Aaron Burr had placed himself in a state of war with his country; was aiming a blow at the vitals of our government and liberty, and that blow could be averted in no other way, I hold that his destruction would have been a virtue; a great and glorious virtue. Affairs, however had not reached that desperate crisis. We have seen the orders, sir, and at a proper time will produce them. The very orders to lieutenant Shaw, which the prisoner has so often mentioned, as having been published in the Natchez gazette; those orders are not as he has described them; they are simply orders to apprehend Aaron Burr, and *if it shall become necessary for that purpose, to destroy his boats.* Those are the bloody orders which have been so often mentioned with looks of such tragic and mysterious import! Suppose the orders were as barbarous as he has described them, and that the emergency did not justify them, they prove the administration wrong; but do they prove, or tend to prove, Aaron Burr innocent? If the president were on his trial, for having issued these orders, it would be necessary to hear the orders themselves, in order to ascertain their merits or demerits. But the question is not now as to the guilt or innocence of the president: it is as to the guilt or innocence of Aaron Burr on the charges of treason and misdemeanor; and whether the president has acted right or wrong, does not and cannot affect the question of Burr's guilt or innocence. The charges against him are to be proved by witnesses on behalf of the United States. If these witnesses do not prove the charges, there is an end of the inquiry: but if they do, I ask whether it be possible that his production of the president's orders, even in his own terms, will remove that evidence of his guilt? Every judgment must answer No: and if so, the orders are clearly immaterial for his defence. But although the affidavit does not attempt to show wherein these orders are material for the prisoner's defence, Mr. Martin has attempted to supply this omission by his argument. It seems these orders were so lawless, that Burr had a right to resist them: and whatever he has done has been in self-defence against these orders. It would be easy, sir, to expose the flimsiness and fallacy of this pretext by a reference to dates. The man cannot have a very chronological head who can impute crimes throughout 1805, 1806, to orders issued in the last month of the last year, or the beginning of 1807: but without stopping to annalyse more minutely this strange anachronism, let us inquire into this doctrine of resistance which Mr. Martin has advocated. I am not an advocate for passive obedience and nonresistance. I do not think, as Mr. Martin has asked, that a man becomes a god when he becomes a president. I think he does not become a god even by becoming a king or an emperor. On the contrary, I think that a man who, in a government like ours, even aspires to become one, approaches, in *point of character, a class of beings very opposite to gods.* But ascending again to our president: he is bound by his oath of office to take care that the laws shall be carried into effect. By the particular act of congress which prescribes the punishment of misdemeanor charged on the prisoner, the president is authorised and required to call the naval and military force of the country to defeat the enterprize. In the present instance he has done so, and given orders for the apprehension of the offender: and we are told that Aaron Burr, instead of submitting himself to the laws and justice of his country, had a right to resist these orders; that Aaron Burr was to be the judge, whether he should obey or not, orders proceeding from the lawfully constituted authorities of his country; and that if he thought them unlawful, he had a right to resist them by force. If this be so, there is an end of government. Every individual in the country, I presume, has, at least, the same rights with Aaron Burr: and if he has this right of submitting to, or resisting the laws and officers of the government, as he pleases, every body else has the same right: then where is the use of our constitution, laws, or officers? We might as well abolish them all, and return to a state of nature. But, sir, neither Aaron Burr nor any other individual carries about him this dispensing power. It is clear, that the very act of resistance, of which Mr. Martin has spoken, was itself an act of treason. Before the orders can be material for his defence, on this ground, it must be determined that he had the right of resistance; but, as I presume it to be impossible, that the court can entertain this latter opinion, I conclude, that the orders in question, cannot be relevant or material to his defence in this light; and no other has been presented, or I believe can be presented. Let us now consider the letter from general Wilkinson to the president, and inquire how that touches either of

the issues in which the prisoner is involved, and how the production of the original letter is to operate to his benefit. If the
letter be material at all, a copy will answer every purpose. The
letter, I presume, from the use made of it by the president, is
a public document, and is lodged in the department of state.
The law of the United States, which establishes this office, contains the following clause :

" And be it further enacted, that the said secretary shall
cause a seal of office to be made for the said department of
such device as the president of the United States shall approve,
and all copies of records and papers in the said office, authenticated under the said seal, shall be evidence equally as the original record or paper." 1 vol. Laws U. S. Chap. xiv. p. 5.

Hence a copy of this letter will answer every purpose
of the original; and it will be no more competent to general
Wilkinson to deny the authenticated copy than the original.
But let us see of what use a copy of this letter can be to
him? We know nothing of this letter except from the message
of the president, to which the counsel on the other side have referred us; and by this message it appears, that it was from this
letter, connected with others, that the president inferred the prisoner's guilt; a letter then, which according to the only account
we have of it, contributes to establish the prisoner's guilt, is required for the purpose of proving his innocence! But this letter we learn, not from the affidavit, but from argument, is required for the purpose of confronting general Wilkinson if he
should trip in his evidence. At present then, there is confessedly no issue to which this letter applies; but one may possibly occur by general Wilkinson's departing in his narrative from
the statements of his letter. Now, sir, suppose a man should
move you for a subpœna *duces tecum* in a civil question, stating,
indeed, that there was at present no suit to which the paper
could apply, but that he apprehended one might be brought,
in which it might be material, would his motion be granted?
Now where is the difference between such a motion and the
very remote probability that general Wilkinson will produce an
occasion for this letter, in contradicting by his parol testimony
the statement of his letter? But let us press this point a little further. No one pretends to know any thing of the details of this
letter; all we know of it is derived from the president's message; and from that all we learn of it is its general character,
that it goes to prove the guilt of Burr. Now, in order to produce any collision between this letter and Wilkinson's parol
evidence, the letter must have an opposite character; that is, it
must go to show the innocence of Burr. If Wilkinson continues to avow the guilt of Burr, there will be no contradiction
between his testimony and his letter, and consequently there
can be no confrontation between them, beneficial to the prison-

er; there can be a confrontation in no other event, than that of his deposing to Burr's innocence. The result of the argument is, that Burr, apprehensive that the evidence of general Wilkinson may be favourable to him, wishes the general's letter for the purpose of destroying that evidence, and proving his own guilt. Again, sir. I have never seen or heard of an instance of this process being required to bring forward any paper, but where such a paper was in its nature evidence; for which either party had an equal right to call, and to use it when produced. But it is obvious that in this case and in the present state of things, we could not use the letter of general Wilkinson as evidence; although the opposite party should obtain his subpœna *duces tecum* for this paper, and would seem thereby to have made it evidence, and introduced it into the cause. Yet after it comes we cannot use it: hence there is no reciprocity in it. The paper is not, at present, evidence, and therefore is not within the principle on which this process is awarded. One more remark on this letter, and I have done with it. I am no more an advocate for the needless multiplication of state secrets, than the gentleman who has preceded me. It looks too much like the mysteries of monarchy; and I hate monarchy with all its mysteries, as I do the mysterious movements of those who are lovers of monarchy. Yet it is obvious, that there may be cases in which the very safety of the state may depend on concealing the views and operations of the government. I will instance in this very letter. I do not know what it contains; but it is from the general who commands on the Spanish frontier. That the state of our affairs was and is with Spain, not the most amicable, is well understood. We know that our affairs in that quarter wear, even at this time, the most lowering aspect. Suppose this letter should contain a scheme of war, a project of attack, would it be proper to divulge and proclaim it even to Spain herself? If the letter contains such a thing, I have no doubt that the president ought and will conceal at least so much of it. This, however, will be a question with him, when the paper shall be called for; and a question which he alone is competent to decide.

From what has been said, I take it to be clear, that the relevancy and materiality of these papers for the prisoner's defence, are not palpable, by comparing the nature of the papers with the nature of the issues; and being neither self-evident nor admitted, I hold that the party is bound to show, at least by his affidavit, wherein they are relevant and material. This he has not pretended to do, in the affidavit offered to the court; for in *that*, he has merely stated, in terms the most loose and vague, that he believes these papers *may* be material for his defence. Sir, he might take the same oath as to any paper in the offices of state, without the possibility of proving him forsworn; for he swears merely to a conjecture, and whether he entertains it or not, can never be decisively known to any one but himself. Will you lay open the public offices to be ransacked by conjectural affidavits? Will you adopt a precedent which will put it in the power of the enemies of the government at any time, and without the hazard of punishment, to explore your offices with the worst of views, and harass the officers themselves at their discretion? Sir, I wish the prisoner to have a fair trial. I wish him to possess every atom of evidence which can contribute to his acquittal; but these papers appear to me not calculated to touch the issue, and still less calculated do the prisoner any good. If he thinks otherwise, where can be the difficulty of his showing, by an affidavit at least, some probability of their doing him service. If he knows the nature of these orders and that letter so well as to have ascertained to his own satisfaction, that they may do him service, where can be the harm of his setting out in his affidavit the character of the papers, and showing how they may be brought to bear upon his case? When he shall have done so, the court will have something for its discretion to act upon; at present they have nothing but the prisoner's faint conjecture, and the discretion would appear to me not very sound which would be determined by a consideration like that.

I can see but one possible objection to the particular affidavit which I require, which is, that the prisoner would thereby unmask his defence. But in the case of the United States against Smith, a particular affidavit was required by judge Patterson, setting out what it was expected to prove by the witnesses; and although it was objected in that case, that by demanding such an affidavit, he compelled the accused to unmask his defence, he nevertheless demanded the affidavit. And in that case, as in this, although the materiality of the evidence was supported by some of the ablest advocates on the continent, the court determined against its materiality, and the cause went on without it: but in the present instance, an objection as to unmasking the defence would be an objection merely of form, because the gentlemen have by their arguments, in fact, taken off the mask, and stated the manner in which they expect this evidence to apply. We have examined their expectations, and I hope found them baseless.

I conclude, sir, that this is an application to the discretion of the court; that justice to the prisoner required only that he should have all papers from the officers of state which he shall show to be material and relevant to his defence; that he has not shown them to be so in this case; and that, therefore, the process should be withheld until he does show them to be so. I know of no other rule which, while it will protect the rights of the prisoner, will also save the offices from needless, wanton and wicked violations.

I cannot take my seat, sir, without expressing my deep and sincere sorrow at the policy which the gentlemen in the defence have thought it necessary to adopt. As to Mr. Martin, I should have been willing to impute this fervid language to the sympathies and resentments of that friendship which he has taken such frequent occasions to express for the prisoner, his *honouraable friend*. In the cause of friendship I can pardon zeal even up to the point of intemperance; but the truth is, sir, that before Mr. Martin came to Richmond, this policy was settled, and on every question incidentally brought before the court, we were stunned with invectives against the administration. I appeal to your recollection, sir, whether this policy was not manifested even so early as in those new and until now unheard of challenges to the grand jury for favour? Whether that policy was not followed up with increased spirit, in the very first speeches which were made in this case; those of Mr. Botts and Mr. Wickham on their previous question pending the attorney's motion to commit? Whether they have not seized with avidity every subsequent occasion, and on every mere question of abstract law before the court, flew off at a tangent from the subject, to launch into declamations against the government? Exhibiting the prisoner continually as a persecuted patriot: a Russell or a Sidney, bleeding under the scourge of a despot, and dying for virtue's sake! If there be any truth in the charges against him, how different were the purposes of his soul from those of a Russell or a Sidney! I beg to know what gentlemen can intend, expect, or hope, from these perpetual philippics against the government? Do they flatter themselves that this court feel political prejudices which will supply the place of argument and innocence on the part of the prisoner? Their conduct amounts to an insinuation of the sort. But I do not believe it. On the contrary, I feel the firm and pleasing assurance, that as to the court, the beam of their judgment will remain steady, although the earth itself should shake under the concussion of prejudice. Or is it on the bystanders that the gentlemen expect to make a favourable impression? And do they use the court merely as a canal, through which they may pour upon the world their undeserved invectives against the government? Do they wish to divide the popular resentment and diminish thereby their own quota? Before the gentlemen arraign the administration, let them clear the skirts of their client. Let them prove his innocence; let them prove that he has not covered himself with the clouds of mystery and just suspicion; let them prove that he has been all along erect and fair, in open day, and that these charges against him are totally groundless and false. That will be the most eloquent invective which they can pronounce against the prosecution; but until they prove this innocence, it shall be in vain that they attempt to divert our minds to other objects, and other inquiries. We will keep our eyes on Aaron Burr until he satisfies our utmost scruple. I beg to know, sir, if the course which gentlemen pursue is not disrespectful to the court itself? Suppose there are any foreigners here accustomed to regular government in their own country, what can they infer from hearing the federal administration thus reviled to the federal judiciary? Hearing the judiciary told, that the administration are " *blood hounds*, hunting this man with a keen and savage thirst for blood; that they now suppose they have hunted him into their toils and have him safe." Sir, no man, foreigner or citizen, who hears this language addressed to the court, and received with all the complacency at least which silence can imply, can make any inferences from it very honourable to the court. It would only be inferred, while they are thus suffered to roll and luxuriate in these gross invectives against the administration, that they are furnishing the joys of a Mahometan paradise to the court as well as to their client. I hope that the court, for their own sakes, will compel a decent respect to that government of which they themselves form a branch. On our part, we wish only a fair trial of this case. If the man be innocent, in the name of God let him go; but while we are on the question of his guilt or innocence, let us not suffer our attention and judgment to be diverted and distracted by the introduction of other subjects foreign to the inquiry.

Mr. WICKHAM appealed to the court if the counsel for colonel Burr had been the first who began the attack; and wished the gentleman to follow his own wise maxims. He observed, that Mr. Wirt had met the question fairly, and conceded several points which had been contended for by his associates. He admitted the granting a writ of " subpœna *duces tecum*" to be a matter of discretion; but insisted, that the opinion of the party applying for it, that the papers might be material, was sufficient. He said that the question in the case of the United States v. Smith, arose on a motion for a continuance.

Mr. WIRT corrected his statement; observing, that the motion was for a continuance and for an attachment against the witnesses at the same time, and both questions were argued collectively.

[The following is but a brief and imperfect sketch of the very ingenious and able argument of Mr. Wickham, in reply to the very eloquent and impressive speech of Mr. Wirt.]

Mr. WICKHAM agreed that such was the case; but contended that the special affidavit was required, because there was a motion for a continuance; and that on a motion of this kind, an affidavit need not be special. He said, that the reason given by judge Patterson, for requiring a special statement of what was intended to be proved by Messrs. Madison and Smith, was, that if they had been present, their evidence (if it only went to prove that the president had sanctioned the expedition) would have been of no consequence; since the president's sanctioning the expedition could not have rendered it lawful.

We are told, said Mr. Wickham, that Wilkinson's letter is not important! Yet he is the pivot on which this prosecution turns. Without his evidence they could not progress with the trial. When he arrives, it will be all important to us to prove the falsehood of his testimony, by proving that he has contradicted himself. His credibility is the point in question; and surely general Wilkinson is not so immaculate as the government. We may allude to his tyrannical and oppressive conduct at New-Orleans; we may demonstrate that his feelings, his interests, his character, require him to secure the conviction of colonel Burr. Under these circumstances, his veracity must be very doubtful, especially if we can show that he has made three or four different and inconsistent representations of the transactions charged to be treasonable. His letter therefore ought to be produced.

As to the inconvenience to which the public offices may be subjected, it ought not to be regarded; for those offices were made for the good of the people, not for the good of the officers. All that colonel Burr is obliged to show, is probable cause to believe that Wilkinson's letter may be material, though he cannot swear that it is material. Mr. Wirt says, he is not an advocate for state secrets; but he *is* in this case without knowing it. He has said too, that the acquittal of colonel Burr will be a satire on the government. I am sorry that the gentleman has made this confession, that the character of the government depends on the guilt of colonel Burr. If I believed him to be correct, I could easily explain, from that circumstance, the anxiety manifested to convict him, and the prejudices which have been excited against him. But I will not believe that this is the case, but will tell the gentleman that we think Burr may be acquitted, and yet the government may have pure intentions.

The writ of subpœna *duces tecum* ought to be issued, and if there be any state secrets to prevent the production of the letter, the president should allege it in his return; for at present, we cannot know that any such secrets exist. And the court, when his return is before them, can judge of the cause assigned. But *I have too good an opinion of the president, to think he would withhold the letter.*

The gentlemen on the other side have said, that we do not wish to unmask our defence; but in withholding the papers which we demand, they show that they have on the mask, and we wish the court to aid us in making them pull it off.

We contend that no affidavit on the part of colonel Burr is necessary. Wilkinson's affidavit, already published, together with the president's communication to congress, prove that the letter in question must be material. It may show, that the treasonable transactions attributed to colonel Burr within the limits of this state, never existed; for as to Blannerhasset's island, the gentlemen in the prosecution *know*, there was no such thing as a military force on that island.

[Here Mr. HAY interrupted him, and said, that it was extremely indelicate and improper to accuse them of voluntarily supporting a cause which they knew to be unjust. He solemnly denied the truth of the charge against him and the gentlemen who assisted him, and declared that they could prove the actual existence of an armed assemblage of men on Blannerhasset's island, under the command of Aaron Burr.]

Mr. Wickham acknowledged that he had gone too far in the expression he had used, and ought not to have uttered what he had said concerning the counsel for the United States, and declared that he meant nothing personal against them. He proceeded to argue the question concerning the production of the president's orders. He denied, as Mr. Martin had done before, the legality of those orders, and contended that colonel Burr had a right to resist them. Mr. Burr was brought here—how he was brought we will not say; but we will say, that resistance to the militia ordered out against him, was resistance to tyranny and despotism."

Mr. Wickham returned to the question relative to Wilkinson's letter. We are told, he said, that the letter is in the department of state, and a copy will be sufficient. If the letter was written to the president of the United States, and not to the secretary of any department, we may presume that the president has it in his own possession. But if a copy were here, Wilkinson might deny that he ever wrote the letter; and although the copy might be faithful, it could not prove that the letter was not a forgery. The original, therefore, will alone answer our purpose.

Mr. Wirt lays down the strange principle, that Wilkinson's letter is not evidence, because it could make only in favour of one side; but that it ought to make in favour of the other side also. Give the gentleman his premises, and his conclusion follows. But his premises are false; for the doctrine cannot be sound, that nothing is evidence but that which makes in favour of both sides of a question. Such reciprocal effect is not essential to the admissibility of evidence.

When Mr. Wickham had finished, the CHIEF JUSTICE observed, that although many observations (in the course of the several discussions which had taken place) had been made by the gentlemen of the bar, in the heat of debate, of which the court did not approve, yet the court had hitherto avoided interfering; but as a pointed appeal had been made to them on this day, (alluding to the speech of Mr. Wirt), and they had been called upon to support their own dignity, by preventing the government from being abused, the court thought it proper to declare that the gentlemen on both sides had acted improperly in the style and spirit of their remarks; that they had been to blame in endeavouring to excite the prejudices of the people; and had repeatedly accused each other of doing what they forget they have done themselves. The court therefore expressed a wish that the counsel for the United States and for colonel Burr, would confine themselves on every occasion to the point really before the court; that their own good sense and regard for their characters required them to follow such a course; and it was hoped that they would not hereafter deviate from it.

The court then adjourned until Thursday morning, eleven o'clock.

Thursday, June 11th, 1807.

The court met according to adjournment.

Mr. Hay addressed the court to this effect: I am happy the court has recommended to the counsel on both sides to adhere more strictly to the subjects in debate. Their admonition will be followed by me, and I wish they would cause it to be followed by others. I regret indeed that it was not made somewhat sooner. Perhaps if it had, we might have been spared the pain of hearing many remarks as unauthorised in point of principle and fact as they are irrelevant; remarks which, as a public prosecutor, as a friend of my country, and a supporter of its constitution, government and laws, I heard with surprise and regret, and with a sentiment which I will not name. I will not imitate this example of my opponents, but endeavour to confine my observations exclusively to the question now in discussion. I am really doubtful however, whether I should not be departing in some degree from this declaration in noticing one argument used by the gentleman who last spoke, (Mr. Wickham). Language so strange, a charge so unjust, I hope, however, I may be permitted to repel.

The gentleman, with a tone of voice calculated to excite irritation, and intended for the multitude, charged us with conceding point after point! He insinuates that we have been catching at every thing to bear down the accused; that we inconsiderately contend for any doctrine, however absurd, which might have the effect of injuring him, and afterwards are obliged to abandon the ground we have too precipitately taken. I will ask, if any occurrence has shown that we are actuated by this spirit? No, sir. The gentleman knows the charge is unjust. But even if it had been true, that we had made concessions, it ought to have been considered as a proof of our candour and liberality, in giving up ground as soon as we thought it untenable, and not as a matter of reproach. But, sir, it is not correct. We have conceded no point that we ever maintained. We admitted that the president might be subpœnaed as a witness, because we always thought so. We never clothed him with those attributes of dignity which gentlemen have accused us of ascribing to him. We know the president is but a man, though among the first of men; he is but a citizen, though the first of citizens. The president too knows, that, like the great Cato, he ought to pay obedience to the laws of his country, and obey the commands of its courts of justice. All this we have uniformly admitted; but have denied, and deny now, that a subpœna *duces tecum* ought to be issued to the president.

Mr. Hay moreover observed, that the objection made the day before to the prisoner's right to make the motion in the present stage of the prosecution was not waived; and that in opposing the motion, he was influenced solely by a desire to keep the accused and his counsel within legal limits; because he had endeavoured to procure for them the very evidence they requested. He proceeded to argue the question upon its merits.

It having been admitted, that this was a motion addressed only to the discretion of the court, it followed, that it ought to be granted only when substantial justice required it; that it is to be granted to a person accused, because his defence when properly conducted requires it. But the accused himself in this case does not say these papers are material in his defence. His affidavit is drawn with great caution. He only says that the papers *may* be material. This is nothing more than the mere expression of an opinion, which may be correct or incorrect. Mr. Hay asked the counsel for colonel Burr, and more especially Mr. Martin, if in the course of their long experience they had ever known such an affidavit? Its language is unprecedented, designedly vague, and equivocal. The letter *may* be material! This *may* depend upon the use intended to be made of it. The object of demanding it may be to give his counsel an opportunity to speak as they have done before; to charge the government with illegal and barbarous persecution, and with endeavouring to crush and overwhelm the accused. All this may be said, and no doubt will be said, and may be a very considerable help to colonel Burr.

The affidavit is truly farcical; because from any thing expressed in it, the letter of general Wilkinson *may*, or *may not* be material. Suppose these words " or may not" had been inserted, would it then have been regarded? The absurdity would then have been too evident. And is it not the same thing in substance as it now stands? If such an affidavit as this is sufficient, and mere curiosity is to be indulged, the president might be required to produce all our correspondence with the Spaniards about our disputed territories; in short, all the papers of government would be laid open to the inspection of Burr. But the court ought not to issue process on speculation only; it ought not to subject the public officers to inconvenience, and the national archives to derangement, unless in a case where justice plainly requires it.

But the affidavit would not have been sufficient if he had said, what he dared not to say, that the papers are material. It should appear *how* they are material. The nature of the evidence ought to be specially stated, that the court may judge of it. Will the court rely on the judgment of the party in this case? Misled as he is by his feelings, his judgment ought not to be trusted.

Even in ordinary cases the court will inquire as to the contents of papers on a motion for a continuance. Which doctrine is recognised in 2 Bl. Rep. 514. The same thing was done in the case of the United States v. Smith and Ogden, in which almost as much clamour was excited as in this. There, the evidence of Mr. Madison and others was sworn to be material; but the court required a specification of its substance, and decided that it was not admissible. The papers required in the present case would probably be so decided, if they were here. I have a knowledge of the orders, and think so with respect to them. The letter I know nothing about. Mr. Wickham's argument, that the court did right in Smith and Ogden's case, because it was *prima facie* presumable that the evidence would not be admissible, turns against him here; for, certainly, it is *prima facie* presumable that general Wilkinson's letter cannot make in Burr's favour, since the orders to intercept him on his passage to the seat of his empire were founded on the information received from that letter.

The conduct of the gentlemen proves, that they feel us to be right. Their involuntary conviction of this is evinced by their endeavouring to supply the defect in the affidavit, and to specify the purposes for which the papers are wanted. The accused has not ventured to swear that they are material, but they assert it, and attempt to show it by argument.

First, as to the letter. Mr. Wickham says, that Wilkinson has written other letters to other persons differing from this. We deny the fact. If it be true, why is it not sworn to? But suppose general Wilkinson had done so, what is the inference? Is his evidence before the jury not to be regarded? It is strange indeed that the gentlemen say they have never seen this letter, and only guess at its contents, yet say, that letters containing different statements have been written! Surely such efforts as these are deplorable; for, whether the assertion be true or not, it is not known to be true.

They next contend that the orders are material because they were illegal, arbitrary, unconstitutional, oppressive and unjust; that Burr's acts were merely acts of self-defence against tyranny and usurpation, and, of course, were justifiable.

Many strange positions have been laid down, but this is monstrous. Mr. Martin will excuse me for saying, that I expected sounder doctrine from his age and experience. These principles were not learnt by him in Maryland, nor are they the doctrines of this place. Considering that he has come all the way from Maryland to enlighten us of the Virginia bar by his great talents and erudition, I hoped he would not have advanced a doctrine which would have been abhorred even in the most turbulent period of the French revolution, by the jacobins of 1794! It is the duty of the president to call out the militia to suppress combinations against the laws, (see L. U. S. vol. 3. page 189.) and particularly to prevent enterprizes against foreign nations in amity with the United States; (ib. page 92.) Yet it is contended, that his orders for such purposes are illegal, and may be resisted by force of arms! I will not say it is treason to advance, or a misdemeanor to believe such doctrines; but deplorable is the cause which depends on such means for support. Suppose, however, the president was misled, and that Mr. Burr was peaceably engaged in the project of settling his Washita lands; will it be contended, that he had a right to resist the president's orders to stop him? I say this would be treason. If congress were to pass an arbitrary or oppressive act, but not unconstitutional, (such as the excise law, for example) it has been decided, that an armed combination to resist it would be treason. Of course, resistance to the execution of the statute, under which the president was acting, would be treason. The president receives information, that a law of the United States is about to be violated; he issues orders to enforce the law in the way prescribed by itself. Is not opposition by violence treason? Will the gentlemen, after seriously reflecting, still contend that Burr had a right to resist? This doctrine is not the growth of this country, nor is it the doctrine of the real friends of human liberty: but this is a new-born zeal of some of the gentlemen, in defence of the rights of man. No wonder, therefore, they are not so well acquainted with the subject as those who have always contended, and always will contend, for them. But admit their inference correct; that Burr had a right to resist an illegal order; (which I utterly deny) will the court issue a subpœna founded on that supposition? Will you insult the executive by saying, that its orders were illegal, and ought on that account to be produced as evidence? especially after you have yourself said, that there was probable cause for committing colonel Burr on the charge of a misdemeanor?

Mr. Hay proceeded to argue another point, that the court ought not only to be satisfied that the letter was material, but that it was a public paper. He said, if it was a public document, the right to a copy of it was admitted, unless there should be something in it, which, in the opinion of the president, the public good forbade to be disclosed. But he denied that the letter was a public paper merely because addressed to the president of the United States. It had been observed, that the president had made it so by referring to it in his message to congress. If this argument is correct, only so much is public as is referred to. [Here Mr. Hay read a part of the president's communication to congress.] He contended, that there might have been a great deal more in that letter than what related to the discovery of Burr's plans; that there might have been information of a private nature, accounts of the disposition of the people in the western country towards the government, and general Wilkinson's thoughts on many important subjects. Will the court say, that all these things shall be made known? If a copy was received, such parts only could be extracted as ought to be made public; but if the original should be granted, the whole would be seen and inspected by the court, by the counsel on both sides, and by the public. He said, that the court ought also to be satisfied, that the president has the custody of this letter. The subpœna ought to be addressed to the person who has it in his custody. It is said to be a public document: if so, it is in the office of the secretary of state. See L. U. S. 1 vol. p. 42, 43.

It is absurd then, as well as indecorous, to summon the president of the United States to bring a paper which he has not. The same observations applied to the copies of orders. The original orders were lodged with the secretary of state, and copies were sent by him to the secretaries of war, and of the navy. To the secretary of state, therefore, the subpœna ought to be issued, if at all.

The court ought also to be satisfied that the party could not obtain, without a motion, the copies of the orders now required. The accused ought therefore to show that he has demanded copies; but he has not done so. He asked indeed, a copy from the secretary of the navy; and because he refused, process is to be issued against the president of the United States, though he was never applied to!

The CHIEF JUSTICE asked Mr. Hay, what was the legal way of getting the paper which the secretary of the navy refused? He answered, " by application to the secretary of state for copies."

Mr. HAY made many other observations which the limits of this sketch will not permit us to insert. In opposition to the argument that general Wilkinson might deny any recollection of his letter if a copy only was produced, he said it was mere presumption, a preposterous supposition; that it would be immaterial whether he denied it or not, since the copy is evidence by the act of congress. He here vindicated general Wilkinson from the attacks which were wantonly made upon him; saying, it was the policy of colonel Burr and his counsel to endeavour to tear down his character before he arrived, and that every principle of propriety was violated by such conduct. He asked, if it was right that a man, high in the confidence of government and of his country, should be thus attacked? and declared he should be sorry for the character of his fellow citizens, if the abuse lavished on him by the accused should have the slightest effect on the event of the trial.

Mr. MAC RAE said it was plainly to be inferred from the president's message to congress, that the letter in question was confidential. It appears, that the president furnished extracts of some of the letters he received relative to colonel Burr. His not furnishing congress with a copy of this or any other part of it, is presumptive evidence that it ought not to be made public.

Mr. RANDOLPH.—May it please your honours: To the observations I shall make, I have no preface nor apology. I beg leave to appropriate to argument the time which falls to my lot in the discussion of the present motion. I did not believe sir, that to-day there would have been a resurrection of the dicussion which took place yesterday; but since the attorney on the part of the prosecution has thought proper to introduce it, I shall not shrink from it, but meet it. I make no appeal to the multitude; it is not my desire to excite the sympathy, or rouse improperly the feelings of the bystanders. I shall simply state the proposition. Why is colonel Burr not entitled to ask the court to issue a subpœna for the production of those papers? Is colonel Burr not now before the court? Is he not here upon his recognisance? Has he not been here a considerable time on the tenterhook of expectation, that when general Wilkinson, that great accomplisher of all things, arrived, an indictment would be preferred against him? But has he, on that account, resigned the rights of defence? Is he to be tongue-tied and hand-tied, without the privilege of defending himself? He cannot be properly defended without the production of these papers, and on that account he now demands the interposition of the court. But, say the counsel for the prosecution, he is not entitled to this privilege until an indictment is preferred, and the grand jury find a true bill. Why did we not hear this objection when the grand jury were empaneled? It was proved yesterday, by several law authorities; it was proved, sir, by invariable practice; and it was proved, by a wish of all our souls, that the accused ought to have this privilege from the very commencement of the prosecution. Wherefore then sir, are we to be vexed and perplexed again with this objection? Wherefore do they say it is premature on the part of my client? I see a corps of worthies around me, to justify what I say. Every man, I assert, who appears on the grounds of a recognisance, stands in the same condition as one on his trial. Are you to shut a man out from evidence, because he is only accused, because his life can only be forfeited? There is a harshness in this; there is a severity in this sentiment, which, however agreeable it may be to the principles of law, I have to thank God, has never been my practice. The principles to which I have been accustomed have always agreed with truth, and the sacred books of the scripture. No bill is yet found; and I trust none ever will. The amendment to the constitution, they say, does not apply to the present case, but to a trial. We do not mean to force this point, although ample authority might be produced in support of it. You, sir, will certainly do what is right in the present motion; this we do not mean to doubt: but you will give me leave to ask, what our situation would be, in what a deplorable dilemma we should be placed, if, at the instant the attorney was pressing us with his testimony, we had to supplicate your honours to grant us the purport of the motion now in question? and if the trial could not be postponed, (which in all probability it would not) we must go to a final decision without it. In that case, even were the sun of innocence ready to shed his beams upon us, we would be cast into utter darkness. No, sir, such can never be the opinion of this court; *justice* must be changed; *law* must be changed; *nature* must be changed, before such sentiments can be heard. I will not trouble you much farther with discussing the propriety of our application, feeling the confidence with which I am certain it is regarded by the court; but I will come directly to the consideration of what are the real points in discussion.

This is not whether a president can be summoned: that part is happily conceded; and I rejoice that we mistook in the commencement of the argument, the sentiments of the attorney on the part of the prosecution on this point. I rejoice, I say, that I did mistake him; because, from that very concession, I will draw every corollary that may be necessary for establishing the great point for which we contend. By admitting that the president of the United States can be summoned, a great canon of evidence is admitted. I must, however, be excused by the worthy gentlemen, if I tell them they are a little inconsistent. In throwing obstacles in our way against obtaining the papers for which we have moved the court to issue a subpœna, they imitate that bad example, which they have imputed to us. What is the nature of the evidence we do ask ? We ask for that sort of evidence which may enable us to confront James Wilkinson with himself. There is not an idea beyond this. We wish to show, that James Wilkinson, in his official capacity, as commander of the army of the United States at New-Orleans, is not the same with James Wilkinson the correspondent of the president. We wish to prove, that James Wilkinson has varied from himself, and that he has varied in most essential points in the greatest degree. Mr. Hay tells us, that every thing depends upon this same James Wilkinson; that he is in reality the *Alpha* and *Omega* of the present prosecution. He is, in short, to support by his deposition the *sing-song* and the ballads of treason and conspiracy, which we have heard delivered from one extremity of the continent to the other. The funeral pile of the prosecution is already prepared by the hands of the public attorney, and nothing is wanting to kindle the fatal blaze but the torch of James Wilkinson. He, is to exhibit himself in a most conspicuous point of view in the tragedy which is fancied will take place. He, James Wilkinson, is to officiate as the high priest of this human sacrifice.

Of James Wilkinson we are not afraid, in whatever shape he may be produced; in whatever form he may appear before this court. We are only afraid of those effects which desperation may produce in his mind. Desperation, may it please the court, is a word of great fitness in the present case. General Wilkinson we behold first acting as a conspirator to insnare others, afterwards as a patriot to betray others from motives of patriotism. What must be the embarrassment of this man when the awful catastrophe arrives, that he must either substantiate his own innocence by the conviction of another, or be himself regarded as a traitor and conspirator, in the event of the acquittal of the accused.

Is it not to be supposed, that general Wilkinson will do many things rather than disappoint the wonder-seizing appetite of America, which for months together he has been gratifying by the most miraculous actions ? If I am not mistaken I have seen it in some of the public prints that he is no longer the vice-gerent of the Upper Louisiana; and if I may be indulged with the slightest power of prophecy, I may predict, that this same general Wilkinson, who has been astonishing the citizens of New-Orleans with plots and conspiracies, will, before many weeks, only figure in the capacity of a private citizen. I shall not say that general Wilkinson would commit perjury; let me not be understood as making such an assertion; but if I know human nature; if I understand the feeling of the human breast; if I have the slightest knowledge of those principles which govern the mind of man; I may be allowed to affirm, that every feeling would be asleep in his breast if he did not use every exertion in his power for the conviction of colonel Burr. Upon the conviction of colonel Burr, upon the guilt I say of colonel Burr, depends the innocence of general Wilkinson. If colonel Burr be proved guilty, then indeed general Wilkinson may stand acquitted with many of his countrymen; but if colonel Burr be not found guilty, the character, the reputation, in short, every thing that deserves the name of integrity, will be gone for ever from general Wilkinson. Sir, in that event, I say, in the event of Burr's acquittal, as sure as man is man, storms and tempests will cover the western glory of general Wilkinson, and gather darkness all around him. We have therefore the justest cause to scrutinize this gentleman's deposition. We have the strongest reasons to examine this gentleman's character, and to trace him in his most confidential walks. From his letters we have already had some glimpse of him; but I should wish, as I have said, to have him confronted with himself; I mean, to have his correspondence with the president of the United States opposed to whatever statement he may deliver here. I shall therefore suppose, by way of illustration, that the president were here, and certain questions were put to him. The president certainly could not dispense with answering these questions. Much as I respect the illustrious character of the president of the United States, yet I should begin to imagine that the sheet-anchor of our government was gone, if the president could be excused more than any other individual before this court, from answering any questions which might be put to him. It is really most extraordinary, that these gentlemen should tell us, after arriving in the porch of the temple, that we shall not go into the *sanctum sanctorum;* that we are at liberty to know part of the correspondence, which has taken place between general Wilkinson and the president of the United States, but not the whole.

The gentleman for the prosecution has to-day, sir, given us an eulogium upon himself and his associate friends. He has pictured to us the zeal and the anxiety he has had for the production of those papers, and has assured us that he has already taken means for having them here. I thank the gentleman for his exertions, but at the same time I must beg leave to remark the equal zeal with which he and his friends combat our application. If Mr. Burr were now asking you for these papers, without showing any probable cause that they were material, this indeed would be a wanton, womanish, feverish curiosity; but it is no such curiosity: we have shown, in the fullest manner, that they are material and of the first importance. It is said, that by their production general Wilkinson, that huge Atlas, on whose mighty shoulders the American world is sustained, is wished to be represented as a man in whom confidence ought not to be placed. But, I say, if the production of these papers were to effect the annihilation of general Wilkinson, that I hope and believe no other visible chasm in the creation would be produced, but in that portion of space at present occupied by his material body. How can the rank and safety of general Wilkinson be concerned in the production of these papers? General Wilkinson is only an organ in the hands of government. As to his glory, I believe its meridian splendor is set, and that he will be no longer worshipped as the political Messiah of America; but even if he were crucified, I trust it would make no æra in our time. Suspicion at all events belongs to him. He stands in that character which is always regarded as odious; that of an approver. He has confessed himself guilty of the most heinous of crimes, for the purpose of entrapping others; of rendering others equally infamous with himself.

We are told, that our motion goes to reveal state secrets; that confidential characters are to be brought into view! State secrets! The very name strikes me with horror! I have heard one of the gentlemen concerned, renounce the idea, and I shall not again be the means of recalling the principle. Sir, I will not say that there ought not to be a limitation with respect to the production of state papers. But in what character is the name of general Wilkinson inscribed in the roll of fame, to entitle his actions to be concealed? Is the safety of this country to be endangered by calling upon him as a witness, who is known and declared to be one of the arch-witnesses of this prosecution? Is the national safety to be endangered by this? A nation stand upon this? a nation which ought only to look to the Almighty for its rule! Shall the people of this country be considered as in danger, though this motion be granted? Should they be in danger, though general Wilkinson were given up to be buffeted? I should be very unwilling indeed, that a single name should be unnecessarily exposed; but are one man's fortune, character and life to be brought into jeopardy in order to conceal the names of others? Is this to be the shield under which general Wilkinson is to be screened? Is the executive bureau to be made a sanctuary of scandal, to protect the fame of general Wilkinson, and when opened at some future period, to display to the citizens of this country, a tale perhaps as horrid as many of those which the red book of France has unveiled? The revealing of confidential secrets has also been objected to. Two cases of this nature were yesterday ably detailed by the counsel associated with me. The case of lord Barrington, and the surgeon, whose evidence was given on the trial of the dutchess of Kingston; but, sir, I have seen within the walls of this house, a case still more affecting; a case in which, if ever confidential secrecy was to be pleaded, it ought then to have been sustained. This, sir, was the case of a young lad of sixteen years of age, who was arraigned at this bar for a criminal offence. His infant mind, and the feelings of his heart, had been unburthened to his father alone. He, led by paternal affection, was anxiously attending at the side of the lad, at the issue of the trial. The attorney for the state, after fruitlessly examining all the evidence for the prosecution, and finding no testimony sufficient to sustain it, at length darted his keen and penetrating eye upon the distressed parent. He immediately made an application to the court to compel him to give evidence against his son. The court were greatly affected; tears streamed from their eyes. I defended him. I do not know that I used any reasoning on the subject; but the close ties of father and son, and the nature of confidential secrecy, were in vain pleaded. The court determined that he was a competent witness, and must be sworn to testify; and were about to compel the father to give testimony against the son, who on this testimony alone would have been convicted. The father approached the book, and was going to swear; but, for the honour of Virginia, the records of the state are not blotted with so sanguinary a sentence. The scene was so truly affecting, that at the recommendation of the court the demand for his evidence was not persisted in. But is general Wilkinson the child of the president of the United States? Is the president to be viewed as the father of general Wilkinson? Is Mr. Jefferson to be placed in the same situation with respect to James Wilkinson, as the parent I have mentioned, with regard to the boy? Are the hearts of Mr. Jefferson and general Wilkinson connected by the same tender ties of sympathy, as those of a father and son! The law is, that every man, who is not interested in the event of a cause, is a witness, and bound to give his testimony when called on, except in cases of professional confidence.

The objection to the insufficiency of the affidavit is unfounded. It is a work of supererogation to make it at all. It was not necessary to entitle us to make the president disclose the paper. It is evident, without it, that he ought to produce it. We proceeded in this by way of frank accommodation to prevent the necessity of his attendance. As they deny, we insist on the right to draw this paper from the president's pocket. [Here he expressed a hope that he had not misunderstood Mr. Wirt, concerning the necessity of the affidavit. Mr. Wirt repeated what his argument had been, and the chief justice stated that the impression of the court was similar.] A man ought not to be precluded from evidence which he *thinks* material, though he does not *know* it to be positively so. If the paper were not in a bureau of office, we should want no subpœna *duces tecum*.

It stands on the same ground as a common subpœna, and we have the same right to have it, as to have a common subpœna. But the object being to obtain the paper only, if it be transmitted and found to be different from what it has been represented to be, the witness would then be excused from attending.

If our affidavit stated the materiality of the paper, and yet the paper should be found to be otherwise, we should then have to encounter the full torrent of Mr. Hay's invectives, for having incautiously sworn to what was incorrect, although the affidavit stated the fact precisely, as Mr. Burr had every just reason to believe it. Mr. Burr desires to obtain this paper, but he knows not its contents: he cannot say what is in it, but we have the holy word of the president himself, that it relates to colonel Burr. This is one of the few things which he has done wrong. The president testifies, that Wilkinson has testified to him fully against Burr. I am absolved from all scruples on this subject. I have a right to demand peremptorily Wilkinson's letter, when it is said that it will prove Burr's guilt. The president's declaration of Burr's guilt is unconstitutional. I deny his right to make such a declaration against any man, or to make such an inference from statements made to him. The constitution gives him no such right; and its exercise by the president would be dangerous. It may and must excite unjust prejudices, and create a powerful influence against a man who is really innocent. The constitution very wisely withholds from the president a power so unfavourable to a fair trial between the public and individuals accused, and so dangerous to the liberties and lives of the citizens. I hope it is no rebellion, but I hope our objection to this dangerous and unconstitutional declaration of the president, will be handed down to posterity, to prevent his conduct in this respect from being imitated. Congress did not call upon him for his opinion. They would have been satisfied with his statement of public transactions, without his opinion. He is to see that the laws be faithfully executed, and to give information with respect to the state of the Union; but he is not to give opinions concerning the guilt or innocence of any person.

A copy of this letter would do in every other sense, or for any other purpose; but the original must be produced to Wilkinson, otherwise he might deny it to be his. If a copy were produced, he might deny that he had written, and on every correct principle of law demand the production of, the original. He would look towards the city of Washington, and consider the consequences of testifying here. He would consider how the government would view his conduct. He might know it to be a true copy, and yet be afraid to say so. Perhaps there might be inducements for him not to deny it: but suppose he were to deny it at the trial, could you discharge the jury till the original was brought? No sir, you could not; and every objection would be made and sustained against reading the copy. Original papers only, have ever been admitted as evidence in penal cases. There is no instance of a conviction, in a capital case, on the copy of a letter as evidence. The case of Smith and Ogden is egregiously misunderstood on this point. [Here Mr. Wirt explained. Mr. Randolph read the case and proceeded.] The affidavit was wanted there to put off the trial. To postpone a trial, the utmost precision (precision *ad unguem*) is necessary; but on a motion to take testimony, belief is sufficient.

I believe that Mr. Jefferson ought to hasten to produce that paper. His regard for the promotion of public justice ought to induce him to do it. His character requires that he should produce it. Lest that character should suffer, I would almost ask it for his sake. Gentlemen say, why do we not rely upon him, and demand it of him? I answer, that without the orders of this court, the prospect of obtaining it is very unpromising, after we have made an application to one of his secretaries, (Mr. Smith) and received from him a positive and peremptory denial, with a declaration that the orders were intended for the officers alone who were to execute. Mr. Van Ness had said, that there had been a promise made to furnish it to colonel Burr's counsel; but the promise has not been performed. The orders could not be secret, since they were published in the Natchez Gazette. Can there be any hopes then of obtaining them from the president himself? Time has been taken, and he has very probably been consulted. Mr. Hay is not authorised to produce the papers, although he has some of them. As then it is probable, that the heads of department have been consulted, in the time which has elapsed since our application was made; as the secretary of the navy has refused to furnish these papers, and the attorney will not permit us even to look at the papers in his possession, I trust we shall be excused for not applying to the president, without the order of this court.

It is again said, that this letter is confidential. I must revert to the president once more. He is but a man, has ears and eyes, and can see and hear like another man; he may be a witness like other men; he has no prerogative to have any secrets, the withholding of which may go to the destruction of the dearest interests of an accused man. Mr. Hay has been pleased to call the affidavit "*farcical*." I wish he had been so good as to tell us how he would have had it drawn. [Here he read it.] Mr. Burr has indications that it is material. The president, in his message to congress, in announcing the doubtless guilt of Mr. Burr, has made himself judge and accuser. The opposition now made to its production justifies the opinion, that the letter contains more than has yet been disclosed; that there is something more behind the curtain. Sir, I contend that when the dearest interests of a fellow citizen are involved, the president's cabinet is not too sacred to be examined and exposed to view in a court of justice. I know that the present president abhors such conduct; but would you permit a future president to hunt down any man by proclamation, declaring him to be guilty of treason, and withholding a part of the facts, on which his opinion is founded? This puts an engine into the president's hands to destroy an enemy, by giving a partial statement of facts, while he publishes the most unfavourable opinion of him. Mr. Hay indulges himself in little verbal criticisms; he says that " *may be material*," is the same thing as " *may or may not be material*." Sir, Mr. Burr believes that they *may* be material. With this impression, he has made the affidavit, which in my opinion is sufficiently explicit, if an affidavit be at all necessary. Something has been said of unmasking our defence. Do you wish us to tell general Wilkinson all the grounds upon which he will be attacked? We only say, that he is grossly inconsistent in his disclosures, and that he will be contradicted. We cannot go further while the contents of his letter are unknown to us.

But Mr. Burr's affidavit is not to be attended to, because he has feelings and may be misled by them! It is the same thing with every other man. Because a man is interested, he is more ready to make known to the world his injuries and assert his innocence. But I must notice that part of the argument, relating to these orders of the government, wherein my friend Mr. Martin was charged with speaking treasonably. This has raised an amazing clamour. I added, the other day, the illegality of these orders, as then understood by me, to the other causes of dissatisfaction with the conduct of the president. But I now learn that these orders were worse than I expected: that they were to burn, kill and destroy the person and property of Mr. Burr and his party. Whether the orders were exactly to this effect or not, I am not sure; but I believe this statement not to be very incorrect, and the refusal of gentlemen to produce them proves that there is something behind; or why does not the attorney produce the copy he has in possession? Mr. Martin never did say (as I understood him) that these orders justified an opposition to the government of the United States. Whatever he did, we shall contend was legal, and not in opposition to the government. But I will say, that if the president had called out a military force, *illegally*, to destroy the person or property of any man, that man had a right to resist. The orders to destroy the person and property of Mr. Burr, if given, were unconstitutional and unjustifiable. If I am wrong in my statement I pray to be set right; but if I recollect the constitution correctly, it does not justify such orders in such a case as this. It only empowers congress " to provide for calling forth the militia to execute the laws of the Union, and to suppress insurrections and repel invasions " The president is sworn " to preserve, protect and defend the constitution, and he is to take care that the laws be faithfully executed." " The United States are to protect each state against invasion and against domestic violence, on application of the legislature or of the executive, when the legislature cannot be convened." The president is to call out a military force only to suppress insurrections or to repel invasions. Was this either? There certainly was no invasion of our country by a foreign nation. If there had been an insurrection, the state governments might have interfered. Was there any application for aid by any state government? There is a third case, it must be admitted, in which an armed force may be resorted to. I mean infractions of the law of nations, by armed vessels. These are the only three cases in which the president is, or can be authorised, by the law of congress under the constitution, to call out a military force; and as none of them occurred, those orders were illegal and unjustifiable.

CHIEF JUSTICE.—Does not the law of congress authorise the president to call out the militia to suppress an expedition against any foreign state in amity with the United States?

Mr. WIRT said, that the act of congress, passed in the year 1794, expressly required the president to employ military force to suppress or prevent any such expedition.

Mr. BOTTS said, that colonel Burr could not say more positively than that " *it may be material.*" That as he did not know what evidence might be adduced against him, it could not safely be otherwise expressed.

CHIEF JUSTICE.—Could not the word be changed to " *will.*"

Mr. BOTTS.—For the sake of precedent I wish it to remain as it is.

Mr. WIRT.—If the word *will* were to be inserted instead of " *may be,*" the objection to the generality of the affidavit would still remain.

Mr. MARTIN.—Agreed; but we will speak of that hereafter.

Mr. WIRT.—Examine the letter; it only goes to the guilt of Burr. How can it confront Wilkinson, if it speaks of the guilt of Burr?

CHIEF JUSTICE.—But there may be contradictory statements of guilt.

Mr. WIRT.—But the *prima facie* evidence of this letter is, that it charges guilt; but there is no evidence of contradiction; there are only vague insinuations. The law of congress authorised the president to act as he did. By the 7th section of this law, " the navy or army of the United States may be called out to take such ship or vessel," and also for the purpose of quelling any force raised for carrying on any expedition against any country with which the United States are at peace.

Mr. RANDOLPH proceeded. The object of requiring the orders to be produced is, to ascertain whether they be conformable to the law; and no power to call out the militia *in the commencement of an expedition*, or in *beginning to prepare the means*, is given by the law. I will suppose, for a moment, what I utterly deny to be the fact, that colonel Burr had actually begun an expedition, had prepared arms, vessels, men, &c.; yet, as penal laws are to be construed strictly, he could only be stopped under this law, when the expedition was actually formed and carried on. But it is insinuated to be improper to ask the president, and not the officers of government, for those papers. The president is the person who must be considered as having refused the papers. All the officers act under him and must obey him. Application should be made to the department of state. The chief justice said that the department of state ought not to be applied to. [See Mr. Hay's argument.] As to the letter, it must be in the president's bureau; for, as far as we can discover, it is directed to him, and he withheld it from the legislature. But it is asked, what is to be done with the letter, if parts of it are not proper to be exposed? This is a most extraordinary objection. Shall we be refused the parts important for our defence, because other parts are improper to be published? An arrangement could easily be made, by which only those parts which are proper to be disclosed, should be used.

Sir, I must make a few remarks with respect to your exhortation, and what was said by gentlemen yesterday and to-day. We have been charged with the policy of exciting prejudices against the administration, rather than defending Mr. Burr. Hints were also thrown out as to popular opinion. Sir, I never defend my client by popular prejudice. I know it would be in vain to attempt it. I know who has got the windward of me. They have the public approbation strongly in their favour. I know how impotent is one individual, when opposed to the power of the government. But I hope the arguments we have been compelled to use, will have their due weight with the court. The gigantic magnitude of the crime charged against us, is diminishing every day; and we have nothing but an interested man, whose all is at stake, to oppose us. We demand justice only, and if you cannot exorcise the demon of prejudice, you can chain him down to law and reason, and then we shall have nothing to fear.

Mr. WIRT.—As to the denial of the law by Mr. Randolph, and the gentleman from Baltimore, I insist that they are mistaken; and that the law is as I have stated it to be. The respect which I owe to this court, would prevent me from asserting for law, that which I do not know to be law. Mr. Randolph has enumerated three cases, in which force could be used, and then sat down majestically and called the giant to be produced at once.

Mr. MARTIN endeavoured to explain, by saying, that he had not said that there was no such law.

Mr. RANDOLPH explained.

CHIEF JUSTICE.—The truth is, that you did not advert to the law.

Mr. BOTTS observed, that Mr. Wirt had said, that the law justified an order to kill Burr and his party, without trial or condemnation.

Mr. WIRT denied it. He had only said that there was such a law. I mentioned it before, said he, and I pointed to it afterwards. I feel my candour impeached by the course which gentlemen have thought proper to take. If the court should doubt, as to the construction of the act of congress, I should wish to be heard further on the subject.

Mr. RANDOLPH said, that he meant nothing personally against Mr. Wirt; but he had said that he knew no law that was applicable; and he now insisted, that the law was as he represented.

Mr. Martin asked leave to speak again; and the court was adjourned till to-morrow. Note. The grand jury was adjourned till Saturday.

FRIDAY, June 12th, 1807.

The court met according to adjournment.

Mr. MARTIN addressed the court to the following purport:

I shall now, may it please your honours, make a few observations, in which I shall endeavour to avoid all extraneous matter. This has been uniformly asserted by the gentlemen for the prosecution, to be a motion addressed to the discretion of the court; and in some degree admitted by the counsel with whom I act. But the practice in the state from whence I came (Maryland) is different. A subpœna *duces tecum* is never applied for in court. It is issued of course by the clerk, acquiesced in by the parties and counsel, approved by the court, and never opposed. According to that practice, (and which gentlemen will excuse me for mentioning, as they have so repeatedly called on me to state whether I had known such a process to issue in such a case) the right of the prosecuting counsel to oppose the demand of the accused is denied; and it is no more competent to them to do this, than to oppose the granting subpœnas for living evidence. It would be deemed highly indecorous to make such an opposition. They ask us the reason why we make this motion. We tell them, that the object of the accused, in demanding the production of general Wilkinson's letter, is, that we may compare its purport with that of communications which he has made to others. If he has made inconsistent or contradictory statements, and we can prove that he has done so, we certainly have a right to avail ourselves of it, to lessen or destroy his credit. But its production is opposed on the ground of its containing state secrets; and that it may expose the names of others presumed to be implicated. Is this exposure to be prevented at the hazard of Mr. Burr's life? Innocence cannot suffer by exposure: guilt ought to be detected. What, sir, shall the cabinet of the United States be converted into a lion's mouth of Venice, or into a *repertorium* of the inquisition? Shall envy, hatred, and all the malignant passions pour their poison into that cabinet against the character and life of a fellow citizen, and yet that cabinet not be examined in vindication of that character and to protect that life? Shall a citizen be privately accused, and the name of his accuser not even made known to him? No more of the letter is sought to be used as evidence than relates to the accused. When the letter is produced the court can judge of it, and withhold from the public any secrets which ought not to be disclosed. The mere possibility of its containing state secrets is no reason why there should be a suppression of what is no secret. Gentlemen tell us, that they are perfectly willing we should get it; and yet they throw impediments in our way to prevent us from getting it!

Mr. HAY declared that he had written for the letter, and had done every thing in his power to obtain it; though gentlemen seemed disposed not to credit him.

Mr. MARTIN.—If we were certain that the gentleman would succeed in his application, we should be disposed not to trouble the court with this motion. But can we depend on his success, when the gentleman tells us, that when the papers come he will not let us look at them. What will be our situation after the trial is begun, if the papers do not come? It will be then too late to move for a postponement; and we shall lose the evidence. We are entitled to it now, and ought to have it. I cannot say that I feel disposed to rely much on the favours of an adverse party. " *Timeo Danaos et dona ferentes.*" I prefer the enjoyment of my certain rights, to the promises of him whose interest is opposed to mine.

But we are told that there ought to be respect between the departments of government; that we ought to respect the president. Is it derogatory from that respect, to issue process to obtain necessary testimony from him? Will the president think himself insulted by the demand of a mere document? Can he possibly think it disrespectful? But suppose he should, is the life of a man, lately high in public esteem, not indeed the first, but the second citizen in our country, to be endangered for the sake of punctilio to the president of the United States? Sir, we appeal to the Supreme Maker, that we only wish justice, and fear only perjury. We approach, with uplifted hands, the sacred altar of justice, as a sanctuary to screen us, not from just punishment, but from unjust, rancorous persecution! and from this sanctuary we confidently expect protection.

But we are told, that a copy will be sufficient. But will the copy show that the original is not a forgery? It may prove, that there is a paper, of which it is a copy, deposited in the office; but it will not prove, that the paper so deposited is the hand writing of general Wilkinson. If general Wilkinson wrote a libel and sent it to the president, would a copy be admitted as evidence against him on a prosecution for the libel? Copies are never admitted as evidence in prosecutions for libels, or in any criminal prosecutions. But gentlemen say, that general Wilkinson would not dare to deny that he had written it, if the counsel agreed that it should be evidence. Would that make it his hand writing? General Wilkinson has already violated his oath, in wilfully and tyrannically violating the constitution which he had solemnly sworn to support. Has he not exercised the most wanton military despotism? Has he not insultingly resisted and trampled under foot the constituted authorities, in disobeying the writ of habeas corpus? Has he not done all these things in open defiance and in palpable violation of the plain letter and meaning of the constitution? He comes here to justify these misdeeds. A man who has done a series of bad acts will not fail to add one more, in order to conceal them from view, and secure himself from punishment. Though he is the pivot on which the prosecution turns, and therefore the counsel for the United States uphold him, colonel Burr has not confidence in the honour or integrity of general Wilkinson, to trust his life to his veracity. But it is said, that if he should deny it, then we can send for the original. He would have no occasion to deny it, till the jury were sworn to try colonel Burr; and if the testimony on both sides were equal, and the scales of justice hanging even, the denial of general Wilkinson put in the scale against us, would preponderate; it would be then too late to send for the original, to confront and disprove his denial; the "*fiat*" of life and death, must be determined by the evidence before the jury; we ought therefore to get the original now.

But the gentleman asserts, that we have made the motion in order to glance at the president. We disclaim such motives. It would be dastardly to make a court of justice the scene of detraction; the means to abuse individuals. We deny such motives; nor are gentlemen warranted in imputing them to us.

But the gentleman has told us, that respect ought to be paid to the officers of government. It is granted. I once thought so. I thought that the officers of government ought to be treated with high respect, however much their conduct ought to be the subject of criticism; and I invariably acted according to that principle. If I have changed my opinion, I owe it to the gentleman himself, and the party he is connected with. They formerly thought differently. That gentleman and his friends so loudly and incessantly clamoured against the officers of government, that they contributed to effect a change in the administration, and are now in consequence basking in the sunshine of office; and therefore they wish to inculcate and receive that respect which they formerly denied to others in the same situation. We have a right to inspect the orders issued from the war and navy departments; because, if they were illegal, we had a right to oppose them. If they were unconstitutional and oppressive, it was right to resist them: but this is denied, because we are not trying the president. God forbid, we should. But we are trying if we had a right to resist. If every order, however arbitrary and unjust, is to be obeyed, we are slaves as much as the inhabitants of Turkey. If the presidential edicts are to be the supreme law, and the officers of the government have but to register them, as formerly in France, (the country once so famed by these gentlemen for its progress and advancement towards liberty); and if we must submit to them, however unjust and unconstitutional, we are as subject to despotism, as the people of Turkey, the subjects of the former "*Grand Monarques*" in France, or those of the despot Bonaparte at this day. If this were true, where would be our boasted freedom? where, the superior advantages of our government, or the beneficial effects of our revolutionary struggles? I will take the liberty of explaining how far resistance is justifiable. The president has certain known and well defined powers; so has a common magistrate, and so has a constable. The president may exceed his legal authority, as well as a magistrate or a constable. If a magistrate issue a warrant and direct it to a constable, resistance to it is at the peril of the person resisting. If the warrant be illegal, he is excused: but if it be legal, he is not. On the same principle, resistance to the orders of the president is excusable, if they be unconstitutional and illegal. Resistance to an act of oppression, unauthorised by law, can never be criminal; and this is all we contend for.

Mr. HAY stated that he was sorry to interrupt the gentleman; but, from his argument it was evident, that the ground taken by himself, and the gentlemen associated with him in the prosecution was entirely misunderstood. He denied that he ever said that the president's orders are invariably to be observed. That such an assertion might justly be considered as incompatible with the principles of our government. Mr. Hay then explained what his argument had been; and what he meant to insist on as correct. That if information had been lodged with the president, that a dangerous conspiracy or insurrection against the government and laws, or an expedition against a nation in amity with this country, was secretly or openly forming, it was the duty of the president to issue orders to suppress the insurrection or prevent the expedition; and if he did issue such orders or precept, it would not be lawful in an individual to oppose them by force: that an act of opposition to his precept so issued, if not treason, would be at least a high misdemeanor; that such a precept was very different from an order to kill or imprison without bail or mainprize, or to raze to the ground and destroy, as gentlemen had represented the orders in question.

Mr. MARTIN appealed to the court and bystanders whether Mr. Hay's assertions or arguments had not been substantially as he had represented them, and then continued. The gentleman expressed his surprise that such doctrines should come from me, who come from Maryland to instruct and enlighten the Virginia bar. I come not to instruct or enlighten. I come to unite my feeble efforts with those of other gentlemen in defence of my friend, whom I believe to be perfectly innocent of the heavy charges against him: but their conduct evinces, that if I were to attempt it, my instructions would be in vain. If, however, I did venture to advise him, it would be, not to accuse us of evil intentions; to mix a little of the milk of human nature with his disposition and arguments; to make his conduct conformable to his professions, and not to be perpetually imputing guilt to us. But the gentleman needs no advice.

I have said, that I believed the orders and letter to be necessary. I will not examine now as to their legality; that will be discussed hereafter; but it is evident that they are material to try whether they were legal or not; and if they were resisted, whether that resistance was legal or not? The president is the proper person to apply to, because all the officers of the governments are under his control. But two objections have been made, which have not yet, within my recollection, been answered: One is in the form of a question, that if his evidence came, what would be done with it? The answer is obvious: that it must be retained by the court till it is wanted. The other objection is, that there is no particular day to which the subpœna is legally returnable: the cause is not set on the docket to be tried on any particular day, and therefore, no particular day is named. But this will produce no inconvenience: in general, process is made returnable on the first day of the term. There the witness can attend as soon as it may be convenient; that is, as soon as possible after the subpœna shall have been served; and it is in the power of the court to make it returnable *when* they think proper. [Here Mr. Martin made a reference to the practice in Maryland, which was not distinctly understood.] I thank the court for their patience in hearing these few observations; whether time has been gained or not, the result will show.

Chief Justice.—The affidavit speaks of an answer to general Wilkinson's letter.

Mr. Burr.—Though I am extremely well satisfied with the arguments of my counsel, as far as they have gone, yet I shall offer a few additional remarks. The counsel for the prosecution are mistaken when they say, that it would be improper to address the subpœna to the president. The public papers are not kept in the department of state, but in the separate departments according to their nature. There is no official communication between general Wilkinson, as a general or commander in chief, and the president, though there may be as governor of Louisiana. The communications from him, as general, are to the department of war. The president's letter does not show where general Wilkinson's letter is deposited. If addressed to him, it continues in his possession. His communication to congress shows that he has it. The course in congress is to apply directly to the president for any papers or documents wanted, and not to the secretaries; because they are all under his control and direction: he can order them to deliver any paper or document in their possession, and they must obey him. Mr. Burr then went more into detail, the substance of which was, that there was no evidence of the commission of treason; that the president, in his communication to congress, and in his proclamation, grounded on general Wilkinson's letter to him of the 21st of October, insinuates nothing of a treasonable nature; that in these he states, that an attack on the Spanish colonies was supposed to be intended: but if there had been any just reason for believing that treason had been committed, the president would certainly have stated it; that he had been denounced by the highest authority in the country; that this denunciation had created a general prejudice against him; that the government ought to furnish all the means in its power to remove the unjust prejudices thus improperly excited against him; that he asked no privilege but what the laws conferred on every citizen. He demanded these papers, not for the purposes of detraction, as had been unjustly asserted; but to discover facts tending to prove his own innocence. He denied, in strong terms, having advised or stimulated his counsel to abuse the administration: that, on the contrary, he had charged them to avoid all irritating reflections. He concluded, by expressing his hopes, that the motion would be granted; that if the court made the order, the papers would be obtained without delay: whereas a previous application for them without such order, if unsuccessful, would produce considerable delay, which he wished very much to avoid; and that the approach of general Wilkinson required a prompt opinion of the court to prevent delay.

Mr. HAY observed, that he was much struck with the boldness of some gentlemen on a subject on which they were not correctly informed. He said, that no opportunity was lost to abuse the administration. He animadverted on the argument of Mr. Randolph the other day : That he had proclaimed loudly that some parts of the orders of the navy department had excited in his mind the most uneasy sensations. He confidently stated, that these orders were most cruel and illegal; that they were to kill and destroy colonel Burr, and burn his property wherever found. That the purpose of gentlemen was easily discerned; that Mr. Martin, in his vehement manner, talked about the hell-hounds and blood-hounds of persecution having been let loose by the president or his instrumentality, to hunt down and destroy colonel Burr. That he was sorry that gentlemen should ascribe such acts to the government as not only it had never done, but as it was incapable of doing. To silence their clamours and put an end to such declamation about cruelty and tyranny, he said, that he would produce a copy of the order from the secretary of the navy, to which all their complaints referred; that he would read it, and it would appear to be legal and proper; and that notwithstanding all the invectives against the administration on account of it, there was no just cause of complaint against it.

The counsel of colonel Burr wished to inspect the paper before it was read. Mr. Hay offered to read it, but refused to let them examine it. They then objected to its being read, and insisted, that it was the undoubted right of counsel, in every cause, to examine all documents intended as evidence before they could be read.

Mr. HAY then observed, that their objection to its being read showed clearly their object, and was a palpable contradiction to their statement; that they used it as a mere pretext. Believing it not to be in court, they loudly demanded it as a document essential to their client, and demonstrative of oppression in the government; but the moment it is offered to be read, they object to it.

Mr. MARTIN vindicated colonel Burr from the charge of having stimulated him to make any severe reflections: that colonel Burr had, in fact, endeavoured to restrain him; but that he was urged by his own feelings to express his sentiments, contrary to the directionsof his client.

Mr. BOTTS vindicated Mr. Randolph (who was absent) from the charge preferred against him by Mr. Hay. He did not believe that Mr. Hay had intentionally misrepresented any thing; but that he was incorrect in saying, that the counsel of colonel Burr had expressed complaints without cause, and exibited charges without any evidence. We are, said Mr. Botts, in a delicate situation: great prejudices have been excited, and the popular voice is raised against us. But we hope that truth and justice will prevail. We do not wish to accuse the executive unjustly; innocence ought to be presumed until guilt appears. We have *prima facie* evidence of what we allege; but still we hope that the honour and character of the government will be found to be unsullied, and that all doubts respecting its conduct will be cleared up. This can be most effectually done by producing freely, without reserve or opposition, all the testimony in its power, which we demand as material to our defence. Colonel Burr wished us not to wander into charges against the administration, unless the proofs of its improper acts were indubitable, and they were clearly connected with this cause.

The CHIEF JUSTICE, after having expressed the regret of the court, at the length of time already consumed in the discussion of this motion, proposed, that no more than the usual number of counsel should speak on incidental points. That the court was unwilling to check gentlemen in their arguments, but it was hoped, that hereafter they would endeavour to avoid repetitions, and the unnecessary waste of time.

Mr. HAY again proposed to read the letter of the secretary of the navy.

CHIEF JUSTICE.—The propriety of reading depends on its authentication.

Mr. HAY.—I suppose that gentlemen wish to see it, though not legally authenticated.

Mr. MARTIN expressed a doubt whether this was the same order; he presumed that there were more orders.

Mr. RANDOLPH (who had returned into court) wished to see it, in order to ascertain whether it was the same which they had seen in the Natchez gazette.

Mr. HAY declared his belief that it was the same, but as gentlemen did not wish to hear it, he put it up again.

Mr. BURR addressed the court. He observed, that this was perhaps the most proper time for renewing the motion which he had made some time ago, about giving more specific instructions to the grand jury, on certain points of evidence. These points he had reduced to writing, in the form of abstract propositions, which he would take the liberty of reading to the court: the following is a list of those propositions, with the authorities cited to support them.

First, That the grand jury cannot, consistently with their oath, find a bill, except on such testimony as would justify a petit jury to find the prisoner guilty. Foster, 232. sec. 8. 3 Institute, 25. 2 Institute, 384. Dalton, 519. Judge Wilson's Works, vol. 2. p. 364. T. W. Williams' Justice, vol. 3. printed 1794. 3 State Trials, 419, 420. and Sir John Hawles' Observations, 4 St. Tr. 133. 4 Black. 302—306. 2 Hale, chap. 8. p. 61., Wilson's edition with Wilson's note. 2 Hale, chap. 22. p. 157., with Wilson's note. Eunomos' Dict. 2d. sec. 39. p. 124, 5, 6. 5 State Tr. p. 3. Foster, p. 232. sec. 8.

Second, That no testimony or witness ought to go to the grand jury, but what is legal and competent to support the charge about which the inquiry is made. Danby's case, Leech 443. c. 187. Dodd's case, Leech, 59. c. 77. Commonwealth of Virginia v. Hopbam, Warles and Daws, before the general court at Williamsburg.

Third, That the grand jury cannot return a bill for treason, for levying war against the United States, unless they have two witnesses who swear to the overt act of the treason laid in the indictment; both which witnesses are believed by them. East's Crown Law, chap. 2. sec. 64.

That both must be believed, 3 State Trials, p. 56.

Fourth, That there must be two witnesses to the grand jury of each overt act, follows also as a consequence from the former position, that they must have such testimony as would be requisite for the petit jury.

Fifth, That the grand jury cannot find a bill for treason in consequence of any confessions made, though proved by two witnesses. Foster, 241,—3. 4 Black. Constitution of the United States, article 3. sec. 3. Graydon's Digest, 11. Judge

Iredell's charge, Fries's Trial, 171, 172. East's Crown Law, 96, 97.

Sixth, That as the grand jury only hear evidence on the part of the state, if upon that evidence they entertain a doubt of the truth of the charge, they ought not to find the bill; as the presumption is ever in favour of innocence. 1 Mac Nally, 2 to 6.

Seventh, No act of a third person can be given in evidence against the accused to prove him guilty of treason, or of a misdemeanor under the law of the 5th June 1794, unless that act is proved to have been committed by the advice, command, direction or instigation of the accused, if done in his absence, or if done in his presence, unless it be proved that the accused was aiding or assisting.

An act shall bind a person connected with the act, but the declaration shall not bind him, because no part of the act. Mac Nally, 615, 616.

Eighth, The declarations of others cannot be given in evidence on the present inquiry to support the charge of treason, or of a misdemeanor under the act of congress 15th June, 1794, unless it be proven that the accused was present and assented thereto.

East, 96. In case of conspiracy, confessions good against him who makes them, but not against others, Peake, chap. 1. Admiss. Hearsay—Kelyng, 18. Mac Nally, 40, 41. Confessions of one cannot be read against others. 3 State Trials, 57.

A relation of what had been done, no evidence. Mac Nally, 616.

Declarations of others are not evidence. 4 State Trials, 192—196.

6 State Trials, 218. In the presence of others, they acquiescing. Mac Nally, 621.

Mr. HAY opposed this proceeding. He contended, that the court had no right to give specific instructions to the grand jury, after they had been once generally charged by the court; that such a course was contrary to all law and all precedent; that not a single instance could be quoted to support it; and that there were cogent, and in this instance, particular reasons why criminal prosecutions should be suffered to progress without these interruptions. He further contended, that the chief justice had anticipated such a situation; and that the language in his charge clearly indicated his expectation, that bills would be laid before the grand jury on the ground of treason; and that under this expectation, the chief justice had dilated on the nature of treason, and given all the information which he thought material; that there was no reason at all, why Aaron Burr should enjoy greater privileges than any other man, or why he should rake up all the old, musty and absurd doctrines of antiquity, and have them enlisted in his service; and that he stood on the very same ground as any other man. That perhaps all the propositions on Mr. Burr's list would not be wanting at all; or if there should be any necessity for them, that these questions might be discussed as they successively arose; that these discussions would necessarily consume much of his own time, as well as the time of the court, which might probably be devoted to more useful purposes; and after all, the grand jury might refuse any instructions, and in that case, how could they be controlled by the court? If the grand jury determined to pay no regard to it, of what avail would be the recommendation of the court? (for it was in fact no more). And if they were to find according to their own opinions, and in the old way, how could the court know of this variation, and how could they rectify it?

Mr. Botts replied. He stated that the gentleman had demanded precedents; and yet it was but the other day when that very gentleman had inquired, why we so constantly resorted to precedents, and why we did not sometimes consult the principles of common sense: that the grand jury were not that lawless mob, which the gentleman had seemed to represent them; and that they would not certainly act against the law, when it was properly expounded to them by the court; that although the chief justice's charge was extremely able, yet it was impossible that it could be so comprehensive as it might now be made, from the information which has since occurred; and that the very necessity of giving any charge at all, showed the propriety of perfecting it; that it was not colonel Burr's desire to consume much time, as it was his most earnest wish to end at once the bonds of recognisance and the public prejudice which surrounded him; and that they were even willing to limit their share of the discussion to a particular time.

The Chief Justice said, that it was usual and the best course for the court to charge the jury generally, at the commencement of the term, and to give their opinion on incidental points as they arose, when the grand jury themselves should apply to them for information; that it was manifestly improper to commit the opinion of the court on points which might come before them, to be decided on the trial in chief; that he had generally confined his charges to a few general points, without launching into many details; one reason was, that some of the detailed points might never arise during the session of the grand jury, and any instruction on them, would of course, be unnecessary; another was, that some of these points might be extremely difficult to be decided, and would require an argument of counsel; because there was no judge or man, who would not often find the solitary meditations of his closet very much assisted by the discussions of others : that he would have had no difficulty, however, in expanding his charge, if he had been particularly requested to do it, or if he could have anticipated any necessity for it, and that he would have no difficulty in giving his opinions at this time on certain points, on which he could obtain a discussion by the counsel, provided he did not thereby commit his opinion on the trial in chief.

Mr. BURR then requested him to inspect the list of propositions, and the authorities referred to in support of them, which he had prepared; he might then determine which of those points would admit of the delivery of his opinion, and which would not.

The court then adjourned till to-morrow.

SATURDAY, June 13th, 1807.

The court met according to adjournment.

Mr. BURR thought proper to mention that his counsel had understood, that a supplemental charge had been written by the court, and put into the hands of the attorney of the United States, and that it was to be shown to his counsel before it was delivered. That for want of time, or some other cause, it had not yet been submitted to them. The court had yesterday requested and obtained a copy of his propositions, that they might judge of their application, and if satisfied on that point, that they might give additional instructions to the grand jury. Though the court might not at first have perceived the necessity of a supplemental charge, yet it must now appear, that each of his propositions must come before the grand jury. If the court were satisfied that they ought, they would have such additional instructions as were necessary; and if they had doubts, they would require an argument. He was ready to demonstrate the truth of every one of them. That he was ready to argue three weeks ago, and was desirous to save time, and would support them by written or oral arguments, as the court might think proper.

The CHIEF JUSTICE stated that he had drawn up a supplemental charge, which he had submitted to the attorney for the United States; with a request that it should also be put into the hands of colonel Burr's counsel; that Mr. Hay had however informed him, in the conversation which he had just had with him, that he had been too much occupied himself, to inspect the charge with attention, and deliver it to the opposite counsel; but another reason was, that there was one point in the charge which he did not fully approve. He should not, therefore, deliver his charge at present, but should reserve it until Monday. In the mean time colonel Burr's counsel have an opportunity of inspecting it; and an argument might be held on the points which had produced an objection from the attorney for the United States.

Mr. E. Randolph.—Is it the wish of the court that the argument should be carried on orally or in writing?

Chief Justice.—I am willing to see the remarks on both sides, in writing.

Mr. Hay objected to this method from the excessive labour which it would impose upon them either way.

The Chief Justice declared that it was perfectly indifferent to him.

Mr. Martin assured the court that it was perfectly convenient to him to argue the point either orally or in writing.

Mr. Wickham stated, that the attorney for the United States wished to object to certain propositions which colonel Burr had submitted to the court; that he was ready to go into the discussion immediately; that the attorney for the United States preferred an argument before the court to one in writing; and that this was in fact, the very course which colonel Burr's counsel had first recommended. Mr. Wickham hoped that this supplemental charge would be given to the jury, before the witnesses were sent up; that the counsel for the prosecution preferred the contrary, but which was, in fact, the most improper course.

The Chief Justice observed, that the court would also have wished that the charge should have been delivered, before the witnesses were sent up: but that it was almost indifferent to him, whether the testimony was submitted to the grand jury before or after the delivery of the charge; that it was often the custom for the petit jury itself to hear the testimony before the law was expounded, and the same practice might extend to the grand jury; for it was extremely easy for them, after they had heard the testimony, to apply the instructions of the court, and distinguish those parts which were admissible from those that were not so. It was not, for instance, absolutely necessary for them to know, previous to the delivery of the charge, that two witnesses were necessary to prove the overt act. When the charge had been delivered, that principle would apply to the testimony which they had actually heard; and that it was desirable that though the charge should precede the testimony, yet it was not so essential as to interrupt the proceedings.

Mr. Randolph conceived it far more important to give the supplemental charge before than after the exhibition of the testimony : that with one set of principles on their mind, the grand jury would frequently ask questions in one point of view, which they would not under other impressions; and that the supplemental, like the original, charge ought to precede the evidence.

Mr. MARTIN observed, that there was this considerable difference between a grand and a petit jury, that when any doubt arose about the propriety of testimony before the petit jury, the court would be present and ready to decide; but the grand jury has not the same aid of the judgment of the court in selecting the testimony.

The CHIEF JUSTICE said, that the necessity of giving a supplemental charge, at this time, was not so manifest; as, in his original charge, he had expressed his ideas on the nature of treason. That he stated this crime to consist in an actual "levying of war," and that of course, the grand jury would have to inquire into the existence of overt acts : that, from this statement, it would readily occur to the jury, that no matter what suspicions were entertained, what plans had been formed, what enterprizes had been projected, there could be no treason without an overt act; and without some overt act, no crime of treason had been committed.

The discussion of this question was at length waived, when the CHIEF JUSTICE delivered the following opinion on the motion to issue a subpœna *duces tecum* directed to the president of the United States :

The object of the motion, now to be decided, is to obtain copies of certain orders, understood to have been issued to the land and naval officers of the United States for the apprehension of the accused, and an original letter from general Wilkinson to the president in relation to the accused, with the answer of the president to that letter, which papers are supposed to be material to the defence. As the legal mode of effecting this object, a motion is made for a subpœna *duces tecum*, to be directed to the president of the United States.

In opposition to this motion, a preliminary point has been made by the counsel for the prosecution. It has been insisted by them, that, until the grand jury shall have found a true bill, the party accused is not entitled to subpœnas nor to the aid of the court to obtain his testimony.

It will not be said, that this opinion is now, for the first time, advanced in the United States; but certainly, it is now, for the first time, advanced in Virginia. So far back as any knowledge of our jurisprudence is possessed, the uniform practice of this country has been, to permit any individual, who was charged with any crime, to prepare for his defence, and to obtain the process of the court, for the purpose of enabling him so to do. This practice is as convenient, and as consonant to justice, as it is to humanity. It prevents, in a great measure, those delays which are never desirable, which frequently occasion the loss of testimony, and which are often oppressive. *That* would be the inevitable consequence of withholding from a prisoner the process of the court, until the indictment against him was found by the grand jury. The right of an accused person to the process of the court, to compel the attendance of witnesses, seems to follow, necessarily, from the right to examine those witnesses; and, wherever the right exists, it would be reasonable that it should be accompanied with the means of rendering it effectual. It is not doubted, that a person, who appears before a court under a recognisance, must expect that a bill will be preferred against him, or that a question, concerning the continuance of the recognisance, will be brought before the court. In the first event, he has the right, and it is perhaps his duty, to prepare for his defence at the trial. In the second event, it will not be denied, that he possesses the right to examine witnesses on the question of continuing his recognisance. In either case, it would seem reasonable, that he should be entitled to the process of the court, to procure the attendance of his witnesses. The genius and character of our laws and usages are friendly, not to condemnation at all events, but to a fair and impartial trial; and they consequently allow to the accused the right of preparing the means to secure such a trial. The objection, that the attorney may refuse to proceed at this time, and that no day is fixed for the trial, if he should proceed, presents no real difficulty. It would be a very insufficient excuse to a prisoner, who had failed to prepare for his trial, to say, that he was not certain the attorney would proceed against him. Had the indictment been found at the first term, it would have been in some measure uncertain, whether there would have been a trial at this, and still more uncertain on what day that trial would take place; yet, subpœnas would have issued returnable to the first day of the term; and if, after its commencement, other subpœnas had been required, they would have issued returnable as the court might direct. In fact, all process, to which the law has affixed no certain return day, is made returnable at the discretion of the court.

General principles, then, and general practice are in favour of the right of every accused person, so soon as his case is in court, to prepare for his defence, and to receive the aid of the process of the court to compel the attendance of his witnesses.

The constitution and laws of the United States will now be considered, for the purpose of ascertaining how they bear upon the question. The eighth amendment to the constitution gives to the accused, " in all criminal prosecutions, a right to a speedy and public trial, and to compulsory process for obtaining witnesses in his favour." The right, given by this article, must be deemed sacred by the courts, and the article should be so construed as to be something more than a dead letter. What can more effectually elude the right to a speedy trial than the declaration, that the accused shall be disabled from preparing for it, until an indictment shall be found against him? It is certainly much more in the true spirit of the provision, which secures to the accused a speedy trial, that he should have the benefit of the provision, which entitles him to compulsory process, as soon as he is brought into court.

This observation derives additional force from a consideration of the manner in which this subject has been contemplated by congress. It is obviously the intention of the national legislature, that, in all capital cases, the accused shall be entitled to process before indictment found. The words of the law are, " and every such person or persons accused or indicted of the crimes aforesaid, (that is of treason or any other capital offence) shall be allowed and admitted in his said defence, to make any proof that he or they can produce, by lawful witness or witnesses, and shall have the like process of the court where he or they shall be tried, to compel his or their witnesses to appear at his or their trial, as is usually granted to compel witnesses to appear on the prosecution against them."

This provision is made for persons accused or indicted. From the imperfection of human language, it frequently happens, that sentences, which ought to be the most explicit, are of doubtful construction; and in this case the words, " accused or indicted," may be construed to be synonymous, to describe a person in the same situation, or to apply to different stages of the prosecution. The word *or* may be taken in a conjunctive or a disjunctive sense. A reason for understanding them in the latter sense is furnished by the section itself. It commences with declaring, that any person, who shall be accused and indicted of treason, shall have a copy of the indictment, and at least three days before his trial. This right is obviously to be enjoyed after an indictment, and therefore the words are " accused *and* indicted." So, with respect to the subsequent clause, which authorises a party to make his defence, and directs the court, on his application, to assign him counsel. The words relate to any person accused and indicted. But, when the section proceeds to authorise the compulsory process for witnesses, the phraseology is changed. The words are, " and every such person or persons accused or indicted," &c. thereby adapting the expression to the situation of an accused person both before and after indictment. It is to be remarked, too, that the person, so accused or indicted, is to have " the like process to compel his or their witnesses to appear at his or their trial, as is usually granted to compel witnesses to appear on the prosecution against him." The fair construction of this clause would seem to be, that, with respect to the means of compelling the attendance of witnesses to be furnished by the court, the prosecution and defence are placed by the law on equal ground. The right of the prosecutor to take out subpœnas, or to avail himself of the aid of the court, in any stage of the proceedings previous to the indictment, is not controverted. This act of congress, it is true, applies only to capital cases; but persons, charged with offences not capital, have a constitutional and a legal right to examine their testimony; and this act ought to be considered as declaratory of the common law in cases where this constitutional right exists.

Upon immemorial usage, then, and upon what is deemed a sound construction of the constitution and law of the land, the court is of opinion, that any person, charged with a crime in the courts of the United States, has a right, before, as well as after indictment, to the process of the court to compel the attendance of his witnesses. Much delay and much inconvenience may be avoided by this construction; no mischief, which is perceived, can be produced by it. The process would only issue when, according to the ordinary course of proceeding, the indictment would be tried at the term to which the subpœna is made returnable; so that it becomes incumbent on the accused to be ready for his trial at that term.

This point being disposed of, it remains to inquire, whether a subpœna *duces tecum* can be directed to the president of the United States, and whether it ought to be directed in this case?

This question, originally, consisted of two parts. It was at first doubted, whether a subpœna could issue, in any case, to the chief magistrate of the nation; and if it could, whether that subpœna could do more than direct his personal attendance : whether it could direct him to bring with him a paper which was to constitute the gist of his testimony. While the argument was opening, the attorney for the United States avowed his opinion, that a general subpœna might issue to the president; but not a subpœna *duces tecum*. This terminated the argument on that part of the question. The court, however, has thought it necessary to state briefly the foundation of its opinion, that such a subpœna may issue.

In the provisions of the constitution, and of the statute, which give to the accused a right to the compulsory process of the court, there is no exception whatever. The obligation, therefore, of those provisions is general; and it would seem, that no person could claim an exemption from them, but one who would not be a witness. At any rate, if an exception to the general principle exist, it must be looked for in the law of evidence. The exceptions furnished by the law of evidence, (with one only reservation) so far as they are personal, are of those only whose testimony could not be received. The single reservation, alluded to, is the case of the king. Although he may, perhaps, give testimony, it is said to be incompatible with his dignity to appear under the process of the court. Of the many points of difference which exist between the first magistrate in England and the first magistrate of the United States, in respect to the personal dignity conferred on them, by the constitutions of their respective nations, the court will only select and mention two. It is a principle of the English constitution, that the king can do no wrong, that no blame can be imputed to him, that he cannot be named in debate.

By the constitution of the United States, the president, as well as every other officer of the government, may be impeached, and may be removed from office on high crimes and misdemeanors.

By the constitution of Great Britain, the crown is hereditary, and the monarch can never be a subject.

By that of the United States, the president is elected from the mass of the people, and, on the expiration of the time for which he is elected, returns to the mass of the people again.

How essentially this difference of circumstances must vary the policy of the laws of the two countries, in reference to the personal dignity of the executive chief, will be perceived by every person. In this respect, the first magistrate of the Union may more properly be likened to the first magistrate of a state; at any rate, under the former confederation; and it is not known ever to have been doubted, but that the chief magistrate of a state might be served with a subpœna *ad testificandum.*

If, in any court of the United States, it has ever been decided, that a subpœna cannot issue to the president, that decision is unknown to this court.

If, upon any principle, the president could be construed to stand exempt from the general provisions of the constitution, it would be, because his duties, as chief magistrate, demand his whole time for national objects. But it is apparent, that this demand is not unremitting; and, if it should exist at the time when his attendance on a court is required, it would be sworn on the return of the subpœna, and would rather constitute a reason for not obeying the process of the court, than a reason against its being issued. In point of fact it cannot be doubted, that the people of England have the same interest in the service of the executive government, that is, of the cabinet counsel, that the American people have in the service of the executive of the United States, and that their duties are as arduous and as unremitting. Yet it has never been alleged, that a subpœna might not be directed to them. It cannot be denied, that, to issue a subpœna to a person, filling the exalted station of the chief magistrate, is a duty which would be dispensed with much more cheerfully than it would be performed; but, if it be a duty, the court can have no choice in the case.

If, then, as is admitted by the counsel for the United States, a subpœna may issue to the president, the accused is entitled to it of course; and, whatever difference may exist with respect to the power to compel the same obedience to the process, as if it had been directed to a private citizen, there exists no difference with respect to the right to obtain it. The guard, furnished to this high officer, to protect him from being harassed by vexatious and unnecessary subpœnas, is to be looked for in the conduct of a court after those subpœnas have issued; not in any circumstance which is to precede their being issued. If, in being summoned to give his personal attendance to testify, the law does not discriminate between the president and a private citizen, what foundation is there for the opinion, that this difference is created by the circumstance, that his testimony depends on a paper in his possession, not on facts which have come to his knowledge otherwise than by writing? The court can perceive no foundation for such an opinion. The propriety of introducing any paper into a case, as testimony, must depend on the character of the paper, not on the character of the person who holds it. A subpœna *duces tecum*, then, may issue to any person to whom an ordinary subpœna may issue, directing him to bring any paper of which the party praying it has a right to avail himself as testimony; if, indeed, that be the necessary process for obtaining the view of such paper.

When this subject was suddenly introduced, the court felt some doubt concerning the propriety of directing a subpœna to the chief magistrate, and some doubt, also, concerning the propriety of directing any paper in his possession, not public in its nature, to be exhibited in court. The impression, that the questions which might arise, in consequence of such process, were more proper for discussion on the return of the process than on its issuing, was then strong on the mind of the judges; but, the circumspection with which they would take any step, which would, in any manner, relate to that high personage, prevented their yielding readily to those impressions, and induced the request, that those points, if not admitted, might be argued. The result of that argument is a confirmation of the impression originally entertained. The court can perceive no legal objection to issuing a subpœna *duces tecum* to any person whatever, provided, the case be such as to justify the process.

This is said to be a motion to the *discretion* of the court. This is true. But a motion to its *discretion* is a motion, not to its *inclination*, but to its *judgment;* and its judgment is to be guided by sound legal principles. A subpœna *duces tecum* varies from an ordinary subpœna only in this; that a witness is sum-

It is not for the court to anticipate the event of the present prosecution. Should it terminate as is expected on the part of the United States, all those, who are concerned in it, should certainly regret, that a paper, which the accused believed to be essential to his defence, which may, for aught that now appears, be essential, had been withheld from him. I will not say, that this circumstance would, in any degree, tarnish the reputation of the government; but I will say, that it would justly tarnish the reputation of the court, which had given its sanction to its being withheld. Might I be permitted to utter one sentiment, with respect to myself, it would be to deplore, most earnestly, the occasion which should compel me to look back on any part of my official conduct with so much self-reproach as I should feel, could I declare, on the information now possessed, that the accused is not entitled to the letter in question, if it should be really important to him.

The propriety of requiring the answer to this letter is more questionable. It is alleged, that it most probably communicates orders showing the situation of this country with Spain, which will be important on the misdemeanor. If it contain matter not essential to the defence, and the disclosure be unpleasant to the executive, it certainly ought not to be disclosed. This is a point which will appear on the return. The demand of the orders, which have been issued, and which have been, as is alleged, published in the Natchez gazette, is by no means unusual. Such documents have often been produced in the courts of the United States, and the courts of England. If they contain matter interesting to the nation, the concealment of which is required by the public safety, that matter will appear upon the return. If they do not, and are material, they may be exhibited.

It is said, they cannot be material, because they cannot justify any unlawful resistance, which may have been employed or meditated by the accused.

Were this admitted, and were it also admitted, that such resistance would amount to treason, the orders might still be material; because, they might tend to weaken the endeavour to connect such overt act with any overt act of which this court may take cognisance. The court, however, is rather inclined to the opinion, that the subpœna, in such case, ought to be directed to the head of the department, in whose custody the orders are. The court must suppose, that the letter of the secretary of the navy, which has been stated, by the attorney for the United States, to refer the counsel for the prisoner to his legal remedy for the copies he desired, alluded to such a motion as is now made.

The affidavit on which the motion is grounded has not been

be a blot in the page, which records the judicial proceedings of this country, if, in a case of such serious import as this, the accused should be denied the use of them?

The counsel for the United States take a very different view of the subject; and insist, that a motion for process to obtain testimony should be supported by the same full and explicit proof of the nature and application of that testimony, which would be required on a motion, which would delay public justice; which would arrest the ordinary course of proceeding; or would, in any other manner affect the rights of the opposite party. In favour of this position has been urged the opinion of one, whose loss, as a friend, and as a judge, I sincerely deplore; whose worth I feel, and whose authority I shall at all times greatly respect. If his opinion were really opposed to mine, I should certainly revise, deliberately revise, the judgment I had formed: but I perceive no such opposition.

In the trials of Smith and Ogden, the court, in which judge Patterson presided, required a special affidavit in support of a motion, made by the counsel for the accused, for a continuance and for an attachment against witnesses who had been subpœnaed and had failed to attend.

Had this requisition of a special affidavit been made as well a foundation for an attachment as for a continuance, the cases would not have been parallel; because, the attachment was considered by the counsel for the prosecution merely as a mean of punishing the contempt, and a court might certainly require stronger testimony to induce them to punish a contempt, than would be required to lend its aid to a party in order to procure evidence in a cause. But the proof furnished by the case is most conclusive, that the special statements of the affidavit were required solely on account of the continuance.

Although the counsel for the United States considered the motion, for an attachment, merely as a mode of punishing for contempt, the counsel for Smith and Ogden considered it as compulsory process to bring in a witness, and moved a continuance until they could have the benefit of this process. The continuance was to arrest the ordinary course of justice; and, therefore, the court required a special affidavit, showing the materiality of the testimony before this continuance could be granted. *Prima facie* evidence could not apply to the case; and there was an additional reason for a special affidavit. The object of this special statement was expressly said to be for a continuance. Colden proceeded: " The present application is to put off the cause on account of the absence of witnesses, whose testimony the defendant alleges is material for his defence, and who have disobeyed the ordinary process of the court. In compliance with the intimation from the bench, yesterday, the defendant has disclosed, by the affidavit which I have just read, the points to which he expects the witnesses who have been summoned will testify.

" If the court cannot, or will not, issue compulsory process, to bring in the witnesses who are the objects of this application, then the cause will not be postponed.

" Or, if it appear to the court, that the matter disclosed by the affidavit might not be given in evidence, if the witnesses were now here, then we cannot expect that our motion will be successful. For it would be absurd to suppose, that the court will postpone the trial on account of the absence of witnesses whom they cannot compel to appear, and of whose voluntary attendance there is too much reason to despair; or, on account of the absence of witnesses who, if they were before the court, could not be heard on the trial." (See page 12 of the Trials of Smith and Ogden.)

This argument states, unequivocally, the purpose for which a special affidavit was required.

The counsel for the United States considered the subject in the same light. After exhibiting an affidavit for the purpose of showing, that the witnesses could not probably possess any material information, Mr. Standford said, " It was decided by the court yesterday, that it was incumbent on the defendant, in order to entitle himself to a postponement of the trial, on account of the absence of these witnesses, to show in what respect they are material for his defence. It was the opinion of the court, that the general affidavit, in common form, would not be sufficient for this purpose; but, that the particular facts, expected from the witnesses, must be disclosed, in order that the court might, upon those facts, judge of the propriety of granting the postponement." (p. 27.)

The court frequently treated the subject so as to show the opinion, that the special affidavit was required only on account of the continuance; but, what is conclusive on this point is, that after deciding the testimony of the witnesses to be such as could not be offered to the jury, judge Patterson was of opinion, that a rule, to show cause why an attachment should not issue, ought to be granted. He could not have required the materiality of the witness to be shown on a motion, the success of which did not, in his opinion, in any degree depend on that materiality; and which he granted after deciding the testimony to be such as the jury ought not to hear. It is, then, most apparent, that the opinion of judge Patterson has been misunderstood, and that no inference can possibly be drawn from it, opposed to the principle which has been laid down by the court. That principle will therefore be applied to the present motion.

The first paper required is the letter of general Wilkinson, which was referred to in the message of the president to congress. The application of that letter to the case is shown, by

the terms in which the communication was made. It is a statement of the conduct of the accused, made by the person who is
declared to be the essential witness against him. The order for
producing this letter is opposed,

First, Because it is not material to the defence. It is a principle,
universally acknowledged, that a party has a right to oppose to
the testimony of any witness against him, the declarations which
that witness has made, at other times, on the same subject. If he
possesses this right, he must bring forward proof of those declarations. This proof must be obtained before he knows, positively,
what the witness will say ; for, if he waits until the witness has
been heard at the trial, it is too late to meet him with his former
declarations. Those former declarations, therefore, constitute a
mass of testimony, which a party has a right to obtain by way of
precaution, and the positive necessity of which can only be decided at the trial.

It is with some surprise an argument was heard from the bar,
insinuating, that the award of a subpœna, on this ground, gave
the countenance of the court to suspicions affecting the veracity
of a witness, who is to appear on the part of the United States.
This observation could not have been considered. In contests of
this description, the court takes no part; the court has no right
to take a part. Every person may give in evidence, testimony
such as is stated in this case. What would be the feelings
of the prosecutor, if, in this case, the accused should produce a witness completely exculpating himself, and the attorney
for the United States should be arrested in his attempt to prove
what the same witness had said upon a former occasion, by a declaration from the bench, that such an attempt could not be permitted, because it would imply a suspicion in the court, that the
witness had not spoken the truth? Respecting so unjustifiable an
interposition but one opinion would be formed

The second objection is, that the letter contains matter which
ought not to be disclosed.

That there may be matter, the production of which the court
would not require, is certain; but that, in a capital case, the accused ought, in some form, to have the benefit of it, if it were really essential to his defence, is a position which the court would
very reluctantly deny. It ought not to be believed, that the department, which superintends prosecutions in criminal cases,
would be inclined to withhold it. What ought to be done, under
such circumstances, presents a delicate question, the discussion of
which, it is hoped, will never be rendered necessary in this country. At present it need only be said, that the question does not
occur at this time. There is certainly nothing before the court
which shows, that the letter in question contains any matter the
disclosure of which would endanger the public safety. If it

does contain such matter, the fact may appear before the disclosure is made. If it does contain any matter, which it would be imprudent to disclose, which it is not the wish of the executive to disclose; such matter, if it be not immediately and essentially applicable to the point, will, of course, be suppressed. It is not easy to conceive, that so much of the letter as relates to the conduct of the accused can be a subject of delicacy with the president. Every thing of this kind, however, will have its due consideration, on the return of the subpœna.

Thirdly, It has been alleged, that a copy may be received instead of the original, and the act of congress has been cited in support of this proposition.

This argument presupposes, that the letter required is a document filed in the department of state, the reverse of which may be and most probably is the fact. Letters, addressed to the president, are most usually retained by himself. They do not belong to any of the departments. But, were the fact otherwise, a copy might not answer the purpose. The copy would not be superior to the original, and the original itself would not be admitted, if denied, without proof that it was in the hand writing of the witness. Suppose the case put at the bar of an indictment on this letter for a libel, and, on its production, it should appear not to be in the hand writing of the person indicted. Would its being deposited in the department of state make it his writing, or subject him to the consequence of having written it? Certainly not. For the purpose, then, of showing the letter to have been written by a particular person, the original must be produced, and a copy could not be admitted. On the confidential nature of this letter, much has been said at the bar, and authorities have been produced, which appear to be conclusive. Had its contents been orally communicated, the person, to whom the communications were made, could not have excused himself from detailing them, so far as they might be deemed essential in the defence. Their being in writing gives no additional sanctity; the only difference produced by the circumstance is, that the contents of the paper must be proved by the paper itself, not by the recollection of the witness.

Much has been said about the disrespect to the chief magistrate, which is implied by this motion, and by such a decision of it as the law is believed to require.

These observations will be very truly answered by the declaration, that this court feels many, perhaps, peculiar motives, for manifesting as guarded a respect for the chief magistrate of the Union as is compatible with its official duties. To go beyond these would exhibit a conduct, which would deserve some other appellation than the term respect.

It is not for the court to anticipate the event of the present prosecution. Should it terminate as is expected on the part of the United States, all those, who are concerned in it, should certainly regret, that a paper, which the accused believed to be essential to his defence, which may, for aught that now appears, be essential, had been withheld from him. I will not say, that this circumstance would, in any degree, tarnish the reputation of the government; but I will say, that it would justly tarnish the reputation of the court, which had given its sanction to its being withheld. Might I be permitted to utter one sentiment, with respect to myself, it would be to deplore, most earnestly, the occasion which should compel me to look back on any part of my official conduct with so much self-reproach as I should feel, could I declare, on the information now possessed, that the accused is not entitled to the letter in question, if it should be really important to him.

The propriety of requiring the answer to this letter is more questionable. It is alleged, that it most probably communicates orders showing the situation of this country with Spain, which will be important on the misdemeanor. If it contain matter not essential to the defence, and the disclosure be unpleasant to the executive, it certainly ought not to be disclosed. This is a point which will appear on the return. The demand of the orders, which have been issued, and which have been, as is alleged, published in the Natchez gazette, is by no means unusual. Such documents have often been produced in the courts of the United States, and the courts of England. If they contain matter interesting to the nation, the concealment of which is required by the public safety, that matter will appear upon the return. If they do not, and are material, they may be exhibited.

It is said, they cannot be material, because they cannot justify any unlawful resistance, which may have been employed or meditated by the accused.

Were this admitted, and were it also admitted, that such resistance would amount to treason, the orders might still be material; because, they might tend to weaken the endeavour to connect such overt act with any overt act of which this court may take cognisance. The court, however, is rather inclined to the opinion, that the subpœna, in such case, ought to be directed to the head of the department, in whose custody the orders are. The court must suppose, that the letter of the secretary of the navy, which has been stated, by the attorney for the United States, to refer the counsel for the prisoner to his legal remedy for the copies he desired, alluded to such a motion as is now made.

The affidavit on which the motion is grounded has not been

noticed. It is believed, that such a subpœna, as is asked, ought to issue, if there exist any reason for supposing, that the testimony may be material, and ought to be admitted. It is only because the subpœna is to those who administer the government of this country, that such an affidavit was required as would furnish probable cause to believe, that the testimony was desired for the real purposes of defence, and not for such as this court will for ever discountenance.

When the chief justice had concluded his opinion, Mr. MAC REA addressed the court to the following effect:

I hope, sir, that I have misunderstood an expression, which has just escaped from your honour; but the opinions of those gentlemen, who are near me, completely confirm my own conceptions. Your honour has declared, if I mistake not, that "if the present prosecution terminate as is wished, on the part of the United States." I hope, sir, that nothing has appeared in my conduct, nothing in the conduct of the gentlemen who are associated with me on the present occasion, and nothing in the conduct of the government, to produce such a conviction in the breast of the court. Permit me, sir, to assure this court, if we feel any sentiment at all, that it is one of a very different description. The impression which has been thus conveyed by the court, that we not only wished to have Aaron Burr accused, but that we wished to convict him, is completely abhorrent to our feelings. We trust, that it has rather accidentally fallen from the pen of your honour, than that it is your deliberate opinion. We wish for nothing, sir, but a fair and competent investigation of this case. It is far from our wishes, that Aaron Burr should be convicted, but upon the most satisfactory evidence. And let me assure this court, that nothing would more severely wound my feelings, than if you or any other man should suppose it possible, that I myself, or the gentlemen with whom I am associated, or the government which we have the honour to represent, should at all events, desire the conviction of the prisoner.

The CHIEF JUSTICE replied, that it was not his intention to insinuate, that the attornies for the prosecution, or that the administration, had ever wished the conviction of colonel Burr, whether he was guilty or innocent; that his assertion was this: " Gentlemen had so often, and so uniformly asserted, that colonel Burr was guilty, and they had so often repeated it before the testimony was perceived, on which that guilt could alone be substantiated, that it appeared to him probable, that they were not indifferent on the subject."

Mr. MAC REA begged leave to point out to the court a considerable difference between the *opinions* and *wishes* of the counsel for the prosecution; that from the testimony which they had examined, they thought it extremely probable, that Aaron Burr was really guilty; but that this was very different from wishing to find him guilty, or to convict him at all events.

Mr. HAY observed, that his own conscience was satisfied with the course which he had pursued in this business; that he should attempt to secure the same sentiment by his future deportment; and, provided he enjoyed that satisfaction, he was completely indifferent to the opinion of others; and he should certainly pursue his own judgment. He asked, whether he might not send up the witnesses to the grand jury?

Mr. BURR then pressed upon the court the necessity of giving the supplemental charge; that it would be of considerable benefit in instructing the jury to separate what was proper in the evidence from what was improper; that if the charge was not delivered for several days, the jury might, in the mean time, be receiving very false impressions; and that their minds might be so completely involved in these impressions, that it would be impossible for them, to separate them from their decisions, even after the delivery of the charge. He conceived that the court ought either to prevent the witnesses from going to the grand jury, or to deliver its supplemental charge.

The CHIEF JUSTICE replied, that on Monday morning he would deliver the charge, if all the necessary preliminary points could be settled.

Mr. HAY then requested the clerk to swear four of the witnesses: Thomas Truxtun, William Eaton, Benjamin Stoddert, and Stephen Decatur, who were accordingly sworn.

Mr. BURR hoped, that the court would immediately take up the supplemental charge to the jury. What was the objection which the attorney for the United States has submitted to your honour, and on which you seemed to entertain some doubts?

CHIEF JUSTICE.—It is, whether the statute of Edward VI. is now in force in this country.

Mr. RANDOLPH.—We are ready on that point, sir.

The clerk then proceeded to call four other witnesses to the book; but when Erick Bollman appeared, Mr. HAY addressed the court to the following effect:

Before Mr. Bollman is sworn, I must inform the court of a particular, and not an immaterial circumstance. He, sir, has made a full communication to the government of the plans, the designs, and views of Aaron Burr. As these commu-

nications might criminate doctor Bollman before the grand
jury, the president of the United States has communicated
to me this pardon (holding it in his hands) which I have already offered to doctor Bollman. He received it in a very hesitating manner; and I think informed me, that he knew not
whether he should or should not accept it. He took it from
me, however, as he informed me to take the advice of counsel.
He returned it in the same hesitating manner; he would neither
positively accept nor refuse it. My own opinion is, that doctor Bollman, under these circumstances, cannot possibly criminate himself. This pardon will completely exonerate him
from all the penalties of the law. I believe his evidence to be
extremely material. In the presence of this court, I offer this
pardon to him, and if he refuses, I shall deposit it with the
clerk for his use. Will you (addressing himself to doctor
Bollman) accept this pardon?

Doctor BOLLMAN.—No. I will not, sir.

Mr. HAY then observed, that doctor Bollman must be carried up to the grand jury with an intimation, that he had been
pardoned.

Mr. MARTIN.—It has always been doctor Bollman's intention to refuse this pardon; but he has not positively refused it
before, because he wished to have this opportunity of publicly
rejecting it.

Several other witnesses were sworn.

Mr. MARTIN did not suppose, that the pardon was real or
effectual; if he made any confessions before the grand jury,
they might find an indictment against him, which would be
valid, notwithstanding the pardon; that the pardon could not
be effectual before it was pleaded to an indictment in open
court.

Mr. HAY inquired, whether doctor Bollman might not go to
the grand jury?

The CHIEF JUSTICE suggested, that it would be better to
settle the question about the validity of the pardon before he
was sent to the grand jury.

Mr. HAY.—I am anxious to introduce the evidence before
the grand jury in a chronological order, and the suspension of
doctor Bollman's testimony will make a chasm in my arrangement. He added, that however it was not very important whether he was sent now or some time hence to the grand jury.

Mr. MARTIN.—Doctor Bollman *is* *not* pardoned; and no
man is bound to criminate himself.

The Chief Justice required his authorities.

Mr. Martin.—I am prepared to show, that a party even possessed of a pardon is still indictable by the grand jury, unless he has pleaded it in court.

The other witnesses were sent to the grand jury, and doctor Bollman was suspended.

Four other witnesses were then sworn.

Mr. Hay.—I again propose to send doctor Bollman to the grand jury.

At this time the marshal entered, and Mr. Hay informed the court, that the grand jury had sent for the article of the constitution and the laws of congress relating to treason, and the law relating to the misdemeanor.

Jacob Dunbaugh was sworn and sent to the grand jury.

Some desultory conversation here ensued between the bar and the court respecting doctor Bollman, when Mr. Hay addressed the opposite counsel: Are you then willing to hear doctor Bollman indicted? Take care in what an awful condition you are placing this gentleman.

Mr. Martin.—Doctor Bollman, sir, has lived too long to be alarmed by such menaces. He is a man of too much honour to trust his reputation to the course which you prescribe for him.

The Chief Justice.—There can be no question but doctor Bollman can go up to the jury: but the question is, whether he is pardoned or not? If the executive should refuse to pardon him, he is certainly not pardoned.

Mr. Martin.—But there can be no doubt, if he chooses to decline his pardon, that he stands in the same situation with every other witness, who cannot be forced to criminate himself.

Some desultory conversation here ensued, when Mr. Hay observed, that he should extremely regret the loss of Dr. Bollman's testimony. He believed it to be material. He trusted, that he should obtain it, however reluctantly given. The court would perceive, that doctor Bollman now possessed so much zeal, as even to encounter the risk of an indictment for treason. Whether he should appear before the grand jury, under the circumstance of a pardon being annexed to his name, might hereafter become the object of a distinct inquiry. In the mean time, he might go up without any such notification.

The counsel of Mr. Burr acquiesced.

CHIEF JUSTICE.—Whether he be really pardoned or not, I cannot, at present, declare. I must take time to deliberate.

Mr. HAY.—Categorically then I ask you, Mr. Bollman, do you accept your pardon?

Mr. BOLLMAN.—I have already answered that question several times. I say no. I repeat, that I would have refused it before, but that I wished this opportunity of publicly declaring it.

Mr. HAY.—If the grand jury have any doubts about the questions that they put to doctor Bollman, they can apply to the court for instructions. I assert, sir, that Mr. Bollman is a pardoned man. I wish the opposite counsel to prove that he is not. I therefore move, sir, that he be sent up to the grand jury, certified by you, that he is pardoned. I make this motion, that gentlemen, who wish to discuss the question, may have an opportunity of adducing their arguments.

Mr. WILLIAMS, counsel for Mr. Bollman.—There are three questions to be decided. 1st, Whether a witness be bound to answer any questions, which tend to criminate himself, or afford a clue to evidence for that purpose? 2d, The operation of a pardon, whether it change the question? but in this case, it having been refused, the court cannot notice it. 3d, Who is to be the judge, the witness or the court, as to the propriety of answering the question?

On the first question Mr. Williams laid down the following propositions: 1st, The rule of law is, that no man shall be bound to answer any question which shall accuse himself.—1 Mac Nally's Ev. 256. 2 Haw. c. 46. 2d, He shall not be bound to answer any questions which shall accuse himself of a misdemeanor.—1 Mac Nal. 256. 3d, He shall not be called upon to calumniate himself.—1 Mac Nal. 256. 2 State Trials, 822. 1017 to 1038, Tabsborough's case. 4th, He is not to defame himself.—1 Mac Nal. 256. 258. 2 State Trials, 439. 5th, Not to answer insnaring questions.—Mac Nal. 256. 6th, To ask a man if he is a Roman catholic is not permitted.—Mac Nal. 257. 9 State Trials, 414. 2 Dougl. 593. 7th, Not bound to answer any question which tends to criminate himself.—Mac Nal. 257. 4 State Trials, 605, 606. 8th, The case of Goosely in this court, upon the trial of Reynolds; he was called as a witness, but not compelled to criminate himself,—had been acquitted the day before by the grand jury. So 1 Black. Rep. 27.

As to the second question, the rule of law is the same, even if the man be pardoned. 1st, A witness, although pardoned, shall not be bound to calumniate himself, for the pardon having placed him in statu quo, no question shall be asked him, which tends to make him contemptible, or do away the benefit of the pardon.—1 Mac Nal. 256. 2 State Trials, 822. 1035. If doctor Bollman were bound to acknowledge himself acquainted with any treason, he was guilty of a very high misdemeanor, and therefore it would do away any benefit from the pardon. But the court cannot notice a pardon, unless it be a pardon by statute: for if under great seal and accepted, yet it would be error in the court to allow it not pleaded.—2 Hawk. ch. 37, sec. 59. 64, 65. 5 Bac. 294. If party only entitled upon pleading it, then if he refuse, court cannot take notice of it. Here party refusing to accept, court must say that he is not pardoned: for until it is pleaded, party liable, is to be punished. For if he plead not guilty, the court will not allow him to plead it afterwards.—2 Hawk. ch. 37, sec. 59. Bac. 294. As to the third question, the witness must be the judge of necessity: 1st, Because he can only know what the answer is, and the bearing it will have. 2d, If the court do decide, they must know what would be the answer; and to get *that* from the witness would criminate himself, which I have shown he is not bound to do.

If it be objected, that by this means, no witness would give evidence against the accused, it may be answered, 1st, The refusal is upon oath, because he affirms, that to answer it would be to criminate himself. 2d, You have the same obligation on him to answer that truly, as to speak truth upon any other subject. 3d, If he perjure himself, in that, he would certainly do it to get clear of giving evidence against the accused. It is his privilege not to answer any question having that tendency. This rule is upon the following authorities : The court in a case, in 1743, in 4 State Trials, 414, note, states, to wit, "If you think it will criminate yourself, you need not answer it."—1 Mac Nal. 257—8. It is put to the witness and not to the court, because he knew what was to be the answer. If it be objected, that nothing is evidence against him, which he may say on his oath, the answer is, that it has been otherwise decided.—2 Doug. 398.

Mr. MARTIN would merely suggest a few additional authorities. Among these were 5 Bac. p. 293. 2 Hawkins, ch. 57, p. 59, 60. 65. Mr. Martin contended, that these authorities demonstrated that there were two kinds of pardons in England: one by parliament, and the other under the great seal. That the first exempted an individual from the cognisance of the court as to the particular crime for which he might stand charged; but that the latter was no bar to a judicial prosecution; and was not indeed effectual, until it had been pleaded and allowed in court. Mr. Martin also quoted an authority from Salkeld to show, inc orroboration of Mr. Williams's position, that no witness, however exempted from the charge and necessity of criminating himself; however responsible on that account to the law; can be made to discredit himself by his own testimony.

Mr. WILLIAMS also quoted another authority, to the same effect, from page 258 of Mac Nally's Evidence.

Mr. MAC REA.—It is extremely uncertain, sir, whether Mr. Bollman will or will not answer the questions, which may be propounded to him by the grand jury. If he be the very honourable man, whom these gentlemen have represented, he certainly will not refuse to answer. But if he do refuse, it can only be upon the ground, that he is really a criminal. It is not, therefore, necessary for us to determine this point at the present time. It is not necessary to decide whether doctor Bollman is or is not a pardoned man. We do sincerely hope, that he will appear in the character of an honourable man; and not refuse to answer the interrogatories of the grand jury. But if he should pursue that course, it will be then timeenough for us to bring this discussion before the court.

Mr. HAY.—The proposition which I had stated, seems to me to be so evident, as to require little argument. I consider Dr. Bollman as a pardoned man; and therefore, I desired, that the court should certify that fact for the instruction of the grand jury. Gentlemen, however, seem themselves to concede the very point for which we are contending. Why do they so much expatiate on the consequences of a pardon, if they do not consider that one has been already established? Why do they wish to screen doctor Bollman, under the plea, that he cannot be made to defame himself, unless they consider him not sufficiently secured by the possession of a pardon? As to the effect of a pardon, it is a distinct question, on which the court may hereafter instruct the grand jury. But at present, I wish the court merely to certify, that he is pardoned.

Mr. MARTIN replied, that if the gentleman had attended to his argument, he would have seen, that most of his authorities had borne upon the existence of a pardon, and not upon the effects of one.

CHIEF JUSTICE.—Have any of you authorities to show *when* the pardon operates?

Mr. MARTIN.—Certainly from the time of pleading.

CHIEF JUSTICE.—You mistake my question: suppose the pardon to be lost, is it then valid?

Mr. MARTIN.—If it be proved, that he had pleaded it to an

indictment, I presume an exemplification of it would answer every purpose.

As another reason, sir, why doctor Bollman has refused this pardon, permit me to say, that it would be considered as an admission of guilt. Doctor Bollman does not admit that he has been guilty. He does not consider a pardon as necessary for an innocent man. Doctor Bollman, sir, knows what he has to fear from the persecution of an angry government; but he will brave it all. The man, who did so much to rescue the marquis la Fayette from his imprisonment, and who has been known at so many courts, bears too great a regard for his reputation, to wish to have it sounded throughout Europe, that he was compelled to abandon his honour through a fear of unjust persecution.

After some desultory conversation, doctor Bollman was sent up to the grand jury without any particular notification. The questions whether he be pardoned, and of course how far he may be called upon to disclose all that he knows, are reserved for future discussion and decision.

Mr. HAY requested leave to inform the grand jury that fatigue alone had prevented general Wilkinson from attending them on that day; but that he should appear before them on Monday.

Mr. BOTTS then observed, that there was one point in the supplemental charge, which he wished to notice. In one part of the charge, the clause of the constitution, relative to treason, is quoted; which clause recognises the necessity of two witnesses to prove an overt act. In a subsequent part, there seems to be an implication that one witness to an overt act is sufficient. How was this seeming contrariety to be explained?

CHIEF JUSTICE.—Though the constitution declares that two witnesses are necessary to produce conviction, yet it may not be so strictly and absolutely necessary to authorise an indictment being found a true bill. My present impression is, that though there must be two witnesses to the general charge of treason, yet that one witness may be sufficient to prove one act, and another to prove another. Chief justice quoted the statute of Edward VI. The law books made this discrimination between a trial and an indictment.

Mr. HAY.—There is one important question worthy of our consideration. In your supplemental charge, sir, you have referred to the statute of Edward VI. But no such statute is now in force here. A general law of the Virginia legislature, passed several years ago, (in the year   ) swept off all the British laws; and then they set to re-enacting such as were congenial with our form of government. But this statute was certainly in force at the commencement of our revolution; and the question is whether, if *it* were in force *then*, it can be so considered *now*. Do gentlemen contend, that we are bound by a statute, which the government has not adopted?

At the close of the court, the CHIEF JUSTICE observed, that he had explained the sense, in which the words, which had been remarked on by Mr. Mac Rae, had been employed; that he had no desire that they should remain in the written opinion; that he did not perceive that they were calculated to excite any feeling, or liable to be so misunderstood; but as it was not his intention to convey the idea, that a conviction in any event, right or wrong, was wished; and as that idea had been inferred, and might hereafter be attached to them, by those who might see the opinion without the explanatory words, he had expunged them.

Some desultory conversation ensued; after which the court adjourned till Monday morning, eleven o'clock.

MONDAY, JUNE 15th, 1807.

The court met according to adjournment.

General Wilkinson was sworn and sent to the grand jury, with a notification that it would facilitate their inquiries if they would examine him immediately.*

Some discussion took place, relative to the form of the oath administered to the witnesses, before the grand jury; which at length was agreed to be proper.

Mr. WICKHAM stated, that as the indictments were now pending before the grand jury, it was necessary to recal to the memory of the court, a circumstance which had been early suggested, that a number of improper papers might be exhibited before the grand jury, which ought to be prevented by the court; that the attorney for the United States had pledged himself to send up no papers which had not previously passed the inspection of the court: but it had since occurred to colonel Burr's counsel, that the witnesses themselves might carry up such papers, which would defeat, and render of no avail, the promise of the attorney; that it would be changing the duties of a witness, which were to give testimony, not to carry papers. Finding that nothing could be done without an application to the court, Mr. Wickham submitted to them, whether they ought not to instruct the grand jury to *receive* no papers, but through the *medium* of the court.

* On the appearance of the general in court, it was said that his countenance was calm, dignified, and commanding; while that of colonel Burr was marked by a haughty contempt

Mr. HAY said, that the witnesses would not *deliver* any papers; that he hoped the court would not act upon a mere suspicion, that the witnesses would carry up improper papers; but that it was extremely probable, that general Wilkinson, in delivering his evidence before the grand jury, might find it necessary to refer to certain letters, which he had received, and to papers and documents, relative to these mysterious transactions, in order to refresh his memory. That he would not produce these as distinct and substantive evidence; but as so many private memoranda, in order to strengthen his recollection of the history of those transactions; and to enable him to give a more connected and full narrative. Mr. Hay hoped, that after the splendid example of patience, which the grand jury had displayed, they would not be interrupted in the examination now commenced; but that he had no objection to the court sending up by word, or by writing, such instructions to them on this subject as might be deemed proper.

Mr. BOTTS confessed, that after what had passed, this opposition surprised him. On a former day, he understood that it was agreed, that no papers should be sent to the grand jury, but such as had been inspected by the court.

Mr. HAY begged leave to explain. He had promised, before the arrival of general Wilkinson, to send up no papers without the inspection of the court. That he had at that time, several authenticated papers, and several affidavits; and that he had an impression (though not a very decided one) that they ought not to be submitted to the grand jury. At that time gentlemen seemed to apprehend, that certain papers and cyphered letters were to be sent up to the grand jury, without any previous motion. He had promised, and he would still pledge himself, to avoid this course. But it might happen that general Wilkinson had various papers to connect, explain, and enlarge his narrative. If general Wilkinson had brought these papers from New-Orleans, and now produced them before the grand jury, in order to refresh his memory, and enable him to explain, and amplify his own evidence, it would be correct; and no departure from his word, to which he had substantially adhered. He hoped, therefore, that gentlemen would not accuse him of a breach of faith, and that Mr. Botts would withdraw his expression of surprise.

Mr. BOTTS.—My surprise continues. I believe the attorney for the United States is incapable of any thing like a wilful breach of promise; but while I am willing to admit his intelligence, fairness and honour, I will say, without intending, and I hope without seeming to cast a reproach upon a character, whose head and heart are inferior to none, that a strong bias has stolen on that gentleman's mind, which ought to be vigilantly watched.

He was still surprised at the gentleman's proceedings, because the very principle which he supports as to the papers, would go to prevent the introduction of witnesses before the grand jury. Papers, he admits, are not proper to go before the jury; and therefore, if witnesses are to carry them, they themselves ought not to go. If Mr. Hay were called before the jury, he would produce no papers but what had passed through the court. But Mr. Hay is not the only prosecutor in this business. There is another equally active, and more deeply concerned. Mr. Hay admits, that this zealous prosecutor may produce his papers before the jury. If he merely produce papers to refresh his memory, any instruction which may go from the court, will be perfectly innocent in its effects; but it is possible that such an instruction may be necessary to repress the introduction of very improper papers, which he might hope to convey to the multitude abroad, through the channel of the grand jury. We are asked, why we suppose, that improper papers will be carried to the grand jury? There was a particular reason to recommend this vigilance. It was understood that a species of plunder had been permitted; that the post-offices had been robbed; and that letters thus improperly obtained, ought not to be laid before the grand jury, without being first examined by the court. It was, in fact, impossible that any papers, obtained by such means, could be legal evidence. Mr. Botts here read as an authority, from the eighth volume of the American Museum, judge Grimpkie's charge to the grand jury, to show that written evidence ought not to be heard by a grand jury; it being a well established principle, that a grand jury ought not to hear such evidence, till it is examined, and declared to be *authentic*, by the court.

CHIEF JUSTICE.—Neither affidavits nor papers, containing distinct substantive testimony against the accused, ought to be sent to the grand jury.

Mr. MARTIN.—Mr. attorney has conceded this in substance; and we admit that any witness may refer to papers to refresh his memory.

Mr. HAY.—I am willing to adhere, in *form* and *substance*, to my promise. I know not what papers general Wilkinson may produce. I was with him yesterday, and saw him in possession of a great many. But which of them he may choose to refer to, I cannot possibly say. If gentlemen wish to know the object of my visit to him, I will tell them.

Mr. MARTIN.—It is unnecessary.

Mr. HAY.—I had said before in this court, that I would not undertake to defend general Wilkinson ; but the result of my conversation with him yesterday is, that it is my duty to defend him; because I am well satisfied that he is an honest man, and a patriot. All my suspicions, imbibed from the mysterious circumstances in the case, have completely vanished; and being convinced of his unsullied integrity, I shall defend him with the most perfect sincerity.

Mr. MARTIN.—The gentleman has taken a good way to remove his unfavourable impressions, if that can be called a good one, which consists in hearing but one side of a cause. He has heard Wilkinson's own story. I wish he would hear colonel Burr's story; perhaps his impressions against him might also be removed.

Mr. HAY.—I have heard his story from his counsel; but they have strengthened my conviction against him.

Mr. WIRT said, that he had perused the authority quoted by Mr. Botts, and that he was satisfied, that the papers referred to by judge Grimpkie, were only affidavits. [Mr. Wirt read quotations to prove his position.] That the distinction was, that where a piece of written testimony was *distinct* and *substantive*, it was not admissible as evidence before a grand jury; but where it was explanatory of *viva voce* evidence, it was proper and admissible. That it was sometimes necessary to resort to written papers as the very best testimony. For example, said he, suppose general Wilkinson should state, that on such a day he received a letter from Burr, by the hands of Bollman or Swartwout: would not Burr's letters, in such case, with Wilkinson's oath, that they were the hand writing of Burr, be evidence even before a petit jury, and of course before a grand jury? Such letters are the best evidence of their own contents. If he were to make a verbal statement of their contents, would not the jury have a right to say to him, " Produce the original, we demand it as the best evidence?" Suppose general Wilkinson were to produce the cyphered letter, would it not be competent to the jury to say, " Produce it; we shall receive it, and explanations of its contents?" This shows, that the objection, as made generally to all papers, is fallacious and cannot be supported by law or reason. There are many different links in the chain of evidence. It is manifest, that written documents are sometimes not only evidence, but the very best, which can, in the nature of things, be adduced.

Mr. WICKHAM.—The counsel said, that he would *send* up no papers. But it is contended that the witnesses may *carry* up papers to the grand jury. It is a distinction without a difference. The object is to prevent the admission of improper evidence; and it is precisely the same thing in substance to receive it from a witness who carries, as from the attorney who sends it. When a petit jury is empaneled, the court inspect the papers before the jury are permitted to see them. The gentlemen have laid down a broad position, that any witness may have recourse to any papers to strengthen his recollection. This is certainly not correct. I beg leave to remind the court of a case (judge Chase's trial), which happened before the highest tribunal in this country, the senate of the United States, where it was decided, that a witness (Mr. Hay himself) was not permitted to read *memoranda*, even to refresh his memory. Mr. Wirt admits that an affidavit may not be read, but that a paper, not on oath, may be read.

Mr. WIRT.—The gentleman is uncandid. I wish he would understand me, and answer me candidly. He puts an absurdity into my mouth, which I disclaim. I wish the gentleman to state his argument against my argument as it was, and not according to his own deductions.

Mr. WICKHAM.—I agree that the gentleman did not state an absurdity in terms: but an absurdity inevitably follows from what he said. The court alone ought to determine what papers are evidence and proper to be at all heard by a grand jury.

Mr. HAY.—I beg leave to make one observation. I care not for the decision in Chase's trial; nor do I know that it was as now stated: but if it were, I assert, that those who made it, knew that it was contrary to law. In the trials of Hardy, Tooke and Thelwal, a contrary principle was determined. A witness, who was a spy of the government, had no memory or recollection of the circumstances he was to prove, but from his reference to written memoranda. Mr. Wickham knew this decision not to be law, but he mentioned it merely because I was the witness in that case.

Mr. BOTTS.—Mr. Hay's observation is the longest I ever heard. The senate did so decide, and perhaps unanimously; and it was composed of the ablest lawyers from all parts of the union.

Mr. HAY contested the fact of decision in that manner; but he was irritated, and did not recollect precisely how it was; but he was informed that it was not decided unanimously, though it might have been so pronounced.

Messrs. MARTIN and WICKHAM stated, that the decision was by eighteen senators against sixteen, (which was the fact).

Mr. BOTTS.—Mr. Hay and Mr. Wirt take different grounds.

Mr. MARTIN contended, that the court was to decide what evidence was to go to the grand jury. He cited Danby's case, where a witness gave a deposition under the statute of William and Mary; he prevaricated before the grand jury, and they sent for his deposition to confront him. The court decided that they should not have it, because it was improper for them to see it.

CHIEF JUSTICE.—There is a difference between the grand and petit jury. The former are to make inquiry; they may send for witnesses; directions ought therefore to be given them in general terms. But I am not satisfied that a court ought to inspect the papers which form a part of a witness's testimony before he is sent to the grand jury. This would render it necessary to examine the witnesses in open court. The chief justice here delivered the opinion of the court, reduced to writing, in order to be laid before the grand jury. Its purport was, to instruct the grand jury not to inspect any papers but such as formed a part of the narrative of the witness, and proved to be the papers of the person against whom an indictment was exhibited.

Mr. HAY objected to this form of instruction. Suppose a paper from a person closely connected with the accused were adduced; as for instance, doctor Bollman. Such a paper may be important to prove to the jury the integrity and proper conduct of general Wilkinson. It may have had a material influence on his mind, even if not genuine.

CHIEF JUSTICE.—Your argument is, that the papers are to be admitted to justify the conduct of the witness; but they ought not to bear upon the accused.

Mr. HAY.—The prejudices in the western and other papers against general Wilkinson's character, representing him as connected with Aaron Burr, make it necessary that his reputation should be vindicated. He comes before the jury as a suspected person. The language of the cyphered letter seems to countenance the conjecture. It may be necessary to exhibit these papers to support the credit of the witness.

CHIEF JUSTICE.—The opinion may therefore be amended, by adding that such papers are also admissible as tend to justify the witness, but not to bear upon the prisoner.

Mr. WICKHAM.—General Wilkinson *is not* on his trial. Their object is not to vindicate Wilkinson, but to accuse Burr, who *is* on his trial. Wilkinson's oath is to be supported by proving papers by his oath; so that he is to support himself. This is not legal testimony, and ought not to be admitted. It is true, that these papers do not criminate colonel Burr directly, but they bear upon him by vindicating Wilkinson; and it is a sound rule of law, that what cannot be done directly shall not be permitted to be done indirectly.

Mr. WIRT.—The court does not contravene that doctrine. On Shaftsbury's trial, the grand jury wished to examine witnesses as to the credibility of a witness. Pemberton rejected such evidence, but that opinion has since been exploded. It is the privilege and duty of the grand jury to judge of the credibility of witnesses. If they have doubts of the credibility of Wilkinson, they ought to inquire into, and be satisfied upon the point. They may call upon him for an explanation as to facts and circumstances, which he can afford by the production of his papers.

Mr. HAY proposed an amendment to the court's instructions; "that any paper might be exhibited which came from the accused, or any other person proved to be an accomplice of the accused, or that formed a part, or was explanatory of the witness's narrative."

Mr. MARTIN.—The proposed alteration suits the gentleman's purpose. There is no paper under heaven, but what might be introduced as part of his narrative; even papers procured by breaking open letters from the post office, or seized by violence or robbery, might be so used under that general definition.

The CHIEF JUSTICE wished to send some specific instructions to the grand jury, to prevent the delay that might arise from their coming into court, when they had a particular paper before them, on which they would wish to obtain the instruction of the court.

Mr. HAY contended, that the alteration he had suggested was proper; and quoted authority to show, that when a man was once proved to be an accomplice or connected with another, what was in proof against the other, was good proof against him: [which see hereafter].

CHIEF JUSTICE.—Is there any authority to show that papers communicated by an accomplice can be used as evidence?

Mr. HAY.—The doctrine is, that " where a man is proved to be an accomplice, his papers may be used against another." In Horne Tooke's trial, pages 86, 87, Erskine conceded, that where the prisoner's connection with a third person was proved, the letters or papers of that third person, relating to the question before the court, were testimony against him. 1 East's Crown Law, page 97.

Mr. WIRT added, that there was no difference between the words or writings of an accomplice as evidence; in support of which he referred to the trials of Hardy, Tooke and Thelwal, [which see hereafter], and to 6th Durnford & East's Reports, p. 527, where it was solemnly determined, on the trial of William Stone, for high treason, that " a letter sent by one of the conspirators in pursuance of the common design, with a view of reaching the enemy, was evidence against all persons engaged in the same conspiracy."

Mr. MARTIN.—The cases mentioned by the gentleman are cases of treason, for a conspiracy to kill the king: it is only in such cases, where the crime consists in the imagination of the mind, " to compass the death of the king," that such testimony is admissible; but where " levying war" is the charge, the declarations or acts of third persons, however connected, cannot be admitted as evidence.

Mr. WICKHAM.—Mr. Wirt's authorities do not apply to the case of levying war. The constitution of the United States says, that no person shall be convicted except by the evidence of two witnesses, or his own confession in open court. Colonel Burr's confession out of court could not be used against him; but it seems by the doctrine of gentlemen, that the confession of others can be adduced against him.

Mr. HAY.—There are several good lawyers on the grand jury. Mr. Martin says it would take him a day to state what he had to say on this subject. It would take him his whole life to prove the distinction he contends for. Modern systems of evidence lay down the doctrine without the distinction. There is much absurdity in the distinction. The same rule ought to prevail in both cases. Levying war against the states, is a higher offence than compassing the death of the king. In the latter case, the declarations of third persons connected with the person accused, are admissible evidence: *a fortiori* they ought to be in the former case. Mr. Wickham says that confession in open court is requisite to convict. He does not understand the doctrine correctly. It is this, sir, that where a party is convicted *on his confession only*, it must be in open court: but where the confession itself is proved as evidence of an overt act, it must be proved by two witnesses. This discussion is an unnecessary waste of time; it may be thus prolonged at gentlemen's pleasure; but it is only proper to tell the jury to *ask advice when they want it.*

Mr. MARTIN thanked the gentleman for enlightening his mind; but insisted that such a construction as that contended for by him, was novel and extraordinary.

Mr. BOTTS, after some facetious remarks on the doctrine of pleas, rejoinders and rebutters, &c. as exemplified in the cause, proceeded to this effect: The declarations of persons connected in a conspiracy, are not to be received in evidence until the conspiracy itself is proved. Previously, the association and the extent of it must be proved. The association itself is not to be proved by such declarations. Such evidence is admissible under very limited restrictions. It is unreasonable and absurd for such evidence to prevail over evidence of a superior nature;

over evidence of overt acts. Neither conspiracy nor intention *is war*. The best evidence which the nature of the case is susceptible of, must be produced on all occasions. You make it out by such an unreasonably dangerous doctrine as this is, that where a guilty intention is once formed, it cannot be forsaken with safety; for if it be admissible evidence, a previous declaration may be proved against a man after he has repented and relinquished his criminal intentions.

Mr. HAY informed the court, that the grand jury had sent for doctor Bollman; that they wanted him to decypher, if he could, a cyphered letter .annexed to Mr. Willie's affidavit, and which he held in his hand. That Mr. Willie, the reputed secretary of Mr. Burr, would prove the identity of the paper, and doctor Bollman, it was expected, would interpret it.

Mr. MARTIN hoped the affidavit would be severed from the letter to which it was annexed.

Mr. HAY consented; and Willie who was absent, was sent for.

The CHIEF JUSTICE declared, that he did not wish to pronounce an opinion on the distinction as to the evidence in the two kinds of treason, without seeing authorities referred to. That he was inclined to think that such a distinction as was stated might exist.

Here the chief justice delivered the instruction, as amended, to the marshal, to be transmitted to the grand jury. It was not read in court.

Mr. HAY wished the expression concerning " *credibility*" to be struck out, as implying a doubt.

CHIEF JUSTICE.—That idea was not suggested by the court; such evidence is deemed inadmissible, except for the purpose of supporting the credibility of witnesses.

Mr. HAY wished the latter clause to be altered, as the grand jury might think themselves bound to make application to the court; and that showed the impropriety of giving such instructions at all.

Mr. BOTTS.—It is indecorous to be consuming time until the grand jury shall have returned; their own excellent understanding will condemn this conduct.

Mr. HAY.—General Wilkinson is not under examination.

Mr. WICKHAM.—Gentlemen think general Wilkinson the sole patron of the cause, but there are other witnesses.

Mr. HAY.—None who are expected to have any papers. Mr. Hay again produced the cyphered letter, annexed to Willie's affidavit, (Willie appearing in court.) He then proceeded;

This is the paper which I wish to transmit to the grand jury. It is addressed, I understand, to doctor Bollman under a fictitious name, and is all in the hand writing of Mr. Willie.

Mr. BOTTS objected to its being sent up to the grand jury; that he understood that no paper was to be laid before them, that was not material to the cause, whether it could or could not be authenticated; and that gentlemen must therefore prove both its *materiality* and its *authenticity*.

Mr. HAY.—A hard proposition indeed, when it is written partly in cyphers and partly in German! I deem it material, because I understand it was either dictated by the accused, or first written by him, and afterwards written by his secretary, and at his request; it is addressed to Henry Wilbourn *alias* Erick Bollman. I wish it to be sent up while doctor Bollman is before the grand jury.

Mr. BOTTS.—Our wishes are at issue.

Mr. WIRT.—May it not be received under the instructions already sent up?

Mr. BURR.—The paper is now in possession of the court; it is not to be sent up to the grand jury, but under the judgment of the courts; and of course the court must be satisfied with the materiality of the paper.

Mr. HAY.—The accused is mistaken in point of fact. The paper is in my possession. Though I considered myself bound to *show* it to the court according to my agreement, I have not yet delivered it, nor am I bound to deliver it.

Mr. WICKHAM.—Why was it offered to the court, if it were not to be put into their possession? If it be merely brought into court that it may be sent to the grand jury, and not considered as in possession, or under the control of the court, any paper may be conveyed to them in the same manner. Mr. Hay asserts, that it is addressed to E. Bollman. But how has it been obtained? Has it not been taken from the post-office? Has it not the post-office mark on it? Has it not been obtained by felony? He wished to see it. Mr. Hay refused to show it, and said that he would know what to do with papers hereafter. [He was understood to deny that there was any post-office mark on it; this however may be a mistake.]

Mr. WICKHAM demanded as a matter of right, that the paper should be delivered to him.

Mr. HAY.—I deny that the paper is in possession of the court, or that it was *offered* by me. If it were, I acted improperly. There is no precedent to justify the doctrine, that I was *com-*

pelled to *offer* it. A paper *offered* to the court is either *delivered* or *read*. I did *neither*. I have a right to send any paper to the grand jury, under the directions already received by them; unless it be explained by Willie and Bollman, it will be no more than an oak leaf. I hope I shall be permitted to pursue the usual and regular course.

Mr. Wickham.—If the paper be not before the court, I wish to know what is the question? Does he offer it to the court? [Mr. Hay. No.] How then can any notice be taken of it? *How* can he send it up to the jury? By the marshal? He is the officer of this court, and bound to pursue its orders. By Mr. Willie? He is but a witness and not bound to carry it. If any paper go from the prosecutor to the grand jury, it must be with the leave of the court. If a witness go up, it is because he is presumed to be a relevant witness; but if it be a paper, how can its relevancy be established, until its contents and materiality are known? If an improper paper be sent to the grand jury, the indictment may be quashed, because founded on illegal evidence. Was not the leave of the court asked? If it were, *that* put it in the power of the court. If it were not asked, the whole is improper and illegal. As to what they say they can prove respecting the paper, let them first prove it. When they *do*, the paper may be proper.

Some ingenious sparrings between Messrs. Wickham and Wirt amused the audience a moment; when,

Mr. Botts objected to the transmission of the paper. It was immaterial, or it was not. If it were immaterial, why embarrass the jury with it? If it contained pertinent matter, it was certainly wicked matter, in which Mr. Willie may be himself concerned. If he be sent to the grand jury with this paper, what would he say about it? Would the court wish him to say any thing that would criminate himself? We have a right, said Mr. Botts, to see this paper. Perhaps we shall find, that it has been filched from the post-office, contrary to the eighth amendment of the constitution, which protects every man's papers from unreasonable searches and seizures. If it has been obtained by such illegal and violent means, perhaps the court would arrest it; even the grand jury would not dirty their fingers with it.

Some desultory conversation ensued, when Mr. Willie was called to the court.

Mr. Williams, his counsel, hoped that no question would be put, the answer to which might tend to criminate himself.

Mr. Mac Rae.—Did you copy this paper?

Mr. Williams, (after consulting with his client)—He says, that if any paper he has written have any effect on any other person, it will as much affect himself.

Mr. WIRT.—He has sworn, in his deposition, that he did not understand the cypher of this letter. How then can his merely copying it implicate him in a crime when he does not know its contents?

Mr. MAC RAE.—We will change our question. Do you un-understand the contents of that paper?

Mr. WILLIAMS.—He objects to answering. He says, that though that question may be an innocent one, yet the counsel for the prosecution might go on gradually, from one question to another, until he at last obtained matter enough to criminate him.

Mr. MAC RAE.—My question is not, " Do you understand this letter, and *then* what are its contents?" If I pursued this course, I might then propound a question to which he might object; but unless I take that course, how can he be criminated?

Mr. BOTTS.—If a man know of treasonable matter, and do not disclose it, he is guilty of misprision of treason. Two circumstances, therefore, constitute this crime : knowledge of the treason, and concealment of it. The knowledge of the treason, again, comprehends two ideas : that he must have seen and understood the treasonable matter. To one of these points, Mr. Willie is called upon to depose. If this be established, who knows but the other elements of the crime may be gradually unfolded, so as to implicate him. The witness ought to judge for himself.

Mr. MAC RAE.—I did not first ask, if he copied, and then understood it? but first, if he understood it? Had he answered this question in the affirmative, I certainly should not have pressed the other question upon him, because, that might have amounted to self-crimination ; but, if he did not understand it, it *could not* criminate him.

Mr. HAY.—I will simply ask him, whether he knows this letter to be written by Aaron Burr, or by some one under his authority?

The CHIEF JUSTICE said that that was a proper question.

Mr. WILLIAMS.—He refuses to answer; it might tend to criminate him.

The court were of opinion, that Mr. Willie should answer upon oath, whether, or not, he thought that answering the proposed question, might have a tendency to criminate himself.

Here a long desultory argument ensued.

CHIEF JUSTICE.—Has the witness a right to refuse to answer?

Mr. WILLIAMS.—The knowledge of the treason, and concealment of it, amount to a misprision of treason.

CHIEF JUSTICE.—The better question *is*, Do you understand it?

Mr. WILLIAMS.—He ought not to have such a question put to him, because he might be obliged to answer " *Yes.*" He ought not to be compelled to answer, if it might *possibly* criminate him. The witness is to judge for himself, though the question may not seem to affect him. He referred to the case of young *Goosely* before referred to by Mr. Randolph.

Mr. BOTTS.—I will give Mr. Hay the benefit of an authority, 1 *Mac Nally*, 257, 258. which shows, that the possibility of *crimination* is sufficient to excuse the witness from answering.

Mr. WILLIAMS.—What the witness says here, tending to his own crimination, may be used as evidence against him on a prosecution. If he answer at all, he is deprived of the privilege given by the law, not to criminate one's self.

CHIEF JUSTICE.—If he be to decide upon this, it must be on oath. He asked Willie, whether his answering the question, whether he understood that letter, would criminate himself? He answered, It may in a certain case.

CHIEF JUSTICE.—I wish to consider the question until to-morrow.

Judge GRIFFIN to Mr. Williams.—The case of Goosely was not as you represented it. It was the court who knew, that the witness was one of those who robbed the mail.

Mr. HAY.—The doctrine is most pernicious and contrary to the public good.

Mr. WILLIAMS.—The public good does not require the conviction of colonel Burr so much as to dispense with the law.

It was then agreed that the point should be argued to-morrow, and colonel Burr's counsel promised to produce their authorities to show, that Willie could not be compelled to answer such questions, as might in his own opinion tend to criminate himself.

The court then adjourned till to-morrow.

TUESDAY, June 16th, 1807.

As soon as the court met, Mr. Hay produced and read the following letter from the president of the United States, in answer to his letter on the subject of the subpœna *duces tecum,* observing at the same time, that he read it to show the disposition of the government, not to withhold any necessary papers, and that if gentlemen would specify what orders they wanted, they would be furnished without the necessity of expresses.

Sir, Washington, June 12th, 1807.

Your letter of the 9th is this moment received. Reserving the necessary right of the president of the United States, to decide, independently of all other authority, what papers coming to him as president, the public interest permits to be communicated, and to whom, I assure you of my readiness, under that restriction, voluntarily to furnish, on all occasions, whatever the purposes of justice may require. But the letter of general Wilkinson of October 21st, requested for the defence of colonel Burr, with every other paper relating to the charges against him, which were in my possession when the attorney-general went on to Richmond in March, I then delivered to him; and I have always taken for granted he left the whole with you. If he did, and the bundle retains the order in which I had arranged it, you will readily find the letter desired, under the date of its receipt, which was November 25th; but lest the attorney general should not have left those papers with you, I this day write to him, to forward this one by post. An uncertainty, whether he be at Philadelphia, Wilmington, or New-Castle, may produce delay in his receiving my letter, of which it is proper you should be apprised. But as I do not recollect the whole contents of that letter, I must beg leave to devolve on you, the exercise of that discretion which it would be my right and duty to exercise, by withholding the communication of any parts of the letter which are not directly material for the purposes of justice. With this application, which is specific, a prompt compliance is practicable; but when the request goes to copies of the orders issued, in relation to colonel Burr, to the officers at Orleans, and Natchez, and by the secretaries of the war and navy departments, it seems to cover a correspondence of many months, with such a variety of officers civil and military, all over the United States, as would amount to the laying open the whole executive books. I have desired the secretary at war to examine his official communications, and on a view of these we may be able to judge what can and ought to be done, towards a compliance with the request. If the defendant allege, that there was any particular order which, as a cause, produced any particular act on his part, then he must know what this order was, can specify it, and a prompt answer can be given. If the object had been specified, we might then have had some guide for our conjectures, as to what part of the executive records might be useful to him. But with a perfect willingness to do what is right, we are without the indications which may enable us to do it. If the researches of the secretary at war should produce any thing proper for communication and pertinent to any point we can conceive in the defence before the court, it shall be forwarded to you. I salute you with esteem and respect.

TH. JEFFERSON.

George Hay, Esqr.

Some conversation ensued, about the specification of the papers wanted from the executive.

Mr. HAY stated, that in his communication to the president, to which this letter was a reply, he had mentioned these papers in the terms by which he thought the opposite counsel would probably have described them. The president, however, did not deem this description sufficient.

Colonel Burr's counsel then stated, that they had sent an express to Washington for these papers, with a subpœna to the president, and that it would appear on the return, whether they could obtain them or not.

The CHIEF JUSTICE recommended a certain order in the debate, and that only two counsel should speak on each side; that it would be the best course on every point of subordinate importance, for the counsel on one side to open the motion or argument, the opposite counsel to reply, and the party who opened, to close the debate, unless some new matter rendered a departure from this rule proper.

Both parties acquiesced in the propriety of this arrangement, except that Mr. Martin said, that as there was no other business before the court, there was no necessity of adhering to the rule, limiting the number of counsel to speak.

Mr. HAY hoped the rule would be observed; it would relieve himself and some other gentlemen. He then begged leave to call the attention of the court to a subject mentioned yesterday; that doctor Bollman had gone up before the grand jury. What his answers were he knew not; but he thought he ought to be sent to the grand jury with Willie, that he might interpret, and Willie could authenticate the cyphered letter; hence arose the necessity of deciding the proposition that he was a pardoned man.

Mr. BOTTS hoped, that they would not be interrupted in the discussion of the question about Willie, which they were about to begin.

Mr. HAY was willing to discuss either point first.

Here a desultory conversation ensued, in which Mr. Hay insisted that doctor Bollman was a pardoned man, and ought to communicate all he knew to the grand jury; which was denied by the other side; when doctor Bollman, addressing himself to the court, said, I have answered every question that was put to me by the grand jury.

CHIEF JUSTICE.—Is there any obligation to ask doctor Bollman if he can decypher the letter?

Mr. MARTIN.—It will be time enough to discuss that question, after the letter shall have been before the grand jury.

Mr. MAC RAE.—I wish the question now put. I asked Willie whether he understood that part of the letter which is in cypher: he could not be criminal, if he did not understand it. I wish the part which is written in German now to be explained, to show that there is nothing criminal in *it*. I wish Bollman to translate that part.

CHIEF JUSTICE.—I had rather proceed with the other point now: how far a witness may refuse to answer a question, which he thinks would criminate himself.

Mr. BOTTS.—I am glad to be relieved from the necessity of showing the versatility of gentlemen, who fly from one point to another. I am sorry they should attempt to drive us from the discussion. The oblique insinuation of Mr. Hay against Willie, seeming to presuppose his guilt from his exercising the privilege of not answering the questions propounded to him, must be answered, though it is painful for me to notice such illiberal attacks. He says, that Willie acts as if he were engaged in the conspiracy. Cannot Willie have another excuse, in seeking exemption from the examination, than conscious guilt? The attorney for the United States sees every object, connected with colonel Burr, through a *jaundiced medium*. With him " trifles light as air, are confirmation strong as proofs of holy writ." How far he might be disposed to involve this young man, upon a confession of having copied a letter in cypher, though of harmless import, I am not prepared to say. But let Willie only commit himself, so far as to make such confession, and then be called by his business to that poor unfortunate, enslaved country Louisiana, and it may be the pretext for oppressing him most cruelly. He may be seized, thrown into a dungeon, or into the hold of a ship in the most rigorous season, and be heard of no more, unless he should have the better fortune of being transported to Washington for trial. An unfortunate ignorant man should be guarded from the penalty of suspicion. The danger to be apprehended from this source is not imaginary. We have not arrived at that part of our inquiry, which is awfully terrible, and apt to rouse the indignation of our country; we shall very soon give you an awful impression

of the miseries of that ill fated territory, under the total surrender of the civil authority to military guidance. I am driven
prematurely to glance at one outrage which may serve as a
sample of the wretched state in which that section of our dependencies is. A citizen of the United States, now within the
hearing of my voice, in a time of profound peace, was seized
in New-Orleans, and, without being charged with any offence,
but merely on suspicion that he could give evidence against colonel Burr in this court, to which he was willing to come, was
committed to prison without bail or mainprize; thrown into a
stinking room with the common felons and negroes confined
there, and only taken out at last to be transported on board of
a vessel to Richmond in custody. He was hurried like a male-
factor on board, without being permitted to go to his lodgings
to get a shirt to put on. He was forced to yield, in the humility
of abject submission, to the arbitrary will of his oppressors.
Are we content to bear such enormities? A man, only *suspected of being a witness*, is subjected to military slavery. Shall
we furnish a pretext against this stranger, now called on to implicate himself, in what are called the treason and misdemeanors of colonel Burr? It has been said, that my client and his
counsel have taken much interest in this privilege. I feel interested to protect the innocence of that young man from the
vengeance of illegal power. My client feels the same anxiety.
He is solicitous that he alone should feel the pressure of unjust
suspicion and persecution.

But how did this letter come here? Foulness and violence
are betrayed in the mode of its acquisition. In the hardest and
most arbitrary times in England, papers which were seized by
force, were brought forward as evidence against the party from
whom they were taken; but succeeding times have abhorred
the doctrine; and papers found in possession of a party have
been deemed the weakest of all evidence. The foulness of that
very mark of 25 cents deserves execration.

Mr. HAY said, that there was no post mark.

Mr. BOTTS.—The " 25" on the back, is the only post-mark
of many of the country post-offices. Mr. Hay did not withhold
it on that account. How came that mark there? Will the gentleman say how the paper was acquired? If the post-office was
robbed, the possession of the paper was gained feloniously.
The constitution has provided against the seizure of papers;
and the act of congress has fixed the offence of stealing from
the post-offices. The means of obtaining the paper are unconstitutional. The end cannot be sanctioned, without maintaining
the means. It is impossible that this most detestable vice, of
the most infamous of European courts, can have been pa-

tronized by the government. By a familiarity of our rulers with such hateful practices the people would be demoralized. I claim from the counsel for the United States, as patriots, their aid to sanction my propositions, and join me in arraigning an act, which will disgrace all who had any agency in it. It must be a dreadful state of society, in which such an offence should be made the means of assisting to prove another. The principal of the government, if here, would join in the denunciation. If it behoove the government to suppress a paper thus unconstitutionally, clandestinely, and illegally obtained, if they cannot use the end without sanctifying the means, I wish, for the honour of the government, that the paper may be suppressed. I hope that in the dignity and generous spirit of Chatham, they will renounce it as unworthy of their use. It will do more mischief than the treason could, were it real.

I come now to the abstract question of law. The question put to Willie is, Do you understand that the original of this letter was written by colonel Burr?

Mr. MAC RAE.—That is not the question last put. It is, Do you understand that part of the letter which is in cypher?

Mr. BOTTS.—Very well. The gentlemen *charge* that this letter contains treasonable matter.

Mr. HAY denied it.

Mr. BOTTS.—Either the letter contains treasonable matter or it does not. If the latter, it is irrelevant and improper for discussion. If treasonable matter be contained in it, the question goes to criminate the witness. If he answer " Yes," he is infamous. The rule is, that you shall not make the witness answer a question which may tend to implicate him in moral or legal turpitude. The witness himself is the judge, how far his answer may affect him. If he were obliged to answer, that the court may judge of its tendency, he would be surrendering his protection in the means of securing it. If the answer should tend to make a single link in the chain of testimony necessary to involve him in suspicion, he has a right to decline it. The link cannot be perceived by the judges to belong to the chain, without an exposure of every other part of it. Suppose another question were put to him, How do you understand it? He must answer it, as he is to tell the whole truth. Half of the truth is not to be told. *Gilbert's Law of Evidence*, p. 134. 9 *State Trials*, 434. Another authority from an able and impartial court, which has been already referred to, shows, that although a question may be apparently innocent, yet a witness is not bound to answer it, if he think that it tends to criminate him. The question was, " What profession are you of?" The witness was a Roman Catholic priest, and the answer would have subjected him to penalties. The court *did not* know what the question would be, or how it would affect him, but the witness *did know*. His right to decline the answer was sustained. What question could, on its face, be more harmless than that resisted by that witness? Unless the witness be made the sole judge of answering, the benefit of the rule is lost to him.

If, as I have already observed, the contents of the letter be not of a treasonable nature, it is irrelevant: we know not the contents of it. Suppose the letter were written by an amorous young fellow to his sweetheart, would it be a proper subject of discussion in this case?

I shall conclude with an admonition, or an *humble* request, that gentlemen will give us a better opportunity to prepare ourselves for the defence of our rights, by possessing the court with any papers they intend to exhibit and letting us see them. It is a matter of right, that when a paper is offered for any purpose, it should be deposited with the clerk. Heretofore we have been prevented from getting a sight of any paper till the moment of discussion, and then obtained it, not without difficulty.

Mr. WILLIAMS, counsel for Mr. Willie.—I lay down two propositions which I deem incontrovertible: first, that a witness is not bound to criminate himself: secondly, that a witness is from necessity the best judge of the tendency of his answers.

To support the first proposition, I refer the court to 1 *Mac Nally*, 256, 7, 8., *Douglas*, 590., Goosely's case, in this court, where, I understand, both points for which I contend were established. If a witness admit that he knows the contents, he is guilty of misprision of treason, and if it only tend to produce that result, he is not bound to answer.

Second, The witness is to be the judge how far he ought to answer. The reason of the rule supports this position. It is given for his benefit; it is a privilege for his protection. The other rule of examining witnesses on the ' *voir dire*' before they are sworn in chief, is explanatory of this rule. A witness is asked whether he is interested in the event of the cause, before he is admitted to give evidence relative to the matter in issue. If the opinion of the person offered as a witness be, that he is interested, he is rejected as an incompetent witness. If his opinion be to exclude him in civil cases, *a fortiori*, ought it to exempt him from giving testimony in a criminal prosecution where his personal safety may be in danger? The witness only knows, what will be the answer to the question. The court cannot know it. It may discharge or criminate him. The witness must tell the court, what his answer will be, before they know it. A bystander who hears him, may be called on to fix guilt on him by his declaration. The interest of the United States cannot deprive him of his right. His saying that he cannot answer without criminating himself is on oath, and if he were to perjure himself upon that point, he would be equally ready to perjure himself on every other point. Whether public justice require an answer, is not the question; but whether the witness ought to be compelled to answer, when he believes it it would criminate or endanger him? To compel him would be a violation of a great and valuable principle of law and justice. No case can be produced wherein it has been adjudged, that a witness is first to say what he does know, and that the court is then to judge of its tendency, whether it will endanger him or not. A man is not bound to produce evidence against himself. 1 *Bl. Rep.* 37.

Mr. MARTIN.—The answer must be, " I do or I do not." Mr. Willie has been considered a secretary of colonel Burr. If he confess that he knew the contents of this letter, and they should prove to be treasonable, his continuing in the service of colonel Burr, will make him a principal in the treason. He may have written to others; the post-offices have been put in requisition.

Mr. HAY —Insinuations ought not to be thrown out against the government without evidence to support them. I am willing to communicate all that I know about that letter. It was transmitted by general Wilkinson, through the hands of Mr. Minnikin, who accompanied Mr. Willie to this place, and it was attached to an affidavit obtained from judge Toulmin. I know not whether Willie ever saw it or not.

Mr. MARTIN.—I do not charge general Wilkinson with plundering this letter, but we will hereafter prove, that they have laid violent hands upon the post-office of New-Orleans. They have a paper and know not how they have come by it. The post-office mark on it, is a presumptive proof of the violation of the post-office. Never will I mince the matter. They would not get Willie to decypher this letter if he could; but other witnesses may be used to decypher it, and it may then be evidence against him, if he acknowledge now that he understands its contents. Do gentlemen produce this letter to criminate doctor Bollman? Let him decypher this letter. If other letters are hereafter found, in the same cypher, his acknowledgment, that he can decypher the one, will make him equally responsible for the rest. By this contrivance, he and doctor Bollman may be made the instruments of their own crimination: the one being used against the other. If a witness refuse to be sworn, he is liable to be committed for a contempt of the court. *Salkeld*, 270. But there is no instance to be found where the court has committed a witness for a contempt, for refusing to answer a question, which he supposed would criminate himself. *Mac Nally*, 837. 2 *State Trials*, 124.

Mr. Botts.—It is important to know how the letter was obtained. I wish Minnikin to be examined.

Chief Justice.—That is foreign to the present discussion.

Mr. Mac Rae.—The question proposed to the witness is, " Do you understand the contents of this letter?" But, before I proceed to demand the answer, I hope we may congratulate ourselves on the situation in which we are placed. The proceedings clearly evince, that it is not our wish to withhold from the accused any, the slightest means of defending himself; and yet, the present is a spectacle very rarely exhibited in a court of justice. The counsel of the accused aiding the counsel of the witness to prevent him from being examined! I am glad, sir, that counsel is employed for the witnesses, *if thereby the accused can be benefited.* I am pleased that they have united in his defence. But I have endeavoured, in vain, to discover, whether any thing, which they have advanced, bears upon the point before the court. These gentlemen have widely wandered from it, and I feel deep regret, that they will not confine themselves to the point of law. Henceforth, I hope that they will do so, and abandon this species of warfare, and address the judgment of the court, instead of the prejudices of the multitude around.

Great part of Mr. Botts's remarks are foreign to the point. Instead of reasoning on the subject, and referring to authors in support of his assertions, he has made some strange conjectures, as to what may happen hereafter to Willie, even if the letter were innocent. That his acknowledging, that he had copied it, though its contents be innocent, may expose him, at some future day, to persecution in some distant territory; or, perhaps, doom him to be thrown into confinement into the hold of a vessel. Is not this mere declamation? can it be called argument? Does it bear at all upon the question? His remarks were certainly improper; and, perhaps, it may be improper to answer them. His observations about a distant territory are irrelevant, as are also all he has said about the manner of obtaining the letter. What connexion has this subject with Louisiana or the manner of obtaining this letter?

As to the robbing of the mail, it is all conjecture. Why has he not specified the name of the post-office, and the name of the officer? A custom prevails in those post-offices to *affix upon a letter* the name of the office, *printed* or *written.* This impression would have been sufficient to have led to the discovery: but there is none such on the back of that letter. The non-observance of the custom, in this case, repels their insinuations. As to the figures "25," they occur very frequently on the face of the letter. On the back of it, they may be a cyphered direction or caution to the person for whom it was intended: and this conjecture is as good as theirs.

Mr. Botts says, that the letter must be fraught with treason, or it is not; and that if it be not, it is perfectly irrelevant to the present case. But ought not the fact to be ascertained? Is it not material to the present inquiry that it should? But, says Mr. Botts, "if the letter be material, and Willie confess that he copied it, he will fix a crime on himself." That is not granted, sir. Willie must also understand it. Even if it be treasonable, it was no offence to copy it, unless he understood its contents. He can neither be accused nor punished for it. All that could be said against him would be, that he had ignorantly done an act, injurious to the public, with an intention to benefit an individual.

The authority in *Gilbert*, 134, cited by Mr. Botts, would apply, if the question were about the credibility of a witness. But that is not the case, and the authority is inapplicable.

They have also quoted a case from 9 *State Trials*, where a popish priest was permitted to elude a question without answering it. According to the English laws, the witness, if he confessed that he was a roman catholic, was liable to certain disabilities. There it was known to the court, as well as to the witness, that there was such a law, and that by such a confession he would subject himself to its operation. The court, therefore, did not press him for an answer. But here, it is contended, that the witness is alone the judge of the law and the fact; whether he ought to answer or not: for both the law and fact are included in the privilege, which they claim for the witness. In the cases cited by them, the court did understand the subject, and saw the danger of the witness: but here, the subject is not understood by the court; and the right of judging, whether the witness be in danger or not, is denied them. Mr. Martin cited authority in support of this principle: that courts had punished a witness for a contempt in not taking the oath, but never where he refused to answer in cases in which he might criminate himself. A court has always a right to understand the ground on which a witness refuses to answer, and every man is liable to give testimony, unless he come within certain exceptions; and in those cases, he must show some law or authority to justify his refusal to answer. Does the court possess the power of compelling a man to make oath that he will give evidence, and yet not possess that of making him comply with it? Surely, this would be preposterous.

In the case of the *voir dire*, it is not sufficient to ask a witness, if he be not interested. If he say, that he is not interested in the event of the cause, inquiries may be made into the ground of his opinion; and, if it can be proved, by other witnesses, that he is interested, he is excluded. It is never referred to the witness only. Every day's practice proves this to be the law.

The court has a right to understand the grounds of the privilege claimed by the witness. Suppose an attorney were called on to give testimony, and he should say, that his knowledge of facts had been derived from confidential communications from his client: he would not be the only judge in that case. The court would inquire, whether they were made to him in his professional or private character? The supreme court have so decided. *Cranche's Reports*, 137. and 1 *Mac Nally*, 255. substantially support this doctrine. The priest, in the case referred to, was compelled to state the ground of his refusing to answer.

The witness objects, that by answering, he may criminate himself; but the court is to judge of the tendency of the question. It *must appear*, that he *may* criminate himself. The question is, Do you understand that part of the letter that is in cypher? Whether he answer " yes," or " no," he cannot criminate himself. If he say " Yes," it cannot criminate him, unless it be coupled with other questions, and his answers to them; and unless, also, he wrote it. He may know the key to the cypher very innocently. It may have been imparted to him for the purpose of carrying on an innocent correspondence. He may know the cypher without having any connexion with its contents; or he may have acquired a knowledge of the cypher long after the letter was written. I wish gentlemen to show how he *can* criminate himself, by answering this question. They have not shown that it *will*, or that it *may*, criminate him: and if the answer will not criminate him, the United States are entitled to his evidence. If he answer " No;" if he be unacquainted with the cypher; he is innocent, and cannot be criminated.

As to the law, there is no difference in opinion. We all agree in opinion, that a witness cannot be made to criminate himself. The only dispute is about the effect of the answer. I hope, therefore, that the court will compel him to answer the question, unless it be shown, that he *will* or *may* criminate himself. I am sorry that so much time has been consumed upon so plain a question.

Mr. HAY.—I did not wish to say any thing on this frivolous question, when a subject so important ought to occupy our time. The effect of the paper is dreaded, for gentlemen discover unexampled solicitude to keep it out of view. I know not its contents. They have repeatedly asserted, that Mr. Burr was persecuted and innocent. If this be true, why do they shrink from the evidence. Integrity walks forth with a bold and erect front before the world. A man, who knows his own innocence, despises the powerless efforts of his enemies. They have consumed a great deal of time unnecessarily; and yet, charge us with wasting it. I have taken up about the fortieth part of the time occupied by the gentleman who spoke first.

I come now to the question. There are, in fact, two questions which we wish to put to the witness. 1st, Do you understand the cypher of that paper? 2d, Did the paper come from colonel Burr? was it written by him, or by his directions? The last question ought to have been first stated. The witness does not say, why the answer to the question will have a tendency to criminate him. The court cannot judge, whether his motive may not be an unwillingness to give testimony against a person to whom he is attached. He ought to answer: the court cannot decide without information from him, showing in what manner it may tend to his crimination. The meaning of the argument offered in defence of his silence, is, that he is connected with colonel Burr, and as deep in the treason as he is. Will his answering the question, " Whether he understand that cypher?" subject him to a prosecution? It certainly will not. His knowledge of the cypher is not inconsistent with perfect innocence. They say, that the question ought to be, *Has it a tendency to criminate him?* The wit of man cannot tell whether any tendency to criminate him can result from answering this question. The great rule of law, of which the cases cited are illustrations, *is this*, that a witness is not to give evidence to accuse himself of a crime, 1 *Mac Nally*, 256. *Hawk.* 609. I venture to affirm, that the gentlemen cannot produce a case, that goes as far as to say, that a witness is not to answer what may *tend* to criminate himself. But this answer will not even *tend* to criminate him, nor will it *tend* to calumniate him. The doctrine of Mr. Williams, about a pardoned man, does not apply. I contend, that a *man is bound to answer every question relating to the point in issue*, unless it subject him to a prosecution. But as to collateral points, he is not bound merely to degrade or calumniate himself. Every case mentioned has been decided on these principles. 1 *Mac Nally*, 258: The authorities there show, that a witness must make answer, unless it directly criminate him; or, what is the same thing, subject him to punishment. The objection now made by the gentlemen *was there expressly overruled.* In the case of the King v. Edwards, the question put was *objected* to, as *tending to criminate himself.* But the objection was overruled by the court; saying, " there was no impropriety in the question; *as the answer would not subject him to any punishment.*" This therefore is a decisive authority in our favour, being precisely the same point. The doctrine, cited from the State Trials, was overruled by the cases in 1 *Mac Nally,* 259. I will not appeal to the candour, but to the ingenuity of gentlemen, to show how the answer to this question can criminate the witness. The question is, " *Do you know* that cypher?" relating to the *present* time. If the letter contained guilt, and he knew it from the beginning, it might implicate him ; but we do not ask how long he has known it.

The other question, which we propose, is not whether he copied or wrote the letter, but whether it were written by Burr or by his directions? This he can say, without saying who wrote it, if Mr. Burr did not.

But it is said, that "the court is not to judge" whether he ought to answer, or whether it tend to criminate him or not. This is one of the wonderful positions in the wonderful cases resorted to by gentlemen. Yesterday they said, that it was a clear case, and that they only wanted time to look for authorities. And what have they found? Nothing to support their position, though I have produced an authority, directly in point, against it. I ask, if this doctrine be not a prostration of the rules uniformly prevailing in all courts of justice? The court ought to judge every point of law arising collaterally or incidentally in a cause. The witness, from caprice or corrupt motives, may refuse to answer the question. Is it not strange that the court should politely say to a witness, " You have been sworn to tell the whole truth, but you *may be silent if you think proper,*" without assigning any reason for it ? I expected something like authorities to prove, that the witness had a discretion to answer or not. *Douglas* 593, stating, that a man was not bound to answer whether he were a roman catholic or not, might as well have been introduced to prove any thing else. The answer there, if in the affirmative, would subject immediately to disabilities, but here it cannot.

As to Goosely's case, I know nothing of it. Judge Griffin and Mr. Williams differ in their statements concerning it; but if that case be contrary to the uniform current of authorities, it is not binding. In Cooper's case the decision is contrary to law, and has been disregarded since.

The CHIEF JUSTICE.—The decision in Cooper's case was only that the accused had not a right to obtain papers from the public offices for certain purposes.

Mr. HAY.—That decision, that papers shall not be obtained from the public offices, does not apply to the present case.

[Here, Goosely's case was produced, and part of it read from the manuscript report of Mr. Daniel Call, (a gentleman well known as an able lawyer and correct reporter) and which case, in substance, is as follows: Goosely was indicted for felony, under the 16th and 17th sections of the act of congress establishing the post-office and post-roads within the United States, for robbing the mail of some bank notes. On his trial, "the attorney for the United States called —— Reynolds, an accomplice with the person, against whom an indictment for the offence had been preferred, but which had been found "not a true bill" by the grand jury. Randolph and Wickham, counsel for the prisoner, objected to his testimony, on the principle, that the witness was not bound to give any evidence which might implicate himself. The attorney admitted the general principle, but denied its application, and insisted that he might give evidence. The court determined, "that he was a competent witness;" but judge Iredell observed, (and judge Griffin concurred) that "he *could not be compelled to answer a question leading to an implication of himself;* and that it was very probable, that the jury would pay but little attention to a fact, which they were satisfied was but partially related." He was asked, whether he knew of any bank notes being taken out of the mail by the prisoner? He answered, none, but what he was jointly concerned in. The court said he was not bound to tell any thing that might "tend to criminate himself." The jury returned a verdict for the prisoner of not guilty, and he was discharged."]

Gentlemen prove a thing which is not denied, and say that they have gained a victory. 4 *State Trials*, 414, seems to countenance the doctrine on the other side. In 1 *Mac Nally*, 258, the court perhaps knew the situation of the man, and that it would criminate him; but it is here decided, that where the court knows not the situation of the witness, or whether his answer would subject him to punishment, they will leave it to the witness.

Mr. Williams says, that the answer itself must be given to enable the court to judge whether it will criminate him. But certainly the court may inquire into the circumstances, to discover why he will be endangered. A man who says that he is interested, even if he be not, is disqualified; because he is under a bias if he think so, whether the fact be that he is or is not interested. In that case, it is an objection to the testimony of a witness who is offered. This, on the contrary, is a question of exemption of privilege, claimed by the witness to excuse him from giving testimony; a duty incumbent on all, except interested persons. In the case of Marbury v. Madison, it was decided, that "*a witness may state his objections,*" and the witness did state his objections and they were sustained; but here the witness refuses to state his objections. He is silent, and refuses to explain.

Mr. Botts says, that the letter is irrelevant. To this I answer, that *this* can only be ascertained by discovering its meaning. The gentlemen declaim about plundering the post-offices. We deny it: let them prove it. I could talk of a detestable plot to plunder a city and rob a bank, as subservient to the execution of projects of unprincipled ambition; but, I will not do it till a future day. They scatter ambiguous words with a view to excite public suspicion and discontent. They insinuate, that this depredation has not only been committed, but that it was countenanced by general Wilkinson, and the president of the United States. But it ought to be proved before they allege it in a court of justice. But suppose the letter had been in the post-office, and it had been voluntarily delivered by the postmaster, on discovering that it contained a treasonable plot, to the commander in chief, in order to prevent the treason; would this have been criminal or improper? It has always been the practice to intercept letters to prevent treason. It is founded on necessity, and dictated by the laws of self-preservation. As to Mr. Martin's position, that a witness may be committed for refusing to be sworn, but not for refusing to answer —

CHIEF JUSTICE.—Mr. Martin's position was, that a witness might be committed for refusing to be sworn; but not for refusing to answer, *when he thinks the answer would criminate him.*

Mr. HAY.—If that be the law, it does not justify the refusal of the witness, in this case, to answer. The cases are not alike. No authority would be found, after their most industrious researches; because no case could be found similar to this case. I trust, therefore, that the witness will not be permitted to judge for himself; but that he must answer our question, as it cannot be shown that it will endanger him.

Mr. WIRT.—Very little is left for me to say, after the able arguments of my respectable associates; but, if I cannot add to their arguments, I will try not to obscure the subject. We ought indeed to render thanks to the gentlemen for keeping us from gaping, by the multiplicity of their motions and interludes. They have made so many points as to form a perfect *chevaux de frise* in the stream of the prosecution, and to place an insurmountable bar between the prisoner and justice. This is the true mode to get the prisoner off at all events; but not the way to get him off with honour. If they wish to remove the blot in his escutcheon, they must submit to a candid examination of all the testimony; they must cease their constant efforts to stifle the evidence that operates against him.

The gentlemen have assumed what is not proved, that Willie is an accomplice. But all their arguments and inferences founded on this assumption must be unavailing. We do not, and will not, admit that he is an accomplice till it be proved: but, if an accomplice may be a witness, *a fortiori* a person who is not an accomplice may certainly be a witness: and that an accomplice may be a witness, can be clearly shown by many respectable authorities. I refer the court to 1 *Mac Nally*, 192, 193, 194. 2 *Hawk*. 608. *Gilb*. 122. Why should the law make an accomplice a witness, unless the court had a power to interrogate him? This man cannot shelter himself from giving testimony, but by showing some legal privilege or exemption. 1 *Mac Nally*, 247. 253, 254, 255. All these authorities are strong and applicable; but the last is directly in point. It is there stated, as clear law, that the " claim of exemption from giving evidence is scrutinized with a jealous eye; and the person relying upon it, must establish his right, by showing a positive law, or express authority." There it was determined, that it was no cause of exemption that the knowledge, which " the witness had of the matter in issue, arose from a confidential communication made to him, in the exercise of his clerical functions; and which the principles of his religion forbade him to disclose;" and that every man is bound to discover what he knows of the matter in " issue unless he be specially exempted and protected by law." They say, that the witness is exempted by a rule of law. I will examine what that rule is. It is laid down in *Hawkins*, 609, *book* 2, *chap*. 46, *sect*. 20. that " it is a general rule, that a witness shall not be asked any question, the answering of which might oblige him to accuse himself of a crime." This, sir, is a narrow rule, which they have blown up into an immense magnitude. If the answer of the witness include guilt, he is not bound to speak. Unless it oblige him to accuse himself of a crime, he must make answer to any question propounded to him; but what are the limits to the rule they contend for? What are the limits of " *a tendency* to *criminate?*" Any question may *indirectly* and *remotely* have a tendency to criminate or to produce any other effect. The rule they insist on, is almighty and boundless: any witness may thereby screen himself from giving evidence against a person to whom he is attached. Like the Cretan labyrinth, it can never be traced nor pursued; and if the witness once get into it, you never can extricate him from it. Does the witness know, that the answer he is to make to this question, has a tendency to subject him to legal prosecution or punishment? I contend, that the precise question put, must contain the criminating matter; and that therefore a question, to which an answer must criminate, must be put before the court can arrest the inquiry. If we put questions, to which answers may be made, without such an effect, the witness must answer them. This question requires no such answer. If we afterwards put a question to which the answer must subject to a prosecution, it will be then time enough to arrest us. If the letter be treasonable, and he were to answer " Yes" to the question, whether he knows the cypher; and if he knew it to be treasonable from the first, he might be endangered; but many links are wanting to make a chain to bind Willie. Accomplices may be witnesses, but they say, they must not be compelled to give evidence that may *tend* to criminate them. *Tendency* unlimited, brings the rule to nothing. But I will meet them plainly. If we ask the witness if he be guilty of treason, and he answer " Yes," his confession cannot be used against him. The " confession in open court," mentioned in the constitution of the United States, applies to confessions on arraignment, and to no other. It will puzzle the learning of Mr. Martin to show a case of a witness being exempted from answering questions applying to the point in issue. The exemption, in the cases they rely on, extends only to collateral points. Cases are frequent in the books, where witnesses are examined to points, to defame or convict themselves, where they are questioned as to the issue. The cases in *Mac Nally*, are always of questions put, not touching the issue. In the trial of *Reading*, 2 *State Trials*, *p.* 802. 806. 822. the question was to a collateral point. It was so in the earl of Shaftesbury's case, in 3 *State Trials*, 418; and so it is in all the cases. They are not permitted to wander out of the track to defame witnesses. A confession by a witness, on oath, does not bind him, because it is not voluntary. 2 *State Trials*, 123. *Christopher Love's case.* Jackson's examination in that case, exactly resembles this of Willie. It proves, too, that he was committed not merely for refusing to swear, but also for refusing to tell the whole truth. If Mr. Martin say it was merely for refusing to take the form of the oath, what benefit would his taking the oath produce, if he were not to answer the questions put to him? That was only the case of an accomplice about to be interrogated as to the point in issue, and a difficulty was raised. This is a very simple point; and the only way to authenticate this letter is by the evidence of this witness. The prisoner is a great lawyer. Is it supposed he did not guard his footsteps? Would he call two witnesses to the letter? We want it not to go to the grand jury, until we prove it his offspring, by this witness, who would not tell one truth against him, if he could help it. They put their hands on his mouth to prevent him from telling any thing he knows; and he is so eager to secure the safety of colonel Burr, that he employs counsel himself, to prevent him from being obliged to reveal what he knows against him. I trust, therefore, that this witness will be compelled to answer our questions.

Mr. MARTIN proposed to go on with the argument to-morrow.

Mr. HAY wished it to go on this evening; that the public

convenience required, that the evidence should be introduced at this time to the grand jury.

Mr. MARTIN.—I will endeavour to answer first, the gentleman who spoke last. He says that we have made more points than ever were made before; to which I answer, that no prosecution was ever conducted like this. He says that we ought to court the fullest investigation. What! without the means of repelling their unjust attacks, and the misrepresentations of their witnesses. The privilege is not colonel Burr's, but that of the witness. As to accomplices being witnesses, they may be, and sometimes are so voluntarily, but never otherwise. As to the witness employing counsel, he is right to do it to protect himself. His own character and life may be endangered, and the counsel for the defendant are not wrong in assisting to protect the witness. A *great lawyer* in the case of Callender did the same; and there is no impropriety in either case; both are proper.

Mr. Wirt said that he would not follow the same track which we had travelled. He has indeed followed different principles. In all the cases which he has cited, the accomplice came forward voluntarily; but he could not have been compelled to give testimony: there the objection went to the credibility not to the competency of the witnesses. The accomplice having confessed, cannot afterwards refuse to answer. He states, also, that an accomplice being a competent witness by law, cannot be privileged from giving testimony, without a special exemption. Now all accomplices are persons expressly excepted by the law, unless they waive their privilege, and voluntarily come forward and swear.

Mr. WIRT.—I deny that Mr. Martin stated my argument correctly. It is not a confession that makes an accomplice a witness. Confession does not prevent his being a witness; but it is not necessary to make him one. This doctrine is that of approvers.

Mr. MARTIN.—All the cases are, where the accomplice comes forward voluntarily.

Mr. WIRT.—Porter's examination, in *State Trials*, was a compulsory examination of an accomplice.

Mr. MARTIN.—That case is not authority. It is an arbitrary doctrine. They have two strings to their bow, or rather two stools to sit on, the treason and misdemeanor; that they may repose on the one, should the other fail them: but we trust that both will fail them. The case of compulsory examination applies to treason only. Lord Audley's was a case of rape, not of treason. I know not why Christopher Love's case was introduced, unless it were to show the coarse language used in those days by prosecutors and judges. There is nothing else remarkable in it. A man refused to swear, and he was committed for it. That a witness may be committed for not swearing, but not for not answering questions, is said to be my argument, and very uncandid deductions are made from what is called my position. I never was so weak as to think or to say, that a witness was obliged to be sworn; and yet that he might withhold testimony, and be silent at *his whim and pleasure*. No, sir, my position was only, that a witness, having a legal reason for refusing to answer, was never committed; and so far is it from being dependent on his *whim*, that he must swear to the existence of this legal reason; and as much reliance is to be put on his oath, on this point, as on any other.

I ask the gentlemen to produce any authority to show, that a witness can be compelled to answer, where he thinks it can criminate him; but no such authority exists. As it was now late Mr. Martin said, that he could not finish his argument to-day, but hoped that the court would adjourn; and that he should be permitted to add some observations to-morrow.

The court then adjourned till to-morrow morning, at the usual hour.

WEDNESDAY, June 17th, 1807.

Mr. HAY stated to the court, that many remarks had been made yesterday, respecting the letter addressed to Winburn (in cypher); that it had been insinuated, that it had been taken improperly, if not feloniously from the post-office; that this was evidently done to affect the character of general Wilkinson, who having been informed of it, wrote him the following note on the subject :

Richmond, June 17th, 1807.

SIR,

The letter addressed to Winburn, was delivered to me by Charles Patton, of the house of " Meeker, Williamson & Patton," New-Orleans; and he informed me, was transmitted in the inclosed envelope. Respectfully I am, sir, your obedient servant,

JAMES WILKINSON.

George Hay, esquire.

Mr. MARTIN requested to know, *who* opened the letter, or *who* first broke the seal?

The court said, that this was a question which was not now before it.

Mr. BOTTS said, that at a proper time, they would bring it before the court, as a substantive and independent inquiry.

Mr. Martin said, that general Wilkinson was not a proper witness to remove suspicions from himself. He then resumed the argument which he left unfinished yesterday.

The great question is not, whether the witness ought to answer or not? But whether he is not the sole judge, whether his answer to the question will criminate him or not? I contend that he is, and if it were otherwise, the provision in his favour would be nugatory. He ought to answer no, question, if it tend or lead to criminate him.

The first gentleman who spoke for the prosecution, on this point, manifested candour. He advised us not to wander from the question. The advice was good; I wish they had followed their own advice. If good advice had been followed, the post-offices would not have been violated. Was their advice given as a caution by these kind indulgent friends? Or was it to excite prejudices against colonel Burr? Many and strong attempts have been made to prevent a fair trial. The newspapers, and party writers, are employed to *cry* and *write him down*. His counsel are denounced for daring to defend him. The passions of the grand jury are endeavoured to be excited against him, and the very judges denounced if they do not decide against him, at all events! The laws of the country, on the contrary, presume every man innocent till he be convicted. How then can such proceedings be justified? On the trial before the petit jury, I admit that they may declare as counsel that Burr is guilty; but at this stage of the proceedings, every observation should be avoided that may create or excite prejudices either on one side or the other. I hope that the zeal of gentlemen will be moderated, and that they will remember the benignity of the law, which declares, that it is better, that ten guilty men should escape unpunished than that one innocent man should be punished.

Gentlemen say, that they are about establishing the relevancy of the paper. They do not know its contents, yet they take it for granted, that it is material, because we oppose it. Heretofore it has been the invariable practice to *know*, in such cases, and to *produce*, evidence both of the contents and the relevancy of such exhibits. Suppose the letter were written in the French language, they must procure a translator before they could read it as testimony. Yet they cannot compel any body to translate it against his will. A person ought to be specially sworn as an intrepreter, to translate truly and faithfully. If they could not translate it themselves, they ought to have procured some person to do it, for the court is not bound to find a translator.

The gentlemen say, that there is this distinction, that a witness is not compelled to answer where the point to which he is questioned is not in issue, but that he must answer where it is in issue. No such distinction exists. " No evidence ought to be admitted to any point, but that on which the issue is joined." This is manifest from *Mac Nally*, *p.* 2, and is the first rule of evidence therein stated. The court is to judge whether the evidence be pertinent to the issue or not.

Mr. HAY.—That is what we want.

Mr. MARTIN.—I am not arguing about that; but demonstrating, that no such distinction exists. I refer the court to *Hargrave's Index to the State Trials*. "A witness is not compelled to answer where it *tends* to criminate him, nor where it does not relate to the issue."

Mr. HAY and Mr. WIRT wished to see the pages referred to.

Mr. MARTIN.—They are cases in the second *State Trials*, and already commented upon. I cite this authority only to show Hargrave's opinion. He certainly is of opinion, that if a witness imagines a question has a tendency to criminate him, or subject him to a penalty, he is not bound to answer it.

Mr. Martin then read Hoffman's argument in the trial of Smith, to show the question put to Ogden, concerning the Leander's destination. He also quoted the question put to Mr. Ogden, relative to his first acquaintance with Miranda; when the court appeared to be of opinion, and admitted the principle, that Mr. Ogden was not bound to answer any question which might criminate himself, but yet declared that he should answer these questions put to him, page 95, 96, 98.; and added, that Talmadge's opinion was of no consequence, but which was not admitted by the counsel on the other side.

Mr. HAY.—It is irregular, to read the arguments of counsel as authority.

CHIEF JUSTICE.—It is regular to read them only as arguments.

Mr. HAY requested Mr. Martin to read the arguments in the same case, on the part of the prosecution.

Mr. MARTIN, after some conversation on this point, read the words of the prosecutor, in the same case, and the argument of Colden, for the defendant, and a part of the arguments of Mr. Edwards, one of the counsel in the same case. There, it was evident that the court was wrong. There was a question refused by Ogden to be answered. From the arguments and observations of counsel, I infer, that they waived their right to enforce the law against Ogden. They declined at that time calling on the court to enforce its decision, in respect to Ogden's answering, but said, that they did not waive the right to call upon him thereafter; but they never exercised it. From which it may be reasonably inferred, that they had not the fullest confidence in the opinion of the court, but thought it erroneous or doubtful.

As to the case of the United States against Goosely, the counsel merely objected from memory; Mr. Wirt only read a part of it from Call's manuscript report of it, p. 140. But why did not the gentleman read the whole of that case? If he had read another part of it, it would have explained the law much more fully, and proved that a witness could not be compelled to answer a question, which might *tend* to implicate or criminate himself. [Here the case of the United States v. Goosely was fully read. *Vide ante, p.* 222.]

Here then is a decisive authority that my position is correct, as far as the opinion of one very respectable judge (judge Iredell) goes.

Mr. Martin then read from *Mac Nally, p.* 258. the authority relied on by the other side, the case of the King against Edwards, accused of grand larceny. One of his bail was asked whether he had not stood in the pillory for perjury? The question was objected to as tending to criminate him, but over-ruled. He said, that both in England and Maryland, and in every state whose laws he had had occasion to investigate, the law exempted in penal cases a witness from criminating himself. This case, in *Mac Nally,* 258. and 4 *Term Reports,* 440. is the only authority relied on as establishing the opinion, that a witness may be examined as to matters that make him infamous. It means, where a witness has been convicted of an infamous crime, and has *suffered* the *execution* of the judgment, that he may be questioned as to that fact. That was a case where bail was called on to justify as to the sufficiency of his property, and the objection was to his credibility, on account of his former infamy, where he had been punished, but could not be subjected to any further penalty. I doubt, however, this authority. The prosecutions for treason in England have been generally conducted with candour and gentleness. These authorities, (or rather this authority, as there is but one case) however they may be justified, are more rigid, than formerly. They are of modern invention. The mild maxim of the law is, " *nemo tenetur seipsum accusare.*" Even after a man is pardoned for a crime, he is not bound to show his own former turpitude or infamy: 2 *State Trials,* 822. An additional authority on this point is 1 *Mac Nally,* 212. rule the sixth, where it is said, that " whenever the competency of a witness is objected to, on the charge of conviction and judgment on an infamous crime, the party making the charge must produce in the court the record of the judgment, *sub pede sigilli,*" which shows, that such evidence could not be extorted from the witness himself. There was no instance of such doctrine until the decision of the King v. Edwards, in 4 *Term Reports.* Until that decision, the rule of law was sacred, that a record was necessary to be produced to prove perjury. The relaxation of the law, with respect to witnesses, is for the benefit of the party, because he does not know what witness will be brought against him. *Peake*, 88. explains this to be the reason. That a witness may be asked, whether he had been convicted and punished? 4 *Term Reports*, 440. was a decision in the year 1791, since the revolution. It may be no authority. We do not know, whether our courts of justice will adopt this law-rule or not. It has not been adopted in Maryland. It has no bearing on the question. The true question is, whether the court has a right to inquire into the circumstances, or whether the witness is the sole judge, whether he ought to answer or not? Let us revert to the authorities before cited by us. *Mac Nally*, 256. " Hilsley, a roman catholic witness, being again asked by Titus Oates, by virtue of his oath, whether the house where he lodged, at St. Omers, was not governed by priests and jesuits ?" That was apparently an innocent question; but as it might be made a link in a chain of testimony, that would criminate him, the chief justice said it was not a question fit to be asked, and told the witness that he was not bound by his oath to answer it. *Mac Nally* has put in, that he was a roman catholic priest, but nothing appears (in the report of the same case in *State Trials*) to the court, of his being a priest. The court determined that they were not to go into the circumstances; because, thereby, facts, criminating the witness, would be disclosed, in order to show how an answer to the question would criminate him, so that by his answer, he would lose the privilege of the law. In the case of the *voir dire*, if a witness think himself interested, he is excused from being sworn. We admit, that in this case, the witness may be sworn; but insist that he is not to answer questions which he thinks may tend to criminate him. His being interested, ought to exempt him from giving evidence, as in the case of the *voir dire*. There is no difficulty in going into circumstances on the *voir dire*. Disclosures can do no injury. But it is not so, if he think himself interested: he is excused, without any examination into circumstances. This rule is laid down explicitly in *Mac Nally*, 140. that " if a witness think himself interested, although, in point of fact, he is not, he should not be examined as a witness." *A fortiori*, in a case where his honour, fame, and life are in question, if a witness think that his answer will criminate him, he ought not to answer. Does it not apply with tenfold force? It would drive men to perjury, if witnesses were compelled to answer in such circumstances; and lord *Mansfield* has always laid it down as a great maxim, that men ought not to be exposed to temptation.

But it is said, that if an attorney be called to give evidence, the court ought to decide whether he ought to be excused, and that he is not judge for himself. By analogy, this is in our favour. The privilege belongs not to the attorney, but to the client. The court in such cases, only asks him, whether his client made the communication to him as an attorney, or otherwise? but the court goes no farther. So in this case they ought only to ask the witness, if he think his answer will criminate him? and it is impossible to obtain from him an explanation of the effect of his answer, without taking away from him the protection of the law.

If he gave it secretly to the judges, they might be compelled to reveal it, however confidentially communicated. The authority in 1 *Cranch*, in the case of Marbury v. Madison, is said to be conclusive in their favour. I thank them for adducing it. It is strongly in our favour, because there, the witness was not compelled to give the evidence required. Gentlemen say, that they disapprove of part of the authority; and so I disapprove of so much of it as declares that the court did not think themselves empowered to issue the mandamus to the secretary of state. They say, that in that case, the witness was bound to state, and did state his objection to answer. We admit it, and we state our objection. The witness says, " It tends to criminate me," and this objection is sufficient.

But gentlemen say, that we have produced no authority in support of our argument. I insist that the opinion of judge Iredell in Goosely's case, and the case referred to from 9 *State Trials*, are conclusive in our favour. The attorney for the United States has told us, that he expected a great deal would be said by us, but it would not produce conviction on his mind. We hope to convince the court, but we do not expect to produce conviction on the impenetrable mind of Mr. Hay, which is harder than Ajax's seven-fold shield of bulls' hides. I do not think it necessary to say more, than once more to express our hopes of a favourable decision.

Mr. WICKHAM.—I shall add a few remarks to what has been already said, and trust that the importance of the subject will be my excuse. I mean, that the principle is of very great importance; for as to the paper, it is of but little.

They contend that colonel Burr is liable for the letters of persons connected with him, however remote the connexion, and whatever may be the contents of the letters. This principle is too general, and more dangerous than it is comprehensive. We do not admit it, either in its application, or in the extent insisted on. It may be construed in the most dangerous manner. Blannerhasset, stated to be connected with him, is said to be imprudent and of a singular turn of thinking. Is colonel Burr to be responsible for all his actual and verbal eccentricities, merely because he was acquainted with him? I thought before, that no man was liable for the acts of another, unless done by his authority or contrivance. Though we do not admit principles contended for by the gentlemen on the other side, (which we sincerely believe to be unjust and unfounded,) yet as it is not impossible but the court may decide against us, it is our duty to oppose them. This is a governing principle which may run through the whole cause, and will apply to every other similar evidence. We deem it our indispensable duty to oppose the testimony now adduced, to affect colonel Burr with the acts of others. Was it fair to sound so much alarm and prejudice throughout the whole country, because we stated and availed ourselves of these legal objections? I am not well acquainted with that branch of the science which is called *criminal* law, and I hope to become less so; but I had always thought, that more protection was necessary, and afforded by the law, for the rights of individuals, in criminal than in other cases. If other prosecutors act like these, I am mistaken. I never knew before, declarations made against any person for standing on the rules of law. I never knew before, that a citizen is to be reviled for adhering to the laws of his country. The court ought to stop gentlemen who make such an objection.

But it is said, that "public prejudice is excited by his mode of defence!" If his claiming legal rights excite prejudice, we need not try him, but convict him at once without a trial. The witness ought not to be compelled to answer. The examination of facts leads to the discovery which he seeks to avoid. He is on his oath. If he commit perjury in answering this interrogatory, he would do so in any other case. The questions asked a (roman catholic) witness, what business he had at St. Omers six years before, and what profession he was of, are innocent questions; yet in both instances, the witness was excused from answering, because he thought it would criminate him.

They tell us, " that this objection admits the guilt of colonel Burr." No, it only admits that he is under prosecution. Does it not endanger this young man of being arraigned, if he own connexion with colonel Burr. Is not an innocent man in danger of conviction by perjury? The whole strength of the government is exerted against the prisoner. The government would not suborn witnesses; but bad men might think to render an acceptable service by swearing falsely against a party under prosecution. The danger is real, though the party accused is innocent.

As to Goosely's case, gentlemen suppose me mistaken. Mr. Wm. Marshall's (the clerk of this court) recollection corresponds with mine. Our remembrance is confirmed by Mr.

Randolph, who was counsel in the cause, and by the judge. Reynolds was an accomplice, and was proved, by the finding of the grand jury on the record, to be an innocent man, and it was determined that he was not bound to give testimony against Goosely, because it might tend to criminate himself. The case is the same here. Willie, the secretary of, is connected with, Burr. They might send up to the grand jury a bill of indictment against him, if they did not think him too insignificant. The witness, like most other men, may estimate his own importance more highly than others might be disposed to do. A question, " where were you on such a day?" is an innocent one; yet, as it might tend to criminate him by being connected with other evidence, the court excused a witness from answering it. The question at present before the court is of the same nature, and his answer may be made, with the aid of other testimony, to criminate him.

As to the authority from *Mac Nally*, that a man is bound to answer the question, whether he had been punished for a crime or not? I shall observe, that a man's answering, whether he had been punished, cannot injure his character, because the punishment is public : if it were private, he would not be compelled to answer. Every man is indifferent until sworn. He ought to refuse to be sworn to any inquiry tending or leading to implicate him. The secret is locked up in his own breast : you cannot know that such a secret exists until he be examined, and you have no right to extort it from him to his own injury. I am sorry that so much time is consumed on so plain a question; but as it is important, as it respects the progress of the investigation, I hope we shall be excused.

Here some conversation ensued between Mr. Wirt and Mr. Martin, respecting the legal authorities referred to by Mr. Wirt, and supposed to have been admitted by Mr. Martin.

After some further desultory conversation, the chief justice asked whether there were any other question before the court?

Mr. MAC RAE requested a decision on Dr. Bollman's case, as he wished to interrogate him about the cyphered letter.

Mr. WILLIAMS was ready to discuss the question.

Mr. BURR.—There will arise some very important questions, affecting the very sources of the jurisprudence of this country. I have several affidavits to produce, to show that improper means have been used to procure witnesses, and thereby contaminate the public justice: when these proofs have been duly exhibited, it will be the province of the court to decide, whether they will not arrest the progress of such improper conduct, and prevent the introduction of such evidence.

Mr. Botts.—I rise to apprise the opposite counsel, that there are three or four questions of considerable importance, which we shall bring forward as soon as possible. Two or three days ago, I commented upon the plunder of the post-offices; and I assure the counsel for the prosecution, that I shall probe that subject to the bottom; as no man can be more anxious than myself, that the stigma which this transaction attaches to the inferior or superior officers of the government, should be wiped off. As a private citizen, or as counsel for my client, I shall be sincerely pleased with a fit opportunity of retracting the expressions which I have employed. The court will at once perceive the necessity of going into this inquiry at a very early period; for if the officers of government have hitherto broken open letters from colonel Burr, they may hereafter resort to the very same expedient; and by thus obstructing the very medium of communication between colonel Burr and his witnesses, prevent him from summoning them, and preparing for his defence. One more remark: yesterday I understood Mr. Hay to charge us with having made certain insinuations against persons not actually named. He demanded, why we had not forborn these charges, until we were prepared to support them? That remark, sir, struck me with peculiar force. I was of the same opinion, that some proof ought to be produced; I immediately rose and professed my wishes to go into an investigation of the case. But, sir, little did I expect that the gentleman would have proceeded to have justified these crimes. Little did I expect that such felonious transactions should have been blazoned into mighty virtues, or that it would have ever been maintained in this court, that the persons who had failed to plunder the post-offices, would have been guilty of a dereliction of their duty. The offer to go into the evidence operated as magic: he justified what he had before denied. I wish, sir, to explore the post-office laws to see whether they do not contain some provision, prohibiting the introduction of testimony, thus illegally obtained.

Chief Justice.—Unless these allegations affected some testimony that was about to be delivered, how can you introduce this subject?

Mr. Hay informed the court, that colonel Morgan was at that time before the grand jury, and they had sent for a letter, from Aaron Burr to him. Should the letter (holding it in his hand) be sent to the grand jury?

Mr. Botts requested to see it. Here, said he, is a small piece of newspaper attached to it, which ought not to accompany it before the grand jury.

Mr. Burr.—I have no objection that any of my letters should be sent up; but I trust, sir, it will be separated from this bit of a newspaper, and this comment which Mr. Morgan has attached to it.

The letter was handed to the Chief Justice; who observed, that the only use of the newspaper was to show, that at that time colonel Burr was at Pittsburg.

Mr. Hay said, it was nothing more than to refresh his memory.

The Chief Justice decided, that it was right to dissever it from the letter: the newspaper itself was no evidence; but if colonel Morgan would wish to refresh his memory, there could be no objection. They were accordingly separated by the directions of the court, one was sent to the grand jury, and the other to colonel Morgan.

Mr. Burr.—The court has very properly demanded some proof of the relevancy of our proposition. Sir, we are ready to prove the violation of the post-office. We are ready to fasten it on individuals now here, and we are ready to name the post-offices, if the court require it, which have been thus plundered. When it comes out, that evidence has been thus improperly obtained, we shall say, sir, that it is contaminated by fraud. I will name three persons who have been guilty of improper conduct, in improperly obtaining letters from the post-office, to be evidence against me. These are Judge Toulmin, of the Mississippi Territory, John G. Jackson, a member of congress, and general Wilkinson. Two of these persons are within the reach of this court. As well as the improper manner in which they have procured affidavits and witnesses against me, I mention these circumstances for two reasons: First, that the facts may be proved to the satisfaction of the court; and, second, that the court may lay their hands on testimony thus procured.

Mr. Botts.—The circumstance of the post mark proves that the post-office was robbed of that letter; therefore it is not evidence.

The Chief Justice said, let the consequences be as they may, this court cannot take cognisance of any act, which has not been committed within this district. That mark is not necessarily a post mark. The court can only know the fact, in a case to which it applies, except to commit and send for trial.

Mr. Hay.—Let some specific motion be made, and the evidence procured; and if there have been any crime committed, let the offenders be prosecuted according to law. These gentlemen know the course; and I most solemnly promise to discharge the duties of my office, whether they bear against general Wilkinson, or the man at the bar. If the crime have been committed, it is not the province of the court to notice it, till after an indictment has been found.

Mr. Botts.—We only wish to prove, and prevent a repetition and continuance of this improper mode of proceeding. The proof will affect general Wilkinson.

Chief Justice.—If it did affect general Wilkinson, it could not prevent him from being a witness.

Some desultory conversation here ensued, when Mr. Burr observed, that he was afraid he was not sufficiently understood, from mingling two distinct propositions together. As to the subject of the post-offices, it might rest for the present; but as to the improper means employed in obtaining testimony, they were at this moment in actual operation. Some witnesses had been brought here by this practice; and it was one which ought immediately to be checked: he did not particularly level his observations against general Wilkinson. He did not say, that the attorney for the United States ought to indict, or that such a crime if committed out of this district was cognisable by the court, unless it be going on while the court is in session, or the cause depending; in those cases improper practices, relative to crimes committed out of the limits of this court, may be examined, and the persons committing them attached. Such practices have been since I have been recognised here, and they ought to be punished by attachment.

Mr. Wirt.—I do not yet understand the gentlemen. What is the object of their motion?

Mr. Botts.—We shall hereafter make it; we have no other object by the present annunciation, than to give gentlemen a timely notice of our intentions.

Mr. Burr.—We have sufficient evidence on which to found our motion.

What motion? demanded Mr. Hay.

Mr. Burr.—I thought, sir, I had sufficiently explained my intentions. I may either move for a rule, to show cause why an attachment should not issue against judge Toulmin, John G. Jackson, and general Wilkinson, or what is sometimes, though not so frequently practised, I may directly move for an attachment itself.

Mr. Mac Rae.—At whose motion?

Mr. Burr.—At the public's.

Mr. MAC RAE.—A pretty proceeding indeed! that the public prosecution should thus be taken out of the hands of the public prosecutor, and that the accused should supersede the attorney for the United States!

Mr. BURR.—A strange remark indeed! As if it were not the business of the injured person himself to institute the complaint.

Mr. HAY.—I wish for further explanation. Let the specific charge, on which their motion is founded, be clearly pointed out and reduced to writing.

Mr. BURR.—The motion will be for an attachment, for the irregular examination of witnesses, practising on their fears, forcing them to come to this place, and transporting them from New-Orleans to Norfolk.

At this moment Mr. RANDOLPH entered the court, and observed, that if he had been present, he would have, himself, opened this motion; which was intended to operate immediately upon general Wilkinson, and ultimately upon some other persons. Mr. Randolph here read the motion which he would have submitted to the court.

Mr. HAY protested against this proceeding; which was calculated to interrupt the course of the prosecution; and was levelled at general Wilkinson alone. He asked, why these hints? Why these mysterious looks of awe and terror, with which gentlemen come into this court, as if they had something to communicate which was too horrible to be told? Was Mr. Randolph (when attorney general, it is presumed he meant) ever interrupted in the midst of one prosecution, by introducing another? Do they wish to intercept general Wilkinson from going to the grand jury? Mr. Hay claimed from the court, a priority for the business of the United States. Let the present prosecution be concluded; and gentlemen may then proceed with their investigation into the conduct of general Wilkinson.

Mr. RANDOLPH.—The gentlemen, sir, will understand this subject much better to-morrow. I understood the motion was to be postponed till to-morrow; but as he asked for some intimation of our designs, I thought proper to accompany it with a few remarks. And, sir, if this affair be really so stupendous, as I conceive it to be, if it be true, [Mr. Hay exclaimed that it was not.] is it not entitled to the most serious inquiry? If this subject bear upon the present case, though it may influence the result of the trial, ought it to be suppressed? Your honour will direct me when to come out; and I assure your honour, that it is not merely conjecture, but fact. I shall come forward with the affidavit of one of the witnessess to support our motion.

Mr. MARTIN.—The gentleman is on his heroics. He will protest where? In the Argus, I suppose. He hopped up like a parched pea, to make his protest against our motion. He insists that we shall postpone it till the trial is over, and the evil is done!! The court and grand jury may be engaged in twenty different prosecutions at the same time. We shall prepare our motion, and make it to-morrow.

Mr. HAY.—I hope the court will decide not to hear it till this business is over. My protest will not have the tenth part of the effect of the *attic wit* of Mr. Martin. I have a great deal of *feeling*, but it is not such as can be excited by the elegant comparisons of that gentleman. Comparisons are always odious. This is expressive of contempt, and is viewed as it ought. Mr. Hay then expatiated at some length. He understood the object of this motion was to affect the credibility of general Wilkinson's testimony; and in what way? He presumed that the court would not notice the pretended transactions which had been alluded to, in any other way, than as amounting to a contempt. As to any other offence against the laws of the United States, the true course would be, to proceed in the way of a presentment, or indictment in the regular way. Now, what are the principles of the law of contempt, in relation to this subject? General Wilkinson is said to have taken the depositions of certain persons in New-Orleans, and then to have brought these reluctant witnesses hither by military force. This is the only ground of the contempt against this court? But how can a contempt be committed? Either by directly insulting this court, or abusing its process, or interrupting its justice. Will it be said, that general Wilkinson's conduct comes under either of those descriptions?

Gentlemen have very often been pleased to put words into our mouths; and on one occasion, they have made us to say that general Wilkinson is the " pivot of the prosecution." And is it this very pivot which they are now attempting to remove or pare down, by this precipitate application? It is my duty to vindicate him from this unjust charge, which is as immaterial as it is unjust. Are the communications between the court and the grand jury to be thus interrupted? Is their examination to be suspended, until general Wilkinson has been put upon his trial? If these suspected transactions do amount to a contempt of this court, it is not my business, officially to notice it. It is of no consequence to them whether they prevail in their motion or not; their purpose is attained; their pompous declamation, that Wilkinson is a despot, and acted tyrannically, is intended to excite prejudice against him.

Mr. Hay then said, that he should move to postpone the motion of gentlemen, until the prosecution was over; for several reasons: because it would necessarily interrupt the business before the court; because it was intended to impeach the credit of a witness; and because this inquiry could be as well conducted after as before the prosecution.

Mr. Mac Rae.—I will affirm, sir, in the presence of this court, and the surrounding people, that the charge now adduced against general Wilkinson, is completely unfounded. I affirm, that no witness has been brought forcibly by general Wilkinson from New-Orleans; one individual came reluctantly escorted; who, refusing to obey the summons of the government, was regularly brought before a magistrate, for his disobedience, and dealt with according to the due course of law; and who is now in the custody of a person before this court. All the rest came as good citizens ought to have done; and the only fault which can possibly be attributed to them, if it be a fault, is, that they came in the United States vessel, in which general Wilkinson was authorised to come.

Mr. Wickham.—May I request the liberty, sir, of making a few remarks upon Mr. Hay's motion? Colonel Burr brought forward his motion in the simplest style possible. There was no imputation; there was no attempt to excite the public feelings. He merely stated his object in the most general terms; he ought to have been understood. The gentlemen, however, misunderstood him. They required a specification of our designs; we gave it to them in writing, and then we promised to bring forward our motion to-morrow. They still insisted upon a more particular explanation of our points; and Mr. Randolph rose and spoke to gratify them. Nothing, however, seems to please those gentlemen. They not only found fault with the motion, but the looks of Mr. Randolph. He will scarcely, however, change his face to please them. It is precisely such as God Almighty gave him.

Mr. Hay, sir, has got into parliamentary habits; and talks very fluently of the previous motion. These things are novel to me, who am a mere lawyer. On this motion, I will make but one remark. The constitution has divided the powers of the government among these great departments; the legislative, executive, and judiciary. These must be kept separate and distinct, not only in their duties, but in their practice. The legislature act upon *expediency*, the judiciary act upon *right*. The gentleman, however, seems to think himself suddenly transported to the legislative hall; and no doubt, would soon think it very convenient to hang colonel Burr. He tramples all our judiciary forms under foot; if we make a motion before the court, he soon trips up the heels of ours with his previous motion; but he has no right to do so. And where is his doctrine to end? We certainly have the same rights which they have; and as they have moved the previous question, we move, sir, that the court shall not hear their motion. This will be ringing the changes without end: it is a new invention. It is better that we send these parliamentary distinctions to the other side of the house, where they ought for ever to remain.

Mr. Hay says, that this motion ought not to be made *pendente lite*, and that he ought to be tried like other people. Sir, colonel Burr ought to have the same justice meted out to him, which is meted to every other person. He stands here on the same footing, and with the same privileges, as any other citizen in his situation. I assert, that any, other man would have a right to this attachment; and that the motion ought to be made *pendente lite*, if at all. " Why, (they loudly ask us) does he make it at this time?" " Why does he not postpone it till after the prosecution?" Why, sir, when colonel Burr is discharged, (and I hope he will shortly be so) he may not be disposed to trouble the court any further. How long this prosecution will last, no one knows: perhaps a week; perhaps longer. It is already gone so far beyond our expectations, that it is impossible to conjecture. Now, sir, may not similar contempts occur? Is it not necessary to restrain certain people, by convincing them, that such practices make them liable to punishment? But they say, that these charges are no foundation for a motion. Our object is not to inflame the public mind: facts will suffice. And what has general Wilkinson done? He has brought witnesses with him from New-Orleans, by military force. He has taken their depositions entirely *ex parte* at the point of the bayonet; yet there is no horror in all this, for the purpose of keeping their testimony straight! I lay down this broad position: that the man, who goes about collecting affidavits upon affidavits, corrupts the fountains of justice. We have already seen a volume of such at this bar. [Mr. Hay. Did they come from New-Orleans?] I did not say from New-Orleans. I might have particularly mentioned Mr. Jackson, who comes here with the depositions of witnesses, who are thus bound hand and foot, thus tongue-tyed, because their depositions had been taken. Sir, I saw them in this very court examining witnesses with affidavits in their hands, and comparing the one with the other: depositions taken not by commission, but *ex parte*. When an interested agent thus goes about collecting depositions, and with ignorant men, shaping them just as he pleases; I aver, that they are contrary to law, and to the spirit and genius of our government; that they are a contempt upon this court, if done during the prosecution, by interfering with the purposes of justice. Such men are liable to an attachment, from the very moment when the government took possession of colonel Burr's person; not from the moment of his first arrest, but from the time when they ordered Perkins to conduct his prisoner from Fredericksburg to Richmond.

The gentleman has enumerated three species of contempt: but the enumeration is certainly imperfect. Does the gentleman know nothing of prosecutions for libels on the court or on the parties? The publication of a handbill against a party is a contempt of the court, because the administration of justice is affected by it. All acts to defeat justice, or to influence the public mind *pendente lite*, are, for the same reason, contempts of the court. Such contempts have been punished in Europe and in this country. I repeat it, that whoever does any act to influence the administration of justice is liable to an attachment. But they say, our object is to affect general Wilkinson. He is a competent witness, however arbitrary he may be. His credibility will be judged of from all the circumstances. Does general Wilkinson shrink from the investigation?

Mr. HAY.—You know he does not.

Mr. WICKHAM.—The attorney for the United States charges us with interrupting the prosecution. Our motion is founded on right, and we will prove its truth. He need not attend to it. If the court have not the right to grant our motion, we shall lament it. We hope the court will hear our motion to-morrow.

The CHIEF JUSTICE said, that the pendency of the prosecution was no objection to hear the motion: but it was another question, whether there were any grounds for it or not; and that the court would not say, that a motion, relating to the justice of the case, ought not to be heard.

Mr. HAY wished it postponed to a later day; and insisted, that admitting the charges were true, they could have no legal effect on the prosecution. He said, he would repeat his motion to postpone the inquiry.

Mr. MARTIN and Mr. BOTTS denied it; and after some desultory conversation, the court adjourned till to-morrow.

THURSDAY, June 18th, 1807.

As soon as the court met, the CHIEF JUSTICE delivered the following opinion, in the case of Willie:

In point of law, the question now before the court relates to the witness himself. The attorney for the United States offers a paper in cypher, which he supposes to have proceeded from a person, against whom he has preferred an indictment for high treason, and another for a misdemeanor, both of which are now before the grand jury; and produces a person, said to be the secretary or clerk of the accused, who is supposed either to have copied this paper by his directions, or to be able to prove, in some other manner, that it has proceeded from his authority. To a question, demanding whether he understands this paper, the witness has declined giving an answer, saying, that the answer might criminate himself; and it is referred to the court to decide, whether the excuse he has offered be sufficient to prevent his answering the question which has been propounded to him.

It is a settled maxim of law, that no man is bound to criminate himself. This maxim forms one exception to the general rule, which declares, that every person is compellable to bear testimony in a court of justice. For the witness, who considers himself as being within this exception, it is alleged, that he is, and from the nature of things must be, the sole judge of the effect of his answer: That he is consequently at liberty to refuse to answer any question, if he will say upon his oath, that his answer to that question might criminate himself.

When this opinion was first suggested, the court conceived the principle laid down at the bar to be too broad, and therefore required, that authorities in support of it might be adduced. Authorities have been adduced, and have been considered. In all of them, the court could perceive, that an answer to the question propounded might criminate the witness, and he was informed, that he was at liberty to refuse an answer. These cases do not appear to the court to support the principle laid down by the counsel for the witness, in the full latitude in which they have stated it. There is no distinction, which takes from the court the right to consider and decide, whether any direct answer to the particular question propounded, could be reasonably supposed to affect the witness. There may be questions, no direct answer to which, could, in any degree, affect him; and there is no case which goes so far as to say, that he is not bound to answer such questions. The case of Goosely in this court is, perhaps, the strongest that has been adduced. But the general doctrine of the judge in that case, must have referred to the circumstances, which showed, that the answer might criminate him.

When two principles come in conflict with each other, the court must give them both a reasonable construction, so as to preserve them both to a reasonable extent. The principle which entitles the United States to the testimony of every citizen, and the principle by which every witness is privileged not to accuse himself, can neither of them be entirely disregarded. They are believed both to be preserved to a reasonable extent, and according to the true intention of the rule and of the exception to that rule, by observing that course which, it is conceived, courts have generally observed. It is this:

When a question is propounded, it belongs to the court to consider and to decide, whether any direct answer to it can implicate the witness. If this be decided in the negative, then he may answer it without violating the privilege which is secured to him by law. If a direct answer to it *may* criminate himself, then he must be the sole judge what his answer would be. The court cannot participate with him in this judgment, because they cannot decide on the effect of his answer without knowing what it would be; and a disclosure of that fact to the judges would strip him of the privilege which the law allows, and which he claims. It follows necessarily then, from this statement of things, that if the question be of such a description, that an answer to it may or may not criminate the witness, according to the purport of that answer, it must rest with himself, who alone can tell what it would be, to answer the question or not. If, in such a case, he say, upon his oath, that his answer would criminate himself, the court can demand no other testimony of the fact. If the declaration be untrue, it is in conscience and in law as much a perjury as if he had declared any other untruth upon his oath; as it is one of those cases in which the rule of law must be abandoned, or the oath of the witness be received.

The counsel for the United States have also laid down this rule according to their understanding of it; but they appear to the court to have made it as much too narrow as the counsel for the witness have made it too broad. According to their statement, a witness can never refuse to answer any question, unless that answer, unconnected with other testimony, would be sufficient to convict him of a crime. This would be rendering the rule almost perfectly worthless. Many links frequently compose that chain of testimony, which is necessary to convict any individual of a crime. It appears to the court to be the true sense of the rule, that no witness is compellable to furnish any one of them against himself. It is certainly not only a possible but a probable case, that a witness, by disclosing a single fact, may complete the testimony against himself; and to every effectual purpose accuse himself as entirely as he would by stating every circumstance which would be required for his conviction. That fact of itself might be unavailing; but, all other facts without it would be insufficient. While that remains concealed within his own bosom, he is safe; but draw it from thence, and he is exposed to a prosecution. The rule which declares, that no man is compellable to accuse himself, would most obviously be infringed, by compelling a witness to disclose a fact of this description.

What testimony may be possessed, or is attainable, against any individual, the court can never know. It would seem then, that the court ought never to compel a witness to give an answer, which discloses a fact that would form a necessary and essential part of a crime, which is punishable by the laws.

To apply this reasoning to the particular case under consideration: To know and conceal the treason of another is misprision of treason, and is punishable by law. No witness, therefore, is compellable by law, to disclose a fact which would form a necessary and essential part of this crime. If the letter in question contain evidence of treason, which is a fact not dependent on the testimony of the witness before the court, and, therefore, may be proved without the aid of his testimony; and if the witness were acquainted with that treason when the letter was written, he may probably be guilty of misprision of treason; and, therefore, the court ought not to compel him to answer any question, the answer to which might disclose his former knowledge of the contents of that letter.

But if the letter should relate to the misdemeanor and not to the treason, the court is not apprised that a knowledge and concealment of the misdemeanor would expose the witness to any prosecution whatever. On this account, the court was, at first, disposed to inquire, whether the letter could be decyphered; in order to determine from its contents, how far the witness could be examined respecting it. The court was inclined to this course from considering the question as one, which might require a disclosure of the knowledge, which the witness might have had of the contents of this letter when it was put in cypher, or when it was copied by himself; if, indeed, such were the fact. But, on hearing the question more particularly and precisely stated, and finding that it refers only to the present knowledge of the cypher, it appears to the court, that the question may be answered without implicating the witness; because, his present knowledge would not, it is believed, in a criminal prosecution, justify the inference, that his knowledge was acquired previous to this trial, or afford the means of proving that fact.

The court is, therefore, of opinion, that the witness may answer the question now propounded.

The gentlemen of the bar will understand the rule laid down by the court to be this:

It is the province of the court to judge, whether any direct answer to the question, which may be proposed, will furnish evidence against the witness.

If such answer *may* disclose a fact, which forms a necessary and essential link in the chain of testimony, which would be sufficient to convict him of any crime, he is not bound to answer it so as to furnish matter for that conviction.

In such a case, the witness must himself judge, what his answer will be; and if he say, on oath, that he cannot answer without accusing himself, he cannot be compelled to answer.

Mr. WILLIAMS (counsel for Mr. Willie) stated, that he had misunderstood him the other day in court, and in a subsequent conversation had obtained more accurate information. He does understand a part of that letter.

Mr. HAY requested, that Mr. Willie should be called into court.

When he appeared, Mr. Hay interrogated him. Do you understand the contents of that letter? Answer, No. Mr. Willie afterwards said, that he understood the part of the letter which is written in Dutch.

Mr. HAY.—Was this letter written by the hand or the direction of Aaron Burr?

Mr. WICKHAM objected to the question.

CHIEF JUSTICE.—The witness and his counsel will consult.

Mr. HAY repeated the question. Mr. Willie. Yes. Mr. Hay. Which? By his hand, or his direction? Mr. Willie. By his direction. It was copied from a paper written by himself.

Mr. HAY.—I wish this paper to be carried to the grand jury. I presume there can be no objection.

Mr. BOTTS.—No objection! We call upon you to show the materiality of that letter.

Mr. HAY.—I deny the necessity of any such thing. Until this letter be decyphered, it will be perfectly unintelligible to me, and to the grand jury. It is no more than a blank piece of paper.

Mr. WICKHAM.—I had always understood before, that the testimony, which is laid before a grand jury, must not only be legal in itself, but proved to be material.

Mr. WILLIAMS begged leave to interrupt the gentleman. Mr. Willie is anxious to be particularly understood. He says, that this cyphered letter was first written by colonel Burr, and afterwards copied. But it is the cypher only, which has been copied from colonel Burr's original.

Mr. HAY.—It is quite sufficient, sir. If colonel Burr wrote the cyphered part, he will be considered the author of the whole.

Mr. WICKHAM.—The gentleman has started a curious proposition indeed! I had always understood before, that the whole included the part; but it seems now, that the part is to comprehend the whole.

Mr. HAY.—The remark of the gentleman may be wit, sir, but he certainly knows, that it is not law.

CHIEF JUSTICE.—Can you get this letter decyphered?

Mr. HAY.—Is Erick Bollman in court? I wish him to be called. These gentlemen demand proof of the materiality of this letter. Is this a question about which the court will interfere? Can the court think it proper to require the materiality of this cyphered letter to be proved, before it is sent up to the grand jury? We may turn the very favourite argument of gentlemen against themselves. This letter is either material to the present case, or it is not. If it be material, how can they object to its production? And if it be perfectly immaterial, what injurious consequences can result from its being sent up to the grand jury?

Mr. BOTTS.—I never supposed that it could be a question, whether an immaterial paper could be exhibited before the grand jury? This question has been frequently decided in the nega-tive. On the trial of Smith and Ogden, judge Patterson solemn-ly decided against such a proceeding. Were papers permitted to be laid before a grand or a petit jury, before their materiality was proved, it would produce an endless confusion, and waste of time. In *Washington's Reports* there is a case, where the court of appeals inferred error, because an inferior court had permitted the introduction of an immaterial paper; and this too, was in a civil case. Even if the grand jury have called for it, it ought not to be sent to them, before its materiality has been shown to the satisfaction of the court.

Mr. MAC RAE.—Would it not be as proper, sir, to compel every witness, before he is sent up to the grand jury, to state the substance of his testimony, as it is to require proof of the materiality of a paper? This inquiry, however, is never made. The only qualification which is required about a witness is, that he should be a legal competent witness; not that he should be sworn to be a material one. The very same principle is applica-ble to this paper. After it is proved to be relevant testimony, is it necessary that an inquiry should be made into its materiality? In fact, how can any such proof be given, when the letter itself is principally in cyphers?

Mr. WICKHAM.—Mr. Mac Rae has demanded authorities; I have prepared none at present, sir, because I could not sup-pose that any were necessary. As to his argument, that no in-quiry is to be made into the materiality of a paper to be sent to the grand jury, because none is made into that of a witness, it does not apply. When a witness is sent up before a grand jury, it is presumed that his testimony is relevant to the case. The only question is, *is* he a competent witness? And it is only on the ground of incompetency, that his testimony is not legal. If com-petent, he is a legal witness; he is sworn, and is forced to an-swer such questions as may be put to him by the grand jury. If, however, he refuse, they then call upon the court to interpose its jurisdiction; and the inquiry will then be, whether the question be material and proper? As to papers, they are not to be received at all, unless they are shown to be relevant to the case. And where is the limit to this species of proceeding? Suppose, in this search after papers, all the private letters of colonel Burr should be brought up; all the most secret actions of his life should be written down, and brought hither to be submitted to public inspection; will the court indulge them in such a wide inquisition?

CHIEF JUSTICE said, he had in some measure anticipated this question, and had reflected upon it; his opinion was this : a paper, to go before the grand or petit jury, must be relevant to the case, even if its materiality were proved. Why send this letter before the grand jury, if it cannot be decyphered? If it can be decyphered before the grand jury, why not before the court? Let it then be decyphered, and its relevancy may at once be established.

Mr. HAY.—Is there no difference between any other paper and a cyphered letter proved to have been originally written by Aaron Burr?

CHIEF JUSTICE.—Still this letter may not be relevant to the present case.

Mr. HAY then directed Erick Bollman to be called into court, that he might be interrogated as to its contents. He requested that the court would indulge him for a short time, until he could execute some important business before the court of appeals.

The court accordingly suspended the prosecution.

At half after one o'clock, the court again resumed the business; but neither doctor Bollman, nor Mr. Hay appeared.

A few minutes after the court had resumed its business, Mr. John Randolph entered at the head of the grand jury, and addressed the court:

May it please the court: One of the witnesses, under examination before the grand jury, has answered certain questions touching a letter in cyphers. The grand jury understand that this letter is in the possession of the court or of the counsel for the prosecution. They have thought proper, to appear before you, to know whether the letter, referred to by the witness, be in the possession of the court?

CHIEF JUSTICE observed, that as the letter was wanted by the grand jury, a witness having referred to it, that was sufficient to establish its relevancy, and directed it to be delivered to them.

Mr. MAC RAE hoped, that before the grand jury retired they would be informed, that a witness had proved that this letter was originally written by Aaron Burr.

Mr. WICKHAM.—And I hope, they will also be informed, that the superscription on that letter has not been proved to have been written by colonel Burr. The witness did not, and would not, say that he knew the superscription to have been written by him.

The grand jury then retired, and the court adjourned till to-morrow, eleven o'clock.

FRIDAY, June 19th, 1807.

As soon as the court met, Mr. BURR addressed them. He stated, that the express, that he had sent on to Washington with the subpœna *duces tecum*, had returned to this city on Wednesday last, but had received no other than a verbal reply from the president of the United States, that the papers wanted, would not be sent by *him;* from which I have inferred, said Mr. Burr, that he intends to send them in some other way. I did not mention this circumstance yesterday to the court, under an expectation that the last night's mail might give us further intelligence on the subject. I now rise to give notice that, unless I receive a satisfactory intimation on this subject before the meeting of the court, I shall, to-morrow, move the court to enforce its process.

CHIEF JUSTICE handed down to the bar a copy of a letter addressed from doctor Erick Bollman to the chief justice. It was not publicly read, and for that reason Mr. Hay declared that he should not make any remarks upon it.

Mr. Burr's counsel called James Knox and Chandler Lindsley, (two of the witnesses of the United States) whose affidavits had been drawn and were intended as the ground of the motion for an attachment against general Wilkinson.

Mr. HAY interrupted the motion, by stating, that he himself had a motion to make to the court; and *that* was, for leave to send up such written interrogatories to the grand jury as he thought proper to put to certain witnesses. His reason was, that some of these witnesses would voluntarily depose to as little as possible; that the grand jury might not always know the particular questions to be proposed to them respectively, and to what point to shape their inquiries; that he himself better knew what they would say, (having seen their depositions); and that his interrogatories might probably aid the jury in their investigation.

Mr. MARTIN.—I shall object to this motion, unless it be qualified by giving us the same privilege. We cannot send up our witnesses to the jury, but we may send up our interrogatories. We will assent to the motion of the attorney for the United States upon the condition that he will assent to ours.

Some conversation ensued upon the motion for an attachment; when the CHIEF JUSTICE asked, if the papers could not be put into his hands, and the argument take place to-morrow; that he wished to consider the question before it was discussed.

Mr. HAY approved of this course. It would prevent the public exhibition of these affidavits, which were drawn up for he sole purpose of defaming general Wilkinson, and thereby making an improper impression on the public mind with respect to the trial of Aaron Burr; and had been obtained from persons who were willing to say any thing to answer the purposes of the accused, but very reluctant to give any evidence on behalf of the United States. That these were voluntary affidavits of these reluctant witnesses, whose connexion with the accused would one day be known. If the *place where*, and *persons by whom* they were dictated, were considered, the court would see that the object was to prejudice the surrounding multitude against general Wilkinson; that they had such deadly hatred against him, that if they could but *sink him*, they were regardless of sinking themselves; but, that the integrity and patriotism of that man would soon be known to all America; that he had merely glanced his eye at a single expression in one of these papers, which was as impudent a falsehood as ever malignity had uttered. The court might compare these papers with the law, and determine whether they would justify an attachment or a rule to show cause, and that the court, if they entertained any doubts, might then direct an argument; but *then* he hoped that the witnesses would be examined in court.

Mr. RANDOLPH spoke at considerable length. He had been disposed to postpone this subject till to-morrow; but, from the moment when he heard Mr. Hay's anticipating speech he was opposed to all delay. He had produced documents to support his motion; and yet, according to Mr. Hay, it was dictated by nothing more than the policy to defame general Wilkinson. Mr. Hay had wandered into the very error which he had charged to us. He had called upon the court to defend the character of general Wilkinson, the defender of his country, who is to come through the fiery furnace purer than gold; and yet he has himself charged the witnesses now before the court with malignity and rancour! That general Wilkinson was subject to the legal consequences of his own illegal acts, and ought to be punished; that the affidavits were to the point, and ought to be read: they would show that he practised a system of tyranny from the commencement.

Mr. Botts.—Why do gentlemen object to the present motion being heard, when they have so often insisted upon their own right to be heard by the court? Why do they reproach us with shrinking from the evidence, when they are attempting to screen their favourite witness, general Wilkinson, from a fair investigation of evidence? The witnesses ought to have been under the protection of the court. Their countenances do not bespeak devils: they are like other men; but they are branded as villains. Does Mr. Hay desire that the characters of these men should be immolated to this saviour of his country? that their fair reputation should be sacrificed to save his? The constitution has recognised the equality of man. Though those gentlemen may not be decked out in the tinsel ornaments of military grandeur, their rights as citizens, and the respect due to their characters, are the same as those of any other men. If Wilkinson be able to go through the fiery ordeal, put him on his trial. If *his* private declarations to Mr. Hay are to be set against *their* oaths, let it be tried. I desire for them to be put on trial as well as general Wilkinson. Put them in one scale, and him in the other. We hope our motion will be heard.

Mr. Mac Rae, at some length, expatiated upon the impropriety of animadverting at this time upon the character of general Wilkinson. The court had already said, that no step should be taken, which would affect the justice of the case; and it was therefore much better for the court to pursue the suggestion which it had thrown out; to examine the papers in private, and see whether the affidavits were relevant to the point, than to prejudice the justice of the case by a public exhibition of these affidavits; that he was prepared to vindicate his character; but this was not the time, and he wished the cause to be conducted regularly; that the motion ought to be reduced to writing, and the court would then decide on it, and the affidavits together.

Mr. Wickham protested against the secret tribunal to which gentlemen wished to resort, for stifling inquiry and murdering character. That gentlemen complained of the waste of time, but they themselves wasted the most by previous questions. The gentlemen who have made these affidavits are upon their oaths. Is it right, said he, for the counsel to charge them with perjury, and yet not give them an opportunity of vindicating their veracity? If an expression escape our lips, we are charged with forestalling the public opinion. In every instance they wander into bold assertions and violent invectives. Is Wilkinson's character too sacred for public investigation? We have a right to be heard, and insist on it.

Mr. Hay denied having made any such assertion. He had merely alluded to one expression in their affidavits, which was too monstrous to be believed. But why all this feeling on the present occasion, when gentlemen have so often charged general Wilkinson with perjury?

Mr. MARTIN.—When did we charge him with any other perjury, than that of violating the constitution which he had sworn to support? Is not this notorious? Are not Swartwout and others here to prove it? We did not say that general Wilkinson was ready to perjure himself; but merely that he had every thing now at stake, and would go almost all lengths to hang colonel Burr.

Mr. WICKHAM insisted on their right to go on with their motion; that the court only wished to get the affidavits to understand their arguments better; but even the court could not deprive them of the right to be heard as advocates.

After some other discussion, Mr. Burr agreed to place the papers in the hands of the court, and to waive his motion till to-morrow.

CHIEF JUSTICE.—Reduce the motion to writing. [This was done.]

Mr. BURR.—It is only upon the affidavits of Knox and Lindsley, that we move for a rule to show cause why an attachment should not issue against general Wilkinson.

Mr. MARTIN hoped, as colonel Burr had postponed his motion, the attorneys for the United States would postpone theirs.

Mr. HAY refused, upon the ground, that the witnesses were now before the grand jury, and that his interrogatories would be necessary to direct their inquiries; that he knew the testimony better than they did, and in saving time, he wished to promote their convenience and to put them on the track to get the *whole truth*.

Mr. BURR.—I instructed my counsel to consent to this motion upon the condition, that I should also be permitted to send counter-interrogatories; and the way to get the whole truth is to send interrogatories on both sides.

Mr. HAY did not feel himself at liberty to acquiesce in such a proposition. He would rather trust to the distinguished intelligence of the grand jury.

Mr. MARTIN said, that in his practice of nearly thirty years, he had never known interrogatories to be sent to a grand jury; that such a practice had never been known in the whole history of jurisprudence.

CHIEF JUSTICE said, that the court was unwilling to declare its opinion before it heard argument on that point; that the practice was uncommon in America, because indictments usually suggest enough to a grand jury; that there was no objection, in principle, to interrogatories, but that the witnesses ought to be fully examined; that witnesses were only on one side, and therefore they should relate *all* they *knew* on both sides.

Mr. WIRT.—Though the practice is unknown in America, yet in Shaftesbury's trial, questions were put by the attorney general, the court, and the grand jury; but the intelligence of this grand jury will save us this trouble.

Mr. BOTTS.—I wish you had found out this before.

Mr. WIRT.—It is time enough.

Mr. RANDOLPH.—The case cited by Mr. Wirt, shows, that interrogatories on one side only are not admissible. The court was counsel for the prisoner.

CHIEF JUSTICE.—I do not recollect whether at that time a prisoner were allowed counsel or not.

Mr. HAY.—If the court allow interrogatories by both sides, to be sent to the grand jury, I am not willing to send any. I never heard of such a case.

CHIEF JUSTICE.—Nor hath the court; but as the grand jury are only to examine witnesses on behalf of the prosecution, if they are to be aided by interrogatories, the principle of equal justice requires, that the witnesses should disclose all they know, on one side as well as on the other, and that the interrogatories should be sent by both sides.

Mr. BURR stated that he recollected no instance of interrogatories sent to a grand jury, except in Kentucky, in the prosecution against himself. That Mr. Davies, the attorney for the United States, had drawn up some interrogatories, which were shown to him, and with some slight alterations suggested by himself, were sent to the grand jury.

Here some conversation ensued relative to the form of the motion for an attachment against general Wilkinson. The counsel for the United States insisted upon a specification of the conduct, for which it was to issue; that if generally expressed as a " contempt of the court," nothing but the spirit of divination could enable him to discover the specific offence charged against him, nor to prepare for his defence; that the precise circumstances which constituted the offence ought to be particularized.

Mr. Burr and his counsel said, that the specification was to be found in the two affidavits, and that it was from delicacy to gentlemen, he had not attempted to make these affidavits matter of record, by introducing them on the face of the motion. The motion reduced to writing, stated the offence to be " for a contempt in obstructing the administration of the justice of this court." The court then adjourned till to-morrow, eleven o'clock.

SATURDAY, June 20th, 1807.

The court met according to adjournment. Present, the same judges as yesterday.

Mr. Randolph rose to proceed with his motion, when he was interrupted by Mr. HAY, who spoke to this effect:

I have a communication to make to the court, and to the counsel of the accused. The court will recollect the answer which I received from the president, to my letter respecting certain papers. He stated in that letter, that general Wilkinson's letter of the 21st October had been delivered to Mr. Rodney, the attorney-general, from whom he would endeavour to obtain it. By the last mail I have received this letter from the president on the same subject.

Washington, June 17th, 1807.

SIR,

In answering your letter of the 9th, which desired a communication of one to me from general Wilkinson, specified by its date, I informed you in mine of the 12th, that I had delivered it, with all other papers respecting the charges against Aaron Burr, to the attorney-general when he went to Richmond; that I had supposed he had left them in your possession, but would immediately write to him, if he had not, to forward that particular letter without delay. I wrote to him accordingly on the same day, but having no answer, I know not whether he has forwarded the letter. I stated in the same letter, that I had desired the secretary at war to examine his office, in order to comply with your further request to furnish copies of the orders which had been given respecting Aaron Burr and his property; and, in a subsequent letter of the same day, I forwarded to you copies of two letters from the secretary at war, which appeared to be within the description expressed in your letter. The order from the secretary of the navy, you said you were in possession of. The receipt of these papers has, I presume, so far anticipated, and others this day forwarded, will have substantially fulfilled the object of a subpœna from the district court of Richmond, requiring that those officers and myself should attend the court in Richmond, with the letter of general Wilkinson, the answer to that letter, and the orders of the department of war and the navy therein generally described. No answer to general Wilkinson's letter, other than a mere acknowledgment of its receipt in a letter written for a different purpose, was ever written by myself or any other. To these communications of papers, I will add, that if the defendant suppose there are any facts within the knowledge of the heads of departments, or of myself, which can be useful for his defence, from a desire of doing any thing our situation will permit in furtherance of justice, we shall be ready to give him the benefit of it, by way of deposition through any persons whom the court shall authorise to take our testimony at this place. I know indeed that this cannot be done but by consent of parties, and I therefore authorise you to give consent on the part of the United States. Mr. Burr's consent will be given of course, if he suppose the testimony useful.

As to our personal attendance at Richmond, I am persuaded the court is sensible, that paramount duties to the nation at large, control the obligation of compliance with its summons in this case, as it would, should we receive a similar one to attend the trials of Blannerhasset and others in the Mississippi Territory, those instituted at St. Louis, and other places on the western waters, or at any place other than the seat of government. To comply with such calls, would leave the nation without an executive branch, whose agency nevertheless is understood to be so constantly necessary, that it is the sole branch which the constitution requires to be always in function. It could not, then, intend that it should be withdrawn from its station by any co-ordinate authority.

With respect to papers, there is certainly a public and private side to our offices. To the former belong grants of lands, patents for inventions, certain commissions, proclamations, and other papers patent in their nature. To the other belong mere executive proceedings. All nations have found it necessary, that, for the advantageous conduct of their affairs, some of these proceedings at least, should remain known to their executive functionary only. He, of course, from the nature of the case, must be the sole judge of which of them the public interest will permit publication. Hence under our constitution, in requests of papers from the legislative to the executive branch, our exception is carefully expressed, " as to those which he may deem the public welfare may require not to be disclosed," as you will see in the inclosed resolution of the house of representatives, which produced the message of January 22d, respecting this case. The respect mutually due between the constituted authorities in their official intercourse, as well as sincere dispositions to do for every one what is just, will always insure from the executive, in exercising the duty of discrimination confided to him, the same candour and integrity, to which the nation has in like manner trusted in the disposal of its judiciary authorities. Considering you as the organ for communicating these sentiments to the court, I address them to you for that purpose, and salute you with esteem and respect.

TH: JEFFERSON.

Accompanying this letter is a copy of the resolution of the house of representatives, containing the exception to which the president refers. I have also received a letter from Mr. Smith, secretary of the navy, containing an authentic copy of the order which was wanted, precisely corresponding with the unauthenticated copy in my possession.

Mr. WICKHAM.—I presume that these must be considered and noted as the return to the " subpœna *duces tecum.*"

Mr. HAY.—So far as they go. When we receive general Wilkinson's letter, the return will be complete. I have also received a letter from the secretary at war, which contains all the orders of his department relative to Aaron Burr. All which papers I shall deposit with the clerk of this court.

The following is the order of the navy department:

I certify that the annexed is a true copy from the records in the office of the department of the navy of the United States, of the letter from the secretary of the navy, to captain John Shaw, dated 20th December, 1806.

In faith whereof, I Robert Smith, secretary of the navy of the United States of America, have signed these presents, and caused the seal of my office to be affixed hereto, at the city of Washington, this 17th day of June, *anno Domini*, 1807; and in the 31st year of the independence of the said States.

(Registered,)   RT. SMITH.
Ch. W. Goldsborough,   Secretary of the Navy.
    Ch. Clk. N. D.

(Copy)
Navy Department, 20th December, 1806.

SIR,

A military expedition formed on the Western waters by colonel Burr, will soon proceed down the Mississippi, and by the time you receive this letter, will probably be near New-Orleans. You will by all the means in your power, aid the army and militia in suppressing this enterprize. You will with your boats take the best position to intercept and to take, and if necessary, to destroy the boats descending under the command of colonel Burr, or of any person holding an appointment under him. There is great reliance on your vigilance and exertions.

I have the honour to be, sir, your most obedient,

(Signed)   RT. SMITH.

Captain John Shaw,
or the Commanding Naval Officer,
    at New-Orleans.

Mr. RANDOLPH.—May it please your honours:

I am now about to commit to your attention the motion of which we gave notice some days past. The general purport of it will be, to award a rule against general Wilkinson, to show cause, why an attachment should not issue against him for attempting to obstruct the free administration of justice. Whether we shall be again charged with an intention to inflame the public mind against general Wilkinson, or to defame him, I know not; but of one thing I am conscious, that my object is essentially different. We do not proceed on mere general surmise; but on plain facts. We shall endeavour to remove all the prejudices which have been excited, and shall rely on plain facts only. We hope to guard the public mind against erroneous impressions, by depending on correct evidence alone; and that it will be manifest to all, that every effort to obstruct the free will of a witness should be punished. If general Wilkinson's character should be incidentally affected, it will not be our fault. If he must take upon himself the legal consequences of his own improper conduct; if he must submit to legal doctrines; he cannot complain. It is due to the United States, to the witnesses themselves, and to the persons accused, that obstructions to the free administration of justice should not pass with impunity. Sir, we shall attach general Wilkinson on specific allegations, and by specific facts. It is his duty, if he can, to repel these by legal evidence; not by illegal testimony, or the protestations of his counsel, that they believe him to be innocent, and an Israelite without guile. I prefer this course, that there may be no more waste of time in passing eulogies on general Wilkinson. There will be a future occasion which will require the concentration of all his *lustre*, and it will be as well that the beams of his glory should not be dissipated till we make the attack that will strike home.

The ground on which we make the motion is this, that general Wilkinson, who is now before the court, in a case depending between the United States and Mr. Burr, deliberately abused the process of the law relative to a witness who has been summoned in this case. He contrived, on his own affidavit, and by his own power, to obstruct the free course of legal testimony, and to intimidate, and coercively bring to this court, a witness, by the abuse of military authority. For this illegal proceeding it is the duty of the court to take notice of general Wilkinson. As the cases ought to be kept distinct, I speak of him only; but it may be necessary to carry the principle into immediate execution as to other persons. The grounds of this accusation are the depositions of James Knox and Chandler Lindsley, which will be read to the court.

Mr. HAY objected to the introduction of these affidavits, be-cause he understood that they had been written and dictated by the counsel of colonel Burr. He did not pretend to say, that they contained any thing which they did not believe to be true, nor did he know their contents; but he understood, that they were introduced for the purpose of strengthening some testi-mony concerning general Wilkinson, or of showing improper conduct on his part; that he understood, that those witnesses had voluntarily gone and given information to the counsel, upon which the counsel had written or dictated the terms of those affidavits; that his idea was, that when affidavits are taken by the opposite counsel, though the court may be perfectly sa-tisfied with the conduct of the counsel in taking them, yet ac-cording to universal practice the court would not permit them to be read; that the legal authorities showed, that a court would never issue an attachment founded on affidavits taken by the agent or attorney of the party applying for it; that this court would admit of no exceptions to this rule; the court of king's bench determined that " it was invariable and founded on the wisest and most obvious principles." Mr. Hay here cited the case of the King v. Wallace, in 3 *Term Rep.* p. 403., where the court had set aside an affidavit that had been sworn to before the attorney for the prosecution, and refused to grant an attachment; that the present case was stronger than that. The objection in that case was, that it was sworn to before the counsel; the objection here is, that it is penned by the counsel, and is therefore stronger and more within the scope of that policy on which the principle of the law is founded; that how-ever he did not mean to reproach gentlemen for the course pursued in this instance; that he was sure that nothing like impropriety was thought of by them, and that perhaps he would have done the same thing in their situation.

Mr. BAKER.—May it please the court. I shall not under-take to say, what Mr. Hay would have done in our situation, nor do I feel much interested in knowing; but I rise solely for the purpose of correcting a mistake, which he has committed. He says, that these affidavits were originally written by colonel Burr's counsel. As to the affidavit of Knox, I know I can say nothing; but as to the affidavit of Lindsley, it was written by himself. The facts are simply these: He called upon me with his affidavit already written, (I had never seen him before) to know whether it were correctly written or not. I read it, cor-rected some inaccuracies in the style, and wrote it over again: it was not sworn to when brought to me. After I had corrected those grammatical errors, and submitted it to Mr. Lindsley's inspection, he said that the statement was perfectly correct.

Mr. Wirt.—Do you know, Mr. Baker, who induced Mr. Lindsley to adopt that course?

Mr. Baker.—Perhaps yourself, sir: I never saw Mr. Lindsley before.

Mr. Mac Rae.—I beg to add one observation to what has been already said on this subject. As the witnesses are now before the court, and can be examined *viva voce*, there is no inconvenience in the objection. If they were at a distance, so that they could not be personally examined, we should have found no difficulty in admitting their affidavits; we should have waived the objection, lest it might seem that we were afraid of them. I hope that it will not be believed, that we feel any such apprehension. I hope that it will seem to the court right, that the affidavits shall not be read, especially as our affidavits were objected to, when our witnesses were at New-Orleans. I hope that gentlemen will not insist on the necessity of discussing this point farther. If they wish to know the whole truth, they will consent to examine the witnesses in open court.

Mr. Wickham hoped that gentlemen would persevere in the course which they had this day begun; and instead of warm and desultory declamation, come at once to the law and authorities. They object to the reading of our affidavits, and the question is, whether in point of law, their objection will be sustained? It happens in many cases, and must happen in the progress of litigation, whether between individuals, or between the public and individuals, that collateral points arise, in which it is necessary that testimony should be heard: but if on every collateral question, *viva voce* testimony were to be introduced, great inconvenience would result; it would lead to an unnecessary confusion and waste of time: and the regular and established practice, therefore, is, when these collateral points occur, not to produce *viva voce* testimony, but affidavits in support of them. These affidavits are made *before* private magistrates; that is the authority by which they are *taken.* These being in writing, must necessarily be written by one of three descriptions of persons: by a magistrate or judge; by the party himself, or his agent; or by the witnesses. With respect to the necessity of their being written by a judge or magistrate, it will not be contended, that they are bound to submit to the drudgery of writing the affidavits, and most of them have no clerks. It is therefore usual to prepare the affidavits before, and for the magistrate to sign them thus previously prepared: and besides, a man may be an able magistrate, but a bad clerk. With respect to the parties themselves, it will not be contended, that they ought to write them, because a very great proportion of them are unable to write them. Who then is to write them? their counsel or agent, or some indifferent person. How can the party get an indifferent person to write his affidavits? The moment he calls for an indifferent person to write them, he becomes his agent, and is incapacitated from writing them: and according to the gentlemen's arguments, these affidavits could very seldom be produced. Hence, from the necessity of the case, a custom has prevailed among lawyers, to write their clients' affidavits; and the gentleman himself admitted fifteen minutes ago, that he has been in the habit of doing so himself.

As to the authority quoted by Mr. Hay, had he considered it but one tenth part of the time he has argued it, he would have seen that it did not apply. In that case, the affidavits, on which the motion for an attachment was founded, were sworn to before Lothian, who was the attorney, or agent, for the prosecution. Here the affidavit was written by the witness himself, and only corrected and copied by the counsel. Does the gentleman suppose, that the actual presence of the attorney would vitiate the affidavit? When a man writes an affidavit, he acts a mere ministerial part; but he who administers an oath, performs the judicial function of a judge, or justice of the peace. It is a sacred rule, that a magistrate who administers an oath, should be disinterested between the parties: and in the case referred to, he who administered the oath was not disinterested, but the attorney for the prosecution. I recollect an instance in this city, where a magistrate, who was also a practitioner of the law, drew an oath and administered it himself, even in his own case: the first was not improper, though the second was. Here Mr. Baker wrote the affidavit, but did not administer the oath. There is a substantial and plain reason, why the oath should be administered with impartiality, but no reason can be assigned why the agent of the party should not, as in this instance, copy, and correct, in point of language, at the instance of the witness, an affidavit prepared by the witness himself. As to the witness being present, it makes no difference. The practice, in such cases, is to read affidavits just as if the witnesses were absent.

Mr. Burr.—If it were perfectly agreeable to you, I should have no objection to an examination of the witnesses in court; although the practice is, on principles of convenience, otherwise: but if the court will submit to the inconvenience, it will be agreeable to me. As to the origin of this business, it is not perfectly understood, and some unfounded insinuations have been made concerning it. James Knox called on me, stated the usage which he had received; and asked, whether any redress could be obtained? One of my counsel, who was present at this interview, concurred in opinion with me, that some notice should be taken of this proceeding. We at first thought of referring him to Mr. Hay; but on reconsideration, we thought that, perhaps, Mr. Hay might think himself disqualified from acting. Mr. Knox's own idea was, that he ought to come into court, and complain, himself, of the treatment he had received.

Mr. WIRT.—Mr. Wickham says, that it is the practice to produce affidavits on such motions: but this practice is founded on expediency, and when it ceases to be expedient, the practice will also cease. The inquiry then will be, whether it will be most expedient to examine a number of witnesses openly, who are now in court, or take their affidavits and read them? The court would wish to come at the true state of facts. I hope the gentlemen on the other side, would also wish the same. You are called on, to make a rule, against general Wilkinson, to show cause, why an attachment should not issue against him; and to support this application, affidavits are offered, and said to be founded on expediency. We contend that *viva voce* testimony is better. Before you grant it, you must be satisfied that it is right. The question then is, which is most satisfactory to your mind, an affidavit taken by the party, or evidence stated by the witness himself? How can the court be satisfied till the witness be examined and fully heard? Was the affidavit written by the witness himself? Did it proceed from him? or, was it advised by him? or, did it contain his words? The counsel, no doubt, endeavoured to draw it as correctly, and as free from bias, as he could; but it was difficult to state it precisely as the witness would have done. The witness states his facts, but he states them in his own *language*. Is it likely, that when it is changed to the words of the attorney, the idea intended to be expressed by the witness, will be precisely retained? If you take the evidence, not from the fountain head, the witness himself, but from a statement taken by another, you run the risk of not being rightly informed: but if you examine the witness, there can be no mistake.

Mr. BOTTS said, that colonel Burr had acquiesced, and consented that the witnesses should be examined in court, though he regretted the departure from usage established on principles of convenience.

Mr. MARTIN.—If the witness be examined, the clerk will reduce what he shall say to writing, so as to give it the effect of an affidavit.

Mr. HAY apologised for frequently misunderstanding colonel Burr. He complained, that from their respective situations he could not hear the accused, notwithstanding his clear and distinct voice, and emphatic manner.

James Knox was then called, when

Mr. MAC RAE addressed the court. He said, that as the business was of considerable importance to general Wilkinson, it was extremely desirable, that he should be present at the examination of this and the other witnesses, who might be introduced on this occasion; that he was now before the grand jury, and he had applied to the gentlemen on the other side to postpone the motion till he could be present, but they objected to any delay. He therefore found it necessary to apply to the court, to suspend the examination for a short time, till the general could be present; that important facts, unknown to the counsel for the prosecution, might be within the knowledge of general Wilkinson, who therefore might materially direct their inquiries in this examination.

Mr. MARTIN said, that the gentleman did not seem to know in what stage of the business they were then engaged; that the question was, whether a rule should be granted to show cause; with which neither general Wilkinson nor his counsel had any thing to do, and were not, in fact, as much as supposed to be present; and that the court would take care that the witnesses should answer correctly.

Mr. WICKHAM complained, that they had been for a considerable time prevented from making the motion, by the delay of the gentlemen on the other side, and of general Wilkinson.

Mr. MAC RAE.—The gentleman from Maryland has said, that we were not present in court. I thought, that all the while he spoke, we were in court. The court were pleased to notice our presence, and we were heard and answered politely and respectfully; and what has the court said? That gentlemen on both sides in court, had a right to argue this question. It is now too late for them to say, that they are exclusively engaged in this motion, which we have an acknowledged right to discuss and oppose; and we shall be perfectly satisfied, if the court will take notice of our observations, although Mr. Martin should not. We hope, that if the reasons for desiring general Wilkinson's attendance appear as strong to the court, as to the counsel for the prosecution, it will consent to this short delay. We mean, with the leave of the court, to put some questions to the witnesses, and also, to produce some testimony ourselves; and we feel confident, that we can satisfy the court, that no just foundation exists for the present motion.

Mr. MARTIN.—I thought I had assigned very sufficient reasons why the business should not be delayed. I knew they were *personally* present. I saw them; and if I had not, they took good care to make us often hear them. They detained us three or four hours the other day, in opposing the motion for a subpœna *duces tecum*, after the court had decided, that they had no right to interfere. It is unfair to take up a great deal of the time of the court, when, in point of legal contemplation, they are not in court. Let the present motion be decided, and when the rule is made, they may bring counter affidavits.

Mr. WIRT.—If presence depend on speaking, Mr. Martin is not only present, but, perhaps, is the only person who is. I am willing, however, to be considered, if he please, as not legally present; but, as *amicus curiæ*, I may make a few observations. These questions may merit the consideration of the court. " Here is a rule which I am required to make on general Wilkinson, to order him to show cause, why an attachment should' not issue against him. Shall I make it on a personal examination of the witnesses, or follow custom, and by taking their affidavits exclude part of their evidence? Shall I use one or two links when I may have the whole chain before me? Where testimony is present, ought I not to take the full benefit of it?" The inquiry will be made, whether the man's interrogatories, when general Wilkinson is present, will not give more satisfaction to the court than his mere affidavit? Will not the court think, that a full view of the evidence will be better? Though not present, he is deeply interested in the event of this motion, when its object is, that he should show cause, why an attachment should not issue against him for a supposed contempt of the court: his character as a man, as well as his credit as a witness, is affected. We are told, that the streams of the prosecution should be kept clear and untroubled. If gentlemen be serious in these admonitions, they will not persist in this mode of exhibiting mutilated testimony; for these *ex parte* affidavits, uncontradicted by general Wilkinson, may unjustly prejudice the public opinion against him. We hope that the court will, for themselves, as well as for general Wilkinson; for expediency and public justice, suspend this examination for a short time, till he can be present. We do not wish a postponement for two or three days or more, but a mere suspension while he is necessarily before the grand jury.

Mr. MARTIN drew an analogy between this motion and the proceedings before the grand jury. Gentlemen, said he, have no more right to interfere, in this stage of the business, than we have to interfere before the grand jury. It is exclusively in the power of the counsel for the prosecution to send witnesses before the grand jury. We have no such right. When the grand jury find a true bill, and the trial in chief comes on before the court, we can introduce what evidence we please, but not before:

the principle is the same here. Gentlemen have no right to introduce testimony when we apply for the rule, but after it is granted, and they come forward to show cause against issuing the
attachment; then they have an undoubted right to adduce what
testimony they think proper, to show that it ought not to issue.
But gentlemen say, that granting the rule may possibly tarnish
the reputation of general Wilkinson. He may, on showing cause
against the attachment, come forward in vindication of his character. We have no right to bring testimony in our exculpation
before the grand jury, where indictments and accusations, committing our character and as materially injuring us as he can be
by this motion, are exhibited. Were we to attempt it, their answer
to us would be, " *You are irregular; you can introduce no evi-*
dence before the grand jury, and if they find any bill against
you, you can wipe off the impression made by their finding, in the
usual and regular manner." As this is the way in which we wipe
off the impression of what is before the grand jury, so he can
wipe off the effect of granting the rule, on showing cause.

Mr. BURR.—It is not my wish to prevent gentlemen from
producing testimony in behalf of general Wilkinson, or to prevent his witnesses from being heard; but this can be done by
introducing their affidavits. I object only to the innovation of
examining them personally on collateral motions like this, instead
of reading their affidavits.

Mr. HAY.—It seems to be conceded that general Wilkinson
may produce testimony in his part. He has been three hours before the grand jury, and in a very short time he may be discharged and appear in court. It is singular that we should, by
their own concession, have the right to appear and interrogate
witnesses after the rule is made, and yet not at this stage of the
proceedings, when we are present to contest it. The party on
whom such a rule is usually made, is absent; and the object of
it is, to bring him forward and to show cause, if he can, why he
should not be attached for his supposed misconduct. No opposition is usually made, because the party happens to be at a distance; yet if he be on the spot, as in the present case, there could
be no sort of reason or justice in preventing him from showing
at once that the charges against him are perfectly visionary and
groundless.

Mr. WICKHAM stated the importance of immediately proceeding with the motion; and that, according to law and practice,
there was no just ground of opposing it; but that if the counsel on
the other side would name a particular hour in the course of this
day, when the motion would be made, they would waive their
right of going on with it now.

Mr. MARTIN hoped, that the court would express in its order, that this postponement was not in consequence of the right
of the gentlemen to demand it, but of the consent of his friend.

CHIEF JUSTICE said, that it was unnecessary to do so. He
stated what the law and practice were, and observed, that if the
motion were to be postponed till Monday, and the witnesses on
both sides were *then* heard, it would answer every purpose; and
it might be considered then as a motion for an attachment, not
for a rule to show cause. This would prevent disputes and delay.

Mr. RANDOLPH.—We shall move then immediately for an
attachment.

Mr. MAC RAE observed, that they only wished the motion
delayed till general Wilkinson could be permitted to attend.

Mr. HAY wished, that in order to save time, gentlemen would
prepare their interrogatories, by reducing them to writing.

Mr. MARTIN said, that this could not be done till it was determined that an attachment would go; but that there would be
no delay on that account.

The examination was then postponed till Monday; and the
court adjourned till that day, at eleven o'clock.

MONDAY, June 22d, 1807.

The court met according to adjournment.

Mr. RANDOLPH, having directed James Knox and Chandler
Lindsley to be called, was proceeding to open the motion which
he had introduced on Saturday —

Mr. MAC RAE had understood that this motion was to be
postponed till general Wilkinson could be present; and that the
moment he was discharged from the grand jury, they should
notify the opposite counsel of it.

CHIEF JUSTICE said, that as this was a motion for an attachment against general Wilkinson, he ought to be heard in his
defence.

Here a desultory discussion took place.

Mr. BOTTS observed, that from a spirit of accommodation,
they had agreed on Saturday, to postpone their motion till this
day; but it was in certain expectation that general Wilkinson
would be here to-day, and that their motion would be no longer
delayed; that if they consented to further delay, it might take
several days before the general would be discharged from the
grand jury; that though he was not present himself, he was ably
represented by counsel; and that considering the hardships and
inconvenience imposed on colonel Burr, by such delays, he hoped

that they would now be permitted to proceed in their motion for an attachment, or a rule to show cause.

Colonel BURR enforced the same principle. He was unwilling to contravene the opinion or wishes of the court; but the subject required a few remarks. On Saturday, he had waived his rights; he had consented to vary the motion, to give general Wilkinson an opportunity to be present, under an expectation that he would be here on this day, and that the motion would certainly be made; but he asked, whether his consent was to be indefinitely extended to any period? It was then in his power to vary the form of the motion once more: but notwithstanding the inconvenience it would occasion to himself, he was ready to waive his motion for the present, if they would but name a certain time to-morrow, when they would be certainly ready.

Mr. WIRT declared that it was impossible for them to say, when the grand jury would finish the examination of general Wilkinson; before which time he could not come into court. We would have thanked gentlemen for the accommodating spirit which they had manifested, if they had not completely wiped away the obligation, by converting it into a topic of reproach. If the rule were granted, general Wilkinson would still be before the grand jury, who would not spare him to the court.

The CHIEF JUSTICE said, that the court would have conceived itself bound to hear the motion for the rule, as it was a motion of course; but now it was varied, partaking of a motion for a rule to show cause, and of one for an attachment. That if general Wilkinson should be in court to-morrow, the motion might go on; that it was not certain that he would be present; but that the testimony of colonel Burr could not be delayed longer than till to-morrow; and that general Wilkinson could cross examine those witnesses when he came into court.

Mr. HAY stated, that this was the very circumstance which they wished to avoid; that those witnesses were brought hither to accuse general Wilkinson, and that he ought to be present to shape his inquiries according to their evidence, and to expose their fallacy.

CHIEF JUSTICE.—General Wilkinson cannot cross examine them till colonel Burr have done with them.

Mr. HAY.—How can general Wilkinson know what questions to put, if he know not what testimony has been given by those witnesses?

CHIEF JUSTICE.—All the questions put to them, and their answers, will be reduced to writing.

Mr. HAY was unwilling that gentlemen should believe that he wished to waive the discussion for a single moment. Perhaps the grand jury would spare him for an hour. He understood that he was then employed in decyphering a letter before them. He suggested that a messenger should be sent up to the grand jury, requesting them to spare him for an hour, if it were compatible with their arrangements.

The marshal was accordingly sent to deliver the message, who returned and informed the court, that general Wilkinson was at that moment under examination. The motion was accordingly postponed till to-morrow, when it was understood that it would certainly be made.

The CHIEF JUSTICE observed, that the attorney for the United States might state to general Wilkinson, the facts which were charged in the affidavit, and which would agree in all the most material points with the interrogatories that would be proposed to the witnesses.

The court adjourned to the usual hour of adjournment.

TUESDAY, June 23d, 1807.

The court met according to adjournment.

General Wilkinson appeared in court, and took his seat among the counsel for the United States.

Mr. BURR rose and observed to the court, that as general Wilkinson was then present, he would proceed with his inquiry. He would have it, however, distinctly understood, that if the charge could not be brought home to general Wilkinson himself, so as to support the motion against him, yet it must attach according to the testimony, to any of his subordinate officers, as Mr. Gaines, or any other.

Mr. HAY objected to this extension of the motion, which he had understood to be confined to general Wilkinson alone; particularly as they had not given any intimation of such an intention before: As no other person had notice of this intended motion, but general Wilkinson, the inquiry should be restricted to him alone.

Mr. RANDOLPH insisted that the evidence to be introduced in support of their motion, must attach to general Wilkinson, or any of his subordinate officers, or any other person, according to what the witnesses should prove. Before the witnesses were examined, he stated briefly the nature of their motion and the substance of the testimony by which he expected to support it. That the charge against general Wilkinson was, that he had, in conjunction with others, used unlawful and oppressive means, under colour and in abuse of the process of this court, to bring James Knox and Chandler Lindsley from New-Orleans to this city; and thus had obstructed the free course of testimony, and the fair and regular administration of justice; and he hoped, that if the evidence would prove the facts as he expected, the court would punish him, his associates, dependents, or others, according to the degree of their misconduct.

The witnesses were then introduced. James Knox was first sworn. His testimony was as followeth:

He says, that he went to New-Orleans some time in March; soon after his arrival, he received a note from general Wilkinson, making some inquiry concerning serjeant Dunbaugh. He waited on the general, who received and treated him handsomely, took him by the hand, and asked him if he were not afraid after what had happened, and what had been said about him. He told him he was not afraid. He asked him, whether he were at liberty to reveal what occurred in coming down the river? The witness said he was at liberty to reveal what he knew; but did not wish to do so. He inquired whether the witness were a freemason? He then began to take notes. The witness stopped him from taking down, and told him it was not his wish to have what he said taken down. He complained of distress; expected to be ruined. Said that there was a great force coming down the river. He asked the witness his circumstances; what money was due to him for his services in coming down? He answered, one hundred and fifty dollars. Asked him if he were in want of money, and offered to supply him, which the witness refused. He said he was very unhappy; had lost his wife; but *all that* was nothing to his trouble on account of the state of the country. The witness said that a subpœna had been served on him about the 12th of May, by Mr. Gaines, to attend this court; that he told him he was not prepared to come round then, but he expected to get money in ten or twelve days, and would then be ready. He went to Gaines's office about four days afterwards; was taken by a sheriff on Sunday evening, who took him to judge Hall's. The judge was from home. He went again, and was told by the judge that he must give his deposition, or go round to Richmond. He answered, that he had no objection to going to Richmond; but having no counsel, would not give his deposition, lest he should commit himself. No person but the sheriff was present. The governor desired the sheriff to take his word, if the judge could not be found: saw the judge, and was bailed until eleven o'clock; gave two securities, bound in five hundred dollars each, to avoid being put in gaol. When he appeared, the judge had before him a number of printed interrogatories. The witness asked the liberty of reading them. He permitted him to do so. The judge asked him if he would answer. The witness refused until he had counsel; but offered to be placed in confinement until he could procure counsel. He afterwards saw, as his counsel, Mr. Carr, who informed him that the judge had no right to demand such answers. The judge still persisted to interrogate him, to some of which interrogatories he answered, in order to save trouble. The witness then related every thing that passed, from Meadville, until his arrival in New-Orleans. Mr. Fort was then sent for and interrogated. He made some observations, and refused to answer (being, he said, about *Tom, Dick,* and *Harry*). After which the judge gave the deputy marshal a note, who put Fort and the witness into gaol, among forty or fifty negroes and criminals. Fort was bailed by his friends; but they required bail of the witness in five or six thousand dollars, and he remained in gaol until the vessel was ready, in which he embarked. He requested leave to get his clothes. Dunbaugh then came with some men with belts and side-arms. The witness asked if they were a guard ? He was answered, no; but that they were some acquaintances. That he has since been told by Dunbaugh, they were a guard. They went with Dunbaugh and himself, to the water edge. The witness asked whether lieutenant Gaines were on board ? They said no, but soon would be. When Dunbaugh came to the gaol, he had an order which was handed to the gaoler. While in gaol, the witness wrote to Lindsley and doctor Mulhollon, to come and see him; and told them if they came to New-Orleans, what they might expect. He was informed by the gaoler that they would be confined. He did not send the note. He did not see Gaines until the next day. When lieutenant Gaines came on board the vessel, he said the witness was in a bad humour; the witness told him he was, and Gaines said that he had better be satisfied, and bear his situation with patience. He asked Gaines for leave to go on shore for his clothes, he did not care what guard was sent with him. Gaines said, that it was not in his power to grant it, but the power was in general Wilkinson. The witness was not permitted to get his clothes, and came without any except what he had on at the time, and except that Lindsley brought him one of his shirts which he had lent him. Gaines, after having told him that he might put him in irons, and bring him round in that manner, offered him forty dollars. The witness said, that if he would let him go on shore, he did not want it, otherwise must take it. It was paid and sent on shore; twenty dollars were paid to his landlord, and the other twenty dollars returned to him by governor Claiborne, who came on board and went with them six or eight miles on the passage. And also, when they came to anchor in Hampton Roads, Gaines asked him if he had any objection to coming to Richmond; he answered that he never had any objection. Gaines said, that he was sent by the authority of judge Hall. General Wilkinson spoke to him next day, and asked him if he had any objection to come to Richmond. He answered he had not, if properly treated; but he had been brought off without clothes or money. General Wilkinson had not heard of his not being permitted to bring his clothes, until that morning. General Wilkinson agreed he was ill treated. Told him that he (witness) must understand, that he was brought round by the direction of judge Hall. General Wilkinson proposed to let the witness go to Richmond upon his parole of honour, which was refused. Wilkinson said, if the witness wanted twenty dollars, he should have it; afterwards he talked with Mr. Lindsley, and returned to the witness and said, if he wanted fifty dollars he might have it. Witness wanting money to purchase clothes, took it. He observed, in the first conversation, that he had twice asked favours of him and Gaines, and would never ask a third favour of any person. He came to Richmond with Moxley, in a pilot boat. Moxley told him that he had orders from general Wilkinson, to take charge of the passengers on board the Revenge, and bring them to Richmond, and there wait his (Wilkinson's) orders.

Cross-examination by the counsel for the United States. Have you any military commission? Answer: None. Where were you born? Answer: In Maryland; left it very young; resided in Pennsylvania, and left it sometime in November last. Left Pennsylvania, (Meadville) for New-Orleans, on the 24th or 25th of November, went down the Alleghany and Ohio to Beaver; went from thence, with about twenty or thirty, to Blannerhasset's island, where he did not recollect to have staid but two days or a day and a half: left that place some time in December, Blannerhasset and another with them, who were the only persons who joined them there. Stopped at Shawnee Town; went with about double the number to Cumberland island, just opposite to the mouth of Cumberland river; staid a day and a half, met with colonel Burr and a few others; the whole number about fifty or sixty, about seven or eight boats, five fire-arms: went thence to Fort Massac; serjeant Dunbaugh met them there with a musket, and after meeting with colonel Burr, he considered himself under his direction. Went to Natchez. Colonel Burr did not accompany them. Went from Natchez to New-Orleans. Some of the boats were chartered and others sold. They arrived at New-Orleans on the 13th or 16th of March. The first notice he had, after seeing general Wilkinson, of the proceedings against him was, when he was carried before judge Hall. He was said to be carried under an affidavit of general Wilkinson before judge Hall. Captain Gaines requested him to write to him on shore, and he would get what he wanted. He was not permitted to send the letter. Never mentioned this to general Wilkinson till they arrived in Hampton Roads. That he was treated as others while on his way; that is, as well as some; not so well as some, and better than others. Arrived at Richmond on Friday evening, put up at the Bell tavern. Three days elapsed before he saw colonel Burr. He mentioned the treatment he had received to colonel Burr, and intended mentioning it to the court, on his first appearance; but was told it was unnecessary. That general Wilkinson used no terror against him; and offered to relieve him if he wanted money. Whilst at the mouth of

Cumberland river, and when colonel Burr made his escape, he was one that took colonel Burr in a wherry, and carried him some distance, and left him in the woods; did not hear him address any one. The note written him by general Wilkinson, and sent by Dunbaugh, was left at his house sealed : the object was to obtain some information about Dunbaugh. No letters. Carried colonel Burr's things to a parson Bruin's, as he was told. They had but few guns, which were traded for as they descended the river. The vessel sailed from New Orleans in half an hour after general Wilkinson came on board. The one hundred and fifty dollars offered him by general Wilkinson, he was induced to believe, was to bribe him to give evidence against colonel Burr, or it might be considered as a bribe. Said he could obtain from colonel Tyler a sufficiency to carry him home under his agreement with that gentleman. This conversation took place before the subpœna was served.

Lieutenant Gaines was then sworn. He stated that he received a letter from the attorney general of the United States, enclosing subpœnas for witnesses against colonel Burr. That he went to New-Orleans in consequence, and arrived there on the 7th of May. Called several times at the house where James Knox staid, with Mr. Lindsley and doctor Mulhollon, and could not find them. He was told by the landlord, that those gentlemen walked out whenever he approached; they supposed he had something against them. He told his business, and at length saw them. They said, that the reason why they endeavoured to keep out of his way was, that they had belonged to Burr's party, and did not wish to appear against him. He told them that the commander in chief offered them a passage in the United States' vessel with him. He desired Knox and Lindsley to say whether they would come or not? Knox said he could not come until he had made some money arrangements (though Lindsley seemed disposed to come on). That he then applied to judge Hall; the judge directed him to obtain an affidavit of the refusal, and that he would take the proper steps. He said, that the subpœna might be served by the marshal or sheriff, and proposed that he (lieutenant Gaines) should be appointed by the marshal, a deputy. He refused, unless he could afterwards be released from any further service in that capacity. Next day the judge told him, that the marshal had left a deputation for him, and asked him if he would act; he answered that he would, on the foregoing condition, and that he should not attend to Knox, at New-Orleans. Knox appeared always ill-natured, which induced him to ask him if he could do any thing for him? He obtained from the United States' agent at that place, forty dollars, and offered it to Knox, which he, after some hesitation, accepted. In reply to his inquiries, whether Knox wanted assistance, he hesitated, and then said, that he wished to go on shore himself, to get some necessaries out of his trunk. He told him that as the vessel was going to sail so soon, he could not; but offered him pen, ink and paper, and requested him to write to some friend on shore, to do what he wanted done; or he would act for him, himself. He was then in a very ill humour, and was so when the witness returned on board. James Knox was under no restraint, from the time the vessel sailed, till they arrived at Hampton Roads. To a question put by Mr. Burr's counsel, by whose authority he acted, lieutenant Gaines answered, that in every step relative to Knox, he acted under the authority of the marshal, at New-Orleans, except that he was authorised by the commander in chief, to offer him a passage in a public vessel. In serving the subpœna, he acted under the authority of the attorney general. When at Hampton Roads, he inquired of Knox, whether he had any disposition to go to Richmond? He said that he wished to come to Richmond, but wished also to leave that vessel. He told him he should leave it, but had not determined how he would be conveyed to Richmond. General Wilkinson told him, all would come in a vessel, except those who would come in the stage. His getting off, gave him no concern; because he supposed that Knox could be caught again in some part of the country, if he attempted to go away. Whilst the witness was on shore, general Wilkinson procured a vessel in which Knox and others were sent to Richmond. He considered Knox under his authority, not as a military officer, but as deputy marshal. That he was committed to his charge, as such, in virtue of a warrant of commitment issued by judge Hall. He did not know the reason why the judge made such an order. That general Wilkinson never attempted to exercise any authority over Knox, on his passage. That the deputation was not of his own procuring. That he had received an order from the department of war, to leave the garrison at which he commanded, under the direction of some other person, and to attend to the orders of the attorney general.

Question by colonel Burr. Had you no previous conversation with general Wilkinson about this deputation? Answer: I had none. I never heard nor had any conception of such a deputation till it was mentioned by judge Hall. He gave to serjeant Dunbaugh an order at New-Orleans to receive from prison and deliver to the commanding officer on board the United States' schooner Revenge, the body of James Knox, and he was accordingly conveyed on board.

Question by Mr. Baker. Was not Dunbaugh a serjeant in the army, and did you not consider him acting as such under you? Answer: I should not have considered any citizen of New-Orleans bound to obey my order; I did not consider serjeant Dunbaugh farther bound than in compliance with his promise. He was called serjeant Dunbaugh, but I did not consider him under my authority as a military officer. I took no oath of office; I gave no bond to perform the duties of a deputy-marshal; I do not know that I shall get any pay; I have no promise of any. General Wilkinson made his affidavit at his own quarters, before Mr. Cenas. I do not recollect whom general Wilkinson consulted; an attorney had been with him. I delivered to general Wilkinson the subpœnas received from the attorney-general of the United States, and among them one for myself, another for Mr. Graham. I always considered myself bound to obey the orders of general Wilkinson. I was bound before the deputation to obey him, and I continued so. I considered general Wilkinson as having the power of controlling myself, and every person belonging to the army and navy of the United States, on board the Revenge, if he chose to exercise that control; but I do not consider that he did exercise such control.

The subpœnas which I delivered to general Wilkinson came into my hands afterwards, but nothing passed between the general and myself on the subject, except that I stated to him the orders I had received, and the power I possessed. My impression was, that general Wilkinson must have been privy to the whole, and perhaps recommended that I should transact this business. I communicated to him what judge Hall had said; that an affidavit must be made of the materiality of Knox as a witness, before he could take any steps to compel his attendance. General Wilkinson knew that Knox was put on board the Revenge unwillingly.

On our way to Virginia we stopped at the Havanna for fresh supplies of water and other necessaries. Some on board were sick; they prevailed on the officers to call. While preparing to go on shore, a shot was fired from the Moro castle, and orders given to come on shore. They went on shore at the request of the sick persons on board made to general Wilkinson and captain Read. They did not land until after four o'clock in the afternoon, and a little after dark they set sail again. Had good provisions, &c. on board. Heard captain Read direct the cook to let those people have their provisions regularly. To a question put by Mr. Burr's counsel, he answered, that general Wilkinson pointed out the witnesses on whom the subpœnas must be served. He, on several occasions, received advice and instructions from the counsel whom he consulted how to act in executing the business in which he was engaged.

Mr. RANDOLPH.—Upon what authority were the forty dollars received from the military agent? Answer: The money received from the military agent was applied for, after several applications from Knox; and general Wilkinson advised me to consult judge Hall, whether it were legal to demand money for him? And was told by the judge that it was regular to advance a reasonable sum; and was also told by the military agent, that general Wilkinson had advised him to advance that sum. The general advised me to consult the attorney-general there, or Mr. Duncan, and the general's own idea corresponded on the su ject.

Mr. Graham being sworn gave the following testimony. A short time after the arrival of captain Gaines at New-Orleans, I was told that he had subpœnas for witnesses, and one for myself; that there was a public vessel that would carry us to Richmond. I then waited on general Wilkinson to know whether I could be accommodated in that vessel? My health was bad at that time: general Wilkinson agreed that I should; and then said, that he understood that there were several witnesses in town, some of whom were unwilling, others unable to come round; and asked me if I knew any legal means or process, by which those who were unwilling could be compelled to come? I told him I did not know, but I supposed the federal judge could inform him. As there was a misunderstanding between the general and the judge, I offered to ask the judge myself, whether there were such process; and I did so. At this, or some subsequent time, general Wilkinson told me to ask the judge, whether there were any impropriety in advancing money to the witnesses, and to what amount? The judge said, that so far from being improper, the witnesses had a right to demand it. The judge said, in answer to the other question, that if the witness refused to enter into recognisance, or to answer such questions as would satisfy him of the materiality or relevancy from the law, (which he showed me) he would be authorised to send such witness round under the care of the district marshal. He saw, a few days after, in an outer room at the judge's, Mr. Knox talking with Mr. Keene, a lawyer; some short time after, when these gentlemen came into the room, the judge asked Knox if he were then willing to answer questions, or enter into recognisance? He declined doing either. The judge had that clause of the law before him. He pointed it out to Mr. Keene, and a Mr. Fort, who was in the same situation with Knox, and advised them to do one of the two; or he should be obliged to act rigidly towards them; that he was very unwilling to act against them; but it was his duty, and he must do it. The same gentleman had a curiosity to know what questions they intended to put to him, and then the printed interrogatories were shown to him. The judge asked Mr. Fort to answer these interrogatories, which he refused to do. The judge then sent for the marshal, and committed both of them.

In the afternoon captain Fort gave security in 500 dollars for his appearance at Richmond, and was released. He understood captain Fort was going in the ship Amity to New-York, in order to come to Richmond; but as Fort told the witness, he could not leave New Orleans without injury to his business, it was his own opinion, that he would not leave that place. Mr. Keene intimated to the judge, that he did not appear as an attorney; but expressed some doubt of the correctness of the proceedings, and of the power of the judge to send Knox round. The ship's stores were good, and the persons treated civilly and not restrained. They slept where he did. They called in at the Havanna on account of bad winds, and being chased close in by a British cruiser. Captain Read, who commands the vessel, Mr. Gaines, Mr. Smith and himself went on shore to procure fruit, &c. Remained there about three hours. His impression was, that if the gun had not been fired from the fort, they should not have gone in. That part of the navy of the United States, which is at New-Orleans, and was formerly under the control of the government, and the officers about New-Orleans, when the country was considered to be in a state of danger, was put under the command of general Wilkinson. He saw no guard on his way to New-Orleans. I went, said Mr. Graham, partly by land, and partly by water. I went down the river with captain Fort, who said, that he was one of a party, whose object was to go against Mexico; of which declaration he made no secret. I do not know by what authority Fort was brought before the judge, but judge Hall said he felt himself bound to act under the law. I advised Fort not to oppose the judge, who was a very determined man. Fort replied, that Mr. Alexander said, that the judge had no right to send him. The judge and Mr. Keene both requested him, to request Mr. Gaines to remove Knox out of the prison to the vessel.

Lieutenant Gaines, upon being called up again, said he is an officer of the United States army, never consulted general Wilkinson about accepting the appointment of deputy-marshal. He understood Fort was included in the same affidavit with Knox. He sailed from New-Orleans in the Revenge; saw general Wilkinson exercise no kind of authority on the voyage.

Mr. Graham said, that general Wilkinson opposed their stopping at the Havanna for two reasons; first, that it would occasion delay, and secondly, that his enemies might charge it against him as an improper act. The gun was fired from the Moro castle.

I understood that the judge had requested Mr. Gaines to accept the deputation. Gaines did not wish to act. He was urged by myself and others to accept it; and he did accept it, I believe from motives of patriotism. General Wilkinson exercised no control over the persons on board; and no restraint was used, except what has been mentioned with respect to the witness Mr. Knox.

After the testimony was closed, a dispute arose between the counsel, which side should begin the argument, both parties claiming the right. After some observations by gentlemen on both sides, it was determined, that the correct distinction was, that he who obtained a rule to show cause should close, and, of course, begin the argument.

The court then adjourned till to-morrow, eleven o'clock.

WEDNESDAY, June 24th, 1807.

The court met according to adjournment.

Mr. Graham was called by Mr. MAC RAE, and questioned, relative to the state of the public mind at New-Orleans, and whether great alarms were not excited by the conspiracy? He answered, that he had not arrived at that place till the month of March, and at that time the public mind was much agitated.

To a question put by colonel BURR, whether general Wilkinson himself had not contributed to excite those alarms by his violent measures? Mr. HAY objected as improper. Colonel BURR insisted on the propriety of his question.

The court was of opinion, that the witness was only bound to answer such questions as directly applied to the subject before them.

Mr. Graham said, that there was a considerable portion of the people at New-Orleans, who believed, that there was another portion unfriendly to the government. He did not know the measures pursued by the executive, at New-Orleans. He was then interrogated as to the post-offices being robbed of letters. He did not recollect that general Wilkinson particularly informed him how letters of information were received by him; only he observed, concerning a letter partly in cypher, that he had received it from a house at New-Orleans; [which Mr. Graham named; but it is not inserted, as he was not distinctly heard] that the practice of opening letters, if it existed at all, had ceased, when he arrived at New-Orleans; that general Wilkinson showed him three or four letters. He did not know how those letters were taken from the post-office, but it was generally said at New-Orleans, that the post-master there had given him those letters.

Colonel BURR asked him, whether a considerable number of letters, directed to himself, or to others, had not been taken from the post-office there? He answered, that he knew not; but there was an impression on his mind, that letters were improperly taken from the post-office; whether by general Wilkinson or not, he knew not. He rather thought not.

Mr. MARTIN.—Did you not understand that general Wilkinson had placed guards on the river, and on the roads, to stop travellers and passengers from passing?

Mr. Graham.—I did understand that he had placed guards at two points, near New-Orleans, for the purpose of arresting suspected characters. I had understood also, that certain persons had been seized.

Mr. MARTIN.—Did general Wilkinson never tell you how he got those letters? Mr. Graham.—He did not.

Captain Murray was then called and sworn.

Being interrogated by colonel BURR, he stated that he was stationed at Ville Grove, two miles above New-Orleans. His orders from governor Claiborne were to stop boats coming down the river, and examine them; to examine papers, but break no seal: but that, from his orders he would have deemed it his duty to have transmitted letters addressed to suspicious persons to the executive at New-Orleans.

Colonel BURR.—Would you have obeyed the governor, since, as an officer, you are strictly bound to obey general Wilkinson?

Captain Murray.—Yes, I should. The orders from governor Claiborne originated with, and always came through, general Wilkinson.

Mr. EDMUND RANDOLPH then addressed the court thus:

May it please your honours: The motion which we so often attempted to bring forward, I hope, will now be submitted and freely argued: the motion to attach general Wilkinson, for endeavouring to prevent the free course of testimony. The immediate object will be to call on him to answer interrogatories, whether improper practices have not been used by him: the ulterior object will be determined afterwards. I believe that, in cases of this kind, where strong suspicions exist, the attachment must go, because it is in the power of the party charged to purge himself on oath. If he refuse, it arises from a consciousness of his own guilt. His innocence is first to be presumed, and every thing is in his own power. If he omit to clear himself, the court will take measures for enforcing obedience to the power and dignity of this tribunal.

Give me leave to open this case as it now appears, from the testimony before the court. It no longer depends, as at first insinuated, on the evidence of James Knox, who has been censured for enmity against general Wilkinson. It has been enlarged and enforced by the testimony of two very respectable gentlemen, brought forward by general Wilkinson himself.

Sir, if we were to have the same command or range of persons that the counsel for the prosecution have, we should lay before you a history of this illegal and oppressive proceeding, far more detailed, and far more strong, than is yet in our power. I judge, that this would be our ability, when you hear so much from his own witnesses, who are supposed by him the best to understand the circumstances which can operate in his favour. And here give me leave to pay a tribute of applause (which I shall always be ready to avow) to the frankness and manliness of those gentlemen, whom he has introduced, in candidly and ingenuously stating all the circumstances known to them. That confidence which I had before in the evidence of James Knox is greatly strengthened and confirmed by the strong and respectable testimony of lieutenant Gaines and Mr. Graham. Mr. Gaines, a lieutenant in the army, was, by words, made a deputy marshal. Sir, I feel a repugnance at the idea. I feel a repugnance at this germ of an alliance between the civil and military authority, when the civil wants not the aid of the military arm. I am not sufficiently versed in the policy of mixing offices of such opposite descriptions together, without necessity. I hope I shall never have occasion to be acquainted with the extraordinary and dangerous policy of joining together such offices.

That a man, owing obedience only to a superior military commander, is to be placed in a civil capacity, for the single purpose of catching and detaining unfortunate men, who may happen to be witnesses in a particular cause, is a dangerous innovation, and ought not to be tolerated. Sir, I do not pretend to recollect the purport of that paper, by the authority of which lieutenant Gaines acted as deputy marshal; but I understand, that its principal object was, to enable him to transport Mr. Knox from New-Orleans to Richmond. It is immaterial, at this time and place, to enter into a specification of his power thus conferred, or attempted to be conferred. It is sufficient that a military man is created a deputy-marshal; not for the general purposes of the office of marshal, but for the single purpose of proceeding and carrying by force, to Richmond, a man apprehended as a witness in New-Orleans. This outrage, whether it be called civil or military, was committed after Mr. Knox was regularly summoned. The inference that I draw from this, is, that something of a military nature was intended in order to effect the object in view by compulsion.

Can you believe, that there were so few men of integrity in New-Orleans, (I believe it abounds with such) that no man could be found by whom this business could have been executed, without this oppressive union of military power with civil authority? It cannot then be justified by the plea of necessity. It was as unnecessary as it was unprecedented and illegal; and whether this appointment was suggested by the judge (who seems to have been infected with the mania excited by Wilkinson,) or whether it proceeded from Wilkinson himself, it was equally improper. He was appointed to an office without the possibility of employment: the subpœna had been served, and he had nothing to do as marshal. Every step taken, after the subpœna was served, was military, coercive and violent; nothing conformable to law. Consider the whole testimony, and say, once for all, whether it were not a contrivance to effect their favourite object, in pretended observance, but in real evasion of the law? It is evident, that in truth and in law, Mr. Gaines was no deputy marshal. He was commanded by the act of congress, to give bond and security before he entered on the duties of his office; nay, more, he must qualify and be duly sworn in the same manner that the marshal himself is sworn; and till he does comply with these requisites, he has no more power as a marshal, than any man whom I now behold in this assembly. [Here Mr. Gaines being called for that purpose, showed his deputation.] But it may be said, that there was no occasion to give bond and security, because he was only appointed for the special purpose of removing a man from New-Orleans to Richmond. But before he could be a marshal at all, these requisites must be complied with. He would not otherwise be a marshal for *any purpose*. Without doing so, he was wholly unauthorised, and intitled to no respect as an officer. He had no civil authority or character: he had no right to take upon himself the office of sub-marshal. Mr. Gaines frankly and candidly tells you, that he was not absolved from military duty; but to comply with the wishes of the general, he was obliged, or found it convenient, to act thus towards James Knox; and he has said, that if commanded by the general, he would have put him in irons. The military genius prevailed over the civil wherever it was seen. But he deemed it necessary to make use of the judge to execute his plan. This man, without any authority, by the orders of his superior officer, and to please him, goes to judge Hall; he has an interview with him; " *How am I to get this refractory man to Richmond?*" " *You cannot do it without an affidavit.*" " How must this affidavit be procured?" The transaction furnishes the answer. It is procured by a communication through Mr. Gaines to general Wilkinson; that this step was necessary for this particular purpose. The affidavit is made by general Wilkinson, knowing that its object was to effect the transportation of James Knox to Richmond. He himself caused his own affidavit to be taken. He tells captain Gaines, a military officer under his command, to transport him. He wilfully then contributed to do an act which he knew to be illegal. Do not let me be told, that it was the act of the judge. The case will not be amended by that refuge; for the judge himself, as is manifested by all the circumstances, was stimulated by Wilkinson, and greatly transcended the limits of the law, to effect the performance of an act to which Wilkinson was not only contributing, but of which he was prime mover. He demanded bail and bond security that Knox would go twelve hundred miles. Sir, if conduct like this in a judge is to be tolerated, there is an end of all law and justice. He could not but know, that there was no law authorising such an act of oppression. What, sir, shall he, from his own arbitrary will, demand bond and security, in a large sum, of a man who is merely summoned to appear at a court as a witness, who is willing to attend, and whose failure to appear legally subjects him only to an attachment? Shall he cast a man thus summoned into gaol, because he cannot give such excessive security as he tyrannically demands? They wished to extort testimony from this man by intimidation and violence; they required bail of him, though a stranger without property, in five or six thousand dollars, in a case where they had no right to require any security, or to molest him at all. Was this man capable of giving bail in so excessive a sum? This judicial outrage of demanding bail, where none was demandable; of casting the man into prison, because this illegal condition was not, and could not be complied with, and this for the purpose of extorting evidence, is an offence of unusual enormity. What a mass of destruction to the rights and privileges of private citizens is here contrived between the judge and general Wilkinson? The illegal design cannot be accomplished without an affidavit. Wilkinson voluntarily makes this affidavit, stating the materiality of the evidence of Knox. After it is made, by what means does it come into the hands of judge Hall? Who was the carrier of it? Not lieutenant Gaines, but general Wilkinson himself. And for what purpose? To enable them to transport James Knox to Richmond. And who is the executioner of this order? This transportation is to be effected, not by a regular marshal or civil officer, but by an officer under his command, unless Knox gives bond and security, in a strange country, to an amount which he could not possibly command; and moreover, this is to be executed on a man already in gaol for the sin of being a witness! Thus general Wilkinson has incorporated himself with all Hall's acts.

But Wilkinson connects himself further in these proceedings, which are all illegal from beginning to end. Stimulated by Wilkinson's oath, his agents put Knox in confinement; and Knox was removed by a *military* order, from an officer under the command of Wilkinson, on board of a vessel under the control of this commander in chief: so that the outrage against Knox was commenced by his imprisonment on shore, and consummated by his imprisonment on sea; and both contrived by Wilkinson. The same commander in chief has drawn money from the military chest, for the purpose of aiding him in these unlawful transactions. Sir, you cannot view any part of this case, without viewing the same military features strongly marked: general Wilkinson as the principal actor, as a military character, and for military purposes. Wilkinson most assuredly considered himself as possessing the most positive power over this vessel; because he authorised captain Gaines to offer him a passage in the vessel; and how could he give such an authority, if Read was not under his command? Wilkinson was the *effective* commander of this vessel. Observe, sir, if you please, the order, which Gaines gives. It is a written order, in a military style, delivered to *serjeant* Dunbaugh, commanding him to take this man into custody. He directs him not as a *deputy marshal*, but as captain Gaines, to take possession of Knox; and he addresses him not as an *individual* obliged to obey a marshal, but as *serjeant* Dunbaugh, bound to obey him as his military superior officer; and no permission is given to Knox to go on shore, but through Wilkinson. The spirit of Wilkinson appears through the whole of this business. The genius of Wilkinson is apparent in every stage of the transaction. I was at no loss at all, when I saw the letter of the attorney general directing so many subpœnas to be put into Wilkinson's hands, to perceive the object. What authority could the attorney general confer on Wilkinson? I had, no hesitation, on reading this letter, to conclude that the intention was, to enable him to effect by force, the removal of such persons as he could not persuade to come voluntarily. I refer to the fact; it is acknowledged and cannot be denied. [Here Mr. Hay interrupted him: he insisted that the letter should be read, and that it would show, that Mr. Randolph was incorrect.] Mr. Randolph waived the reading of the letter; but appealed to the facts, and insisted that his inference was justified by the testimony. He then proceeded. Is it not singular, that subpœnas in a *civil* case, should be confided to the military commander in chief? Did it not seem to tell him, that he was to use these subpœnas with some degree of authority, and did he not at least arrogate that authority to himself? Why did general Wilkinson mention to Mr. Gaines the necessity of summoning Mr. Knox, in recommending to him to find out who were witnesses? Who, I again ask, carried the affidavit of Wilkinson to judge Hall? Mr. Gaines has stated that he did not; who then carried it but general Wilkinson himself? Does not this still go to show, that there was not the minutest thing that general Wilkinson would omit for this purpose? There was a military temper, a military spirit displayed by general Wilkinson, throughout the whole transaction. Why did he consult an attorney? Was he a marshal?

Was military money put into his hands to employ a lawyer? No, sir, but because he viewed the subject in a military form. Gaines tells us that Wilkinson must have known that Knox was carried on board unwillingly; yet, notwithstanding he knew this, and that Knox was anxious to come on shore, he suffers him to remain in the pinnace of a ship—in the hold; perhaps to mess with degraded people: torn from his family and his private concerns, without the common comforts usually prepared for a sea voyage; an exile from his country, without money, without friends. Mr. Gaines states, that he, Wilkinson, had observed to him, that there were some unwilling witnesses, (such as he must coerce by military rigour); and Mr. Graham tells you, that he consulted him on the means of sending forward unwilling witnesses. See, then, the solicitude of Mr. Wilkinson, through the whole of this business! He began; he consummated every thing. Dunbaugh was applied to, for the liberty of Knox, and it was refused. But Wilkinson took his parol of honour, from him at Hampton: none but Wilkinson could give him liberty. We have seen him in the character of a military tyrant. We shall now find him using the blandishments of a courtier. He is particularly complaisant and friendly; offering him money, and any services in his power, in order to relieve his wants. At one time he asks him " Are you not afraid of seeing me, after what has happened to many?" At another, he asks him in a familiar way, if he were not a free mason; and thus profaned that institution, by attempting to impose on him the seal of secrecy. Terror was used to frighten him; and when he was found too firm and stubborn, cajoling and complacency were used. The means of operation were changed as he found it expedient. It is immaterial in what order these things took place. It is certain that they all took place. Various passions played in his breast; sometimes softness, sometimes severity.

Sir, I beg to deduce from these facts, this conclusion: that general Wilkinson caused the arrest and imprisonment of Mr. Knox; that Wilkinson executed it; and that it was done for the purpose of compelling Knox to give testimony. Though he was privileged as a witness, Wilkinson, by his own authority, had him again imprisoned on board the vessel; and this, also, for the same purpose of compelling him to give testimony, and of interrupting the free course of evidence. These are the principal facts upon which an attachment ought to issue against general Wilkinson. Sir, I will not stop to look at the insinuations against Knox. He had been summoned by the United States, and was waiting to arrange his private affairs, to enable him to depart for this place. The account which Knox has given, is just, candid, and unexceptionable; and shows that he was very much disposed to give his evidence. It is truly a hard case, that he should be solicited by the United States to come as a witness, and when he does come, that his character should be assailed as participating of something criminal. Facts, then, are fixed as to general Wilkinson. But it may be asked, what motives general Wilkinson could have for his conduct? It was said the other day, that he was the *pivot* of the prosecution. The prosecution was not hazarded before his arrival; not a single witness was sent to the grand jury till he came. The grand jury had to wait several weeks for his arrival. We have already had occasion to notice the stake which general Wilkinson had in the issue of this prosecution. Sir, the truth is, and it cannot be concealed, that the names of Wilkinson and Burr are *antipodes* to each other by the act of Wilkinson himself. Wilkinson declares, and the fact is, that he never will regain his meridian brightness, unless he can throw Mr. Burr into darkness. It is his duty to take care, that like some mock god, he fall down from his imaginary glory, tumbling among ruins, and into a chaos of rubbish, which he himself has created.

Thus we have established what Wilkinson has done, and what were his motives. Let me now show, that these facts do amount to a contempt of the court. From the authorities which I will read, it will appear, that no force or violence should ever be unnecessarily used, in making arrests; and of course, every species of unnecessary force, in compelling witnesses to attend to give depositions, or in executing any other process, amount to a contempt of the court. *Hawkins, in book* 2. *sec.* 2. lays down this general principle, that " it seems clear from the general reason of the law, that all courts of record have a discretionary power over all abuses by their own officers, in the administration or execution of justice." And in *sec.* 3. he lays down these general principles, that " it is every day's practice to grant attachments for misdemeanors of this kind; as, *for using needless force, violence and terror, in making an arrest;* or by breaking open doors, where, by law, it is not justifiable, and there is no plausible excuse for doing it; or treating the persons arrested, basely and inhumanly, or keeping them in custody, till they pay money; or *making an arrest without due authority."* And in the twelfth section of the same book, after having spoken of punishing by attachment, the misconduct of attorneys, he says: " Where the court may proceed in the manner above mentioned, against other officers of the court, there being *scarce* any thing of this kind to be met with in the books; I shall only observe, that it *seems clear* from the *general reason of the law,* which gives all courts of record a kind of discretionary power in the government of their own officers, that *any such court may proceed in such manner,* [He is speaking of the process of attachment] *against any such officer,* not only for refusing to execute its commands, or *for executing them irregularly, remissly,* or *oppressively;* but *also for all kinds of oppression or injustice done by them in the execution of their offices, or by colour of them.*" And in section 41. of same book, he says, that " making use of the process of the court in a vexatious manner"—and, in section 42. that " using it to serve the purpose of oppression or injustice, are both punishable by an attachment." Here, then, is a universal principle, that for all *kinds of oppression* or *injustice,* done by the officers of courts of justice, either in the actual execution of their offices, or by *colour of them,* they may be proceeded against by attachment. If we do not produce a case in point, it is for the reason mentioned by Hawkins, that there is scarce any thing of this kind to be met with in the books, and therefore the general principle must be resorted to. Where the public necessity, and the cause of justice require, that a party should be *arrested* by an officer, the officer must use no violence or terror, in making the *arrest;* he must be guilty of no act of oppression in any case. If no violence or oppression ought to be used, where an arrest is authorised, how much more must the law discountenance such violence and oppression, towards those who are not liable to be arrested? The oppression practised upon Mr. Knox, in this case, has been by colour of the process of this court; and those guilty of it ought, on the principles here laid down, to be punished for it. This is a more violent case, than any mentioned by this author. What would Hawkins have said to this case, where we see a man, who was regularly summoned as a witness, to attend a court of justice, seized at New-Orleans, upon the affidavit of a military officer, dragged before a person, who is called a magistrate, for the express purpose of being held to bail; required by this magistrate to give bail, for his appearance next day, in an enormous sum, in a place where he is unknown; then thrown into gaol and confined for three days, in a sultry climate, among negroes and felons; then taken out by a military authority, placed under a military guard, and by a man, who, though a military officer, had the name of a deputy marshal conferred on him, for the purpose of executing this tyrannical act, and that gentleman, himself, acting in this double capacity under the authority of general Wilkinson; then forced on board a vessel, and continued under restraint, till he gets within a few miles of Richmond! and *all this,* without so much as the pretence of any cause or crime, and under the control of Wilkinson? I ask, what would Hawkins, or other eminent Engglish writers, have said of a case of such flagrant oppression? Is not this the use of needless force, violence, and terror? Was not this an act of inhuman treatment to Knox? Was not the process of this court abused, for the purpose of oppression and injustice? Was not vexation practised under colour of this process? And do not the offences committed, come completely within the definitions of Hawkins, as punishable by attachment? Is not this arbitrary and illegal arrest, contrary to all practice and experience, in cases of witnesses in that country? There has been no example, in this country, of confining a man for the purpose of compelling him to give testimony. He only enters into a recognisance to appear in court to give testimony. No compulsion or influence is to be exercised over a witness; it is forbidden by the law. All temptation to perjury is taken away, as neither threats nor promises, rewards nor punishments are permitted by law. In the examination of a witness, no force is to be used. On the contrary, when a witness has been summoned, and has not failed to attend, there is no presumption or anticipation, that he will not obey the summons; there is, consequently, no compulsion to be exercised on him. Voluntary affidavits cannot be restrained. They are not free from exception, because they are liable to be abused; and are not legal evidence on a regular trial, because taken *ex parte;* but many people will go before a magistrate of their own accord, and make such affidavits. No person can prevent it. But when these *ex parte* affidavits are spoken of, it is always meant, that they are *voluntary.* A *forced* affidavit never was heard of before. Let us look at the power which the marshal has on such occasions. The 33d section of the judicial act points it out.—1 *vol. Laws of the United States,* p. 73: " If such commitment of the " offender, or the witnesses, shall be in a district other than that " in which the offence is to be tried, it shall be the duty of the "judge of that district where the delinquent is imprisoned, " seasonably to issue, and of the marshal of the same district to " execute, a warrant for the removal of the offender, and the wit- " nesses or either of them, as the case may be, to the district " where the trial is to be had." What is the power which the magistrate has by this clause? It is unnecessary to inquire into the extent of it. He had no such power as is here contended for. The party accused was not committed *by him,* nor brought *before him,* nor imprisoned in his district. He had, therefore, no right at all to confine the witness for the purpose of transporting him to the district where the trial was to be had: and yet, that was done by Mr. Hall, notwithstanding the plain and explicit terms of the law, that the duty of " the judge of the district, *where the delinquent is imprisoned,* is to issue a warrant, and of the *marshal of the same district to execute it,* for the removal," &c. This judge Hall well knew, that the accused was not imprisoned in his district; that he had not committed him; and that, therefore, under this law, he had no right to issue such a warrant, and as he could not *lawfully grant*, so the marshal could not *lawfully execute* such a warrant. The act was, therefore, unlawful, and every person knowingly and actively concerned in it or otherwise contributing to it, was participating in the offence, and guilty of a contempt of the court.

I am astonished at the boldness of this judge, in supporting the arbitrary military order of the general; for such it assuredly was. Affidavits, sir, they called for as gluttons: their greediness is never to be satisfied. But why did they ask for them? What was their object in so doing? Was it not to entangle their prisoner, by compelling him to make an affidavit, which he could not afterwards retract? The witness once committed by his oath, struggles to adhere to what he has sworn to. The printed interrogatories pin him down to a particular point. Whatever may be his wishes or feelings, he must adhere to them. Great strength and presence of mind, are not always to be expected in a person, placed as Mr. Knox was at New-Orleans. That strength of mind, which will adhere to the exact truth under every pressure and difficulty, is not to be found in every man. The witness is not to be always at hand to explain his affidavit. Mr. Knox was in a strange country friendless, in want of every thing, and subject to the military despotism of general Wilkinson. From his situation it might be supposed, that the affidavit which he would give would be different from what it would be, if given in a court of justice, where law and order are preserved, and testimony is not extorted at the point of the bayonet. This was the object of the printed interrogatories; and of obtaining the affidavit of Mr. Knox: for they calculated, that a regard for his own reputation, would prevent him from contradicting any fact to which he had previously deposed. He might hesitate between the love of truth, and a regard for his character. He might greatly prefer a candid detail of facts; when by showing him his former testimony, and reminding him that want of uniformity in his evidence would expose him to public contempt, his real regard to the truth would be shaken, so as to make him confirm his former extorted statement. Sir, there is not a more dangerous power, that can be exercised on the part of the government, than that of forcing a man to give an affidavit taken *ex parte*, by a man who will not be careful to state facts as intended by the witness, but as tending to establish the object, or to favour the views of those who take it. He may wish to retract; but when his deposition is brought before his eyes, he will be unable. Sir, what must be the force of that man's mind, who, unskilled in courts, unskilled in the world, can give a correct statement of facts, when confronted in court with his declarations before committed to paper, and can firmly explain and give a narration different from it? Who can be safe, if proceedings like these should be tolerated? We are told, that the bill of rights gives to the accused the right of being confronted with his accus rs and witnesses. That privilege would be evaded in a case like this. The witness would be unequally matched in meeting the terrors of a slanderous world. Yes, he would be terrified by the censures of an inconsiderate and defamatory world. As long as the law could not reach him, he would not hesitate between adhering to his former deposition, and what he would know secretly within himself to be correct. I trust, that whatever may be the fate of this motion, you will not suffer such encroachment on the privileges of witnesses; that you will not suffer them to be intimidated, and overawed by art and dexterity, from telling the real truth; or compelled to give colouring to circumstances contrary to their meaning. Sir, we cannot do better than to adopt in the law, the principle in the Lord's prayer: "Lead us not into temptation." This improper mode of extorting *ex parte* testimony, will cause a man to have a conflict in his own mind, between the truth of which he is conscious, and what he may have hastily been made to declare. We contend, that neither the proceedings in a cause, nor the witness should be interfered with, and that to do either amounts to a contempt of the court. In support of these principles we adduce several respectable authorities.—*5th Viner's Abridgment, p.* 444, 445, 446. In *2d Atkin,* 469. it was determined to be a contempt of the court, to publish a libel against a party, or an advertisement reflecting on the witnesses in a cause. And it was observed by that great chancellor, Lord Hardwicke, "That nothing was more incumbent on courts of " justice, than to preserve their proceedings from being misre- " presented; that nothing was of more pernicious consequence, " than to prejudice the minds of the public against persons con- " cerned as parties in a cause before it was finally heard." It was also observed by him, that "to abuse the parties in a cause, or to " prejudice mankind concerning it before it was heard, was a " contempt of the court as well as to scandalize the court itself." And in *2d Vezey,* 520. it was adjudged, that to publish an advertisement concerning proceedings in court was a contempt of the court. In the case here referred to, a man was committed for offering 500l. to prove a fact, though the court had already decided the point. The principle is the same in the case now before the court, as in those cases. Why is the publication of a libel against a party in a cause depending in a court of justice, or of an advertisement reflecting on the witnesses, deemed a contempt of the court? Why are all publications to inflame or prejudice the public mind prohibited? Because they tend to prejudice the public mind against the parties, or the proceedings in the cause; because they obstruct the free administration of justice; because it may influence the minds of the jury, who may have to try the cause, and, consequently, may occasion an unjust determination. Why are such rules of caution adopted in taking evidence, but to prevent false swearing? Why are needless force and violence in making arrests forbidden, and why is force towards a witness censured by the law? Because, in these cases, the mind is not left free, though it ought to be free. Compare these cases with the severity practised in this case. The minds of the public may not be prejudiced, but the mind of the witness was not free: he was under temptation to adhere to what he had said. He may, indeed, not have been under terror; perhaps the firmness of his mind may have supported him, and prevented him from being alarmed: but terror was rigidly employed by military authority. He was arrested and thrown by a military officer into gaol; was escorted by a military officer; forced on board a military vessel, under the command of the same military officer, and there for a long time restrained by the same military officer. If there can be a case of greater enormity than this, it has eluded my search. If there were nothing in this case more than the improper and unjust effort to obtain the affidavit of Mr. Knox to commit him, it would be sufficient to constitute a contempt of the court, and would be punishable by attachment: but it is rendered further criminal by the force used to obtain it. The liberty of the witness was invaded. A free citizen of the United States is dragged by corporeal force and thrown into gaol, for the crime of being a witness; and this within the knowledge, and at the instigation of general Wilkinson. I hope I shall not be told, that there was an association with certain conspiracies, which rendered these rigorous measures necessary and proper. There was no connexion proved between Knox and any conspiracies. Why insidiously attack a man as a witness, who is to be denounced as a criminal? I hope that no man, who is not guilty of a crime, will be caught and cooped as a gaol-bird, and compelled to receive crumbs of bread through the grate of a prison, at the will of a military commander, especially when I recollect what is to be superadded: that he is to be transported twelve or fifteen hundred miles, not for trial or suspicion of an offence, but for the iniquity of being supposed to be a witness, accidentally acquainted with facts. What are to be the consequences, if such doctrines as these are to be tolerated? That it is only in the breast of a military commander to transport any, the most peaceable citizen, if he be only supposed to be a witness, on board of a vessel, under military restraint, at any season of the year, however inclement, and any distance, without a crime, or the suspicion of a crime? We, who have so often seen and read the declaration of independence, must feel indignation at the oppression practised upon Mr. Knox. This is one of the acts of oppression, we are told, that the British government had committed against us. "Transporting us beyond seas, to be tried for pretended offences," is stated in the declaration of independence, as one of the principal acts of misrule, which roused us to resistance, and to declare ourselves independent. To be free from such aggression on our rights was a fundamental part of the basis of our independence. This was not a mere ebullition of patriotism for the purpose of exciting popular phrensy; nor one of those artifices used to increase the public discontent, or to swell the catalogue of the crimes committed by Great Britain. No, sir, this particular injury alleged in the declaration of independence was a real, an enormous grievance, which was execrated by the wisest men of our country. Exemption from it was founded in human rights, and was one of those blessings of liberty to which we had by nature a right, and which having secured, we ought ever to be jealous of preserving. This invaluable privilege we claim as citizens. It is a demand which we make of the government for protection, and it must be guarded by the court, unless some of those doctrines, which we have long reprobated in a military despotism, shall be sanctioned to destroy our rights. Even *then*, when criminals were transported, the innocent were left unmolested. What shall we say to this aggravated case, when the gentlemen themselves must admit, that this man is innocent?

I will not enter into those feelings that might be described, but I feel horror when I reflect that an individual, innocent and inoffensive, engaged in locating lands for the subsistence of himself and family, should be stopped from completing his laudable undertaking, and taken up far from his home, his family and friends, and transported as a witness twelve hundred miles, to the injury and derangement of his views and domestic concerns. I hope, sir, that transportation will be reserved for the guilty. If these things be done and tolerated in the green tree, what shall not be tolerated in the old? What is to be the effect of a precedent like this? Who can foresee the consequences if it be not repressed? This particular case may lead to dreadful events, and by artificial means become a tempest. But remember, sir, you have foresight, and can judge of the practical effects of injurious precedents; and if the unjust proceedings on this case be not severely censured and punished, though we may not suffer, our children will repent of it. But this act is said to have been extra-territorial, and that Wilkinson was not engaged in the whole of it; and therefore it is pretended without the control of the court. This is true, as far as Mr. Hall is concerned. We cannot operate on him here. If it were so at the beginning, see how it has passed from New-Orleans to Richmond.

Wilkinson was engaged in it at the beginning, at the second stage, and at James' river itself. The spirit of Wilkinson pervades the whole. He is every where seen, not merely as an integral part, but as the first cause of the whole. Is this court to suffer its witnesses to be abused without its jurisdiction? But I say, that it was not without the limits of the jurisdiction of this court. There must be a power in every court, to procure the attendance of witnesses; and wherever that power extends, the witnesses are protected by it; particularly if the man who has abused them, be present before the court. General Wilkinson is present and may be animadverted on. I will not pretend to say, what effect this may have on his character, nor can it affect the right to examine into his conduct; because he ought to have preconceived the consequences before he committed the acts. The man who interposes the sword, in support of the civil authority, ought to have the patriotism to acquiesce under the consequences, let them be what they may. The prying world may ask, whether Wilkinson is to be supported in such outrages? In practising on the necessities, fears, and terrors of the witnesses? Whether he is to be supported in the duress which prevailed on land and water? and in (what will be more fully discussed hereafter) the improper if not felonious taking of letters from post-offices? These questions will be asked after the testimony is known. The answers will be awful to him. The consequences of his violent and outrageous conduct must be awful to him. He will find himself devested of his military array and parade with which he used to be surrounded at New-Orleans, to stand here like a common individual. He must then answer those questions and account for his invasions of the rights of his fellow citizens. The magnitude of the offence calls for exemplary punishment. I insist on the motion that I have made, that an attachment do issue against general Wilkinson, for the various reasons I have stated. He is here himself, and if he be innocent, he can answer and purge himself on oath, of the guilt imputed to him; and if guilty of abuse of power, let him be punished in the proper manner.

Mr. MARTIN said, that he would make a few additional observations; that he would not enter into a general detail of the subject *then*, but would adduce some additional authorities to show, that the acts at New-Orleans were illegal, and that the magistrate had no authority for what he did. If it were pretended that the act of congress justified it, gentlemen were much mistaken. [He then read *Graydon's Digest of the Laws U. S.*] The 33d section of the judicial act, must be that on which they relied; that witnesses examined under the circumstances there stated may be committed, but that this law extended only to the magistrate before whom the arrested person was brought to be examined; that it says, " it shall be the duty of the judge of that district where the delinquent is imprisoned, to issue a warrant, &c." that Hall did not commit colonel Burr, who was seized and transported more than a thousand miles, was brought hither, examined here, and recognised to appear this term; that the magistrate had no power to examine the witnesses at all, except where the accused person was brought before him to be examined. That 2 *Hale's Pleas of the Crown, p.* 51, and 285., and *Mac Nally,* 314. prove that Hall had not this authority. Those authorities state, that where a crime is committed in the county of B., and the criminal is arrested in the county of C., the magistrate before whom he is brought to be examined in the county of C. has really no original jurisdiction over him, nor can his examination be read on his trial, though from the necessity of the case, and to preserve the peace, he has a consequential jurisdiction; and can examine and commit him in order to be sent to the proper county. But that here, as the party accused was not brought before *Hall,* he had no power whatever. He had neither original nor consequential jurisdiction. Every thing he did at New-Orleans, at the request of general Wilkinson, was perfectly *illegal* and *extrajudicial;* but that perhaps it might be said, that state-necessity would justify what the law did not authorise. On this subject he referred the court to what was said by one of the most celebrated judicial characters of the British judiciary, lord Cambden, 3 *State Trials,* 320. He referred also to 1 *State Trials, vol.* 7. 180.

Mr. HAY.—He is anticipating arguments which we shall never use.

Mr. MARTIN quoted 3 *State Trials,* 8th article of the impeachment of Sir Robert Beckley. 1 vol. 709, 710, 711. 716, 717. 2 *State Trials,* 306. *vol.* 12. 7 *State Trials,* 306.

Mr. WIRT.—I shall not trouble you to take notes. The short question is, whether general Wilkinson be guilty of a contempt, and ought to be attached? We proposed that the court should decide at once without any observations on either side; but gentlemen insisted on an argument, and they have had it. Our impressions are, that the evidence is perfectly clear; and we are willing to submit the question on the argument already heard.

Mr. BURR's counsel insisted to speak further.

Mr. WICKHAM.—All questions are very plain to counsel on their own side. They may be mistaken. Though it may not be perfectly clear on our side; yet I think I can convince the court, that on an examination of the law and the facts, the attachment ought to issue.

Mr. Mac Rae.—I regret that so much of the time of the court is to be consumed on every point. I confess that my hopes were, that our offer, to submit the case without discussion, would have been agreed to; but as they insist on an argument, they must be gratified. I hope that I may be permitted to say, that in the whole course of my short practice, I never read or heard of a case similar to that now before the court. The motion as to its foundation is "*sui generis!*" No motion of a similar character or nature can be found in the annals of forensic proceedings, either in England or in this country. If there be any record of any such motion, I have been unable to find it, after the most industrious researches. Mr. Randolph, sensible of this, thought proper to read a passage from *3d Hawkins*, to show, that such cases might occur, for which no precedent could be found; and that in such cases, the court was to decide "*according to the general reason of the law.*"

It was deemed proper to state, as some kind of an apology for the unmerited attack on general Wilkinson, that no precedent could be found to justify this application to the court. Before I shall reply to the animadversions on his character, I beg leave to observe, that general Wilkinson is doubly protected by the law of the land from any danger from this motion, even admitting that the charges against him are true, which is utterly denied. The charge against him is, that he has obstructed the administration of justice in the cause of the prisoner. He is said to have obstructed the administration of it, by two distinct acts: First, by extorting testimony from Knox, on this subject: Secondly, by forcibly bringing him round from New-Orleans to this city, to give evidence here. If these charges were both true, they would not warrant the motion to attach general Wilkinson. I shall *by* and *by*, prove them to be untrue. But suppose them, for the sake of argument, to be true. If the offence have been committed at all, according to the allegations of those who have made this motion, it has been committed at New-Orleans. For any real offence committed at New-Orleans, a person is not answerable before this court; because that place is not within its jurisdiction. I should deem it an insult to this court to dwell on such a topic, or to use much argument to prove, that an offence, committed out of the jurisdiction of this court, cannot be judicially noticed by it. But suppose the offence to be done within the limits of Virginia, and of course within the jurisdiction of this court. General Wilkinson, even in that event, would not be answerable in this form; because he appears as a witness before the court, in obedience to its subpœna, and a witness is privileged from arrests: he cannot be arrested for any act of this description.

In the 1*st vol. of the Laws of the United States, p.* 74, it is enacted, " That the laws of the several states, except where the constitution, treaties or statutes of the United States, shall otherwise require or provide, shall be regarded as rules of decision, in trials at common law, in the courts of the United States, in cases where they apply." There is no particular direction given in the laws of the United States, as to the privileges of witnesses; of course, whenever they come in question, it will be proper to inquire in the acts of the legislature of Virginia, how extensive their privileges are. In the *revised code of the Laws of this state*, *p.* 278, it is enacted, " That witnesses shall be privileged from arrests, *in all cases except treason, felony, and breaches of the peace,* during their attendance." The only cases in which a person who is a witness can be arrested, are treason, felony, and breaches of the peace. Here we might safely rest his defence; but every step he takes, as a soldier and patriot, he travels on solid ground. I trust that this court will say, that instead of obstructing the administration of justice, or deserving the smallest censure, for what he has done in this case, he has deserved well of his country, and merits the highest encomium. When he looks back to these transactions, and the part he acted, as well towards Knox as to others, he will see no cause to blame himself for any thing he has done in public or private; but will feel that pride which conscious innocence never fails to inspire. He has risked his fortune, his life, and his fame, to save his country from audacious treason, which but for him, might have ended in the subversion of the government, and destruction of the liberties of his country. I trust, and he expects, that his country and this court will examine and appreciate his conduct, and will bestow on him that reward of praise, which his praiseworthy deeds demand.

Sir, Mr. Randolph let out an important secret. The gentleman finding that there is no evidence to bear them out in their illiberal attack on the character of general Wilkinson, intimates, that they will resort for testimony against him, to the very man who is thus attacked; that they will call on him to answer their interrogatories. Is this correct? Has Mr. Randolph's extensive reading taught him, that, instead of proving general Wilkinson's guilt, he shall be condemned out of his own mouth?

Here Mr. WICKHAM interrupted Mr. Mac Rae, and informed him, that he had misunderstood Mr. Randolph, (who was then absent), who had taken the course pointed out by the court, and the chief justice explained it thus: that the attachment must go, if the testimony were sufficient to prove that it ought to be granted; and *then* the defendant must answer interrogatories; but that without sufficient evidence, an attachment could not be granted in any case.

Mr. MAC RAE.—I have examined authorities, and understand the regular course; but I understood Mr. Randolph to have said, that if the evidence amounted only to suspicion, general Wilkinson must be called on as a witness against himself, which would be illegal and a violation of a sacred right. Here Mr. Mac Rae referred to 1*st Dallas's Reports*, 328, in the case of the Commonwealth v. Oswald, and read part of the argument of the counsel, and the opinion of the court, approving thereof; and contended that the contempt must be proved by disinterested witnesses; and that this proof must be clear and full; after which proof, the defendant has the privilege of purging himself from the imputed offence. He then proceeded: The question then is, has he committed this offence or not? Mr. Randolph says, that not merely the evidence of Knox proves this contempt, but that two witnesses, whom we have ourselves improvidently introduced, have confirmed it. This conclusion is wholly unsupported by evidence. Destitute of proof from beginning to end, the gentleman has been reduced to the hard and cruel necessity of heaping conjecture on conjecture, till he has conjectured that this court will, without a particle of proof, conjecture and grant their motion. Though I shall be followed by gentlemen of unexampled talents and excellent memories, I venture to affirm, that they will not be able to show, that this motion ought to be granted, or even to excite doubts. I must pass over some of that gentleman's conjectures, without feeling any kind of disrespect for him, (I am disposed to treat him and every other gentleman to whom I am opposed with respect). I feel myself compelled to do so, because they do not appear to me to merit a serious refutation. I shall, however, notice a few of them. First, he states a very important circumstance which he trusts will be conclusive with the court; that a military man was made a deputy-marshal; and that this was the result of a concert between judge Hall and general Wilkinson: that they were secretly plotting together to make it appear a civil, when in fact, it was a military power. When Mr. Randolph formed this conjecture, he unfortunately forgot, that when he and Mr. Graham were deliberating on the way of bringing reluctant witnesses to this place, to give testimony in support of the violated laws, he was only doing what he was bound to perform in duty as an honest man. That he desired to compel their attendance by legal means only; that he consulted Mr. Graham how to proceed; that it was suggested to him by Mr. Graham, that it would be proper to see judge Hall, and consult him; and that Mr. Graham, knowing that there was a misunderstanding between judge Hall and general Wilkinson, offered to consult the judge himself, and did so. What then becomes of the concert which is urged to have taken place between them? For it is said, that all were to be directed by general Wilkinson. Did Mr. Randolph recollect this? Or did he suppose that the court would attend to his statement of secret plots and contrivances without proof to support it? You find that the fact is, that there was no concert between them; that they were separated by a previous misunderstanding; and that judge Hall acted upon the application of Mr. Graham. Away then goes this conjecture; in truth, so all must go; for he has no proof to support any. But " a military man was made a marshal." What of that? Who made him so? You recollect the interrogatory put yesterday to Mr. Gaines. " Would you have accepted of the deputation unless you knew that it would be agreeable to general Wilkinson?" Gaines said three times on oath, that he had no previous communication with general Wilkinson on the subject; that he was advised by Mr. Graham. Did not Mr. Graham say, that he had urged him to accept it; and that it was much against his inclination that he did accept it? This conjecture also falls to the ground. It is a poor prop; but like the rest of the props, weak and useless.

But " captain Gaines acted contrary to law." Suppose we admit, (but which is not admitted), that captain Gaines did act contrary to law. What is that to general Wilkinson? Is he answerable for it? It was thought in days of yore, a hard rule, when they visited the sins of the fathers upon the children, to the third and fourth generation; but it would be still harder to make general Wilkinson responsible for the supposed misconduct of Gaines. I have shown that there was no sort of connexion between them. Gaines has declared there was none. Gentlemen seem to wish to prove, that Gaines has done what is unlawful, and then to impute without proof, the whole to general Wilkinson. I believe the spirit of the law justified what captain Gaines did. [Here he read *Graydon's Digest* of the laws.] The words are such as might have fairly induced the judge and captain Gaines to have acted as they did. The words are extremely broad, and comprehensive enough to cover this very case. It is not certain, but it is at least extremely questionable, whether the law did not authorise what they did. But whether it did or not, is not material. General Wilkinson and captain Gaines are two distinct men; and general Wilkinson is not bound to answer for the offences or errors of another man.

Mr. Randolph then skips to judge Hall; and his judicial outrage is repeatedly charged to general Wilkinson. Why, sir, there was a misunderstanding between them. The judge acted at the instance of Mr. Graham, and not at that of general Wilkinson, who therefore cannot be answerable for it. After proving this error or judicial outrage, as it is called, of the judge, they ought to show a connexion between them, to have existed before. But, sir, Mr. Randolph discovers a very important secret. He says, that the act of congress compels the removal of the party accused and the removal of the witnesses together;

that in giving power to the judge to remove the witnesses, it requires him at the same time, to remove the party accused that both must be removed together. But if the party accused had been removed before, ought not the witnesses to be removed afterwards? Because it does not come within the *letter* of the law, would he not have a right to send on the witnesses? I doubt whether *that* would be a correct interpretation of the act of congress. It cannot be reasonably supposed, that as the removal of the witnesses was as much intended as that of the party accused; that if the accused were removed first, the witnesses should not be removed afterwards. I should suppose, that the judge might remove both, at different times; that if he sent on the accused before, (from necessity or convenience) he might send on the witnesses afterwards. But whether the judge committed an outrage or not, is unimportant to general Wilkinson. He was not bound to attend on every step which judge Hall had taken; and if the judge may send on the witnesses without the party accused, it is to be intended, that he has fully executed the law, until the contrary appear in a cause of his own, in which he is a party, called on to account for his conduct, and in which he shall have an opportunity to vindicate himself. But whether his construction of the law be correct or not, is immaterial. Wilkinson is not amenable to this or any court, for any act of judge Hall, or any other officer.

But Mr. Randolph has discovered a great secret, which no body else has discovered; which the most *astute* men in the commonwealth could not find out: " That it was a military order which was given by Gaines to serjeant Dunbaugh, to remove Knox from gaol to the vessel; and this is thought a proof that the whole was contrived by general Wilkinson; and that the order emanated from him. This is in the very teeth of the evidence. Mr. Gaines being called on to say, whether he had not given it as a military order to Dunbaugh, answered explicitly in the negative; that he had not given it in that capacity. I saw the gentlemen looking attentively at the order; and I understood their motive to be, to discover whether Gaines had signed it as captain; but when this order is seen, there is no signature of " *captain*" to it. He merely annexed his own name " *Gaines;*" which proves that he was not acting in a military character. It is very probable that if he had been acting in that character, he would have signed his military title. It is customary, I believe, to sign military orders, with the title or rank of the officers who give them; and an officer of his rank would have signed the order as " *captain.*" If there were any doubt before, that doubt could no longer exist, after captain Gaines has declared before the court, not only that he did not give a military order, but that he never did act under general Wilkinson, in that whole transaction. He was called on repeatedly to say, whether he had not given the order to Dunbaugh as his serjeant, and in his military character; and he as often denied that he had commanded him as serjeant, (though he understood him to be a serjeant) but because he had obtained his promise before to execute the order; and if he had not, he would have got some other person to do it. Sir, if Gaines had been acting as a captain, and signing as a military commander, would he have proceeded to ask a favour as he did? Would a gentleman who understood his duty, have gone to him and asked him, "*Will you be pleased to do so?*" No, sir, he would have *enjoined it as his duty:* and his not doing so, proves that he acted in a civil capacity; and this disproves this conjecture also.

But general Wilkinson is a great criminal, because he consulted the attorney general of the district. The *outcry* which had been raised against this valuable citizen and soldier, gave him sufficient warning, in order to avoid reproach, never to do an act of this nature, but by the advice of persons learned in the law. Of course, when general Wilkinson, instead of giving advice himself, mentioned to those who were engaged to act for the public, that they should advise with the attorney general and another lawyer how to act; it showed a disposition to have nothing done but what the law warranted. Why are their acts charged against him? Is not this enough to show, that the charge of violence and oppression is wholly unfounded? If such conduct as this be censured, I should suppose that it would be better to be silent, than to give judicious and friendly advice. As Wilkinson was not himself a lawyer, he told those gentlemen, " Consult the attorney general, and other gentlemen learned in the law, who will advise you how to act." Is it indeed criminal to aid the government in a case where the government and all America are interested ; and, instead of giving advice to the persons called upon to act for the public, to refer them to the best source of legal information, the attorney general, and another lawyer? I never expected to hear such an objection urged against general Wilkinson. This part of his conduct is strong and conclusive to show, that he was determined that the laws of his country should be the rule of his conduct. But it is not to be wondered at, that sinking without evidence or law to support them, they should catch at this straw; for there is nothing but assertion and suspicion: all conjecture, and no proof.

But my friend Mr. Randolph, forgetting that he was addressing this honourable court, and feeling as he does sometimes, when he addresses gentlemen ill informed about the laws of their country, endeavours to excite sympathy, and tells you without proving it, that general Wilkinson threw him (Knox) into a ship; that he was torn from his family and friends, and transported hither. But he forgets the facts. What family had he in New-

Orleans, and how long had he been there? He stated, that he went with colonel Tyler down the river. [Here Mr. Mac Rae repeated the substance of Mr. Knox's own testimony, relative to his going down the river to New-Orleans and staying there.] You will observe, sir, that I am only stating what he himself said yesterday. He was dragged away from *his* country, and transported. What country? He only staid two short months at New-Orleans. But, alas! alas! He has suffered all these dreadful calamities. This is the melancholy statement made to help them out; but all without proof. We fear not its effects. But, sir, general Wilkinson is a curious sort of a man. He sometimes uses all the blandishments of a courtier; sometimes he is the most cruel savage that ever existed. Sometimes he talks of free-masonry; and all by fits and starts. By fits he is very kind; and by fits very cruel. But what evidence is there to prove all this? Has Knox said that general Wilkinson treated him cruelly? Does Mr. Graham say so? No, sir. Was he maltreated on shore or on board? The ship's provisions were very good; and he was treated on board like other people. Has captain Gaines said that he treated him very cruelly? Where did Mr. Randolph find this evidence? I hope he misunderstood the witnesses. Your honours, who have listened patiently to the testimony, know that these are only bold conjectures. Well, then, after going through all these conjectures, and refuting them, we come to another; that Wilkinson put him on board, transported him, and brought him to Richmond; and this conjecture is equally destitute of proof. These acts ought to be proved, before gentlemen indulge in this freedom of speaking to the court, of violence, oppression, and tyranny. I do not wish to tire the court by a recapitulation of all the evidence; but I will briefly repeat the principal facts, to show, that general Wilkinson had no agency in them. How was Knox first taken in custody? Was it by general Wilkinson? No: by the sheriff at New-Orleans. Before whom was he taken? Before judge Hall; a man, who, we are told, was at variance with him. By whom was he committed? By a warrant from the same judge Hall, executed by captain Gaines, in his civil capacity. Was this done by the direction of general Wilkinson? There is no evidence whatever of this fact. By whose orders was he carried on board the vessel? By the same deputy-marshal's request to serjeant Dunbaugh. By whom was he brought to Norfolk? By captain Gaines, who has the honesty to confess that he did it. Is it sense, or law, to attach general Wilkinson for an act which another confesses he has done, without having consulted general Wilkinson on the subject?

But it is a most important object to affect general Wilkinson; because he is summoned as a witness against the prisoner. It has been often said by the counsel of the accused, that he is a most important witness; and if the course pursued by those gentlemen can justify conjectures on our part, we may perceive that *they* think him an *all important witness;* for there is no step taken without some obloquy cast on this respectable man. It was rumoured all over this town, that he would never dare to come to it; that he would tremble to appear before Aaron Burr. This soldier and patriot has shown, that he can confront Aaron Burr or any other man. The report before, and the proceedings had against him since, his arrival, have but one object; and that is, to excite suspicions against his character. From the delay in his coming, even honest men began to think, that perhaps there was some truth in what was said against him. But now, that he has come, and that this cloud of prejudice has been dissipated, another must be conjured up. Not content with attacking him for his own acts, they attack him for the acts of others, in which he had no agency or concern. Does not the court see the object of attacking general Wilkinson? Has he done any thing to obstruct the administration of justice? Does the court believe that the gentlemen themselves believe, that he has done any act to obstruct the administration of justice? His great crime, forsooth, is, that he did presume to advise with proper and well informed persons, in order to *make the law his guide,* in endeavouring to procure material evidence for his country, in a case deeply affecting its interest; and for this high sin, he is charged with obstructing the administration of justice. Whether he have done so or not, the court will decide. I am confident they will decide fairly and correctly.

The court is entitled to admiration for having so very patiently heard all the arguments which have been delivered. It is right to hear every thing that can be said on both sides of every question brought before the court. I wish it to be known, let the event be what it may, that there never was a case, in which there was less of persecution, than this case against Aaron Burr. He has had privileges that never were extended to any other man. I rejoice that he has had those privileges; and we wish it to be known, that it is our desire, that he may continue to have the benefit of all the privileges to which he can possibly be entitled; because it will completely repel the unjust imputation of persecution.

Sir, shall I add any thing more? Is it necessary? But let me ask, why has the prisoner made this motion? Has he taken out a subpœna, that general Wilkinson or any other person has prevented from being served? Has any witness summoned for him, been prevented from attending? Justice has been strangely obstructed in this case; not by stopping witnesses, but by bringing hither a man who has been with Aaron Burr, and appeared to be a material witness. There are many motives for believing, that this man was an important witness. The court will recollect what he has already said. He was with the accused, and was, from his situation, one of those to whom the accused might have communicated some of his projects. It has been said, that there was no evidence of Knox's materiality, though general Wilkinson made an affidavit to that effect. The information given by Knox himself, and the circumstances of the case, justified that affidavit; and in my conscience I believe him to be material, and that when on his oath hereafter, on the trial, he will give material testimony, if he disclose all he knows.

Mr. Randolph may move for attachments to confine all the people in gaol, in defence of Aaron Burr, while he walks the streets unmolested. I do not know how many motions are to be made, if this motion succeed; and they have already apprised us, that they had several others to make. The next motion, I suppose will be against Mr. Perkins, for taking up Aaron Burr. Even for such a motion, there would be more ground than for that now before the court.

I hope, sir, that for the length of time that I have trespassed on the patience of the court, I may be excused; and that I may be also excused, if, by any inadvertent expression, I have wounded the feelings of any gentleman; which was far from being my intention. I merely obeyed the impulse of duty, and I cheerfully submit the case to the court.

Mr. BENJAMIN BOTTS then addressed the court as follows:

The charge, on which our motion is founded, is, that illegal means, invading the privilege of witnesses, tending to the corruption of evidence, and materially to affect the justice and dignity of the court, in the present prosecution, have been practised by James Wilkinson, within the jurisdiction of this court, so as to subject him to process of contempt.

The first description of these illegal means, consisted in rifling the post-offices, and the seizure of private papers, upon searches, some of which are attempted to be used against colonel Burr; and others are believed to have deprived him of the means of preparing for his defence, through the mail. These acts of oppression would, in England, have subjected any man to the heaviest pains and penalties of the law. In the time of lord Camden, that great supporter of the rights of the subject against the assumptions of power, upon solemn argument, declared, that such seizures violated the first principles of social union, and that the law of England admitted no pretext of state-necessity, to justify acts so subversive of the dearest rights of the people. He enumerated the multiplied abuses to which it had led, and clearly proved, that the power was utterly incompatible with the exemption of the accused from giving evidence against hims , and with those privileges which *Magna Charta* had secured. The constitution of the United States, provides against searches upon warrants;

but the present case reaches beyond the evil to which the convention looked; for Mr. Wilkinson thought the form of a warrant unnecessary. The act of congress inflicts high pains and penalties for taking or breaking a letter, after it has been put into the post-office. The postmasters, and all other agents in the establishment, are subject to punishment for violating the mail; no exception is made in cases of insurrection, rebellion, or invasion; though assuredly these events must have been within the view of the national legislature, as possible ones. Private property and commerce, the innocent and the guilty, will be at the mercy of principal and deputy plunderers, as long as the practice obtains. I never can reflect on this subject, without feeling strong emotions. I cannot forbear again to remind you of the part acted by the prosecutor when I first introduced this subject to the court, the other day. He complained that I should insinuate the perpetration of high crimes like these, without proof. His honest bosom seemed to swell with indignation at the injustice I was doing. I felt the impropriety of making such heavy charges, without the exhibition of testimony, and called for proof. Instantly the scene was changed. The man was lost in the lawyer. What a minute before was a crime, then became a subject of eulogy. The second class of illegal means practised by general Wilkinson, we contend, consisted in attempts to *extort* and *inveigle* partial testimony against colonel Burr.

There are two characters of craft in this branch of his misdeeds. The one acts upon *fear* in all cases; the other generally on *hope*. We see this man in all his power and splendor, inviting an obscure stranger to his quarters; he proposes several questions. Knox shows reluctance in answering them; he then tenders Knox his service, his influence, patronage, and finally, one hundred or one hundred and fifty dollars. Finding all these unavailing, he resorts to the influence of terrors. He is interrogated by Hall, who threatens imprisonment and transportation, in case of disobedience. A list of printed interrogatories is exhibited, and Knox is required to submit to examination on them.

This evil and corrupting practice of affidavits is but little understood. My friend Mr. Wirt stigmatized them justly, the other day, as tending to the worst of purposes, always containing the language and the colouring of a biassed draftsman, and never telling the whole truth. When a witness is examined *ex parte* by counsel, every thing that makes for his employer is carefully culled out and committed to writing, without the dross of what may be for his adversary's advantage. If a witness should know much for the accused, and nothing for the government, he would be passed by of course. These affidavits are sent to the attorney. He is armed now with a gre   bundle of them. So many daggers put to the bosoms of the witnesses, as they successively appear, could not

be more inauspicious to truth. Should a witness be cross-examined, to give a different complexion to a fact contained in his affidavit,
the terrifying writing needs only to be held up at the bar, and the
naked exhibition of such spectacle eloquently proclaims his destiny, if he vary in the least from that fatal paper. He is told,
" *if you go a step out of this paper, perjury is the consequence,
and your ears shall come off.*" The important right of cross-examination is useless in such a case. To be confronted by the accused, is nothing, when the witness is confronted by his affidavit.

The other means practised by general Wilkinson appertain
to the privilege of the witness, and the liberty of the citizen.
This work of unprovoked tyranny, began on a Sunday. Under
colour of law, Knox was imprisoned and transported for the
crimes of having eyes to see, and ears to hear. He was not permitted to obtain from his lodgings the clothing necessary to
cleanliness and health. The sagacious and patriotic judge had
as much reason to drag Wilkinson from the pinnacle of his great-
ness and pomposity, and to commit and transport him after he
had hung back, until " his friends trembled for his fame," as Mr.
Knox.

The *habeas corpus* act in England, was produced by the unlawful transportation of offenders for trial. That measure has been
marked by all the great measures of the resisting colonies and of
the old congress, as one of the most usual and most grievous con-
comitants of arbitrary authority. The legislature of Massachusetts,
in 1769, were excited to, what were said in the mother country to
be, seditious resolutions, against the use of such an expedient by
parliamentary authority. The articles of confederation; the various addresses of congress to the people of England, Ireland,
and to the Canadians; the petitions to the throne, and the re-
monstrances to the parliament; the declaration of independence,
and the preamble to the constitution of Virginia; all enumerated
among the acts of royal misrule, justifying revolt, the oppressive
one of transporting *offenders* for trial. The nation waded
through blood and slaughter, to rescue us from this power; but
now it is exercised as an act of course, not indeed in all cases,
upon a *criminal* by legislative authority, but upon a witness at
the pleasure of a military chief, whose delinquency in attendance
was real, while Knox's was imaginary.

But why all this complaint about poor Knox? He is nothing
but a poverty-stricken, obscure individual. The vague and whimsi-
cal phantasy of equality, that kindled enthusiasm in former times,
is now too ridiculous for our cares. The abuses of Knox are of
no moment. The sun rises and sets as usual. General Wilkinson takes his coffee in the morning, and reposes himself on his
sofa in the evening. We are happy and content at our homes,

and things in general go on as before. It is a mortifying thought, that the enemies of our happy form of government, may now triumph in the acquiescent surrender of the rights, which it was instituted to secure. They may boast that liberty has been scourged with relentless fury and perseverance; that the revolution has been shorn of the brightest of its beams, with the heartiest applauses of those, in whose presence the offences of a tyrant have been presented for punishment. I feel more pain and solicitude on this subject, as a friend to the present administration, than I do as counsel for colonel Burr. I could humble myself to beg of the gentlemen in the prosecution, to save the glory of our executive from the tarnish of praise and impunity to general Wilkinson. If they will not grant my prayer, I must address it to you, sir. I hope and believe, that the chief magistrate of our country is a stranger to what has passed and is passing here. His generous manly soul would surely disdain all the pettylarceny means which have been used to kidnap testimony, betray confidence, and induce perjuries; it would equally revolt at the wanton violation of the most sacred of our laws and chartered rights. Such a system cannot characterize the noblest administration that ever existed.

Let but this daring act pass unpunished, and we cease to be what we were. If a citizen could be imprisoned for three days, he may for three years. If he could be transported to Richmond, he may to India. If one man can be so imprisoned and transported, so may a thousand.

A witness was asked, whether Knox had not his liberty on the voyage? Yes, was the answer. How precious the boon! He was perfectly at liberty to jump into the sea whenever he pleased!

The attempt to make Mr. Gaines the scape-goat of this confederacy (he deserves a better fate) is only equalled by the atrocity of the confederacy itself.

We find that Mr. Wilkinson was inquisitor and transporter general, without scruple or disguise, until he was about to come to the United States. To borrow an idea from Mr. Mac Rae, the noise that had been made about his misdeeds, had taught him cunning. In the courts of New-Orleans, he could make the tribunal bow and tremble, by a parade of magnificent nonsense. To avoid his own humiliation in a freer climate, this farce, in which a mock-judge and a military-civil-sea-marshal, without oath, bond or compensation, were to perform their parts, was devised. It is too clear that Wilkinson was the wire-worker behind the curtain, by which the wicked catering and gambols of mimic magistracy were played. I pity the condition of a subordinate military officer bound to passive obedience. Mr. Gaines was a worthy, duped young man. I was fond of the honest appearance he made. The candour of his testimony made it more a subject of grief and indignation, that the contrivance should be to put the whole responsibility on him. The introduction of the lawyer, to complicate the disguise, is another feature in the picture. I hope, for the honour of the profession, that there is some mistake as to the part he acted. Wilkinson is to be discerned through every part of the cobweb. He makes the affidavit; he sets the lawyer to work; his military officer becomes a deputy of the marshal to leave his situation *without the leave of the commander in chief;* a serjeant is the deputy of that deputy; the captain on board is under the direction of the general; to his care captain Gaines commits Knox through the serjeant; the military purse yields the money given to the witness; the vessel taken up by Wilkinson conveys him, and Mr. Gaines owns, that if the general on the passage had directed Knox to be put in irons, the order would have been instantly obeyed. What, a deputy marshal, *as such,* to obey the orders of a military commander! The insidious attempt at Hampton Roads, first involuntarily made by Mr. Gaines, and afterwards repeated by general Wilkinson, to seduce an acknowledgment, that the civil authority had transported the witness, may be connected with the other proofs. But the demand, by general Wilkinson of Knox's parol of honour to come to Richmond as the condition of his enlargement, would be decisive on the present question, if it admitted of doubt.

But you are gravely asked by Mr. Mac Rae to pronounce, that general Wilkinson deserves well of his country for all these his patriotic acts. What, in other times, and in other places, would subject a man to be suspended between the heavens and the earth, from whence his spirit should flee for ever, now calls forth the highest panegyric. I heard a compliment like the present from the counsel, when general Wilkinson was here on yesterday. I looked upon him and witnessed a smile, when the occasion was better adapted to a groan. It was a smile of the ghastly kind. It seemed to be of that convulsive sort which distorts the face of the dying. Perhaps general Wilkinson took a retrospect and felt the compliment to be a reproach. Thus prejudice leads gentlemen to praise acts of atrocity. This subject has been treated with singular levity, by the gentlemen in the prosecution. They have not ventured to justify the commitment of Knox. The farthest that Mr. Mac Rae ventured, was to risk the supposition, that the act of congress was of doubtful application, and might possibly apply. He in this tacitly yields, that there is no justifying the conduct pursued in the commitment. The gentleman who spoke last, reminds us, that " the sins of the fathers ought not to be visited on the children." I say then, that the sins of the principals ought not to be visited on the subalterns.

Mr. Mac Rae concludes with reminding the court, that colonel Burr had enjoyed privileges that no one under prosecution before him had ever enjoyed. He said too, that you were perfectly right to hear us on this question. I submit to him whether the first remark were just or respectful to the court? In the latter point he differs from another gentleman on the same side, who has struggled much to prevent us from address. ing you.

It only now remains for me to prove that your jurisdiction is commensurate with our purpose. The 14th sect. of the judicial act authorises the court to issue all writs not specially authorised, for the more perfect exercise of the powers vested in it. The power of compelling attendance and securing privilege, cannot be exercised in perfection without a power of attaching for contempts in the one case or the other. The district courts of Virginia constantly exercise this right of overlooking the purity of the streams of their justice, through all its branchings, without the district as well as within. The right of attachment overreaching the limits of the state, must result as incidental to the emanation of the subpœna to other states. But the rioting of lawless power continued from New-Orleans to Richmond. When it entered on the seas it was within the regular limits of your authority.

In a view to the privilege of the witness this motion must be sustained, if we be deceived in all our other grounds. What means the privilege, unless it be, that he shall have protection from abuse? Is it to assist in this privilege to imprison him? Is the privilege to exclude him from all his rights, and put him at the mercy of land and sea gaolers? If this be the enviable advantage of privilege, general Wilkinson will *deserve well of his country* for assisting to maintain it.

Knox was summoned before any of this violence was used towards him. From the *moment* that he was summoned, he was under your protection. The naked service of a summons must have proved, that your powers reached not beyond a summons until there were default. It was absurd to suppose, that what this court could not do for itself, a magistrate, no way connected with it, could unasked and officiously do for it.

I refer the court, without comments, to *Supplement to Viner's Abridgment*, 225. and 3 *Hawkins*, 275. on the subject of contempts of the court.

When Mr. Botts was speaking, [being about two o'clock] the grand jury entered, and Mr. Randolph, the foreman adress. ed the court; and stated, that they had agreed upon several indictments; which he handed in at the clerk's table. The clerk read the endorsements upon them in the following terms:

An indictment against Aaron Burr for treason—" A true bill."

An indictment against Aaron Burr for a misdemeanor—" A true bill."

An indictment against Herman Blannerhasset for treason—" A true bill."

An indictment against Herman Blannerhasset for a misdemeanor—" A true bill."

Mr. RANDOLPH then continued: May it please the court, Although the grand jury have returned these bills; they have still other subjects for their consideration, and have adjourned themselves to meet to-morrow at ten o'clock.

After Mr. Botts concluded his argument, Mr. BURR addressed the court and observed, that as bills had been found against him, it was probable, the public prosecutor would move for his commitment; he would, however, suggest two ideas for the consideration of the court: the one was, that it was within their discretion to bail in certain cases, even when the punishment was death; and the other was, that it was expedient for the court to exercise their discretion in this instance, as he should prove, that the indictment against him had been obtained by perjury.

Mr. HAY moved for the commitment of Aaron Burr. He stated, that if the court had the power to bail, by the 33d sect. of the judicial act, it was only to be exercised according to their *sound discretion;* and that the prisoner was not to demand bail as matter of right, because the court was authorised to grant it, but by his making out an adequate case, and showing that he was entitled to it. He quoted 4 *Blackstone's Commentaries, p.* 298. to prove that this discretion ought to be deliberately and cautiously exercised.

Mr. MARTIN.—The counsel for the prosecution have then admitted the right of the court to give bail, according to its discretion.

Mr. MAC RAE did not understand from the judicial act, that the discretion was to be exercised at this stage of the business, but only at the time of making the arrest.

Mr. MARTIN.—I can hardly suppose that this court has less power than the court of king's bench in England, which certainly possesses this authority, according to 2 *Hale, p.* 129. 134.

Mr. WIRT was extremely solicitous to do any thing, compatible with his duties, which might soften the situation of the prisoner, and if the court had the discretion, he did not wish them to restrict it; but he did not perceive the analogy which had been drawn between this court and the court of king's bench. The powers of that court grew out of the common law of England, whereas the powers of this court were defined by a statute of our country. What says the 33d section of the judicial act? " Upon all *arrests* in criminal cases, bail shall be admitted; except where the punishment may be death, in which case it shall not be admitted but by the supreme or a circuit court, or by a justice of the supreme court, or a judge of a district court, who shall exercise their discretion therein, regarding the nature and circumstances of the offence, and of the evidence and the usages of law." Is not this inquiry by the court stopped, said Mr. Wirt; is not the *evidence* and testimony stopped, when it is now locked up by the finding of the grand jury? Would it be right for this court to go into all the merits of the case, which this clause evidently requires, before the court can exercise this discretion? Will the court go into the investigation of the evidence, and thus throw itself into collision with the grand jury? It is obvious from these considerations, as well as from the words of the law, that such a discretion does not exist at this stage of the business, but only at the time of arrest.

Mr. WICKHAM.—The counsel for the United States express their readiness to accommodate colonel Burr, yet act otherwise. If the court of king's bench possess this authority, shall it be contended that this court is without it? Shall it be said, that the liberties of the people of this country are not as well secured as those of Great Britain? that a British subject has greater privileges than an American citizen? It is said, however, that this court grows not out of the common law, but out of our statutes; but will it be said, that, when this court has once been constituted, it does not proceed according to the established jurisprudence; that is, the common law? There can be no question but that a state district court can bail, even in capital cases. Will this court, it is asked, place itself in opposition to the grand jury? No, sir, it will not; and Mr. Wirt certainly forgets that the court is to hear both sides of the evidence; whereas, the grand jury heard one side only, and indeed a part only of that side; for had the United States' attorney sent up all the witnesses, whose names appear at the foot of the indictment, very different would have been the result of their inquiries. The ground which we take is this: that the grand jury have found their bill upon the testimony of a perjured witness; and if the court were to bail colonel Burr, would it not be justly inferred, that they had not set themselves up in opposition to the grand jury, but that they had been furnished with lights, which had been denied to that jury? "Upon arrests," signifies in all cases, where there has been an arrest. The case in *Dallas* comes fully up to the point.

Mr. BOTTS said, that if the common law did not enable the court to bail, it did not enable them to commit.

CHIEF JUSTICE.—Mr. Martin, have you any precedent, where a court has bailed for treason, after the finding of a grand jury, on either of those grounds; that the testimony laid before the grand jury had been impeached for perjury, or that other testimony had been laid before the court, which had not been in the possession of the grand jury?

Mr. MARTIN said, that he had not anticipated this case, and had not, therefore, prepared his authorities; but he had no doubt, that such existed.

Mr. BURR.—Two distinct questions have been blended in this discussion, which ought to have been kept separate: First, Whether this court have the right to bail according to its discretion; and secondly, Whether it were expedient to exercise its right in the present instance? If the court have no discretion, it is unnecessary to produce evidence. That question ought, therefore, to be previously settled.

Mr. HAY observed, that when he first addressed the court, he was of opinion, that the circuit court had this power, having been misled by a very transient conversation with the chief justice, on the first examination of Mr. Burr; that he had however, considered this subject more maturely, and the more he thought of it, the more he was convinced, that Aaron Burr was not privileged to demand bail. That he would feel no regret if the court could bail, but he thought they could not; that it was incumbent on the prisoner to show the law which authorised his being bailed; that the question was to be decided by the common law, by the acts of congress, or by the acts of Virginia. It could not derive the authority from the common law, because this court is of a recent origin, deriving its power not only from a late law, but a lately created government; and it has no authority but from an established law. Does then, (said Mr. Hay,) the law which established this court, expressly convey this power? [Here he read the 33d section of the judicial act.] Now, how are the court to attend to the nature and circumstances of the case and of the evidence? Will they require all the evidence to be before them, which has just occupied the attention of the grand jury for seven or eight days? Mr. Wirt's argument on this point is conclusive. The law too is applicable to a prisoner only at the time of his *arrest*, and not of an indictment being found against him; in the last case, the situation of the accused becomes still more precarious; the danger which he apprehends, comes nearer and nearer, and the temptation to violate his recognisance, becomes much greater than at the earlier steps of the prosecution. [Mr. Hay then referred to the case of Bedinger v. the Commonwealth of Virginia, decided by the court of appeals, where that court refused to review the errors of a district court, in criminal cases, because no act of assembly gave them the power.]

No man will contend, that the common law is in force in the courts of the United States. As soon might you assert the validity of the laws of the Cape of Good Hope or of Turkey. It was therefore ridiculous to compare the organization of the court of king's bench with that of the present court. As to the complaint of Mr. Wickham, that by this doctrine an American citizen would stand on worse ground than a British subject, it is unavailing. Perhaps courts of justice would even be more disposed to bail for treason under such a government as that of Great Britain, than under our own, where the power of the government falls so rarely and so lightly upon the people. Were even the common law in force in the United States, it would have no relation to the organization of our courts.

The power of bailing is neither derived from the common law, nor the act of congress; nor is it deducible from the laws of Virginia. In cases affecting life, the prisoner is not entitled to bail by our laws. *Rev. Code*, 63. 83. 411. In the two former pages, two judges of the general court have the power; but it cannot be inferred that this court therefore has it.

Mr. WIRT.—I have stated, that the powers of the court of king's bench are not applicable to this case, because, that court is the creature of the common law, whose powers are of ancient date, and have been growing up from time to time; whereas this court is recent, and its powers fixed and defined by law. There is another great difference. The powers of the court of king's bench take their origin in a fiction. It is supposed to be held *coram ipso rege!* In its origin, the king himself sat there, and he is still supposed to sit. Treason was a crime against his dignity; he might bail for it; and the same power belongs to the judges who represent his person. But how is it with us? Treason is an offence against the people of this country. And have the people ever sat here for the administration of justice? Are the judges of this court invested with the powers of the people? But on the supposition that this fiction does exist, is not the power of bailing removed by a positive law? Does not the act of congress expressly take it from the court? By the laws of Virginia, in cases of offences punishable in life and limb, bail is only admitted where there is but a light suspicion of guilt. If some of the witnesses be perjured, that does not prove that the indictment is found on their evidence. There has never been an instance of bailing after a true bill found. The act of congress enables the court to bail only on arrests, after examination of the circumstances, the evidence and law of the case. Can you bail therefore on a partial view of the evidence?

Mr. WICKHAM.—Two indictments have been found for treason; one against colonel Burr, and the other against Blannerhasset. If the latter were now to come into court, he would be bailed, according to Mr. Wirt's distinction, because not previously arrested; whereas colonel Burr would be devested of the very same privilege, though he was indicted for the very same crime.

Mr. HAY said, that the judges of the general court in Virginia have a copy of the record, with evidence included, before them, to enable them to judge whether they ought to bail in certain cases; but that this court, if they had the power, could not let to bail without examining all the witnesses.

Mr. RANDOLPH expatiated on this subject at considerable length, and with great ingenuity. He particularly contended, that the power of admitting to bail was incident to every court; that the power was implied in the term " court." That it was as absolutely necessary for the happiness of the people, that courts should possess this power, as it was, that they should have the right of committing persons accused, for their safe keeping, in order to be regularly tried. That the common law must be received to a certain extent; that every judge and court had the right to bail persons indicted before them; and that it would be an extreme hardship to confine in a dungeon, a person who could clearly prove that he was not guilty of the offence charged against him. That the counsel for the prosecution occasioned this lengthy discussion, by moving to commit colonel Burr; and that *time* was of no consequence compared to *liberty*.

Mr. MARTIN protested against the ingenious *fiction* of Mr. Wirt, as he called it. He challenged him to name any king, from the days of king Arthur to the present time, who either did, or would, sit in the court of king's bench. That the act of congress only defined the powers of individual magistrates out of court, but took away no power from them as a court. That bailing was incident to commitment, and coextensive with the jurisdiction of the court over crimes.

After a considerable desultory discussion on this point, the CHIEF JUSTICE declared, that the act of congress, in express terms, enabled the court to bail a prisoner arrested for treason. That there was no distinction between treason and other criminal cases, *as to the power to bail upon arrests;* but, that an *arrest* might be after a finding by a grand jury; in which case, the finding of the grand jury would be the evidence on which the court would have to judge whether the party arrested ought to be bailed. That they were to exercise their discretion " according to the *nature and circumstances of the offence, and of the evidence and usages of law*." That " usages of law" were to be found in the common law, and the practice of courts; but that he doubted extremely, whether the court had the right to bail any person, after an indictment for treason had been found against him by a grand jury; especially in a case like the present, where the government was ready with its testimony, and there was no extraordinary circumstance, (as an *alibi* clearly proved) to repel the effect of the finding of the jury, and that he wished authorities produced to satisfy the court that it had the power.

Mr. Burr said, that if the court thought it had the power to bail in any case after a bill found, it would be then necessary to show that it ought to exercise its discretion in this instance. That the finding of the jury was founded on the testimony of a *perjured* witness. That general Tupper would prove, that there had been no such resistance to his authority as had been stated by that witness; and that though this circumstance had been mentioned to the prosecutor by general Tupper, he had not been sent up to the grand jury.

Mr. Mac Rae.—General Tupper has made no such communication to me.

Mr. Hay.—Though I had a conversation with general Tupper, I do not exactly recollect what it was. The truth is, that I have carefully avoided conversing with the witnesses of the United States, (except general Wilkinson). General Tupper made application to me for permission to go away; but I said, that I would, for no consideration, submit to the imputation of consenting to the departure of any of the witnesses. He was not sent up to the grand jury, because he was not considered as a material witness.

Mr. Wirt.—He has made no such communication to me; and I take it upon me to assert, that the resistance to general Tupper was not the treason, on which the indictment has been found.

Mr. Wickham.—Suppose a man were indicted for murder, committed at some distance from this city, and a grand jury had found a true bill against him; but it could be proved, by every man in the city, that he was at the moment when the offence was said to have been committed, walking in the streets: would such a finding by the grand jury preclude a court from bailing him? The *constructive* murder in that case is of the same stamp as the *constructive* treason of colonel Burr in this case, who is indicted for an act said to be done in Blannerhasset's island, where he was said to be present, although he was at a considerable distance from the place.

Mr. WIRT.—Why should evidence be produced to prove the perjury of a witness? why look to the indictment itself for a proof of its own fallacy, when the requisitions of the court have not yet been satisfied? The court wanted authorities to prove, that in *such* a case as this, it had a discretionary right to bail " according to the *usages of law*."

Mr. BURR wished to know, whether the court would go into testimony extrinsic to the indictment.

The CHIEF JUSTICE had never known a *case* similar to the present, where such an examination had taken place.

Mr. MARTIN would produce authorities, if he had time allowed to him.

Mr. RANDOLPH drew an analogy between this and the case of a coroner's inquest.

Mr. WIRT said there was no apposite analogy between them.

The CHIEF JUSTICE insisted upon the necessity of producing adjudged cases, to prove that the court could bail a party, against whom an indictment had been found.

Mr. BURR did not wish to protract the session of the court to suit his own personal convenience. There was no time at present to look out for authorities.

The CHIEF JUSTICE observed, that he was then under the necessity of committing colonel Burr.

Mr. BURR stated, that he was willing to be committed, but hoped that the court had not forestalled its opinion.

CHIEF JUSTICE.—I have only stated my present impressions. This subject is open for argument hereafter. Mr. Burr stands committed to the custody of the marshal.

He was accordingly conducted to the gaol of this city, and the court adjourned till to-morrow.

THURSDAY, June 25th, 1807.

After a writ of habeas corpus was granted to bring up the body of colonel Burr, General Andrew Jackson from Tennessee, and sundry other witnesses were sworn, and sent to the grand jury.

Mr. HAY addressed the court.—We were reluctant the other day to discuss this subject. (It is not a question; for it does not deserve to be so called.) We wished the court to decide on the testimony; but counsel would have an argument. We have repeatedly proposed to them to close the arguments. I thought, and still think, this motion an obstruction to public justice. I wish to go on with the business of the court, and this motion prevents me. Gentlemen have determined to persevere; but, they have not stated the object; they have not specified the act of which they complain. If they had stated in their motion the fact said to be an obstruction of justice, the absurdity would have been apparent. By avoiding a specification they get over the difficulty, and are enabled to go at large on every topic for the public ear. But a fair examination of facts will satisfy the court that there is no foundation in law, nor justice, nor even in policy for this motion.

Before I examine the merits of this motion, I cannot forbear to express my surprise, that it should be made by the counsel for the prisoner. It is called a contempt of the court. In what manner can any of the acts charged, be tortured into a contempt of the court. Is this motion made by order of the court itself? The court would never have thought of it. Is it made by the United States, or their officers? No. Nor is it made by a party injured. Burr cannot justly say that he was injured by bringing a witness to this place, who was one of his own associates, and who quitted his wife, children, home and business, to join him.

What then can be their motive in making this motion? The solution is obvious. It is not with a view to clear away obstructions of justice; but to make an impression on the public mind, that general Wilkinson, whose evidence is important, was guilty of violence and injustice. The motion itself is a contempt of the court, by obstructing public justice.

CHIEF JUSTICE.—Mr. Hay, the court will hear any motion which you may have to make, or which any other gentleman may wish to make.

Mr. HAY.—I cheerfully withdraw the remark, and to save time, I will discuss this motion first. I will state as briefly as I can, the evidence of the only witness introduced in support of this motion to attach general Wilkinson, James Knox.

He says, that general Wilkinson sent for him, conversed with him about Burr, and his plans, as he wished him to be a witness at the expected trial. Knox complained to him of the want of money to carry him home. General Wilkinson offered him money. He knew, that if Knox were summoned as a witness on the part of the United States, he would be entitled to money for his attendance. It is only a conjecture of Knox, that general Wilkinson's motive for offering him money was to induce him to be a witness. I think this conjecture infinitely more probable: that, knowing his evidence to be material, and that he would be entitled to his expenses for his attendance, which might be prevented by his want of money, Wilkinson thought he might, very properly and innocently, obviate that difficulty by advancing money from the treasury of the United States, to the amount that he would probably be entitled to. Knox said, that he was afterwards arrested, and carried as he understood, before judge Hall; committed to prison, and carried on board the schooner *Revenge*, by what he conceived to be military authority; that he answered some questions, which, according to his own statement, were artfully put; but that he declined going through his evidence before general Wilkinson: notwithstanding, he is declared, in presence of this man, to be a military despot, keeping the whole western world in awe and terror. The witness himself expressly declares, that Wilkinson never used threats nor promises to him; and yet gentlemen have frequently mistated the notes, taken by general Wilkinson, to be an affidavit extorted from him. Now, sir, admit for a moment, that this man was brought here under a mistake of the law; admit more than he states, that he was brought by military authority, and the orders of general Wilkinson, and forcibly brought into this court. Suppose merely, that the general thought, that as the military commander he had a right to bring reluctant witnesses to this country; and had brought Knox to this court, because he knew him to be a material witness. I ask the court, whether this evidence, on principles of common sense, could justify the motion now before the court? This would be an illegal act, and for which Knox might recover damages; but certainly it could not be called a contempt of the court, without a perversion of terms, and confusion of ideas. It would *promote*, rather than *obstruct*, justice. There is one species of treatment which might be offered to a witness, that might be called such a contempt. Suppose a witness were coming to this capital with a subpœna in his pocket, which had been served on him to attend and give testimony in this cause, and he were forcibly prevented from coming to court, that would be a contempt of the court. In that case, the streams of justice would be interrupted, and the court ought to punish the party guilty of such unjustifiable conduct; and if the court would punish an offender for stopping a witness from coming to court, it would not act absurdly, blow hot and cold at the same time; and punish a person for bringing a man to court to tell all he knew in this cause. If to prevent a witness from attending the court, be a violation of private right, and a contempt of the court, for which the offender ought to be punished; on principles of common sense, an act diametrically opposite, cannot be the same offence. Admitting the conception of the witness to be correct, that he was brought hither by military authority proceeding from general Wilkinson, this is conclusive to show, that it is not a contempt of the court. Therefore, according to the testimony of the only witness brought forward in support of this motion, and allowing it the utmost latitude of construction, general Wilkinson is not guilty of a contempt of the court, for which he ought to be attached, or for which even a rule to show cause against it, should be granted.

But, sir, what is the real history of the conduct of general Wilkinson? Why, sir, the mountain of which gentlemen have talked so much dwindles to a mouse: nay, more, it disappears; not even a shadow is left behind. The cause, about which so much has been said, and by means of which so much obloquy has been attempted to be thrown on general Wilkinson, is this: Mr. Gaines was requested, by the attorney general of the United States, to serve subpœnas on such witnesses as should be indicated to him. General Wilkinson has the honour and glory of being the man, by whom a dreadful explosion was prevented. He knew facts and the particular state of things better than any other man. The subpœnas were, therefore, very properly transmitted to him, to be filled up with the names of the witnesses. Mr. Gaines did serve the subpœna on Knox, who said he was unwilling to attend; and he served it on him, because he was previously pointed out to him by general Wilkinson, to whom Knox had made some disclosure. Though he had not made a full disclosure, yet he had told enough to show that he was a material witness. I have, in my possession, the notes of his evidence, taken by general Wilkinson which, though neither sworn to nor signed, would have been sufficient to show his materiality; as he had come down the river with the party, and had some opportunity of knowing their views and objects. With a knowledge of this man's materiality, general Wilkinson made an affidavit, that he was a material witness for the United States, and it was sent, we do not know by whom, (perhaps by a servant); it is certain he did not carry it himself. I will make a single reflection in this place. If general Wilkinson had been under the influence of those diabolical designs which are ascribed to him, how came it to pass, that he intrusted this business to a man with whom he was at variance? This evinces a great deal of fairness and candour on his part. The judge issues his precept to take this man up, requires a recognisance of him; he gives no security; the judge deliberates on the subject; examines the laws of his country, (with the examination of which he was intrusted); gives his opinion, and expresses his extreme reluctance to act against him. He refers to the clause of the act of congress in question; to the counsel who was present; and *after all*, he said, that he thought it his duty to secure the attendance of this man as a witness. He committed him, not to military authority, but to the marshal. He issued his warrant to the marshal of that district, and the marshal authorised Mr. Gaines to act as his deputy; and here is the warrant, (showing it) which authorised Mr. Gaines to act as deputy marshal.

Mr. Botts denied that there was any order conferring such an authority. [Mr. Gaines was then sent for.]

Mr. Mac Rae offered to prove the respectability of judge Hall, as he had been attacked; and said he could amply establish that he was a man of character and talents, and incapable of being used as a tool.

The Chief Justice said, that nothing would be more improper than to go into such proof; that his character was not arraigned; and that, therefore, a vindication of it was unnecessary.

After a few desultory remarks, Mr. Botts said, that he had not attacked him except as to this business; but his opinion was, that if a lawyer in Virginia had given such an opinion, and acted as judge Hall did in this transaction, his licence ought to be revoked; but that he had understood from the best authority, that he was a man of unimpeachable character.

Mr. Hay.—Gentlemen may do as they please with judge Hall. It is not my business to vindicate him; they may lay him down in dust and ashes. It cannot affect general Wilkinson, nor the question before the court, unless they prove a connexion between them. I said, that the judge had committed Knox to the custody of the deputy marshal; that he directed the warrant to the marshal, requiring him to bring him to this place. The marshal executes a deputation to Gaines, who arrests him, puts him in custody, then puts him on board the vessel, and brings him as a witness to Richmond. General Wilkinson, so far from manifesting contempt of the civil authority, was fearful that Gaines might do wrong, and recommended to him to apply to the attorney of the United States, and to other counsel to know how to proceed. I deem this a very important point: because general Wilkinson had not the slightest expectation, that he would be the subject of public animadversion, or that Burr would be the public accuser for what he was then doing. Therefore, his recommendation to Gaines to apply to counsel, demonstrates the habitual reverence of his mind for the constituted authorities of his country. It is impossible that he could have done so, for the purpose of shielding himself from this attachment; for without inspiration from above, he never could have guessed that such a motion as this would be made. This conduct, in my mind, demonstrates, in the clearest manner, that those imputations, that he is a *military*, *lordly*, *despotic*, character, and holds in contempt the civil authority, are absolutely groundless. How far general Wilkinson was justifiable in time of great danger, when he was threatened by traitors without and within, in acting as he did at New-Orleans, or what he ought to have done on that trying occasion, is a question not now to be determined. I am inclined to believe, (though I do not certainly know) that the decision will not only be favourable to him, but that ultimately, the part he took will be honourable, in the highest degree, to his character.

The declaration made by general Wilkinson to Knox, who was complaining to him of the want of money, that he might have so much, if duly considered, was proper and correct. Now, sir, take up the subject as it really appears; even on the witness's own statement, it appears to be almost nothing. His ordering the military agent to pay money to the witnesses, shows his reason for offering money to Knox. When, therefore, we consider the case as fully stated by Gaines, it appears to be less than nothing; because general Wilkinson did what was perfectly consistent with law, and dictated by every principle that ought to influence a man of integrity and patriotism.

Gentlemen say, that it was his interest and his object, in all his plans, to destroy colonel Burr for his own salvation. If this were true, would he not have used the most decisive means to force the witnesses hither? What did he do in this critical situation? He receives subpœnas from the attorney general, and tells the agent of the government, that he must apply to counsel, and act in the business according to law. I ask, whether general Wilkinson has done any thing for which he or his friends ought to blush, or the accused to complain? All he did was to make an affidavit, that the witness was material; and every thing which *he* did, stopped there. After the affidavit, every thing which was done was the act of the judge and of Mr. Gaines. Will gentlemen contend, that, if my representation be correct, Wilkinson is to be blamed for these acts? I know they have too much respect for the court and for themselves to say so: but they will say, that the military and civil authority were united for this purpose. I ask, where is the evidence of a combination between general Wilkinson and the judge? What temptation was there to induce the judge to violate his oath, and prostrate his judicial character? Was it only for the purpose of gratifying general Wilkinson, with whom he had no intercourse, and with whom he was at variance? It is incumbent on them to prove a previous connexion between them before they can affect general Wilkinson. They have not deigned to do this. But we have a witness on our part, whose testimony proves, that such a connexion was highly improbable. I wish Mr. Randolph had pointed out the grounds on which he so boldly denounced general Wilkinson for the acts of the judge. Knox, who made a voluntary representation to Burr, has no right to complain. He could maintain no action against general Wilkinson. Suppose he were to sue him for false imprisonment. Could he recover damages against him for making the affidavit, that he was a material witness? No, sir. The connexion between him and the judge, and an improper and corrupt decision by the judge, must be proved. The witness could have no action against general Wilkinson, admitting the conduct of judge Hall to be illegal and oppressive. I think this ought to be conclusive. If there can be no right of action, there can be no contempt. But how strange does this proposition appear before the court? Knox was summoned to attend here as a witness. Suppose he had not attended, he would have been liable to an attachment for not coming; because the process of this court (in the name of the president of the United States) had been served on him, and it was his duty to obey it. He would, therefore, have been liable to be attached for not coming, and yet general Wilkinson is to be liable to an attachment for making him come!! Is not this to blow hot and cold at the same time? This may be law; but no man in the world would say, that it bears the least resemblance to common sense.

The gentlemen have never defined a contempt of the court. It is stated in *5th Viner*, 442.

The very definition of the offence excludes the possibility of its application to the act now complained of.

How then can there be any thing by way of contempt, unless gentlemen will seriously say, that general Wilkinson himself has brought the witness hither, and that bringing a witness to the court is a contempt of it?

The case in 2 *Viner*, 234, *pl.* 56. referred to by Mr. Martin, has no application to this case : it is not like it. The contempt there consisted in keeping a juryman from attending the court. I will trouble the court by referring to 4*th Blackstone's Commentaries*, *p.* 283. He states that the contempts punishable by attachment are " either direct, which openly insult or resist the powers of the court, or the persons of the judges who preside there; or else are consequential, which (without such gross insolence or direct opposition) plainly tend to create an universal disregard of their authority." He further enumerates in the two next pages, the instances of the different kinds of contempts by officers, witnesses and parties, and other persons; all of which come within the same definition, of disregarding the authority of, or disobeying, treating with disrespect, or abusing, the process of the court. I believe it has been observed, that there never was an author on any subject, either law or any other science, more distinguished for precision than *Blackstone*. This is a character which he so well deserves, that I believe that an act that does not come within the scope of his definition, is not a contempt, and ought not to be so construed. Motions for contempts are questions between the court and individuals. In ninety-nine cases out of a hundred, they have no influence on the private rights of individuals. Yet the judges are but men, and they may sometimes think there was a contempt, when none was intended; and, under the influence of feelings, of which they are not themselves conscious, may decide accordingly, and punish a party for an offence never intended, and of course not committed. This is an observation for which I am indebted to one of the ablest judges under the government of Virginia. Its propriety struck me with great force. Notwithstanding I presume that this is a fact, under such a high-toned government as that of England, the counsel who opened the motion acknowledged, that a case in point could not be found. Contempts in Great Britain have been frequent, and they have been uniformly punished; but in this country very few instances have occurred, and these were mostly by drunken men. I ask then, whether it be not wonderful, if their motion be regular, that in all the volumes in the English laws, which treat on the subject of contempts, not a single instance can be adduced, by the industry of all the counsel on the other side, of an attachment for such conduct as is now complained of? But it can be readily accounted for: it is because no such motion as this has ever been known in Great Britain. Though the doctrine of contempts has been too much extended in that country, yet no motion was ever attempted to punish a man for promoting justice by bringing forward a witness to give evidence in a court of justice. But I deny that this has been done by the party now accused. Is there a single circumstance in the conduct of general Wilkinson, showing a disregard for the authority of this court? An attachment is a summary proceeding, by which a man is taken up instantaneously, brought before the court, and unless, as in the present case, long speeches happen to intervene, he is immediately punished or discharged; and the case is determined with as much rapidity, as the fate of those suspected persons, who were formerly sent to the revolutionary tribunal in France. Need I say to you, that however justified on the score of necessity, this mode of proceeding is not perfectly congenial with the spirit and principles of our constitution and laws. I do not mean to say, that this power is improper, and ought to be cut up by the roots by the legislature; but that it ought to be exercised with caution, and in cases of real necessity. 1st *Bacon*, 181. & 4 *Blackstone's Commentaries*, 286, show, that attachments are issued on the ground of necessity. If it be a doubtful case, since he is not tried in the usual manner, but interrogated to give evidence against himself, the court ought not to stretch the doctrine, but confine it within those limits which sound discretion requires. Even if an officer of the court acted improperly, yet *Bacon* has laid it down as the law, that an attachment ought not to be issued against him, if there were no palpable corruption in his conduct. If this be the law, is it not irresistible and conclusive to show, that admitting that general Wilkinson did bring Knox to this place, yet if he were not actuated by palpable corruption, and if no extraordinary circumstance of misconduct appeared on his part, the court will not proceed against him in that way. If this caution be used in exercising this extraordinary power in Great Britain, is not this caution ten times more applicable to, and more desirable in, a government like ours? I will mention a case which occurred in Fredericksburg, which has been communicated to me by judge Roane. Some men were charged in that district court with murder; the grand jury found a true bill against them. The court told the gaoler to look to them; accordingly the man took them out of court; but it was understood next day, that he had permitted them to escape. The court thought it a contempt of the express order of the court, and the question was, in what manner a gaoler should be punished for suffering men indicted for murder to go at large. The gaoler was willing to encounter the punishment of the law, and the men came back. Judge Tucker thought it certainly a contempt of the court; but did not sit to give a judicial opinion. Judge Roane, recollecting the general power of courts, and the practice in such cases, and that he was himself a party in the cause, was unwilling to use the power which this law of England conferred, and ordered a jury to be impaneled, to determine, whether a contempt were intended? The point was tried, and the gaoler was found not guilty. I do not mention this as authority; but to show, with how much caution this summary mode of proceeding is used in this country. In Great Britain they have no fixed constitution, containing fixed principles, by which their parliament is to be regulated. But in this country we have a constitution which regulates the duties of the different departments of government, and defines the rights of the people. The seventh article of the amendments, adopted as parts of the constitution of the United States, provides, among other things, that " no person shall be subject for the same offence, to be twice put in jeopardy of life or limb, *nor shall be compelled in any criminal case, to be witness against himself.*" This amendment is not directly applicable to this subject, but it shows its regard for the great and important rights of the people, and that they are not to be interfered with, but with the utmost respect and caution. What cannot be done *directly* in a criminal prosecution, ought not be attempted indirectly by an attachment. I shall add, on this point, one more observation. General Wilkinson is attending this important prosecution, under the authority of this court. A subpœna, obliging him to attend here, has been served upon him. I do not say, that there is a provision in the constitution and laws of the United States, by which witnesses attending their courts, are put on the same footing as witnesses attending courts under the state authority; but I have understood, that the practice in the federal courts is precisely the same. It is, perhaps, grounded on that clause of the judicial act, which makes the laws of the several states the rule of decision in the courts of the United States, in trials at common law, in cases where they apply. In pages 122. and 278. of the *Revised Code* of Virginia, the privileges of witnesses are stated. In the former page they are exempted from ordinary process. In the latter, they are privileged from all arrests, except for treason, felony, or breaches of the peace.

I did not suppose, when I saw the extreme solicitude of gentlemen to bring forward this motion, their chagrin at delay, and their eagerness to rush into the combat, that they would have come forward on such feeble trembling ground, as they have done.

Mr. Randolph said, that suspicion was a sufficient ground for their motion. This is a plain admission, that he had no facts to support it; for if he had evidence, he would have relied on the facts he could prove, and never have called the attention of the court to suspicion. It is one of the last cases in which suspicion ought to be indulged. This is not a rule to show cause, but a motion for an attachment. Probable ground might be sufficient to induce the court to grant a rule to show cause; but not to grant an attachment. To grant an attachment against a man, to have him taken up, brought before the court, and compelled to give evidence against himself, not on evidence, but on merely probable ground, or what is the same thing, *suspicion*, is incompatible with every principle of law and of human rights. The evidence which it is incumbent on them to produce, in support of their motion, ought to produce not suspicion, but conviction. When Mr. Randolph says, that suspicion may be the ground for an attachment, he goes on a slender basis, which is occupied by the previous rule to show cause. This rule is always granted on showing probable cause. If an attachment were grantable on mere suspicion, what could support a rule to show cause? It must be less than suspicion!

But I am wrong to blame Mr. Randolph, because it is the best and strongest ground he could take; for, with respect to the fact which he ought to prove at this stage of the business, it is so far from being established, that it is clearly disproved. I know, sir, why the motion was made. If I may use another very homely expression; he " *let the cat out of the bag.*" He became more animated, his voice more loud, and his arms more extended, and then he told us of the dreadful union between the civil and military authority. This is bad enough. It is terrible enough to make strangers to our institutions think it an extraordinary mixture of powers. When we hear of this union of the civil and military authority, and the complaint comes from Mr. Randolph, it must excite surprise. Those who never heard of it before, as foreigners, must think that this business is strangely managed in this country. I am surprised to hear Mr. Randolph speak in such a manner. Why, sir, he knows that this identical union of the civil and military authority exists in our own government. The civil and military authority are joined by the constitution of the United States. The president is commander in chief of the army and navy of the United States: yet this constitution, which we all revere, and which we have all sworn to support, contains the very doctrine which Mr. Randolph so eloquently denounced. Even in this humble government of Virginia, where liberty is secure, and where no man apprehends oppression from the government, the head of the executive, is the head of the military. The governor is the commander in chief of the militia when brought into service: yet Mr. Randolph puts on his best countenance, voice, and gesture, to warn the people of this country, of a dreadful attack on their liberties, by giving this commission to a lieutenant to serve a subpœna!

He ought to have recollected another thing. He is not only a lawyer, but a politician. He knows that it is to this very identical union of the civil and military authority, that we are indebted for our liberties in their origin, and since in their preservation. If they were distinct, and exercised by different hands, we should soon see the military have the ascendency.

But suppose that lieutenant Gaines's undertaking to serve the subpœna was wrong, is it a matter of consequence to general Wilkinson, who did not know that Gaines had put off his military dress, *and assumed, instead of it, that of a civil officer?* Gaines swears that he never had any previous communication with general Wilkinson on the subject; and never knew any thing of it, till the deputation was offered to him. General Wilkinson never advised it; but if he had advised him to accept it, it cannot be charged as a crime to general Wilkinson. He is able and willing to bear the imputation without shrinking. There could be no impropriety in advising him to do what was perfectly consistent with the law.

But Gaines did not give bond for the performance of the duties of his office. What is the result? That the marshal was authorised to take assistance, and Gaines might innocently have assisted him; and this was all done, not under the military, but under the civil authority.

[Mr. Hay then referred the court to *Graydon's Digest of the Laws, p.* 264, to show, that his observations on this part of the subject were correct.] But, sir, the word " *military,*" is formidable in the ears of those who attend courts of justice. It is therefore used. It is true, that he acted in taking and keeping Knox, till he secured his attendance here. But had gentlemen attended to the evidence, they would have seen that this was done under the authority of the judge. But we hear distinctly those parts of the evidence which favour our own side of a cause, and turn a deaf ear to those parts which are against us. It is only on this principle, that I can account for Mr. Randolph's preference in asserting that Gaines acted as a military character; whereas it is evident that he acted in his civil capacity, in pursuance of his commission from the marshal, and in obedience to the order of the judge. In this statement, he is corroborated by Graham, and not contradicted by any one. He not only says so, but he produces the deputation from the marshal, and the warrant of the judge, for the removal. But if Gaines did act as a military man, general Wilkinson is not responsible for it, any more than the major or colonel, who were also his military superiors; and if he were liable to the party in a civil action, yet not for a contempt of the court. Yet, says Mr. Randolph, "he is incorporated with judge Hall, in all his acts;" and one fact is particularly insisted on as incorporating them, that of his making the affidavit, that Knox was a material witness: and the result is, that if judge Hall put a wrong construction on the law, general Wilkinson is responsible for it. Suppose Wilkinson had gone before Hall, and made an affidavit to the materiality of the witness, could Wilkinson be considered as responsible for any illegal conduct of the judge, after the affidavit was made? Making such an affidavit is a lawful act. On what principle can a man, who does a lawful act, be amenable for the subsequent unlawful acts of another? Will they contend for so monstrous a proposition? Suppose an individual goes before a magistrate, and makes an affidavit, that he has lost something, which he believes to be in the possession of another; and the magistrate, not knowing his duty, issues his warrant for the purpose of taking up the person suspected, to hang him; would the individual, thus submitting his case to the magistrate, be responsible for the conduct of the magistrate? What does he do? He goes to the magistrate and asks for the interposition of the law, according to the law. Is the applying, but innocent, individual to be accountable for the mistakes and errors of the magistrate? The position cannot be maintained. It was not advanced in so many terms, but it was strongly insinuated in their arguments, or plainly to be inferred from them.

But another circumstance is relied on. Wilkinson was the commander of the vessel. This is disproved. For it is clearly proved, that Franklin Read was the commander, who had a commission to that effect. Though the naval forces were for a time put under the command of general Wilkinson at New-Orleans, he had no control over this vessel at this time. It was natural that general Wilkinson should have offered a passage to the witnesses, if they chose to come in the same vessel that he came in himself. He manifested the same disposition when he came to Hampton. He got a vessel for their accommodation and its cheapness. It only proves his humanity and his disposition to oblige them, and make their passage as comfortable as possible.

Yet, said Mr. Randolph, with an increased emotion, and elevation of voice, that would have surprised me if I had not known his object, " why were subpœnas sent to him, if not to be used with military authority?" Suppose it *was* correct, that the attorney general had sent a number of subpœnas with a view to be used with military authority, and that the commander in chief receives them. What does he do? What would any man suppose he would do, or had done, if he were to form his opinion from what has been said of his character here? He would suppose that he had called about him his janizaries and his mamelukes; that he had sent one detachment to one part, and another to another, through the whole country, to search for, and seize all persons, who had the misfortune to be witnesses; that this military despot had sent out his myrmidons and military men, and without any regard to law or justice, had seized, confined, and transported as many as his arbitrary caprice required. This, and worse he would have done, if his character were such as it has been depicted. But what did this mighty lord of the west do, with all these witnesses? He gave the subpœnas to Mr. Gaines to serve them, and told him, that if there should be any difficulty, to apply to a lawyer for advice how to act. And this is the mighty complaint against Wilkinson and Gaines!

Do gentlemen think that they make a favourable impression on the public mind, when things in themselves so innocent, are represented as acts of the highest enormity? When things so white are thus discoloured? If they do, they are mistaken in all their calculations.

But sir, general Wilkinson is guilty again, because he ventured to ask Knox, if he were not afraid after what had happened. After what? " After I have arbitrarily seized and sent people to a great distance." What right had Mr. Randolph to put these things in his mind, or these words into his mouth? I will venture to say, that they do not express his real intention. It is obvious that his meaning was, " *Are you, who are an associate of Burr, and have been of his party, not afraid to appear before me?*" I will ask, whether it be right to ascribe to general Wilkinson sentiments which are not his own, and then to condemn him for the sentiments thus improperly imputed to him? Yet, this is the deplorable necessity to which gentlemen are driven!

Mr. Randolph says, that Burr and Wilkinson are antipodes to one another. Indeed they are; but in what sense they are so is a consideration which I need not mention.

But, says Mr. Randolph, " it is the intention of Wilkinson to ruin Burr. He must perish unless the other fall." We were charged with going too far, in drawing unauthorised conclusions and inferences; but Mr. Randolph has gone much further than any of us, and has substituted assertion for proof. He has stated, what is an unsupported assumption, that the reputation of Wilkinson depends on the destruction of Burr. I will not retort the charge; but I will say, that it is more important to Burr to destroy Wilkinson's reputation. He knows how important it is to the accused to batter down the reputation of general Wilkinson. The accused knows it, and professes it by his conduct; because, from the commencement of the prosecution till this time, the object of every step taken, and motion made, was to beat down the character of general Wilkinson: but if they were to accomplish it, it would be the same to their client; it could not save him. But they would say, that if it would not be victory, it would at least be revenge. The arguments of Mr. Randolph are so irrelevant, and the cases he adduced so inapplicable, though plain and not denied by us, that I shall not take up time to worry myself and the court, in proving points which are too plain to admit of controversy; but I will trouble the court with a few more observations, without noticing his law authorities. I shall boldly contend, that there was not only not a single precedent among them, but that there was not even the least justification for the present motion; that they have no real bearing on the subject. They were either general principles, which are not denied, but which do not apply to this subject, or relate to the conduct of the officers of the court, in serving criminal and other process. But he stated with great solemnity, that " any force to swerve a witness from the right statement of facts, was illegal and improper." In order to apply this, he is obliged to put down his own witness. The objection is, to the taking testimony from the witness. But the witness said, that there was no coercion used in taking his evidence; on the contrary, that he was treated with courtesy. The objection operates equally against them; for they have taken his affidavit in this city. Admitting there was no degree of terror or force used. This has no sort of application.

But Mr. Randolph says, that " no force is to be used in getting a witness to attend." This is not law. If the accused had been committed in the same district where the witness resided, and the judge had sent forward the accused, he would have been authorised to compel the witness to come, and if he did not enter into a recognisance, he would have put him in gaol. The spirit of the law is, that a witness who is material, and refuses to enter into a recognisance, may be removed by force. These are the provisions of the act of congress. *Force* may *be and is used.* The law directs that it *shall be* used. But the position, if it were correct, does not apply to general Wilkinson, because he did not bring the witness.

It was said by Mr. Randolph, that it was a " most dangerous power in any government, to extort testimony *ex parte.*" Is general Wilkinson responsible for all illegalities committed in the western country? Mr. Jackson, they say, has been guilty of great impropriety in taking evidence. But notwithstanding this blame, which they so eagerly attempt to attach to general Wilkinson, he has not taken any evidence at all. All he did, was, to make inquiry and take notes of Knox's evidence. But they ask why were these notes taken? To satisfy his own mind, that he was a material witness.

But there was one observation which Mr. Randolph used, with great warmth and solemnity, that " a citizen of the United States was thrown into gaol by corporal force, and transported for the crime of being a witness." Is it not surprising, that they take such ground as this? Is it not strange to hear gentlemen of great experience, who have been intrusted with the management of important business, gravely speaking in this way? to hear Mr. Randolph say, that " a citizen has been thrown into gaol and transported?" These are sounding and imposing words. Does not the court know, that these are things that may be done by law? The court well knows, that under the law of congress it is the business of a judge to recognise witnesses, and if they refuse to enter into a recognisance, or fail to attend, to commit them and transport them by land or water, as may be most convenient, to the place of trial. Is not this power expressly given by the words " it shall be the duty of the judge of that district where the delinquent is imprisoned, seasonably to issue, and of the marshal of the same district to execute a warrant for the *removal* of the offender *and the witnesses* or *either of them,* as *the case may be* to the district in which the trial is to be had?"

Mr. Randolph, without a single tittle of evidence, and without any principle of law to support him, prays in vain for a favourable decision. All the authorities which he introduced are extremely vague; they do not show, in the smallest degree, that the facts alleged, if proved, would amount to a contempt of the court. Superadded to all this long catalogue of black crimes, you are told, with great solemnity, that a citizen of a free country has been transported by military authority; not for a violation of the laws of his country, but because he was a witness. Sir, I will not animadvert on his mode of conducting a cause; I will only remark, that those observations, when made, were introduced with the utmost solemnity, expressed with the strongest and most forcible voice, heard by every person within the walls of this house, and were certainly intended by the speaker to excite indignation against general Wilkinson, and sympathy for the accused; and after all, it amounts only to this, that a witness may be compelled to attend, if he do not do it voluntarily.

The next observation was urged with precisely the same view. He seems to tremble when he fancies, that he sees the prostration of all our rights and of our independence; when with uplifted hands and eyes, and elevated voice, he tells you of the military sporting with the rights of the citizens! If it were mere sport, he need not be so much alarmed. But what was this military sport, against which he so loudly declaimed? It was simply this, that a *captain*, with the permission of his *general*, and after a deputation by the marshal, served a subpœna on a *witness*, and brought him with him, being himself a witness and obliged to come! I am not surprised, that gentlemen wander from the point, because otherwise there would be very little ground for them to stand upon.

He talks of the robbery and plunder of the post-offices. For what purpose? Suppose the fact to be as it is assumed without the slightest proof. Let general Wilkinson, or any other person, who has committed the act, be prosecuted according to law. Let the parties injured apply to the law, and the parties who are guilty be punished. But though the acts thus ascribed to general Wilkinson were clearly proved, they could not be considered as a contempt of the court. Every thing is ascribed to general Wilkinson, in order to furnish a sort of pretext for denouncing him to the world.

Being fatigued myself, and believing the court to be so also, I shall not trouble it with any further observations. I trust that the court will render a correct judgment, according to the evidence and law.

While Mr. Hay was speaking, the grand jury entered, and their foreman, Mr. Randolph, addressed the court to the following effect:

May it please the court:

The grand jury have been informed, that there is in the possession of Aaron Burr a certain letter, with the post mark of May 13th, from James Wilkinson, in cyphers, which they deem to be material to certain inquiries now pending before them. The grand jury are perfectly aware, that they have no right to demand any evidence from the prisoner under prosecution, which may tend to criminate himself. But the grand jury have thought proper to appear in court to ask its assistance, if it think proper to grant it, to obtain the letter with his consent.

Mr. BURR rose, and asked whether the court were about to give an opinion?

The CHIEF JUSTICE stated, that the court was about to say, that the grand jury were perfectly right in the opinion, that no man can be forced to furnish evidence against himself: he presumed that the grand jury wished also to know, whether the person under prosecution, could be examined on other questions, not criminating himself?

Mr. BURR declared, that it would be impossible for him, under certain circumstances, to expose any letter which had been communicated to him confidentially; how far the extremity of circumstances might impel him to such a conduct, he was not prepared to decide; but it was impossible for him even to deliberate on the proposition to deliver up any thing which had been confided to his honour; unless it were extorted from him by law.

Mr. RANDOLPH.—We will withdraw to our chamber, and when the court has decided upon the question, it will announce it to the grand jury.

The CHIEF JUSTICE knew not that there was any objection to the grand jury calling before them and examining any man as a witness, who laid under an indictment.

Mr. MARTIN said there could be no objection.

Mr. RANDOLPH said, he was afraid that the object of the grand jury had been misunderstood by the court. The grand jury had not appeared before the court to apply for the person of Aaron Burr, to obtain evidence from him, but for a certain paper, which might or might not be in his possession; and upon that paper being or not being in his possession, and upon its being possible or not possible to identify that paper, it might depend, whether Aaron Burr himself were or were not a material evidence before them. And then the grand jury withdrew.

When Mr. HAY had concluded his argument, Mr. MAC RAE addressed the court. He was solicitous, he said, to lay a communication before it, on a circumstance, which had lately transpired. The grand jury had asked for a certain letter in cyphers, which was supposed to have been addressed by general Wilkinson to the accused. The court had understood the ground on which the accused had refused to put it in their possession; to be an apprehension lest his honour should be wounded, by his thus betraying matters of confidence. I have seen general Wilkinson, sir, since this declaration was made. I have informed him of the communication which has thus been made; and the general has expressed his wishes to me, and requested me to express those wishes, that the whole of the correspondence between Aaron Burr and himself, may be exhibited before the court. The accused has now therefore a fair opportunity of producing this letter: he is absolved from all possible imputation; his honour is perfectly safe.

Mr. BURR.—The court will probably expect from me some reply. The communication which I made to the court, has led, it seems, to the present invitation. I have only to say, sir, that this letter will not be produced. The letter is not at this time in my possession, and general Wilkinson knows it.

Mr. MAC RAE hoped that notice of his communication would be sent to the grand jury.

Mr. MARTIN hoped that colonel Burr's communication also would go along with it.

The CHIEF JUSTICE was unwilling to make the court the medium of such communications.

Mr. MAC RAE hoped that the court *would* notify his communication to the grand jury, and for an obvious reason. When the grand jury came into court to ask for the paper, what did the accused say? Did he declare that it was not in his possession? No: he merely said that honour forbade him to disclose it. The inference undoubtedly was, that he had the paper, but could not persuade himself to disclose it. And what then must have been the impression of the grand jury? A cloud of suspicions must have fastened itself upon their minds; suspicions unjustly injurious to the character of general Wilkinson; and which the present communication may at once disperse. It is but justice, therefore, to general Wilkinson, to whom the inquiries of the grand jury may at present relate, to give them the benefit of this information.

Mr. BURR.—General Wilkinson, sir, is extremely welcome to all the eclat which he may expect to derive from this challenge; but as it is a challenge from him, it is a sufficient reason why I should not accept it. But as the remarks of the last gentleman seem to convey some reproach against me, (which no man who knows me can believe me to deserve) it may be proper to say, that I did voluntarily, and in the presence of a witness, put the letter out of my hands, with the express view, that it should not be used improperly against any one. I wished, sir, to disable any person, even myself, from laying it before the grand jury. General Wilkinson knows this fact.

The CHIEF JUSTICE then reduced these communications to writing, and transmitted them to the grand jury.

Mr. Burr.—Let it be understood, that I did not put this letter out of my possession, because I *expected* the grand jury *would* take up this subject; but from a supposition that they *might* do so.

Mr. Wickham, about to speak, was interrupted by the entrance of the grand jury; when Mr. Randolph their foreman, informed the court, that they had agreed upon some presentments; which he then delivered into the hands of the clerk. The clerk read as follows:

The grand inquest of the United States, for the district of Virginia, upon their oaths, present, that Jonathan Dayton, late a senator in the congress of the United States, from the state of New-Jersey; John Smith, a senator in the congress of the United States, from the state of Ohio; Comfort Tyler, late of the state of New-York; Israel Smith, late of the state of New-York; and Davis Floyd, late of the territory of Indiana, are guilty of treason against the United States, in levying war against the same; to wit, at Blannerhasset's island, in the county of Wood, and state of Virginia, on the 13th day of December, 1806,

Upon the information of

William Eaton,	Erick Bollman,
Peter Taylor,	Jacob Allbright,
Charles Willie,	John Graham,
Samuel Swartwout,	George Morgan,
John Morgan,	Thomas Morgan,
Elias Glover,	D. Woodbridge, junr.
David C. Wallace,	Edmund B. Dana,
John G. Henderson,	Alexander Henderson,
James Wilkinson,	Hugh Phelps,
Jacob Dunbaugh,	John Monholland,
Chandler Lindsley,	James Knox,
William Love,	Thomas Hartly,
Stephen Welch,	James Kinney,
Samuel Moxley,	David Fisk,
Benjamin H. Latrobe,	

JOHN RANDOLPH, foreman.

The grand jury, continued Mr. Randolph, have no farther presentments to make. He then delivered two papers which they had received from the court. The one was a cyphered letter, addressed to H. Winbourn; the other was the letter to colonel Morgan.

Chief Justice.—Mr. attorney, have you any thing more for the grand jury?

Mr. Hay.—I can have all the indictments ready to be laid before them to-morrow.

Mr. Taylor (from Norfolk). Is it not customary for the attorney to file informations upon these presentments? Is there any necessity for detaining the jury?

Some objection was made.

Mr. Randolph. May not the bills be laid before another grand jury, as the parties presented are not now in custody?

Mr. HAY.—That course would be productive of great inconvenience. All the witnesses are now here; and they will not, perhaps, appear before another grand jury, and the present jury are already in possession of all the evidence.

Mr. Randolph had hoped, that they would be discharged. He was not anxious on his own account, but there was one of the jury peculiarly and delicately situated; who wished to return to his family.

Mr. Taylor observed to the court, that a very afflicting circumstance, of a domestic nature, made him peculiarly anxious to return home.

Mr. HAY was extremely sorry that he could not gratify the wishes of the jury; but the interest of the United States forbade him. He would have the indictments ready at any hour in the morning, that the jury would name. Nine o'clock was mentioned, and the jury were then adjourned to that hour.

Mr. WICKHAM then addressed the court to the following effect:

I should envy the gentleman, last up, the peculiar felicity of never being in the wrong; and that happy ductility of judgment, which enables him to apply other gentlemen's arguments to suit his own purposes, and to view every thing on his own side as perfectly clear. The praise of general Wilkinson is his great object. His pure virtue and disinterested patriotism constantly excite his utmost zeal, and form the theme of his finest eulogies. Of this object he has never lost sight; but his own argument did not make much impression on his own mind: the farther he went on, the weaker it was. Whether this were produced by some supervening *doubts* on the subject, or because what is deemed clear requires no argument, I will not undertake to determine. It would however save much time if the gentleman would introduce a short *formula*, referring to his former arguments in praise of general Wilkinson, instead of perpetually repeating them. On what ground has the gentleman on the other side gone to argue so elaborately and zealously, if he think the case so perfectly plain? If it were so perfectly clear as he affects to consider it, why did he address so long an argument to the court? Did he believe so much labour necessary to satisfy the minds of your honours that the case was so very plain?

But, waiving all these considerations, I mean to confine myself to the point. It is to the court and the court alone, that I mean to address myself. The gentleman on the other side insists, that we have made no specific charge against general Wilkinson. We cannot help it if he do not understand us; but we have stated a specific charge in terms as plain, as any in the English language. If he do not comprehend it, perhaps it is because our arguments have not as much weight with him as his own. It is extremely difficult to conquer prejudice. Our charge is, that there have been acts in the highest degree illegal, done by general Wilkinson, under colour of the process of this court; that a citizen has been dragged by military force one thousand two hundred miles, for the crime of being a witness, and having a subpœna served on him. We contend, that this is a direct invasion of the liberty of the citizen; an abuse of the process, and a contempt, of the court; and deserves a most severe punishment, if we can bring it home to general Wilkinson, of which we have no doubt. We have supposed, that the judge's warrant was *merely* a void act; because it was illegal. We have supposed, that calling on the judge, an officer without authority, to make out a warrant, which was neither legal in form nor substance, but a mere attempt to give the semblance of legality to what they knew to be illegal, was an aggravation of the offence.

Gentlemen say, that it was only a judicial act, in which a judge may be mistaken, without being liable for his mistake. Will the gentlemen contend, that an illegal warrant, issued by a magistrate having no authority to act, can have any effect? Whatever he does, without having jurisdiction, is void, and has not the least validity: if he err, his mistakes are not excused. But if he have jurisdiction, and a right to act on the subject, he is not responsible for errors of judgment. There is nothing better settled, than that distinction between cases where a magistrate has authority to act, and cases where he has not. In the former, his mistakes of judgment are excused; but in the latter, he is personally responsible for his acts, and his misconception of the law does not in the least excuse him.

Another observation is, that in the lowest as well as in the highest offences, all are principals. Every person concerned in an illegal act is equally guilty, in the eye of the law, with the person most active. The question then arising on this particular case, is, whether this act of violence, this abuse of the process of this court, were procured or aided by general Wilkinson, or were assented to by him; either before or after the imprisonment complained of? If he acquiesced in the mischief done, or assisted in it, he is as guilty as if he had first contrived it. Every person who assents to, or aids in, the *completion* of an *illegal* act, is a *trespasser ab initio.*

Instead of wandering into the wide field of declamation, to palliate or justify those illegal acts, gentlemen ought candidly to have said, " We admit the guilt of those inferior agents, by whom the acts were committed, but we insist that general Wilkinson is innocent." No sir, not choosing to rely on his innocence, they undertake to show, that the act itself, if not innocent and justifiable, is at least excusable ; and they censure us for making this motion, as if we had no interest in it. They tell us, that " the United States have not been injured, and make no motion." Sir, if the officer of the United States do not choose to resent this indignity to the court, which goes to sap the foundation of justice, is *that* a reason why the party injured should not lay it before the court? This is the cause of the United States ; it is the cause of every man who comes forward as plaintiff or defendant. Every man feels an interest to keep the fountain of justice pure and uninterrupted.

They ask, " was the witness brought here to speak truth?" I hope this man did say the truth. I am sure he did say the truth; because the witnesses they relied upon, to exculpate general Wilkinson, proved, that every thing he said was true. They confirmed not only all he said, but supplied every omission in his chain of evidence. But sir, has fear no effect? Has it no operation on the human mind? If this man had nerves strong enough to bear such treatment, are we sure that the fortitude of others will not be shaken? If the court sanction the practice of bringing witnesses to the bar as criminals, will it not have the practical effect, in many instances, of preventing impartial evidence? Can we expect from a man dragged as a felon, that manly disclosure of facts, which distinguishes a firm and independent mind; and which neither the fear of offending, nor the hope of pleasing any party, however powerful, can prevent from exculpating or criminating according to truth and justice? Was not hope as well as fear used? On one side you have a sum of money and other emoluments; on the other, ruin and disgrace. On the one hand you have every prospect of advantage; on the other of being dragged in chains! Can it be doubted, that if this practice be tolerated, a witness, allured by hope on one side, and alarmed by fear on the other, will deviate from the truth? If there be a deviation, it is on the side of the prosecution; for which way they wish it cannot be doubted. The man who avows maxims of this sort, for the attainment of any end, will not be scrupulous as to the means which he employs to secure it. But another view in which this subject ought to be placed is this : Colonel Burr in *justice* and law stands on an equal footing with his accusers. He ought, if possible, to be so in fact; but we know that it is impossible; that every disadvantage operates against every man who is a prisoner; and that every advantage is in favour of the prosecution. On one side all the means of procuring evidence are restricted; on the other the means of commanding testimony for the prosecution are unrestrained and abundant. An officer appointed by the government, and liable to be turned out of office at its pleasure, summons the witnesses. If he be a firm and independent man, determined to do his duty correctly, at all hazards, so much the better; but if not, we know how his bias will be. The public treasury may be emptied in collecting witnesses and employing affidavit-men : and, in addition to all these means, if there be unwilling witnesses, or any who suggest doubts, they are brought by force to give evidence. But, if we have unwilling witnesses, who can testify the truth in our favour, we have nothing but the naked process of subpœna to compel their attendance. There are great advantages on the part of the prosecution, which ought not to be carried any further. This is an unfair advantage to the prosecution, which this court ought to take from them. But, " we have made this motion, in order to make impressions on the public mind." I will not waste the time of the court in inquiring who have wasted most time. We have been obliged to follow the gentlemen in this course. It will be recollected by the court, that they have repeatedly attempted, in this court, to advocate and foment those strong prejudices, which have been industriously, and but too successfully excited against colonel Burr in the country. They still continue their efforts to create and increase those prejudices. I ask, whether it were to the public or to the court that those remarks were addressed? What has the court to do with motives? But if motives be discussed, did they not wish to influence the public mind, at the very moment when they accused us of it? Colonel Burr is not obliged to account for his motives. We are correcting that influence on the public mind, which has been improperly produced. But there is a motive, and a very powerful one, to justify this motion. We know not how long this prosecution may be continued. We know not how long this practice may be continued. We wish this court to put its *veto* upon it, and act *in terrorem*, to prevent such oppressive and unjustifiable practices hereafter. For as long as the prosecution lasts, this offence may be repeated, and therefore ought to be repressed.

But, " suppose general Wilkinson to be the man who has dragged a citizen, by military force, from one end of the country to another, it is only a mistake of the law." Does the gentleman forget the legal maxim, that " *Ignorance of the law excuses no one?*" But if this were not the law, and ignorance were an excuse, can it be believed, that this was a mistake proceeding from ignorance? General Wilkinson is in possession of the highest military office under the government. Can a man, in his elevated station, be so ignorant as to believe, that he can drag a man, as a felon, twelve hundred miles for the crime of being a witness? If he be this ignorant man, and if he commit acts in the highest degree tyrannical, through ignorance, what shall we say of the government which appointed him? Sir, the government knew that he was a man of talents, and had no right to believe, that he would do these things; or, if he should, that he would not be personally responsible for them. No man will believe that the government thought, or that he himself thought, that he could assault or imprison any man lawfully or with impunity. There is hardly a boy out of his hornbook, that does not know better than that such acts could be legal. I hope we shall hear no more of the ignorance of general Wilkinson.

But we are told, that we are guilty of a contradiction that cannot be reconciled. The gentleman says, " if Wilkinson had stopped Knox and prevented him from attending as a witness it would have been a contempt of the court;" and we are asked, " if it be a contempt to stop him, how it can be a contempt to bring him, as the acts are opposite in their nature?" This is a most singular argument. Things may be opposite, and yet be wrong. Extremes are frequently wrong. It would be a strange thing if general Wilkinson could have carried this man from Richmond to Norfolk, by force, and be liable for his conduct; and yet if he carried him, in like manner, from Norfolk to this place, that he should not be equally liable. These acts are opposite in their nature, and are equally contrary to law. Suppose Knox had been brought in irons, and used cruelly; (for Wilkinson used no more cruelty than suited his purposes) would he not be responsible for so maltreating a witness, under the protection of the court?

But the gentleman says, that it was stated to be an attack on the liberty and privileges of a citizen; but that " it shrinks into nothing :" that the offence was only to compel an unwilling witness to attend! And does the gentleman seriously contend, in this country, and in this court, that it is a venial offence to cast a man into prison, and to force him to come twelve hundred miles, with only the authority of a subpœna? Are the liberties of the people of this country dependent on so fine a thread, that any man, clothed with military authority, can use his power or force over any citizen of the United States, if he have a subpœna in his pocket? Any party having a cause in court, may have a subpœna to summon any other person. I remember, the other day, that these gentlemen admitted, that a *subpœna* might issue against Mr. Jefferson, and that his high station, of chief magistrate, did not exempt him from it; that all the citizens of this country were on grounds of perfect equality. We agree that their doctrine is correct. Let us see the application of it. If all the people be on terms of equality, they were so when the process which issued, requiring the president to give testimony, was served. Suppose it had been put into the hands of half a dozen myrmidons, and that after serving it, they had dragged him by force from Washington to this place; what would have been said of such conduct? Would it not have been an offence that ought to be severely punished? Yet there is no difference between Mr. Jefferson and Knox, with respect to their legal right of exemption from such acts of violence; and yet they contend, that the treatment of Knox was correct and lawful. Are gentlemen serious, when they urge arguments like these? I come now to the inquiry, What are the facts which are said to justify or excuse the ill treatment complained of? And first, as to Mr. Hall, whose warrant, though null and void, is brought forward to bolster up general Wilkinson. He is the mere puppet of Wilkinson. They say, that he and general Wilkinson were at variance. It is very probably true; and general Wilkinson might be at variance with every man at New-Orleans, except his own immediate dependents. Was there no motive to operate on judge Hall? Was there not such a passion as fear? Hall knew what Wilkinson had done, and what he could do; and when he sent him a message, to devise some process to bring Knox by force to this court, Hall knew, that the requests were commands. Observe how the transaction originated. Wilkinson's motives are too obvious to admit of a doubt. He sends for Knox; treats him with particular courtesy; offers him his services; asks him if he wanted money, and a number of questions concerning Burr; and takes down his evidence in writing, differently from the facts, and not as he told them. These are all done by general Wilkinson, without the intervention of any other human creature. It is obvious, that general Wilkinson did not go directly to the object he had in view, but amused him at first with some observations about Dunbaugh; about all of whose measures he knew more than the witness himself. After this solicitude shown to get testimony from the witness (and such only as suited his purposes) we find the process of this court used. Lieutenant Gaines, who commanded at Fort Stoddert, one hundred, or perhaps two hundred miles from New-Orleans, in pursuance of an order from the secretary at war, (a military order, gentlemen will admit) is directed, after serving some of the subpœnas, sent to him, on some persons under his own command, to go to general Wilkinson, and to deliver him the subpœnas; and some how or other, they get from general Wilkinson's hands into his own. We have brought the case of Knox before the court, in order to try the principle, and to ascertain, whether such practices are to be tolerated. General Wilkinson tells Gaines that Knox is an important witness and must be summoned. He *recommends* to him to summon him. Is not a recommendation from a military superior a command? and was not this command, to have this man summoned? It was found, that he would not go. What was the next step? He did not order Gaines to go and consult a lawyer, to know what was right and ought to be done, as gentlemen allege in his defence; but how Knox was to be brought, and how his own illegal purposes were to be effected. Gaines refers to lawyers; they give advice how this purpose is to be attained. Wilkinson then gives him further *orders*. He *advises* him to go and consult Mr. Hall, and obtain his advice and assistance. A subordinate officer is bound to obey his master's commands. He therefore goes and takes the advice of Mr. Hall. After getting his advice and directions, he goes to the witness, who is a little sulky; and in order to put him into good humour, in this pleasant situation, he is thrown into gaol; and then forced by a military guard on board the vessel, which was under the control of general Wilkinson; for *he* only gave them permission to take a passage with himself. After the witness is deprived of the means of getting his clothes and other necessaries, and sent on board by Dunbaugh, some money is wanted; forty or fifty dollars must be had. Where is this sum to be got? Did general Wilkinson give Gaines any order respecting it, and what? He orders him to take the money out of the military chest. This proves, that it was for a *military*, and not a *civil*, purpose. Why was he recommending, advising, ordering, and referring, this inferior officer, unless he were performing a military service? I mean no disrespect to lieutenant Gaines, but the contrary. For it is evident, that he must have felt himself in a disagreeable situation; but he was compelled by the authority of his superior officer to execute this *request*. He obeys; and when all this had been done, it was not sufficient. There must be a marshal to execute this process. Lieutenant Gaines, from being an officer of honour, is turned into a bailiff. He was told, " The marshal has already appointed you; here is a deputation by which you are constituted his deputy to perform this business. It may be unpleasant for you, as an officer, to do this dirty business. You are to have the paper in your pocket that authorises you to do it; but you need not do it yourself. You can employ a serjeant or a soldier to do it."

There was an evident perplexity in Mr. Gaines's testimony. It was a perplexity arising from the interference of civil with military duties. He found himself obliged to wear over his military garb the *disguise* of a *catchpole*, which, as an officer, must have been extremely repugnant to his feelings. The perplexity was not in his narrative, but arose from the situation in which he was placed by general Wilkinson.

It would be a waste of the time of this court to show, that general Wilkinson was the *prime mover* and contriver of all these rigorous and oppressive proceedings. The gentlemen attempt to devolve the responsibility on judge Hall, who is said to be a man of honour and respectability. You may judge how honourable his situation must have been, when he was forced to obey general Wilkinson in manifest violation of law! Must he not have felt himself degraded, by being compelled to give an oppressive construction of the law, against his own judgment? The judge could not be mistaken as to the law. It is written in plain terms. Can it be supposed, that so respectable a judge as he is represented to be, could believe, that he had a right to send a witness, as a prisoner, to *any place*, and in *any manner*, he pleased; and that a witness loses the rights of a citizen the moment he is summoned? The *eulogium* pronounced on judge Hall, disproves every argument they use on the subject.

But " Mr. Wilkinson asked Mr. Graham to consult Mr. Hall." Mr. Graham, delivered his evidence in a most correct and proper manner, and free from perplexity. He proves every feature in the cause, that was not proved by Knox and Gaines. *They* rely on Mr. Graham's testimony. To *me*, it is most marvellous, that gentlemen cannot perceive, that his testimony goes directly to fix the guilt, if there be guilt, on general Wilkinson. He says, that he was directed by Wilkinson, to ask judge Hall, if there were any legal means of compelling this man to attend as a witness? The evident meaning of this inquiry was this, " *Compel him, by legal means if you can, but in any event, compel him to attend.*" Every illegal warrant is void. He must have known it to be so. Is it not evident that this communication between Graham and Hall, was made at the instance of general Wilkinson, and with a view to shelter himself under the forms of law?

But " if he were a military despot, he would not have regarded them!" When did this happen? In May 1807. He must have known what had been done in the United States, and that his conduct had excited universal horror and indignation throughout the country. He is the *prime mover*, and every act, done by others, is imputable to him. They were under his control, and compelled to act as they did; and perhaps they deserve rather the pity, than the censure of the court. He therefore was desirous at this time, to shelter his acts under the forms and apparent sanction of the law.

But this is not all, as I had occasion to observe before. A man who sanctions an illegal act, though not the first contriver of it, subjects himself to all the consequences of it. When Knox came on board the vessel, the question is, whether general Wilkinson knew that it was reluctantly? General Wilkinson knew, most assuredly, that he was put on board against his will, by a military guard, and yet he did not assist him; for he knew that it had been done in pursuance of his own well understood wishes and orders. The evidence of Mr. Gaines, collectively considered, proves this clearly. Gentlemen say, that the vessel was commanded by Mr. Read. I have seen the young gentleman, and I hope he deserves the character which the gentleman gives him; but it is clear, that he was ready to obey the superior commands of general Wilkinson, and that he knew it to be his duty. Mr. Gaines said, that he was obliged to apply to general Wilkinson, and not to Franklin Read for a passage on board the vessel. It was the same case with Mr. Graham. When several different commanders, as a military and a naval commander are together, the inferior in rank acts under the command of the superior, and all the navy of the United States at New-Orleans was under the command of general Wilkinson.

But what was done at Hampton? Mr. Gaines, in every thing relative to this transaction, only obeyed his superior officer. He therefore told Knox, "You are to understand, that you are brought *here* by virtue of a deputation from judge Hall to me, and not by the military orders of general Wilkinson. You are to understand, that this was really the case." Why? Because general Wilkinson recommended it. These were terms of mere civility. I dare say, that Bonaparte, when he gives orders, uses civil language; whenever he gives particular orders to any of his officers, he may say, "You will oblige me, by taking such a place." "You will oblige me, by seizing such a party." "You will oblige me, by conquering such a territory." Or, "by accomplishing any other achievement." Suppose the officer thus ordered, were to disobey and excuse himself by saying, "I misunderstood you; you only said you would be obliged to me, if I would do so." Would he not be instantly punished or shot for disobedience of orders?

Mr. HAY.—That is only the rule on military subjects.

Mr. WICKHAM.—*This* was not a *civil* transaction certainly. But, sir, this was really not so bad after all, because Knox had counsel. That counsel only expressed his *doubts* to judge Hall. It is the custom at New-Orleans for lawyers to respect and obey judges; (it was *once* so *here*); and this was a respectful expression of his opinion. The judge directed the measure, and the counsel acquiesced. He knew that his doubts would be of no sort of consequence, and that Knox would be sent round. He knew that Wilkinson directed and controlled all. The gentleman then went on and assumed as a *postulatum*, that if no action would lie for this treatment to Knox, there could be no contempt of the court, for which an attachment would lie. It would be a most extraordinary doctrine, that the process of this court could be obstructed by the application of force, or even by the *fear* of violence, and yet that the court could not punish it by an attachment. But I will admit, for the sake of argument, that an attachment for a contempt will not lie, if no action can be maintained by the party injured. But what then? Will the admission strengthen his argument? Has the party aggrieved no redress? If to be taken up, confined, and transported as a felon, from one part of the country to another, for no crime, will not support an action, then our courts of justice may as well be shut at once. If an action could not be maintained for such treatment, for what would it lie?

" But he had good provisions." That is not the point at issue. " But he was at liberty after he was on board." He was not permitted to go on shore, and if he were not satisfied with his situation in the vessel, he was at liberty to walk overboard. The only sort of liberty which he had, was that of jumping into the sea, if he thought proper.

I will not go into the law of the case, because I am perfectly convinced it is unnecessary. We rely on the broad principle, that whenever the process of the court is abused, it will interfere. But you are advised to imitate the judge, who some time ago at Fredericksburg, directed it to be decided by a jury, whether a contempt of the court were intended. I will not undertake to undervalue the benefit of the trial by jury on any account; but there would be a disadvantage to general Wilkinson, in submitting it to a jury. It would not be a boon, but a probable injury. If he be in contempt, how is he to be exonerated? By his own oath, and not by the oath of a jury. He comes in and answers interrogatories on oath, and if he deny the facts charged, he is acquitted; or if he explain them to the satisfaction of the court, he is equally cleared; but if he refuse to answer, or if he admit the facts as charged, *then only* is he to be punished. But he is referred to his *own oath*, and to his *own judgment*, for a complete exoneration. Is this an advantage or a disadvantage? Is it not more beneficial than to refer it to the judgment and the oath of a jury. There can be no doubt that a motion for an attachment is sustainable, for the abuse of the process of the court, in any place where it can lawfully issue.

There is one difficulty which the gentlemen on the other side did not mention, and it is this; that the acts were not done in this district, and that perhaps this court has no cognisance over them. But part of them was done in this district; force was used at Hampton; Knox was there continued on board against his will, and that gives the court jurisdiction.

But, sir, the process of attachment is auxiliary to that of subpœna. The process of subpœna goes throughout all parts of the United States; and that of attachment ought to be commensurate with it. It is in vain to give the power *to issue* process, without the power to *enforce* it; and wherever it is abused or improperly executed, the court can notice it and punish the party for not executing it according to law. This doctrine, I think, was sanctioned by the opinion of judge Patterson, in the case of Smith and Ogden, in the district of New-York. In the case of William Smith, a subpœna had issued, to summon the secretary of state, and the secretary at war. They failed to attend, though the process had been duly served on them. A motion was made to issue an attachment against them, for their contempt, on various grounds, explained by his counsel. The court differed in opinion. One of them, (I believe judge Patterson) was of opinion, that a rule to show cause, why an attachment should not be issued aginst them; ought to be granted. But it is unnecessary to dwell on this point, as the gentlemen on the other side took no notice of it. In every point of view, therefore, our motion for the attachment is sustainable, and I pray the court to award it.

Mr. HAY.—I will set Mr. Wickham right as to one fact. He had attended so much to what he was going to say himself, that he did not attend to what we had said. Mr. Mac Rae did press the objection, and he was answered by Mr. Botts. My own opinion, however, is, that the power of the court to attach is commensurate with its process; and that those gentlemen who were summoned, would be liable to an attachment for not attending. I incidentally admitted the doctrine.

Mr. MARTIN. I shall make some few observations in addition to what has been said by the gentleman who preceded me. I shall endeavour to show, that it was a military transaction from the beginning, till the arrival of Mr. Knox at this place; and that its direct tendency has been to prevent justice. Let us examine the rights of parties in a court of justice, and the cause as between man and man. Each man has a right to compel the attendance of witnesses, to give evidence in support or defence of his rights, in any cause depending therein; one party has no more right than another, to compel the attendance of witnesses. How is the law in this respect, as between the United States and individuals accused of crimes? Suppose a person charged with an offence is arrested; the magistrate, before whom he is brought, is to hear the statement of the United States, and of the prisoner, and to examine the witnesses brought before him for the purpose of determining, whether the prisoner ought to be committed or not. He is then to bind the witnesses in a recognisance to appear before the proper tribunal, at the time appointed for the trial of the prisoner. But if a witness refuse to enter into such recognisance, he is to be committed to custody till the time of trial, in order to secure his evidence. But this can only be done by the examining magistrate; and this is all that can be done by the United States, with respect to the witnesses who happen to be present at the examination. But if the United States wish to have the privilege of further testimony, they are to apply to that court of justice, before which the trial is to be had, for subpœnas. These subpœnas must issue, be served, and returned executed. After which, if they fail to appear on the return-day, an attachment may be issued against them. This is the whole process in behalf of the United States. How is the defendant to get his evidence? His privileges are the same. He is to send subpœnas in like manner, for his witnesses; and if they do not attend after they are summoned, they are to be attached. They stand, in point of law, on equal terms; but the United States have superior advantages over the defendant, if they be compelled to resort to the same means of enforcing obedience. The power and influence of the United States command much greater diligence and alacrity on the part of the officers, who are to execute the process, than the means of any individual, labouring under the disadvantages of a public prosecution, can possibly procure. Whatever means are illegally used to procure witnesses for the United States, prevent the stream of justice from flowing purely; it is as much an interference with the equal administration of justice, as it is by illegal means to keep a witness away from the court. The law only ought to be resorted to on the part of the government and on the part of the prisoner: and it is as inconsistent with the law, that testimony should be brought by coercion, as that it should be illegally kept away. It is an act injurious to the prisoner, and if we examine which is the more oppressive and destructive to personal rights, we shall find, perhaps, that the former is more so than the latter. It is said to be " a singular case." It is indeed a singular case. I think on my conscience, that such a case was never heard of before; and that such pains were never taken to destroy a person who was charged with a crime. In addition to the means directly used by the government, many persons in order to ingratiate themselves with it, have used all the efforts in their power for the attainment of that object.

The secretary at war wrote a letter to lieutenant Gaines, who was the commander of a fort, directing him to quit it and execute this business. It was a *military command* from the secretary at *war*, ordering him to undertake a *military journey* for civil purposes; to go to general Wilkinson; to deliver him a letter; to serve subpœnas, after filling up the names of the witnesses which he should point out; to obey the instructions of the attorney general, and then to come to Virginia. It was by a *military command* that he received and executed the subpœnas. It was by a *military command* that he was to *summon himself*, and obey the instructions of the attorney general at New-Orleans. Did he serve the subpœnas as a civil officer, or in obedience to the orders of the secretary at war? Did he receive information and directions from the attorney general at New-Orleans, as a civil officer, or pursuant to the directions of the secretary at war? By whose orders did he quit his garrison? To whom was he referred? To the same person to whom general Wilkinson was referred. Who is this attorney general? A man probably of respectability, but ready to be displaced unless he obeyed the government, and assisted in facilitating to the means of causing the witnesses to be brought hither.

General Wilkinson in the next place was to fill up the names of the witnesses. There have been complaints against Mr. Jackson for taking affidavits, but he did not *compel* men to give testimony; *that* was general Wilkinson's province at New-Orleans. He was to find out who were witnesses, and fill up the blanks in the subpœnas with their names. Has not Mr. Knox told us that *Hall* had a number of *printed* interrogatories? That he and Mr. Fort were called on to answer them on oath? And that their declining to answer them, was the cause of sending them to gaol? Knox has further informed us, that it was on Sunday evening that they were carried before the magistrate. It is well understood that Sunday is not a legal day for such purposes. As Knox declined answering those questions, he was committed that night to the custody of the sheriff, who was to bring him back on Monday morning, and to whom he gave security for his appearance accordingly. Knox says further, that the next day they appeared and were both interrogated; that he answered some of the questions, but with respect to the other interrogatories, he begged an opportunity to consult a lawyer, lest he should commit himself. Fort refused to answer any of them, and both were put into gaol with negroes and felons. It was by the warrant of the judge, that the sheriff carried him to gaol. And for what reason? Was it because he refused to appear before this court, to give testimony, or for refusing to answer the printed interrogatories before him? It was certainly for the latter. Did the subpœna by which he was summoned to appear, before this court, require him to answer interrogatories before that judge? No, sir, nor had the judge any legal authority to act as he did. Afterwards an order was given to the marshal to transport him hither to give evidence.

Let me, in a few words, state the improper manner in which the government, or its agents, proceeded. Wherever they suspected any person of being able to give information, they carried him before a magistrate, and forced him to give testimony, all on one side; and wickedly interfered with the purity of the stream of justice. What, sir, would a court of justice permit *ex parte* testimony to be read? A witness, who can give testimony on the side of the defendant, and for that reason does not suit their purpose, is passed by and never heard. They take the evidence for the prosecution in such manner as they think proper, and designedly trammel and shackle the witnesses so as to be bound by their own *ex parte* testimony, when confronted with it on their examination in court. I heard one of the gentlemen, who prosecute, (Mr. Wirt.) the other day, with great delight, expatiate on the nature of *ex parte* evidence. He made a most eloquent and correct speech, to prove, that such evidence is not dictated by the witness, but by the person who takes the depositions, and that it ought not to be trusted. If *ex parte* testimony be so improper, when only a motion is made, or when trivial collateral points are discussed, how much more improper must such testimony be in an all-important case, where the honour, reputation and life of an individual are at stake? Was it for the sake of the government that general Wilkinson did all this? I will admit, that holding an important and lucrative office under the government, he might think, that he would retain his present advantages and obtain future favour by this conduct. But this was not his only motive. He had every thing at stake himself. He was most deeply interested. All those acts of tyranny and oppression, which he committed: the violation of the constitution, the prostration of the judiciary, the arbitrary imprisonment and transportation of individuals, are to be justified, by such testimony, against the gentleman for whom I am now concerned. Would he not, when thus interested, procure testimony in so garbled a state, that he would be able to prevent the disclosure of the whole truth on the cross-examination of the witnesses?

Then, sir, having shown that all these acts had a tendency to obstruct and divert the pure stream of justice, let us see what were the immediate and direct acts of general Wilkinson. He invites Knox to his own house. Serjeant Dunbaugh told him that he had invited him. Dunbaugh was surprised that this great god of New-Orleans, who trampled on their rights, and who confined and transported suspected persons, should condescend to converse with such a man as Knox. He thought that it would be an intrusion for such a man as Knox to approach so august and sacred a presence. Knox at first declines going; but afterwards goes. Wilkinson invites him to take a seat, and began by asking him if he knew Dunbaugh; not that he really wished to know any thing about Dunbaugh, whom he already knew well, and concerning whom he knew it was probable that Knox knew nothing; but he used it as an introduction. He then proceeded in an insinuating manner, about his coming down the river. "Have you got your money yet?" "No." "How much is due you?" "One hundred, or one hundred and fifty dollars." "Well, I can oblige you with as much money myself." Kind affectionate man! What was all this for? To make interest with Knox, and to induce him to favour his views. "Well, what did you know in all your trip coming down?" Knox answered, that this was not the business he came on. He wants Knox to show him all he knew, and offers him one hundred or one hundred and fifty dollars as a bribe. It was a direct attack on the honesty of the man; to be sure, it was done very *smoothly*, as general Wilkinson does every thing, when he chooses. A charming opportunity of getting one hundred and fifty dollars, for only telling a few lies!

Mr. Mac Rae. I hope the gentleman does not mean to insinuate, that general Wilkinson solicited him to say an untruth; there is no evidence whatsoever to that effect.

Mr. Martin. I state facts, and insist that its direct tendency was to get him to swear to what was untrue. I do not say, that general Wilkinson said, in downright plain terms, "*I will give you one hundred and fifty dollars for telling what is untrue;*" but that the direct tendency of his conduct was, to induce him to swear to a falsehood, if he were capable of such baseness; and Knox declares, that the offer was made in such a manner, that he considered it as a bribe. He begins again to ask him about his affairs; he takes pen, ink, and paper, and notes down what he said; but so differently from the real meaning of Knox, that he disapproved of it, and would not proceed further.

The next thing we hear is, that he receives subpœnas, to fill up the names of the witnesses. That he requests lieutenant Gaines to find out Knox and summon him; and that he did summon him under a military order. When summoned, did Knox attempt to refuse to come hither? He was willing to come, and made no other objection, except that the notice was too short; that in his situation, he was not prepared to set off on a journey of twelve hundred miles, and that he had no money, but expected to get some soon, and then he would come. He only refused on account of his want of preparation, and of money. Was this criminal in poor Knox? Because he does not wear a sword and epaulets, and wants the means to enable him to come, he is to be treated as a felon! (It was not then known that the military chest was to be drawn upon, for the purpose of hiring witnesses to come.) Why did not general Wilkinson come sooner? He had been subpœnaed before Knox. Why did he not obey the process of the court promptly? He takes his own time; and only comes when he finds it convenient. Was there any attachment sent against him after his great delay? The court, grand jury, and all of us, must wait from day to day to suit his convenience and pleasure; but poor Knox, because his convenience was to be a little attended to, was treated like a felon, thrown into gaol, with negroes and criminals; from whence he is sent on board a prison-ship, as soon as it is ready to sail, and brought hither by force. All these are general Wilkinson's acts. *He* filled up the subpœ-na with Knox's name, and therefore caused him to be summoned. Here there is a chasm in the chain of the evidence; but it is easily supplied. We find him, in the next place, in the hands of the sheriff. How he came into that situation is not absolutely certain; but no person who hears me can doubt, that it was by general Wilkinson's contrivance; as also that he was carried on Sunday before judge Hall, who found him in the hands of the sheriff, and the next day put him into gaol, because he refused to answer the printed interrogatories. General Wilkinson applies to judge Hall, to know how to compel Knox to come to this court. The answer was, that some person must make an affidavit, that he was a material witness for the United States; and this affidavit is made by general Wilkinson. The very man who is endeavouring to bring him by force, is the person who does the act, that was said to be necessary to carry that purpose into effect.

It is said, that general Wilkinson directed Mr. Gaines to consult the attorney general and some other lawyer. The attorney general is the person whom general Dearborne, the secretary at war, directed Gaines to obey. The other lawyer consulted, is Mr. Duncan, general Wilkinson's aid-de-camp; who marched before him when he went into a court of justice and bade defiance to the civil government; insulted and resisted the judicial authority of his country, and placed the laws at the feet of the military. Mr. Gaines found Knox in jail among thieves, felons, and negroes, and placed under a guard. It is said, that Gaines took out Knox in his civil garb, and acted as a deputy marshal; but in truth his military garb hid it all. The gentlemen express doubts whenever rights are to be supported, but on all other occasions, they entertain no doubts at all; indeed I was astonished, that they did not get up and say, it was the clearest case in the world, that the commitment of Knox was legal. We know *who wanted* to bring him to this place. It is said, that on the subject of acting as deputy marshal, Gaines had no previous communication with general Wilkinson. I believe it, because Gaines says so. But the marshal had given a deputation to Gaines for the very purpose of bringing Knox to this place; and therefore it is reasonable to presume, that it was contrived by Wilkinson. They say, that a deputy is not obliged to give bond; but I say, that in the first place, a deputy marshal is bound to give a bond for the faithful performance of the duties of his office, and in the next place, to take the same oath that the marshal takes. It is required by the act of congress, (See *Graydon's Digest of the Laws, p.* 247.) that before a deputy marshal acts, he shall take the same oath with his principal, and must give bond. Gaines was unwilling to do it himself, and he was informed that he might do it by another. Now no principle is more clear, than that a deputy cannot make a deputy, and this act being performed by Dunbaugh was therefore illegal. But it is said, that there was no collusion, but on the contrary a variance, between Wilkinson and Hall. This was the strongest reason in the world, to make Hall dread to give Wilkinson offence; a man, who but a short time before came into a court of justice and looked proudly around to the court, insulted the judges, set at defiance the writ of *habeas corpus*, and told them, that every man whom he suspected, he would take up and transport in like manner as those, whom he refused to release in obedience to the writ; and denounced two gentlemen of the bar, as traitors to their country, because he knew that they were the most able and determined to oppose his military usurpation. Judge Hall had therefore great reason to dread his displeasure, and a repetition of the same treatment.

Now let us see how this poor fellow got out of gaol. It was by a deputation by deputy Gaines to serjeant Dunbaugh. The counsel for the prosecution examined the order in court, and they say, that Mr. Gaines did not sign it in his military, but in his civil character as deputy marshal, because he did not sign himself " *captain*" at the bottom. The order to Dunbaugh is not signed by him as deputy marshal; on the contrary it commanded him. " You are hereby requested and *commanded* to take &c." not " you will oblige me by taking, &c." It is addressed " to *serjeant Dunbaugh*," and it *commands* him, and being from captain Gaines to him as serjeant, it must be in his military character. The order authorised and commanded him to take Knox out of goal and carry him on board the vessel. If ever there were a military order in the world this is one. Let us examine the civil and military character blended. As deputy marshal, general Wilkinson had no right to order Gaines to do any thing; he was as free from his authority as I am. As a citizen of the world, he had no right to order him, except he chose to exercise an illegal power. Dunbaugh was as free, as a citizen, from the authority of Gaines in his character of lieutenant, as any other citizen of the United States; and, as a serjeant, he was as free from his authority as deputy marshal, as I am; (and God knows what I should have been if I had been then at New-Orleans,) and yet lieutenant Gaines told us, that he was so much under the command and in the power of Wilkinson, that if he had ordered him to put Knox in irons he would have done it. What sort of civil authority was it, by which a military officer was employed to bring the witness to this court, and that officer bound to put him in irons if his general ordered it? Was it not under that authority that he was brought round without a shirt, except a borrowed one? These are thé methods by which testimony is to be obtained! Instead of using the legal means of subpœna and attachment to obtain evidence, witnesses are thus illegally forced to come and give testimony in a court of justice! Has not this a direct tendency to destroy the purity of trials?

But it is said, that this court has no right to take cognisance of the offence, because it happened at New-Orleans. If general Wilkinson, after having committed this offence, had not come hither, this court could punish him, the first time it could find him within its jurisdiction for affecting a cause depending here. His interfering with the pure principles of the administration of justice was a contempt of the court. It is a principle of law, that every interference with the administration of justice is a contempt of the court, and punishable wherever its process can reach. Why is it improper and punishable by attachment to insult a judge sitting in court? Because it tends to intimidate him and prevent an impartial judgment. Why are publications in news-papers concerning any cause depending in a court prohibited by law? (This has been lately done in this very place.) Because it tends to make impressions unfavourable to one of the parties, and its immediate tendency is, to obstruct the pure sources and channels of justice. Most of these things had happened at New-Orleans; and the offence was incipient there, but was not completed till they arrived here. It was a continued act. Knox wished, but was not permitted, to come on shore to get clothes, and not to be brought into a court of justice like a dirty beast.

But serjeant Dunbaugh went on shore with him, confessedly to prevent him from missing his way, but in reality because they did not choose to trust him alone; so that he still was confined, for they would not trust him by himself. The conduct of general Wilkinson in the first movement was most artful. He asks him, " Why Mr. Knox, are you not afraid to appear before me?" Why should he be afraid of him, unless he referred to his military despotism? for he had nothing to do with him; and as to his being with colonel Burr, it was the civil magistrate that he should have been afraid of: he could not be afraid of Wilkinson, for any thing of this kind; but he might fear to be imprisoned and transported like others, contrary to law and justice.

But the gentleman has said, that there was no danger in the union of the civil with the military character in one person; and asks us if the president of the United States have not those powers blended in him? What civil authority has the president? It is much circumscribed. He must apply to a magistrate before he can arrest any person suspected of any crime. He is not a conservator of the peace, though he is commander in chief of all our troops, (which are not many.) He has nothing to do with the civil, that is the judicial authority; yet this is the inference, that the civil and military authority were united in the president.

We have been told by the gentlemen, that " the court had shown great indulgence towards us, lest it should be censured, and not for the sake of doing justice." I took it down from his mouth as he spoke.

Mr. Mac Rae denied positively that he had ever said so.

Mr. Martin insisted that he had taken it down from his *mouth* as he had spóken the words.

Mr. Mac Rae replied, that he had taken it from his own head.

Mr. Martin.—I dare say the gentleman has forgotten it; his mind having been occupied by great things: by general Wilkinson. Sir, he said, that great indulgence had been granted to colonel Burr, for which he complimented the court. I wonder if he will recollect another thing that he said, that we wished to imprison all the people for the sake of Aaron Burr, while he was stalking through the streets. I cannot help congratulating the gentleman, that he may now walk at large, without having his eyes offended by seeing Aaron Burr at *liberty*.

But the gentleman said, that unusual mildness had been shown to colonel Burr. Persons have been tried for treason before in the United States. John Fries was tried before that *Jeffries* Samuel Chase. Was the treasury of the United States thrown open and lavished to employ other counsel, in addition to the attorney for the United States, to prosecute? No persons were then employed to forestal the truth, by taking *ex parte* affidavits; and Mr. *Rawle*, the attorney for the United States, who prosecuted according to general usage, without any aid, was a man whose mildness and benignity resembled an angel of mercy; and the United States sent for no other witnesses than those summoned in the usual course. But this trial took place " *in the days of terror,"* under that old dotard John Adams. Let us contrast it with the proceedings under the enlightened reign of philosophy and philanthropy. Money has been taken out of the treasury to employ two eminent lawyers to aid in the prosecution; compulsive affidavits have been taken; affidavit-men employed to take them, and witnessess brought by force, without relying on the process of the court as sufficient.

Mr. Martin concluded, by expressing his firm persuasion, that the whole transaction was *military*, and contrived by general Wilkinson; that it was clearly a contempt of the court, and that he hoped he would be punished for it by an attachment.

The court then adjourned till to-morrow morning, at nine o'clock.

FRIDAY, June 26th, 1807.

The court met about nine o'clock, and, about ten o'clock, the grand jury entered, and Mr. Randolph, their foreman, presented ten indictments, found true bills; that is, one indictment for treason, and another for a misdemeanor, against each of the following individuals, viz. Jonathan Dayton, John Smith, Comfort Tyler, Israel Smith, and Davis Floyd.

The CHIEF JUSTICE then made a short address to the grand jury, expressed in elegant and appropriate terms; in which he complimented them upon the great patience and cheerful attention with which they had performed the arduous and laborious duties in which they had been so long engaged; and concluded, by discharging them from all further attendance.

The court then adjourned till twelve o'clock. As soon as it met again,

Mr. BOTTS requested the court to remove Mr. Burr from the public gaol, to some comfortable and convenient place of confinement. He depicted in very strong terms the miserable state of the prison, where he was then confined. The grounds of this motion are to be found in the following affidavit made by some of Mr. Burr's counsel, and laid before the court:

We, who are counsel in the defence of colonel Burr, at the suit of the United States, beg leave to represent to the court, that in pursuance of our duty to him, we have visited him in his confinement in the city goal: that we could not avoid remarking the danger, which will most probably result to his health, from the situation, inconveniences and circumstances attending the place of his confinement; but we cannot forbear to declare our conviction, that we ourselves, cannot freely and fully perform what we have undertaken for his defence, if he remain in the gaol aforesaid, deprived, as he is, of a room to himself; it being scarcely possible for us to consult with him upon the various necessary occasions which must occur, from all which we believe, that he will be deprived of that assistance from counsel, which is given to him by the constitution of the United States; unless he be removed.

EDMUND RANDOLPH,
JOHN WICKHAM,
BENJAMIN BOTTS.

Sworn to in open court, by Edmund
   Randolph, John Wickham, and
   Benjamin Botts, esquires. June
   25th, 1807.

WILLIAM MARSHALL, *Clerk.*

The counsel for the prosecution were perfectly silent on the motion.

After a long and desultory argument by Mr. Burr's counsel the court determined that the prisoner should be removed to his former lodgings near the capitol, provided they could be made sufficiently strong for his safe keeping, being of opinion, that the act of congress authorised it, on the foregoing affidavit, to make the order of removal.

Mr. Latrobe, surveyor of the public buildings of the United States, was requested to inspect them; and upon his report the court passed the following order:

Whereupon, it is ordered, that the marshal of this district, do cause the front room of the house now occupied by Luther Martin, esq. which room has been and is used as a dining room, to be prepared for the reception and safe keeping of colonel Aaron Burr, by securing the shutters to the windows of the said room by bars, and the door by a strong bar or padlock. And that he employ a guard of seven men to be placed on the floor of the adjoining unfinished house, and on the same story with the before described front room, and also, at the door opening into the said front room; and upon the marshal's reporting to the court that the said room has been so fitted up and the guard employed, that then the said marshal be directed, and he is hereby directed, to remove to the said room, the body of the said Aaron Burr from the public gaol, there to be by him safely kept.

Mr. HAY.—My only wish is, that this prosecution should be regularly conducted. Is it not the usual practice to read the indictment first and then move for the venire?

Mr. BURR.—I have been furnished with a copy of the indictment; I have perused it; and I am ready to plead not guilty to it.

Mr. WIRT.—The usual form requires the actual arraignment of the prisoner; however the court may dispense with it, if it think proper.

Mr. HAY was indifferent about the form, if the law could be substantially executed. He supposed that a simple acknowledgment of the prisoner was sufficient, without the customary form of holding up his hand.

CHIEF JUSTICE.—It is enough, if he appear to the indictment, and plead *not guilty*.

The clerk then read the indictment against Aaron Burr, for treason against the United States; which specifies the *place* of the overt act, to be at *Blannerhasset's island*; and the *time*, the 10th *day of December* 1806.

When he had concluded, Mr. BURR addressed the court: " I acknowledge myself to be the person named in the indictment: I plead *not guilty;* and put myself upon my country for trial."

Mr. HAY then addressed the court on the venire that was to try the issue between the prisoner and the United States. He said that he thought there was an apparent incompatibility on this point, between the twenty-ninth section of the act of congress called the judicial act, and the eighth amendment to the constitution. It was not certain that this act was in force. It was passed on the 24th of September 1789, and it provides that " In cases punish- " able with death, the trial shall be had in the county where the " offence was committed, or where that cannot be done without " great inconvenience, twelve jurors at least shall be summoned " from thence." Subsequent to this, a constitutional provision was made, requiring that the trial shall be held before " an im- " partial jury of the state and district, wherein the crime shall " have been committed." If then, this law be in force, there must be twelve petit jurymen summoned from Wood county, which would make it impossible to have the trial at any early day. Here then was the difficulty. The act was passed in 1789; the amendments to the constitution were not ratified before the 15th December 1791. Does then the constitution repeal this law? Had this eighth amendment formed an original part of the constitution, no more would have been requisite than an impartial jury from the state and district where the crime was committed. Had congress passed this law, after the constitution was thus amended, would it not have been a violation of it? Had it then any force at this time?

Mr. MAC RAE quoted the 2 *vol.* of the act of congress *page* 226, *section* 3, to show that the first law was considered to be in force, notwithstanding this amendment to the constitution.

The CHIEF JUSTICE said, that he had no difficulty on the subject. He saw no incompatibility between the law and the constitution. He had no doubt that the law was still in force.

Mr. BURR had not considered the question maturely; but at present saw no inconsistency between them; however, as this law was most probably intended for the benefit of the accused, he consented to waive the right.

Mr. WIRT.—But there is another consideration, sir: Can consent, take away the error? In England, in the celebrated case of Alexander Kinloch and Charles Kinloch, he consented to draw one of the jurymen, and afterwards pleaded this error in arrest of judgment. After a long and elaborate argument, the court rejected his plea, though there was a division among them.

Mr. MARTIN.—In that case, (or what is the same, Weddiburn's case) there was but one dissentient judge.

Mr. HAY.—In the case of Hardy or Tooke a question was made, whether the jury must be kept together during that long trial? Though the prisoner at the bar consented to waive that right, the court nevertheless instructed the sheriff to keep them together.

Mr. BOTTS protested against the delay and inconveniences which would ensue, from summoning the venire from Wood county.

The CHIEF JUSTICE believed that the provision was not absolutely obligatory, if both parties would waive the right; but it was as much so, if the United States insisted upon the right, as if the prisoner himself had done so. If the United States insisted upon its execution, the law must be executed, unless there were sufficient evidence to satisfy the court, that such a measure would violate the amendment to the constitution, which requires a trial to be held by an impartial jury of the state and district; unless both sides therefore consented, it was his opinion that the court was bound by this law.

Mr. HAY said, that he felt no disposition to delay the trial; but he could not think of pledging himself to such a measure without due deliberation. He would consult with the gentlemen associated with him, on this point; and would inform the court of the result.

The counsel for the prosecution then retired from the bar, and after a few minutes consultation returned. Mr. HAY informed the court, that they could not assume the responsibility of consenting to such a proposition; the law seemed to be imperative in its language, " twelve petit jurors at least *shall be* summoned." He must therefore request the court to direct a venire of twelve men at least, to be summoned from Wood county.

The Chief Justice inquired what number should be summoned? Different numbers were named, and there appeared to have been a great difference in the practice. The common practice required forty-eight; and cases were cited, where not less than sixty, or seventy-two jurors had been summoned.

The court finally decided that the entry should be made for a venire of forty-eight jurors; twelve of whom, at least, were to be summoned from Wood county.

A long conversation ensued upon the time when this process was to be made returnable; or in other words, when the trial in chief was to commence. Some contended that twenty days would be sufficient to summon the venire from Wood county; others, that thirty five would be necessary. The general opinion seemed to be in favour of an adjournment till the first Monday in August.

The Chief Justice said that he would have preferred the shortest possible day in consideration of the expence and inconvenience which would result from the delay; unless, indeed, more important circumstances should have recommended a longer period; such as the necessity and advantage of obtaining witnesses from distant parts of the country. No time was determined upon. The decision was postponed until to-morrow. The orders were to be made out for summoning a venire, and the time of the return to be left blank and filled up to-morrow.

Mr. Hay informed the court that the clerk was doubtful whether the parties last indicted, should be brought before the court, by a capias or a summons. He should now move for a capias.

The Chief Justice replied there could be no difficulty on the subject, for that a capias must certainly issue. The court then adjourned.

Saturday, June 27th, 1807.

The Chief Justice delivered the following opinion on the motion, for an attachment against general Wilkinson:

The motion now under consideration was heard at this time, because it was alleged to be founded on a fact which might affect the justice of the case in which the court is about to be engaged, and because, while the bills were depending before the grand jury, the court might, without impeding the progress of the business, examine into the complaint which has been made.

The motion is to attach general Wilkinson for a contempt of this court, by obstructing the fair course of justice, with regard to a prosecution depending before it. In support of this charge, has been offered the testimony of Mr. Knox, who states a conversation between general Wilkinson and himself, previous to his being served with a subpœna, the object of which was to extract from him, whatever information he might possess, respecting the expedition which was the subject of inquiry in this court; and who states also, that he was afterwards summoned before judge Hall, who examined him upon interrogatories, and committed him to gaol, whence he was taken by order of the deputy marshal, who was a military, as well as civil offieer, and put on board the Revenge, in which general Wilkinson sailed, for the purpose of being brought from New-Orleans to Richmond.

That unfair practices towards a witness who was to give testimony in this court, or oppression under colour of its process, although those practices and that oppression were acted in another district, would be punishable in the mode now suggested, provided the person who had acted therein came within the jurisdiction of the court, is a position which the court is not disposed to controvert; but it is also believed that this mode of punishment ought not to be adopted, unless the deviation from law could be clearly attached to the person against whom the motion was made, and unless the deviation were intentional, or unless the course of judicial proceeding were or might be so affected by it, as to make a punishment in this mode obviously conducive to a fair and correct administration of justice.

The conversation which took place between general Wilkinson and the witness, on the arrival of the latter in New Orleans, was manifestly held with the intention of drawing from him any information which he might possess, relative to the expedition which was then the subject of inquiry. In this intention, there was nothing unlawful. Government and those who represent it, may justifiably and laudably use means to obtain voluntary communications, provided those means be not such as might tempt the person making them, to give an improper colouring to his representations, which might afterwards adhere to them, when repeated in court. The address stated to have been employed, the condescension and regard with which the witness was treated, are not said by himself to have been accompanied with any indications of a desire to draw from him more than the truth. The offer of money, if with a view to corrupt, could not be too severely reprehended. It is certainly a dangerous species of communication between those who are searching for testimony, and the person from whom it is expected. But in this case, the court cannot contemplate the offer as being made with immoral views. The witness had a right to demand from those he was expected to accuse, a small sum of money sufficient to subsist him on his return to his home. He was asked, whether on receiving this sum, his objections to giving testimony would be removed. This was certainly a delicate question, but it might be asked without improper motives, and it was pressed no further. This is not shown to be an attempt to contaminate the source of justice, and a consequent contempt of the court, in which it is administered.

The imprisonment of Mr. Knox, and the order for conveying him from New-Orleans to Richmond were the acts of judge Hall. Whether his proceedings were legal or illegal, they are not shown to have been influenced by general Wilkinson, and this court cannot presume such to have been the fact; general Wilkinson therefore is not responsible for them. They were founded it is true, on an affidavit made by him; but there was no impropriety in making this affidavit, and it remained with the judge to decide, what the law would authorise in the case.

All the subsequent proceedings were directed by the civil authority. The agents who executed the orders of the judge were indeed military men, who most probably would not have disobeyed the commander in chief; but that officer is not responsible, in this way, for having failed to interpose his authority, in order to prevent the execution of the orders of the judge, even if those orders ought not to have been given.

Upon a full view of the subject, the case appears to have been this. General Wilkinson was desirous that the testimony of the witness should be obtained; and aware of the accusations which had before been brought against him, for the use he had made of the military power, he was desirous of obtaining the testimony by lawful means, and therefore referred the subject to a judge of the territory, under whose orders all subsequent proceedings were taken. Whether the judge did or did not transcend the limits prescribed by law, those ministerial officers who obeyed his orders, cannot be supposed to have acted with a knowledge that he had mistaken his power. Should it be admitted that this would be no defence for them in an action to obtain compensation for the injury, yet it furnishes sufficient evidence, that no contempt was intended to this court by general Wilkinson, that he has not been guilty of any intentional abuse of its process, or of any oppression in the manner of executing it.

It is said that captain Gaines the gentleman whom the marshal appointed as his deputy for this particular purpose, had not taken the oath of office, and was therefore not legally qualified to act in that character. However correct this observation may be in itself, it does not appear to the court to justify an attachment against general Wilkinson. The person who sees in the possession of another, a commission as deputy marshal, and sees that others are acting under that commission, ought not to be subjected to a process of contempt for having made no inquiries respecting the oath which the law requires to be taken.

The attachment will not be awarded because general Wilkinson cannot be considered as having controlled or influenced the conduct of the civil magistrate, and because in this transaction his intention appears to have been not to violate the laws. In such a case, where an attachment does not seem to be absolutely required by the justice due to the particular individual against whom the prosecution is depending, the court is more inclined to leave the parties to the ordinary course of law, than to employ the extraordinary powers, which are given for the purpose of preserving the administration of justice in that purity which ought to be so universally desired.

The court made the following order on the postponement of the trial.

Aaron Burr, late of the city of New-York, and state of New-York, attorney at law, who stands indicted for treason, was this day brought to the bar in custody of the marshal of this district, and thereof arraigned, and pleaded, Not guilty to the indictment, and for his trial put himself upon God and the country; whereupon he is remanded to gaol. And as the trial of the said Aaron Burr cannot be had in the county of Wood, where the offence is alleged to have been committed, without great inconvenience, it is ordered, that a *venire facias* issue, to the marshal of this district to be directed, commanding him to summon forty-eight fit persons qualified as the law directs, twelve of whom, from the said county of Wood, to appear here on the third day of August next, as a *venire* for the trial of the said Burr.

The court then adjourned till Monday next.

MONDAY, 29th June.

Mr. HAY laid the following order of the executive council before the court:

IN COUNCIL, June 29th, 1807.

The board being informed that an affidavit has been filed in the circuit court of the United States, for the Virginia district, which states, that the gaol for the county of Henrico and city of Richmond is inconvenient and unhealthy, and so crowded with state offenders and debtors that there are no private apartments therein, for the reception of persons charged with offences against the laws of the United States: it is therefore advised, that the governor be requested to tender the said court, (through the federal attorney of the district of Virginia) apartments in the third story of the public gaol and penitentiary house for the reception of such persons as shall be directed under the authority of the United States to be confined therein.

Extract from the Minutes.
DANIEL L. HYLTON, Clerk of the Council.

The following was the order of the court on this subject:

" Which tender the court doth accept for the purpose above mentioned."

The final decision of the motion to commit Aaron Burr to the penitentiary was postponed till to-morrow.

TUESDAY, June 30th.

After the court met, the motion to commit Aaron Burr to the penitentiary was renewed.

It was objected to by his counsel on the ground, (and an affidavit was made by them to the same effect) that in so important a case, it was essentially necessary for the most uninterrupted intercourse to subsist between the prisoner and his counsel; but that the distance of the penitentiary, combined with their own professional avocations, would necessarily narrow and interrupt this intercourse. It was also said, that by particular regulations of the penitentiary, the custody of the prisoner would be transferred from the marshal to the superintendent; and that the communications of the prisoner with his counsel would be limited to the very same short period which was allowed to the other visitants; that is, from eleven to one o'clock.

The attorney for the United States repelled these objections.

The CHIEF JUSTICE said, when there was a public gaol not unreasonably distant or unfit for the reception of the prisoner, and when the court was called upon on the part of the United States to commit a prisoner to its keeping, that he conceived himself bound to comply with the requisition; that when he had given the order for his removal from the gaol to his own lodgings, it was under an expectation, that the trial would be prosecuted immediately, and that the intercourse between the prisoner and his counsel would be necessarily incessant; but as a postponement had taken place, such an intercourse would not be absolutely necessary; under such circumstances therefore, he should direct the removal of the prisoner to the penitentiary, if he were still to continue in the possession of the marshal, and if his counsel were to have a free and uninterrupted access to him.

Some difficulty having thus occurred on these points, the executive council was immediately convened. In a short time the following letter was submitted to the court:

COUNCIL CHAMBER, June 30th, 1807.

SIR,

In pursuance of an advice of the council of state, I beg leave, through you, to inform the circuit court of the United States now sitting, that any persons who may be confined in the gaol and penitentiary house, on the part of the United States, will be considered as in the custody, and under the sole control of the marshal of the district; that he will have authority to admit any person or persons to visit the confined that he may think proper; and that he will be authorised to select for the purposes aforesaid, any apartment in the penitentiary, now unoccupied, that he may deem most conducive to safety, health and convenience.

I am, with great respect,
Sir, your obedient servant,
George Hay, Esquire. Wm. H. CABELL.

The court then came to the following order:

In consequence of the offer made by the executive of apartments in the third story of the penitentiary and state prison, for persons who may be confined therein under the authority of the United States, and of the foregoing letter from the governor of this commonwealth, it is ordered, on the motion of the attorney for the United States, that so soon as the apartments in the third story of the public gaol and penitentiary shall be fit for the reception and safe keeping of Aaron Burr, that he be removed thereto and safely kept therein by the marshal, until the second day of August next, when he shall be brought back to the prison where he is now placed, there to be guarded in like manner as at present, until the further order of the court.

CITY OF RICHMOND,

Monday, August 3d, 1807.

On this day the circuit court of the United States for the fifth circuit and district of Virginia was held according to adjournment.

Present the Chief Justice of the United States:

George Hay, William Wirt, and Alexander Mac Rae, esquires, counsel for the prosecution.

The prisoner was brought into court from his apartment near the Swan tavern, to which he had been removed on Saturday.

Edmund Randolph, John Wickham, Benjamin Botts, John Baker, and Luther Martin, esquires, appeared as his counsel.

The court assembled at twelve o'clock. An immense concourse of citizens attended to witness the proceedings of this important trial.

Mr. Hay observed, that he could take no steps in this business until he had ascertained, whether the witnesses summoned on the part of the United States were present; he therefore requested, that their names might be called over: they were more than one hundred in number. Their names were accordingly called in the following order:

*Thomas Truxtun, *Stephen Decatur, *BenjaminStoddert, *William Eaton, *William Duane, *Erick Bollman, *Peter Taylor, *Jacob Allbright, *Charles Willie, *John Graham, *Samuel Swartwout, *Julien Dupiestre, *P. H. M. Prevost, Israel Miller, *Samuel Skounten, *George Morgan, *John Morgan, *Thomas Morgan, *Nicholas Perkins, *Robert Spence, *George Harris, *Cyrus Jones, *Thomas Peterkin, Elias Glover, *Simeon Poole, *Dudley Woodbridge, *David C. Wallace, *Edmund B. Dana, James Reid, *John G. Henderson, *Alexander Henderson, *Hugh Phelps, Jacob Dunbaugh, *Chandler Lindsley, *John Mulhollon, *James Knox, *William Love, David Fisk, *Thomas Hartley, *Stephen S. Welch, *James Kinney, *Samuel Moxley, *Edmund P. Gaines, *Ambrose D. Smith, George Peters, Abner L. Duncan, Lewis Kerr, John A. Fort, *Benjamin H. Latrobe, Cowles Meade, Thomas Fitzpatrick, Thomas Butler, Robert A. New, Thomas T. Davis, Silas Dinsmore, Owen Aston, William Davis, F. Kibby, Theodore Brightwell, John Callier, Dr. Bennett, Earl Sproat, Robert Wallace, Walter Putnam, John Dana, Alexander Ralston, Mrs. Vanhorne, Henry Jacobs, Ransome Peale, Hamlin Hicks, Phelow Wooster, John Blair, James M'Dowell, Samuel N. Luckett, Stockley D. Hayes, Samuel W. Butler, Walter C. Davidson, John Barry, Thomas H. Cushing, Nathaniel Evans, Jacob Jackson, William Piatt, William White, Jerard Brooke, Morgan Nevill, Thomas Callis, Mr. Peterson, Lieutenant Swearingen, Mr. Weaver, colonel Osmund, major M. Porter, J. B. Walback, Mr. Vanhorne, Dr. Carmichael, Dr. Alston, colonel P. Read, John Wilkins, Stephen Woolberton, David M'Key, Hugh Allen, William Davis.

[Those were present whose names are printed in *italics :* the rest were absent. Such as have an * prefixed to their names were recognised at the former meeting of the court. The rest were not. Of course, all those whose names are placed *after* that of Benjamin H. Latrobe have been subpœnaed *since* the adjournment of the court.]

Mr. HAY begged leave to mention, that he had nothing more to submit to the court this day. There were many of the witnesses, of whose places of residence he was ignorant: several had not appeared; many had been merely pointed out to him by the attorney general of the United States. He observed, that, therefore, he had not yet been able to furnish colonel Burr with a list of the witnesses, and a statement of the places of their residence, as the law requires; that, as many of those, who had been summoned and recognised, had failed to appear, he was not ready to proceed with the trial immediately. He also informed the court, that a list of the venire had been delivered on Saturday to colonel Burr, but had since been discovered to be inaccurate. It became therefore necessary (an act of congress having directed this to be done at least three days before the trial) to deliver a correct list on this day; and of course, the trial would be postponed until the requisite time should have elapsed.

The CHIEF JUSTICE inquired then to what day it would be proper to adjourn the court.

Mr. HAY could not positively state by what day he should be able to prepare his lists.

Mr. BURR observed, that it was not very probable, that he should avail himself of any privileges which he might derive from any delay which had occurred in not furnishing him with the list of the jurors; and therefore the court might adjourn itself to any day, which was convenient to the attorney for the United States. Neither was it probable, that he should avail himself of any objections, which might be made to any incorrectness in the names of the jurors, or the places of residence, as stated in the list; unless certain circumstances might occur after the production of the list, on which he ought to found objections to it.

A short conversation then ensued upon the day of adjournment, when Mr. Burr observed, that as it would seem, in some measure, to depend upon his own consent, he should not hesitate to consent to an adjournment, provided it did not extend farther than Wednesday. Mr. Hay had no objection to that day.

Mr. HAY observed, that it might be proper to have the names of the *jury* called over, though not to impanel them at present. It would be premature now to impanel them, as the opposite counsel had not yet possessed a sufficient time to examine the list, and as the witnesses for the United States were not present.

The names of the jurors were accordingly called.

The names of the jurors summoned from Wood county to appear before the judges of the court of the United States, for the fifth circuit in the Virginia district, on the 3d day of August, 1807, for the trial of colonel Aaron Burr, are

Hezekiah Bucky, Jacob Beeson, James G. Laidly, William Prince, James Henderson, Nimrod Saunders, James Compton, Thomas Creel, Hamilton Morrison, Anthony Buckner, Yates S. Conwell, David Creel.

Wood county, district of Virginia,

JOSEPH SCOTT, Marshal, V. D.

List of the petit jurors for May circuit term, 1807, continued.

Names of he jurors summoned from the body of the district of Virginia for the trial of colonel Aaron Burr:

John Horace Upshaw of Essex county, William Pope of Powhatan, Peyton Randolph of Richmond city, John Bowe of Hanover, John Roberts of Culpeper, Joshua Chaffin of Amelia, Jervis Storrs of Henrico, Miles Selden of ditto, Lewis Truehart of Hanover, William Yancey of Pittsylvania, Thomas Prosser of Henrico, John Staples of Albemarle, Edward C. Stanard of Albemarle, Richard B. Goode of Chesterfield, Nathaniel Selden of Henrico, *Esme Smock of ditto, William Wardlaw of Richmond city, Richard E. Parker of Westmoreland, John W. Ellis of Hanover, Thomas Starke of ditto, William White of ditto, William B. Chamberlaine of Henrico, David Lambert of Richmond city, Randolph Harrison of Cumberland, William Hoomes of Caroline, Overton Anderson of Richmond city, Hugh Mercer of Spottsylvania, David Bullock of Richmond city, Jerman Baker of Cumberland, *Edward Carrington of Richmond city, Robert Haskins of Chesterfield, William R. Fleming of Goochland, George W. Smith of Richmond city, Armistead T. Mason of Loudon, Dabney Minor of Albemarle, William M'Daniel of Stafford.

JOSEPH SCOTT, Marshal, V. D.

[The two whose names are marked with an * were absent: all the rest were present]

Mr. HAY then requested the marshal to deliver, as soon as possible, a correct copy of this list to the opposite counsel.

Mr. Peyton Randolph inquired, whether this were a proper opportunity for any man on that panel to state his objections to the service.

The CHIEF JUSTICE answered, that it would be better to waive any objections, until the jury were about to be impaneled.

Mr. HAY wished, such of the witnesses, as had not appeared before, to be recognised as the others had been. And accordingly Messrs. Duncan, Nevill, M'Dowell and Peters, were recognised by the clerk.

The deputy marshal was then about to adjourn the court, when Mr. BURR recalled to the recollection of the court, the motion which he had made, on a former occasion, for a subpœna *duces tecum* addressed to the president of the United States. That motion had been partly complied with. He wished to know of the court, whether it were not a matter of right for him to obtain a subpœna *duces tecum*. If it were not, he should then lay a specific motion before the court.

The CHIEF JUSTICE did not believe it to be the practice in

Virginia to obtain such a subpœna upon a mere application to the clerk. The motion must be brought before the court itself.

Mr. HAY said, that he would say nothing on this subject, until he understood the object of the application: that if it were to obtain the letter which was not formerly furnished, he would inform the opposite counsel, that he had it now among his papers, and was ready to produce it.

Mr. BURR.—That is one object of the application. Another is, to obtain a certain communication from general Eaton to the president of the United States, which is mentioned in his deposition.

Mr. HAY said, that he was not certain, whether he had that communication, but believed that it was among his papers. If it were there, he would certainly produce it.

Mr. BURR.—But if, after a search, the gentleman find that he has not that paper, will he consent out of court, to issue a subpœna to the president of the United States, under the qualification I have mentioned? I wish not at the present exigency, to derange the affairs of the government, or to demand the presence of the executive officers at this place. All that I want, are certain papers.

Mr. HAY said, that he could not consent to it; he would rather that a regular application should be made for it to the court.

Mr. BURR.—Then, sir, I shall move for a subpœna *duces tecum*, to the president of the United States, directing him to attend with certain papers. This subpœna will issue as in the former instance. I shall furnish the clerk with the necessary specification of the paper, which I require.

The court was then adjourned till Wednesday, twelve o'clock.

WEDNESDAY, August 5th, 1807.

The court met according to adjournment.

Present, JOHN MARSHALL, chief justice of the United States.

Mr. HAY requested that the names of the witnesses might be called over, who had not appeared on Monday, and of whose arrival he was not yet informed.

The following witnesses *answered* to their names: Charles Willie, John Graham, Samuel Swartwout, Julien Dupiestre, P. H. M. Prevost, Israel Miller, William Eaton, George Morgan, Cyrus Jones, Simeon Poole, Dudley Woodbridge, John G. Henderson, Samuel Moxley, Ambrose D. Smith, John A. Fort, and Hugh Allen.

The names of the witnesses being called over, Mr. HAY observed, that the court would perceive that the number of the witnesses attending, was greater than it had been on Monday; that he presumed the whole of them would be here in a few days; that he had no doubt they would go into the trial during the present term; but that he could not now furnish the accused with such a list of the witnesses as was required by law; for though he knew their surnames, yet he was ignorant of the christian names of many, and their places of residence. He was not certain to what day the court might properly adjourn.

CHIEF JUSTICE.—It will make no sort of difference to the court, whether it adjourn from day to day, or to a certain day.

After a short conversation between the counsel on both sides, it was agreed that a list should be furnished of the witnesses, and of their places of abode, so far as they had been ascertained; and that a postponement should take place until Friday.

Mr. HAY proposed an arrangement, as to the mode of conducting the trial, the object of which was to save time. He said, that the course pursued in Great Britain on such occasions, is for the counsel for the prosecution, to open his case and examine all his witnesses, before any thing is said on the other side; for the prisoner's counsel, afterwards, to state the case on his part; to proceed to examine his witnesses, and to make such observations upon the whole of the testimony as he should think proper; and for the counsel for the prosecution to terminate the arguments by a reply. This he said, was a convenient and expeditious method. But, in Virginia, the practice is as follows : the attorney for the United States, or for the commonwealth, states the case on the part of the prosecution, and the counsel for the accused, also makes a statement on his part; after which the evidence is gone through on both sides; beginning with the witnesses against the prisoner. This being done, the counsel for the prosecution commences the argument, is answered by the counsel for the prisoner, and then concludes the debate. Mr. Hay observed, that this mode was much more tedious than that which prevails in Great Britain; and therefore ought particularly to be avoided in conducting the trial of Aaron Burr, in which the number of counsel employed, and of witnesses to be examined, is so great; especially as other trials equally tedious are about to take place; Herman Blannerhasset being now in custody, and Jonathan Dayton, known to be in this neighbourhood.

Mr. WICKHAM wished time to consider the subject; not being prepared to determine whether the counsel for colonel Burr, would accede to the proposal ; as this was a new mode of proceeding, to which they were not accustomed, they wished to consult their client, who, on this day, was not in court.

Mr. HAY said, he did not think this a matter of consent; the court ought to fix the practice.

The CHIEF JUSTICE observed, that it would be better to bring on this question on Friday; since gentlemen, in the mean time, might settle it among themselves; saying, moreover, that he should feel a difficulty in departing from the settled mode of practice in this country; though he thought the English mode better than ours. The best mode appeared to him to be this: that the case should be opened fully, by one of the gentlemen on the part of the United States; then opened fully, by one of the counsel on the other side; that the evidence should next be gone through; and the whole commented upon, by another of the gentlemen, employed by the United States; who should be answered by the rest of the attorneys for colonel Burr; and one only, of the counsel for the United States, should conclude the argument.

This mode was not approved of by Mr. HAY, as there were to be several trials; he feared that it would impose too much labour on the counsel for the prosecution.

Some further conversation passed, but no arrangement was determined on.

The court adjourned till Friday, twelve o'clock.

FRIDAY, August 7, 1807.

The court met according to adjournment.

Present, JOHN MARSHALL, chief justice of the United States, and CYRUS GRIFFIN, judge of the district of Virginia.

The witnesses were again called over, and several who had not been present before, appeared, and were recognised to attend until discharged by the court.

The counsel for the United States, however, not being as well prepared to go into the trial, as they expected to be, (many of their witnesses being still absent) the trial was farther postponed, and the court adjourned until Monday next, at twelve o'clock.

In the course of this day, a difficulty was suggested by major Scott, the marshal of the Virginia district, as arising out of the order of the court, by virtue of which colonel Burr had been removed from the penitentiary house, to his present lodgings. He stated, that he had been informed from good authority, that the secretary of the treasury had declared, that he would not allow his charge of seven dollars per day, for the guards employed for the safe-keeping of the prisoner; and, therefore, he might lose that sum, which he had hitherto been advancing out of his own pocket.

The CHIEF JUSTICE declared, the firm conviction of the court, that the order, heretofore made, was legal and proper; that the payments made in pursuance thereof, would be sanctioned by the court, and ought to be allowed by the secretary of the treasury. He could not believe that the secretary would finally disallow those items in the marshal's account. But as the officer of the court ought not to be subjected to any risk in obeying its directions; and, if the secretary should refuse to allow him a credit for the money paid, the court had no power to compel him to do so; and the situation of the marshal was such, that he dared not enter into a controversy with the secretary; the court was disposed to rescind the order, unless some arrangement could be made by colonel Burr and his counsel, for the indemnification of the marshal.

Colonel BURR declared, that an offer had already been made on his part, to indemnify the marshal, and that he was still ready and willing to give him satisfactory security, that the money should be paid him, in once the secretary of the treasury should refuse to allow the credit.

Some desultory conversation ensued, but nothing positive was agreed upon; but it appeared to be understood, that security was to be given to major Scott, and that colonel Burr was to remain in his apartment near the Swan Tavern.

MONDAY, August 10th, 1807.

The court met according to adjournment.

After the court met, Herman Blannerhasset was brought into court.

The following gentlemen appeared, and were recognised. Return J. Meigs, Maurice P. Bellnap, Charles Duvall, James Taylor, Tunis ———, Bennett Cook, Hezekiah Lewis, and G. B. Vanhorne.

Mr. WIRT moved the court to discharge Dr. Wardlaw, one of the *venire.* His wife was in extreme danger, and required the assistance of a sea voyage. The vessel would sail to-morrow.

CHIEF JUSTICE.—Is the court to understand that there is no objection to this motion?

Mr. BURR.—If the remark be addressed to me, sir, I can only say, that I shall remain passive. Dr. Wardlaw was then dismissed.

Mr. MAC RAE also moved the discharge of Mr. Randolph Harrison, whose extreme indisposition was attested by a certificate from Dr. Adams. Mr. Harrison was accordingly dismissed in the same manner.

Mr. HAY moved, that Herman Blannerhasset be arraigned for treason; which,

Mr. BOTTS opposed, on the ground that he had not been furnished with a copy of the indictment three days previously. After some desultory conversation on this circumsance,

Mr. BOTTS requested that Mr. Blannerhasset be reconveyed to the penitentiary, as he was extremely indisposed, and the heat nearly overpowered him. No opposition was made, and Mr. Blannerhasset was accordingly reconducted to his prison.

At Mr. HAY's request, the panel of the jury was called over by the deputy marshal, and also at Mr. Burr's request, the list of the witnesses, whom he had subpœnaed, for the purpose of investigating the qualifications of some of the *venire*.

Mr. HAY read a certificate from Dr. Upshaw, stating that Mr. James Henderson is sick of a bilious fever, and incapable of attending.

Mr. MAC RAE then read a certificate from Dr. Greenhow, showing, that David Bullock, esq. one of the *venire* was prevented by indisposition, from discharging his duties. Mr. Bullock was accordingly excused.

The clerk informed Mr. Burr, that he was at liberty to challenge such of the *venire* as he might object to.

Mr. BURR begged leave to inform the jurors, who were within hearing, that a great number of them may have formed and expressed opinions about him, which might disqualify them from serving on this occasion. He expected that as they came up, they would discharge the duties of conscientious men, and candidly answer the questions put to them, and state all their objections against him.

The deputy marshal then summoned first, Hezekiah Bucky.

Mr. BOTTS.—We challenge you for cause. Have you ever formed and expressed an opinion about the guilt of colonel Burr?

Mr. Bucky. I have not, sir, since I have been subpœnaed.
Question. Had you before?
Answer. I had formed one before in my own mind.

Mr. HAY wished, that the question of the opposite counsel could assume a more precise and definite form. If this question were proposed to this man, and to every other man of the panel, he would venture to predict, that there could not be a jury selected in the state of Virginia; because he did not believe that there was a single man in the state, qualified to become a jury-man, who had not, in some form or other, made up, and declared an opinion, on the conduct of the prisoner. The transactions in the west had excited universal curiosity; and there was no man who had not seen and decided on the documents relative to them. Do gentlemen contend, that in a case so peculiarly interesting to all, the mere declaration of an opinion is sufficient to disqua-lify a juryman? A doctrine of this sort, would at once acquit the prisoner; for where is the jury that could try him? Such a doc-trine amounts to this: that a man need only to do enough to draw down the public attention upon him, and he would immediately effect his discharge. Mr. Hay concluded with a hope, that the question would assume a more definitive form; he should not pretend to decide the form in which it should be proposed, for that was the province of the court; it was a privilege to which every court is entitled; and one which the court had exercised in the case of James T. Callender.

Mr. Botts considered it as a misfortune ever to be deplored, that in this country, and in this case, there had been too gene-ral an expression of the public sentiment, and that this generality of opinion would disqualify many; but he had never entertained a doubt, until the gentleman for the prosecution had avowed it, that twelve men might be found in Virginia, capable of deciding this question, with the strictest impartiality. He still trusted that the attorney for the United States was mistaken; that the ca-tastrophe was not completely fixed; and that every man in the state had not pledged himself to convict colonel Burr, whether right or wrong. He was not present at the trial of James T. Callender; but all America had heard the question which was then propounded to the jurymen; and that was, whether he had made up and expressed an opinion respecting the guilt of the prisoner.

Mr. Hay said, that he would put Mr. Botts right as to matter of fact. The court would recollect that on the trial of Callender, the question was, not whether the jurymen had formed and ex-pressed an opinion on that case generally; but on the subject matter that was to be tried, and contained in the indictment. The question then in the present case should be, have you for-med and expressed an opinion on the point at issue; that is, whether Aaron Burr be guilty of treason? On the trial of Cal-lender, the court would particularly recollect, that Mr. John Basset having objected to himself, because he had read the libel-lous publication, was actually overruled; because it was not on the book itself, but on the subject matter of the indictment, that he was called upon to say, whether he had ever expressed an opinion?

Mr. BURR declared, that there was a material distinction between that and the present case. Mr. Basset's acknowledging that he had seen the book did not disqualify him from serving on the jury; in the same manner, the person who had seen a murder committed, would not be an incompetent juror in the prosecution for that crime. But if a man pretended to decide upon the guilt of a prisoner, upon mere rumour, he would manifest such a levity and bias of mind, as would effectually disqualify him. Mr. Bucky, however, has not yet come out completely with his declarations. Let him be further interrogated.

Mr. HAY observed, that the question would still be too general and vague, if it were even to be " Have you expressed any opinion on the treason of Aaron Burr?" for the case stated in the indictment was infinitely more specific. It was treason in levying war against the United States at Blannerhasset's island. Unless this particular allegation be proved, it defeats all the other parts of the accusation; and it was, probably, on this point that the juror had never made up any opinion.

Mr. MARTIN contended, that it was the duty of every juryman to come to the trial of any case with the most perfect impartiality; and more particularly one where life and reputation were at stake; that it was a libel upon Virginia, a blot upon the whole state, to assert, that twelve men could not be found to decide such a case, with no other knowledge than what they had picked up from newspapers: that there was a material distinction between this and Callender's case; the libel was a book in every man's hand; but does any juryman in the present case pretend to know the testimony on which this charge depends? The gentleman proposes to ask the juryman, whether he have made up an opinion on colonel Burr's treason? But it is extremely probable, that most of them know not what treason is; and though they may decide upon the guilt of colonel Burr, they may be ignorant, whether it come under the name and description of treason.

Mr. BOTTS quoted authorities in support of his opinion, but they are not all inserted here, because the same question was afterwards very fully argued, and many authorities cited. The *Trials of Smith and Ogden* in New-York, and the opinion of judge Iredel, on the *Trial of John Fries*, in Pennsylvania, were particularly referred to.

The CHIEF JUSTICE observed, that it might save some altercation, if the court were to deliver its opinon at the present time; that it was certainly one of the clearest principles of natural justice, that a juryman should come to a trial of a man for life, with a perfect freedom from previous impressions; that it was clearly the duty of the ourt to obtain, if possible, men free from such bias; but that if it were not possible from the very circumstances of the case; if rumours had reached and prepossessed their judgments, still the court was bound to obtain as large a portion of impartiality as possible; that this was not more a principle of natural justice, than a maxim of the common law, which we have inherited from our forefathers; that the same right was secured by the constitution of the United States, which entitles every man under a criminal prosecution, to a fair trial by " an impartial jury." Can it be said, however, that any man is an impartial juryman, who has declared the prisoner to be guilty and to have deserved punishment? If it be said, that he has made up this opinion, but has not heard the testimony; such an excuse only makes the case worse; for if the man have decided upon insufficient testimony, it manifests a bias that completely disqualifies himself from the functions of a juryman. It is too general a question, to ask whether he have any impressions about colonel Burr. The impressions may be so light, that they do not amount to an opinion of guilt; nor do they go to the extent of believing, that the prisoner deserves capital punishment. With respect to Mr. Basset's opinion, it was true he had read " The Prospect before Us;" and he had declared that it was a libel; but Mr. Basset had formed no opinion about James T. Callender's being the author. It was the same principle in the present case. If a juryman were to declare that the attempt to achieve the dismemberment of the union, was treason, it would not be a complete objection or disqualification; but it would be the application of that crime to a particular individual; it would be the fixing it on Aaron Burr that would disable him from serving in this case. Let the counsel then proceed with the inquiry.

Mr. Botts.—Have you said that colonel Burr was guilty of treason?

Mr. Bucky.—No. I only declared that the man who acted as colonel Burr was said to have done, deserved to be hung.

Question. Did you believe, that colonel Burr was that man?

Answer. I did, from what I had heard.

Mr. Hay.—I understand then, that the question proposed in Callender's case is to be overruled?

Chief Justice.—My brother judge does not recollect whether it particularly went to the indictment or not.

Judge Griffin.—I think the question was, " relative to the matter in issue."

Mr. Hay.—The very position that I have laid down.

Chief Justice.—The simple question is, whether the having formed an opinion, not upon the evidence in court, but upon common rumour, render a man incompetent to decide upon the real testimony of the case?

Mr. WIRT, (addressing Mr. Bucky.) Did I understand you to say, that you concluded upon certain rumours you had heard, that colonel Burr deserved to be hung?

Mr. Bucky.—I did.

Question. Did you believe these rumours? Answer. I did.

Question. Would you, if you were a juryman, form your opinion upon such rumours? Answer. Certainly not.

Mr. MAC RAE.—Did you form and express your opinion upon the question, whether an overt act of treason had been committed at Blannerhasset's island?

Answer. It was upon other rumours, and not upon *that*, that I had formed an opinion.

Mr. MARTIN submitted it to the court, whether he could be considered an impartial juryman.

The court decided that he ought not to be so considered and he was accordingly *rejected*.

James G. Laidly stated, that he had formed and expressed some opinions unfavourable to colonel Burr, that he could not pretend to decide upon the charges in the indictment, which he had not heard; that he had principally taken his opinions from newspaper statements; and that he had not, as far as he recollected, expressed an opinion, that colonel Burr deserved hanging; but that his impression was, that he was guilty. *He was therefore set aside.*

James Compton being challenged for cause and sworn, stated, that he had formed and expressed an opinion from hearsay, that colonel Burr was guilty of treason, and of that particular treason of which he stood charged, as far as he understood. *He was rejected.*

Mr. BURR observed, that as gentlemen on the part of the prosecution had expressed a willingness to have an impartial jury, they could not refuse that any juryman should state all his objections to himself; and that he had no doubt, in spite of the contrary assertions which had been made, that they could get a jury from this panel.

Hamilton Morrison upon being called, said, that he had frequently thought and declared, that colonel Burr was guilty, if the statements which he had heard were true; that he did not know whether they were so; but only thought from the great clamour which had been made, that it might be possible that they were true; that he had not passed any positive opinion; nor was he certain that he had always qualified it by saying,

" if these things were true;" that he does not recollect to have said, that colonel Burr ought to be punished, without stating at the same time, " if he were guilty." *Mr. Morrison was suspended for further examination.*

Yates S. Conwell had formed and expressed an opinion, from the reports he had heard, that colonel Burr must be guilty of high treason. *He was accordingly set aside.*

Jacob Beeson declared, that he had for some time past formed an opinion, as well from news-paper publications, as from the boats which had been built on the Ohio, that colonel Burr was guilty; and that he himself had borne arms to suppress this insurrection. *He was therefore set aside, as incompetent.*

William Prince declared, he had nearly the same impressions as Mr. Beeson; that he too had borne arms; as well on Blannerhasset's island, as on descending the river, in search of Blannerhasset. *He was set aside in like manner.*

Nimrod Saunders declared, that he had expressed an opinion previously to his being summoned on the jury, that the prisoner had been guilty of treason. *He was therefore set aside as incompetent.*

Thomas Creel had no declaration to make, and was challenged for cause. Upon being interrogated, he stated, that he had never asserted that the prisoner ought to be punished, that he had said, that he was a sensible man; and if there were any hole left, he would creep out of it; that he had conceived that colonel Burr had seduced Blannerhasset into some acts that were not right; that he had never positively said, that colonel Burr was guilty; that he had said, that Blannerhasset was the most blamable, because *he* was in good circumstances, and *well off in life;* whereas colonel Burr's situation was desperate, and that he had little to lose; that he had not said, that colonel Burr had directly misled Mr. Blannerhasset, but through the medium of Mrs. Blannerhasset; in short, that there was no determinate impression on his mind respecting the guilt of the prisoner.

The Chief Justice did not think, that this was sufficient to set him aside, and *suspended his case for further examination.*

Anthony Buckner had frequently said, that the prisoner deserved to be hung. *He was therefore set aside.*

David Creel had formed an opinion from the statements in the newspapers, and if these were true, the prisoner was certainly guilty. He had expressed a belief that he was guilty of the charges now brought against him, and that he ought to be hanged. *He was therefore rejected.*

Jurors from the body of the district.

John Horace Upshaw declared, that he conceived himself to stand there as an unprejudiced juryman; for he was ready to attend to the evidence, but that as he had formed opinions hostile to the prisoner; (if opinions they can be called, which are formed from newspaper testimony,) and had, he believed, frequently expressed them; that he was unwilling to subject himself to the imputation of having prejudged the cause.

Mr. BURR.—We challenge Mr. Upshaw for cause.

Mr. HAY.—Then, sir, I most seriously apprehend that we shall have no jury at all. I solemnly believe, Mr. Upshaw is an intelligent and upright man, and can give a correct verdict on the evidence; and I will venture to assert, (whatever credit my friends on the other side will allow to my assertion,) that I myself could do justice to the accused; I believe that any man can, who is blessed with a sound judgment and integrity. We might as well enter at once a *nolle prosequi*, if he is to be rejected.

Mr. WICKHAM.—Then according to the gentleman's doctrine, any honest man, no matter what his impressions may be, is a competent juryman. Is this agreeable to the principles of law? Does the gentleman mean to insinuate, that when we object to a juryman, it is for his want of honesty? No, sir, every man is subject to partialities and aversions; which may conscientiously sway his judgment. Mr. Upshaw does no doubt deem himself an impartial juryman; but Mr. Upshaw may be deceived.

After some desultory argument between Messrs. Hay and Wickham, Mr. WIRT proceeded to ask Mr. Upshaw, whether he had understood him to say, that notwithstanding the hostile impressions he had taken up from newspaper reports, these impressions had not received that determinate character which might entitle them to the name of opinions?

Answer. I have received *impressions* hostile to colonel Burr, and have expressed them with some warmth; but my impressions have not been induced by any thing like evidence. They were predicated on the deposition of general Eaton and the communications of general Wilkinson, to the president of the United States. I had conceived that the prisoner had been guilty of some criminal act against the public, and ought to be punished, and I believe also, that I went on further to vindicate the conduct of those gentlemen who would appear as the principal witnesses against him; and also of the government in the measures which it had taken to suppress his plans. After some further and animated discussion on this point, Mr. Upshaw's case was *suspended for subsequent examination.*

William Pope declared, that his impresssions were nearly the same with those of the gentlemen, who had preceded him; that he had thought at first, from newspaper representations, that it was colonel Burr's intention to make his fortune in the west by the settlement of lands; that when 'he had afterwards understood that he had formed a union with Wilkinson to proceed to Mexico he had regarded the prisoner's conduct in such a light, that if he had proceeded to Mexico he would have considered it as an excusable offence, but when he had afterwards understood that there was treason mixed with his projects, it was impossible for him to view his conduct without the deepest indignation; if these impressions could be called prejudices, he trusted that he should always retain them; what other sentiments could he feel against such a crime perpetrated against the very best government on the surface of the earth? But Mr. Pope declared that from his heart he believed, that he could divest himself of these unfavourable impressions, and give colonel Burr a fair and honourable trial. He would add, that in pursuance of the spirit manifested by the constitution which required two witnesses to an overt act of treason; he should think it necessary, that the evidence for the United States, should be so strong as to make the scale preponderate.

Mr. WICKHAM.—You will not misunderstand me, Mr. Pope, when I ask you whether you have not been a candidate for your county, and whether you be not now a delegate?

Answer. Yes.

Question. In canvassing among the people, have you not declared, that the government had acted properly in commencing this prosecution?

Answer. Yes; I believe I have said generally, that I thought colonel Burr was guilty of high treason. *Mr. Pope was therefore set aside.*

Peyton Randolph declared, that it had never been his wish or intention to shrink from the discharge of a public duty; but that he had peculiar objections to serve on this occasion; one of which only, he shôuld state. He had been enrolled and was qualified as a lawyer in this court; and he would submit it to the court, whether this did not exempt, if not disqualify him from serving?

CHIEF JUSTICE admitted Mr. Randolph's privilege, unless there were an express interposition on the part of the prisoner, to retain him and others of the venire who had privileges; for this would call a conflicting privilege into operation.

Mr. Burr said, that he should be passive.

John Bowe did not recollect to have said, that the prisoner was guilty of treason; but of something hostile to the peace and happiness of the United States. Upon being interrogated he observed, that he was a delegate from the county of Hanover; that there had been a competition at the last election; that he had had occasion to speak at that time, of the views of the prisoner; but had always done it cautiously; had never asserted that he ought to be hung, but that he was guilty of something unfriendly to the peace of the United States.

Mr. Wickham.—You have said that the prisoner was guilty?

Answer. Yes.

Chief Justice.—Did you ever make up an opinion about his levying troops and making war against the United States.

Answer. Yes : but I have never expressed it.

Mr. Burr.—Take the whole together, and it amounts to an opinion of treason. Mr. Bowe has *said*, that colonel Burr was guilty; and of what? Of that which in Mr. Bowe's mind amounts to the definition of treason. *He was therefore set aside.*

John Roberts had thought and declared, from the reports in the public newspapers, that the prisoner was guilty of treason, though he had no doubt, that his opinion might be changed by the production of other testimony. *He was set aside as incompetent.*

Joshua Chaffin *excused from indisposition.*

7. Jervis Storrs observed, that the state of his mind was like that of the gentleman who had gone before him (Mr. Bowe); he was in the habit of reading newspapers, and could not but examine their statements relative to these transactions. If he could believe general Eaton's assertion, that the prisoner had threatened to turn congress out of doors, and assassinate the president, he had said, and would still say, that colonel Burr was guilty of treason. If general Wilkinson's letter were true, he had surely been guilty of something in the west, that was hostile to the interest of the United States. He did not know, whether in the multifarious conversations he had had on this subject, he had always expressed this opinion of his guilt with that reservation. He had *very often* communicated his impressions, that he was plotting some hostile designs against the United States. Mr. Storrs confessed that he might be prejudiced against the prisoner; and that he might be judging too highly of his own mind, to entertain the belief, that he could divest himself of all his impressions; and upon the whole, he expressed a wish not to serve. *He was then rejected.*

8. Miles Selden declared, that it was impossible not to have entered into the frequent conversations which had occured on this topic, and to have declared some opinion; that he had always said, that colonel Burr was guilty of something, and that if he were guilty of treason against such a government as that of the United States, he would deserve to be hung; that he could not assert that he had always accompanied his opinions with this reservation; but that he was not afraid to trust himself in the rendering of a verdict.

Upon being interrogated, he said that he had frequently jested on this subject; and particularly recollected to have said in a sportive conversation with colonel Mayo, that this was a federal plot and that Burr had been set on by the federalists. *Colonel Selden was therefore suspended for further consideration.*

9. Lewis Truehart had said, that if the reports were correct, colonel Burr had been guilty of something inimical to the country, and that he always qualified his opinions in that manner.

Colonel Tinsley was then called in as a witness, who stated, that from a conversation with Mr. Truehart, he thought that he had discovered that he had a general prepossession against colonel Burr. He did not expect to be called on, and had no very distinct recollection of the particulars; that this was before any of the proceedings of the trial; and when he heard that he was summoned as one of the *venire,* he then recollected their conversation and happened casually to mention it. *Mr. Truehart suspended.*

William Yancey had expressed an opinion on newspaper testimony that colonel Burr guilty; that he had frequently said that he would believe the statements of newspapers till the contrary were proved; but that he had no doubt he should entertain a different sentiment, if other testimony were produced. *He was set aside.*

Thomas Prosser was next called. He said that he had made numberless declarations about colonel Burr; that he had believed him to be guilty of a treasonable intention, but not of the overt act; on this point he had suspended his opinion, but he was rather inclined to believe that he had not committed it.

Mr. MARTIN.—Can this gentleman be considered as an impartial juryman, when he thus comes with his mind made up on one half of the guilt? *He was suspended for further consideration.*

John Staples had been under the same impressions, which had been described by others; that he dared to say, that he had said colonel Burr was guilty of levying troops and making war upon the United States. *He was set aside.*

Edward C. Stanard acknowledged that his prejudices against colonel Burr had been deep-rooted; that he had no doubt of the criminality of his *motives*, but that he had doubts of the commission of an *overt act;* he regretted that a man of his talents and energetic mind, should be lost to his country. Upon being interrogated he observed, that he had doubts as to the overt act, because he believed him to be a man of such deep intrigue as never to jeopardise his own life, till thousands fell before him. *He was rejected.*

Richard B. Goode was then called.

I have never seen, neither do I believe, that I have heard correctly, the evidence in this prosecution. From common report, and newspaper information I have formed an opinion unfavourable to colonel Burr: that opinion has been strengthened by what I have heard from the lips of colonel Burr in this court; but without arrogating to myself more virtue than belongs to other men, if I know myself, I have formed no opinion which cannot be altered by the evidence.

Mr. BAKER.—Did you not endeavour to displace Mr. Heth as captain of the Manchester cavalry, for becoming the bail of colonel Burr?

Answer. I never did. (Here sundry witnesses were directed to be called.)

Mr. Goode.—I will state the circumstance to which you allude, unless you prefer to prove it.

The Court.—Do so, if you please.

Mr. Goode.—On the 4th of July, 1806, I was a member of a committee with captain Heth, appointed to prepare toasts to be drunk on that day by the Manchester cavalry. I profess to be attached to the present administration of the general government, and wished to express such a sentiment. Captain Heth declared, that he had not confidence in the executive, and rather than express such a sentiment he would resign his commission. At that time, I thought captain Heth and myself differed only as to measures, and not as to principles; and that it was an honest opinion. But in a few months after, when I understood that captain Heth had become bail for colonel Burr, and was his zealous friend, with whom he was neither connected nor acquainted, but a stranger, who, three years ago, would have been consigned to the grave by captain Heth, and those thinking with him upon political subjects; and when I recollected the charge preferred against colonel Burr, I confess that the declaration and conduct of captain Heth made such impressions upon my mind, that I refused to trust my person with him as a military commander, and I would do it again.

Colonel BURR.—Pray, sir, did you not write a letter to captain Heth?

Answer. I did; and I have reasons to believe, that that letter is in your possession or in the possession of your counsel. You are at liberty to show it to the court, or I will repeat that part of it, which relates to captain Heth and yourself.

The Court.—Do so, sir.

Mr. Goode.—A few weeks past, I received a letter from captain Heth, *commanding* me to appear at a certain time and place, in order to take my proper command in the troop. I wrote him, in answer, that my post as a soldier would never be abandoned, and that my duty as a citizen forbade that I should silently approve of the conduct of those who had extended a favour to a traitor, which the justice of my country denied to an unfortunate debtor, or words to that effect.

Mr. Goode *was then rejected.*

Nathaniel Selden stated, he had formed an opinion, particularly from general Eaton's deposition; that the intentions of the prisoner were hostile to the United States; but that he had also said he had seen no evidence to satisfy him that he had been guilty of an overt act. *He was suspended for further consideration.*

16. Esme Smock declared, that he had formed and expressed an opinion that colonel Burr had treasonable designs.

CHIEF JUSTICE.—To what time did your opinion relate?

Mr. Smock.—I have formed my opinion from newspaper publications and common report; but I have constantly conceived that colonel Burr's intentions were treasonable throughout.

Mr. WICKHAM.—Have you ever formed an opinion, that colonel Burr was guilty of treason?

Answer. I have in my own mind. *He was set aside.*

Richard E. Parker said, that he had, like every other person, formed an opinion on that case, on newspaper statements; but he had heard very little of the evidence that may be adduced on this occasion. He had declared, that if these newspaper statements were true, colonel Burr had been guilty of some design contrary to the interest and laws of the United States. As to the doctrine of treason, he had not formed a conclusive opinion.

Mr. BURR.—I have no objection to Mr. Parker. *He is therefore elected.*

A desultory argument here ensued, about the propriety of swearing one juryman at a time. The counsel for the prosecution opposed, the counsel for the prisoner advocated, the doctrine. The court decided, that it would adhere to the practice of Virginia; and swear four jurymen at a time.

John W. Ellis said, that he had no doubt that the prisoner had been guilty of having treasonable designs; whether he had proceeded to acts, he had doubt. *He was suspended.*

Thomas Starke, without any expectations of being summoned as a juryman, had stated his opinion to his neighbours, who had asked him questions on the subject, that colonel Burr had been guilty of high treason. *He was set aside.*

William White stated, that he had been in the western country, in May last; and from colonel Burr's character and from the representations he had received of his conduct, he had been induced to say, that he was guilty of treason, and that he ought to be hanged, or that hanging was too good for him. *He was set aside.*

William B. Chamberlaine stated, that he stood in a very peculiar situation; if, as Mr. Wickham declared, any man were unfit to be a juryman who had asserted colonel Burr to have been worthy of death; he was ready to confess that he himself came under this restriction. He had said, uniformly, that he had treasonable designs; but he did not now believe that colonel Burr had committed an overt act of treason; though he believed him to be guilty of the intention. He however believed that he could do him justice; and that he could conscientiously pass between him and his country. *He was rejected.*

David Lambert wished to be excused on account of his indisposition; but the court rejected his plea. On being interrogated, he declared, that he did not recollect to have formed an opinion, for or against colonel Burr. *He was elected.*

William Hoomes had no hesitation in saying, that he had often declared his opinion, that colonel Burr was guilty of treasonable intentions, and perhaps he might say, of treason itself. He had imbibed his impressions from every thing he had seen, heard or read. He had understood that colonel Burr's counsel had made preparations to prove, that he had disqualified himself, by his own declarations. He should thank them to develop their objections.

Mr. Burr.—I assure you, sir, no such preparation has been made. *He was set aside.*

24. Overton Anderson said, that he had often expressed an opinion, that colonel Burr's views were inimical to the United States; these opinions he had principally formed upon newspaper statements; he did not recollect that he had ever asserted him to be guilty of treason; but he had sometimes given credit to the representations, which he had heard, without particularly defining the degree of guilt in which they might involve the pri-

soner; and thought him guilty of the charge against him, though he would not say it was treason. *He was rejected.*

Hugh Mercer, upon being called, said, that it was his duty to state, that an opinion, which he had for some time past entertained, of the character of colonel Burr, was unfriendly to a strictly impartial inquiry, into his case; that he was entirely uninformed as to the testimony which would be introduced, and that he did not recollect to have ever expressed a positive opinion, either as to his guilt or innocence. *He was elected.*

Jerman Baker had entertained opinions unfavourable to Aaron Burr, which he had repeatedly expressed. He had spoken them with warmth, for it was his nature to be warm. He had no doubt, that the prisoner had formed very unfriendly designs against the United States; but from his ignorance of the evidence, he could not venture to say, that they had ripened into an overt act.

Mr. BURR.—What opinion have you formed of me?

Answer. A very bad one; which I have expressed often when called upon; and often when not. *He was set aside.*

Edward Carrington, next called, said, that he had formed an unfavourable opinion of the views of colonel Burr; but these opinions were not definitive. Some had said, that colonel Burr's object was to invade the Spanish territories; others, that it was to dismember the union: his own opinion had not been definitely fixed. There was another subject connected with this trial, on which he had also expressed his opinions; and that related to the measures taken at New-Orleans. His own opinion had been, that it was impossible for any one at this remote scene, to determine upon the state of affairs in that city; but if general Wilkinson did seriously believe what he said had been represented to him as the views of colonel Burr, that he ought to consider it as an extreme case, and take extreme measures, and act somewhat in the manner that general Wilkinson had done. This has been the state of his mind for twelve months.

Mr. BURR.—Have you, colonel, any prejudice of a more settled kind and ancient date against me?

Colonel Carrington.—None at all.

Mr. BURR.—*He is elected.*

Mr. Parker said, that perhaps he had been misunderstood by the court, and colonel Burr; perhaps he was disqualified, and he wished to be distinctly understood. He said, that he had expressed no deliberate opinion on the subject, yet he had believed, that colonel Burr had some designs contrary to the interest of the United States; that he had formed no opinion of the truth of those depositions, but if they were true, his designs were treasonable. Mr. Parker *was returned as a juror.*

The four jurymen that had been elected, were then called to the book, and sworn, viz. Messrs. Parker, Lambert, Mercer, and Carrington.

Robert Haskins had expressed an opinion, that colonel Burr was guilty; but does not recollect to what extent he went. He went so far as to say, he was guilty of an intention of treason, but not of an overt act. He might have said, that he deserved to be hung. *He was set aside.*

William R. Fleming had formed, and frequently expressed, an opinion, that colonel Burr was guilty of treasonable intentions; and might have made a general declaration, not only as to intentions, but to acts. *He was set aside.*

George W. Smith suggested a right to the same exemption, which had been granted to Mr. P. Randolph. The court said, that this privilege would be incontestible, unless the prisoner should urge his conflicting privilege. Mr. Burr then requested Mr. Smith, to attend to-morrow. Mr. Smith wished to be excused, as he had some important business in another court, to attend to. He should, however, attend on the trial to-morrow; but it might now be proper to state the general impressions which he had received, from these transactions. He had generally been solicitous to avoid an expression of his opinions; and as in such cases, where the government commences a prosecution against an individual, there is always a preponderance of prejudice against him; he himself, had not only been solicitous, not to declare, but even not to form, an opinion. No one can, however, avoid reading representations of these things, in the public papers : and he had formed, and declared, his impressions, that colonel Burr had entertained designs, offensive to the peace and laws of the United States. What was the species of guilt, he had not pretended to define; but he had concluded from the newspaper reports, and the testimony which he had heard in the other end of the capitol, that his designs were of a military nature, and that they might amount, at least, to a misdemeanor. *He was suspended for further consideration.*

31. Armistead T. Mason had formed no deliberate opinion, in regard to the actual commission of treason. But it was his deliberate opinion, that colonel Burr had designed, if not to subvert the government, at least to divide the country. *He was suspended for further consideration.*

32. Dabney Minor had often said, that colonel Burr's intentions were unfriendly to the United States ; that he had said, that if he were guilty of what was charged against him, he ought to be hanged; but had heard no positive testimony.

Some conversation here ensued, between Mr. Minor and Mr. Botts, when Mr. Minor *was suspended until to-morrow.*

Thus, then, of the whole *venire* that appeared, four only were elected and sworn, and nine were suspended, till arguments should be heard on the subject, in order to aid the court, to form an opinion, whether they were competent jurymen or not.

Here a discussion of considerable length took place, on the propriety of confining or not confining, in the custody of the marshal, the jurors already sworn, till the other eight should be sworn.

The court then decided, that there was no necessity for delivering the jurymen, who had been, or should be sworn into the custody of the marshal, until the whole number had been impaneled and sworn.

Adjourned till Tuesday, eleven o'clock.

TUESDAY, August 11th, 1807.

The court met according to adjournment.

Present, the CHIEF JUSTICE and Judge GRIFFIN.

The CHIEF JUSTICE informed the counsel engaged in the cause, that the court was ready to hear any observations on the question before them yesterday, which they might think proper to make.

Mr. MARTIN.—We are ready to say something relative to the situation that a juryman ought to be in, to enable him properly to pass upon the case of a prisoner.

Mr. George W. Smith was the first of the jurors, suspended yesterday for subsequent examination, who was called. He said, that he supposed himself entitled to exemption, from his profession as a practising lawyer in this court: that by the law of the land, as long as he behaved with respect to the court, and diligence to his client, he ought not to be obstructed in the pursuit of his professional duties: that though there was no express statute exempting him, yet he was exempted by the reason of the law.

Mr. BURR observed, that, as some real or fictitious difficulty had occurred in the selection of jurymen, he should be extremely sorry, if such as were impartial should object to themselves. If Mr. Smith, however, raised such objections, he himself should submit to the decision of the court, as he wished to be perfectly passive.

Mr. Smith did not know whether he deserved such an encomium on his impartiality; but as the arrangement of his professional business, in other courts, (though not in this court at this particular time) would not permit him to attend the trial with any convenience, he should claim the privilege of exemption, to which, in his opinion, he was entitled by law.

CHIEF JUSTICE said, that this privilege would certainly exempt Mr. Smith, unless his attendance were claimed by the prisoner; and as colonel Burr waived this right, Mr. Smith was excused from attending.

James Henderson, of Wood county, who was absent yesterday, was next called; he was challenged for cause. On being examined by Mr. Botts, he admitted that he was not a freeholder, and was consequently *set aside*.

Mr. Hamilton Morrison was the next of the suspended jurymen who was called. He declared that it was with pain he should serve on the jury; that he did not wish to serve on it; that it was still more disagreeable to him, as the defendant seemed to have such imaginary thoughts against him; that he had not meddled with the prisoner's transactions, though *perhaps* he might have done so, had it been profitable to him. James Henderson and Mr. Neale were both examined as to what they might have heard him say on this subject, and both declared that they had heard him say nothing material.

Mr. BURR.—Have not these rumours excited a prejudice in your mind against me?

Answer. I have no prejudice for or against you.

Mr. BOTTS.—Are you a freeholder?

Answer. I have two patents for land.

Question. Are you worth three hundred dollars?

Answer. Yes: I have a horse here that is worth the half of it.

Question. Have you another at home to make up the other half.

Answer. Yes: four of them. [Here the court said, that sufficient cause had not been shown against his being a proper juror.] I am surprised why they should be in so much terror of me. Perhaps my *name* may be a terror, for my first name is *Hamilton*.

Colonel BURR then observed, that *that* remark was a sufficient cause for objecting to him, and challenged him. Mr. Morrison was therefore *set aside*.

This was the first peremptory challenge which the prisoner made, of the thirty-five to which the law entitles him.

Thomas Creel, another of the suspended jurymen from Wood county, was next *set aside* by the court; because, he said, that he had both formed and expressed sentiments unfavourable to the prisoner.

John H. Upshaw was next called up. He stated, before he

was interrogated, that he had received strong impressions against colonel Burr, but that he believed he could find a verdict according to testimony.

The CHIEF JUSTICE wished to know, whether those impressions related to the general charge of treason against the prisoner, or to what happened before, or to what circumstances?

Mr. Upshaw answered, that they related to the transactions in the western country; and added, " my opinions have changed as the lights of evidence seemed successively to appear. It was my first impression, that he had nothing more in view than the settlement of the lands on the Waschita. I next supposed that he intended to attack Mexico; but that as a mean of effecting that object, he intended to attack New-Orleans: and last of all, that his plans were of a more *complicated* nature; but that he never thought, till after his leaving the mouth of Cumberland, that Burr had treasonable designs; but that he could not recollect *particularly*, the times, *when* he formed, or changed these opinions.

Mr. WICKHAM asked him, whether, as the result of all these impressions, he did not consider colonel Burr a dangerous man? He answered, that *that* was his impression.

Mr. MAC RAE.—Have you formed or delivered an opinion, that he has committed an overt act of treason, as charged in the indictment?

Answer. I have not.

Mr. MARTIN said, that he should state, whether there were any *bias* on his mind, although he did not believe that an overt act had been committed; for if he had such *bias*, he was unfit for a juryman.

Mr. BAKER.—Have you not, in your own county, argued in conversation, to show, that colonel Burr was guilty, and that there was strong presumptive evidence against him?

Answer. I have done so; and not only supported such opinions, but have gone on to vindicate the propriety of the measures taken by the government.

Mr. BURR said, that enough had appeared to show, that Mr. Upshaw had taken up strong prejudices against him.

Mr. HAY asked, whether such testimony as that could disqualify him as a juryman?

Mr. Upshaw said, that he had been in the habit of impressing on others his prejudices, or opinions, that Burr was a dangerous man to the community.

Mr. MAC RAE.—I beg leave to ask, whether personally you

have any prejudices against him? Have you any other prejudice against him, except that he has entertained treasonable designs?

He answered explicitly, that he had not.

Mr. BURR.—Had you not, anterior to those transactions rumoured in the western country, formed an unfavourable opinion of me?

Mr. Upshaw answered, that he had before (with other persons) formed rather an unfavourable opinion against him, during the presidential election (of 1801,) though he had no positive evidence on that subject.

Here Mr. Upshaw was *suspended*, till the general question on the doctrine of challenges should be argued.

Mr. MARTIN rose to proceed with his argument. He stated, that it was one of the soundest principles of law, that every man had a right to be tried by an impartial jury: that this right extended to all cases, civil and criminal; but that in criminal cases it was secured by the constitution in a positive and sacred manner, so that all altercation as to the meaning of the terms was rendered unnecessary.

Mr. MAC RAE apologized for interrupting Mr. Martin, but suggested that it would be a saving of time, first, to know the objections to all the jurors, and then to have one general argument, as to all, instead of having an argument on each particular case as it might occur; that he wished to economize time, and that the experience of yesterday showed the propriety of saving time as much as possible. Evidence is now heard as to this case, and if it be argued, the court must hear arguments in the case of every other juryman: he did not see the necessity of holding twelve arguments instead of one, where the cases were precisely similar. He did not wish to prescribe to gentlemen the course of proceeding, but he really supposed that one argument would suffice for all the cases.

To this the CHIEF JUSTICE assented.

Mr. MARTIN.—I have been repeatedly interrupted by the gentlemen; and they have found out in their infinite wisdom, that we are to hold twelve arguments on this point. They talk, sir, of economy of time: they have shown a happy instance of this economy of time, when I was here on a former occasion. I know what kind of economy they wish. They wish us to be silent; they would, if they could, deprive colonel Burr's counsel of an opportunity of defending him, that they might hang him up as soon as possible, to gratify themselves and the government.

Mr. Mac Rae.—That is a most unprincipled and most unfounded assertion.

Mr. Burr said, that he thought the gentlemen for the prosecution were not altogether so wrong. Generally the question was whether those gentlemen who said, that they were convinced that he had treasonable intentions were impartial and proper jurymen? They had avowed their conviction as to these intentions in court; that one argument would apply to all; and if the principle were once fixed, it would not be necessary to renew it in the case of each gentleman; that they had entered into the argument because they wished the principle to be settled, and then it could be applied to the particular cases.

Mr. Hay.—We wish the argument to proceed without hearing ourselves grossly insulted; without making accusations against us that are malicious and groundless. We said nothing that could give offence to the feelings of any gentleman. The gentlemen cannot say with truth, that we wish to deprive them of the right of defending their client. The charge is unjust. I wish him to have a fair trial, and justice to be done with all my heart; but I feel myself hurt, and grossly insulted, when the gentlemen on the other side charges me with feelings that are disgraceful to humanity. I trust, therefore, that the arguments will no longer be conducted with such indecorum.

The Chief Justice had hoped, that no such allusions would have been made; that the government ought to be treated with respect, and that there was a delicacy to be observed on that subject, from which he hoped there would be no departure hereafter.

Mr. Burr.—I rose to stop the progress of such language when up before. I had made sufficient apologies, if any were necessary, for any expressions which had been used, and I had hoped, that no allusions would have been made to the subject. It will be recollected, that I have constantly manifested my displeasure at such expressions. I have carefully avoided such myself, and imposed similar restraints on my counsel; and urged, that the government should be treated with the utmost delicacy, though there was great provocation from the gentlemen on the part of the prosecution, which would have justified harsh terms. I hope these things will cease. On the part of my counsel I am sure they will cease.

Mr. Martin.—I have no wish to hurt the feelings of a single individual, but they have no right to hurt our feelings; and when I am so often interrupted and charged with wasting the public time, and the gentlemen still persist in their observations, I cannot repress mine.

As to the point before the court, what I am about to adduce will show unequivocally, that these gentlemen are not proper jurymen. The emphatic language of the constitution is, that jurors shall be free from all bias and prejudice. The constitution of the United States requires, that every criminal shall be tried by an "impartial jury;" that is, a jury that must be perfectly indifferent, and have no prejudice whatever on their minds; that every juror shall receive his impressions from the evidence which shall be adduced in legal form, and under the sanction of an oath. But those gentlemen come with minds already prepossessed against the prisoner, and it will require stronger evidence to eradicate those previous impressions; whereas, according to the constitution, there ought to be no impression against a criminal, except what arises from the facts proved against him in court, according to the rules of law on the subject. To this effect, I will take the liberty of reading *Reeves' History of the English Law*, *vol.* 1. *p.* 329. to show the rigid impartiality required by the law of England. [Here Mr. Martin read it.]

Every objection that is valid against a juryman is valid against a witness, but not *vice versa*. The credibility of a witness may be questioned though he be admitted to be sworn, but a juror must be free from every objection; exempt from every thing that may possibly give a bias to his mind or judgment. He must have no enmity against, or friendship with the party, whose cause he is to try. That even a great or particular familiarity, or being constantly at the same table with him, will disqualify him from being a juror. *See* 2*d vol. Reeve's English Law*, *p.* 446. The general principles herein stated, show how particularly cautious the law is, that jurors should, in all cases be free from all impressions and influence, and not liable to be suspected.

In confirmation of this doctrine, I will refer your honours to *Care's English Liberties*, *p.* 245. a work of very considerable merit. He states here the great benefits of the trial by jury; that "no man's life shall be touched for any crime whatsoever till found guilty on two trials; that no person shall suffer death but by the verdicts of *twice* twelve men against him, or two juries: one to find the bill or charge to be true, and the other on the merits, to decide on full and legal proof, adduced on both sides, all of which jurors must be honest, substantial, impartial men." In page 248. he tells us what he means by an impartial man: "that he ought to be least suspicious, that is, to be indifferent as he stands unsworn;" that his mind should be free from every cause of suspicion. In page 249. the author is still more explicit. Among other qualities, he says, "that jurors must be *free* of and from *all manner* of *affections*, *relations* and *prejudices*." This is a general proposition extending to all cases whatsoever, civil as well as criminal; and if a man to be a proper juror, must be divested of all affection for, and all relationship to, the parties in a civil case, how much more essential is it that he should be in this situation in a case of life and death? He must be also " free from all prejudices," and come into court in that situation; that all his impressions are to be received from legal evidence, delivered in open court, under the sanction of an oath. His mind must be totally *indifferent* in every respect. As to the idea of a person charged being guilty or innocent, it is one of the most sacred as well as humane maxims of the law, that it presumes every man to be innocent, till an impression·by the evidence is made on the minds of the jurors to remove that presumption. I do not understand this quarering and halving of prejudices, and partialities. It is not sufficient that one man should have only a quarter of the prepossession of another; or that *this* man should only have one half, or three fifths, or four sevenths of the prejudice of *that*; but the law requires, that he shall not be biassed *at all;* that he shall be *perfectly impartial.* The constitution has secured to us a privilege so sacred, that no law, nor this court of justice can take it from us. Sir, so jealous were the citizens of the United States of their rights, that they were dissatisfied with the constitution in its original form, because it did not expressly provide, that there should be a trial of every offence " *by an impartial jury.*" They therefore chose to have it secured by the constitution, so that there should be no possibility of being deprived of an "*impartial jury-trial.*" The eighth amendment of the constitution provides, that " in all criminal prosecutions the accused shall enjoy the right to a speedy and public trial by an impartial jury of the state and district wherein the crime shall have been committed."

This provision in the constitution, which secures this sacred right, is binding on every judge, sitting on the trial of every criminal. It forbids him to force upon him any juror that is not perfectly indifferent. Gentlemen may say, that we must take such men or have no trial at all. Gentlemen do not understand the subject correctly. They take it for granted, that colonel Burr *must* be tried at all events, and hung, if an impartial jury cannot be had! But I contend, that if an impartial jury cannot be found to try him, he cannot be tried at all: because the constitution says, that he "shall be tried by an impartial jury." But I do not believe what has been said, that an impartial jury cannot be found in Virginia! I have no doubt, that many impartial juries can be found in Virginia. The plea of necessity of trial insisted on by the gentlemen is not founded on fact. I can see no such necessity as to render it compulsory on the court to try him in any event, whether an impartial jury can be obtained or not: because the constitution on the contrary declares, that no person shall be tried till he can be tried " by an impartial jury." But let us see what has been done in such cases in that country from which we have derived our system of laws. It is not thought necessary there, that a man shall be tried by a partial jury, rather than that he should not be tried at all. 2d *Mac Nally*, *p*. 667. a trial was put off on an affidavit, that the public mind was so prejudiced by recent publications, as to prevent a fair trial: because those publications had so poisoned the public mind, that a fair trial by an impartial jury could not be obtained. To the same effect, and in the same page is the case of the *King v. the Dean of St. Asaph*, and the case of the *King v. Robinson, Brooks, and others*, where the court thought it correct to decide, that the trial should be postponed till another term, lest certain recent publications, giving an imperfect statement of the evidence, should influence the public mind. If such be the humanity of the law, that it requires that jurymen shall be selected from the public, who are without bias, and persons were deemed improper jurymen in that case, on account of a trifling and temporary bias produced by such publications, how much stronger is the objection against a man being a juryman, who has had a bias on his mind for years and declared that bias? In that case, there was propriety in putting off the trial, because of the impossibility of selecting a proper jury at that time, out of that public whose minds had been poisoned by the publications.

On the present occasion let us examine the situation of the gentlemen called to serve as a jury. They are to determine on the guilt or innocence of the accused, arising from, and depending on certain transactions in the western country. Do they come hither with a bias, or do they come perfectly indifferent as to the innocence or criminality of colonel Burr? The crime consists in intention and act. The intention constitutes the most important part of the crime. The act of itself may be innocent; but treasonable views or designs annex guilt to it. These gentlemen say, " We are perfectly satisfied as to the treasonable intentions, designs and purposes of the accused." To have believed that his purposes were immoral or dangerous, would suffice to exclude them from serving on the jury, because the court is to give a *name* to these crimes; but when they go so far as to assert, that his designs were treasonable, the objection against them is stronger. When they come forward with a full conviction on their minds, that he has been engaged in practices dangerous to the community, do they come forward with impartial unbiassed minds? Their minds are already half made up, and that half the most material part. Twenty or thirty men on Blannerhasset's island, and eight or ten of them armed, may have been perfectly innocent, as if they came together with an intention to shoot game, or for any other lawful and innocent purpose. The witnesses may tell them "We have not a thought that he has committed treason, or that his mind had treasonable designs; we know of no evidence to that effect." But what do these gentlemen say? That they have come to hear witnesses prove such and such acts, for they have already settled the intention in their own minds to be treasonable. What do the constitution, and common reason, and common justice require? Certainly that a juryman must be free from impressions both as to the *intention* of the accused, and as to the *act*. The intention constitutes the most important part of the crime; and their minds ought to be as free from impressions as to the *intention* as they ought to be as to the *act*. But it may be said, that they do not consider, that he did the act at Blannerhasset's island; but your honour does know, that it has been said, and it will be again said, that if the act be done at the persuasion of colonel Burr, it must be considered as committed by him. Let me familiarize this case with the common case of burglary, which is the crime of breaking and entering a house in the night time with an intention to steal. Suppose a person is charged with the crime of burglary, and a juryman called to act on his trial says, that he has his mind perfectly made up that the person indicted intended to steal; but, that he is not sure that he got into the house. Then it is proved that he did enter the house, and the only question is, with what *intent* he did enter the house? (because he may have gone in with a mind perfectly innocent, without intending to take any thing.) Could such a juryman be truly said to be impartial? Most certainly he could not. When a man is indicted for burglary, the juror to try him must be as free from the belief that he intended to commit burglary, as that he went into the house. He must be free from every impression when he comes to be sworn. These observations I have made to show, that on principles of common law and justice, every juryman in every case, especially in criminal cases, ought to be without any prejudice. How can *they* be said to be free from prejudice who *say*, that they believe that colonel Burr had treasonable designs? Do they not come with minds ready to listen to whatever may confirm his guilt? and will they not listen with great reluctance to arguments used to drive away their prejudices from their minds? It is to be lamented, that the public mind is in the state which gentlemen have described, but it certainly is not so to the extent which is represented. I do not consider the forty-eight gentlemen, who have been summoned, as an accurate specimen of the people of Virginia. To the honour of this populous state, I will say, that I believe that a great many impartial juries might be selected, and I should think it strange if one out of a hundred had imbibed prejudices. It implies some degree of malice in any man, judge or juryman, to suffer his mind to be thus poisoned against a person accused, when the law presumes his innocence. How came these impressions to be on the public mind? Did we busy ourselves to mislead or influence it? Was not the Alexandria Expositor and other papers, under the influence of our rulers at Washington, constantly occupied in throwing out dark hints on this subject, long before the proclamation of the president appeared? Have not great pains been taken by inflammatory publications to impress the minds of the people with a belief of his guilt? Those who have done it have to answer for it; and if they have created such a prejudice, that colonel Burr cannot be rightly tried, they alone are to blame. I am sure, that the respectable gentleman on the other side, (though I do not charge him with having done so designedly,) has contributed to increase this prejudice. Has he not frequently declared himself satisfied of the guilt of colonel Burr? The zeal which he has manifested in the prosecution was well calculated to create prepossessions, as he must be presumed to be well acquainted with the evidence against him. When gentlemen, who have set their hearts on the success of the prosecution declare, that they have no doubt of his guilt, other people will be misled by their declarations, and conclude that he is guilty. I submit the case to the court, and have no doubt those jurymen will be deemed improper to serve on this jury, because the constitution requires, that the mind of a juror shall be as free from bias, as if he had never heard any thing of the cause before. Can the gentlemen conscientiously say, that they stand indifferent? Can the court say so? But if they be excluded from serving, it is not the court which says, that they shall not be sworn on this jury, but the constitution of our country which prescribes, that every person accused "shall be tried by an impartial jury."

Mr. Botts observed, that every crime consisted of a great many constituent parts; and that the question was, when a crime was analysed, and a juryman confessed, that he had made up his mind on a number of those component parts, and said, that there were two or three of those parts out of a multitude upon which he had not committed himself, could such a man be regarded as impartial in the subject he is to investigate? Is he, said Mr. Botts, without bias on the question? Is he free from prejudice? The man who has made up his mind on part of the crime, is not without a bias and some degree of predetermination. What portion of the crime the intention may make, cannot be exactly computed; but it is, at least, an important feature of it. Fix on twelve jurors who have made up their minds as to the intention, and you deprive us of half of our defence. We have a right to be tried by a jury, unprejudiced, as to every part of the crime. Colonel Burr has a right to insist, that he is not guilty either of the intention, or of the act; and if there should be complete evidence of the one, yet it will not suffice without full proof of the other. If you fix on twelve jurors, who have made up their minds as to the intention, and prove an act to them, they may find a verdict of guilty; when twelve jurors, who had not made up their minds as to the intention, might be perfectly satisfied, that no crime had been committed, although an act were proved to them; because, without an intention, there can be no guilt. With what face could colonel Burr's counsel stand before a jury, predetermined as to the intention, and urge on their minds an innocent intent? With what face could we stand before a jury, who had made up their minds as to the act, and insist, that no act was committed? It is of no sort of consequence, what description of intention should be associated with the act, nor what act is to be associated with the intention; it is sufficient that the intention is an ingredient of the crime. Yesterday, when we took an exception to a juror because he said, that the accused ought to suffer punishment, he was rejected, because his meaning might have been, and probably was, that the accused deserved death, if he ought to be punished at all. Could we offer any argument to the gentleman, who had expressed this sentiment, to convince him that the prisoner ought not to suffer any punishment? There is no kind of question; but the only inquiry with him, would have been, what kind of suffering he ought to be subjected to? We should have been precluded from investigating, with any rational expectation of success, the general principles of innocence. When the public mind is so infected with rancorous prejudice, it is necessary to select a jury entirely unbiassed; for he might as well be condemned at once, without a trial, as to be tried by a jury prepossessed against him.

Colonel BURR said, that he rose to narrow, and not to extend, the argument; not to add any thing more, but to throw out of the discussion, what had been accidentally and irregularly introduced. The question, said Mr. Burr, is not whether great prejudices exist in the public mind, or what produced them, but whether these jurymen ought or ought not to be regarded as *impartial?* I sincerely hoped, that this point would not have been introduced. Certain analogies had been taken from the crime of treason to other crimes. I wish the discussion of these analogies, at present, to be omitted; for they may hereafter, though only discussed in a collateral manner, be construed into opinions. The inquiry is, whether in civil or criminal cases, a juryman who has made up his mind on part of the subject matter in controversy, ought to be considered as impartial? It is evident, however, that no man can be considered as impartial, who has made up his mind as to the intention. Suppose the case of slaying a man; the act of killing may be differently construed. It may be justifiable, excusable, or clergiable; or it may be murder. Suppose on the trial of the party accused of the murder, that several jurymen come forward and say, " We have no doubt of the *murderous intent* of the prisoner, but we do not know, whether he killed the deceased or not;" would such jurymen be considered as impartial, or be permitted to be sworn to try him? Would not the intention in that case, constitute the principal part of the offence? But I hope that these public impressions, and analogies from treason, will not be drawn again into this discussion.

Mr. MAC RAE.—It was never my wish, in any period of all the various discussions which have taken place before the court, in this case, to travel out of the way, for the purpose of making any observations calculated to defend a government, which in my opinion requires no defence, or to say any thing to wound the feelings of the prisoner. It has been invariably my wish to confine myself to those points only which were under consideration. I have most studiously and constantly avoided making any remarks to wound the feelings or to excite the resentment of the opposite counsel. Frequent as have been the occasions, when I was tempted to deviate from this course, and to follow the example set before me, I carefully avoided availing myself of it, except on one occasion, when the nature of the case was such, that I could not perform my duty without following the example, and repelling an unmerited and unprovoked attack. I will so far respect the admonition of the court, that I will not comment upon it, but will pursue the course that it may think proper, and confine myself to the subject under consideration. But I must, at the same time, be permitted to remark, that I shall not for ever do this, if the admonition of the court, reiterated over and over again, will not be regarded by the gentlemen on the other side. If they make undeserved attacks, I will retort them with the force with which they ought to be retorted, on the quarter from which they come. This I will do in every case, but more especially in cases of this description. It will be unnecessary to state what my feelings and what my wishes in this case are. But perhaps it may be a duty, which in some degree I owe to myself, after considering the quarter from whence the attack came, and the manner in which it was made, to declare to this court, to this people, and to the God of my being, that I have never felt that inhuman, that infamous, and worse than diabolical disposition, to wish that the blood of the prisoner, or of any other fellow being, should be shed. That man is a stranger to me, who thinks that I have such a heart and disposition. I wish that the prisoner may have a fair trial, before an unprejudiced jury. I do not wish that a single man should be impaneled on it, who is not impartial. If there be a single individual on this panel, who is not, within the precise meaning of the constitution, impartial, and fit to decide between the United States and Aaron Burr, I pray the court to reject him. I would unite, with the counsel of the accused, for the sake of the community and posterity, in praying, not for the sake of justice to him only, but to every person, who may be in his situation in future, that such jurymen may be excluded from serving on this jury. But if nothing said by themselves, or by the witnesses called on to show their incompetency, shall satisfy the court, that they are unfit to be jurors, I trust, that as they ought, they will be admitted by the court.

It was unnecessary to read the authorities, which the gentleman adduced; the principles therein stated, are not controverted; but we deny their application to the case now before the court. If any of those gentlemen whose case is now before the court, be partial or biassed, with respect to this cause, or have really an ill will to the party accused, then their case comes within the objection. Is there one of these jurymen who feels an ill will against Aaron Burr? Does any of them entertain a *personal* prejudice against him? Is there one of them who says, that his mind has received a bias, on the question, whether he be guilty of treason or not? There is nothing which goes to justify the opinion, that they have a settled bias, on the question submitted to the court; which is that sort of prejudice, which the law recognises as a valid objection against the competency of a juryman. It is true, that most of them say, that they have formed an opinion as to his intentions; but the question is, whether he have committed treason or not? And they have received no information to enable them to form any opinion at all on this question. Indeed, if I mistake not, some of them have gone so far as to declare their opinion to be, that the prisoner had never committed an overt act. Now what is the argument of gentlemen on this point? It is this; that this crime is made up of several ingredients, as intention and act; and that having formed an opinion on any one of these component parts, disqualifies a man for a juror, as much as if he had formed his opinion on the whole. This does not appear to me to be sufficient to produce the disqualification contended for. They must go infinitely beyond this point: as that they believe that Aaron Burr had formed treasonable intentions, in connexion with individuals, who had committed an overt act. Does any of these gentlemen say, that his opinion extended so far? Those intentions may have related to other acts than those charged in the indictment, to acts committed out of the district, in some other state than Virginia. According to my best recollection of their answers, the treason of which they spoke, related to acts, intended to have been perpetrated not in Virginia, but in a different state, (as Tennessee or Kentucky) and which, therefore, are not now before the court. Some of these gentlemen show, that they have adverted to this distinction, because they have referred to the opinion of one of the judges now on the bench, formerly pronounced on this point. It has been stated from the bench, that these dangerous designs, may have been entertained, but that to constitute treason, they must have been matured into acts. If it be not a bias in this court, if such a prejudice do not exist in the minds of the judges, why should it exist in the minds of the jury? They may have heard the opinion of the court, that various criminal projects may have been revolved in the minds of the accused, but that this was not sufficient to constitute treason, without the commission of an overt act; and paying *respect* to *that* opinion, they may have formed an opinion themselves, that there were treasonable intentions, but they may have considered the *rest* of the opinion of the court, that an act and an intention joined were necessary to constitute treason, and that designs may have been formed by a person who could not be charged with any actual offence. With respect to the question, whether the accused have conceived intentions, which have been matured into treason by open acts, all of them have declared, on that point, that they do not think that an overt act has been committed. Suppose then, that having heard the opinion delivered by the court, they have, in fact, adverted to the distinction, that the formation of designs in the mind, without the commission of an overt act, will not constitute or amount to treason, will they not find a verdict of acquittal, if the necessary overt acts be not legally proved before them? If they declare that they have no ill will or personal hatred against him, will the mere expression of an opinion, that he had entertained treasonable designs, disqualify them from acting as jurors? We wish, sir, that he may have a fair trial, that he may be tried by persons as capable of trying him impartially, as if they had never heard of the question now before the court. In short, by such a jury as the constitution of the United States has secured. I trust it will never be said, that any of us wished to deprive him of any privilege to which he is justly entitled. But if these jurymen will declare, that they have formed no opinion on the actual commission of the crime, that they are unprejudiced and have no ill will against the accused, it does appear to me, and I trust that it will also appear to the court, that they are competent to serve on the jury, who are to try the accused.

Mr. HAY.—The opposite counsel reminded the court, with a frequency that surprised me, that they were entitled to an impartial jury. Nothing is more true. By the constitution of the United States, by the principles of common law, common sense and common justice, the accused has a right to be tried by an impartial jury.

But a question occurs, about which he has not been pleased to say one single word, *Who is an impartial juror?* This is a question, which I conceive, has already been determined by the law. I wonder that the gentleman's extensive learning has not enabled him to give a correct exposition of it. I cannot subscribe to his doctrine on this point. Impartial they may be said to be, who entertain the common sentiments and feelings of a great majority of the people, and who are taken from the mass of the community. According to my judgment, such a jury may be said to be impartial. Who shall say that it is not an impartial jury? Will this court undertake to pronounce its opinion, that the majority of this district are unfit for jurors, and not to be trusted to decide on plain facts; or on the true construction of the circumstances and transactions in the west, within the meaning of this part of the constitution? I believe the court would be very unwilling to say so of all the people of this district. It would be to pronounce a libel on the state. The majority would very truly return the compliment, by saying, that the opinion was one which ought not to have been given, and by a person not competent to give it. " You, who censure us in this manner, show the prejudices by which you are yourselves actuated." What say these jurymen? That they have attended to newspaper publications, which have given them information on a subject, which has excited universal attention. Every man in the community has formed some opinion on it. I will venture to say, that there is not a man in Virginia, however humble or obscure his situation, or supine his disposition; or however much occupied in business, who has not taken some opinion or impression on this subject, and communicated it to others. But these things have been innocently done, without any sentiment of ill will to the accused. The great majority of the people have received impressions of those transactions from newspaper publications, without any prejudice against, or even knowledge of the accused. Is it reasonable then to suppose, that the majority of the people, without any personal ill will against the accused, without even the least personal knowledge of him, are by these general and slight impressions, rendered incapable of deciding fairly and impartially? Can it be reasonable, that the accused should have it in his power, to object to the great majority of the people, as partial and incompetent, on such slight and trivial grounds as these? What is that *impartiality* which the law requires in a juror? It is a disposition of mind to hear the evidence on both sides, and decide thereon according to the immutable principles of natural reason and justice. To exclude from serving on his jury, such an immense majority of the people, on such slender grounds, would probably secure impunity to the accused. There may perchance be some ignorant and obscure individual, some solitary hermit, shut up in the hollow of a tree, or in an inaccessible cavern, secluded from all human concerns, who has received no impression on this subject, because the history of these transactions has never penetrated to his solitude. But those who have intercourse with their fellow citizens, must have heard, in common with the rest of the community, the many reports of a deep laid plot and conspiracy against the peace and union of these states; that the accused had formed some great ambitious scheme for his own personal aggrandisement, to accomplish which, he felt no hesitation in hazarding, no remorse in producing, all the horrors of a civil war. We are divided into parties who have different opinions on political subjects. I do not say, that they are exactly arranged, or united to a man, as to this question; but I know that different sides have been taken: that every man in this community has taken his side, and formed an opinion either favourable or unfavourable on the subject. But still the great majority of the people stand on ground of perfect neutrality, as to the actual guilt of Burr and his associates. The impression which they may have received from reports, and newspaper publications, will vanish like air, as soon as they hear the evidence, on which they will be sworn to decide. I think this is the language of common sense, and that it must convince the court, however it may be disregarded by the gentleman who began the arguments on this point.

He has produced some authorities from *Reeves* and *Mac Nally*, which do not bear on the subject in the least degree: but I shall cite two that do apply to this case. The first was a decision in the case of Callender, of which however, I did not then, nor do I yet, approve. I do not think that in Callender's case judge Chase pronounced the law correctly. I do not see, any difference between *forming an opinion, and forming and expressing an opinion.* A juryman ought to be excluded from serving on the jury, if he have *formed an opinion*, though he may not have communicated it to any person. It is the *formation*, and not the *expression* of his opinion, that indisposes him to attend to the evidence. However it was not my business then, nor is it now, to settle the law; but I thought it *then settled*. The question put to the jurymen, was, " Have you *formed* and *delivered* an opinion on the subject matter of this indictment?" There was nothing said as to men's impressions in relation to the acts of the accused, or their indulging prejudices against him. There was not a man among the jury who tried him, who had not the strongest prejudice against him, for his improper conduct; and very justly. It was pronounced to be the law, that it was a libel. I never heard it controverted before these remarks; but that is not the question now, but a question which is general, indefinite, and vague; a nice metaphysical disquisition, How far a man's mind, by impressions, founded on mere reports, is rendered incompetent to decide impartially on legal evidence? The question ought to be decided by the court, whether a juryman be in that state of neutrality between the United States and a prisoner, which will enable him to decide impartially. According to *Caliender's case*, it was sufficient to establish the competency of a juryman, if he had not formed and expressed an opinion on the subject matter of the indictment; and, according to that decision, all these gentlemen are admissible, because none of them have formed, much less formed and expressed such an opinion. In 2 *Hawkins, chap.* 43. *sect.* 29. on the subject of challenges, it is stated to be law, " that it hath been adjudged to be no good cause of challenge, that, the juror hath found others guilty on the same indictment; for the indictment is in judgment of law, severally against each defendant; for every one must be convicted by particular evidence against himself;" and in the 28*th section*, he says, that " it had been allowed to be a good cause of challenge, on the part of the prisoner, that a juror has declared his opinion before hand, that the party is guilty or will be hanged or the like; *yet it hath been adjudged, that if it shall appear that the juror made such declaration from his knowledge of the cause, and not out of any ill will to the party, it is no cause of challenge.*" Here it is decided, that if a juryman say, that the party accused will be hanged, or is *guilty* not of the intention, *but of the act*, yet if he made this declaration from his own knowledge of the cause, and not from *ill will* to the prisoner, he is a proper juror. But these gentlemen have not declared as much; they have not declared their belief that the accused is guilty of the *act*, but have merely stated as the result of their reflection on the transactions in the western country, that he *intended* to commit the *act*. According to the authority of this case, therefore, these gentlemen are competent jurymen. I do not say that this is law positively, but I find it here written, and it appears to me to be founded in good sense. According to the doctrine in the other section just read, several men may be comprehended in the same indictment; all of whom may be tried separately; and the same juror who has found a verdict against one of them, is competent to try another on the same indictment. His former verdict is no cause of challenge. But the evidence which is admissible against one, may be so against the other. To have already decided on that evidence, is to declare that the party is guilty of the offence, both as to intention and act: and yet this circumstance of having pronounced a verdict on the same testimony, does not furnish grounds of challenge against him. Many more cases might be produced, but these are sufficient to show, that these are proper jurymen, if they be not under the influence of malice or *ill will* against the accused, whatever general impressions their minds may have received. I admit, that if any of them had made up his mind, that the accused was guilty of treason, it would be a good cause of challenge; but that is not the case with any of them. Mr. Martin has made a quotation from *Mac Nally*, to show that the court would postpone a trial, because the public mind had been improperly excited by recent inflammatory publications, touching the cause depending before it. I will only observe, that if this were a motion to postpone the trial, this argument might apply, if the facts of such publications existed; but have they manifested any disposition or wish to obtain a postponement of the trial till another term? Why then do they urge such an argument, while they fail to move for a postponement? They wish to avail themselves of a principle, without performing the act, which would justify its application. But another observation of Mr. Martin may deserve particular notice; that it would be proper to postpone the trial, till a fair and impartial jury could be had.

Here Mr. Martin and Mr. Hay differed as to the precise import of the terms which he had used, and Mr. HAY proceeded. He stated, that the community was divided into parties; that there was an immense preponderance on one side; but that both parties had ascribed certain designs to Mr. Burr, and had taken certain impressions; that these were only the common sentiments and feelings of the country; and that to exclude from the jury all those who had these sentiments and feelings, would amount to a declaration, that the great majority of the people ought not to be trusted with a decision, which might possibly be equal to an acquittal.

Mr. WIRT.—It is much to be wished in this case, and in every case, that a jury could be found of those pure materials which Mr. Martin has desired. He seems to expect, that in every case, and more especially in the important case which now occupies the attention of the court, the jury should come without any impression, with minds as pure as the unsoiled snow on *Dian's* lap. But is this practicable? Does the experience of the world justify the hope, that such a jury can be found? The case cannot exist, and the law does not require it. The authorities relied on by Mr. Martin, are elementary and abstract; and are, I conceive, not to be trusted, when a question of practice is to be decided by the court. They deal in generals; and when they descend to particulars, they all express a distinct reference, and point directly to the person of the accused. If these books were fit to be trusted, and did not their generality exclude them from familiar use, the language used in the specification is clearly expressive of enmity or ill will against the accused. I beg leave to mention another authority to show, that these books are unfit to be trusted as authority. In *Reeves*, it is stated, that any friendship for, or familiarity with the person accused, is a proper ground of objection to a juror; but these general phrases are not sanctioned by practice. For in *Tooke's Trial*, an objection was made to John Thompson as a juror, because an intimacy of thirty-four years continuance had subsisted between him and Mr. Tooke; but the objection was overruled by the judge. These two cases are contradictory. It is important in every case, that the principles of law should be fixed. It is important to the people of every nation, that their rules of action should not be continually floating on the waves of uncertainty, but that they should be known and settled, in order that men should know how to steer their course. I trust that they will be always so in this country. Permit me to advert to a decision in our own country; the case of Callender. I adduce it for the sole purpose of comparing it to the doctrine now in discussion. When Mr. John Basset, one of the jurymen, was called, he challenged himself, because he had seen and read the book (*The Prospect before Us*), for the publication of which he was prosecuted, and made up his mind, that it was a libel; but he had not made up his mind as to Callender being the publisher of the libel. His objection was overruled, and he was sworn on the jury; though he had made up his opinion, that the publication was a libel, which I conceive to be the principal point. He only did not know *who* was the author. But what is the great question of libels in England? Is it *who* is the author? Is it about the mere fact of publication, that the brightest tears of eloquence are shed? The question in every case is, *libel* or no *libel*. The inquiry always is, whether it be a libel or not? The fact of publication is a question of a comparatively trivial nature. Then when Mr. Basset was admitted on the jury, according to the idea of one of the counsel on the other side, Callender was robbed of half of his defence as to that juror; for the great question had been previously settled in his mind. The fact to be ascertained was unimportant. Apply the principle of this decision in that case to this case. We will *suppose* it to be the fact, that these jurymen may have said, that the assemblage of men on Blannerhasset's island was high treason in the parties composing it; but they knew not, and this would not prove, that colonel Burr was there or connected with it. Here the two cases would be very similar.

These gentlemen would have made up their minds, that the assemblage was treasonable. John Basset made up his mind, that the publication was a libel. The great facts would be fixed in the minds of the jurors in both cases, and nothing would remain, but to trace the facts to the party accused. But the present case falls far short of that. These gentlemen say, that they have taken up some impressions from newspaper publications, that Burr had treasonable designs; but they have not said, that the assemblage on the island was treason, which consists of *intention* and *fact;* and if they had said so, they would be good jurymen, according to Basset's case. He had made up his mind on the *great fact*, that the *book* was a *libel;* and in this supposed case, these jurymen would have concluded, that the act of meeting armed, on the island, was treason; but as they have not gone so far as Basset, and he was received as a juror, the court, I presume, will receive them as jurors. In another point of view, Callender's case was stronger than this. In that case, there was no possibility of counteracting the impression that Basset had of the fact, that the book was a libel. His opinion was formed upon the book itself; and there was no other evidence to produce, to change that opinion. But these gentlemen have seen nothing but the statements in the newspapers. They have received no such fixed impressions; their conviction is commensurate with the evidence. They say, that their conviction has gone as far as the depositions, which have been published, seemed to justify, but not farther; that they were willing to hear other evidence, and to retract their opinions. But Basset's opinion was fixed, and admitted of no conflicting evidence. If then colonel Burr would be stripped of one half of his defence by the admission of these gentlemen on his jury, Callender was stripped of much more than half of his defence by the reception of Basset on his.

I said, when I first rose, that the kind of jury which Mr. Martin contended for, could not exist. Necessity has given the law in other cases; and whenever that necessity appears, submission to it must invariably follow. Such a jury could not exist unless it had fallen from heaven. But this is not the only case in which a purely impartial jury could not possibly be obtained, from the very nature of things. Consider the English rebellions of the year 1715 and 1745. Recollect when the great national question between the pretender, and the house of Hanover which occupied the throne, was so warmly agitated. The people took up different sides of the question, not only with zeal and ardour, but even with phrensy. Their gazettes and magazines were filled with it. Every man in the nation was animated with the utmost enthusiasm, which carried him beyond the bounds of reason and propriety. They not only wrote, but they fought for it; and that in so little a kingdom, the very clang and din of the battle of *Culloden* was heard in every part of it. Was this a case in which an impartial jury could have been expected? Could they find any who had not formed an opinion on the cause of the pretender, and on the nature of the rebellion? Every man in the kingdom had made up his mind on the great facts; yet the rebels of the years 1715 and 1745 were tried, by parties who knew these facts, and hanged. Those of the latter were tried, perhaps, by jurors who had met and fought them on the plains of Culloden. Do you believe that the question, whether they believed that the pretender had an intention to seize the throne, was put to those jurors who tried his adherents? His intention, and that of his followers, were facts of public notoriety. The rule of Mr. Martin is a good rule, as it exists in the mind of a good man, or perfect philosopher. It is a good rule for Utopia, or for Arabia Happy, or as a standard of theoretic perfection. But on those who have human passions, it is in vain to expect it to operate. Look at the trials in the year 1794 of *Tooke, Hardy, Thelwall*, and others. Were the jurors who tried these men entirely without impressions? Did the causes of their prosecution produce no excitement? Look at the trials in Ireland of men who fought at the battle of Wexford. Were they tried by men who were entirely indifferent; who had received no impressions from the great events in their country? Had these created no interest, no feeling? Thus it was in the case of Hamilton Rowan: men who were at the very *focus* of public illumination on that occasion, were to sit on his trial! Could such men have come into the jury box, as if they had never seen the books, nor heard of the causes on which the prosecutions were founded; as if they had come from another planet? No such thing could be rationally expected. You will find that the principle, laid down by *Hawkins*, is correct. " That if a juror have declared before hand, that the party is guilty, or will be hanged, or the like, and *made such declaration* from his knowledge of the cause, and *not out of any* ILL *will to the party*, it is no cause of challenge." It is justified by the reason and experience of mankind. Impressions from the public prints, unconnected with any *ill will* to the accused, cannot therefore be a cause of challenge.

From the plains of Culloden and Wexford, let us come to our own country. There have been no battles in this country lately; but there has been a subject which has agitated every part of the country; in which every citizen must have felt a warm interest. A man heretofore distinguished, has been charged in all the public prints, with a crime so destructive of the peace and happiness of this country, that he who could peruse these prints for the last twelve months, with adamantine indifference; he who could read the affidavits of generals Eaton and Wilkinson without some emotion, cannot be a man. No man could see these things without feeling. I put it to your hearts to determine, whether any man who has a soul, that could grace the bosom of a man, could do it. There is not that base frigidity in the American character which is insusceptible of impressions on subjects of great moment. Look at one of the very jurors whom the accused has selected. No man acknowledges with more pleasure than I do, the correct conduct of that gentleman. I have long known and respected him. No man can be more conscientious. Yet he declares, that from the statements in the newspapers, he had some impressions of the views of the accused. Could less have been expected from any man? This was the source from whence his impressions were derived; and not hostility to the person of the prisoner himself.

In England, we see from the authority of *Hawkins*, that if a person summoned as a juror, have declared, that the party accused is guilty, or will be hanged, and made this declaration *from his knowledge of the cause*, and *not from ill will to the party*, it is no cause of challenge; and *if he have found another man guilty under the same indictment, it is no cause of challenge*. As this is the law, how can it be a cause of challenge, that these jurymen have received some impressions from the public prints? It may perhaps be said, that a juror who had found another man guilty under the same indictment, must have made up his mind on the whole evidence in the cause; and that therefore he ought not to be challenged by another party prosecuted in that indictment. Nothing can be more manifest than the absurdity of this reasoning. It amounts to this: He is a good juryman, if he have seen and heard the whole evidence; but if he have only heard some slight circumstances, a small portion of the evidence, then he cannot be admitted as a juryman! Because his mind is locked up for ever by his former verdict, he is a good juror; but a mere fleeting impression disqualifies him entirely! This, surely, is not even the semblance of an argument. Take the other ground mentioned by *Hawkins*, that "it is no cause of challenge to a juryman, that he had declared from his own knowledge, and not from ill will to the prisoner, that he is guilty, or will be hanged," and apply it to this case. To have made such a declaration *from his own knowledge*, means, that he made it *on the evidence of his own senses*. As in the case of murder: suppose a juryman, had by accident, *seen* the person accused actually commit the murder, but has no ill will against him, he is a good juror; because it is impossible to change his opinion. But if a gentleman of respectability will say, that he has a slight impression on his mind from mere reports, or newspaper statements, he is not a good juror at all. Because a man's mind is locked up against evidence and argument beyond the possibility of persuasion he is an impartial juryman: yet he whose mind has only received a trivial impression, and is open to evidence and conviction, must be rejected as partial and improper. This is the substance of their argument.

I trust, that whether you take the authority of this court, or the practice in England into consideration, you will find, that these gentlemen, having no ill will against the accused, and but a slight impression relating to the cause, and not to him personally, ought not to be rejected. They have stated themselves, that they had but *a slight* impression on their minds. If the question therefore depended on the depth of their impressions, these gentlemen could not be excluded. When a man, who has read some reports in the newspapers, professes himself ready to hear further evidence, his mind is open to conviction, he is a fair juror, and cannot be challenged as partial; for as to a slight impression, it was impossible even to hear of treason against their country, without some emotion. I trust, therefore, that these gentlemen will be considered as proper jurors.

Mr. WICKHAM spoke to the following effect. I will endeavour to show, that the observations of the gentlemen on the other side, and their construction of the law, are incorrect. Their whole arguments rest on the basis of necessity; but the gentleman last up, has placed it in a greater variety of views. I heard him with great pleasure. His eloquence, which is at all times pleasing, was at this time particularly interesting; but he used so many tropes, and scattered so many flowers, that he reminded me of a Roman epigram on a lady, who was so completely enveloped in decorations, that she was the smallest part of herself. It was precisely so with the gentleman's argument. It was so perfectly ornamented and covered with figures and graces, that it constituted the least part of itself: and it was only by lifting a flounce here, and a furbelow there, that you could discover the argument. What does he state? That from necessity, and the nature of things, there can be no jury obtained, without some impressions. How does he prove it? The gentleman has hurried us to England and the battle of Culloden, with as much ease as if he had waved the wand of a magician, and told us, that the din of arms was so loud, that it might be heard six or seven hundred miles! He has compared the judicial decisions in that country, at the period of the rebellion, to the case now before this court, without having attended to the natural and manifest distinction between them. It was clear to every man in England, that there was a rebellion in the country. An army traversing the country in military force and array: places taken, and battles fought. Lords Balmerino, Kilmarnock, and Cromartie, and many other men of distinction, were known to be engaged in the cause of the pretender, and concerned in those transactions. Every man in the country could reason upon the case; the basis of his decision was a chain of historical facts, known and recorded, which could neither be distorted by prejudice, nor destroyed by falsehood. How did the courts decide, that there was a jury to be found in England, which could try the prisoners impartially? The existence of the rebellion was an historical fact known to every man before the trials; but whether the particular individuals accused were actively concerned in it or not, depended on the evidence against each of them. The case now before the court would have been precisely similar, if it had been founded on historical facts. If it had been established, that colonel Burr, with twenty or thirty thousand men, and a number of gun boats had descended the Ohio; that he had taken New-Orleans, had fought several battles with general Wilkinson, and had been brought before this court for trial, the jury would have to decide, not upon their own prejudices, but on historical facts, and the evidence against each person accused. But where are the established facts in this case? The president has declared, that there is no sort of doubt of his guilt. It is not pretended, that *he* could know the facts himself, and he is liable to the deception of others. Is his *word* to be taken as evidence in a court of justice, and that adduced not even on oath? But general Wilkinson has said so also. But *his* credibility may be hereafter impeached; he is only a witness to prove certain facts; but does he say, that colonel Burr is guilty of treason? The supreme court has decided, that his evidence was not relative to the charge of treason. This whole tale then is referred to the affidavit of general Eaton, an *ex parte* witness. It rests on that alone; of which I will say, though we may not be disposed to assert, that it is untrue, yet that it must be admitted, that his tale is marvellous, and not reconcilable to itself. Is this accusation then founded on historical facts? Is it a piece of history that is known to every man in the country? This story, which has excited so much alarm and interest in every part of the United States, is reduced to the testimony of a single witness, who tells a most wonderful tale. How then can he draw a comparison between this case, and that of the rebellions in England? The gentleman certainly did not consider the cases well, or he would not have thought of such a parallel. The battle of Culloden, for instance, was a matter of public and universal notoriety; it was known to every man, woman and child, in England; and it could have formed no part of the inquiry, on the trial of the rebels, whether such a battle had been fought or not.

There is not a single deposition to prove that treason has been committed. The president's letter, though it confidently ascribes guilt to colonel Burr, does not say, that he was guilty of treason. If *one* of these jurymen be not disqualified by a preconceived opinion of colonel Burr's treasonable intentions, the rule will apply to the *whole jury;* and if *one* of those gentlemen who think he had treasonable designs, can be sworn to try him, *twelve* of them *can.* What then would be our situation as his counsel? Twelve jurors are impaneled, all of whom believe him guilty of treasonable intentions. The crime of treason consists of *intention* and *act.* In what attitude should we stand before such a jury, to vindicate the innocence of colonel Burr's intentions? What course could we take? Their minds would be satisfied already as to his intentions; it would be in vain to urge evidence or authorities, to show that he had no treasonable designs. Would we attempt to make an impression on such marble? We might as well abandon at once the cause of our client. The jury would be made of such stubborn and impenetrable materials, that he would be sure to be sacrificed. As an aggravation of this evil, it is to be observed, that their belief respecting colonel Burr's intentions, has an influence and direct operation on the question, whether an act have been perpetrated or not. They will listen more attentively to evidence that will confirm, than to testimony that will contradict it. Suppose there are two witnesses, one who thinks there was an overt act committed, and another who thinks there was not; the juryman who has made up his mind, as to the intentions of the accused, will very probably believe the testimony which maintains the intention, and will not believe the man who swears to the fact in opposition to the intention; because the act is made more probable by the intention, which is the first step towards it: but a juror who had not believed that the accused had criminal designs, would very probably not believe either of the witnesses, as their testimony was contradictory, or might believe him who swore that there was no overt act. I insist, that twelve jurors, with impressions fixed as to the intention, though an honest, could not be an *impartial,* jury; because the intention has a direct operation, not on a part only, but on the whole cause; it bears directly on every point of the cause. *That* juror must be more than man, who believing the accused guilty as to intention, will be able to stop at the point of sober investigation, and not permit his judgment to be influenced by it with respect to the commission of an overt act. The man whose belief is made up as to the intentions of colonel Burr, cannot be said to be impartial on any point in the cause. Let us suppose a very possible case; that six jurors are impaneled, who say, that they believe he had treasonable intentions, but they know nothing of an overt act; and six more are called up and sworn, who admit that they have an impression as to an overt act having been committed, but as to the intention, know nothing. Six have taken up one opinion and six another. Their opinion on the whole is unfavourable to the prisoner. How could his counsel address them on either of those points? If they address them on the intention, six of them are adamant on that point; and if they address them on the other point, it will be in vain, because six of them are equally obdurate. On either side, they would meet with prejudice and resistance. It would be like the case mentioned in Tristram Shandy, of the abbess and nun, where it was necessary to pronounce a certain criminal word, to make their mules move with their carriage; it would have been a sin for either of them to utter the entire word, but they divided it into two parts; one articulated one part and the other the other, and thus effected their purpose, and avoided all the sin of the expression. One half of the jury think the intention existed, the other think the fact was perpetrated; and by dividing the transgression between them, and compromising the intention and act, they may find a verdict of guilty. Those who have made up their minds as to the *design*, will readily concur with those who think that the *overt act* is *unquestionable;* and those who think the overt act *notorious*, will require but little persuasion to believe, that the intent was criminal. But on many occasions, there is no doubt, but the whole crime consists in the intention; and the whole inquiry is, whether there were a criminal intent or not?

I will now proceed to answer the arguments of counsel in their order. Mr. Mac Rae says, that the standard with respect to the competency of jurors, depends on whether they have a personal prejudice or ill will against the accused or not? What is meant by the word *personal?* Is it a dislike to the appearance, the countenance, or features of a man? If it depended on this, colonel Burr would stand a better chance than most of his counsel; perhaps than most men. But if you believe him guilty of a crime, is it not prejudice against him? Is it not prejudice to entertain such a belief against any man? The usual ground of prejudice against a man is, that he is guilty of criminal conduct.

But it is said by Mr. Mac Rae, that it would be necessary, in order to exclude them as jurors, that they should have said, that they thought colonel Burr had been guilty of treason in connexion with Blannerhasset. We have nothing to do with Blannerhasset. They are not joined together in the indictment. The complaint is not now before the court. Some of these gentlemen say, that they believe, they intended to take New-Orleans. It should have been a joint indictment against them: and they could then know the charge in the indictment, and meet it with the necessary defence; but there is nothing in it about New-Orleans, and joint treason with Blannerhasset.

But " Callender's case is directly in point, where Mr. Basset was determined to be a proper juryman." What was it? Did he pronounce any opinion on the intention of Callender? He said the book was a libel. That was not an *opinion*, but a *fact*. But did he say, that Callender was the author or publisher of it? Suppose he had been called on for a definition of sedition. What would he have said? Did he say, that he had made up his mind, that Callender was guilty of *intending* to publish a *seditious* libel? Callender was defended by several learned counsel of this bar. Did *they* attempt to deny that it was a libel? Did Mr. Randolph, or the other gentlemen, who managed the impeachment of judge Chase, in the senate of the United States deny that it was a libel? It ought, also, to be recollected, that this very senate of the United States decided by a majority of eighteen against sixteen, that the decision of judge Chase, in not rejecting Mr. Basset as a juror, because he said, that he had made up his mind from the extracts said to be taken from the book, that it was a libel, was illegal. Sixteen, out of thirty-four, thought it correct, and eighteen thought it corrupt*. This was the case, if I recollect right. I then thought, and still think, the opinion which he gave, was law. It was *palpable* and *manifest* to every person, that *the book was a libel;* and the declaration of that fact, is not like imputing a criminal design to the party accused; and therefore the admission of Mr. Basset as a juror, though correct and proper, ought not to be considered as a precedent for the admission of these gentlemen on this jury. If these gentlemen came forward and gave a correct definition of treason, they would be improper jurymen. They ascribe such intentions to the accused, as may support the charge of treason.

But these jurymen say, that they think they can give a fair verdict. I mean no reflection on the gentlemen, by saying, that they may be mistaken. I am confident they have no intentional prejudice. But what is prejudice? Do not most men believe their own opinions to be correct? Is it easy for every man to discern and retract his erroneous opinions? If a man were to go so far as to say, that he could conquer prejudice, still it ought only to be admitted, that he believes so: the frailty of human nature, forbids complete confidence in such cases; his belief ought not to be depended upon, however respectable he may be.

But Mr. Hay has given us a definition of an impartial juryman, which neither Mr. Martin nor I would ever have thought of. What was it? That the common sentiments and feelings of a majority of the people of any country, form the criterion of impartiality and truth! Take this position to be correct, let this new principle be adopted, and the study of the law will be ren-

---

* This was immediately discovered to be a mistake. The second article of the impeachment was for overruling Mr. Basset's objection. On this article, ten senators only voted guilty, and twenty-four not guilty.

dered very easy and short; and to some gentlemen, very pleasant. It would save a great deal of time and trouble. A student,
instead of poring over the black letter in his own closet, and
wearying his faculties for years in search of principles and scien-
tific knowledge, need only go about to barbacues, horse-races,
cock-fighting, and other public meetings and places of amusement,
to learn the common sense of mankind! A lawyer would consult
his law books, but Mr. Hay would go about collecting the sense
of the nation. Mr. Wirt has given us another and a better rule,
to which most men would give the preference. He has told us,
that the principles of law ought to be *certain*, and not continually
floating on the ocean of uncertainty. But he is contradicted by
Mr. Hay. *He* advises us to follow the principles of law, but
Mr. Hay prefers the popular opinion; the sentiments of a majority of the people to be ascertained, I presume, by officers appointed to collect them in every district.

Mr. HAY denied that he expressed such a sentiment, and insisted, that his words and meaning were misrepresented.

Mr. WICKHAM proceeded. The gentleman did say, that an
impartial juror was one who had the common sentiments of the
mass or majority of the people. Compare this sentiment with
those of Hale, Hume, Robertson, and other eminent writers,
and see how very different they are. I understood him distinctly,
that impartiality in a juror, depended on his concurrence with
the public sentiments. That is the true meaning of what he
said. I follow it up to its consequences, and if the result be absurd, he is not, for that reason, at liberty to deny his position. Is
every man in the community to be consulted? Is there then to
be an "*appel nominel*," as there was in France, when the
French people were asked, "Shall Napoleon be emperor of the
French?" The public opinion cannot be truly ascertained. I do
not believe that the opinion of the jurymen, whose case is under
consideration, is this public opinion which is so much referred
to; but if public opinion, and sentiment, and feeling, were to be
resorted to as the true test of impartiality, what would he do with
the passions of the turbulent, the lawless, and the violent? Has
he any motive for establishing this public opinion as the rule
of justice and fairness? Has he been scattering and fomenting
these popular prejudices, and spreading declarations of the guilt
of the accused all over the country? He has repeatedly declared,
that he has no doubt of his crime. I hope that there is no connexion between his criterion of impartiality, and his frequent
declarations of colonel Burr's guilt. Mr. Hay agrees, that if they
attempted to make proselytes, it would justify their rejection.
Several of these jurymen did acknowledge that they had publicly
argued to inculcate a belief of colonel Burr's guilty designs, and

justified the measures adopted by the government against him. On the gentleman's own admission, therefore, they are not proper jurors. I mean no imputation against these gentlemen; they had a conviction on their own minds, of his evil designs, and they wished to communicate it to others: they are to be respected because they acted under a conviction of the truth. But this argument proves too much; that if every one of these jurymen had declared, that colonel Burr was guilty of an act of treason, it would make no difference, but they would *all* be impartial jurymen; because it happened to agree with the public opinion. It would prove every thing. It might prove, that the sentiments of every man who did not conform to the public opinion, when it was under a different direction from what it is at present, were then wrong; and that those who do not now subscribe to what is called public opinion, are as culpable as those in the minority were formerly; so that what is right one day, may be wrong another.

The gentleman has candidly informed us, that the country is divided into two classes; and that every man has taken his side of this question. I should hope that the gentleman's position was not correct, at least not invariably. If it were so, it would be unfavourable to truth and justice. The majority always possess sovereign power in the United States; but the majority change. He who has had the happiness of thinking and acting formerly with the great majority of the people of the United States, finds himself now decidedly opposed by such a majority. The public opinion is continually fluctuating; and what was law under the administration of John Adams, is not law under the administration of Thomas Jefferson. What was public opinion *then*, is not public opinion *now*. In fact, it is impossible to know what public opinion is. So that, according to the gentleman's doctrine, the impartiality of a juror, instead of being founded on correct, immutable, and permanent principles, would be continually floating on the waves of uncertainty; an evil which is so much and so justly deprecated by his colleague.

But it is said, on the authority of *Hawkins*, that a man may be a proper juror to try a person accused, although he *knows* the fact on which the prosecution is founded. Does any one of these gentlemen say, that he knows the fact? Not one of them pretends to such knowledge. What then can be said of an authority that has no application? It is not necessary to acknowledge or deny the validity of this authority.

But the gentleman says, "that it is impracticable, or something approaching an impossibility, to obtain an impartial jury, if the objection against these jurymen shall prevail. We deny this impossibility; we have already obtained four jurors, and have no doubt the rest can easily be got. I will say nothing of the panel being composed of men, of whom so many had made up their minds. I have no doubt that it was accidental, and that the marshal intended to discharge his duty with fidelity and propriety.

Mr. Wirt says, that these elementary writers, *Hale*, *Hawkins*, *Reeves*, and others, are not to be regarded; that they are not always the test of truth. It may be admitted, that they are not uniformly so, but it is certain that they are, and ought to be generally so considered. Some of these elementary authors, such as *Lord Coke*, are of inestimable value.

As to the variance stated by Mr. Wirt, between one of the elementary principles of *Reeves*, and a case determined by chief justice *Eyre*, the case of *Horne Tooke;* a reference to the report of that trial will shew, that that case had not been accurately stated to this court. I have too high a respect for Mr. Wirt, to say, that he has wilfully *misrepresented* the case; but he has certainly misunderstood the opinion of the court. Thompson, the juryman, was not in court. He had exercised the discretion of absenting himself; and the excuse made for him was, that he had been too long and too intimately acquainted with the prisoner. Was it a question, whether he were to be received as a juror or not? Was it a question put to the prisoner in court, " *Do you like this man or not?*" It was not. The chief justice said, that "it was no excuse." No excuse for what? Not from serving on the jury, but for not appearing at all in court. The expression of chief justice Eyre, was very mild, in answer to the apology made for the absence of the witness.

Mr. Wirt here interrupted Mr. Wickham, and said, that he would submit it to any candid mind, which of them gave the correct interpretation of the passage. He read it and made some comments on it.

After some observations by both gentlemen, the CHIEF JUSTICE said, that he had no doubt, that each of the gentlemen had stated, what was the conviction of his own mind; but that he thought it immaterial to the question now in discussion, which of them was correct.

Mr. Wickham.—I shall make one single remark. We came here to try colonel Burr on the law and the evidence, and not by the public opinion. The life of no man would be secure, if he were to be tried, not according to the known rules and principles of law, but the caprice and levity of what is deemed public opinion. A trial by a prejudiced jury would be nothing but a mockery. What was the meaning of the provision in the constitution, but to protect persons accused from the unjust violence of popular opinion? Was not the security of innocence against unjust persecution, the object of the amendment of the constitution?

Was it not known to the framers of our constitution, who had the volume of human nature before them, that the time would at length arrive, when some individual would be held up as a mark to public indignation, and sacrificed as a victim to popular phrensy, and political jealousy? Was it not to prevent this, that the constitution, originally forbade the legislature to change the law of treason, by fixing it within precise and well defined limits? Was it not for this cause, that a subsequent amendment was introduced, declaring, that " *in all criminal prosecutions, the accused shall enjoy the right to a speedy and public trial by an impartial jury?*" I contend, that all these salutary precautions have been taken to guard against the pernicious effects of this public opinion, and that these gentlemen being prejudiced against the accused, cannot be considered as impartial within the meaning of the constitution.

Mr. RANDOLPH, at the request of the court, read judge Chase's answer to the second article of the impeachment against him, which arraigns his decision in the case of Basset. See appendix to the *Trial of Judge Chase*, pages 19, 20, and 21.

Mr. RANDOLPH then observed, that he had not intended to say any thing on the subject now discussed, because he expected, that objections would have been made to particular individuals only; but that he had since seen, that a most serious blow was meditated at the whole system of jury-trial. For, said Mr. Randolph, whether accident, or Heaven have given us this boon, it is our duty to preserve pure and perfect, and transmit unimpaired to posterity, this only *palladium* against oppression. Vain will be all this parade about the trial by jury, if a judge will calmly sit on the bench, and connive at its violation. If the courts do not defend this sacred right, can it be said that any man's life is safe? The trial by jury is not a beneficial reality, but a mere fiction of law. Away with justice; away with courts: tell me not that I am safe in my own habitation, if a doctrine like this be to prevail. It is a mockery sir, to talk of the benefits of the trial by jury, if men whose minds are impressed with prejudices against a person accused, shall decide his fate! Can *they* be impartial, who on a charge consisting of several points, have made up their minds against him on all, except a little fragment? Would it be conformable to the equal administration of justice, to force such a jury on him?

Analogies have been stated between other crimes and the charge now before the court. Other gentlemen have quoted the cases of murder and burglary. To these I shall add the crime of uttering false money, knowing it to be false. If a man brought forward as a juror on the trial of a person charged with this offence, were to state, that he knew not whether the accused passed the money or not, but that he was certain, he must have known it to be false, would he not be rejected as an incompetent juror?

But we are told, on the authority of *Hawkins, chap.* 43. *sec.* 28. that by the law of England, it has been adjudged, that " if a juror has declared before hand, that the party is guilty, or will be hanged, or the like, it is a good cause of challenge; but if the juror made this declaration from his knowledge of the cause, and not out of any ill will to the party, *it is no cause* of challenge;" and in *sect.* 29. " that it hath been adjudged to be no good cause of challenge, that the juror hath found others guilty on the same indictment."

Sir, does not this doctrine strike your mind with astonishment? Not if you advert to the reference made in support of it. He has taken a posterior doctrine in preference to an anterior; so that it would seem, that the latter had been a revocation of the former. But examine it. What does he refer to? To the year books in the time of Henry the 7th, when liberty had not been established in England. This very *Hawkins*, in whose bloody doctrine confidence is now placed, instead of advocating the more liberal doctrines of his own day, on the subject of juries, refers to the reign of the Tudors, when not a spark of liberty existed. Were he correct in his assertion, that this was the law of England, what influence ought it to have on the practice in this country; where the terms of the constitution are so explicit and imperative, that *the accused shall enjoy* the *right* to a *speedy* and *public trial* by an *impartial jury?* Will our courts subscribe to his inferences? He had advanced a contrary doctrine in a preceding section. Will you say that he shall be justified in supporting and drawing contradictory principles and conclusions? If he maintain positions which are perfectly inconsistent, ought they not to be tried by a critical examination of the authorities to which he refers? and if the court find that his assertions are not fairly deducible from the authors relied on, will they not put him aside and declare that he has no authority on this point? If the gentleman who quoted him, had looked at the 27th section of the same chapter, he would have found all the doctrines on which he commented so fully, entirely destroyed. He there says, that " this exception against a juror, that he hath found an indictment against the party for the same cause, hath been adjudged good; not only upon the trial of such indictment, but also upon the trial of another indictment or action, wherein the same matter is either in question, or happens to be material, though not directly in issue." So that wherever it is the same question, on which he decided in a former indictment, or happens to be a material point, he is to be excluded. Is it not all-important, what the intention is? Is it not a material point? According to this section, if it be a material point, he is to be excluded as a juror, because he had made up his mind before on the same subject. It is not merely that if he decided on the *whole*, but if he have only decided a *material point* of the same cause, he is incapacitated from serving as a juror.

Mr. Wickham has anticipated me, in shewing the effect of different jurors acting on a conviction of different parts of the guilt; that one juror having formed his opinion on one point, and another on another, they may compromise, till by mutual complacency and acquiescence, they make the accused the victim, by a verdict of condemnation.

I will make one observation on the case of *Horne Tooke*, to shew that Thompson did not attend the trial, and that the construction which gentlemen put on it, is incorrect. If Thompson had been present, the law applying to the case, was different from what they contend it to be. It is said, that a friendship or intimacy with a party in a suit, is not a cause of exception to a witness, though it always is to a juror. Some books say, that if a juror be returned by a party, he is disqualified from serving. The law with respect to the admission or exclusion of a juryman, must vary according to the circumstances, and the nature of the influence, which a party in a cause has over his mind. They suppose the question before the judge to have been, " Shall he be excused from serving as a juror or not?" It was not so. It was, whether he should be excused for non-attendance? A mere acquaintance with another for thirty-four years, does not exempt a man from being on a jury to try that other; but if the intimacy and friendship be so great, as to create an influence over him, he would be rejected of course.

I shall not detain the court any longer, but shall conclude with a hope, that you will preserve the purity of jury-trial from violation; that you will take more than common pains to preserve it free and unfettered. I appeal to the volume of human nature; I appeal to the human heart. I could appeal to Mr. Hay's great tribunal itself, to determine, whether there ever were a man who could dispassionately and impartially try a cause, one half of which he had already prejudged?

Mr. MARTIN then observed, that in *Tooke's* case, no challenge was stated to have been made to Thompson the juror, by either the king or the prisoner; and of course the question could not have occurred, whether he should be excused from serving on the jury.

The CHIEF JUSTICE then delivered the following opinion.

The great value of the trial by jury, certainly consists, in its fairness and impartiality. Those who most prize the institution, prize it because it furnishes a tribunal, which may be expected to be uninfluenced, by any undue bias of the mind.

I have always conceived, and still conceive, an impartial jury as required by the common law, and as secured by the constitution, must be composed of men, who will fairly hear the testimony which may be offered to them, and bring in their verdict, according to that testimony, and according to the law arising on it. This is not to be expected, certainly the law does not expect it, where the jurors, before they hear the testimony, have deliberately formed and delivered an opinion, that the person whom they are to try, is guilty or innocent of the charge alleged against him.

The jury should enter upon the trial, with minds open to those impressions, which the testimony and the law of the case ought to make, not with those preconceived opinions, which will resist those impressions.

All the provisions of the law are calculated to obtain this end. Why is it that the most distant relative of a party cannot serve upon his jury? Certainly the single circumstance of relationship, taken in itself, unconnected with its consequences, would furnish no objection. The real reason of the rule is, that the law suspects the relative of partiality; suspects his mind to be under a bias, which will prevent his fairly hearing and fairly deciding on the testimony which may be offered to him. The end to be obtained is an impartial jury; to secure this end, a man is prohibited from serving on it, whose connexion with a party, is such as to induce a suspicion of partiality. The relationship may be remote; the person may never have seen the party; he may declare that he feels no prejudice in the case, and yet the law cautiously incapacitates him from serving on the jury; because it suspects prejudice; because in general, persons in a similar situation, would feel prejudice.

It would be strange if the law were chargeable with the inconsistency of thus carefully protecting the end from being defeated by particular means, and leaving it to be defeated by other means. It would be strange if the law would be so solicitous to secure a fair trial, as to exclude a distant unknown relative from the jury, and yet be totally regardless of those in whose minds feelings existed, much more unfavourable to an impartial decision of the case.

It is admitted, that where there are strong personal prejudices, the person entertaining them is incapacitated as a juror; but it is denied that fixed opinions respecting his guilt constitute a similar incapacity.

Why do personal prejudices constitute a just cause of challenge? Solely because the individual who is under their influence, is presumed to have a bias on his mind, which will prevent an impartial decision of the case, according to the testimony. He may declare that notwithstanding these prejudices, he is determined to listen to the evidence, and be governed by it; but the law will not trust him.

Is there less reason to suspect him who has prejudged the case, and has deliberately formed and delivered an opinion upon it? Such a person may believe that he will be regulated by testimony, but the law suspects him, and certainly not without reason. He will listen with more favour to that testimony which confirms, than to that which would change his opinion: it is not to be expected that he will weigh evidence or argument as fairly as a man whose judgment is not made up in the case.

It is for this reason that a juror who has once rendered a verdict in a case, or who has been sworn on a jury which has been divided, cannot again be sworn in the same case. He is not suspected of personal prejudices, but he has formed and delivered an opinion, and is therefore deemed unfit to be a juror in the cause.

Were it possible to obtain a jury without any prepossessions whatever, respecting the guilt or innocence of the accused, it would be extremely desirable to obtain such a jury; but this is perhaps impossible, and therefore will not be required. The opinion which has been avowed by the court, is, that light impressions which may fairly be supposed to yield to the testimony that may be offered; which may leave the mind open to a fair consideration of that testimony, constitute no sufficient objection to a juror; but that those strong and deep impressions, which will close the mind against the testimony that may be offered in opposition to them; which will combat that testimony and resist its force, do constitute a sufficient objection to him. Those who try the impartiality of a juror, ought to test him by this rule. They ought to hear the statement made by himself or given by others, and conscientiously determine, according to their best judgment, whether in general, men under such circumstances, ought to be considered as capable of hearing fairly, and of deciding impartially, on the testimony which may be offered to them; or as possessing minds in a situation to struggle against the conviction which that testimony might be calculated to produce? The court has considered those who have deliberately formed and delivered an opinion on the guilt of the prisoner, as not being in a state of mind fairly to weigh the testimony, and therefore as being disqualified to serve as jurors in the case.

This much has been said relative to the opinion delivered yesterday, because the argument of to-day appears to arraign that opinion, and because it seems closely connected with the point which is now to be decided.

The question now to be decided, is, whether an opinion formed and delivered, not upon the full case, but upon an essential part of it, not that the prisoner is absolutely guilty of the whole crime charged in the indictment, but that he is guilty in some of those great points, which constitute it, do also disqualify a man in the sense of the law and of the constitution from being an impartial juror? This question was adjourned yesterday for argument, and for further consideration.

It would seem to the court, that to say, that any man who had formed an opinion on any fact conducive to the final decision of the case, would therefore be considered as disqualified from serving on the jury, would exclude intelligent and observing men, whose minds were really in a situation to decide upon the whole case according to the testimony, and would perhaps be applying the letter of the rule requiring an impartial jury, with a strictness which is not necessary for the preservation of the rule itself. But if the opinion formed, be on a point so essential as to go far towards a decision of the whole case, and to have a real influence on the verdict to be rendered, the distinction between a person who has formed such an opinion, and one who has in his mind decided the whole case, appears too slight to furnish the court with solid ground for distinguishing between them. The question must always depend, on the strength and nature of the opinion which has been formed.

In the case now under consideration, the court would perhaps not consider it as a sufficient objection to a juror, that he did believe, and had said, that the prisoner at a time considerably anterior to the fact charged in the indictment, entertained treasonable designs against the United States. He may have formed this opinion and be undecided on the question, whether those designs were abandoned or prosecuted up to the time when the indictment charges the overt act to have been committed. On this point, his mind may be open to the testimony, although it would be desirable that no juror should have formed and delivered such an opinion, yet the court is inclined to think, it would not constitute sufficient cause of challenge. But if the juror have made up and declared the opinion, that to the time when the fact laid in the indictment is said to have been committed, the prisoner was prosecuting the treasonable design with which he is charged, the court considers the opinion as furnishing just cause of challenge, and cannot view the juror who has formed and delivered it as impartial, in the legal and constitutional sense of that term.

The cases put by way of illustration, appear to the court, to be strongly applicable to that under consideration. They are those of burglary, of homicide, and of passing counterfeit money, knowing it to be counterfeit; cases in which the intention and the fact combine to constitute the crime.

If, in case of homicide, where the fact of killing was admitted or was doubtful, a juror should have made up and delivered the opinion, that, though uninformed, relative to the fact of killing, he was confident as to the malice; he was confident that the prisoner had deliberately formed the intention of murdering the deceased, and was prosecuting that intention up to the time of his death; or if on the charge of passing counterfeit bank notes, knowing them to be counterfeit, the juror had declared, that though uncertain as to the fact of passing the notes, he was confident that the prisoner knew them to be counterfeit, few would think such a person sufficiently impartial to try the cause according to testimony. The court considers these cases as strikingly analogous.

It has been insisted, that in *Callender's case*, an opinion was given different from that which is now delivered.

I acknowledge, that I had not recollected that case accurately. I had thought, that Mr. Basset had stated himself to have read the book charged as a libel, and to have formed the opinion that the publication was a libel. I find by a reference to the case itself, that I was mistaken; that Mr. Basset had not read the book, and had only said, that if it were such a book as it had been represented to him, he had no doubt of its being a libel. This was going no farther than Mr. Morris has gone, the challenge against whom has been overruled. Mr. Morris had frequently declared, that if the allegations against the prisoner were true, he was guilty, and Mr. Morris was determined to be an impartial juror.

With respect to the general question, put in *Callender's case*, the court considers it as the same with the general question put in this case. It was, " Have you made up and delivered the opinion, that the prisoner is guilty or innocent of the charge laid in the indictment?" That is in substance, " Have you made up and delivered the opinion that the prisoner has been guilty of publishing a false, wicked, and malicious libel, which subjects him to punishment, under the act of congress, on which he is indicted?" The same question is now substantially put. Explanatory questions are now put when they are necessary; and certainly explanatory questions might have been put in *Callender's case*, had they been necessary.

Had the case of Mr. Basset even been such as I thought it, had he read " The Prospect Before Us," and thought it a libel without deciding who was its author, he would have gone no further than to have formed an opinion, that certain allegations were libellous, which is not dissimilar to the opinion, that certain acts amount to treason. If, for example, a juror had said, that levying an army for the purpose of subverting the government of the United States by force, and arraying that army in a warlike manner, amounted to treason, no person could suppose him on that account, unfit to serve on the jury. The opinion would be one in which all must concur; and so was the opinion that " The Prospect Before Us" was a libel. Without determining whether the case put by *Hawkins, b. 2. ch.* 43. *sec.* 28. be law or not, it is sufficient to observe, that this case is totally different. The opinion which is there declared to constitute no cause of challenge, is one formed by the juror on his own knowledge; in this case, the opinion is formed on report and newspaper publications.

The argument drawn from the situation of England during the rebellions of 1715 and 1745, with respect to certain prominent characters, whose situation made it a matter of universal notoriety, that they were the objects of the law, is founded entirely on the absolute necessity of the case; and the total and obvious impossibility of obtaining a jury, whose minds were not already made up. Where this necessity exists, the rule perhaps must bend to it, but the rule will bend no further than is required by actual necessity. The court cannot believe, that at present, the necessity does exist. The cases bear no resemblance to each other. There has not been such open notorious war, as to force conviction on every bosom respecting the fact and the intention. It is believed, that a jury may be obtained, composed of men, who, whatever their general impressions may be, have not deliberately formed and delivered an opinion, respecting the guilt or innocence of the accused.

In reflecting on this subject, which I have done very seriously since the adjournment of yesterday, my mind has been forcibly impressed by contemplating the question precisely in its reverse. If, instead of a panel composed of gentlemen who had almost unanimously formed and publicly delivered an opinion, that the prisoner was guilty, the marshal had returned one composed of persons, who had openly and publicly maintained his innocence; who had insisted, that notwithstanding all the testimony in possession of the public, they had no doubt that his designs were perfectly innocent; who had been engaged in repeated, open, and animated altercation to prove him innocent, and that his objects were entirely opposite to those with which he was charged; would such men be proper and impartial jurors? I cannot believe they would be thought so. I am confident I should not think them so. I cannot declare a juror to be impartial, who has advanced opinions against the prisoner, which would be cause of challenge, if advanced in his favour.

The opinion of the court is, that to have made up and delivered the opinion, that the prisoner entertained the treasonable designs with which he is charged, and that he retained those designs, and was prosecuting them when the act charged in the indictment is alleged to have been committed, is good cause of challenge.

The suspended jurymen were then called. John H. Upshaw was asked by the court, whether he conceived that the prisoner had pursued his treasonable designs to the time charged in the indictment? Mr. Upshaw answered in the affirmative. And the Chief Justice observed, that he was not qualified to serve as a juryman.

J. Bowe, Miles Selden, Lewis Truehart, William Yancey, Thomas Prosser, Nathaniel Selden, John W. Ellis, Armistead T. Mason, and Dabney Minor were successively set aside, after having been further interrogated; because having formed an opinion as to the criminal intentions of the accused, they came within the principle of exclusion just established by the court.

Mr. Hay then moved the court to award a new venire, to consist of a sufficient number, to secure a certainty of supplying the deficient jurymen. He thought, and referred to the authority of *Hawkins*, in support of his opinion, that the " *tales*" might exceed the number of the original panel. He supposed, that one hundred and fifty would not be too few. Were it not for the expense, he would move for five hundred: that every man in the community who had read and believed general Eaton's deposition, must believe, that the accused had treasonable intentions; that as so much difficulty had already occurred in obtaining only four jurors, he was very solicitous that a sufficient number should be directed to be summoned at once.

Mr. Burr said, that he was sorry that such inferences had been made; that he thought a different conclusion ought to be drawn from the experience already had; that a very great majority of the forty-eight first summoned, had publicly and frequently declared the most injurious opinions respecting his intentions; but when it should be manifest, that the officer of this court was really disposed to seek proper jurymen, the number could easily be completed.

Mr. Wirt hoped, that when insinuations were thrown out against the marshal of this court, a man of as respectable a character as any in the state, he might be called into court to justify himself.

Mr. Wickham objected to his panel; that it contained too many members of assembly, and candidates for public favour and office; that the marshal should have selected the jury from those who were less in the habit of expressing their political opinions than those gentlemen; for that, however respectable they might be, the frequent and public discussion of their opinions, had a tendency to create an involuntary bias on their minds.

Mr. Botts said, that it ought not to be understood, that the motives of the marshal were to be questioned; that he was a respectable man, who certainly meant to act faithfully and conscientiously.

Mr. Wirt appealed to the panel itself, as the best proof of the intelligence and integrity of those who had been selected; that they were as respectable men as any in the whole community; that it had been announced from the bench itself, that some abstruse and complicated doctrines of treason, were to be investigated during the trial; that it was therefore natural, that the marshal should have looked out for the most enlightened men, and that the selection should have comprehended some of those very persons, whom the people had before chosen, for the management of their public concerns; but as only four jurors were obtained out of the forty-eight, such a " *tales*" should be awarded, as would be certainly sufficient to produce the remaining eight jurors.

The Chief Justice stated, that the difficulty of getting jurors, was now in some measure removed, as the opinion of the court was known; that the marshal would not summon a man whose opinions he might have previously understood, although he ought not to interrogate him on the subject; that he would have a good reason for not placing on the panel, any man, who should inform him, that his opinions were strongly in conflict with the test established by the court.

After some desultory conversation, the court awarded a panel of forty-eight, and adjourned till Thursday next.

Thursday, August 13th, 1807.

As soon as the court met, Mr. Burr observed, that just before coming into court, he had received a copy of the panel last awarded; that it was defective, in not having the places of residence annexed to the names of the jurors; that he should, perhaps, require till the day after to-morrow, to examine it, which was a less time than the law allowed him for that purpose.

Some conversation ensued, respecting the subpœna " *duces tecum*," when Mr. Hay stated, that he had found general Eaton's letter, among certain papers, transmitted by Mr. Rodney, and had filed it with the clerk; that he had not found among them, general Wilkinson's letter, of the 21st October, but would seek for it.

Three of the jury summoned on the second *venire*, were discharged by the court, viz: General Pegrom, because he was then necessarily engaged in military business; in giving the necessary orders, to the officers of his brigade, to get in readiness, its due proportion of this state's quota of troops, required by the president's proclamation, pursuant to the act of congress. Mr. Lewis, because he owned no freehold in the state of Virginia; and Mr. Moncure, on account of his indisposition.

It was understood, that the marshal should summon three substitutes; and that the prisoner should accept them. So that the venire was still to consist of forty-eight.

The court then adjourned till Saturday, eleven o'clock.

Saturday, August 15th, 1807.

The court met according to adjournment.

Present, Chief Justice Marshall, Judge Griffin, absent.

The jurymen summoned by the marshal, were severally called, and answered to their names in the following order, except seven absentees.

Jacob Michaux, of Powhattan; William Randolph, of Surry; John Edmunds, of Sussex; George Minge, of Charles City; William L. Morton, of Charlotte; Christopher Anthony, of Goochland; John Darricot, of Hanover; Washington Truehart, of Louisa; Martin Smith, of Prince Edward; Benjamin Tate, of city of Richmond; Christopher Tomkins, of do.; Benjamin Branch, of Dinwiddie; Thomas Branch, of Chesterfield; James Sheppard, of city of Richmond; Gabriel Ralston, of do.; Micajah Davis, of Bedford; Reuben Blakey, of Henrico; Miles Selden, of Sussex; Walter Blunt, of do.; Richard N. Thweatt, of Petersburg; John Fitzgerald, of Nottoway; Robert M'Kim, of city of Richmond; Benjamin Graves, of Chesterfield; William M'Kim, of city of Richmond; Robert Hyde, of do.; Thomas Miller, of Powhattan; Thomas Branch, of Chesterfield; Robert Goode, of do.; Henry Randolph, of do.; Miles Bott, of do.; Henry Bridgewater, of do.; Edward Hallam, of city of Richmond; Anderson Barret, of do.; Henry E. Coleman, of Halifax; Edmund Bailey, of city of Richmond; Holder Hudgins, of Matthews; William H. Hudgins, of do.; John Price, of Henrico; Isham Godwin, of do.; William S. Smith, of do.; George Blakey, of do.; Gray Carrol, of Isle of Wight; Isaac Medley, of Halifax; Richard Curd, of Henrico; Edward Munford, of Powhattan; Samuel Allen, of Buckingham; John M. Sheppard, of Hanover; John Curd, of Goochland. Of whom, there were seven absent.

On motion of Mr. Randolph, Mr. Benjamin Tate was excused from serving on the jury, on account of his bad state of health. Henry Randolph wished to be discharged, because he was engaged in collecting the public revenue. The court would not, however, admit the validity of the excuse.

Mr. Burr then addressed the court, and observed, that the panel was now reduced to forty; and as it would be exceedingly disagreeable for him to exercise the privilege of making peremptory challenges, to which he was entitled, he would lay a proposition before the opposite counsel, which would prevent this necessity, and would save one or two hours, that might be otherwise unpleasantly spent. He would select eight out of the whole venire, and they might be immediately sworn, and impaneled on the jury.

The Chief Justice said, that if no objection were made, it might be done, and that they might be placed at the head of the panel.

Mr. Hay observed, that there could be no utility in objecting to it, as the prisoner could challenge peremptorily, and that he had no objection to this arrangement, as it would be easy for him to examine the qualifications of the eight who were selected, when they were once known.

William S. Smith, then requested to be excused, on account of his indisposition.

Mr. Burr observed, that Mr. Smith was one of those whom he had selected; but he would be sorry to impose such a burden upon any invalid. Mr. Smith was *discharged*.

When Christopher Anthony was called, he observed to the court, that he had uttered some expressions since he came to town, which he had been told, would certainly disqualify him from serving, according to the rules said to have been laid down by the court. On being interrogated, as to what words he had spoken,

Mr. Burr said, perhaps the words were used through levity. Do you think they would be sufficient to warp your judgment?

Answer. No.

Mr. Burr.—Then, sir, you are not disqualified.

Mr. Mac Rae.—State the tenor of those expressions.

Anthony. When I first arrived here, I met with an intimate friend, to whom I observed, that I had come to town with a hope of being placed on this jury, and if I were, I would hang colonel Burr at once without further inquiry.

Mr. Mac Rae.—Did you say so, knowing that such expressions would disqualify you?

Answer. I did not; for I never expected to be put on this panel.

Question. Were you serious?

Answer. Far from it. I spoke in the utmost spirit of levity.

Question. Have you been in the habit of reading the newspapers? Answer. I have.

Mr. Mac Rae proceeded to make further inquiry of him. He asked him, whether he had read the depositions of generals Wilkinson and Eaton? He answered in the affirmative. He then asked him, whether those depositions had made no impression upon his mind? Hereupon, both colonel Burr and Mr. Martin, objected to this inquiry as improper.

Mr. Mac Rae contended, that this examination was in vindication of the rights of the United States, and perfectly proper and correct, and was no more than had been done repeatedly by the prisoner.

Mr. Martin.—You have no right to disqualify any juryman for us.

Chief Justice.—Certainly the counsel for the United States may challenge for cause.

Mr. Mac Rae.—We are entitled to the same rights, which the opposite counsel have exercised, as to the former venire. When the jurymen were successively called before the court, did not the opposite counsel in every case, challenge for cause? Did not the prisoner make some general observations, that were intended for the ears of the jury; in which he spoke of his right of challenge, and requested every juryman who was conscious of prejudice, to object to himself? Did they not, in several cases, without exercising the right of challenge, previously inquire of the jurymen, whether they had no declarations to make? Did not the counsel for the prosecution, suggest some doubts about the propriety of this course? and did not the prisoner reply, that no juryman ought to lock up in his own bosom, the prejudices which he had conceived, and that he ought to declare himself? Did not Mr. Botts frequently interrogate the jurymen, whether they had nothing to state? Mr. J. Baker's case will be particularly recollected; for that gentleman positively replied, that he had no observations to make, until he had been challenged; and not until this step had been taken, did any declarations fall from Mr. Baker. We wish to pursue the same course now, that was adopted on that occasion. We wish to challenge no juryman for cause, until he have previously made declarations of his state of mind. The same justice is due to the United States that was awarded to the prisoner; and they have the same right to know whether a juryman be as perfectly impartial in relation to the prosecution, as to the prisoner. As to the jurors themselves, they would certainly be willing to give all the information in their power.

Mr. Hay was willing to take the persons selected; for he entertained no doubt of the integrity of the gentlemen who were summoned. He was willing to take them, provided they should be asked by the bench, whether they were conscious of any cause, which should disqualify them from serving. If they themselves were satisfied, he should be also satisfied. No man on this panel who had definitively made up his mind, would conscientiously think to lay his hand on the book, and solemnly avow himself an impartial and qualified juryman.

The CHIEF JUSTICE understood then, that these selected eight, were to pass without challenge, unless they challenged themselves. If the court were required to say, as seemed to be the wish of the prosecution, that any impressions however slight, were sufficient cause for challenge, he would ask, where they could obtain a jury? The United States had precisely the same rights as the prisoner had, and were entitled to make the same challenges for good cause. He then addressed those eight jurymen who were placed at the head of the panel, thus:

" Gentlemen, if you have made up, and expressed any opinion, either for, or against the accused, you ought to express it."

Mr. BURR.—The law presumes every man to be innocent, until he have been proved to be guilty. According to the rules of law, it is therefore the duty of every citizen, who serves on this jury, to hold himself completely unbiassed; it is no disqualification then, for a man to come forward, and declare, that he believes me to be innocent.

CHIEF JUSTICE.—The law certainly presumes every man to be innocent, till the contrary be proved; but if a juryman give an opinion in favour of the prisoner, he must be rejected.

When Christopher Anthony was called to the book, he stated, that he was in court the other day, when the first venire was investigated; that it would be extremely unpleasant to serve on the jury; and, that his general opinions had been precisely the same that had disqualified (as he understood), several other gentlemen. Mr. Anthony's objections were overruled.

John M. Sheppard. I too feel myself disqualified for passing impartially between the United States, and Aaron Burr. From the documents that I have seen, particularly the depositions of generals Wilkinson and Eaton, I have believed, and do still believe, that his intentions were hostile to the peace and safety of the United States; in short, that he had intended to subvert the government of the United States. It would be inflicting a wound on my own bosom, to be compelled to serve under my present impressions. Mr. Sheppard observed, that considerations of a private nature, had also borne upon his mind: for he had a child at home, extremely sick.

Mr. BURR.—Notwithstanding Mr. Sheppard's impressions, I could rely upon his integrity and impartiality. As to his private considerations, I do not wish wantonly to wound his feelings. I must request him, therefore, to sit down for a moment, until we shall ascertain, whether we can make a jury without him.

Mr. HAY.—Has the court understood the extent of Mr. Sheppard's declarations?

CHIEF JUSTICE.—If the prisoner's counsel waive the right of challenge, there is an end of it.

James Sheppard was then called; who made no further declarations.

Reuben Blakey. I have made up no opinions either way, positively, on this subject.

Doctor John Fitzgerald. It is incumbent on me, to state to the court, that I have formed and delivered an opinion unfavourable to colonel Burr. My opinion has been founded upon the depositions of generals Eaton and Wilkinson, and other newspaper publications; and it is, that colonel Burr's intentions were hostile and treasonable against the United States. On which account, I am very unwilling to serve, lest I should possess that bias upon my mind, which is unbecoming a juryman. Mr. Fitzgerald was requested to sit down for a few moments.

Miles Bott. From the affidavits of generals Wilkinson and Eaton, my opinion has been completely made up for several months past.

Mr. MARTIN.—I suppose you have only taken up a prejudice on the supposition, that the facts stated were true.

Mr. Bott. I have gone as far as to declare, that colonel Burr ought to be hanged.

Mr. BURR.—Do you think that such declarations would now influence your judgment? Would not the evidence alter your opinion?

Answer. Human nature is very frail; I know that the evidence ought, but it might or might not influence me. I have expressed myself in this manner, perhaps, within a fortnight; and I do not consider myself a proper juryman.

Mr. BURR.—It will be seen, either that I am under the necessity of taking men in some degree, prejudiced against me, or of having another venire. I am unwilling to submit to the further delay of other " *tales*," and I must therefore encounter the consequences. I will take Mr. Bott, under the belief that he will do me justice.

Four jurymen then having been selected, three were sworn. Mr. C. Anthony affirmed.

When Henry E. Coleman was called, he stated, that he had conceived and expressed an opinion, that the designs of colonel

Burr were always enveloped in mystery, and inimical to the United States; and when informed by the public prints, that he was descending the river with an armed force, he had felt as every friend of his country ought to feel.

Mr. BURR.—If, sir, you have completely prejudged my case—

Mr. Coleman. I have not. I have not seen the evidence.

Mr. BURR.—That is enough, sir. You are *elected*.

Mr. HAY then suggested to the court, the propriety of not swearing all the jury this day; as it would subject them to the inconvenience of an unnecessary confinement in their own room to-morrow, (Sunday). Would it not be better for Mr. Marshall (the clerk), to swear three only out of the remaining four? The court might then impanel the whole on Monday, and proceed immediately to business.

Mr. BURR had no objections to this measure; but hoped that the court would enjoin them not to hold any conversations on the subject of the trial.

John Curd, upon being called, stated, that he had no prejudices, for or against the prisoner; but that he was bound in candour, to inform the court, that he was afflicted by a disorder, (a palpitation of the heart), which was irregular in its attacks, but was sometimes very sudden and violent, and rendered him entirely incapable of business; and if he were sworn on the jury, it *might* interrupt and delay the progress of the cause. He was *excused*.

Isham Godwin had formed and declared a uniform opinion of colonel Burr's guilt. If he were impaneled, he should be under a strong impression, that colonel Burr was guilty of treason. *Suspended*.

Samuel Allen, had, for several months, made up an opinion unfavourable to the prisoner. *Suspended*.

Benjamin Graves had not formed an opinion; and gave a long history of his domestic and family engagements, to excuse himself from serving. He was asked, whether he could not make some arrangements of this business, between this time and Monday, calculated to remove all the inconvenience of his serving? Mr. Graves could not positively say.

Mr. BURR then observed, that the two jurors who had been selected, might be sworn; the other two might be selected on Monday. And Messrs. Coleman and Graves were accordingly sworn.

Mr. BURR hoped, that the marshal would direct all the necessary preparations to be made for the accommodation of the jury, who would be confined to their own chamber after Monday.

Colonel Thomas Branch was then excused from serving, because he was engaged in military business.

The CHIEF JUSTICE requested the jury and the remaining members of the venire, to attend on Monday, at twelve o'clock; and enjoined them to hold, in the mean time, no communication on this subject with any person.

Mr. HAY stated, that he was satisfied, from some expressions which he had heard from Mr. Munford, of Powhatan, at the moment of his summons, that the prisoner would himself object to him.

Mr. BURR was satisfied with the attorney's word; and Mr. Munford was accordingly discharged.

Mr. BURR was sorry to be importunate; but he was under the necessity of mentioning once more the letter of the 21st October. He wished to know, whether the attorney had yet found it amongst his papers, or whether he could point to any other means of obtaining it.

Mr. HAY had examined two bundles of papers transmitted to him by Mr. Rodney; but he had not found it. There were other papers which he had yet to examine. He had, however, a copy of the original letter.

Mr. BURR.—Where is this copy from? From Washington, or from general Wilkinson?

Mr. HAY.—It is from general Wilkinson. He has, however, written it from the original.

Mr. BURR.—I shall not accept of his copy: but I will state this proposition to the attorney. If he do not find this lettter by Monday, will he consent that I obtain a subpœna *duces tecum?*

Mr. HAY.—I have no objection.

CHIEF JUSTICE.—I suppose an order may be made to issue a subpœna *duces tecum* addressed to the attorney general of the United States, in case the letter be not found.

Mr. HAY.—I have no objection.

A desultory conversation ensued between Messrs. HAY and BOTTS, on the arraignment of H. Blannerhassett. Mr. Hay was averse to interrupting the jury after it had once been impaneled for the trial of Mr. Burr: he was therefore anxious to have Blannerhassett immediately arraigned, and if possible, to have some day fixed for his trial.

Mr. BOTTS did not think it possible for the court to fix on a particular time for his trial, or for the attorney to furnish any means for calculating it. Mr. Blannerhassett was not prepared for his trial: but he was then preparing a brief for the information of his counsel, which might enable them to give a definitive answer on this subject.

Mr. HAY was willing to grant them any accommodation they might require. At all events, the court would only have occasion to meet one hour sooner on some day, to arrange it.

Mr. BOTTS promised, that he would notify the attorney some day in the next week, for this purpose.

The court then adjourned till Monday, twelve o'clock.

MONDAY, August 17th, 1807.

The court met according to adjournment.

CHARLES LEE, esq. appeared as counsel for the prisoner.

Doctor Bennett, of Mason county, a witness on behalf of the United States, was called and recognised.

Mr. HAY stated some little difficulty which had occurred between Mr. Botts and himself. He had furnished the prisoner with a list of the names of such witnesses, with their places of residence, as had come to his knowledge. He had likewise proposed, and Mr. Botts had consented, that all such witnesses should be examined, whose names should be furnished to the prisoner, before the commencement of the trial. He had furnished the names of three on Saturday, viz. Messrs. Neil, Goodwin, and Jones; which Mr. Botts did not think ought to be accepted, because they were not furnished previous to the trial. For his own part, he did not think that the trial could be said to have commenced, before the jury were sworn and impaneled; the prisoner might at any time before the jury were sworn, move for, and obtain a continuance of the cause; if he could satisfy the court that he was entitled to it.

Mr. BOTTS said, that he had no doubt Mr. Hay thought that he had stated facts to the court, relative to their supposed agreement; that however he was mistaken, and he mentioned some circumstances to convince him that he was so; but that as there had been a mistake, he would, as a matter of voluntary favour and grace, agree to the introduction of those three witnesses.

Mr. HAY solemnly expressed his belief in the accuracy of his statement: but as he was at liberty to introduce these three witnesses, he would let the subject rest where it was.

The names of the selected jurors and of the venire, were then called over. After which, John M. Sheppard, and Richard Curd were selected to complete the panel, and sworn.

The following is, therefore, a complete list of the petit jury.

Edward Carrington,	Reuben Blakey,
David Lambert,	Benjamin Graves,
Richard E. Parker,	Miles Bott,
Hugh Mercer,	Henry E. Coleman,
Christopher Anthony,	John M. Sheppard,
James Sheppard,	Richard Curd.

Proclamation then having been made in due form, the prisoner standing up, the clerk addressed the jury in the usual form, and read the indictment in the words following:

VIRGINIA DISTRICT:

In the circuit court of the United States of America, in and for the fifth circuit, and Virginia district.

The grand inquest of the United States of America, for the Virginia district, upon their oath, do present, that AARON BURR, late of the city of New-York, and state of New-York, attorney at law, being an inhabitant of, and residing within the United States, and under the protection of the laws of the United States, and owing allegiance and fidelity to the same United States, not having the fear of God before his eyes, nor weighing the duty of his said allegiance, but being moved and seduced by the instigation of the devil, wickedly devising and intending the peace and tranquillity of the said United States to disturb; and to stir, move and excite insurrection, rebellion and war against the said United States; on the tenth day of December, in the year of Christ one thousand eight hundred and six, at a certain place called and known by the name of Blannerhassett's island, in the county of Wood, and district of Virginia aforesaid, and within the jurisdiction of this court, with force and arms, unlawfully, falsely, maliciously and traitorously, did compass, imagine and intend to raise and levy war, insurrection and rebellion against the said United States; and in order to fulfil and bring to effect the said traitorous compassings, imaginations and intentions of him the said Aaron Burr, he the said Aaron Burr afterwards, to wit, on the said tenth day of December, in the year one thousand eight hundred and six aforesaid, at the said island called Blannerhassett's island as aforesaid, in the county of Wood aforesaid, in the district of Virginia aforesaid, and within the jurisdiction of this court, with a great multitude of persons, whose names at present are unknown to the grand inquest aforesaid, to a great number, to wit, to the number of thirty persons and upwards, armed and arrayed in a warlike manner, that is to say, with guns, swords and dirks, and other warlike weapons as well offensive as defensive, being then and there unlawfully, maliciously and trai-

torously assembled and gathered together, did falsely and traitorously assemble and join themselves together against the said
United States; and then and there with force and arms did falsely
and traitorously and in a warlike and hostile manner, array and
dispose themselves against the said United States; and then and
there that is to say, on the day and in the year aforesaid, at the
island aforesaid, commonly called Blannerhassett's island, in the
county aforesaid of Wood, within the Virginia district and the
jurisdiction of this court, in pursuance of such their traitorous
intentions and purposes aforesaid, he the said Aaron Burr with
the said persons so as aforesaid, traitorously assembled and armed and arrayed in manner aforesaid, most wickedly, maliciously
and traitorously did ordain, prepare and levy war against the
said United States, contrary to the duty of their said allegiance
and fidelity, against the constitution, peace and dignity of the
said United States, and against the form of the act of the congress
of the said United States in such case made and provided.

And the grand inquest of the United States of America, for
the Virginia district, upon their oaths aforesaid, do further present, that the said Aaron Burr late of the city of New-York, and
state of New-York, attorney at law, being an inhabitant of, and
residing within the United States, and under the protection of
the laws of the United States, and owing allegiance and fidelity
to the same United States, not having the fear of God before
his eyes, nor weighing the duty of his said allegiance, but being
moved and seduced by the instigation of the devil, wickedly devising and intending the peace and tranquillity of the said United
States to disturb; and to stir, move and excite insurrection, rebellion and war against the said United States; on the eleventh day
of December, in the year of our Lord one thousand eight hundred and six, at a certain place called and known by the name
of Blannerhassett's island, in the county of Wood and district of
Virginia aforesaid, and within the jurisdiction of this court, with
force and arms unlawfully, falsely, maliciously and traitorously
did compass, imagine and intend to raise and levy war, insurrection and rebellion against the said United States; and in
order to fulfil and bring to effect the said traitorous compassings, imaginations and intentions of him the said Aaron
Burr, he the said Aaron Burr afterwards, to wit, on the said last
mentioned day of December in the year one thousand eight
hundred and six aforesaid, at a certain place commonly called
and known by the name of Blannerhassett's island in the said
county of Wood in the district of Virginia aforesaid, and within
the jurisdiction of this court, with one other great multitude of
persons whose names at present are unknown to the grand inquest aforesaid, to a great number, to wit, to the number of
thirty persons and upwards, armed and arrayed in a warlike man-

ner, that is to say, with guns, swords and dirks, and other war-like weapons, as well offensive as defensive, being then and there unlawfully, maliciously and traitorously assembled and gathered together, did falsely and traitorously assemble and join themselves together against the said United States; and then and there with force and arms did falsely and traitorously and in a warlike and hostile manner array and dispose themselves against the said United States; and then and there, that is to say, on the day and in the year last mentioned, at the island aforesaid, in the county of Wood aforesaid, in the Virginia district, and within the jurisdiction of this court, in pursuance of such their traitorous intentions and purposes aforesaid, he the said Aaron Burr with the said persons so as aforesaid traitorously assembled, and armed and arranged in manner aforesaid, most wickedly, maliciously and traitorously did ordain, prepare and levy war against the said United States; and further to fulfil and carry into effect the said traitorous compassings, imaginations and intentions of him the said Aaron Burr, against the said United States, and to carry on the war thus levied as aforesaid against the said United States, the said Aaron Burr, with the multitude last mentioned, at the island aforesaid, in the said county of Wood within the Virginia district aforesaid, and within the jurisdiction of this court, did array themselves in a warlike manner, with guns and other weapons, offensive and defensive, and did proceed from the said island down the river Ohio in the county aforesaid, within the Virginia district and within the jurisdiction of this court, on the said eleventh day of December, in the year one thousand eight hundred and six aforesaid, with the wicked and traitorous intention to descend the said river and the river Mississippi, and by force and arms traitorously to take possession of a city commonly called New-Orleans, in the territory of Orleans, belonging to the United States, contrary to the duty of their said allegiance and fidelity, against the constitution, peace and dignity of the said United States, and against the form of the act of the congress of the United States in such case made and provided.

HAY, Attorney of the United States,
for the Virginia district.

Indorsed—" A TRUE BILL—JOHN RANDOLPH."
A Copy. Teste,
WILLIAM MARSHALL, *Clerk.*

After the indictment was read, Mr. HAY requested that the jury should be furnished with implements necessary to enable them to take notes on the evidence, and also on the arguments if they should think proper; that as the cause was important, and would require all their attention, it would be proper to afford them this assistance. This was accordingly done.

Mr. HAY then opened the case in the following speech:

May it please the court, and you gentlemen of the jury: In the preliminary stages of the prosecution in which we are now engaged, many observations were made extremely derogatory to the character of the government under which we live, and injurious to the feelings of the counsel concerned in the prosecution. Among other things, gentlemen of the jury, it was said, that we had indulged an intemperate zeal against the prisoner. which transgressed all the limits of moderation and humanity: that we were anxious to convict him even if innocent, and to deprive him of those means of defence which justice and law direct. I do not know, gentlemen of the jury, whether you heard this charge, or if you did, whether it made any impression on your minds; but if it did, it is my duty to efface that impression. But how, gentlemen? By professions of moderation, candour, liberality and humanity? professions easily made and as easily forgotten! No. I will prove, gentlemen, that this charge is unjust, by the course which I shall pursue in the very management of this prosecution. We come now to a serious and interesting crisis in this inquiry; on the result of which the life of a man, and of a fellow citizen, who once stood high in the estimation of his country, must certainly depend. It is alleged, that his life is forfeited to the offended justice and violated laws of his country. It is my duty to support that allegation: but, gentlemen of the jury, if I know myself, if I can venture to express what my own feelings dictate, I shall support that allegation only, by facts which I believe to be true, and by arguments which have already produced my own conviction.

The prisoner at the bar, is charged with treason in levying war against the United States. To this charge, he has pleaded not guilty. It is your high and solemn duty to decide whether the charge be true or not; and you have sworn to decide it according to the evidence which shall be laid before you. If you attend to the obligation and the words of your oath, any admonitions from me, with respect to the course which you ought to pursue, will be entirely superfluous. If you decide according to the evidence, you will divest your minds of every bias, of all political prepossessions produced by extraneous statements and rumours which you may have seen and heard. You will enter upon the case with impartial attention, and a firm determination to do justice between the U. States and the prisoner. But, gentlemen, if, after that patient investigation of the evidence, which the importance of the case requires, and which I am sure you will bestow, you be not satisfied of the guilt of the accused, it is your duty to say, that he is not guilty. This, gentlemen of the jury, is the language of the law, of humanity and of common sense. If you doubt on the subject, and cannot bring your minds to a positive determination, that he is guilty, you must declare him to be innocent. But gentlemen of the jury, there is one distinction made sometimes by jurymen, to which I will for a single moment call your attention, which seems to me to be a distinction without a difference, and founded in wickedness and folly. It is this : that they were satisfied as individuals that the prisoner was guilty; but yet, that they were not satisfied as jurymen. This appears to me to be a miserable fallacy. A juryman may entertain a belief, founded on what he has heard out of doors, which would not be warranted by the legal evidence before him in court, on which alone he ought to decide; but if the belief once exist in his mind, from the evidence, that the prisoner has committed the crime alleged, he is then guilty of treachery to his God, to his country, and to himself, if he do not pronounce a verdict dictated by that belief.

This indictment contains two counts : one for levying war against the United States, at Blannerhassett's island, in the county of Wood. The other contains precisely the same charge, but goes on with this addition, that in order to levy it more effectually, he descended the Ohio and Mississippi, with an armed force, for the purpose of taking New-Orleans. If either charge be supported by evidence, it will be your duty to find a verdict against him.

In Great-Britain, there are no less than ten different species of treason; at least that was the number when Blackstone wrote, and it is possible that the number may have been increased since. But in this country, where the principle is established in the constitution, there are only two descriptions of treason; and the number being fixed in the constitution itself, can never be increased by the legislature, however important and necessary it should be, in their opinion, that the number should be augmented. By the 3d section of the 3d article of the constitution of the United States, " Treason against the United States shall consist only in levying war against them, or in adhering to their enemies; giving them aid and comfort." With respect to the latter description, there is no occasion to say any thing, as the offence charged in the indictment is "levying war against the United States;" but it adds that " no person shall be convicted of treason, unless on the testimony of two witnesses to the same *overt act*, or on confession in open court." The offence being thus constitutionally defined, the only question which presents itself to your view, at this stage of the inquiry, is, What shall constitute an overt act of levying war against the United States? Treason consists

in levying war against the United States : the question then
is, What is, in the law, an overt act of "levying war" against
the United States? It is obvious, that the interval between the
first movements towards a conspiracy, and actual hostilities,
or a battle fought, is immense. There may be a conspiracy to
"levy war;" but this is not treason. Individuals may meet together and traitorously determine to make dispositions to bring
forces into the field, and levy war against their country; this is
a conspiracy, but not treason. The conspirators may go a step
further; they may not only project a plan for "levying war,"
but they may inlist troops for the purpose of prosecuting their
traitorous designs; but this is not an *overt act*. It hath been
decided by the supreme court of the United States, that the
persons concerned in this conspiracy, may yet take one step
further, and be on the safe side of the line, which separates conspiracy from treason. It has been adjudged that the individuals
engaged in the treason, may proceed to a place of rendezvous.
But gentlemen, common sense and principles founded on considerations of national safety certainly require, that the crime
of treason should be completed, before the actual commission
of hostilities against the government. If force must be employed, before treason shall be said to be perpetrated, what is the
consequence? Why, that the traitor will so take his steps, as not
to strike a blow, till he be in such an attitude, as to be able to
bid defiance to the government, and laugh at your definitions
of treason. If he be a man of common understanding, he will
not hazard a blow, till his arrangements be so complete, that
the blow shall be fatal. It will then be a matter of very little
consequence to him, what may be the definition of the crime
which he has thus committed. What then is the point at which
a treasonable conspiracy shall be said to be matured into treason? What shall be said to be an overt act of treason in this
country? The answer is this, gentlemen of the jury, that an assemblage of men convened for the purpose of effecting by force
a treasonable design, which force is intended to be employed
before their dispersion, is treasonable; and the persons engaged
in it are traitors. The answer which I have thus given, is not
literally that which is furnished by the decision of the supreme
court of the United States; but it is substantially the same, and
is given in conformity to what I understand to be the spirit of
that decision. This is precisely the question which was fully
discussed before the supreme court of the United States; and
as the opinion of that court, on this question, was pronounced
after great deliberation, no other judicial tribunal within the
United States ought to support a doctrine contrary to the principles of that decision; and that opinion was, that a bare assem-

blage of men, met to carry into forcible execution, before their separation, a treasonable design, was an overt act of levying war against the United States. I refer to the opinion delivered by the chief justice, in the case of Bollman and Swartwout, on the 21st of February, 1807; in which the following words occur. "It is not the intention of the court to say, that no individual can be guilty of this crime, who has not appeared in arms against his country. On the contrary, if war be actually levied, that is, "*if a body of men be actually assembled for the purpose of effecting by force, a treasonable purpose, all those who perform any part, however minute, or however remote from the scene of action,* and who are actually *leagued in the general conspiracy, are to be considered* as *traitors*: but there must be *an actual assembling* of *men, to constitute a levying of war.*" If therefore war be levied in this manner, if a number of men collect together for the purpose of effecting a treasonable purpose, all are traitors. The construction which I have thus given, comes within the words and meaning of the decision of the supreme court, pronounced by yourself. The same idea is expressed in perhaps ten or fifteen other parts of this decision: "To complete the crime of levying war against the United States, there must be an actual assemblage of men, for the purpose of executing a treasonable design. There is the utmost precision of language in every part of this judicial sentence. Again:

"A design to overturn the government of the United States at New-Orleans, by force, would have been unquestionably a design, which, if carried into execution, would have been treason; and the *assemblage of a body of men, for the purpose of carrying it into execution, would amount to levying war against the United States;* but no conspiracy, for this object, no inlisting of men to effect it, would be an actual levying of war." If then the accused and his associates, had met together for the purpose of effecting by force, a dissolution of the government of the United States, at New-Orleans, though no force had been used, or battle fought, to accomplish it, they would have been guilty of treason. Again, gentlemen, the same idea occurs in these other passages: "It cannot be necessary that the whole army should be assembled, and that the various parts which are to compose it, should be combined, but it is necessary that there should be an actual assemblage." "The meeting of particular bodies of men, and their marching from places of partial to places of general rendezvous, would be such an assemblage." "It would certainly be an overt act of levying war." I think therefore, gentlemen, that I may with confidence say, that I am warranted in the construction which I have given, by an express and solemn adjudication of the supreme judicial tribunal of this country.

Perhaps, gentlemen of the jury, in opening this cause, I may take more time than you think necessary, or than I myself, strictly speaking, may think necessary; but justice to the accused requires, that I should explicitly communicate the ground and principles on which the prosecution is meant to be maintained, that his counsel may prepare for his defence. I must solicit your attention, while I state for your consideration, those reasons which have induced me, in giving this exposition of the words " *levying war*," to omit two circumstances, both of which may be deemed by the counsel for the prisoner, to form essential parts in the definition of treason. In the definition which I have just examined, no notice is taken of arms or military weapons; nor have I stated, that any actual force or *hostility* has been employed, for the purpose of effecting the treasonable designs; because I think neither of them essential, according to the constitution and laws of this country.

On the first point I shall offer but a few remarks. But before satisfying you of the legal propriety of the omission, permit me to examine the question on principles of common sense; for it must be admitted, that in legal discussion, we do not always carry common sense along with us, from beginning to end. Let us then consider this case, not as it would be presented to us by lawyers and judges, but by the sound principles of common sense and national policy. I say that it is not necessary that the conspirators thus assembled, should be armed, to make them traitors; but that their treason may be complete, though they have not a single gun, nor even a sword, in the whole transaction. Let us suppose a case: There has been a time, when ten or fifteen thousand stand of arms were deposited under the roof of this capitol: suppose that four or five thousand unarmed men, should meet together, within a few miles of this city, with a deliberate, preconcerted design, to march to the capitol, take possession of the public arms, disperse the legislature, and usurp all the powers of the government: suppose ten thousand men unarmed should come within a few miles of this city, where they knew they could get arms, for the purpose of carrying into effect their treasonable designs : let us suppose, what is not unreasonable to suppose, that the infantry and cavalry of this city, should gird on their armour, and resolve, as good honest citizens and brave soldiers, to disperse these conspirators, before they carried their treasonable purposes into effect: they arm, they march, and these conspirators, apprised of their approach, and conscious of their own guilt, disperse and fly in every direction. I ask whether they would not be traitors? They had assembled and marched for the purpose of subverting the government of their country, but before they got possession of the arms which it was their intention to seize and turn against their country, they were dispersed and effected their escape. Could any man say, that these men thus assembled, were not, to all intents and purposes, traitors to their country? Or, gentlemen, suppose that a number of men should assemble on Blannerhassett's island, in the county of Wood : suppose, what I do not believe was the fact, that they have no arms : they descend the Ohio and Mississippi, with an intention to take New-Orleans and plunder it, and divide the union. They calculate on meeting their leader at the mouth of Cumberland river, and when at Baton Rouge, to obtain arms on the river. Their numbers increase as they go on, and we are told, that when they arrive there, they will get arms by the aid of the Spanish minister. Would the simple circumstance of their being unarmed, lessen their guilt? Would it not be an absurdity and a violation of common sense, to say, that the moment before they got possession of arms, they were not traitors; but that the instant they put their hands on the muskets they became traitors? It appears to my mind that the description of treason given by the supreme court, was correct, when in one passage it is silent as to the necessity of possessing arms to constitute treason; and in another part, if I am not greatly mistaken, it has expressly disclaimed it. If, gentlemen, this point were not to be so determined, what would be the result? Why this, that the conspirators would take care never to touch arms, till they were ready to strike a blow. Their arrangements would be made in such a manner, that they would have military weapons placed within their reach, but they would not lay their hands on them till their organization were complete.

It is not essential therefore, on principles of common sense or national policy, that they should have arms before they could be said to have committed an overt act of treason. And what says the law? In the case, gentlemen of the jury, decided by the supreme court, you find that there is not a single syllable said, from beginning to end, with respect to the necessity of arms being in the hands of the persons assembled in order to perpetrate the crime of treason; and in the trial of *Fries, p.* 197. one of the judges of the supreme court, (Judge Chase) embraces this opinion; he says, " That the *court* are of opinion, that military weapons, (as guns and swords mentioned in the indictment) are not necessary to make such *insurrection*, or *rising*, amount to *levying war;* because numbers may supply the want of military weapons, and other instruments may effect the intended mischief. *The legal guilt of levying war may be incurred without the use of military weapons, or military array.*" It is remarkable too, that this very doctrine is admitted by the counsel of the accused, (Mr. Dallas, *p.* 108). I do not state it as authority, but it affords a strong presumptive argument, that the law was against him; for the counsel of a prisoner never makes a concession, unless the law be extremely clear against him.

In Great Britain, there is a statute which passed many years ago, in the 25th year of the reign of Edward the 3d, in which treason is described in the very identical words of our *constitution*, in the *3d section* of the *3d article*. This statute makes " levying war" against the king, to be treason. When, therefore, the framers of our constitution, many of whom were lawyers of distinguished talents, defined " treason" in the very words by which it had been defined many years ago in that country, and which had been so often the subject of discussion and adjudication, it is to be fairly presumed, that they used those words in the same sense which has been annexed to them by the judges in Great Britain. An observation of a judge of the court of the United States on this subject, who is now no more, but was very respectable, (judge Iredell) amply confirms this remark. In *Fries's Trial, p.* 167. that able judge says, " Now, I must confess, as these able and learned framers of our constitution, borrowed the act in terms, from the British statute alone, an authority with which they were familiar, that they certainly at least meant, that the English authorities and definition of those terms should be much respected." The only purpose for which I have made the reference to the British laws, is, to shew that the decision of the supreme court on this subject, in the *case of Bollman and Swartwout,* is not an innovation, not a new doctrine, but is an exact counter-part of, and taken from, the decisions of the English judges. To prove this, I refer to *Foster's Crown Law, p.* 208. where speaking of being armed and arrayed in a warlike manner, he says that " the merits of the case have never turned singly on any of those circumstances." " In the cases of *Demaree* and *Purchase,* which are the last printed cases that have come in judgment, on the point of constructive levying war, there was nothing given in evidence of the usual pageantry of war; *no military weapons,* no *banners* or *drums,* nor *any regular consultation, previous* to the rising: and *yet the want of those circumstances, weighed nothing with the court;* though the prisoner's counsel insisted much on that matter. The *number of the insurgents supplied the want of military weapons,* &c. The true criterion therefore, in all these cases is, *quo animo,* did *the parties assemble?* For if the assembly be on some private quarrel, or to take revenge of particular persons," then it is not treason. But if the cause of the assembly be an object in which the nation itself is concerned, as taking possession of New-Orleans, the key of the western world, then according to common sense, the opinion of the English judges, or of the supreme court, it is treason.

The opinion of judge Foster, is quoted in *East's Crown Law, vol.* 1. *p.* 67. He concurs in the opinion of judge Foster, and thinks, that arms and military array are not essential to constitute treason.

I have thought it my duty to enter into this tedious exposition of the law on this point, though it did not appear to me to be absolutely necessary; because our own courts have decided this question, in language too plain to be misunderstood by mortal man. Another circumstance which perhaps rendered this discussion unnecessary, is this; that the persons assembled on Blannerhassett's island, were actually armed for offensive, as well as defensive purposes.

I have thus endeavoured to satisfy you gentlemen, that I was correct, in omitting in the definition of treason, that they were armed or in military array. I submit to you gentlemen, how far I have succeeded in justifying the propriety of this omission.

I stated to you a second omission, that the persons assembled are not stated to have employed any actual force, or committed any hostilities. I contend that treason may be committed, though no battle be fought, and though no act of violence or force whatsoever be done.

I trust, that I have shewn, that the treason is completed the very instant that they assemble together with a treasonable design. It will perhaps be said on the other side, (though I can hardly persuade myself that it will), that *arms* must be *used*, that *force* must be *employed*, before war shall be said to be levied. If they should contend, that the conspirators must have arms, and must employ force, before they can incur the guilt of treason, observe the embarrassment in which their doctrine will involve them. If ten thousand men were to assemble together and march to the city of Washington, for the express purpose of sending the president to Monticello, turning congress out of doors, taking possession of the capitol, and usurping the powers of the government, they would not be guilty of treason; because they had not yet struck a blow. They advance and proceed; they meet no opposition; the members of the government disperse through fear; and yet this is not treason! I should suppose, that it would be acknowledged to be usurpation, and that the persons who had thus assembled and proceeded to the capital of the union, with a determined intention of subverting the government, were traitors. No violence has been used, no opposition has been encountered, and they effected their object, because the terror and dismay inspired by their numbers, rendered resistance impossible; yet they are not traitors! The doctrine that makes force, or the actual exertion of arms, an essential ingredient in the composition of treason, is, in my estimation, the most dangerous and most fatal that can be conceived. It is the very doctrine which traitors themselves, assembled together, for the purpose of devising laws for their own security, would be most disposed to recognise. For if they were not traitors till they struck a blow, they would have nothing else to do, but to be on their guard, and never to lift their arm till the blow should take full effect. The doctrine for which I contend, is completely and unequivocally confirmed by the decision of the supreme court of the United States. There is not a single word in it, from which it can be reasonably inferred, that, in order to commit treason, actual hostility or force must be employed.

I do not know whether the counsel for the accused, will take shelter under some expressions used by the judges in the *case of Fries, p.* 197. and I candidly admit, that there are some expressions used by judge Chase, from which it may be inferred, that force must be used, to complete the crime of treason. If they should think proper to rely on those expressions, to prove that force is necessary, I have only to remark, that it is but the opinion of a single judge, or of the judges of a subordinate court, and cannot be opposed to the decision of the supreme court. But this opinion cannot be considered as authority, for two reasons. First, it will be recollected, that the opinion on that point, is extrajudicial; by which I mean to say, that it was not such a point, as was necessary to be settled in the case then before the court. He was speaking on a subject not immediately before him, and which he decided only incidentally. The question before him, was not, whether force did enter into the composition of treason; for in the *case of Fries,* there was no sort of doubt, that every kind of force was used. It was a case of an actual opposition to the laws of the United States; and nothing is considered as an authority, but a decision of the court, on the very point which brings the question before it: the opinion was therefore extrajudicial.

But 2dly, the opinion delivered by judge Chase, will be found on an accurate inspection, not to be consistent with itself; for, in some parts of it, he contends for the doctrine which I now maintain, and expresses himself in very different language from those relied on. I do not say this by way of detracting from the intellectual powers of the judge; but such is the infirmity of human nature, that it is difficult for the ablest man to be always consistent in argument. In his definition of treason, in the same *case, p.* 196. he says, that " any insurrection or rising of any body of people, within the United States, to attain or effect, by force or violence, any object of a great public nature, or of public and general (or national) concern, is a levying of war against the United States, within the contemplation and construction of the constitution." Thus excluding from his definition, the two circumstances which I have omitted in mine; military weapons, and the actual employment of force. In the next page, he expressly states, that military weapons, &c. are not essential in the consummation of treason; and yet in the course of the same charge, and in the same page, he seems to think, that some force must be employed, before the crime can be legally complete. In the former page, he lays down the doctrine for which I contend; which is the very same that was delivered in the *case of Bollman and Swartwout;* that is, that an assemblage of men for the purpose before described, is a "levying of war." After stating this in terms as precise as any in the English language, he says in the next page (197), that "some actual force or violence must be used, in pursuance of such design to levy war; but that it is altogether immaterial whether the force used be sufficient to effectuate the object; any force connected with the intention, will constitute the crime of levying war;" and however other parts of this opinion may be reconciled to each other, that part where he says, that the persons assembled must *use some force,* is incompatible with another part, where he declares, that *any insurrection* or rising of any body of *people,* to attain or effect by force, any object of a great "public nature, &c. is a levying of war," &c. In the one, some *actual force* is requisite; in the other, only an *insurrection or rising* of a body of the *people,* for the purpose of effecting their object by force, is deemed sufficient. I stated to you before, gentlemen, that the opinion, that they must have arms, is inconsistent with the principles of national policy, and opposed to the opinion of the supreme court.

It is only a mere *dictum* of judge Chase, in a case not necessary to be decided. The truth is, that he did not express himself on this subject, with the precision which he would have displayed, had the question before him, been what it was before the supreme court, and what it is here. In *2d Dallas's Reports, p.* 335, judge Patterson lays down the law on this subject, in exact conformity to the opinion of the supreme court; and does not think warlike weapons necessary to constitute an act of treason. Let me also refer to the argument of Mr. Lewis, who appeared as counsel in the defence of Fries, with as much zeal and professional ability, as any man could have done. I do not know him, but he is said to be a man of great ability and legal erudition. He would make no concession injurious to his client; and yet, in his elaborate argument, he says not one word about the employment of force, or the actual commission of hostilities. If they assemble without the employment of force, but for the purpose of effecting a treasonable design before their separation, they are traitors. Such is the law as defined by the supreme court, and admitted by a most able and zealous defender of a person prosecuted for treason.

These opinions and decisions are in conformity to the most respectable authorities and adjudications on criminal law, in

England. Treasons in that populous country are generally accompanied by force; but that the actual use of force, where the traitorous design of an assemblage of men is clearly proved, is not necessary, is, in my judgment, indisputably certain. *Foster*, in *p.* 211. says, that "all insurrections of a public and general concern, which in judgment of law are intended against the king, to dethrone or imprison him, to oblige him to alter his measures of goverment, or to remove evil counsellors, &c. amount to levying war within the statute, *whether with the pomp and open circumstances of war or no.*" The words here used, "levying war," are the very words adopted in the *constitution of the United States.* In *page* 218. he is still more explicit: "An assembly armed and arrayed in a warlike manner, for any treasonable purpose, is "*bellum levatum,*" though not "*bellum percussum:*" war levied, though not struck. See, also, *East's Crown Law, p.* 67. before referred to. After stating the same words, he adds, "*inlisting* and *marching* are *sufficient overt acts,* without coming to an actual engagement; in the same manner as cruising under an enemy's commission, though no act of express hostility be proved, is an adherence to the king's enemies." It shews, that according to the exposition of the law in England, it is not necessary that force should be employed before the act of treason shall be said to be completed. But whether I be correct in my exposition of the English law or not, is perfectly immaterial; because in our own country, the judges of the supreme court have placed this point beyond the reach of controversy; and I hope you are perfectly disposed to respect that opinion, which was in fact pronounced by yourself.

If, according to the decision of the supreme court, neither arms nor force be essential to constitute treason, I will ask, whether an assemblage of men on Blannerhassett's island, convened with a traitorous design, to be executed before their separation, were not treason against the United States?

You will be told, gentlemen, that *certainty* in criminal law is important, and, in that part which relates to treason, essential to public liberty. Perhaps you will be reminded of an observation of a celebrated writer, that uncertainty on this single point, is sufficient to convert a republican into a despotic government. This observation, though made by Montesquieu, is not admitted to be applicable to the government of this country, dependent as it is on the people; nor to our people, informed as they are of their rights. But suppose it to be so, it does not apply to the subject now under your consideration. The answer is as conclusive as it is obvious, that by the decision of the supreme court, the law is rendered certain. The decision of that court has pointed out to the people of the United States, the line beyond which they cannot go, without subjecting themselves to the consequences of the commission of treason. The court has said that conspiracy to levy war is not treason; that inlisting of men is not treason; that marching from a place of partial, to a place of general rendezvous is not treason: but that an assemblage of men convened to effectuate forcibly a traitorous intent, is traitorous; and all concerned in it are traitors. Every man may know the situation in which he stands, and at what point to stop, if he wish to avoid the imputation and the guilt of treason. You will probably be told, also, of the danger of constructive treasons. It may be observed, that in Great Britain, this doctrine has produced much oppression; and you may be asked, why we should be exempted from the same evils in this country? *Blackstone, in vol.* 4. of his *Commentaries, p.* 75. describes constructive treason thus: "to raise, by forced and arbitrary constructions, offences into the crime and punishment of treason, which never were suspected to be such;" of this, some terrible examples exist in the earlier periods of English history, when the people were ignorant, and the judges entirely dependent on the king.

It is admitted, that the doctrine which shall let in treasons, not defined by the constitution, by mere arbitrary constructions, influence or analogy, as in England formerly, ought not to be countenanced. But it will not be said, that there is in this country, any danger to be apprehended on this subject; where the government depends so much on the will of the people, and the people know so well their rights, and how to support them. I believe no danger from this consideration, is ever to be experienced here. It may serve as a topic of declamation, but the apprehension of real mischief from this source, is absolutely visionary.

But this is not a question arising on constructive treason, but on the constitution. The inquiry is, what is the meaning of the words used in the constitution? It is the business, no doubt, of the court to construe what is meant by the words " levying war." These words do not present to the mind, a precise and distinct idea, like the words " *murdering a man,*" or " *stealing a horse.*" If the question, what is "levying war?" were propounded distinctly and separately to every individual composing this assemblage, very few, even of the most intelligent among them, would have the temerity to answer, without great hesitation and doubt. The answer would be variant; perhaps as many opinions as men. Necessity therefore requires, that the courts should ascertain the construction of these words. It is their duty to do so. It is a task they have undertaken, when they became judges, and they have performed that task, by giving a reasonable construction of the meaning of the words used in the constitution, as descriptive of treason. This will not be called a constructive treason. It would be absurd to apply that term to it;

because it is absolutely necessary to define the offence. On this point, permit me to refer to the opinion of judge Peters, on *Fries's Trial, p.* 206, 7. " The doctrine of constructive treason, has produced much real mischief in another country; and it has been for an age, the subject of discussion, among lawyers, other public speakers, and political writers. The greater part of the objections to it, are totally irrelevant here. The subject of them is unknown, and may it ever remain so in this country. I mean the compassing the death of the king. It will be found, that the British judges, since the days of political darkness and bigotry have passed away, are to be found among the most able and decided opposers of the abuses of this doctrine. They do not follow decisions and doctrines rooted in bad times, because they find them in their law books. On the contrary, on a fair investigation, it will be proved, that those contrary to justice, reason and law, are rejected. It is not fair and sound reasoning, to argue against the *necessity and indispensable use* of construction, from the *abuses* it has produced. What is there among the best of *human* (and I wish I could not add divine) systems, which has not been perverted and abused? That there must be some *defined sense* and *interpretative exposition*, made of the terms ' *levying war*,' and *when* and in *what circumstances* it is *levied*, *against* the *United States*, cannot be denied. The able counsel in this case, who has said the most on this subject, and travelled the farthest into the gloomy, dark, and tyrannical periods of the British history, and jurisprudence, for melancholy and disgusting proofs of atrocious abuses, and even crimes, committed under colour of law, has unavoidably himself furnished also *proofs* of the *necessity* we are under, of some constructive or interpretative expositions. He at first confined these expositions to three cases. Now, if there be a necessity of *one*, it shews, that without *supplementary interpretation*, the law would be a mere dead letter: aware of the dangerous lengths to which the abuses of construction have been carried, courts and juries should be cautious in their decisions; but not so much alarmed about *abuses*, as to refrain from the *proper* and *necessary use* of interpretation." It is true, gentlemen, that there was a time, when the courts admitted any thing to be treason, which the king of that country wished to be treason: acts in themselves innocent, and which had no relation to treason, were construed to be treason; as coining money, where the party accused, had no idea of the commission of treason, but merely to perform the act of coining. Surely, gentlemen will not say, that constructive treason has been introduced into this country, because the judges are obliged to interpret this part of the constitution. If, gentlemen of the jury, the law thus established by the supreme court, shall be said to be a constructive treason, the inference is, that the judges ought to give no opinion on the meaning of the constitution on this subject; which would be absurd; for it is their solemn duty to construe the constitution and laws of the general government. Another inconvenience, that would result from the inability of the judges to expound the constitution, is, that the law would be perfectly uncertain, on the most interesting of all legal subjects; which would be a most grievous mischief, as juries would be under the necessity of taking upon themselves, the correct exposition of the law, or it must be conceded that the opinion of the supreme court is erroneous. The latter, I presume, is a position, which the counsel for the prisoner will hardly undertake to support.

If, however, they do undertake to shew, that the opinion of the court is incorrect, and that the crime of treason cannot be committed in this case; that, an assemblage of men with a traitorous design is not sufficient, but that actual force must be employed, and hostilities commenced before the treason is complete; the constitution is a dead letter: No man can be pronounced to be a traitor, till, by striking a blow, he be, or conceives himself to be, beyond the reach of the law, or have overthrown your government.

Perhaps it will be said that the decision of the supreme court is not correctly understood or stated by me. I may be incorrect in my exposition of it, but the language of the court is as definite and perspicuous, as any that can be conceived. If we do not understand it correctly, it is in vain to look into reported cases for evidence of the law, or to inquire what the law is. In every part of its judicial opinion, the ideas which it has expressed are perfectly consistent; and you will not find, from beginning to end, a sentence, or even a word, which implies, that any thing more is necessary for the completion of treason, than an assembly of men, convened for the purpose of executing a traitorous design.

I should therefore take it for granted, that the law is as I have stated it to be, and that the overt act of treason was complete, if there were an assemblage of men on Blannerhassett's island, in the county of Wood, whether they were armed or not, and whether they used force or not. It is incumbent on those who prosecute, to shew, 1st, That there was a treasonable design; and 2d, That there was an assemblage of men, for the purpose of effectuating that design. It will be proved to you, gentlemen of the jury, that the design of the prisoner, was not only to wage war against the Spanish provinces, but to take possession of the city of New-Orleans, as preparatory to that design; to detach the people of that country from this, and establish an independent government there, and to dismember the union, separate the western from the eastern states, making the Allegany mountains the boundary line. You will perceive from the evidence, that he intended to take possession of New-Orleans, to excite the people there to insurrection, and to take advantage of the hostile sentiments, which prevailed to the west of the Allegany against the Spaniards. If either of these be proved; if it be established that his design was to separate the states; or after seizing New-Orleans, to invade the Spanish provinces, he is guilty of treason. If in fact, it be proved, that he intended to take New-Orleans at all, he is completely guilty of treason; whether he designed to take possession of the whole or of a part, he is equally guilty of treason. It would be absurd, to suppose, that a man who had revolved in his mind, a scheme so gigantic as this, would communicate it to many persons. But he did disclose it to a few; and fortunately for our country, he was mistaken in his opinion of those persons in whom he confided; and the evidences of his design have been disclosed to our government. I am warranted in saying, gentlemen of the jury, that evidence the most positive and direct, and circumstances numerous and conclusive, will prove to your satisfaction, that the intentions of the accused were precisely such as I have mentioned.

For the purpose of accomplishing these great designs; of establishing an empire in the west, of which New-Orleans was to be the capital, and the accused was to be the chief, he made two long visits to the western country. He went to Ohio, Tennessee and Kentucky, in fact to all the western world, and travelled in various directions, till he went finally to New-Orleans. Wherever he went, he spoke disrespectfully of the government of his country, with a view to facilitate the consummation of his own designs. He represented it as destitute of energy to support or defend our national rights against foreign enemies, and of spirit to maintain our national character. He uniformly said, that we had no character either at home or abroad. To those in whom he confided, he asserted, that all the men of property and influence were dissatisfied with its arrangements, because they were not in the proper situation to which they were entitled: that with five hundred men he could effect a revolution by which he could send the president to Monticello, intimidate congress, and take the government of the United States into his own hands; that the people of the United States had so little knowledge of their rights, and so little disposition to maintain them, that they would meanly and tamely acquiesce in this shameful usurpation. This is the very language of the prisoner, about the government and people; representing the one as totally destitute of all energy and talents, and the other of all patriotism and virtue. But he confined this language to the people of the east; he spoke a different language to the people of the west. He told them, that they were in a state of colonial dependence on those of the Atlantic states, and annually paid millons to the government of the United States, for which they derived no benefit whatever; for which they received no protection, no return. The people on the other side of the Allegany were told, that a separation was necessary and would unquestionably take place; that it was not likely to take effect by the operation of natural, of moral and political causes, but as determined by a particular chain of events; that the destiny of the republic was fixed, and that this revolution would be accomplished in less than two years. I thank God that this prediction has not been fulfilled, and I hope our posterity to the latest generation will thank God that it has not been fulfilled before their time! Such was the language of the accused; such the sentiments which he avowed, and the doctrines which he endeavoured to propagate. He said every thing to dissatisfy them with their brethren of the east, though all this time he pretended that his objects were of a purely agricultural nature. Nor did he confine himself to conversation with intelligent men only; there were writings published that came from the pen of the person who is indicted, as connected with him, calculated to scatter disaffection among the people and prepare them for his plans.

To accomplish these plans, in the summer and fall of 1806, men were actually inlisted, boats were built on the waters of the Ohio, provisions purchased to an enormous amount, and arms and ammunition provided, as if the object was meant to be carried into effect in a foreign nation; and as if some hostile expedition were on foot. Some of these men, about 40 in number, assembled with arms, on Blannerhassett's island, in order to descend the river. Burr was not there then; he had been there only a short time before, and intended to return, but was warned not to return; but his absence at the time when the people assembled is totally immaterial. A man may " *levy war*" against his country, when not present. A man may " *levy war*" against a country, though three thousand miles distant. This we may probably have an experience of in the course of a very few months. But this principle has been sufficiently established by the decision of the supreme court. " If war be actually levied, all those who perform any part, however minute, *or however remote from the scene of action*, and who are actually leagued in the general conspiracy, are to be considered as traitors."

These troops on the island, seeing the country alarmed, and apprehending that they would be attacked by the militia of

Wood county, made a precipitate retreat by night, in company with Blannerhassett, and went down the Ohio to the mouth of Cumberland river, where the accused joined them and took the command. By this time their numbers increased to about one hundred. These men under the command of Burr and Blannerhassett, descended the Mississippi to Bayou Pierre, a point not far from Natchez. It was here, gentlemen of the jury, that he first learned that all his schemes would be frustrated by the exertions of the commander in chief; that his letter in cypher had been communicated to the president; and it was here that in the first moment of surprize, he expressed to another person his astonishment and indignation, at being (as he said) thus betrayed. Finding that the commander in chief, had baffled all his schemes, by communicating his letter to the president, he entered into a kind of capitulation with Cowles Meade, was bound to appear before a tribunal at Natchez, from whence, it is said, he came off without leave of the court, in violation of his recognisance, and in his flight was taken by Perkins.

It will be proved to you, by express and direct evidence, that a settlement of lands on the Washita, was merely a cover to conceal the *real design*, which was to separate the union, take possession of New-Orleans, and attack the Spanish provinces. But the utmost mystery and circumspection prevailed on this subject. To the world at large, and to those with whom he had not tampered, the object was held up to be, the settlement of lands up the Red river. To some, intimations were dropped, of an approaching rupture with Spain, against whose provinces the expedition was intended, and the conquest of Mexico was alluded to; his language varied according to the character of the man with whom he conversed. To a few only his real design was developed; but to all he said that there was a great scheme in view. All were told, that the design was just and honorable; known and approved by the government; in which the cooperation of the army was to be expected; in which great wealth was to be acquired, and that it would be developed as soon as the proper time for the disclosure arrived. The time, however, never did arrive. At Blannerhassett's island, they were told, that it was not the time, but that when they came to the mouth of Cumberland, they should be informed. When there, some of them, whose intentions were really honest, who were not disposed to violate the laws of their country, and who were induced to join him by the expectation of acquiring wealth, by laudable and honorable enterprise, were anxious and endeavoured to know, what was the real design: but circumstances, they were told, were such, that it could not yet be communicated. Ignorant people were led away from their homes, under a belief that they would be speedily informed of the whole project. The information was promised, but never imparted. The consequence was, that when Mr. Burr was apprehended, they were left to find the way back to their own homes, by any means in their power.

Chimerical as this project was, there was only one single thing wanting to its accomplishment; the cooperation of the commander in chief, and of the American army. If general Wilkinson had acted as some have represented, if he had acted the part of a traitor instead of performing the character of a patriot, I ask what would have been the situation of this country at this moment? There would have been a civil war raging in the west; and the people of the United States, united as they are, by interest, by sympathy and blood, would have been involved in a sanguinary contest with one another; while our eastern coasts would have been insulted and ravaged by an insolent and rapacious foe, in consequence of their knowledge of our divided situation. From this calamity in the west, we have been protected by the vigilance and integrity of the commander in chief. I care not how my declaration may be considered; but I will venture to assert, that from the adoption of the federal constitution, till this time, no man has rendered more essential service to the people and government of the United States, than general Wilkinson has done, by counteracting and defeating this project. Yet, for this service, eminent and important as it is, he has been as much censured, abused, and calumniated, as if he had joined in it.

It is not for me to anticipate the defence which will be made for the accused, but I presume I may speak of the defence which he *has* made. He stated himself, while under examination, that his scheme was peaceful and agricultural. If this ground shall be again taken, it will be extremely easy to satisfy you, by a variety of circumstances, that this was not the scheme contemplated by those engaged in that expedition. I intend hereafter, if necessary, to enter into an enumeration of those circumstances, but at present I feel myself too much exhausted to detail them.

I have observed, that you would enter upon this inquiry with candour and patience, and I must hope too with firmness. You will contemplate and decide this question, on the same principles, under the same laws, and in the same manner, as if the question were between the United States and the most ignorant and deluded of those concerned in the scheme. It is true, that the prisoner has been vice-president of the United States; he has been the second in office in the government of this country, and perhaps the second in the confidence and affection of the people; and that he possesses talents and energies, which at the approaching crisis, might have been employed most honorably for himself, and most usefully for his country: but these circumstances rather aggravate than extenuate his guilt, if he be guilty. In other countries, a discrimination may be made between different classes of the community; it is not often that the laws of society operate upon men of this stamp in those countries. Lord George Gordon, the miserable fanatic, who marched at the head of the rioters in London in the year 1781, was discharged, while eighteen or nineteen of his poor deluded followers paid the forfeit of their offences, and were punished for *his* crimes. I call upon you, gentlemen of the jury, to disregard all such distinctions in this land of liberty, equality and justice; and to view this case, in the same light in which you would regard it, if any other man in the community were brought before you. I call on you to do justice and to decide the cause according to the evidence which will be produced before you.

After Mr. Hay concluded, some desultory observations were made by the counsel on both sides, with respect to the accommodation of the jury, and the times of meeting and adjourning the court, during the trial. Some arrangements were proposed for the jury; that they were to occupy convenient rooms in the capitol at night, and in the recess of the court; that for the sake of exercise, they might walk out in a body or separately, if accompanied by the marshal or one of his deputies; that they might send or receive letters, if shewn to the marshal: but that all letters should be laid before the court, which should appear to relate to the trial, and be designedly sent to influence their verdict. These arrangements were not adopted at this time, but their consideration postponed, all parties being desirous to accommodate the jury as much as possible, consistently with the necessity of keeping them together, secure from intrusion.

On the question, how long the court ought to be occupied every day during the trial, colonel Burr expressed a wish, that the court, should for the sake of expediting business, meet at as early and adjourn at as late an hour as possible. He referred to trials in England, where the court sat twelve and sixteen hours every day; and proposed that the court should sit ten or twelve hours each day. This was opposed as too long, fatiguing and oppressive in such warm weather.

The CHIEF JUSTICE said, that the court had no wish on the subject, but was willing to consult the convenience of the gentlemen of the bar, and the accommodation of the jury.

It was then proposed, that the court should meet at nine o'clock in the morning, and sit till four in the afternoon; this was finally determined.

Mr. HAY proceeded then to the examination of the witnesses summoned on the part of the United States; general William Eaton was sworn, when

Colonel BURR rose and objected to this order of examining the witnesses. He said Mr. Hay had not stated the nature of Mr. Eaton's testimony; but he presumed that it related to certain conversations said to have happened at Washington; adding, that the propriety of admitting any other testimony, depended on the previous proof of an overt act.

Mr. HAY.—Our object is to prove by him, what is contained in his deposition, which has been published.

Mr. BOTTS, Mr. WICKHAM and Mr. MARTIN, then called on them to prove (what they said the court had already determined to be the proper course of proceeding) an overt act. They presumed that, if the decision of this court were to be respected, gentlemen should call on the witnesses to prove facts before declarations. But if gentlemen did not admit that this point had been already sufficiently determined by the court, it would be their duty to go into a recapitulation of the arguments, and quotation of the authorities heretofore referred to, unless the court would say, that the question had been already decided. Their object was to save the time of the court; they knew that there had been a great deal of war in the newspapers: but they also knew from actual experience and positive knowledge, that there had been no war in fact in this country; and knowing that there has been in fact no war, are we, (they asked), to be entertained by this and that idle story; to waste several weeks at great expence and trouble; detain from their homes, the court, counsel and jury, and keep the prisoner in a very unpleasant situation; and all for no useful purpose, in the discussion of points entirely irrelevant to the question in issue? Shall we be told in justification of this great waste of time, and this immense trouble, that they mistook the law and the testimony; that they *expected* to prove an overt act, but were disappointed?

They further contended, that the material fact on which all the merits of the controversy depended ought first to be proved in every case; that it would be irregular, irrational and illegal to admit corroborative testimony, before proof was adduced of the principal fact, which it was intended to confirm. They admitted that it was usual, in most criminal prosecutions, to call on the prosecutor to begin his proof in support of either point, fact or intention, as he might deem proper; but, they said, there were two reasons for this practice. First, every prosecutor, learned in criminal law, began with proving the fact on which principally the charge was founded. Or, secondly, the fact was known to be susceptible of clear proof, and therefore, there was an acquiescence on the part of the accused with respect to the commission of that fact. As in the case of a prosecution for murder: the fact of killing ought certainly to be first proved; but it is generally so well known to have been committed by the accused, that there is no question made on that point; and the defence arises from the motives or inducement to the perpetration of the act whether justifiable or excusable. In such a case, it would be ridiculous to inquire into the causes or circumstances of the killing, till the death were proved; but in all other cases of a similar nature, where the fundamental fact was denied, it must be proved before any confirmatory proof should be admitted. And wherever a prosecutor, from inadvertence, want of experience, or any other cause, began at the wrong end of the prosecution, and the accused himself did not see cause to acquiesce, he had a right to apply to the court, to require proof of the principal fact. They argued with great ingenuity and at considerable length in support of this principle; that the court ought not to admit corroborative testimony, in anticipation of the principal fact, to corroborate which, it is sought to be introduced. They referred to the former decision of the court, relative to this same point, on the motion to hold colonel Burr to bail in a greater sum of money, than had been at first required, and insisted that the order of evidence was part of the law of evidence; that the court was to judge of the competency of testimony, and had a right to stop any evidence which it deemed immaterial; that it was of no avail to prove intentions or designs before an *overt act*, an *open deed of war*, had been established; that, as in a writ of ejectment, it would be ridiculous to begin with proving the boundaries before the *title* was proved, so, it was improper to begin with the declarations of colonel Burr, or any conversations, until the overt act were shewn; that these declarations could only be admitted as confirmatory evidence; that it would be peculiarly hard on any individual, to ransack and expose all the transactions of his whole life in a court of justice; that nothing was more repugnant to justice, than to discuss, misrepresent, and torture every conversation, however innocent, which he had held, and every declaration, however loose and inadvertent, which he had made at any time, and on any occasion, before it was known, whether any actual crime could be proved against him; that if the prosecutor would thus proceed to develop the intention only, the court had a right to stop him, and require the production of evidence, of the act itself. They made many other observations to the same purport. They cited *Foster, p.* 246. and Judge Iredell's opinion on *Fries's Trial,* the *Case of Smith and Ogden,* and *Hardy's Case.* Their arguments on this doctrine are considerably condensed; because it was afterwards, with other points, very fully and elaborately discussed on the motion made by Mr. Wickham, to arrest the evidence.

Mr. WIRT addressed the court on this subject, as follows:

After expressing his regret at the unnecessary waste of so much time, by so many motions and obstacles thrown in the way of the prosecution, by the accused, he contended, that the opposition made to the introduction of this testimony, and to the arrangement of the attorney for the United States, was unprecedented; that from the first foundation of courts to this day, it had been the practice for the prosecutor to display the evidence in his own way; and that it manifested a disrespect to the attorney, to require a departure from it, in this instance. I defy, said Mr. Wirt, the gentlemen to produce a single example, from all the English authorities, from the whole history of their jurisprudence, where the attorney general, or the counsel for the crown, has been arrested in the introduction or arrangement of the evidence, by the counsel of the defendant, and put on a different course. I defy them to produce a single example, of any interference with the course adopted by the prosecutor. It depends on himself, who knows the evidence best, to state and exhibit it according to his own judgment. If the whole evidence be adduced, the result will be the same, in whatever manner it may be arranged; but the chronological order which the attorney was about to pursue, unfolding events as they occurred, is no less conformable to law and reason, than sanctioned by uniform experience. It develops this conspiracy from its birth to its consummation; unravels the plot from its conception to its denoument, and traces Aaron Burr step by step as he advanced and became more bold, till the act was consummated, by the assemblage on Blannerhassett's island. Is not this the lucid order of nature and reason? Would you begin to narrate a tale at the end of it? If you were to write a history of the late revolution, would you begin at the siege of York? We wish to display the history of facts as they happened, not only because it is the most luminous mode of communicating them to the jury, but because it is our duty to vindicate it as the right of the attorney, as consistent with universal practice in prosecutions, both in our own, and every other civilized country. Examples of a contrary practice, might be found in England, if it ever existed; but no case can be shewn in the courts of Great Britain, where the counsel for a prisoner has been permitted on a trial, to invert the order of chronology for his own purposes. I refer the court to the *Trial of Hardy, pages* 95, 96, 97. Though that case is not directly applicable to the case now before the court, I introduce it, to shew the independence of the attorney general of England, in conducting prosecutions, and introducing testimony as he thinks proper; and to prove that the opposition now made to our evidence, is unusual in that country. He introduced many letters and papers against Hardy, and *declarations* of his associates. In *p.* 95, " Then followed the correspondence between Mr. Hardy as secretary to the corresponding society, and Mr. Gerald and Mr. Margarot, two of the delegates at the convention in Edinburgh; most of these papers were printed also in the appendix to the report of the committee of secrecy." They were produced by a witness of the name of Gurnell. These papers being all read by the officer of the court, Mr. Bowen said, " My lords, *we now propose, on the part of the crown, to read the proceedings* of the *convention itself.*" To this, Mr. Erskine, for the prisoner, objected; because, though the society had been formed, the object of its formation had not yet been heard of by evidence; that if Margarot and Gerald had exceeded the letter and spirit of their instructions, the prisoner could not be affected by it; that he was charged with no act of the convention at Edinburgh. " He is charged," said Mr. Erskine, *p.* 96, " with having encompassed the death of the king; to prove that he had that wicked intention, the evidence should be clear, and refer tò the act itself; *but no act can be given in evidence*, that *does not go to shew, that the prisoner had that encompassing in his own heart at the time the act was committed.*" This shews his conviction, that proof of the intention may precede that of the acts; *p.* 97. " I must take care that the rules of law are preserved inviolate. All that I mean to say, is, that if Mr. Hardy knew of the proceedings of this convention in Edinburgh, then my objection falls to the ground in this respect." The lord president agreed that the evidence proposed, could not be adduced *immediately* against the prisoner. He observed, however, that it might be let in; but that the application of it was another thing. At all events, the prisoner might afterwards object that the delegates had exceeded their commission, and that objection would be valid so far. Mr. Bower. " Yes, my lord, *we mean to shew*, in many instances, *the prisoner's subsequent approbation of the proceedings of the British convention.*" The lord president. " *That declaration is enough to let in the evidence*, the application of it will depend on what will further appear."

Now, sir, how were the proceedings of this convention admitted as evidence? The court decided, that they should be first read, and applied afterwards by other testimony, to Hardy. Did the court tell the prosecutor, " *you shall stop*, till *you shew a previous connexion between them*, and *his subsequent approbation;*

you shall not read these proceedings?" The attorney told the court
" *I will adduce evidence to let the testimony in. I will prove, his
approbation subsequently."* The attorney's *declaration,* of his *intention* to prove the approbation of Hardy, was respected by the
court, and those proceedings were permitted to be read. Now
here was an evident perversion of the rule, for which the gentlemen contend. For according to it, the subsequent approbation of
Hardy ought to have been proved before the proceedings of the
convention; the admissibility of the latter depended on the'proof
of the former. If this approbation could not have been proved
afterwards, the reading of the proceedings would have been illegal and the time employed in it lost. But the court did not stop
the attorney. It told him, *on your declaration that you will
bring it home to Hardy, you may read the evidence now.* Yet this
was a direct perversion of the doctrine which gentlemen wish
now to establish. Why should not the same respect be paid to
the declarations of the attorney for the United States in this
case? If you permit us to proceed in the way we propose, we
shall neither violate principle nor waste time. Can there be an
overt act of treason without an intention to commit it? Can any
assemblage, however large, armed or arrayed, however disorderly and tumultuous, commit an act of treason without intending it? and ought not their intention be proved? The rule of law
excludes whatever does not touch the issue; but the intention
is an important feature in that issue. Every transaction derives
its character principally from the intention. It is the great point
in every case. Yet we are stopped from explaining the intention
by a pretended difficulty; that its premature introduction tends
to fetter the minds of the jury, as if the proof of the intention
preceding that of the act, did not present an unity of action from
the birth to the consummation of the design. But we are to be
stopped. The objection manifests a want of respect for the attorney, as if he knew not, better than any other, the nature and
bearing of the evidence, and how to unfold it, in the most regular way. It is improper not only for this reason, but because
the mode we propose, is the most luminous and correct; it is
the order of nature itself, as it traces the transactions from beginning to end. We insist on its correctness for another reason;
because the method they propose, cannot produce a single
good effect. Gentlemen say, that if we prove the *overt act* first,
we can be permitted to shew the design afterwards. They say
that none is yet proved. Suppose we prove no overt act in the
opinion of the court, how are the jury to be disposed of? Could
you send them out to deliberate or could you discharge them?
If the prosecutor state that he is about to proceed to prove the
intention, can the court say that it does not prove the overt act,
and that therefore they will send the jury out without hearing the

evidence respecting the intention? The court has no such pow-ers. The only power which the court possesses is, not to direct the order in which the evidence shall be introduced, but to instruct them on the law; to direct whether the evidence be *competent* or *incompetent* to be laid before the jury: to determine its *weight* or *sufficiency* to prove the overt act is the exclusive province of the jury. The court cannot withhold from them any evidence touching the issue. Will the court stop us? Will the court or the jury decide on the issue? All the authorities of the law concur in this, that the *whole testimony* shall come before the jury; that they have a right to hear the whole and decide on it.

The only inquiry now is, as to the order in which it shall be introduced. We insist that the mode which we propose, is the most luminous, and most favourable to a complete comprehen-sion·of the subject; and that that which they maintain, is the most confused and worst calculated to attain that end.

I will·refer you to the sentiments delivered by judge Iredell, on the *Trial of Fries, pages* 174, 175: Mr. Lewis having stated a question, whether the overt act laid in the indictment in a cer-tain county, must not be proved to the satisfaction of the jury, both as to fact and intention in the same county; or whether the overt act did not include both fact and intention? Judge Iredell replied, " that he considered *Foster's Crown Law*, as settling that point. When two witnesses are produced, who prove the overt act laid in the indictment, there might then be evidence from other counties, respecting the intention. This is the opinion of judge Foster, and it is my opinion. But there is another thing. It goes to a point which is inadmissible; *it is not for the court to say, whether there were a treasonable intention or act as charged in the indictment; that is for the jury to determine, we have only to state the law. We therefore should have no right to give an opi-nion upon it.* Again, if no evidence could regularly be admitted out of the county, until both the fact and intention were esta-blished, where the crime is laid, the consequence would be, that there ought to be some way of taking the opinion of the jury, whether they believed that the crime was committed at Bethle-hem, before the court could proceed to extraneous testimony! This cannot be done. A *jury must give a verdict on all the evi-dence collectively:* if the evidence be admitted, then the jury is bound to respect the weight of it; *the competency of that evi-dence is for the court to decide; but the jury must estimate its weight.*" You cannot stop the prosecutor after he has given a part of the evidence. The jury must hear the whole, and make up an opinion on the whole. Neither the court nor the gentle-men can stop us. If we prove an act in the course of the whole evidence, it will suffice. If we prove either first, we must go a step beyond that, and prove the other, so as to shew that it is a complete overt act of treason.

Mr. Botts has referred to the opinion of judge Iredell, but certainly it cannot be interpreted in his favour. The judge is not contemplating the *order* of evidence; he speaks of the evidence to the jury. The point before him was, not the *order* of the evidence, but the propriety or impropriety of its introduction at all. The inquiry was, whether the prisoner were guilty of levying war against the United States, at Bethlehem, in Northhampton county, and whether the evidence supported that charge? and the judge told the jury, that, if the prisoner went to the place where the act was committed, with treasonable intentions, the treason was complete. He investigated nothing but the *propriety* of the evidence. Of its *order*, nothing was said. The court cannot stop the inquiry. Who is to judge of the evidence of the overt act? The court? Will the court tell the jury *when they* are satisfied, that the overt act has been proved? *When* are we to be stopped? Is the court to decide at what stage of the evidence we are to be stopped? If the court stop us before we adduce all our evidence, they usurp the power of deciding on the evidence. Is this a part of your functions? I think not. The whole evidence must be laid before the jury; the court taking care not to let in any but what is legal. The authority quoted by Mr. Botts, from *Foster*, 216. has no sort of application to this point.

The principle of the decision in *Vaughan's case* is not against us. The indictment against captain Vaughan, was for adhering to the king's enemies on the high seas; and the overt act laid was his cruising on the king's subjects, in a vessel called the " *Loyal Clencarty.*" The counsel for the prosecution offered evidence to prove, that he had some time before, cut away the custom house barge, and had gone a cruising in her. This evidence was opposed by the prisoner's counsel, and rejected by the court; " *for were it true*, it is no sort of proof, that the prisoner had cruised in the Loyal Clencarty, which was the only fact he was then to answer for." This case only proves, that on a trial on an indictment for any *specific* treason, evidence of a previous intention to commit a distinct substantive treason, is inadmissible; or in other words, that the evidence must prove the charge; it being a principle universally correct, that an offence different from that which is charged, shall not be proved. It was merely the rejection of evidence foreign to the point in issue. It only proves that no evidence of what is a different and distinct substantive treason of itself, shall be admitted to support any indictment. This doctrine ought to have more effect in England than in this country, since the abuses against which it is intended to secure, might there be more extensively injurious than here: but the same court allowed other overt acts to be given in evidence, for the purpose of shewing the intention of the prisoner. It is, indeed, as Foster says, a sound and just rule, that all evidence *without the issue*, should be rejected: but how can testimony, shewing the intention of Aaron Burr, be said to be without the issue? It goes directly to prove the treason in the indictment.

The doctrine in *Smith and Ogden, p.* 82. explains the danger of going out of the statement in the indictment, and shews the necessity of preserving the principle, " that the evidence must be pertinent to the issue." The exhibition of proof of Aaron Burr's intentions is within the rule established in the English courts, and the decision in *Smith and Ogden.*

Mr. Wirt further remarked, that the former decision of this court on this point, which gentlemen had thought proper to refer to as decisive in their favour, could not be rightly so considered: that two material circumstances would justify this conclusion. First, the court at that time wished to avoid such a discussion and display of the evidence as might prejudice the public mind. Second, the court then decided on the law and the fact, and performed the duties of judge and juror. It might decide when it was proper to stop or proceed; he satisfied with the testimony already introduced, or require more. But that now the jury were to decide on the guilt or innocence of the accused, the court had only to state the law on the different points arising in the course of the trial.

Mr. Lee in substance contended, that the act, *an open deed of war*, committed in the full view of the world, on the 10th day of December, on Blannerhassett's island, if it ever existed, was susceptible of clear proof; that the time, place and manner of committing the offence, as laid in the indictment, were material to be proved; that it was not pretended that the counsel for the prosecution, had any right to exhibit proof of any other treason than that specified in the indictment; that the *effect* of the facts to be proved, must be discussed hereafter, but that the *proof* of them, as preliminary to, and the foundation of, other testimony, was indispensably requisite; that it was difficult to describe the absurdity to which the admission of other evidence, before proof of the acts authorising that admission, would lead; that it would be almost as inconsistent and improper, as to attempt to make the effect precede its cause, or according to the vulgar phraseology, to put the cart before the horse; that it would be changing the rules of law; that a great deal of time might be occupied in adducing a great deal of testimony, to charge a man accused of murder, with malignant intentions, when the person said to be murdered, *was actually alive;* or of arson, when the house alleged to be burnt was standing; that the act existed, or it did not. If it existed, it ought to be immediately proved: if it did not exist, they ought magnanimously to yield, as they could not produce that testimony which might render all other evidence applicable.

Mr. Lee further dilated with great force and ingenuity ; but for the reasons before mentioned, his arguments are necessarily condensed.

Mr. MARTIN spoke to the following effect:

I shall take the liberty of adding a few observations, to what has been already said.

The great question is, whether the prosecutors must not prove an overt act in the first instance, before any other evidence can be introduced? We contend that they must, and that law and reason support us. They admit that colonel Burr must be proved to have committed one or more overt acts; and that the court and jury must be satisfied, that these acts were committed with a treasonable design; that he *levied war* against the United States, with intent to destroy the constitution and government thereof. This is the true construction of the words " *levying war*." There can be no " levying war," unless the object and design be the subversion of the government of the United States. It is admitted that both these things must be proved, before he can be found guilty. The question which results necessarily is, which of them is first to be proved? The very eloquent and ingenious counsel admit, that it is not of much consequence, in which order these facts are to be established; but insist on proceeding as they have done, for two reasons; first, because it is the most correct and usual mode; and secondly, because it is a mark of disrespect to the attorney of the United States, to interfere with his arrangement of the evidence. As to the second cause, which I think proper to answer first, I will only say, that we cannot conceive, why they should have construed the performance of a professional duty, into a manifestation of disrespect for the gentleman. We exercised a right and discharged a duty to our client, in opposing what we deemed an illegal proceeding. How then can he consider himself treated disrespectfully? He certainly has no right to view it in that light. We had no such intention; and I will say further, that if he conduct himself with that mildness and decorum, which ever becomes a public prosecutor, he shall receive from us every mark of respect. As to the first and principal reason urged by gentlemen in support of this mode of conducting the prosecution, that it is the most correct order of proceeding; it might be proper, if it were an indictment for a conspiracy to commit treason, to proceed in the first instance, to prove the intentions: but in this prosecution for treason for " *levying war*," I confidently say, that the most natural order of proceeding, is, to begin with proving the material act, without which, all other evidence whatsoever, would be irrelevant and improper. In Great Britain, a conspiracy to commit treason is made treason by a particular statute; that is, " compassing the death of the king," is made high treason. In that particular instance, the intention, the *mere act of the mind* is rendered, what it is in no other case without an act in pursuance of it, criminal and punishable. In that case, which is in fact a conspiracy to commit treason, the intention of the heart, the formation of the design in the mind is the very crime; and the correct mode of procedure on a trial for it, would be to begin to shew the conspiracy, the number of persons engaged in it, the *time when*, and *place where*, they did conspire, and other circumstances connected with the conspiracy: but this applies only to a prosecution on an indictment for compassing the death of the king. In every other case, where a *material* act constitutes the crime, the prosecutor must begin by proving that act, either by positive testimony or strong circumstances, to shew that the party accused committed it. In a prosecution for treason for " *levying war*," after the cause is opened, proof of the act should be adduced, as is done in every other criminal case. On a trial for murder, the act of killing must first be proved, if not admitted; in a prosecution for burglary, the nocturnal breaking into the house must be proved; in larceny, the taking and carrying away must be proved; and in a prosecution for robbery, it is necessary to prove the taking by force and violence from the person, before any testimony can be admitted respecting the felonious intention. The true and natural order in all prosecutions is to shew first that the principal act on which the charge depends has been committed.

The gentleman who opened the cause argued it on the principles of common sense, which he says is sometimes in discussion not adhered to by lawyers. Let us examine whether he has himself verified this sentiment, and how his doctrine applies to this case. Does not common sense require, that the act which is the very foundation of the charge, should be proved in the first instance? Would it not be absurd to go into evidence to shew that the *act* was committed with a treasonable *intent*, without any testimony to prove that the act was committed at all? Is it rational to inquire into the design and intention with which an act has been performed, without proving that it *has been performed?*

The gentleman who spoke so eloquently against our motion, says, that the jury must judge of the weight of evidence, and that the court cannot stop the prosecutor in his examination of witnesses, and command the jury to find such a verdict as it pleases to require! The general principle is not controverted by us, but we deny the inferences which he has drawn from it. The jury are certainly to decide on the *weight* of evidence, but the court is to pronounce the law, on *what is* or *is not legal evidence.*

Suppose only one witness were introduced to prove the overt act, and it were candidly declared by the counsel for the prosecution that he could prove it by no other witness, would he be permitted then to proceed to examine the intentions of the party accused? Would it not then be the duty of the court to stop him, and tell the gentlemen of the jury, that there was no evidence to convict the accused; that it would be in vain to proceed farther, since it was admitted, that the constitutional requisition of two witnesses to prove the overt act, could not be complied with? We do not contend, that the court has a right to tell the jury, " you *must acquit* the party;" but it is undoubtedly its duty to expound and enforce the law, and this is all we want to be done.

Permit me again, to recur to the case of a trial for murder. A great deal of the time of the court might be taken up to prove malice on the part of the person indicted, when in truth no *act* could be proved, when it *did not* and *could not* appear that the man supposed to have been murdered was actually dead! This would be a fruitless waste of time. If there be no evidence that the man is dead, there ought to be no inquiry into the design inducing the commission of the overt act, the act of killing. If the death be proved, then the intention and other circumstances are to be examined, and the jury must decide whether he be guilty or not. This is the natural and legal order of proceeding in criminal prosecutions. Hardy's case confirms and establishes the propriety of this mode of proceeding. The first inquiry on that trial was respecting the act charged in the indictment.

Thus, if A. were indicted for killing B. would the legal order be to prove, in the first instance, that long and frequent animosities had existed between them? The counsel for the prosecution must first prove, that B. has been killed by some body. If there be any doubt as to the person who killed him, it must be proved who did kill him. If it be proved that A. killed B. then, and not till then, more evidence is necessary to explain the motives and circumstances of the killing; because the law presumes *prima facie*, that a man who kills another, does it with malice prepense, and therefore he must take off by his proof, this presumption of the law. In the case of larceny, as for instance, for horse stealing, you prove the horse to have been taken from the owner, and found in possession of the party accused. After proving the principal fact, you go into evidence of the intention with which the horse was taken. Does the public prosecutor go into proof of the felonious intention, before proving that the horse has been taken? So in the case of burglary, is it the natural order of testimony, to prove that the accused intended to break and enter into the house, in the night time, to steal or to commit any other felony? Is it not the most natural order, to prove first, that he did actually break and enter the house, and then by evidence to shew, that he entered with no other view than to commit a felony. So on a trial for treason, for importing false or base foreign coin, knowing it to be such, does the prosecutor first call witnesses to prove, that the prisoner knew the coin to be base? Does he not first prove the importation? Would it not be preposterous to go into proof of his knowledge of its baseness, without proving that he imported it? The same remark applies to a prosecution for passing false or counterfeit coin, knowing it to be false or counterfeit. Would not the prosecutor first prove, that he passed it, and then shew by testimony, that he knew it to be base when he passed it? In both cases, he first proves the principal fact, without which all other testimony would be useless; and then proves the circumstances which shew that the prisoner must have known the money to be base when he imported or passed it. They charge us with having committed treason in *" levying war"* against the United States. This charge is too vague, and must be supported by full testimony according to the well known principles of the law. Here let me mention, that the question, whether any other act committed at a time and place different from those stated in the indictment can be introduced in evidence on this trial, is a distinct question from that now before the court; which is merely, what is the proper order of introducing the evidence in support of the indictment?

Let me advert to the case of Hardy. It was an indictment for compassing the death of the king, which as I have already mentioned, is distinguishable from all other cases, in this, that the *intention* constitutes the crime. In that case, " what is the natural and *lucid* order" of evidence, is expressly laid down. There were several persons prosecuted in the same indictment. It charged them " First, with a conspiracy to compass or effect the king's death. Secondly, with endeavouring to effect that object, by means of an insurrection, or inciting the insurrection with that settled design." The court determined, that the legal order of proceeding and admitting evidence, after having proved the existence of the conspiracy, was to prove the connexion of the person accused with the conspirators; and then to charge him with the acts of the conspirators; that after proving his connexion with them, he was liable to be charged with any of their acts. In that case, the *intention constituted the crime*, and the connexion between the conspirators was first proved, before the acts of one were admitted to be given in evidence against another. But this mode of proceeding, is only admitted in the case of a conspiracy, or an indictment for *imagining* and compassing the king's death. But in an indictment for " *levying war*," the *acts* of one person have never been admitted to be given in evidence against another; the overt acts must be proved against every individual accused. This distinction has been established by a series of determinations of the most able and correct judges. But if the acts of one cannot be charged or given in evidence against another, much less can his words or declarations. Sir, the declarations of the party accused are not legal evidence against him. Here they have brought witnesses, from remote parts of the union, to prove the declarations of colonel Burr. I contend, that till an act of war shall have been proved, these declarations are utterly inadmissible against him. The gentlemen admit themselves, that they are improper, unless as corroborative evidence; because the constitution requires, that the confession of the person accused shall be in open court, before a conviction shall follow. I am convinced, that all the declarations in the world can only be received as corroborative evidence of facts proved within the dictrict. I do not wish to enlarge the question, or to waste the time of the court in discussing questions touching acts committed out of the district, or declarations explanatory of them. If any such evidence should be offered in the progress of this investigation, the court will of course stop it.

I agree with the attorney of the United States, in expressing my approbation of some parts of the opinion of judge Iredell, on the trial of Fries, which applied immediately to the case before the court. I shall agree, with heart and hand, that no words or declaration of a person accused of this crime, ought to be admitted in evidence, unless they are preceded by proof of facts. One part of his opinion has an immediate application to the question now before the court, where he says, " that *after* the overt act laid in the district is *proved* by *two witnesses*, it is proper to go into evidence to shew the course of the prisoner's conduct at other places, and the purpose for which he went to that place where the treason is laid, and if he went with a treasonable design, then the act of treason is conclusive." But still this evidence is improper, till *after* the overt act is proved. From another part of the same opinion, which immediately follows, in pages 171, 172, of that trial, he says, " We now come to the confession of the prisoner, voluntarily made before judge Peters. Here is a point of law relied on by the prisoner's counsel, that no man should be convicted of treason, but on the evidence of two witnesses, or *upon confession in open court*. This is the provision in England as well as here, and the meaning is, that no confession of the prisoner, *independent of two witnesses*, or *without the facts have been established by two witnesses*, should *be sufficient to convict him:* but if *two witnesses have proved a fact, the confession of the party may be received by way of confirmation, of what has before been sworn to.* In former days, in England, it was allowed, that confession out of court, and the proof of the witnesses should be sufficient to warrant a conviction, *but happily*, *our constitution would not admit it, if an hundred* would swear to it; that danger is wisely avoided. Evidence may sometimes be given, which may be doubtful, and want corroboration." " But if the confession of the prisoner go to confirm the evidence, *if sworn to by two witnesses at least,* it *may be received:*" He then adds, what seems to be decisive on this point: " *but unless it do go to corroborate other testimony, I do not think it admissible.*" This shews clearly, that the testimony now offered, is not admissible, as no act has been yet proved; and that his conduct at other places, and the intention with which he went to the place where the imputed treason is laid, is not proper to be adduced in evidence. " Confessions out of court were formerly admitted;" " *but that danger is now wisely avoided.*" I am sure, that if we were to go into an inquiry as to the admissibility of this evidence, the plain words of the constitution ought to satisfy us at once, that " *no person* shall be convicted of treason, unless on the *testimony of two witnesses* to the *same overt act,* or on *confession in open court.*" No language can be more explicit. An insuperable objection to this kind of evidence, is, that acts committed out of the district might be introduced by it. We have said, that general Eaton's testimony does not relate to any *acts* committed any where, but to mere declarations out of the district. We sincerely wish to avoid any anticipation of his evidence, but since gentlemen will impose it on us, and they admit it to be similar to his ex parte deposition which has been already published, it is our duty to insist that the attorney for the United States, shall produce no evidence of declarations or corroborative testimony of any kind, till he shall first prove the material facts which admit of this confirmation. It is neither reasonable nor constitutional, that acts out of the district should be given in evidence. It might be a mere waste of the time of the court, jury, counsel and witnesses, to enter into a long and elaborate examination and discussion, which would be totally irrelevant, if no act could be proved. As the relevancy of all other testimony depends on the proof of the act, every principle of reason and law requires, that it should be first used as the foundation of the rest.

On the trial of Fries, the first witness who was sworn, was interrogated as to the act of " levying war;" whether he had been at Bethlehem, at the time laid in the indictment? and whether he had seen the acts committed? that is, the rescue of several persons lawfully in the custody of the marshal, and other acts of violence connected with the rescue. Every other witness was interrogated in like manner; first, as to the acts committed; and having established the fact, that the accused had committed the overt act, then other evidence of a corroborative nature was introduced. In page 37, the examination of colonel Nichols the marshal is stated; and he particularly describes the acts committed by the prisoner. The testimony now offered would be at present immaterial, because the act of war to which it applies is not proved.

On this point, I beg leave to refer to the sentiments of judge Foster, in his *Crown Law, p.* 246, which have been commented on already. After stating, that on the trial of Vaughan for treason, for adhering to the king's enemies, and cruising in a vessel called the *Loyal Clencarty*, the court rejected evidence to prove, that he had, some time before, cut away the custom-house barge, and had gone a cruising in her: he says, that " the rule of rejecting all manner of evidence, in criminal prosecutions, that is fo reign to the point in issue, is founded on sound sense and common justice. For no man is bound at the peril of life or liberty, fortune or reputation, to answer at once and unprepared, for every action of his life. Few even of the best of men, would choose to be put to it." Judge Patterson, on an occasion very much like this, speaks with peculiar force and propriety. On the trial of William Smith, when the defendant's counsel moved to postpone the trial on account of the absence of some witnesses said to be material, " The evidence, (says he), which is offered to a court must be pertinent to the issue, or in some proper manner connected with it. It must relate and be applied to the particular fact or charge in controversy, so as to constitute a legal ground to support, or a legal ground to resist the prosecution. For it would be an endless task, and create inextricable confusion, if parties were suffered to give in evidence to the jury, whatever *self-love* or prejudice or whim or a wild imagination might suggest. This is an idea too extravagant to be entertained by reflecting and candid men; as it would, if carried into practice, quickly prostrate property, civil liberty, and good government. Law would become a labyrinth, a bottomless pit; and courts would be perverted from their original design, and turned into instruments of injustice and oppression. *A line must be drawn—a line has been drawn* on *such occasions*, which it becomes the duty of judges to pursue. If there be no line, *any thing and every thing may be given* in evidence. Where shall we stop? What is the rule which we find to be laid down for our guidance? *The evidence must be pertinent to the issue;* the *witnesses must be material.* If the *evidence be-not pertinent,* nor the *witnesses material,* the court *ought not to receive either.*"

A reason given by other respectable authors, for this doctrine is, that the jury may be embarrassed and perplexed by evidence not pertinent to the issue; and that the accused would be unapprized and without notice of the charges to be thus exhibited against him, and consequently unprepared to meet the evidence which he is to resist. He cannot, as Foster says, be prepared to answer at once for every action of his life. This objection applies most forcibly in this case, where the complicated evidence of one hundred and thirty-five witnesses is to be introduced and considered. Notwithstanding the prejudices and alarm which have been excited in this country, are you sure that they were not all without any cause to justify them? If colonel Burr's plans were most meritorious, predicated on principles of an honourable war, and only to be carried on in the event of his country being engaged in it, and with a view to the emancipation of millions who are now in bondage, with a design to take the bonds of slavery off many millions, he would have merited the applause of the friends of liberty and of posterity. This I contend was the case; but his friends may now pray that he may not meet the fate that Washington himself would have met, if the revolution had not been established. If you should permit the witnesses to go into complicated tales of schemes and plots of severing the union, resting solely on the imputed intentions of the accused, (and yet the result of a long and elaborate inquiry would be, that there was no act of war,) it would be worse than a mere waste of time, and would expose, without any possible useful object, the private views and intentions of the accused; prejudices would be increased; the intention would be taken for the deed, under the influence of impressions not to be resisted, when the act itself was incomplete. The jury ought not to be troubled with evidence, which is wholly immaterial till the overt act be proved. I will ask, whether on principles of common sense, any objection can be urged against the production of the evidence which we call for, if it can be produced? What do we ask? Do we ask any thing that will embarrass the prosecution? Not the slightest inconvenience can arise from their producing proof of the act, if there ever were such an act. The witnesses, who know the act, can be called on, and their testimony will be distinct from all the other evidence. What will be their alternative after a solemn argument? If we sustain our position, that the order of evidence is part of the law of evidence, and that before the intention, the act itself must be established, is it their purpose to go into evidence of the intention before the act, or knowing it not to exist, because it is the wish of the court that it should be otherwise? I cannot suppose this to be their purpose; I have too good an opinion of the gentlemen, notwithstanding appearances, to suppose, that they intend to do so. But if it be so, the court will decide without anticipating such conduct; expecting that if the act exist, they will prove it, or if not, that they will yield as they ought.

The principles of law and of convenience, and the natural reason of every man, all concur in requiring, that the first part of the evidence to be proved, should be the act. If it be first proved, no inconvenience will result from it. The rules of law should be general. If this principle of reason and convenience be departed from in this instance, it may in every other; and the most manifest and dangerous inconveniences in other cases (if not in this) must result, if the court will permit gentlemen to indulge, what judge Patterson calls " self-love, prejudice or whim, or the suggestions of a wild imagination."

I will not omit another authority, which may not be directly applicable to the distinction now before the court; but if applicable, it maintains the same principle, in directing the order of the evidence. 1st *East's Crown Law*, *p.* 96, 97. " In this, as in other cases, founded on conspiracy, the conspiracy or agreement among several, to act in concert together, for a particular end, must be established by proof, before any evidence can be given of the acts of any person, not in the presence of the prisoner, and this must be generally done by evidence of the party's own acts, and cannot be collected from the acts of others, independent of his own." " When the connexion between the parties is once established, of which the court must in the first instance judge, previous to the admission of any consequential evidence to affect the prisoner by the acts of others, to which he was not a party or privy, then whatever is done in pursuance of that conspiracy, by one of the conspirators, though unknown perhaps to the rest, at the time, is to be considered as the act of all." This, at least, ascertains that the order of evidence is part of the law of evidence; and that facts may be important and material in one part of a prosecution, which, in another may be entirely inadmissible. As in the case of a conspiracy, before you can introduce any testimony against a prisoner, of the acts of any other of the conspirators, you must prove an association between them: so in this case, before you are permitted to introduce evidence of the intention being treasonable, you must prove an act of war. Before you speak of a treasonable intention, you must go on to prove the act which makes it so. The overt act must be proved by direct evidence, and confirmed by confirmatory evidence.

Mr. Martin referred to 3 *Gilbert*, 816, and to several other authorities, to shew that " when levying war" is the charge laid in an indictment for treason, the rule of proceeding is the same as in murder, larceny and burglary, where the evidence must rise out of the facts first proved, if not admitted. He again referred to the case of the King *v.* Vaughan, who was indicted for treason in adhering to the king's enemies, by cruising against his subjects, in the vessel called the *Loyal Clencarty*, and whose acts, Mr. Martin said, were proved before any evidence of any other kind: he also cited the case of Demaree and Purchase, who were indicted for treason, in pulling down meeting-houses, 8 *State Trials*, 219, and the case of the King *v.* Messenger and others, for pulling down bawdy-houses, 2 *State Trials*, 585. The first proof adduced in both cases, was the act of pulling down the houses: in the former case, the overt act was beginning to pull down *all conventicles or meeting-houses;* and in the latter, beginning to pull down and destroy *all bawdy-houses.* The *universality* of the intention, constituted this crime, which is a species of treason in "*levying war.*" The design to pull down and destroy *all conventicles* and *all bawdy-houses*, evidenced by the open deed of beginning to pull down and destroy, was made treason by the statute; and although there could be no treason without this universal intention, yet no proof of their intention, or of their declarations on the subject, was ever attempted to be introduced, till the fact of beginning to pull down and destroy, was first established. Mr. Martin insisted, that nothing was more consonant to common sense, than to prove the *act* before the " *quo animo;*" that until the overt act were established, and the time and place of its commission were fixed, it was impossible for the court or jury to determine with correctness and propriety, the " *quo animo,*" or design wherewith it had been done. He therefore hoped that the prosecutor would not be permitted to proceed further till he proved some overt act.

The court then adjourned till to-morrow morning, 9 o'clock.

TUESDAY, August 18, 1807.

The court met according to adjournment.

The CHIEF JUSTICE pronounced the following opinion, on the question last argued, relative to the order of evidence.

Although this is precisely the same question relative to the order of evidence, which was decided by this court, on the motion to commit, yet it is now presented under somewhat different circumstances, and may, therefore, not be considered as determined by the former decision. At that time, no indictment was found, no pleadings existed, and there was no standard, by which the court could determine the relevancy of the testimony offered, until the fact to which it was to apply, should be disclosed. There is now an indictment specifying the charge which is to be proved on the part of the prosecution, there is an issue made up which presents a point to which all the testimony must apply, and consequently it is in the power of the court to determine, with some accuracy, on the relevancy of the testimony which may be offered.

It is contended in support of the motion which has been made, that, according to the regular order of evidence and the usage of courts, the existence of the fact on which the charge depends, ought to be shewn, before any testimony explanatory, or confirmatory of that fact can be received. Against the motion, it is contended that the crime alleged in the indictment consists of two parts; the fact and the intention: that it is in the discretion of the attorney for the United States, first to adduce the one or the other; and that no instance has ever occurred of the interference of a court with that arrangement which he has thought proper to make.

As is not unfrequent, the argument on both sides appears to be, in many respects, correct. It is the most useful and appears to be the natural order of testimony to shew, first, the existence of the fact respecting which the inquiry is to be made. It is unquestionably attended with this advantage; there is a fixed and certain object to which the mind applies with precision all the testimony which may be received, and the court can decide with less difficulty on the relevancy of all the testimony which may be offered: but this arrangement is not clearly shewn, to be established by any fixed rule of evidence, and no case has been adduced in which it has been forced by the court, on the counsel for the prosecution.

On one side it has been contended that by requiring the exhibition of the fact in the first instance, a great deal of time may be saved, since there may be a total failure of proof with respect to the fact; and this argument has been answered, by observing, that should there even be such failure, they could not interpose and arrest the progress of the cause, but must permit the counsel for the prosecution to proceed with that testimony which is now offered.

Levying of war, is a fact, which must be decided by the jury. The court may give general instructions on this, as on every other question brought before them, but the jury must decide upon it as compounded of fact and law. Two assemblages of men not unlike in appearance, possibly may be, the one treasonable and the other innocent. If, therefore, the fact exhibited to the court and jury, should, in the opinion of the court, not amount to the act of levying war, the court could not stop the prosecution; but must permit the counsel for the United States to proceed to shew the intention of the act, in order to enable the jury to decide upon the fact, coupled with the intention.

The consumption of time would probably be nearly the same, whether the counsel for the prosecution commenced with the fact or the intention, provided those discussions, which respect the admissibility of evidence would be as much avoided in the one mode as in the other. The principal importance which viewing the question in this light, would seem to attach to its decision, is the different impressions which the fact itself might make, if exhibited at the commencement or close of the prosecution.

Although human laws punish actions, the human mind spontaneously attaches guilt to intentions. The same fact, therefore, may be viewed very differently, where the mind is prepared by a course of testimony, calculated to impress it with a conviction of the criminal designs of the accused, and where the fact is stated without such preparation. The overt act may be such as to influence the opinion, on the testimony afterwards given, respecting the intention; and the testimony respecting the intention, may be such, as to influence the opinion on the testimony, which may be afterwards given respecting the overt act.

On the question of consuming time, the argument was placed in one point of view by the counsel for the defence, which excited some doubt. The case was supposed of only one witness to the overt act, and a declaration that it could be proved by no other. The court was asked, whether the counsel would be permitted then to proceed to examine the intentions of the accused, and to do worse than waste the time of the court and jury, by exposing, without a possible object, the private views and intentions of any person whatever?

Perhaps in such a case the cause might be arrested; but this does not appear to warrant the inference that it might be arrested, because the fact proved by the two witnesses did not appear to the court, to amount to the act of levying war. In the case supposed, the declaration of the law is positive, and a point proper to be referred to the court occurs, which suspends the right of the jury, to consider the subject, and compels them to bring in a verdict of not guilty. In such a case, no testimony could be relevant, and all testimony ought to be excluded. Suppose the counsel for the prosecution should say that he had no testimony to prove the treasonable intention: that he believed confidently the object of the assemblage of men on Blannerhassett's island to be innocent: that it did not amount to the crime of levying war: surely it would be a wanton and useless waste of time to proceed with the examination of the overt act. When such a case occurs, it cannot be doubted that a nolle prosequi will be entered, or the jury be directed, with the consent of the attorney, to find a verdict of not guilty.

It has been truly stated, that the crime alleged in the indictment, consists of the fact and of the intention with which that fact was committed. The testimony disclosing both the fact and the intention must be relevant. The court finds no express rule stating the order in which the attorney is to adduce relevant testimony, nor any case in which a court has interfered with the arrangement he has made. No alteration of that arrangement therefore will now be directed.

But it is proper to add, that the intention which is considered as relevant in this stage of the inquiry is the intention which composes a part of the crime, the intention with which the overt act itself was committed; not a general evil disposition, or an intention to commit a distinct fact. This species of testimony, if admissible at all, is received as corroborative or confirmatory testimony. It does not itself prove the intention with which the act was performed, but it renders other testimony probable which goes to that intention. It is explanatory of, or assistant to, that other testimony. Now it is essentially repugnant to the usages of courts, and to the declarations of the books by whose authority such testimony is received, that corroborative or confirmatory testimony should precede that which it is to corroborate or confirm. Until the introductory testimony be given, that which is merely corroborative is not relevant, and of consequence, if objected to, cannot be admitted without violating the best settled rules of evidence.

This position may be illustrated by a direct application to the testimony of general Eaton. So far as his testimony relates to the fact charged in the indictment, so far as it relates to levying war on Blannerhassett's island, so far as it relates to a design to seize on New-Orleans, or to separate by force, the western from the Atlantic states, it is deemed relevant and is now admissible: so far as it respects other plans to be executed in the city of Washington, or elsewhere, if it indicate a treasonable design, it is a design to commit a distinct act of treason, and is therefore not relevant to the present indictment. It can only, by shewing a general evil intention, render it more probable that the intention in the particular case was evil. It is merely additional or corroborative testimony, and therefore, if admissible at any time, is only admissible according to rules and principles which the court must respect, after hearing that which it is to confirm.

The counsel will perceive how many questions respecting the relevancy of testimony, the arrangement proposed on the part of the prosecution will most probably produce. He is however at liberty to proceed according to his own judgment, and the court feels itself bound to exclude such testimony only, as at the time of its being offered, does not appear to be relevant.

General William Eaton was then called to give his evidence. He inquired, whether he might be permitted to have a recurrence to his notes?

CHIEF JUSTICE.—Were they written by yourself?

Mr. Eaton. They were taken and copied by me from others, which are at my lodgings.

Mr. Burr's counsel objected, unless he had the original notes.

Mr. WICKHAM.—At what time were they taken?

Mr. Eaton. At different times.

Mr. BURR.—What is the nature of them?

Answer. They are nothing but memoranda taken from notes, which I made of the conversations between you and myself, at the times when they passed.

The court decided, that they were not admissible.

Mr. Eaton. May I ask one further indulgence from the court? I have been long before the public. Much stricture and some severity have passed upon me. May I, in stating my evidence, be permitted to make some explanation about the motives of my own conduct?

CHIEF JUSTICE.—Perhaps it would be more correct for the court to decide upon the propriety of the explanation, when the particular case occurs. Some cases may require it; and if any objection be made to your explanation, then the court will decide upon it.

Mr. Eaton. Concerning any overt act, which goes to prove Aaron Burr guilty of treason, I know nothing.

Mr. HAY.—I wish you to state to the court and jury, the different conversations you have had with the prisoner.

Mr. Eaton. Concerning certain transactions which are said to have happened at Blannerhassett's island, or any agency which Aaron Burr may be supposed to have had in them, I know nothing. But concerning colonel Burr's expressions of treasonable intentions, I know much, and it is to these, that my evidence relates.

Mr. MARTIN.—I know not how far the court's opinion extends.

CHIEF JUSTICE.—It is this; that any proof of intention formed before the act itself, if relevant to the act, may be admitted. One witness may prove the intention at one time, and another may prove it at another; so as to prove the continuance of the intention throughout the whole transaction; and therefore the proof of very remote intentions may be relevant to this particular act.

Mr. MARTIN.—I trust, that when he speaks of a treasonable intention not applicable to this act, the court will stop him.

Mr. WICKHAM.—If I understand the opinion of the court correctly, it relates to treason charged to be committed in Virginia, and evidence of acts out of it, is inadmissible.

CHIEF JUSTICE.—The intention to commit this crime, to erect an empire in the west, and seize New-Orleans, may be shewn by subsequent events to have been continued; and facts out of the district may be proved, *after the overt act*, as corroborative testimony.

Mr. Eaton. During the winter of 1805, 6, (I cannot be positive as to the distinct point of time; yet, during that winter), at the city of Washington, Aaron Burr signified to me, that he was organizing a military expedition to be moved against the Spanish provinces, on the south western frontiers of the United States: I understood under the authority of the general government. From our existing controversies with Spain, and from the tenor of the president's communications to both houses of congress, a conclusion was naturally drawn, that war with that power was inevitable. I had just then returned from the coast of Africa, and having been for many years employed on your frontier, or a coast more barbarous and obscure, I was ignorant of the estimation in which colonel Burr was held by his country. The distinguished rank he held in society, and the strong marks of confidence which he had received from his fellow citizens, did not permit me to doubt of his patriotism. As a military character, I had been made acquainted with none within the United States, under whose direction a soldier might with greater security confide his honour than colonel Burr. In case of my country's being involved in a war, I should have thought it my duty to obey so honourable a call, as was proposed to me. Under impressions like these, I did engage to embark myself in the enterprise, and pledged myself to colonel Burr's confidence. At several interviews, it appeared to be his intention to convince me by maps and other documents, of the feasibility of penetrating to Mexico. At length, from certain indistinct expressions and innuendoes, I admitted a suspicion, that colonel Burr had other projects. He used strong expressions of reproach against the administration of the government: accused them of want of character, want of energy, and want of gratitude. He seemed desirous of irritating my resentment by dilating on certain injurious strictures I had received on the floor of congress, on account of certain transactions on the coast of Tripoli; and also on the delays in adjusting my accounts for advances of money on account of the United States; and talked of pointing out to me modes of honourable indemnity. I will not conceal here, that colonel Burr had good reasons for supposing me disaffected towards the government: I had indeed suffered much, from delays in adjusting my accounts for cash advanced to the government, whilst I was consul at Tunis, and for the expense of supporting the war with Tripoli. I had but a short time before been compelled ingloriously to strike the flag of my country, on the ramparts of a defeated enemy, where it had flown for forty-five days. I had been compelled to abandon my comrades in war, on the fields where they had fought our battles. I had seen cash offered to the half vanquished chief of Tripoli, (as he had himself acknowledged), as the consideration of pacification.

Mr. WICKHAM.—By whom?

Answer. By our negotiator, when as yet no exertion had been made by our naval squadron to coerce that enemy. I had seen the conduct of the author of these blemishes on our then proud national character, if not commended—not censured; whilst my own inadequate efforts to support that character were attempted to be thrown into shade. To feelings naturally arising out of circumstances like these, I did give strong expression. Here I beg leave to observe, in justice to myself, that however strong those expressions, however harsh the language I employed, they would not justify the inference, that I was preparing to dip my sabre in the blood of my countrymen; much less of their children, which I believe would have been the case, had this conspiracy been carried into effect.

Mr. MARTIN objected to this language.

I listened to colonel Burr's mode of indemnity; and as I had by this time begun to suspect, that the military expedition he had on foot was unlawful, I permitted him to believe myself resigned to his influence, that I might understand the extent and motive of his arrangements. Colonel Burr now laid open his project of revolutionizing the territory west of the Allegany; establishing an independent empire there; New-Orleans to be the capital, and he himself to be the chief; organizing a military force on the waters of the Mississippi, and carrying conquest to Mexico. After much conversation, which I do not particularly recollect, respecting the feasibility of the project, as was natural, I stated impediments to his operations; such as the republican habits of the citizens of that country, their attachment to the present administration of the government, the want of funds, the opposition he would experience from the regular army of the United States, stationed on that frontier; and the resistance to be expected from Miranda, in case he should succeed in republicanizing the Mexicans. Colonel Burr appeared to have no difficulty in removing these obstacles. He stated to me, that he had in person, (I think the preceding season), made a tour through that country; that he had secured to his interests and attached to his person, (I do not recollect the exact expression, but the meaning, and I believe, the words were), the most distinguished citizens of Tennessee, Kentucky, and the territory of Orleans; that he had inexhaustible resources and funds; that the army of the United States would act with him; that it would be reinforced by ten or twelve thousand men from the above mentioned states and territory; that he had powerful agents in the Spanish territory, and "as for Miranda," said Mr. Burr, facetiously, "we must hang Miranda." In the course of several conversations on this subject, he proposed to give me a distinguished command in his army; I understood him to say, the second command. I asked him who would command in chief. He said, general Wilkinson. I observed, that it was singular, he should count upon general Wilkinson: the distinguished command and high trust he held under government, as the commander in chief of our army, and as governor of a province, he would not be apt to put at hazard for any prospect of precarious aggrandisement. Colonel Burr stated, that general Wilkinson balanced in the confidence of his country; that it was doubtful whether he would much longer retain the distinction and confidence he now enjoyed; and that he was prepared to secure to himself a permanency. I asked colonel Burr, if he knew general Wilkinson. He said, yes; and echoed the question. I told him that twelve years ago I was at the same time a captain in the wing of the legion of the United States, which general Wilkinson commanded, his acting brigade-major, and aid-de-camp; and that I thought I knew him well. He asked me, what I knew of general Wilkinson? I said, I knew general Wilkinson would act as lieutenant to no man in existence. "You are in an error," said Mr. Burr, "Wilkinson will act as lieutenant to me." From the tenor of much conversation on this subject, I was prevailed on to believe, that the plan of revolution meditated by colonel Burr, and communicated to me, had been concerted with general Wilkinson, and would have his cooperation; for colonel Burr repeatedly, and very confidently expressed his belief, that the influence of general Wilkinson with his army, the promise of double pay and rations, the ambition of his officers, and the prospect of plunder and military achievements, would bring the army generally into the measure. I pass over here, a conversation which took place between colonel Burr and myself, respecting a central revolution, as it is decided to be irrelevant, by the opinion of the bench.

Mr. HAY.—You allude to a revolution for overthrowing the government at Washington, and of revolutionizing the eastern states.

I was passing over that, to come down to the period when I supposed he had relinquished that design, and adhered to the project of revolutionizing the west.

Mr. Wickham.—What project do you mean?

Answer. A central general revolution. I was thoroughly convinced myself, that such a project was already so far organized, as to be dangerous, and that it would require an effort to suppress it. For in addition to positive assurances that colonel Burr had of assistance and cooperation, he said, that the vast extent of territory of the United States, west of the Allegany mountains, which offered to adventurers with a view on the mines of Mexico, would bring volunteers to his standard from all quarters of the union. The situation which these communications, and the impressions they made upon me, placed me in, was peculiarly delicate. I had no overt act to produce against colonel Burr. He had given me nothing upon paper; nor did I know of any person in the vicinity, who had received similar communications, and whose testimony might support mine. He had mentioned to me no person as principally and decidedly engaged with him, but general Wilkinson; a Mr. Alston, who, I afterwards learned, was his son-in-law; and a Mr. Ephraim Kibby, who I learnt was late a captain of rangers in Wayne's army. Of general Wilkinson, Burr said much, as I have stated: of Mr. Alston, very little, but enough to satisfy me that he was engaged in the project; and of Kibby, he said, that he was brigade major in the vicinity of Cincinnati (whether Cincinnati in Ohio or in Kentucky, I know not,) who had much influence with the militia, and had already engaged the majority of the brigade to which he belonged, who were ready to march at Mr. Burr's signal. Mr. Burr talked of this revolution as a matter of right, inherent in the people, and constitutional; a revolution which would rather be advantageous than detrimental to the Atlantic states; a revolution which must eventually take place; and for the operation of which, the present crisis was peculiarly favourable. He said there was no energy to be dreaded in the general government, and his conversations denoted a confidence, that his arrangements were so well made, that he should meet with no opposition at New-Orleans; for the army and chief citizens of that place were now ready to receive him. On the solitary ground upon which I stood, I was at a loss how to conduct myself, though at no loss as respected my duty. I durst not place my lonely testimony in the balance against the weight of colonel Burr's character; for by turning the tables upon me, which I thought any man, capable of such a project, was very capable of doing, I should sink under the weight. I resolved therefore with myself, to obtain the removal of Mr. Burr from this country, in a way honorable to him; and on this I did consult him, without his knowing my motive. Accordingly, I waited on the president of the United States, and after a desultory conversation, in which I aimed to draw his view to the westward, I took the liberty of suggesting to the president, that I thought colonel Burr ought to be removed from the country, because I considered him dangerous in it. The president asked where we should send him? Other places might have been mentioned, but I believe that Paris, London and Madrid, were the places which were particularly named. The president, without positive expression (in such a matter of delicacy) signified that the trust was too important, and expressed something like a doubt about the integrity of Mr. Burr. I frankly told the president, that perhaps no person had stronger grounds to suspect that integrity than I had; but that I believed his pride of ambition had so predominated over his other passions, that when placed on an eminence, and put on his honor, a respect to himself would secure his fidelity. I perceived that the subject was disagreeable to the president, and to bring him to my point in the shortest mode, and at the same time, point to the danger, I said to him that I expected, that we should in eighteen months have an insurrection, if not a revolution, on the waters of the Mississippi. The president said he had too much confidence in the information, the integrity, and attachment to the union of the citizens of that country, to admit any apprehensions of that kind. The circumstance of no interrogatories being made to me, I thought imposed silence upon me at that time and place. Here, sir, I beg indulgence to declare my motives for recommending that gentleman to a foreign mission at that time; and in the solemnity with which I stand here, I declare that colonel Burr was neutral in my feelings; that it was through no attachment to him that I made that suggestion, but to avert a great national calamity which I saw approaching; to arrest a tempest which seemed lowering in the west; and to divert into a channel of usefulness those consummate talents, which were to mount " the whirlwind and direct the storm." These, and these only, were my reasons for making that recommendation.

About the time of my having waited on the president, or a little before, (I cannot however be positive whether before or after) I determined at all events to have some evidence of the integrity of my intentions, and to fortify myself by the advice of two gentlemen, members of the house of representatives, whose friendship and confidence I had the honor long to retain, and in whose wisdom and integrity, I had the utmost faith and reliance. I am at liberty to give their names if required. I do not distinctly recollect, but I believe, that I had a conversation with a senator on the subject. I developed to them all Mr. Burr's plans. They did not seem much alarmed.

Mr. MARTIN objected to the witness stating any of the observations of other persons to himself.

After some desultory conversation between the counsel on both sides, the chief justice said, that though more time was wasted by stopping the witness, than by letting him tell his story in his own way, yet if it were required, he must be stopped when he gave improper testimony. He then told the witness, "You are at liberty to vindicate yourself, but declarations of other gentlemen are not to be mentioned, because that certainly would be improper."

Mr. Eaton. I did ask indulgence of the court to make such explanations, because perversions of my conduct were before the public: but I waive this indulgence; contented with meeting these perversions at some other time and place.

CHIEF JUSTICE.—You have used that indulgence.

Mr. Eaton. Little more passed between colonel Burr and myself, relevant to this inquiry, while I remained at Washington, though I could perceive symptoms of distrust in him towards me, he was solicitous to engage me in his western plans.

I returned to Massachusetts, to my own concerns, and thought no more of colonel Burr, or his projects, or revolutions until in October last, a letter was put into my hands at Brumfield, from Mr. Belknap, of Marietta, to T. E. Danielson, of Brumfield, stating that Mr. Burr had contracted for boats which were building on the Ohio.

Mr. BURR.—Have you that letter?

Mr. Eaton. No.

Mr. BURR.—It is improper then to state it.

Mr. HAY.—It is immaterial. Mr. Belknap is here.

Mr. Eaton. As to letters, I have had no correspondence with colonel Burr. I was about to state, that I had made a communication, through Mr. Granger, to the president of the United States, stating the views of colonel Burr; and a copy of the letter from Belknap was transmitted to the department of state.

Questions by the prosecution.

Mr. WIRT.—Was there any conversation between you and the prisoner, in which you spoke of the odium attached to the name of *usurper?*

Mr. Eaton. That conversation was excluded by the opinion of the court, as relating to the central project.

Mr. HAY.—Did you mean to state that the *honourable indemnity* proposed to you by the prisoner was to be included in this plan?

Mr. Eaton. I understood it to be included in the perpetual rank and emolument to be assigned me. In his conversations he declared that he should erect a permanent government, of which he was to be the chief; and he repeated it so often that I could not have misunderstood him.

Cross-questioned.

Mr. MARTIN.—Do you recollect when you arrived in Washington?

Mr. Eaton. I said that I did not recollect particularly. But the principal part of these conversations must have been between the middle of February and the latter end of March, 1806. I arrived here in the latter end of November, 1805, at Philadelphia; and in December, went to New-England, and afterwards returned; these conversations happened after my return.

Question. Did you go any remote distance till you came back? Were you as far as Baltimore? (To these questions no answers were made, or if made, were not heard.)

Question. Do you recollect any particular conduct of yours, calculated to put an end to colonel Burr's importunities?

Answer. Yes. At some of our last interviews, I laid on his table a paper containing the toast which I had given to the public, with an intention that he should see it, but I do not know that he did see it, but I believe it. " The United States: palsy to the brain that should plot to dismember, and leprosy to the hand that will not draw to defend our union."

Question. Where was that toast drunk?

Answer. I cannot say. This question was made to me from authority. It was sent with other toasts I had corrected, to a paper at Springfield. I laid this paper on colonel Burr's table.

Question. Was it drunk at any distant place? At Philadelphia?

Answer. I do not recollect. I thought at first it was at Philadelphia, but on reflection, it could not have been there; but I had received many hospitalities throughout the union; many of my toasts were published; and in the hurry of passing and repassing, I have completely forgotten.

Mr. BURR.—Do you recollect when you left Washington?

Answer. About the 5th or 6th of April.

Question. Can you not be certain where this toast was drunk? At Washington, or at Philadelphia?

Answer. I am not certain *when or where* it was drunk, but I am certain it was not at Washington, because I gave another there when called upon.

Question. Did you say, that all these conversations happened between the middle of February and the last of March?

Answer. No: I did not say so. I said the principal part of these conversations passed in that interval.

Mr. BURR.—Did you say the paper containing that toast was laid on my table in March?

Answer. I cannot tell; it cannot be material; from that time our intercourse became less frequent; you expressed some solicitude to keep me at your house.

Question. You say that this toast was printed at Springfield?

Answer. I did.

Question. Have you in your possession a paper containing that toast?

Answer. I have not here.

Mr. MARTIN.—Did you transmit the toast for publication, and to what printer?

Answer. I do not recollect distinctly.

Question. You mentioned something about a communication which you made to the president, through the post master general. Look at that paper. Is that your signature?

Answer. It is; and I must give a short account of that paper. I went to Springfield about twenty-five miles distant from my place of residence. Mr. Granger was there; I went to see him; on my arrival there, in the evening, I understood that he had gone out of town to his seat in the country; but that he had taken notes concerning those transactions. Next morning I went to his house; he put into my hands notes which he had got from Mr. Ely.

Question. Whom were the notes written by?

Answer. By Mr. Granger; they were subscribed by him if I have a correct recollection. Mr. Eaton then mentioned that the notes on the two first pages were drawn up by Mr. Granger, from conversations which had passed between Mr. Granger and Mr. Ely, on certain communications made to Mr. Ely by Mr. Eaton, respecting colonel Burr's plans; that he had seen Mr. Ely at Northampton, at the session of the court of common pleas, at the time when they had first heard of the building of boats on the Ohio. The notes on the last page, in

Mr. Granger's writing, and subscribed by himself, were from subsequent conversations between him and Mr. Granger.

Question. How many days' travelling is it by the stage from Springfield to Washington?

Answer. Not more than five.

Mr. BURR.—You spoke of accounts with the government. Did you, or the government, demand money?

Answer. They had no demand on me; I demanded money of them.

Question. Did they state in account a balance against you?

Answer. I expended money for the service of the United States, when employed as consul at Tunis; an account of which being presented to the accounting officers of the treasury, they, I was told, had no legal discretion to settle it. As there was no law to authorise this adjustment, I did refer to the congress of 1803, 4. A committee had reported on my claims, favourably, as I supposed; then my accounts were left; when I went however to the coast of Barbary, and when I returned after eighteen months, I renewed my claim to the congress. I found that new difficulties had occurred to prevent an adjustment. Leaving out the sums I had advanced, the government had a considerable balance against me. Some comments were made by a member from New-York, which I thought derogatory to my character; but the balance was in my favour. The last session of congress left them to the accounting officers to settle according to equity. It has been since settled and paid.

Mr. MARTIN.—Did not colonel Burr confine his plans to attack the Spanish provinces, for the most considerable part of the time, to the event of a war with Spain?

Answer. Not for the most considerable part of the time, but for some time.

Mr. MARTIN asked him some questions relative to his having seen him accompanied by his step-daughter and another lady and a gentleman, at George-Town and Alexandria, about the time he had spoken of; and whether he had given the toast then, when together in the same room?

He admitted that he had seen him when so accompanied. but was not positive when or where the toast was given.

Mr. MARTIN.—What balance did you receive?

Answer. That is *my* concern, sir.

Mr. BURR.—What was the balance against you?

Mr. Eaton (to the court). Is that a proper question?

Mr. Burr.—My object is manifest; I wish to shew the bias which has existed on the mind of the witness.

Chief Justice saw no objections to the question.

Mr. Eaton. I cannot say to a cent or a dollar: but I have received about 10,000 dollars.

Mr. Burr.—When was the money received?

Answer. About March last.

Question. You mentioned Miranda. Where did you understand he was gone to?

Answer. On the benevolent project of revolutionizing the Spanish provinces.

Question. What part of them?

Answer. Caraccas. I had some reason too to know something of that project; because I too was invited to join in *that*. He too was to have been an emperor; he might have been troublesome to us; and of course when I asked you what was to be done with him, you observed, " hang him."

Question. Did you understand, that I was to do all at once; to execute the central project too as well as those in the west?

Answer. I have no objection to answering that; but it will be nothing in your favour. When colonel Burr was speaking of a central revolution, not much was said about his revolution in the west. Had the other been effected, I doubt much whether you would have been willing to have separated that part.

Question. You spoke of a command?

Answer. You stated, what I have already mentioned, that you were assured, from the arrangements which you had made, that an army would be ready to appear, when you went to the waters of the western country. I recollect particularly the name of Ephraim Kibby, who had been a ranger in general Wayne's army. You asked me about his spirit. You gave me to understand that his brigade was ready to join you, and that the people also in that country were ready to engage with you in the enterprise. You spoke of *your* riflemen, *your* infantry, *your* cavalry. It was with the same view, you mentioned to me that that man [pointing to general Wilkinson, just behind him] was to have been the first to aid you; and from the same views you have perhaps mentioned me.

Mr. Martin objected to the witness interposing his own opinions in this manner.

Mr. Hay.—Some allowance is to be made for the feelings of a man of honour.

Mr. Eaton, bowing, apologized to the court for the warmth of his manner.

Mr. Burr.—You spoke of my revolutionizing the western states. How did you understand that the union was to be separated?

Answer. Your principal line was to be drawn by the Allegany mountain. You were persuaded that you had secured to you the most considerable citizens of Kentucky and Tennessee; but expressed some doubts about Ohio; I well recollect *that* on account of the reason which you gave; that they were too much of a plodding, industrious people to engage in your enterprise.

Question. How was the business to be effected?

Answer. I understood that your agents were in the western country; that the army and the commander in chief were ready to act at your signal; and that these, with the adventurers that would join you, would compel the states to agree to a separation. Indeed, you seemed to consider New-Orleans as already yours, and that from this point you would send expeditions into the other provinces; make conquests, and consolidate your empire.

Question. Was it after all this that you recommended me to the president, for an embassy?

Answer. Yes; to remove you, as you were a dangerous man, because I thought it the only way to avert a civil war.

Question. Did you communicate this to me, and what did I say?

Answer. Yes: you seemed to assent to the proposition.

Question. What had become of your command?

Answer. *That* I had disposed of myself.

Question. Did you understand that you had given me a definite answer?

Answer. No: after you had developed yourself, I determined to use you, until I got every thing out of you; and on the principle that, " when innocence is in danger, to break faith with a bad man is not fraud, but virtue."

Question. Did you think that your proposition, as to a foreign embassy, which was so incompatible with my own plans, would be received by me with indifference, had I abandoned the project?

Answer. You seemed to me to want some distinguished place: as to the mode, you were indifferent: and you seemed to acquiesce in the plan of a foreign embassy

Mr. HAY.—You said that you received about 10,000 dollars from the government, in consequence of a law passed for the purpose. The act of congress did not give you a definitive sum.

Answer. The act of congress gave the accounting officers the power of settling with me, on equitable principles, under the inspection of the secretary of state; under whose department I had served, and the settlement was accordingly made.

Commodore Truxtun was then sworn.

Mr. HAY.—Were you present when the court delivered its opinion?

Answer. I was. I know nothing of overt acts, treasonable designs or conversations, on the part of colonel Burr.

Here Mr. HAY, the attorney for the United States, *seemed* to doubt whether the evidence of the commodore applied to this charge, and to be indisposed to examine him.

Mr. WICKHAM then observed, that he would put two questions to him. 1st, Whether he had not frequent and considerable conversations with colonel Burr, concerning the Mexican expedition? 2d, Whether in any of those conversations he ever heard him say any thing of a treasonable design?

Mr. HAY objected to his examination at this time, and Mr. Wickham insisted on it.

Mr. WIRT contended that the attorney had the right to examine the witness or not, at this time, as he thought proper; that the court would recollect, that there were two indictments against the prisoner; the one for high treason, now in discussion before the court, and the other for a misdemeanor (under the act of congress) for preparing an expedition against the Spanish provinces; that the witnesses were summoned promiscuously to support both charges; that the attorney could not ascertain what witnesses supported each indictment without inquiring of themselves; and what he now asked the witness, ought to be considered merely as an inquiry to which of the two indictments his evidence related; and that his evidence was deemed very material on the second indictment, though not on the first.

Mr. HAY said, that on reflection he had no doubt the testimony of commodore Truxtun would have a direct bearing on the subject now before the court, when connected with the other evidence in the cause; that it would appear that there was an intimate connexion between the two projects, the seizure of New-Orleans and the attack on Mexico; he would therefore examine him now and propound this question. Have you not had several conversations with the accused concerning the Mexican expedition?

The commodore proceeded thus:—About the beginning of the winter 1805—6, colonel Burr returned from the western country to Philadelphia. He frequently, in conversation with me, mentioned the subject of speculations in western lands, opening a canal and building a bridge. Those things were not interesting to me in the least, and I did not pay much attention to them. Colonel Burr mentioned to me that the government was weak, and he wished me to get the navy of the United States out of my head; that it would dwindle to nothing; and that he had something to propose to me that was both honourable and profitable; but I considered this as nothing more than an interest in his land-speculations. His conversations were repeated frequently. Some time in July 1806, he told me that he wished to see me unwedded from the navy of the United States, and not to think more of those men at Washington: that he wished to *see* or *make* me, (I do not recollect which of those two terms he used) an admiral: that he contemplated an expedition to Mexico, in the event of a war with Spain, which he thought inevitable. He asked me if the Havanna could be easily taken in the event of a war? I told him that it would require the cooperation of a naval force. Mr. Burr observed to me, that, *that* might be obtained. He asked me if I had any personal knowledge of Carthagena and La Vera Cruz, and what would be the best mode of attacking them by sea and land? I gave him my opinion very freely. Mr. Burr then asked me, if I would take the command of a naval expedition? I asked him if the executive of the United States were privy to, or concerned in the project? He answered *emphatically* that he was not: I asked that question, because the executive had been charged with a knowledge of Miranda's expedition: I told Mr. Burr that I would have nothing to do with it; that Miranda's project had been intimated to me, but I declined to have any thing to do with such affairs. He observed to me, that in the event of a war, he intended to establish an independent government in Mexico: that Wilkinson, the army, and many officers of the navy would join. I told Mr. Burr that I could not see, how any officer of the United States could join. He said that general Wilkinson had projected the expedition, and he had matured it: that many greater men than Wilkinson would join, and that thousands to the westward would join.

Question by Mr. HAY. Do you recollect having asked him whether general Wilkinson had previously engaged in it?

Answer. He said yes, and many greater men than Wilkinson.

Question by Mr. HAY. I will ask you whether at that time, you were in the service of the United States?

Answer. I was declared not to be.

Mr. HAY. I do not wish to hurt your feelings, but merely to shew to the jury the state you were in.

Commodore Truxtun then proceeded :—Colonel Burr again wished me to take a part and asked me to write a letter to general Wilkinson; that he was about to dispatch two couriers to him. I told him that I had no subject to write about; and declined writing. Mr. Burr said that several officers would be pleased at being put under my command. He spoke highly of lieutenant Jones, and asked me if he had sailed with me? I told him that he had not, and that I could give him no account of Mr. Jones, having never seen him to my knowledge. He observed that the expedition could not fail; that the Mexicans were ripe for revolt; that he was incapable of any thing *chi-merical*, or that would lead his friends into a *dilemma*. He shewed me the draught of a periauger or kind of boat that plies between Paulus-Hook and New-York, and asked my opinion of those boats, and whether they were calculated for the river Mississippi and the waters thereof; and I gave him my opinion that they were. He asked me whether I could get a naval constructor to make several copies of the draught? I told him I would. I spoke to a naval constructor and delivered it to him, but as he could not finish them as soon as colonel Burr wished, the draught was returned to him. Mr. Burr told me that he intended those boats for the conveyance of agricultural products to market at New-Orleans, and in the event of a war, for transports. I knew, and informed him, that they were not calculated for transports by sea, nor for the carrying of guns; but having determined to have nothing to do with the Mexican expedition, I said very little more to him about those boats; but I very well recollect what I said to him in our last conversation towards the end of July. I told him that there would be no war. He was sanguine there would be war. He said, however, that if he was disappointed as to the event of war, he was about to complete a contract for a large quantity of land on the Washita; that he intended to invite his friends to settle it; that in one year he would have a thousand families of respectable and fashionable people, and some of them of considerable property : that it was a fine country, and that they would have a charming society, and in two years he would have double the number of settlers; and being on the frontier, he would be ready to move whenever a war took place. I have thus endeavored to relate the substance of the conversations which passed between us, as well as I can recollect. Though it is very possible that I have not stated them, after such a lapse of time, *verbatim.*

Question by Mr. MAC RAE. Was it in your first conversation that he told you, that you should think no more of those men at Washington?

Answer. It was in several.

Question by the same counsel. Was it not in July, that he told you, that he wished to see you unwedded from the navy of the United States, and to make you an admiral?

Answer. That conversation happened in July. He wished to *see* or *make* me an admiral; I cannot recollect which.

Question by Mr. HAY.—Did not those conversations take place, after it was declared, that you were no longer in the service of the United States?

Answer. They did.

In answer to a question by colonel Carrington, one of the jury, he again stated, that the latter conversation was in July.

Question by Mr. MARTIN.—Was it not to the event of a war with Spain, that these conversations related?

Answer. All his conversations respecting military and naval subjects, and the Mexican expedition, were in the event of a war with Spain. I told him my opinion was, that there would be no war, and he seemed to be confident, that there would be war.

Mr. MAC RAE.—Did he mention general Eaton in any of those conversations?

Answer. He mentioned no person but general Wilkinson and lieutenant Jones.

Mr. HAY.—Had you not expressed your dissatisfaction at the declaration of your not being in the service of the United States?

Answer. I had. The misunderstanding between the secretary of the navy of the United States and myself took place in March 1802.

On cross examination, the commodore further stated, that he had had several (he did not know how many) conversations with Mr. Burr; and that as well as he could recollect, it was about the latter end of July, that he informed him, that he was about concluding a bargain for the Washita lands, and wished also to see him unwedded from the navy of the United States. He added, colonel Burr said, that after the Mexican expedition, he intended to provide a formidable navy, at the head of which he intended to place me: that he intended to establish an independent government, and give liberty to an enslaved world. I declined his propositions to me at first, because the president was not privy to the project. He asked me the best mode of attacking the Havanna, Carthagena, and La Vera Cruz; but spoke of no particular force.

Question by colonel BURR.—Do you not recollect my telling you of the propriety of private expeditions, undertaken by individuals in case of war; and that there had been such in the late war, and that there is no legal restraint on such expeditions?

Mr. HAY objected to this question as improper.

Colonel BURR insisted on its propriety, and that the gentlemen for the prosecution had set an example far beyond it.

Commodore Truxtun answered: You said that Wilkinson, the army and many of the officers of the navy would join, and you spoke highly of lieutenant Jones.

Colonel BURR.—Had I not frequently told you, and for years, that the government had no serious intention of employing you, and that you were duped by the Smiths? and do you not think that I was perfectly correct in that opinion?

Answer. Yes: I know very well I was.

Colonel BURR.—Were we not in terms of intimacy? Was there any reserve on my part, in our frequent conversations; and did you ever hear me express any intention or sentiment respecting a division of the union?

Answer. We were very intimate. There seemed to be no reserve on your part. I never heard you speak of a division of the union.

Colonel BURR.—Did I not state to you, that the Mexican expedition would be very beneficial to this country?

Answer. You did.

Colonel BURR.—Had you any serious doubt as to my intentions to settle those lands?

Answer. So far from that, I was astonished at 'the intelligence, of your having different views, contained in newspapers received from the western country, after you went thither.

Question. Would you not have joined in the expedition if sanctioned by the government?

Answer. I would most readily get out of my bed at twelve

o'clock at night, to go in defence of my country, at her call, *against England, France, Spain*, or *any other country.*

Mr. HAY.—Did the prisoner speak of commercial speculations?

Answer. He said they might be carried on to advantage.

Question. Did he, in his conversations, speak of commercial establishments, in which he or his friends were to have an interest?

Answer. He spoke of settling that country, and sending produce therefrom to different parts of the world, New-Orleans particularly.

Mr. WIRT.—Did he speak of an independent empire in Mexico having an advantageous connexion with this country?

Answer. I understood him so.

Mr. MAC RAE.—Did he wish to fill your mind with resentment against the government?

Answer. I was pretty full of it myself, and he joined me in opinion.

Mr. WIRT.—On what subject did Burr wish you to write to general Wilkinson?

Answer. General Wilkinson and myself were on good terms, and he wished me to correspond with him; but I had no subject for a letter to him, and therefore did not write to him.

Mr. HAY.—Suppose we were to have a war with Spain, would not New-Orleans be a proper place from whence to send an expedition against the Spanish provinces? Is it not more proper for that purpose, than any other place in the western parts of the country?

Answer. Certainly it is; but large ships cannot come up to New-Orleans; small craft or vessels must take the expedition down the river.

Question by Mr. Parker, one of the jury. Did you understand for what purpose the couriers spoken of were to be sent by Mr. Burr to general Wilkinson?

Answer. I understood from him, that there was an understanding between himself and general Wilkinson, about the Mexican expedition.

Mr. Parker. Was this expedition only to be in the event of a war with Spain?

Answer. Yes: In all his conversations with me, he said that this expedition was to take place only in the event of a war with Spain.

Mr. Parker. Was there no proposition made to you for such an expedition, whether there was war or not?

Answer. There was not.

Colonel BURR said, that enterprises by individuals, are lawful and customary in cases of war; and asked, whether there were not preparations making in Philadelphia now for that purpose.

Answer. Preparations are making at New-York, as to gun boats and fortifications. The merchants of Liverpool, in expectation of war, build ships for privateers, and if there be no war, they convert them into Guineamen.

Question by Mr. MAC RAE.—Are not the preparations going on openly at New-York? Has any commander been appointed independent of the government?

Answer. No.

Question by colonel BURR.—Did I not say, that I had never seen lieutenant Jones?

Answer. I do not recollect that, but you spoke highly of him.

Question by Mr. HAY.—When he proposed to make you an admiral, did not the thought strike you, how he was to accomplish this?

Mr. BOTTS denied that commodore Truxtun had said that Mr. Burr had promised to make him an admiral.

Commodore Truxtun.—Mr. Burr told me he wished to make or see me one, I do not particularly recollect which was his expression.

Question by Mr. HAY.—From what quarter of the world was the expedition by sea to go?

Answer. I do not know. I did not ask him where it was to go from.

Question by the same. Did you not understand that you were to command the expedition by sea?

Answer. I declined the offer, and asked no questions particularly on the subject.

Mr. BOTTS.—Can ships be built secretly in a corner?

Answer. No.

Peter Taylor was next sworn.

Mr. HAY asked him to state every thing he knew concerning the assemblage on Blannerhassett's island.

Mr. BOTTS objected to this mode of examination; and though he was willing to accommodate Mr. Hay so far as to let the witness tell his story in his own way, yet he would not consent to his introducing completely illegal testimony; he had no objection to the witness stating, what colonel Burr *had said*, or the facts which happened on the island, though both were, strictly speaking, improper evidence: but he would not agree to his speaking of the declarations of Mr. and Mrs. Blannerhassett.

Colonel BURR said he waived the objection at present.

Mr. HAY.—This witness will directly prove the connexion of Burr with Blannerhassett, and with the assemblage on the island.

Peter Taylor. The first information I had upon this subject, was from Mrs. Blannerhassett, when Mr. Blannerhassett and Mr. Alston were gone down the river. The people got much alarmed concerning this business, and Mrs. Blannerhassett sent me to Lexington after Mr. Blannerhassett, with a letter to prevent colonel Burr from coming back with him to the island. I went to Chilicothe, but I did not find Mr. Blannerhassett there, and I then went on to Cincinnati. I was directed to call at Cincinnati, at Mr. John Smith's, where I would find Mr. Blannerhassett. I called at Mr. Smith's store, where I saw his son. I asked if Mr. Smith was at home, he said yes. I said I wanted to speak to him. His son went and told him, a man wanted to see him. When Mr. Smith came out, I inquired for colonel Burr and Blannerhassett, to see whether he could give any account of them. He allowed he knew nothing of either of them. He allowed I was much mistaken in the place. I said no, this was the right place: " Mr. John Smith, storekeeper, Cincinnati." Says I, " don't you recollect a young man, who came here some time ago for colonel Burr's top-coat?" [great coat]. I said, " Sir, I have lived with Mr. Blannerhassett for three years." When Mr. Smith heard me talk so, he knew me, and took me up stairs to talk with me. He wanted to know the news up our way. I told him the people had got alarmed. I told him that every thing was in agitation; that they talked about new settlements of lands, as they told me. He seemed surprised. He asked what was said about general Wilkinson? I said, I knew nothing about it. He asked me if I would carry a letter from him to Blannerhassett? I told him I would carry any thing, so as it was not too burthensome; so he sat down and wrote a letter. He asked whether I wished to drink? for he charged me not to go to any tavern, lest they should be asking me questions. He gave me liquor and I drank; and then he shewed me a stable, and told me to go and get my horse fed by the ostler, but not to go into the tavern. I asked him where I should find colonel Burr and Blannerhassett? He said, he expected they were at Lexington. I told him, I supposed at Mr. Jourdan's. He said, that was the very house. When I got to Lexington, it was Saturday, about one o'clock. Mr. Jourdan happened to be in the street and knew me. He said, " Peter, your old master, as you call him, is not in town." But he said, before I asked him, he expected him either that night or to-morrow early. He asked me, what news in our parts? and I told him. I asked him, what I was to do with my horse? He said that he was to be put at the livery stable. He then went up stairs, and he opened a door, and made a motion with his hand, I suppose to colonel Burr. I went in, and *there* was colonel Burr. Colonel Burr wanted to know the news in our parts. I began to tell him, that my business was to prevent colonel Burr from going back to the island.

Question. Did you know colonel Burr at that time?

Answer. I did not. He had been on the island three times; but I did not see him. When I told colonel Burr *that*, says he, " I am the very man involved in this piece of business; and you ought to tell me all you know." I said, " if you come up our way, the people will shoot you." I told him, it was my sincere opinion, that it was not safe for him to come up our way. I told him, that I had heard several declare, that they had rather shoot him than let it alone, if they had a good chance. He seemed surprised, that they should have such a thing in their heads. I told him, I could not tell why; and then I told him about the land-settlement, but the people said all *that* was a *fib*, and that he had something else in view. Then colonel Burr asked me, what letters I had? I said, two; one was from Mrs. Blannerhassett, and the other from John Smith, of Cincinnati. He asked me, if he might open the letter from John Smith to Blannerhassett, for he expected it was for him? I told him, I supposed it made no difference between him and Blannerhassett, and he might. He broke the seal open, and shewed me there *was* a letter inclosed for himself. He asked me about my wife. I asked him, whether I might not go about the town. He said I might, and then I went down stairs, and left the opened letter with him. I then went to Mr. Jourdan, and asked him, whether I was to stay at his house, or go to a tavern? He said I was to go to a tavern, and he would pay for me. Mr. Jourdan wished me to go next day to Millersburg, after the saddle-bags, left there by Mr. Blannerhassett. I told him, I would, and I did go. I left Mrs. Blannerhassett's letter with Mr. Jourdan, expecting Blannerhassett to get there before me. I got back on Monday by one o'clock; and then Mr. Blannerhassett was come and preparing to go home. We started and came ten miles that night. We stopt at a tavern. I went to see after the horses, and he went into the house. There were people in the house who wanted to know his name. He told them his name was Tom Jones. He came out and told me, the people in the house had asked, and he had told them his name was Tom Jones, and I must mind and not make no mistake, but call him Tom Jones too. So he passed by that name till we got to the Mudlicks. He then told me he was known there, and I must call him by his own name.

Question. When did these things happen?

Answer. All this was in October 1806, I believe. He then began to inquire for young men, that had rifles; good orderly men, that would be conformable to order and discipline. He allowed that colonel Burr and he and a few of his friends, had bought eight hundred thousand acres of land, and they wanted young men to settle it. He said he would give any young man who would go down the river, one hundred acres of land, plenty of grog and victuals while going down the river, and three months' provisions after they had got to the end; every young man must have his rifle and blanket. I agreed to go myself, if I could carry my wife and family, but he said he must have further consultation upon that. When I got home I began to think, and asked him, what kind of seed we should carry with us? He said we did not want any, the people had seeds where we were going.

Mr. WIRT.—Of what occupation were you on the island?

Answer. A gardener.

Mr. WIRT.—I put this question, that the jury might understand his last observation.

I urged that subject to him several times; at last he made a sudden pause, and said, " I will tell you what, Peter, we are going to take Mexico; one of the finest and richest places in the whole world." He said that colonel Burr would be the king of Mexico, and Mrs. Alston, daughter of colonel Burr, was to be the queen of Mexico, whenever colonel Burr died. He said that colonel Burr had made fortunes for many in his time, but none for himself; but now he was going to make something for himself. He said that he had a great many friends in the Spanish territory; no less than two thousand Roman catholic priests were engaged, and that all their friends too would join, if once he could get to them; that the Spaniards, like the French, had got dissatisfied with their government, and wanted to *swap* it. He told me that the British also were friends in this piece of business, and that he should go to England, on this piece of business, for colonel Burr. He asked me if I would not like to go to England. I said I should certainly like to see my friends there, but would wish to go for nothing else. I then asked him what was to become of the men who were going to settle the lands he talked about? Were they to stop at the Red River, or to go on? He said, "O by God, I tell you, Peter, every man that will not conform to order and discipline, I will stab; you'll see how I'll fix them;" that when he got them far enough down the river, if they did not conform to order and discipline, he swore by God he'd stab them. I was astonished: I told him I was no soldier, and could not fight. He said it made no odds; he did not want *me* to fight; he wanted me to go and live with Mrs. Blannerhassett and the children, either at Natchez, or some other place, while he went on the expedition. I talked to him again, and told him the people had got it into their heads, that he wanted to divide the union. He said colonel Burr and he could not do it themselves. All they could do was to tell the people the consequence of it. He said the people there paid the government upwards of four hundred thousand dollars a year, and never received any benefit from it. He allowed it would be a very fine thing if they could keep that money among themselves on this side the mountains, and make locks, and build bridges, and cut roads. About two weeks after I got home, he sent me to doctor Bennett's, of Mason county, with a letter. He wanted to know if doctor Bennett *would'n't* sell him the arms belonging to the United States, which were in his charge? If he could sell them and keep himself out of danger, *he'd* give him a draft upon his friend in Kentucky for payment: if he could not sell them without bringing himself into a hobble, he must send him word *where* they were kept, and he would come and steal them away in the night. I delivered the letter. He gave me directions to get it back and burn it, for it contained high treason. I was not to give the letter to doctor Bennett, until the doctor promised to deliver it back, for me to burn it; for that it contained high treason. I did burn it; the doctor was present.

The doctor read the letter, and said he was unacquainted with the plot, and *could'n't join in it.*

Mr. HAY.—Were you not on the island when the people were there?

Answer. Yes.

Question. When did the boats leave the island?

Answer. It was contemplated to sail on the 6th of December; but the boats were not ready; they did not come till the 10th, (Sunday.) Mr. Knox and several other men were with him, and they sailed on the Wednesday night following.

Question. How many boats were there?

Answer. Four.

Question. How many men from the boats came ashore?

Answer. About thirty.

Question. What did the men do, who did not belong to the boats?

Answer. Some were packing meat; and some were packing other things.

Mr. MAC RAE.—Who went off on Wednesday night?

Answer. Mr. Blannerhassett and Mr. Tyler, and the whole of the party.

Question. At what time in the night?

Answer. About one o'clock.

Question. Did all that came down to the island go away?

Answer. All but one, who was sick.

Mr. HAY.—Had they any guns?

Answer. Some of them had: some of the people went a shooting. But I do not know how many there were.

Mr. J. M. Sheppard (a juryman.) What kind of guns; rifles or muskets?

Answer. I can't tell whether rifles or muskets. I saw no pistols but what belonged to Blannerhassett himself.

Question. Was there any powder or lead?

Answer. They had powder and they had lead both; I saw some powder in a long small barrel, like a churn; but I was so employed I could not notice particularly. Some of the men were engaged in running bullets; but I do not know how many.

Mr. MAC RAE.—What induced them to leave the island at that hour of the night?

Answer. Because they were informed, that the Kenawa militia were coming down there.

Question. Did you carry some boxes to the boats?

Answer. I carried half a bushel of candles and some brandy; several boxes were carried, but I knew not what they contained, and a great many things besides, of which I knew nothing.

Mr. HAY.—Were you on the island, when they went off?

Answer. Yes. They held a council at the foot of the pier, to determine which was the best way to go. Mr. Blannerhassett said, that they had better go together; if he went in a canoe, he would be an easy prey. I said to them, " best stick together;" and so they determined to stick together. They went off in great haste.

Question. Why did they go in a body?

Answer. I suppose for security.

Cross-questioned.

Mr. WICKHAM.—You saw general Tupper and Mr. Woodbridge that night?

Answer. Yes.

Question. Was colonel Burr there?

Answer. No. I did not see him.

Question. Did you understand whether he were in that part of the country at that time?

Answer. I understood not: never saw him on the island.

The court then adjourned till to-morrow.

WEDNESDAY, August 19th, 1807.

The court met, according to adjournment, at the usual hour.

General John Morgan was then sworn, and gave the following testimony.

Some time in August last, about this time twelvemonth, my father put a letter into my hands, signed Aaron Burr, in which he said that himself and colonel Dupiester would dine with him the following day. My father requested me and my brother to go and meet colonel Burr; which we did, about seven miles distant. After a few words of general conversation, colonel Burr observed to me, that the union of the states could not possibly last; and that a separation of the states must ensue as a natural consequence, in four or five years. Colonel Burr made many inquiries of me, relative to the county of Washington; particularly the state of its militia; its strength, arms, accoutrements, and the character of its officers. These conversations continued some time, besides other things, which I cannot recollect, because I did not expect to be called upon in this way. After travelling some miles, we met one of my workmen, a well-looking young man. Colonel Burr said, he wished he had ten thousand such fellows. At my father's table, during dinner, colonel Burr again observed, that the separation of the union must take place inevitably, in less than five years. Shall I give the answers that were made?

Mr. WIRT.—Perhaps it may serve to connect your narrative better.

I recollect that it was my father who answered him, God forbid! Colonel Burr in the course of conversation at the dinner table, observed, that with two hundred men, he could drive the president and congress into the Potowmac; and with four or five hundred he could take possession of the city of New-York. After dinner, he walked with me to my brother's, about one mile distant; and in the course of the walk, spoke of military men, and asked me, if either of my brothers had a military turn? He said he should like to see my brother George at the head of a corps of grenadiers; he was a fine, stout looking fellow. These circumstances induced me to speak to my father: I warned him to beware of colonel Burr, and told him, that in the course of that night, colonel Burr would attempt to have an interview with him, and would make a requisition of my brother Tom, to go with him; and that I suspected something was going on, but what I did not know. The next morning I rode with colonel Burr to the town of Washington, about nine or ten miles. We had a good deal of conversation, principally on military affairs; on the state of the militia; the necessity of attending to military discipline. He told me the effect it had in New-York; that in New-York, the militia were in good order, which was brought about by the influence and exertions of a single individual (colonel Swartwout.) Colonel Burr asked me, if I thought I could raise a regiment in Washington county; or whether I could raise one with more facility in New-Jersey.

Mr. WIRT.—You have lived in New-Jersey?

Answer. Yes.

At Washington, we took a walk; colonel Burr, colonel Dupiester and myself, down the town; and I pointed out to him the house where Mr. Bradford lived, who had been at the head of the western insurrection. He inquired about Mr. Bradford. (He was at Baton Rouge.) I told him his son was in town, and colonel Burr expressed a wish to see him. Colonel Burr mentioned to me, that he had met with several, who had been concerned in the western insurrection; and particularly a major in the North-Western Territory (whose name I do not recollect) who had told him, that if he were ever engaged in another business of the kind, he pledged himself it should not end without bloodshed. He said that he was a fine fellow. It was on these circumstances, that I advised my father to apprise the president of the United States, that something was going on.

Questioned by the prosecution.

Mr. HAY.—Which way did he go?

Answer. I saw him leave Washington for Wheeling.

Mr. WIRT.—Were the separation of the union and military affairs the predominant subject of his conversations?

Answer. Our conversation was very general and mixed, never very long; but these seemed to be the leading subjects.

Mr. HAY.—Do you recollect any thing he said, about Brad-ford's qualifications for conducting such an enterprise?

Answer. I recollect it well. He said that Bradford was very incompetent to such an undertaking; and that in such a case, there ought to be the utmost confidence in the leader.

Mr. WIRT.—At what time in the month of August was this visit?

Answer. Somewhere between the 20th and 25th.

Mr. HAY.—Perhaps the date of this letter (from the prison-er to your father) may shew. This letter is dated on the 21st.

Mr. Parker (one of the jury.) Did he approve or condemn that sentiment of the major's which you have quoted.

Answer. I do not recollect.

Question. Did he make any further remarks respecting him?

Answer. He only said that he was a fine fellow, or words to that effect; that he was very fit for business of that kind.

Cross-examined.

Mr. BURR.—You spoke of a letter from me to your father. Do you know whether he wrote me, some time before, a letter of invitation to his house?

Answer. Yes: He had written about a year before, to you at Pittsburg. That letter is yet unsealed, in my brother Tom's bureau.

Question by the same. Do you remember that it was com-municated to me, and that that was the cause of my coming to visit him?

Answer. Not by myself or my brother, in my hearing.

Question by the same. Do you remember the manner in which I introduced the subject you allude to. Was it in the course of a lively conversation? Was there any thing very serious in it?

Answer. You only mentioned it in a lively or careless manner.

Question. Did your father communicate to you, next morn-ing, our night's conversation?

Answer. Yes.

Question. Before we rode?

Answer. No.

Question. Do you recollect of my having made several in-quiries also about the seminaries of learning; and of one that was projected in your neighbourhood, and of my suggesting the necessity of encouraging it?

Answer. You spoke much too on that subject.

Question. Did I seem to know any thing of Bradford, before you told me?

Answer. You seemed to know a good deal about the insurrection.

Question. Did you not tell me that Bradford was a noisy fellow?

Answer. I did not. I have no objections to give my opinion of Mr. Bradford. I mentioned him to you as a mere lawyer.

Question. Did I seem to know that Bradford lived at Washington, before you mentioned it and pointed out his house?

Answer. You did not seem to know it.

Question. Who were at dinner at your father's?

Answer. My father, mother, wife, sister, colonel Dupiester, Mr. T. Ewell and my brother Tom.

Colonel Morgan was then sworn, and was proceeding, when

Mr. BURR remonstrated against this kind of evidence, consisting of conversations and previous declarations. He did not mean to interrupt the inquiry, but to prevent the time of the court from being wasted. Some desultory conversation ensued upon this point, when

The CHIEF JUSTICE said, that he understood the same objections would hereafter apply as well to the consideration as to the introduction of testimony; that these objections might be *hereafter urged;* and that it was impossible for the court to know the nature of the evidence before it was introduced.

Mr. HAY.——If the gentlemen will only have a little patience, they will find that other circumstances will come out to prove the materiality of this testimony, and will also prove the most perfect connexion between the different parts of the conspiracy. This witness will prove what was the state of the prisoner's mind in August last.

Mr. LEE.——I hope, then, the jury will distinctly understand, that they are not to infer from the court's declining to interfere on the present occasion, that every thing which drops from the witness is to pass without objection, which may be made at any time.

Colonel Morgan (the father of the last witness). There has been a long acquaintance between colonel Burr and myself. He had introduced to my notice, two of his nephews, by the name of ————, and a third, by the name of Edwards, Pierrepont Edwards's son. I had received many civilities from colonel Burr, and had received many civil letters from colonel Burr, from New-York, in consequence of my civilities to those gentlemen. After these things had passed, I had formed such an attachment to him, that I never should have forgotten it, had not this late business taken place. About three years ago, colonel Burr was under considerable and, as I thought, unjust persecution. I had then a younger son (who is now here) studying law at Pittsburg. I wished to make him known to colonel Burr, and in consequence of my friendship for him, and of the great rage of persecution against him, I invited him in that letter, to come to see me at Morganza. In all probability, I should have done the same thing, from the attachment which I had conceived for him. Colonel Burr, however, had left Pittsburg before my letter reached it, and it remains now in my son's bureau at Pittsburg. On the 24th of last August, I received a letter from colonel Burr, dated at Pittsburg, informing me, that he should dine with me next day.

Here Mr. HAY handed the letter to colonel Morgan, who said, that the letter was dated on the 21st, and that he had not for some time seen it, as he had inclosed it to the president of the United States, as introductory to his communication to him.

This letter was handed to me by a man who called himself Count Willie, one of his attendants. I believe my son did not call on me that evening; but next morning I informed him, that from my great affection for colonel Burr, if I was able, I should certainly go and meet colonel Burr; and I requested him and his brother to do it, with a letter of introduction, explanatory of their names and their intention. What conversation took place between him and my son I know not. Colonel Burr mentioned to me in conversation, colonel Dupiester, as one of the first military characters of the age. I shall pass over the conversation and incidents during dinner. After dinner I spoke of our fine country. I observed, that when I first went there, there was not a single family between the Allegany mountain and the Ohio; and that by and by we should have congress sitting in this neighbourhood, or at Pittsburg. We were allowed to sport these things over a glass of wine. " No, never," said colonel Burr, "for in less than five years, you will be totally divided from the Atlantic states." The colonel entered into some arguments to prove, why it should and must be so. The first reason was, the produce of the sale of the western lands being carried to the Atlantic states, and that the people to the west should not be tributary to them. He said that our taxes were very heavy; and demanded, why we should pay them to the Atlantic parts of the country? By this time I took an opportunity to observe, God forbid! I hoped that no such things would ever happen, at least in my time. This observation terminated the conversation as to that particular point. It then turned upon the weakness and imbecility of the federal government.

Mr. WIRT.—Who started that subject?

Answer. Colonel Burr started it. I don't recollect saying any thing on the subject; but began to think that all was not right. He said, that with two hundred men, he could drive congress, with the president at its head, into the river Potowmac; or that it might be done; and he said with five hundred men, he could take possession of New-York. He appealed to colonel Dupiester, if it could not be done: *he* nodded assent. There was a reply made to this by one of my sons, that he would be damned, if they could take our little town of Cannonsburg with that force. Some short time after this, colonel Burr went out from the dining room to the passage, and beckoned to my son Thomas. What their conversation was, I cannot say. Soon after, a walk was proposed to my son's mill, and the company went. When they returned, one (or both of my sons) came to caution me, and said, " You may depend upon it, colonel Burr will this night open himself to you. He wants Tom to go with him." After the usual conversation, colonel Burr went up stairs, and as I thought to go to bed. Mrs. Morgan was reading to me, (as is usual, when the family have retired) when about eleven o'clock, and after I had supposed he had been an hour in bed, she told me that colonel Burr was coming down, and as she had heard my son's conversation, she added, " You'll have it now." Colonel Burr came down with a candle in his hand. Mrs. Morgan immediately retired. The colonel took his seat by me. He drew from his pocket a book. I suppose it was a memorandum book. After looking at it, he asked me, if I knew a Mr. Vigo, of Fort Vincent, a Spaniard. I replied, yes; I knew him; I had reasons to know him. One was, that I had reasons to believe that he was deeply involved in the British conspiracy in 1788, as I supposed; the object of which was to separate the states; and which general Neville and myself had suppressed. I called it a nefarious thing to aim at the division of the states. I was careful to put great emphasis on the word ' *nefarious.*' Colonel Burr finding what kind of man he had to deal with, suddenly stopped, thrust into his pocket the book which I saw had blank leaves in it, and retired to bed. I believe I was pretty well understood. The next morning colonel Burr and colonel Dupiester went off before breakfast, without my expecting it, in company with my son; and from that time to this, I have not seen him but in this place. I well remember some explanatory circumstances. My son agreed with me, that I should apprise the president of our impressions, and point out a mode by which colonel Burr might be followed step by step.

Mr. MAC RAE.—After your son's observation about the town of Cannonsburg and the subsequent conversation, did the prisoner draw any comparison between the people of the eastern and western country?

Answer. He said, "keep yourself on this side of the mountain, and you'll never be disturbed." By which I understood, that there was an attempt to be made, to effect a disunion. There is one more circumstance which I must state to the court. The Sunday after, the judge of our circuit court dined with me. I requested him to mention the circumstances to general Neville, and invited him to come the following Sunday to dinner, with judges Tilghman and Roberts, for I had business of the first importance to communicate. The court being longer engaged than was expected, they did not dine with me on that day; but they did on the following Sunday. These gentlemen wrote a joint letter to the president, informing him of my communications to them.

Cross-examined.

Mr. BURR.—What sort of a book was the one I had in my hand?

Answer. It was a small book like this. [A pocket book.]

Question. Was it bound?

Answer. It was not so large as this; I do not recollect whether it was bound, as it would not be very polite in me to take particular notice of such things, when gentlemen are at my own house.

Question. When you spoke of a nefarious plan, to what transaction did you allude?

Answer. To Vigo's plan, which I conceived was intended to dissever the union.

Question. Who were present when judge Tilghman saw you?

Answer. General Neville and judge Roberts and my son.

Question. Was there any other from Pittsburg?

Answer. None.

Question. Your conversation at dinner, then, was jocular about the moving of congress to Pittsburg? Was not part of the conversation jocular?

Answer. My manner might have been jocular, but not my meaning.

Question. Did you not once live on the Mississippi; or go to that country with a design to settle there?

Answer. I *did*, with the approbation of my country, in order to take up and distribute lands to all my countrymen to the west of the Mississippi.

Question. Did you acquire any lands there?

Answer. I am told I have a right to some lands there.

Question. Where was it that you lived on the Mississippi?

Answer. At New-Madrid.

Question. On which side of the Mississippi?

Answer. The west.

Question. In the Spanish territories?

Answer. With the approbation of the Spanish government.

Question. How long did you live there?

Answer. About forty days. I went from that place to New-Orleans, where I detected a British spy.

Question. In what year?

Answer. In 1788.

General Morgan was then called in at the request of the prisoner.

Mr. Burr.—In what state of mind was your father when general Neville and judge Tilghman were there?

Answer. He had lately had a fall, which had done him considerable injury.

Question. I mean as to his capacity. Did you not make some apology to judge Tilghman for the state of his mind?

Answer. I did tell judge Tilghman, that my father was old and infirm; and like other old men, told long stories and was apt to forget his repetitions.

Mr. Mac Rae.—What was the prisoner's reply to your ....?

Answer. When colonel Burr said that with two hundred men he could drive the president and congress into the Potowmac, I must confess that I felt myself hurt, and replied with some warmth, " I'll be damned, sir, if you could take the little town of Cannonsburg with that force." Colonel Burr replied, " Confine yourself to this side of the mountain, and it is another thing."

Question. Do you recollect whether any thing were said concerning the people on the eastern and western sides of the Allegany.

Answer. He answered, " Confine yourselves on this side of the mountain and it is another thing."

Mr. BAKER objected to this examination by Mr. Mac Rae, as improper.

Question by Mr. BURR.—Do you recollect that the probability of a Spanish war was mentioned?

Answer. It was a general subject of conversation between colonel Burr and myself.

Thomas Morgan was next sworn: His evidence was as follows:

On the evening of the 21st of August, my father received a letter from Pittsburg, by the hands of some person, the signature of which was Aaron Burr. In that letter the writer communicated his intention of dining with my father on the following day: he also mentioned that he should take the liberty of introducing a friend. My father requested my brother and myself to meet him, which we accordingly did. Nothing of importance occurred during our ride in my presence. Colonel Burr rode generally with my brother; colonel Dupiester was often with myself, and sometimes we were promiscuously together. Whilst we were at and after dinner, colonel Burr emphatically, as I thought, confidently and with great earnestness said, that we (meaning the people of the west) would be separated in five years from the Atlantic states; the Allegany mountain to be the line of division. He said that great numbers were not necessary to execute great military deeds: all that was wanting was a leader, in whom they could place confidence, and who they believed could carry them through. This conversation occurred during dinner. He said that with five hundred men, New-York could be taken; and that with two hundred, congress could be driven into the Potowmac river.

To the last observation, my brother, I think, indignantly replied, " By God! sir, with that force you cannot take our little town of Cannonsburg." Colonel Burr's reply to this observation was, " Confine yourself to this side of the mountain, and I'll not contradict you;" or words to that effect. Colonel Burr withdrew from the room where we dined, and on reaching the door leading into the entry, invited me, by a nod, to go with him. When we had arrived at the back door of the entry, out of hearing of any other person, colonel Burr inquired what my pursuits were. I informed him that I was studying the law.

He tnen said, he was sure I could not find employment for either body or mind; but he did not further explain himself. He said that there were, or asked, if there were not, a number of young men in Pittsburg similarly situated. He said that under our government there was no encouragement for talents; that John Randolph had declared on the floor of congress, that men of talents were dangerous to the government. He asked me, how or whether I would like a military expedition or enterprise? (I cannot recollect which, but it was some such expression.) My answer was, " It would entirely depend upon the object or cause for which I was to fight." I think previously, or certainly soon after, he said, " I wish you were on your way with me." After asking colonel Burr concerning a young man (Mr. Duer) living at New-Orleans, with whom I had a slight acquaintance, he said he was doing well; and he then spoke of Duer's brother, of whom I knew nothing, who was also doing well, as a lawyer, but he had much rather be at the head of a military corps. Mr. Morgan then proposed to state the steps which his father had taken to defeat A. Burr's projects, when he was stopped by the court.

Cross-examined.

Mr. BURR.—Had you ever spoken to me before?

Answer. Never.

Question. Did you not mention, with some complaints, the neglect which your education had received?

Answer. No.

Question. Did you not complain about wasting your time?

Answer. I recollect nothing on that subject, but your remark, that I could not surely find employment for either body or mind.

Mr. WIRT.—Do you recollect your answer to colonel Burr's observation, that he would like to see you on your way with him?

Answer. I do not recollect except what I have stated already. Here our conversation ended.

Mr. HAY.—Do you recollect, when you said that your liking a military life would depend on the object or cause in which you were engaged, whether any thing more was said by colonel Burr?

Answer. No.

Examination of Jacob Allbright.

Mr. HAY.—Our object is to prove by *his* testimony the actual assemblage of men on Blannerhassett's island, and it goes of course to prove directly the overt act.

Jacob Allbright. The first I knew of this business was. I was hired on the island to help to build a kiln for drying corn; and after working some time, Mrs. Blannerhassett told me, that Mr. Blannerhassett and colonel Burr were going to lay in provisions for an army for a year. I went to the mill, where I carried the corn to be ground after it had been dried. I worked four weeks on that business in the island. Last fall (or in September) after Blannerhassett had come home (he had been promising me cash for some time) I stept up to him. He had no money at the time; but would pay me next day, or soon. Says he, " Mr. Allbright, you are a Dutchman." But he asked me first and foremost, whether I would not join with him and go down the river? I told him, I did not know what they were upon; and he said, " Mr. Allbright, we are going to settle a new country." And I gave him an answer, that I would not like to leave my family. He said, he did not want any families to go along with him. Then he said to me, " You are a Dutchman, and a common man; and as the Dutch are apt to be scared by high men, if you'll go to New-Lancaster, where the Dutch live, and get me twenty or thirty to go with us, I will give you as many dollars." New-Lancaster was some distance off. I went home then, and gave him no answer upon that. In a few days after the boats came and landed at the island. The snow was about two or three inches deep, and I went out a hunting. I was on the Ohio side; I met two men; I knew they belonged to the boats, but I wanted to find out; and they asked me whether I had not given my consent to go along with Blannerhassett down the river? As we got into a conversation together they named themselves colonel Burr's men, belonging to the boats, landed at the island. When they asked me, whether I had not consented to go down with Blannerhassett, I put a question to them. I told them I did not know what they were about; and one of the gentlemen told me, they were going to take a silver mine from the *Spanish*. I asked the gentlemen, whether they would not allow, that this would raise war with America? They replied, no. These were only a few men; and if they went with a good army, they would give up the country and nothing more said about it. I had all this conversation with the two men. These men shewed me what fine rifles they had, going down the river with them. Then I went to the island and Blannerhassett paid me off in Kentucky notes. People however did'nt like these notes very well, and I went over to the bank at Kanhawa to change them. I got two of the notes changed; and one, a ten dollar note, was returned to my hand, for which I wished to get silver from Blannerhassett. I went to the island the day the proclamation came out. But before I went to Blannerhassett's house, I heard he was not at home, but at Marietta. I went on the Virginia side, where I met three other men, belonging to the boats, with three complete rifles. They made a call upon me, to take them to the island in my canoe, and I *accepted* [excepted or refused] to it; but afterwards I carried the third man, who stood close by my canoe, over to the island. After being some time on the island, I went down to the four boats. Blannerhassett was not at home yet; and I met some of the boat people shooting at a mark. They had a fire between the bank and boats. I saw this in the day time.

Mr. HAY.—How many boats were there?

Answer. Four.

I waited at the house till Blannerhassett came home. He appeared very much scared. One of the boat-men came up to him for something, and he told him, " Don't trouble me, I have trouble enough already." He went up to his chamber; and I saw no more of him. I asked an old gentleman who was there, and with whom I was well acquainted, to go up to his chamber, and change my note for silver. He did go, and brought me silver. By and by I heard that they were going to start that night. Thinks I, " I'll see the end of it." This was the night of the very day that Blannerhassett got back from Marietta. He got back before night. When night came on, I was among the men and also in the kitchen; and saw the boat-men running bullets. One of them spoke out to the others, " Boys, let's mould as many bullets, as we can fire twelve rounds." After that, I saw no more till after twelve o'clock at night. Then Blannerhassett came down from the chamber, and called up some of his servants; he had four or five trunks. There were not trusty hands enough to carry them to the boats; and some person called after my name, and asked me to help them; and I carried one of the trunks and moved along with them. When we got down, some person, I don't particularly know who, but think it was Blannerhassett himself, asked me to stand by the trunks, till they were put in the boats. When the last of them went off, I saw men standing in a circle on the shore. I went up to them; perhaps they were five or six rods from me. The first thing that I noticed, was their laying plans and consulting how Blannerhassett and Comfort Tyler should get safe by Galliopolis. One Nahum Bennett [perhaps *Bent*] was called forward, and when he came, Blannerhassett asked him, whether he had not two smart horses? Nahum Bennett answered no; he had but one. Then Blannerhassett told him to go to captain Dennie, and get his sorrel horse; and Nahum Bennett told him, that the sorrel horse had no shoes on; and Blannerhassett said, the roads were soft and would not hurt the horse. Blannerhassett told Nahum Bennett to meet him and Comfort Tyler with the horses, some where about Galliopolis: Bennett inquired how he was to find him out, should he inquire for him? " No." " Have you no friends there?" " No." Mrs. Blannerhassett then came forward, and she told Blannerhassett and Comfort Tyler, that they must take a canoe and get into it before they got to Galliopolis, and sail down the stream of the Ohio; for no body would mind a couple of men going down the stream. She said " *she'd*" pay for the canoe. Blannerhassett told Nahum Bennett to take the two horses and pass round Galliopolis before day, and then they might surround [go round] Galliopolis. After that, a man by the name of Tupper, laid his hands upon Blannerhassett, and said, " Your body is in my hands, in the name of the commonwealth." Some *such words* as that he mentioned. When Tupper made that motion, there were seven or eight muskets levelled at him. Tupper looked about him and said, " Gentlemen, I hope you will not do the like." One of the gentlemen who was nearest, about two yards off, said, " *I'd as lieve as not.*" Tupper then changed his speech, and said he wished him to escape safe down the river, and wished him luck. Tupper before told Blannerhassett he should stay and stand his trial. But Blannerhassett said no; that the people in the neighbourhood were coming down next day to take him, and he would go. Next day after, I saw the Wood county militia going down. The people went off in boats that night about one.

Question. All?

Answer. All but one, who was a doctor. All belonging to the boats had some kind of arms. Some of the boats were on the shore and some not.

Mr. HAY.—How many men were there in all?

Answer. About twenty or thirty: I did not, however, count them. Every man belonging to the boats that I took notice of, had arms.

Mr. Coleman (one of the jury.) What day, month, or year, was this?

Answer. In the fall of the year. I don't recollect the month or particular time, but there was snow on the ground.

Mr. HAY.—Do you recollect whether it snows in September?

Answer. I do not know.

Mr. Sheppard (one of the jury.) Was Tupper a magistrate or officer?

Answer. I know not.

Question. Where had Blannerhassett been?

Answer. In Kentucky.

Mr. WIRT.—Had you seen colonel Burr on the island?

Answer. Yes.

Question. Was he there before Blannerhassett went to Kentucky?

Answer. He was.

Question. Did you speak of the boats under the command of Tyler?

Answer. I did.

Question. Did the boats quit the island at the time of hearing about the proclamation?

Answer. Yes.

Question. Did the Wood county militia go there next day?

Answer. Yes.

Question by Mr. Parker (one of the jury). Did you hear Peter Taylor give advice?

Answer. I did not.

Question by Mr. Parker. Did you see Peter Taylor converse with Blannerhassett that night?

Answer. I do not recollect, I was busy about the boats.

Question by the same. How long did Aaron Burr remain on the island?

Answer. I do not recollect.

Question by the same. How long had he been there before the departure of the boats?

To this question, he *first* answered, that he did not know; and that Mr. Burr never returned back to the island: but after some reflection he said, that he had been there about six weeks before the departure of the boats.

Mr. Sheppard (one of the jury.) How long was Blannerhassett absent?

Answer. I don't know. I did not live on the island.

Cross-examined.

Mr. BURR.—Was that Mr. Tupper called general Tupper?

Answer. He was.

Question. Did you know general Tupper?

Answer. Yes.

Question. Is that the gentleman? [pointing to general Tupper, who was present in court].

Answer. Yes.

Question. When the muskets were levelled at him, did they seem to have a mind to hurt him?

Answer. Yes. A gentleman near me said, " *I'd as lieve* shoot *as not.*"

Mr. BURR.—You said differently on a former occasion. Don't you recollect making a statement in which nothing was said about levelling guns at him? and that it looked like exercising?

Answer. I do not.

A desultory conversation here ensued between the opposite counsel.

Mr. BURR professed that it was his intention to degrade the witness, by invalidating his credibility.

Mr. HAY said, that it was very probable, if this man had at different times stated what *seemed* to be contradictory, he did it through ignorance; and Mr. Burr insisted, that an error through ignorance might be as injurious to him, as an error through immorality; he cared not which; that the consequences to him were in both cases the same.

Mr. BURR.—Have you not been examined before?

Answer. Yes.

Question. By whom?

Answer. By Mr. Jackson.

Question. Had he not printed questions in his hand?

Answer. He had a paper in his hand.

Question. Did he set down your answers?

Answer. Yes.

Question. How long after the guns were pointed at general Tupper, before the men went to their boats?

Answer. I do not recollect. Any thing that I am not certain of, I cannot speak to.

Question. Was Mrs. Blannerhassett there when the guns were pointed?

Answer. Yes.

Question. Was Tupper inside of the circle?

Answer. Yes.

Question. Was she too?

Answer. I don't recollect.

Question. Did you see Mr. Woodbridge there?

Answer. I don't know him. He lived in the state of Ohio.

Question. How long did you work with Blannerhassett?

Answer. Six weeks.

Question. At what time was it that you saw me there?

Answer. I do not recollect.

Mr. BURR.—The counsel for the United States know, I presume, this circumstance, and have testimony to ascertain it.

Mr. HAY.—We have not, as far as I am informed.

Mr. BURR.—If they have no objection, I will state *when* I was on the island.

Mr. HAY said he had not.

Mr. Burr then said, that it was on the last day of August, and the first of September, that he was on the island.

Question. Were the boats in the stream, or close to the land, when general Tupper wished them good luck?

Answer. In shore.

Mr. Anthony (one of the jury.) Did you see any powder?
Answer. No.

Mr. HAY.—Were you in the boats?

Answer. I was not.

Mr. BURR.—Where does general Tupper live?

Answer. In Marietta.

Question. Does he not belong to the state of Ohio?
Answer. Yes.

Question. When did you first know him?
Answer. Last fall.

Question by Mr. Parker. Where did you live before you went to work on the island?

Answer. About a mile from the island.

Mr. BURR then asked the clerk for the statement, which he had taken of Allbright's testimony, when it was submitted to the court on a former occasion, on the motion for binding himself in a higher bail.

The clerk handed him the copy, and the prisoner proceeded with the examination.

Question. You said before, that the men who raised their muskets against general Tupper, were not in earnest?

Answer. That was a piece of my opinion. I did not know whether they were in earnest; as there was no quarrel among them, and no firing afterwards.

Mr. Carrington, (one of the jury), reminded him of an expression of one of the party: " I had as *lieve as not shoot*," which shewed that they were in earnest.

Mr. Burr.—I beg the court to call on the prosecution, for the deposition of this witness, taken before John G. Jackson.

Mr. Hay said, that he would not let gentlemen have access to his port folio when they pleased; that he must be satisfied by reasons assigned, or required by the order of the court, before he produced it.

The Chief Justice was not satisfied, that the court had a right to call for the affidavit.

Mr. Wickham said it was obvious, that there were certain suspicions attached to the credibility of the witness; and that it was their desire to compare his present testimony with his former affidavit.

Mr. Hay observed, that Mr. Jackson might not have taken down the testimony of the witness in his language, but couched it in his own; hence there might be an apparent variation between the present evidence and the affidavit; but that there was no real variance: that the object of Mr. Jackson's taking his affidavit was merely to ascertain, whether he were possessed of any useful information, and to know whether he ought to be summoned as a witness or not: that this was the object in taking all the testimony which had been collected: that his affidavit was therefore general; but that the man, after finding that he was to be summoned as a witness, had revolved the subject in his own mind, and recollected many circumstances which had not before occurred to him.

Mr. Burr.—We have a right to coerce this paper. If gentlemen will not surrender it, I may at all events avail myself of their refusal. My object is to prove such a diversity between the statements of the witness at different times, as may destroy all faith in his recollection.

Mr. Hay.—Then, sir, although I might retain this paper, the gentlemen are welcome to make all the use of it they can. Take it.

Mr. Burr then proceeded. When you said that all had guns, did you mean to say, that *all in the circle*, or *all of them together without exception had arms?*

Answer. There were seven or eight who had guns, and there were other arms; but there might be more men than guns.

Question. How many were in the circle?

Answer. I did not count them.

Question. What kind of guns had they?

Answer. Rifles and short guns.

Question. Did you see any guns with bayonets?

Answer. I saw none.

Mr. MAC RAE.—When did you see most arms? in the day, or in the night?

Answer. I saw more arms in the day; but it was in the night that I saw most armed men.

Mr. Parker (one of the jury.) Why did you think that *all* of them had arms?

Answer. Because I was with them almost all night. In the day, I saw some of them shooting at marks; and I saw other arms at that time lying upon the beach.

Mr. WICKHAM.—Did you *see them all with arms at once?*

Answer. No.

Question by the same. How many arms did you see *in the whole*, or *at any* one time and place together?

Answer. I cannot tell.

Question by the same. Did you know the men who had arms?

Answer. I did not,

Question by the same. Did you know the names of the other men?

Answer. No.

Question by the same. Would you know any of them if you saw them?

Answer. I would not. They are all strangers to me.

Question by the same. How could you distinguish the arms seen in the day-time, from those seen late in the evening, or at night?

Answer. I cannot answer.

Question. How then are you certain that you did not see the same arms at different times, in the hands of different persons?

To this question he made no answer.

Peter Taylor was then called, and

Mr. HAY asked him, whether he had not seen Mr. Burr on the island?

He answered that he had not.

Mr. BURR.—If gentlemen have now done with the overt act, or when they have done, I will thank them to inform me; for then we shall have some considerations to offer to the court.

Mr. HAY.—We have other additional testimony to offer on this very point: the assemblage of men on the island.

Maurice P. Belknap was called, but did not answer.

William Love was then sworn.

Mr. HAY.—Were you on Blannerhassett's island?

Answer. Yes: but I was not there at the time when colonel Tyler's boats arrived there. I was then at Marietta; and it was on Sunday that I went down in a skiff with two barrels of salt.

Question. How many boats were at the island?

Answer. Four.

Question. How many men?

Answer. I cannot tell you; but I suppose *about betwixt* twenty and twenty-five belonging to colonel Tyler's boats. When I arrived on the island, Blannerhassett met me.

Question. Did you see any arms?

Answer. I saw the men and rifles. I know that Mr. Blannerhassett took away with him one brace of horse pistols, a brace of pocket pistols and a dirk. Some fusees were put in the boat; but not more than three or four, all belonging to him.

Question. And what arms had Tyler's men?

Answer. Pistols, dirks and rifles, they brought there; but all were not armed with rifles. I know not whether they were armed with different things. Some of the men had guns, some had dirks. Being, as how, Mr. Blannerhassett's servant, that is, his groom, I went down the river with him.

Question. Did you see Taylor and Allbright there?

Answer. I knew Peter Taylor very well. I saw him there the morning of the day I went away: and I saw Allbright also. I saw Mr. Woodbridge too.

Question. What time did you set sail?

Answer. We were the last to embark; and we started between twelve and one, as well as I can recollect. We parted with general Tupper in the greatest friendship, so I understood from others. I do not know that I saw him. I was the last man who went into the boat.

Question. Did you see the prisoner on the island?

Answer. I never saw colonel Burr on the island. I first saw him at Natchez about two and a half years ago.

Question. What took place after you left the island?

Answer. That night was very cold. The next morning we stopt and made fires. Mr. Blannerhassett and colonel Tyler went ashore and called the company together; and the best I could make out was, I understood that the governor of Ohio, had uttered state-warrants against Mr. Blannerhassett and Tyler; and that they wanted to make their escape as fast as possible. I went down with the party to Bayou Pierre, where . . . . .

Mr. Burr expressed a wish, that the attention of the witness should be *at present*, confined to the transactions on the island. He said that gentlemen ought to confine themselves to evidence of the overt act; that they would submit the question to the court; that it would be too late to discuss the question, whether the evidence ought to be submitted to the jury, after it should have been all heard.

Mr. Martin.—Gentlemen had better confine themselves to facts within the district of Virginia. When they travel beyond the district, we shall have some important questions to bring forward. We shall object to the production of such evidence.

Mr. Hay acquiesced for the *present*, in this arrangement.

Cross-examined.

Mr. Burr.—Were not some of Mr. Blannerhassett's clothes put up in the boats?

Answer. Yes.

Question. Did you not assist in putting those things in the boats?

Answer. Yes.

Question. Were not his books put in boxes and trunks?

Answer. None that I ever saw.

Question. How long had you lived with Blannerhassett?

Answer. Ten or twelve days before we started.

Question. How many guns had the party?

Answer. I do not know: many of the young men that came down with Tyler were out a gunning.

Question. Did you see any thing like military appearance?

Answer. The men were in a state of preparation to defend themselves, because they expected people from the mouth of Kenhawa, to attack Blannerhassett and the island. And to the best of my opinion, they did not mean to be killed, without some return of the shot. It was said at Marietta, that the people of Kenhawa were to attack him; and I suppose they would have done their best to defend themselves. I should be sorry if a man slapped me on my face, without returning the blow.

Question. Was there no disturbance among the party on the island?

Answer. None: I did not part with my friends in England more comfortably than in parting with the people on the island.

Question. Were they in fear of being attacked when they first met together?

Answer. Not till Tyler's boats came down. I do not recollect to have seen general Tupper there.

Mr. Parker (one of the jury.) Did you ever see all the men with arms?

Answer. I cannot say. When I got to the mouth of Cumberland river, I saw a chest of arms opened.

Mr. MAC RAE.—Were any chests of arms put into the boats when you left the island?

Answer. Not that I know. They might or might not have been put on board without my seeing them. Many things were put into the boats before I got in.

Mr. Parker (one of the jury.) Had you no conversation with Blannerhassett about the expedition?

Answer. Only that if I did not choose to go with him, he would recommend me to some travelling gentleman as a servant; or, if I went to the Washita, he would make me a present of a piece of land.

Mr. BURR.—Did you see any arms but those belonging to Blannerhassett?

Answer. I did not.

Question by the same. Did you see any guns presented?

Answer. I did not.

Question. Were they mostly young gentlemen who came in the boats?

Answer. They looked like young gentlemen in that country.

Mr. WIRT.—Why did they go away in the night?

Answer. They were afraid of being taken by warrants issued by the governor of Ohio.

Mr. MAC RAE.—Was the chest which you saw opened at the mouth of Cumberland, the same as those that you saw go from the island?

Answer. No.

Question. What did you think of this business?

Answer. I understood the object of the expedition was to settle Washita lands.

Mr. HAY.—What kind of looking men were they?

Answer. They looked like gentlemen, such as live upon their own property.

Question. Did they look like men used to work?

Answer. They did not.

Question. When did you see Mr. Blannerhassett that night down at the beach?

Answer. Late that night: it was a very cold night, raining and freezing: it was generally expected that the people would come and destroy Blannerhassett's house.

Mr. Parker (one of the jurymen.) Did you see any bullets run?

Answer. Yes: but I do not know how many. I was a servant in the house, but could not mind my own business and other people's too.

Dudley Woodbridge was next sworn.

Mr. HAY.—Were you on the island when the boats left it?

Answer. I slept there that night.

Mr. WIRT.—What party do you mean?

Answer. I allude to the four boats with Comfort Tyler, Mr. Smith and others.

Question. Were you at the boats?

Answer. I passed them about dusk.

Question. Did you see any of the men?

Answer. I came to the island about dusk. I saw five or six standing about the boats. I went directly up from the landing to the house and saw fifteen or twenty men in one of the rooms of Mr. Blannerhassett's house.

Question. Had they any arms in their hands when you saw them?

Answer. I recollect to have seen no arms, but two pair of pistols on the bureau of the room where I slept, which were gone in the morning.

Mr. HAY.—Had you no communication with Mr. Burr or Mr. Blannerhassett about this expedition? Will you inform us what you know on this subject?

Answer. About the beginning of September or last of August, Mr. Blannerhassett, (with whom I had been connected in commercial business for six or eight years past, under the firm of Dudley Woodbridge and Company) called with colonel Burr at our counting house at Marietta. Mr. Blannerhassett observed that colonel Burr wished us to purchase a quantity of provisions. I am not positive that Mr. Burr was present when he *first* mentioned the subject, but I think he was. Colonel Burr then went into an inquiry about the prices of different kinds of provisions, and the expense of boats best calculated to carry provisions up and down the river. After his making a number of inquiries and receiving such information as I could give him, he left a memorandum of such provisions as he wanted, and of the boats which he wished to have built. They were to be on the Schenectady model, such as are used on the Mohawk river. The number ordered was fifteen; only eleven were completed.

Question. What were their dimensions?

Answer. Principally ten feet wide and forty feet long; five were to be ten feet longer.

Question. What provisions were ordered?

Answer. Pork, flour, whiskey, bacon and kiln-dried meal; but no article was purchased but pork, the prices in our market being much higher than those limited in the memorandum. I immediately made a contract with colonel Barker to build the boats, and proceeded to make arrangements for purchasing provisions. The boats were built up the *Muskingum*, about seven miles above Marietta, and were to be delivered on the 9th of December. On that morning when they were to be brought down (the 9th of December,) I saw six or eight armed men of the militia going to take possession of the boats. I set off for Blannerhassett's island, but met Mr. Blannerhassett, Comfort Tyler, Mr. Smith and some young men from Belpré going up to take down the boats. I informed them of the proceedings at Marietta, and advised Mr. Blannerhassett not to go up. After some consultation, he determined not to go up, and returned to the island. I went back to Marietta to get some money and papers, and returned that evening to the island, after getting the papers.

Mr. HAY.—On what terms was the contract for the boats made?

Answer. I made the contract for the boats with colonel Burr and agreed to take a *draft* on New-York. When Mr. Blannerhassett handed me the draft, I expressed my dissatisfaction at the long sight at which it was drawn (being ninety days,) observing, that it would not become due, until after the time in which the boats and provisions were to be delivered, and that I wished to run no hazard. Mr. Blannerhassett, with some warmth, asked me if I doubted colonel Burr's honour? When I repeated that I wished to run no risk, he said that *he* would guarantee the draft and be answerable himself; and that in the event of its not being paid, I might charge it to him. The draft was drawn by Mr. Burr on Mr. Ogden of New-York. These were the boats which Smith, Tyler, Blannerhassett and the young men were going up to receive.

Mr. HAY.—Do you recollect *where* the boats were to be delivered by the contract.

Answer. Colonel Barker undertook to bring them, but there was no contract to deliver them at any particular place.

Mr. Parker. Did you say that it was the 9th day of December that the boats were to go away?

Answer. The boats were to be delivered on the 9th, but those that were at the island went away on the 10th. When colonel Barker was bringing them to Marietta, they were taken by general Buel, as I understood, by order of the governor of Ohio.

Mr. MAC RAE.—State what occurrences took place on the island.

Answer. I arrived about dusk, and immediately inquired about Mr. Blannerhassett. I stated to him that I was ready to adjust our partnership-concerns, and that I had brought down the money and papers for that purpose. We went up stairs; we were two hours engaged in the business; after settling which, I set off to go across the river home, and met Mr. Belknap at the shore. He asked me to go back with him, that he had business to do. I returned with him. We went both to bed at nine o'clock at night, where I remained, and did not, as the witness Peter Taylor states, go to the shore with the party when they went off. His saying that I was there then is a mistake, as this gentleman [Mr. Belknap] can prove.

Mr. HAY.—State to the court and jury, for whom the boats were built. Was the contract made for the company?

Answer. Yes; it may be so considered; but it was not particularly specified. Mr. Blannerhassett first introduced the subject, and Mr. Burr then spoke. As to the use for which these boats were intended, Mr. Blannerhassett made some communications to me respecting it. Shall I now state to the court these communications?

[He was requested to proceed.]

Late in August or early in September, Mr. Blannerhassett mentioned to me, that he had embarked in an enterprise with colonel Burr; that general Eaton and some others were engaged in it; and that the prospects were flattering. Our first conversation lasted but a few minutes. The next week I was at the island, when he went into further particulars. From what he stated, the inference I drew, was, that his object was Mexico. He did not positively say so, but I inferred it from several circumstances, particularly from a map of that country which he shewed me. He spoke highly of the country; stated its advantages, wealth, fertility and healthiness. He asked me if I had a disposition to join? I evaded his question. but could not forbear telling him that I preferred my situation to an uncertainty, (which was the same as declining it.) On the way up to Marietta, he observed, that he did not wish me to say any thing about his conversations on this subject. This is the substance of my testimony.

Mr. HAY.—Do you recollect any further detail of the plan or object of the expedition?

Answer. I do not.

Mr. HAY.—What became of the boats and the pork you purchased?

Answer. The pork was taken and sold by order of the president or government; it was sold, as I understood, by general Buel. The boats, or a part of them, were afterwards fitted out by the government for transports to convey troops from Marietta to St. Louis.

Colonel BURR.—Do you recollect that I told you, that I wanted the description of boats used in the Mohawk river; and were they not made for shoal water, and to go up the stream?

Answer. You did. The boats were to be calculated for shallow water.

Colonel BURR.—You know Mr. Blannerhassett well. Was it not ridiculous for him to be engaged in a military enterprise? How far can he distinguish a man from a horse? Ten steps?

Answer. He is very near sighted. He cannot know you from any of us, at the distance we are now from one another. He knows nothing of military affairs. I never understood that he was a military man.

Question by the same. What became of his library?

Answer. Part of it was carried down by Mrs. Blannerhassett; the residue was left behind, and has been since sold.

Question by the same. Do you recollect when I was at Marietta? Was it not about the last of August or first of September?

Answer. I left Philadelphia about the middle of August, and on my return, I saw you about the time you mention. I have never heard that you have been there since.

Question. What became of the draft on Mr. Ogden for two thousand dollars?

Answer. It was paid.

Question. What quantity of pork did you purchase for me?

Answer. About one hundred barrels.

Question. At what price?

Answer. It cost about twelve and was charged at thirteen dollars per barrel.

Question. What became of it?

Answer. I stored it in Mr. Green's cellar, adjoining our store: it was taken and sold by general Buel, by order of the government, as already mentioned; that is as I understood.

Question. Did you demand it of Mr. Green?

[The answer to this question was not heard.]

Question. To whom did you consider the pork as belonging when seized? Whose loss was it? Yours or mine?

Answer. It may hereafter become a dispute.

Question. What were the boats estimated to be worth?

Answer. Colonel Barker's bill for the eleven boats, amounted to twelve or thirteen hundred dollars.

Mr. MARTIN.—Were you at any time that evening on the water's side, with Mr. or Mrs. Blannerhassett?

Answer. I was not.

Mr. WIRT.—You were asked, sir, about Mr. Blannerhassett's military talents? Permit me to ask you what were his pecuniary resources; what was the state of his money matters?

Answer. I believe they are not as great as was generally imagined. I gave him six thousand dollars for one half of his profits of our business; he had about three thousand dollars in stock in our company's concern. His fortune is much less than is generally understood. He had not over five or six thousand dollars in the hands of his agent at Philadelphia. His island and improvements cost about forty or fifty thousand dollars. It would not however, sell for near that sum, except to a person of the same cast with Mr. Blannerhassett. After building his house, his property exclusive of the island and five negroes amounted probably to seventeen thousand dollars.

Question by Mr. Coleman (the juror.) Explain again if you please; in what did that property consist, and how much money could he command?

Answer. He had nine thousand dollars in my hands in stock and profits already stated, and about one thousand dollars on another account, and the money in his agent's hands, besides his island and negroes.

Question. Had he no foreign funds?

Answer. I think he had none. They were vested in American stock some years before.

Question. What was the amount of property he had in these funds?

Answer. I believe the property left him by his father amounted to twenty thousand pounds sterling, which he vested in British three per cent. stock.

Mr. WIRT.—Is he esteemed a man of vigorous talents?

Answer. He is; and a man of literature. But it was mentioned among the people in the country, that he had every kind of sense but common sense; at least he had the reputation of having more of other than of common sense.

Question. What are his favourite pursuits?

Answer. Chemistry and music.

Mr. HAY.—Was colonel Burr to have returned to the island

Answer. I believe so; I expected him to have returned in about two months, the time for the delivery of the boats.

Mr. HAY.—Had you received any money from Burr before the presentation of the draft by Blannerhassett?

Answer. The draft was at so long a sight, that I objected to letting the property out of my hands, till I was secured by the responsibility of Mr. Blannerhassett. The balance over the two thousand dollars (the amount of the draft on Ogden) was to be paid by Mr. Burr on his return. He was to return in two months and to complete the payment when the property was delivered.

Mr. HAY.—Did Mr. Blannerhassett bring you the draft?

Answer. He did; but Burr made the contract with me.

Mr. HAY.—Do I understand you correctly in supposing that Mr. Burr contracted to pay two thousand dollars in one draft, and the balance on his return?

Answer. You do.

Mr. LEE.—How many acres of land are in the island?

Answer. Mr. Blannerhassett owned about one hundred and eighty acres, which was about half of the island, and cost him about five thousand dollars; but with the house and all, cost him forty or fifty thousand dollars as already observed.

Mr. Hay——Was not one of the boats fitted up for Mrs. Blannerhassett and family?

Answer. One of the large boats was. Mr. Blannerhassett had taken a keel boat, belonging to the firm, up to colonel Barker's to be fitted up for his family; but by colonel Barker's advice, he concluded to have one of the large boats prepared for that purpose, on account of its superior accommodation. This was accordingly done.

Mr. Hay.—Had not the delivery of the boats been interrupted by the armed men, would they not have been delivered to Blannerhassett?

Answer. I suppose they would have been delivered at Marietta, where he would have received them.

Mr. Martin.—Was not the contract made by colonel Burr with your firm?

Answer. It was.

Question by the same. Do you understand that colonel Burr has received any consideration for this sum of two thousand dollars thus paid?

Answer. I do not know.

Mr. Wirt.—If the delivery of these boats had not been prevented, would they not have been delivered to Blannerhassett or Burr?

Answer. They would have been delivered to either. The company contracted for them.

Mr. Hay.—If delivered to Mr. Blannerhassett, would you not have considered yourself as delivering them to one of Burr's associates?

Answer. I cannot say what I should have thought.

Colonel Burr.—How came you to suppose yourself authorized to deliver the boats to Blannerhassett, since I gave the draft?

Answer. I should in any event have considered myself justified in delivering the boats to him, as he guaranteed the payment for them, and he had property to a larger amount in my hands; and besides these considerations, early in September Blannerhassett had mentioned to me his having joined colonel Burr.

Mr. Baker.—Did you make any stay upon the beach, on the night of their departure?

Answer. I did not; for I returned immediately to the house with Mr. Belknap.

Mr. BOTTS.—Were the people peaceable on that night?

Answer. Yes.

Question by the same. Did you hear any noise, like that of war, the roaring of cannon or the rattling of small arms?

Answer. None.

Mr. WIRT —Did you hear any alarm in the evening about the militia from the Ohio side?

Answer. There was some alarm in the evening.

Mr. Parker. Did Mr. Burr leave the island, before Mr. Blannerhassett communicated to you his being joined with him?

Answer. I do not precisely recollect the *time* of the communication; but I knew that Blannerhassett had connected himself with him in the same enterprise, and I would therefore have delivered the boats to him.

Mr. Coleman. Was Mr. Blannerhassett's determination to go away, the effect of your having told him of the armed men going to take the boats?

Answer. That information might have operated with other circumstances.

Mr. Parker. Did you see the president's proclamation on that day?

Answer. No; *that* was Wednesday, and it came next Friday by the mail. It was handed to me by the postmaster. I did not hear of its being sent otherwise. I might have heard of it before but I am not absolutely *certain.*

Mr. MAC RAE.—Did you hear *any thing* of it before?

Answer. I do not recollect distinctly. I believe that the printer at Marietta, who had been at Pittsburg, had brought some information about a proclamation; I have some idea that he might have mentioned that he had seen it.

Mr. HAY.—Did you hear any thing of a state warrant?

Answer. No. I did hear that the legislature of the state of Ohio were sitting with closed doors, in consequence of something communicated by Mr. Graham, and that it was probable that the boats would be stopped, and that they would suppress the enterprise.

Mr. WICKHAM.—Did you understand, that Blannerhassett's boats or the people on the island would be taken?

Answer. I did not suppose that they would go to Virginia; but that they would only stop the boats that were built pursuant to his contract up the Muskingum.

Mr. HAY.—What was the cause of his precipitate flight? Did you hear any particular observations from any of the party on the island?

Answer. Mr. Blannerhassett told me that he would go off in three or four hours; and I heard Comfort Tyler say, that he would not resist the constituted authorities, but that he would not be stopped by a mob.

Mr. WIRT.—At the time he said so, was the legislature of Ohio understood to be in session, with closed doors?

Answer. It was; and I *saw* the militia of Wood county assembled the next day or the day after.

Mr. BURR.—Was there not some danger of being stopped by the ice, if they had not gone off as soon as they did?

Answer. I thought so; and that it was also hazardous for Mrs. Blannerhassett to go. Tyler was detained two days by Blannerhassett.

Mr. MAC RAE.—Did Blannerhassett that night communicate his apprehensions to you?

Answer. He did not.

Mr. BURR.—Were Tyler's party disorderly?

Answer. They were not.

Question. Did they do any mischief? Were they guilty of any misconduct?

Answer. None.

The court then adjourned till to-morrow at the usual hour.

THURSDAY, August 20th, 1807.

The court met at the usual hour, when a desultory discussion took place, in which

Colonel BURR and his counsel insisted, that the counsel for the prosecution should produce all the evidence which they had, relative to the overt act, before they attempted to offer any collateral testimony: and again reminded them, that as soon as all their testimony on that point was introduced, they had certain propositions to submit to the court.

The counsel for the prosecution said, that they had some more evidence to introduce on this point, and

Simeon Poole was then sworn.

Mr. HAY.—Be so obliging, as to say what you know, with respect to the men on Blannerhassett's island.

Simeon Poole. I never was on the island at that time; but was opposite to it. I saw boats and men there, if I mistake not, on the 10th of December. I arrived opposite the island about dusk, at the distance of about one hundred and fifty, or two hundred yards from it. I do not know how many boats there were. I saw people walking about in the evening; and in the course of the night, they kindled a fire, and I saw some persons by the light, that appeared to be armed, as if they were sentinels.

Mr. HAY.—Why did you think they were so?

Answer. I don't know that they were; but they appeared so to my view. I don't know positively what they were, but they appeared to have guns, and looked like sentinels. I did not go over that night, nor did I offer to go. Boats were passing and repassing during the night from the island to the mainland.

Question. To whom did these boats belong?

Answer. I do not know, but I presume to the island. There were large boats at the landing, but these were small boats. I did not speak to them. I stood as much undiscovered as possible, as I was authorized by the governor of Ohio, to apprehend Blannerhassett: I went for that purpose.

Mr. HAY.—Do you recollect any indications of arrangements about a watch-word?

Answer. Yes. In the course of the evening, I saw that some boats crossed; and when a particular word was given, I observed there were some that did not cross. I heard others that were hailed across and a word given. They would hail for a boat. The people on the island would ask, " What boat?" If the answer was, *I's* boat, the boat immediately put off.

Mr. Parker. On what occasion was the watch word used?

Answer. When the people on the Ohio side wanted to go across, they would hail, or call for a boat; the people on the island would ask, " What boat?" and if the answer were *I's* boat, the boat would immediately put off.

Cross-examined.

Mr. BURR.—Till what hour did you stay out that night?

Answer. I imagine it was as late as ten o'clock.

Question. Was it not cold enough to render a fire pleasant?
Answer. It was.

Question. Is it not usual for boats to build fires on the bank, when it is so cold?

Answer. It is. There seemed to be a considerable number of men on the island that evening, going up and down, to and from the house. The witness further observed, that lanterns were passing during the night, between the house and boats, as if there were business between them; that he could not say, whether the persons whom he had called sentinels, were not merely loitering around the fire; that he thought it likely, that, if he too had used the watch-word, the boats would have put off for him; that he lived on the Ohio side; that he could not distinguish well, but he apprehended, that some of them had guns; but most of the people were without guns.

Mr. Burr.—Do you not commonly hail boats when you wish to cross the river?

Answer. It is not common to give a *word*. There were several boats hailed by people, who did not use that word; and these people were not sent for; but there was no instance where the boat was not sent for the party hailing, where that *watch-word* was used.

Maurice P. Belknap was then sworn.

Mr. Hay.—Will you tell us, sir, what you saw on the island?

Mr. Belknap. On the evening of the 10th of December, I was at the island of Mr. Blannerhassett. I arrived there between eight and nine o'clock in the evening. I hailed a boat, and they asked my name. Having given it, a skiff was immediately sent over with two of Blannerhassett's servants. Having crossed, I met with Mr. Woodbridge, who returned to the house with me. When I went into the house, I observed in the room, when I first entered, a number of men, who, from the promiscuous view I had of them, might have been about twenty.

Mr. Hay.—What were they doing?

Answer. The two or three I noticed near the door, had rifles, and appeared to be cleaning them. These were all the arms I saw: for I merely passed through the room where they were. Near the place where I landed, there appeared to be two or three boats, and people about them. It was a dark evening, and the *lights* in the boats *was* the only circumstance which made me notice them.

Mr. Burr.—Did you give a watch-word when they brought you over?

Answer. I gave no watch-word, I only gave my name; but they brought me over.

Edmund P. Dana was next sworn.

Mr. Dana. I never saw colonel Burr on the island.

Mr. Hay.—Will you state what you know about their number and arms?

Answer. On the evening of the 10th of December, I understood that the boats were to start with Comfort Tyler and his men down the river. Two other young men and myself were determined to cross over from Belpré, where I live, to the island. We went down to the landing opposite the island about dusk, took a skiff and landed at the upper part of the landing. We then went up to the house. Tyler's boats lay below our own about seven or eight rods. I heard some person talking on board, but it was dark, and I could not distinguish any one. We went into the hall, a large room, where there were a number of men. I remained but a short time and did not count them. I cannot say how many there were, but I should judge there were about fifteen or sixteen. One of them was running some bullets; and there was nothing but *hub-bub* and confusion about the large fire. I was then introduced into a chamber, where there were colonel Tyler, Blannerhassett, Mr. Smith of New-York as they said, and three or four other gentlemen. I was introduced to Mr. Smith and Doctor M'Cassley (or M'Castle) who had his lady, if I mistake not, there. I had been introduced to colonel Tyler the day before.

Mr. Randolph.—Were you a perfect stranger to the people in the hall?

Answer. I was.

Question by the same. Was there any alarm on your going in?

Answer. They did not appear to be alarmed.

Mr. Coleman (one of the jury) addressed the court. Is it proper to ask any questions about the conversations which took place with those gentlemen?

Chief Justice.—It is left to the consent of the accused.

Mr. Burr.—If any of the jury think proper, I have no objection. The inquiry was not pressed.

Before the examination of Mr. Belknap and Mr. Dana, an interesting and animated discussion took place at the bar.

Colonel Burr and his counsel objected strongly to the introduction of collateral evidence, and insisted strenuously, that the counsel for the prosecution should adduce, without further delay, all the testimony which they had, relating to any overt acts alleged to have been committed; that they had already submitted to too much irrelevant evidence; that it could not be denied, that colonel Burr was at a great distance, in the state of Kentucky, when these acts were alleged to have been committed on Blannerhassett's island; and that the relevancy or irrelevancy of the collateral proof offered, depended entirely on the existence of those acts. They insisted, that notwithstanding the numerous efforts and prejudices which had been so artfully and zealously excited, and so industriously spread throughout the country, there had not been any act of war, tumult or insurrection, nor even the semblance of an overt act; that they had a right to have the opinion of the court on the subject, and would insist on exercising it, as soon as the testimony, relating to the overt acts of this pretended war, was all introduced; and if gentlemen had any more such, they insisted on its immediate production, or that they would proceed to make their intended application to the court.

The counsel for the prosecution opposed this mode of proceeding. They contended, that it was unusual, irregular and improper; that the whole evidence should be submitted to the jury, whose province it was to decide whether, according to the exposition of the law by the court, there had been war or not; that the counsel for the accused might, when the whole should have been laid before the court, move the court to instruct the jury on the law, or make such other motions or propositions, as they might deem proper; that to decide whether overt acts had been committed or not, was an inquiry of fact, not of law; that though the court had a right to expound the law, and explain what in law constituted an overt act, yet it could not stop the prosecution, and say to the jury, that no overt act was committed; that it was evident that the object of attempting thus to arrest the inquiry, was to prevent the public from seeing and knowing what had been done, and which ought to be known; that the question was not, *where* the accused was when the treason was committed, but whether he *procured it* or *had a part in it?* and that as the objection of the accused to the evidence offered by the prosecution was irregular and improper, it ought to be disregarded by the court.

It was admitted that colonel Burr was in Kentucky at the time when the acts charged in the indictment were committed. It was stated that several witnesses were present ready to prove it.

After some further desultory remarks at the bar,

The CHIEF JUSTICE said, that there was no doubt that the court must hear the objections to the admissibility of the evidence; that it was a *right*, and gentlemen might insist on it: but he suggested the propriety of postponing their motion.

Mr. HAY admitted their right to object to the introduction of evidence; but contended, that the course they now adopted was irregular. He stated that they had some other witnesses to examine on the same point, whom they wished to introduce.

As soon as Messrs. Belknap and Dana were examined,

Mr. Botts moved the court to direct the marshal to make payment daily of their allowance to about twenty witnesses, summoned for the accused, most of whom were so poor, that they could not subsist without it. He had hoped the marshal would have paid them without this application. Colonel Burr thought them material, and summoned them from the best information he could obtain; and when the United States even imprisoned witnesses to compel their attendance, those of the accused ought at least to be supplied with the means of subsistence.

The marshal said that as the number of witnesses was so great, and many of them were said to know nothing of the subject in controversy, he was cautioned by the attorney for the United States, not to pay them till their materiality was ascertained, or till the court ordered him.

Mr. Hay said that the expenses were so enormous, that they would be felt by the national treasury, though it was full. This justified the caution alluded to; and the laws contemplated to pay the witnesses as soon as they gave their evidence.

Colonel Burr said, that when the attorney cautioned the marshal, it was supposed that he had summoned between two and three hundred witnesses, whereas the truth was, that they did not exceed twenty; that they were material; that some of them were summoned to repel what might be said by the witnesses for the United States; that the United States had many advantages in commanding the attendance of their witnesses, which he had not; that he would not acquiesce in the establishment of a principle that might prove injurious to others; that the witnesses ought to be paid, and he hoped that there would be no more difficulty made on the subject.

After some more desultory observations, as the witnesses were stated and considered to be material, the court directed the payment to be made by the marshal.

Mr. Wickham then renewed the subject of objecting to the evidence; and again urged the gentlemen who prosecuted, to adduce, if they could, any more testimony in support of what they deemed the overt acts.

Mr. Hay objected to their course of proceeding, but added, that he had only one or two more witnesses on that point, who were then absent, and if gentlemen were determined to make their motion, they might proceed.

Mr. WICKHAM then addressed the court.

May it please the court: The counsel for the prosecution having gone through their evidence relating directly to the overt act charged in the indictment, and being about to introduce collateral testimony of acts done beyond the limits of the jurisdiction of this court, and it not only appearing from the proofs, but being distinctly admitted, that the accused, at the period when war is said to have been levied against the United States, was hundreds of miles distant from the scene of action, it becomes the duty of his counsel, to object to the introduction of any such testimony; as according to our view of the law on this subject, it is wholly irrelevant and inadmissible.

It is not without reluctance that this measure is resorted to. Our client is willing and desirous, that at a proper time, and on a fit occasion, the real nature of the transactions which have been magnified into the crime of treason, should be fully disclosed: and unless he be greatly mistaken, it is now in his power to adduce strong and conclusive testimony in direct opposition to that which has been relied on in behalf of the prosecution. But if we may calculate from the time that has been already consumed in the examination of the small number of witnesses that have yet been introduced, out of about one hundred and forty, that have been summoned on the part of the United States, it is hardly possible, that an opportunity will be afforded him of calling a single witness before this jury. Weeks, perhaps months, will pass away, before the evidence for the United States is closed; and at this unfavourable season, nothing is more likely than that the health of some one, and perhaps more of the jury will be so far affected by the climate and confinement, as to render it impossible to proceed with the trial. Should such an event happen, the cause must lie over, and our client, innocent, as we have a right to suppose him, may be subjected to a prolongation of that confinement which is in itself a severe punishment. The jury too are placed under very unpleasant restraints, and it would be an act of injustice to them, as well as him, to acquiesce in a course of proceeding, which would draw out the trial to an immeasurable length; and which we conceive to be neither conformable to the rules of law, nor consistent with justice.

Hitherto the counsel for the United States have taken frequent occasions to declare their belief of the guilt of the accused. On the motion I am about to make, arguments drawn from this topic will have no application. The question will turn on abstract principles, which will neither be changed nor affected by his innocence or guilt. The foundation on which this prosecution must rest, and which I should hope had not been seen or attended to by the counsel for the United States themselves, will be exposed to view; and it will be for them to determine, whether it shall be abandoned, or maintained by doctrines incompatible with our republican institutions, and utterly inconsistent with every idea of civil liberty.

In combating these doctrines, we shall, so far as we are able, support the cause, not of our client alone, but of every citizen of the United States, and of future generations; for as to the establishment of the principle, it ought not to be considered as his cause alone, but as the cause of every member of the community and of posterity.

The first position I shall lay down, is, that no person can be convicted of treason in levying war, who was not personally present at the commission of the act, which is charged in the indictment as constituting the offence.

The 3d section of the 3d article of the constitution of the United States, declaring that " treason shall consist only in *levying war* against them, or in adhering to their enemies, giving them aid and comfort" and that " no person shall be convicted, unless on the testimony of two witnesses to the same overt act," there can be no doubt, if the words be construed according to their natural import, that it is necessary, in order to fix the guilt of the accused, to prove by two witnesses, that he committed an act of open hostility to the government, at the place charged in the indictment.

But artificial rules of construction, drawn from the common law and the usages of courts in construing statutes, are resorted to in order to prove that these words of the constitution are to be construed, not according to their natural import, but that an artificial meaning, drawn from the statute and common law of England, is to be affixed to them, totally different.

In the first place, I deny that any such rules of construction, however just they may be when applied to a statute, can be properly used, with reference to the constitution of the United States.

This instrument is a new and original compact between the people of the United States, embracing their public concerns in the most extensive sense; and is to be construed, not by the rules of art belonging to a particular science or profession, but, like a treaty or national compact, in which the words are to be taken according to their natural import, unless such a construction would lead to a plain absurdity, which cannot be pretended in the present instance.

It being new and original and having no reference to any former act or instrument, forbids a resort to any other rules of construction than such as are furnished by the constitution itself, or the nature of the subject. If I be correct in this, there is an end to all further inquiry. It is not necessary to resort to artificial rules of construction. The words of the constitution, " *levying* (or making) war," are plain and require no nice interpretation: and with respect to the other clause, " adhering to their enemies," &c. it is a matter of no consequence here what may be its correct exposition, for the commonwealth has no enemies. The counsel for the United States will not contend that the words, used in their natural sense, can embrace the case of a person who never himself committed an act of hostility against the United States, and was not even present when one was committed.

But they will insist, that these words in the constitution are to have an artificial meaning, such as they contend has been given them in the courts in England; and that in that country, all persons aiding and abetting others in the act of levying war against the government, are guilty of treason, though not personally present.

I shall contend *first*, That, notwithstanding some *dicta* of law-writers to the contrary, no such rule has practically obtained in that country; and that the decisions, entitled to any respect, lead to an inference directly contrary.

And secondly, That if I be wrong in this, the principle adopted there cannot apply to treasons under the constitution of the United States.

I shall admit that lord Coke and, after him, other writers who are deservedly revered, have laid down as a general position, that there are no accessories in treason either before or after the fact, but that all are principals.

But no adjudications, in the case of an accomplice in the nature of an accessory before the fact, bear them out in it, except that of sir Nicholas Throgmorton, reported 1 *State Trials p.* 63 to 78; and the conduct of the court on that occasion was so obviously contrary, not only to the rules of law and justice, but even to those of decency, that I persuade myself the counsel on the other side will not rely on it as an authority.

A very faithful and correct account of it is given by judge Tucker in his appendix to 4*th Blackstone's Commentaries, note a. p.* 44. He contests the doctrine advanced at this day, " that whatever will make a man an accessory in felony, will make him a principal in treason." He shews that it is derived from three original cases only and then proceeds thus, " This doctrine appears to have slept from the year 1488, to the year 1554, when it was revived upon the trial of sir Nicholas Throgmorton, in the first year of the reign of queen Mary. He was indicted first, for conspiring and imagining the death of the queen: 2. For levying war against her within the realm: 3. For adhering to her enemies within the realm, giving them aid and comfort: 4. For conspiring and intending to depose the queen: 5. For traitorously devising and concluding to take the Tower of London. Upon his trial, Stanford, author of the **Pleas** of the Crown, and Dyer, afterwards chief justice, assisted in the prosecution, as queen's sergeants. Bromley, chief justice of England, who appears to have been another Jefferies, and sir Nicholas Hare, master of the rolls, a fit associate for him, and sir Roger Cholmley, one of the same stamp, were among the number of his judges, and managed the trial. At this trial, the doctrine of constructive treason in its fullest extent was insisted on by the counsel for the prosecution, and sanctioned by the judges, notwithstanding the prisoner reminded the court of a statute, passed not six months before, whereby it was declared, that no offence made treason by act of parliament should thereafter be held to be treason, except such as were so declared by the statute 25 Edw. 3. which statute he desired might be read to the jury. The court told him there should be no books brought at his request; they knew the law sufficiently without book; it was not their business to provide books for him, neither did they sit there to be taught by him. If any thing more be requisite to shew the respect due to the decisions of the court, it may not be amiss to mention, that they ordered a person, whom the prisoner called as a witness, on his behalf, out of court. That one Vaughan, who was under sentence of death, and whose execution was respited that he might be present at this trial, was admitted as an evidence against him. That the confessions of one Winter and one Crofts, then alive and in custody, were read in evidence against him, the witnesses themselves not being produced in court. These words of the statute 25 Edw. 3. ' and be thereof attainted of open ' deed *by people of their condition*,' which sir Edward Coke, and every other writer on criminal law from his time to this, expounds to mean, by *verdict of a jury of their peers*, were thus expounded by the chief justice addressing himself to the prisoner: ' You deceive yourself, and mistake these words *by people of their condition;* for thereby the law doth understand the discovering of your treasons. As for example, Wyatt and other rebels, attainted for their great treasons, already declare you to be his and their adherent, in as much as divers and sundry times you had conference with him and them about the treason; so as Wyatt is now one of your condition, who as the world knoweth, hath committed an open, traitorous fact.' The word ' *enemies*' was likewise expounded to mean *traitors* within the statute. And lastly, when the jury brought in a verdict of acquittal (for there was no evidence against the prisoner on either point) the court immediately committed them all to prison, and some of them were fined two thousand pounds, some one thousand pounds, and the lowest paid three score pounds a-piece, before they were discharged from their imprisonment.

Stanford, who was active in the prosecution, was afterwards promoted to the bench, and published his Pleas of the Crown, in 1560, six years after, in which he has laid down the doctrine at large, as it is received at this day, but cites the case 3 H. 7. 10. before mentioned in support of it. Abington's case was resolved, when sir Edward Coke was attorney-general, in the fourth year of James the first, when the spirit of persecution was at its height, from the terrors of the powder-plot, in the guilt of which the prisoner was involved, by receiving one Garnett, a jesuit, knowing him to be guilty of the powder treason. It is not improbable however, that this doctrine was aided in its progress, by the statutes which passed in the reign of Hen. 5. and Hen. 6. and the numerous acts of attainder, passed in those of Edw. 4. and Rich. 3. and the multiplied treasons created in the reign of Hen. 8. and his successors, whereby the aiders, counsellors, consentors, abettors, maintainers, procurers, comforters, receivers, relievers, and so forth, of persons guilty of any such treasons, are repeatedly declared to be principal traitors also. These parliamentary declarations and statutes must, I conceive, have had a strong influence over the judges, in those days, when parliaments and courts were equally devoted to the will of the ruling monarch.

" I should not have taken the trouble of this scrutiny, had not the same judge [judge Chase] who declared, that the English authorities were not to be regarded as precedents in our courts, on the same occasion, declared the law to be, ' that in treason all the *participes criminis*, are *principals;* that there are no accessories in that crime, and that *every act*, which in case of *felony* would render a man an *accessory*, will in the case of *treason* make him a principal.' If the learned judge rejects the authority of the English precedents, where can the law be found? And if he relies upon those precedents, where can the reason of the law be found?"

In that case it was perfectly clear, that the prisoner was not present at the only scene of action. I can find no case, where a person who was not present at the scene of action, or where a procurer or aider of treason *before the fact*, was convicted or even *brought to trial*, except the case of Mary Speke. In Tremaine's *Pleas of the Crown, p.* 3. I find an indictment against her for treason, in *aiding* the duke of Monmouth and others in levying war, *with provisions;* neither *before* nor *after*, but *at* the time when the treason was committed by the principals. She was not an accessory in fact, but an " *aider*" in the commission of the treason, it comes within the definition of "an aider or procurer," and belongs to the class of accessories before the fact. But I cannot learn how the case was decided; whether according to common sense or justice, or in what manner determined, neither history, nor any report of the decision of the court (as far as I have been able to discover) informs us. It was in the fourth year of the reign of James 2d, when the spirit of persecution was very high, and was probably one of the cases decided by the execrable Jefferies, on the occasion of Monmouth's rebellion. Whether he carried this doctrine to the utmost length or not, I cannot say; but I presume the counsel for the United States would not rely on it as a precedent even if it applied.

After a diligent and painful research, I have been unable to find any other decisions that go to this point, with respect to accomplices in the nature of accessories before the fact, to treason in "levying war." I cannot find, and I am confident the gentlemen cannot shew any solemn decision subjecting the procurer, before the fact, to the pains and penalties of treason. The other great branch of treasons, that strikes directly at the existence of the government, that of compassing the death of the king, does not admit of an accessory before the fact, as distinguished from a principal. We all know that that crime consists in the intention. The agreement to do the act constitutes the crime itself. It is impossible that there can be an aider or procurer in this case, because every person concerned is party to the agreement, and therefore, from the nature of things, is a principal. It will not be contended by the counsel on the other side, that an agreement to levy war amounts to levying war. They themselves admit that they who conspire to levy war only become traitors by relation when the war is actually levied. With respect to treason for compassing the death of the king, where the mere agreement to do the act does itself constitute the crime, I thank God, that in this country, we have no subject to which it applies; and our constitution forbids that the intention alone, which is so liable to be misunderstood and misrepresented, should in any case be construed into treason.

In the lesser treasons, such as counterfeiting the coin, I have not met with any instance of a conviction of an accomplice before the fact.

It is admitted that there are to be found in England a number of convictions of receivers of traitors and other aiders in the nature of accessories *after* the fact; and I admit the correctness of the inference, that if these decisions were proper to be considered as precedents, the principle would apply to aiders and abettors before the fact. But it becomes proper before they ought to be regarded as precedents worthy of imitation, to inquire in what times and under what circumstances, those cases were decided. I have not found any of them since the revolution of 1688, when the principles of civil liberty and enlightened jurisprudence began to be better understood than before; and most of those previous to that event, were decided by Jefferies: such as the case of lady Lisle, reported in 4 *State Trials*, *p.* 106. John Teurnley's case, *ibid. p.* 131. and Elizabeth Gaunt's case, *p.* 142. They were all cases of receivers of traitors or accessories *after* the fact. With respect to the former, which served as a prototype of the others, I trust there is only one opinion among us. I will only refer the court to Mr. Hume's account of this atrocious legal murder, and of the case of E. Gaunt, in his 8*th vol. of the History of England, p.* 233. (octavo edition); which is as follows:

" Of all the executions during this dismal period, the most remarkable were those of Mrs. *Gaunt* and lady *Lisle*, who had been accused of harbouring traitors. Mrs. Gaunt was an anabaptist, noted for her beneficence, which she extended to persons of all professions and persuasions. One of the rebels, knowing her humane disposition, had recourse to her in distress, and was concealed by her. Hearing of the proclamation, which offered an indemnity and rewards to such as discovered criminals, he betrayed his benefactress, and bore evidence against her. He received a pardon as a recompense for his treachery; she was burnt alive for her charity.

" Lady Lisle was widow of one of the regicides, who had enjoyed great favour and authority under Cromwell, and who having fled, after the restoration, to Swisserland, was there assassinated by three Irish ruffians, who hoped to make their fortune by this piece of service. His widow was now prosecuted for harbouring two rebels, the day after the battle of Sedgemoor; and Jefferies pushed on the trial with an unrelenting violence. In vain did the aged prisoner plead, that these criminals had been put into no proclamation; had been convicted by no verdict; nor could any man be denominated a traitor, till the sentence of some legal court was passed upon him: that it appeared not by any proof, that she was so much as acquainted with the guilt of the persons, or had heard of their joining the rebellion of Monmouth: that though she might be obnoxious on account of her family, it was well known that her heart was ever loyal, and that no person in England had shed more tears for that tragical event, in which her husband had unfortunately borne too great a share: and that the same principles which she herself had ever embraced, she had carefully instilled into her son, and had at that very time, sent him to fight against those rebels whom she was now accused of harbouring. Though these arguments did not move Jefferies, they had influence on the jury. Twice they seemed inclined to bring in a favourable verdict. They were as often sent back with menaces and reproaches, and at last were constrained to give sentence against the prisoner. Notwithstanding all applications for pardon, the cruel sentence was executed. The king said that he had given Jefferies a promise not to pardon her. An excuse which could serve only to aggravate the blame against himself."

These cases and decisions (Throgmorton's and lady Lisle's), I admit, are precedents, if they choose to rely on them, and they can find no other.

Since the revolution of 1688, though the doctrine has been admitted by writers to be true, yet all the decisions of the court, that I can find, which bear upon the subject, lead to a directly opposite conclusion. The most numerous class of cases relate to convictions which took place before judges of a very different stamp, whose decisions are entitled to the highest respect. The occasion on which there was the greatest number of prosecutions for treason, in levying war, was the rebellion in the year 1745; and no one can doubt the accuracy of the reports of the decisions at that period, or the ability of the judges who presided, and the counsel who conducted the prosecutions. We all know the history of those times, and what cruelties the late duke of Cumberland committed after the victory of Culloden. His name is held in general detestation by the people of that part of the country from parent to child. Yet there was not a single instance of a conviction for assisting or harbouring the traitors. History mentions the wonderful escape of the pretender, and his concealment and protection, by the unexampled courage and fidelity of Miss Macdonald. Yet no attempt was made to convict her of treason, or others who aided him, or even to prosecute them. Though he was a long time concealed, and in eluding the vigilance of his pursuers was favoured by many, yet it is remarkable, that no person who assisted him in his distress, was attempted to be punished. But let us not draw any inference from the silence and inactivity of the officers of the crown, but advert to what was actually done.

The fact of the pretender's raising an army in Scotland, with a view of seating himself on the throne of Great-Britain; his giving battle to the king's troops, defeating them several times, and marching into the heart of England, could have been proved by thousands of witnesses. If the doctrine, that persons absent and not in arms might be charged with the overt acts of others with whom they were connected, were admitted, nothing would have been more simple and easy, than the mode of conducting the prosecutions on this occasion. The prosecutors would have had nothing to do, but to charge an overt act in some county through which the pretender's army had passed, no matter which; to prove the fact of his having done so (a fact as notorious, as that the places themselves were in existence) and then to prove, that the person charged, was connected with the rebellion, and assented to it; whether he had ever been in the county where the act was charged upon him, or had even raised a finger in opposition to the government or not, was a matter of no importance. His conviction followed as a necessary consequence.

But did the courts and prosecutors proceed in this manner? A reference to their decisions will prove, that the courts proceeded on the contrary doctrine; and that the judges, as well as the counsel for the prosecutions, thought that they could only be sustained by bringing the overt act home to the person himself, by establishing the fact, that the *accused was present*, and *personally committed the overt acts charged in the indictment.*

Justice Foster, in his *Crown Law, p.* 3 to 6, gives the form of the indictment, and says that " it was used against *all* the rebels who were tried in Surry (except one, for reasons explained); " *that the overt acts were laid in different counties of England or Scotland, as the cases respectively required; that the fact of taking and possessing the city and castle of Carlisle, was not charged on those who were not concerned in that part of the rebellion.*"

According to the doctrine of the gentlemen on the other side, what necessity was there of varying the overt acts from one county to another? Why charge them in different counties, if any one might be charged with the acts of others wherever committed? For what purpose was the act of taking Carlisle not charged on those who were not concerned in that part of the rebellion? If this doctrine be correct, it was no matter whether they were present or absent; if they were concerned, they were all, in the eye of the law, present on the spot. Was not judge Foster talking nonsense, when he stated different modes of charging the overt acts, if their doctrine be correct? One mode would have done for all whether they were present or absent. But this is not a loose expression put down incautiously by judge Foster, but an opinion on which the court acted.

In Deacon's case, *Foster's Crown Law, p.* 9, 10. it was insisted for the prisoner, that as the overt acts were laid in Cumberland, evidence of an overt act in Manchester should not be given; but the court determined, " *that it was indeed necessary, that some overt act laid,* be *proved on the prisoner in Cumberland; but that being done,* acts of treason, tending to prove the overt acts laid, though done elsewhere, might be given in evidence." It is evident from the *expressions* " *proved on the prisoner,*" and "*that being done,*" as well as the whole context, that the court required *proof* of an act in Cumberland, and that the prisoner himself *had in person committed the overt act charged,* and that *no evidence short of this was sufficient.*

If gentlemen doubt the propriety of this construction, there is another authority in the same book, page 22, which confirms it.

In sir John Wedderbourn's case, the overt acts were laid at Aberdeen; it was proved by two witnesses, that he was with the rebels at Aberdeen; and then proof was offered of an overt act elsewhere, which was objected to by his counsel; but "this objection was overruled, upon the reasons before given, in the case of Deacon."

What necessity was there to prove that he was with the rebels at Aberdeen? If their doctrine be law, proof that the *rebels* had *been there*, was sufficient; and that fact being as well known as that there had been a rebellion, no evidence of *any overt act*, of *any sort*, at *any place*, done by the accused, was wanting; *proof of any act however secret*, and *however remote from the scene of action, was all that was requisite.*

In the trial of lord Balmerino, reported in 9th *State Trials*, *p.* 605. one of the overt acts charged was his marching into, and taking possession of the city of Carlisle, and holding it for the pretender. He denied, that in point of fact, he was present at the taking of the city. This objection was met by the counsel for the crown, among whom was the late lord Mansfield, by a reference to the testimony; proving that he marched in with the rebels after the surrender, and to the other charges in the indictment which had been clearly proved; so that it was unimportant whether this was established or not. Neither lord Mansfield, sir John Strange nor any of the other great lawyers who were counsel for the crown, thought of the objection now urged by the gentlemen on the other side. They exerted themselves merely to shew, that the *day* was im*material;* and that the subsequent entry of the prisoner into the city, and remaining in it with the rebels, was sufficient for his conviction, exclusive of the other acts proved. Had they understood the law to be, as the counsel for this prosecution understand it, they would have at once replied, " *Whether the prisoner were personally present at Carlisle or not, is of no consequence; others with whom he was connected were there, and did the act charged on him, and as all are principals in treason, their acts are his.*" But they urged no such doctrine; it was reserved for the ingenuity of future ages to discover it. It is evident that they thought it necessary to prove that he was present and an actor in the scene where the overt act was laid; or that this charge in the indictment must be abandoned. This has uniformly been the rule, nor can any instance be shewn, where a party who was not present himself where the act was done, but a mere procurer, has been subjected to the punishment of treason.

In opposition to these decisions, (given at a time when there was certainly no partiality in favour of the accused, but as much learning and virtue on the bench, and as great a portion of talents at the bar as in any period of English history, and which are not opposed by a single case since the revolution, when the independence of the judiciary, and the principles of a free government were first established and confirmed) the counsel for the prosecution may quote lord Coke, Stanford and other eminent law writers, since the age of Henry the 8th. If this be so, it proves nothing, except that the theory was one way, and the practice the other; and as this is a practical question, we ought to abide by the precedents established by the courts on this law, as they occurred, and not the *dicta* of men however eminent, who appear to have written without due consideration, and to have done little more than to copy *verbatim* the speculative opinions of their predecessors.

For the history of this opinion, I beg leave to refer to judge Tucker's very able treatise on the subject. He has traced it to its source, and shewn how error is begotten by error. See *Tucker's Blackstone, 4th. vol. appendix, note a. p. 40 to 47.* After having shewn the important effect of the word " *only,*" in the constitution, " as the strongest term of limitation and restriction in our language, that its obvious meaning is, that " *treason shall consist in these two cases,*" (levying war and adhering to their enemies, &c.) *and no other cases whatever,* he proceeds:

" And here it may not be improper to repeat the remark, that this definition *creates,* as well as *limits,* an offence which had no previous existence ; whereas the *statute 25 Edward* 3. did not create, but only defined an offence already known to the common law. 'That statute, said Stanford, (afterwards chief justice of the common pleas), is but a declaration of certain treasons, which were treasons before at the common law.' Will any man presume to advance, that there is any treason against the United States by the common law? that a limited federal republic of yesterday hath already appropriated to itself all the foul corruptions of despotism, collected from time immemorial. To infer that the courts of the United States, are left to range at large, in the boundless field of *construction,* in search of *other cases* of treason against the United States, seems, to my apprehension, to be a doctrine equally unfounded, awful, and dangerous.

" If, then, we are not at liberty to reject this important word ' *only,*' we must assign to it some determinate signification, and if that signification be that which I have ascribed to it, to wit, ' *these cases and no other whatsoever,*' its necessary operation and effect must be, to *cut up all constructive treasons, root and branch.* If a single scion be left, it will be the parent of ten thousand others, shedding like the ' *Buonas Upas,*' their baneful influence far and wide, poisoning and desolating the whole region where they are permitted to take root. Faction and factious men are not confined to any one party in a republic: and when such men have the command of the purse, the sword and the scales of justice, the lives of their opponents will not weigh a feather in competition with their own advancement, or that of their party. This, the framers of the constitution must have considered, and therefore endeavoured by the strongest terms, and the strictest limitation, to restrain within the narrowest limits. And this should serve as the polar star of construction to judges and all others, who may be called upon to administer the government.

" Thus having sought, and, I trust, discovered not only the literal sense and meaning of the word ' *only*,' but also its proper interpretation, according to the true spirit of our federal constitution, I shall now inquire into its effect and operation in certain cases, which might have been supposed to be treason had it been omitted.

" In England, it is now generally admitted, that ' in treason, all the *participes criminis* are principals;' there being, as it is said, no accessories to that crime; and that every act which, in case of felony, would render a man an accessory, will in case of treason, make him a principal.*

" This doctrine was laid down by judge Chase, in his charge to the jury, on the trial of *Fries;* but as I conceive it to have been extrajudicial, for reasons already mentioned, I shall take the liberty now to inquire, whether it be not also questionable. But before I do this, I shall endeavour to trace this copious branch of constructive treason to its fountain head, and shew how small a portion of that fatal torrent flows from an uncorrupted spring. In doing this, I shall begin with the latest authorities, and conclude with the most ancient. This doctrine is advanced by judge Blackstone, (4th *Com.* 35, 36.) for which he cites 3 *Institutes*, 138. 1 *Hale's P. C.* 613. and *Foster*, 342. The latter cites 3d *Institutes*, 9. ‡ and 138. and 1 *Hale*, 235, 237, 328, 376. *Hale* himself cites 3 *Inst.* 16, and 138. *Stanford's P. C.* 32. and the year book, 1 *H.* 6, 5. of which last case, I shall make particular mention by and by.

" Sir *Edward Coke*, 3 *Inst.* 16, and 138. cites *Stanford, P. C.* 3. and the year books, 19 *H.* 6, 47. and 3 *H.* 7, 10.

" *Stanford, P. C.* 3 and 32. 40 and 44. cites the same identical cases from the year books, that sir *Matthew Hale* and sir *Edward Coke* had cited before. From *these three original cases*, 1 *Hen.* 6, 5. 19 *Hen.* 6, 47. and 3 *Hen.* 7, 10. we must consequently derive the doctrine in question.

* The *ancient* law of England was, that they who were present and abetting others to do the act, were accessories and not principals. Per Bromley, C. J. Plowden, 97, 98. See Plowden's note thereon, ib. 99, 100. whereby it seems the law was changed *tempore* Henry 4. 1 Hale, 437.

† Fries's Trial, 198.

‡ This is a mistaken reference in Foster; it should be 16.

" The case of 1 *H.* 6, 5. (A. D. 1422.) is thus mentioned by *Stanford, p.* 32. A man was outlawed of felony, was imprisoned in the king's bench, and indicted and attainted of breaking prison, and releasing certain persons confined for treason, and this was adjudged petit treason.

" Upon what principle this case could be judged petit treason, it might puzzle any man at this day to conjecture, and creates a presumption, that the case is not very accurately reported. But there is another principle of the common law, on this particular subject of breach of prison, which will probably lead us to under-stand it. It is this: If there be felons in prison, and a man know-ing of it, breaks the prison and lets out the prisoners, though he knew not that there were felons there, it is felony; and if traitors were there, it is treason. Now if the persons released in the case here referred to, were imprisoned for petit treason, instead of high treason, this judgment would be regular: but by no rule of law, could they be deemed guilty of petit treason, in any other case. And, if this were the case, it would prove that there was no distinction in principle, between treason and felony; inasmuch as the releasing a felon from jail is felony, in the same manner as releasing a traitor from jail is treason. And it appears from Stanford, that a stranger rescuing one indicted for felony, was in-dicted and tried, and found guilty for that offence, before the principal felon was tried. But sir Michael Foster gives us a fur-ther clue to the understanding of this case; for in speaking on this subject, he observes with great reason, that the forcing of prison doors may be considered *as overt acts of ' levying war;'* the species of treason for which Benstead, of whom he was speaking was indicted. And this might have been the case in this instance. These cases confirm the conclusion, that the law made no distinction at that time, between treason and felony. A statute was made in the year after this case was adjudged, 2 H. 6. c. ult. cited by Stanford, whereby it was declared to be treason in any person imprisoned, to break prison. All which circumstances united, create a strong presumption, that this case is not correctly reported, nor the grounds of the judgment perfectly understood.

" The second case occurred thirteen years after, in the year 1441, and is thus mentioned in Brooke. A man was indicted for forging false money, and another at the same time: one confesses and approves, and has a coroner assigned him; the other pleads not guilty, and it was found that he was consent-ing and aiding in forging the false money, and so guilty. Stan-ford mentions the case in the like manner, and it is evident from this state of it, that the defendant was *present*, aiding and assisting, and so would have been a principal in felony as well as in treason, which is confirmed by Stanford, who proceeds thus: 'It is the *same case in rape, where one does the act, and another assists him to commit the rape;* he *is by this a ravisher.'* The law is the same in felony as well as in treason, that all present, aiding and assisting *at* the fact are principals. Neither of these cases, therefore, justify the doctrine advanced at this day, that whatever act will make a man an accessory in felony, will make him a principal in treason.

"The next case is 3 *H.* 7, 10. and is relied on by Stanford and sir Edward Coke, as establishing the doctrine abovementioned: it was thus; one Cokker was indicted and attainted of making false money, and afterwards one J. B. was indicted for traitorously and knowingly entertaining and comforting him; and was found guilty, and the question was, whether he would be deemed an accessory to Cokker? Brian justice, said he might be accessory, for such counterfeiting was felony before the statute and is not cut off by it; and in every treason, felony is implied, &c. '*et tamen Hussey Cap:* Inst: *dixit quod in hoc quod factum est proditio, non potest esse accessarius felonicè et proditorie non potest esse accessarius,'* for which doctrine he refers to the preceding case of 19 *H.* 6. 47. Here then we have this opinion of two judges in opposition to each other; and we find the latter supporting his opinion by a reference to the very case, which, we have already shewn, does not authorize it.

"These are all the ancient authorities referred to either by Stanford, sir Edward Coke, sir Matthew Hale, or any writer on the subject; and it requires very little discernment, I apprehend, to discover that the two former do not warrant the latter, and that the latter is the *dictum* of a single judge. And Brooke cites it in that manner: '*Nota, P. Hussey C. I. que accessary ne poet este a treason; le recotment de traitor, ne poet este tantum felony, mes est treason.'* Had this been the established doctrine of the common law, we might have expected that the laborious and indefatigable sir Edward Coke (under whose auspices it was brought to maturity as we shall see hereafter) would have referred us to the *Mirror, Bracton, Britton, Fleta,* or *Glanville,* in some of which, it would most certainly have been found."

In page 47, he adds, "Both common law and common sense have been able to perceive, and draw a distinction between the actual perpetration of a crime, and the bare *advising,* or even procuring the perpetration of it, without being present when it is perpetrated; they have also been able to distinguish between the perpetration of a crime, and the receiving and comforting one, who has been himself the perpetrator, knowing him to be such: it was reserved for the astute reason of judges appointed by the crown, to discover, that there was no distinction between these cases, when the sacred majesty of their master's head was in danger, or supposed to be so: it was reserved for them to declare, that to give a meal's victuals to one guilty of treason, was a crime of the same malignity as levying war against the throne, or as aiming a dagger at the heart of the monarch."

An additional reason may be drawn from the law of treason in compassing the king's death. There, as the crime consists in the intention, *all* are principals, and the aider or procurer in the first instance is guilty, and this rule has been transplanted or extended by theorists, to the other great branch of treason, "levying war" against the government. Lord Coke was very fond of quaint expressions; of these one was, that " in the highest and lowest offences all are principals." That in them there are no accessories. As a general principle, can this be correct? Apply it to the lowest offences; apply it to the case of an assault and battery. Suppose a man, having an enmity against another, is determined to gratify his vengeance against him; he does not act himself, but employs a *bravo* to assassinate or severely beat him. A. thus advises and procures B. to beat C., but is not present at the beating: will it be contended that an action or an indictment will lie against A., who was absent, for this assault and battery? The authority of Hawkins in his *Pleas of the Crown*, book 2d, chap. 29th, section 4th, is decisive on this point. " It seems agreed that whosoever agrees to a trespass on lands or goods, done *to his use*, thereby becomes a principal in it. But *that no one can become a principal in a trespass on the person of a man by any such agreement.*" Also it seems agreed " that no one shall be adjudged a principal in any common trespass, or inferior crime of the like nature, for barely receiving, comforting and concealing the offender, though he knew him to have been guilty and that there is a warrant out against him, which by reason of such concealment cannot be executed."

Could it be supposed that gentlemen would have denied this to be law? It never can be admitted that the procurer or adviser of a trespass is punishable as a principal. No man can be a trespasser against the person of another who is not present and acting or assenting to it.

Mr. HAY here insisted, that if a man procure another to beat a third, the procurer is a trespasser, and will be liable to an action or indictment.

Mr. WICKHAM. I insist that the law is otherwise; and I refer to the authority I have already produced. They can adduce none to oppose it, and were it necessary it could be confirmed and fortified by others. To be liable for the trespass on the person, he must be present. If a man in Frederick county advise another to beat a man in *Henrico*, and he does beat him accordingly in Henrico, where the adviser never was, an action or a public prosecution will certainly never lie against the adviser.

But, admitting that both the theory and practice in the English courts concur in establishing the doctrine which the gentlemen contend for, and that any man, connected in any manner with the traitors, is himself a traitor; yet I contend that it cannot be law in this country, where the constitution of the United States has pointed out and established a different rule. The statute in England, on which all the indictments are founded, is well known to be that of 25 *Edw.* 3. It does not create any new treasons of which the punishments are pointed out, or enlarge the doctrine of treasons; but on the contrary was intended to narrow the legal definition of this crime, which was punishable at common law.

In construing the statute therefore, the judges considered it as made in affirmance of the common law, except, where the restraining clauses were permitted to operate: it was construed according to the course of the common law, and the doctrine, that all are principals in treason, if it rest on any foundation, can have no other than the common law. 1 *Hale P. C.* page 76 to 87. proves that this stat. 25 *Edw.* 3. was made to confine and limit the crime of treason, " which was *before* that statute *arbitrary* and *uncertain.*" In page 85 he calls it " the *great boundary of treason;*" and shews that its object was to prevent *constructive treasons.* This salutary statute is also spoken of by Hume, as a very popular act passed to narrow, define and limit treasons known at common law.

Under the federal constitution, I presume, it will hardly be contended by the counsel for the prosecution, that we have any common law, belonging to the United States at large. I always did believe and still believe, that we have no common law for the United States, especially in criminal cases. The only ground on which the common law becomes a rule of decision, in the federal courts, is under that clause in the judiciary law, (*Laws of United States, vol.* 1. *chap.* 20 *sect.* 34. *page* 74.) which makes the laws of the several states a rule of decision, as far as they respectively apply. The common law is part of the law of Virginia, and the act of congress has adopted the laws of Virginia as the rule of decision in cases where they apply.

With respect to crimes and offences against the United States, which must be punished in an uniform manner, throughout the Union, it seems clear for the reason already given, that none such can exist at common law, as the United States have in that character no common law, and that they must be created by statute. Unquestionably the gentlemen will not deny this uniformity; they will not contend that what is treason in Maryland is not treason in Virginia, or vice versa. If it exist at all, it must be uniform, embracing the whole of the United States. I do not know whether gentlemen will admit, but I presume they will not deny, that treason against the United States is only punishable by virtue of the act of congress, under the constitution of the United States, and that no indictment would lie against any person for such an offence till it passed; and the crime being punishable by a general statutory regulation, extending throughout the United States, the mode in which that regulation operates must be uniform. The act of congress does not admit of different constructions in different states. To illustrate this position by a familiar case, I will mention the late sedition law. One party thought it unconstitutional; another party thought it consistent with the constitution, and that a person guilty of the offence, could be punished in each state, by the common law in such state. It was a question of jurisdiction, but all parties agreed, that if the constitution did authorize (or did not prohibit) the congress to legislate on the subject, no person could be punished for such an offence, till they passed an act creating the offence; because there was no general common law pervading the United States. The party who thought it constitutional, were of opinion that the offence was punishable as soon as the law passed. The other party of course thought otherwise.

That the United States have no common law, and that offences against them must be created and prohibited by statute, is the opinion of the learned judge Chase; and I believe that this opinion received the unqualified approbation of those who thought most unfavourably of his opinions, and judicial conduct on other occasions.

Now, as there is no general common law of the United States, the act of congress must be construed without any reference to any common law, and treason is to be considered as a newly created offence, against a newly created government.

In England *treason* and *felony* are classes or descriptions of offences at common law; they are generic terms; aiders and abettors are punished in the former *if you will*, as principals, in the latter as accessories.

It is a rule of law there, that, when a statute is made in affirmance of the common law, or to supply the defects of the common law, it should be expounded according to the common law, see 10 *State Trials*, 436. M'Daniel's case; *Hob. Rep. p.* 98.

It has therefore been held, that if an act, criminal at common law, be declared by a statute to be felony or treason, it being made to supply the defects of the common law, its prototype, the same consequences follow, as if it were felony or treason by common law. It becomes therefore unnecessary to mention accessories, or even to define the punishment; and accordingly there are acts of parliament which go no further than to declare, that the offences mentioned in them shall be felony, without even mentioning the punishment.

This rule may be questioned on this ground, that penal statutes should be construed strictly; but it is generally considered as law in England, that when a felony is created by statute, accessories to it, though not named in the statute, are punishable; and that all legal consequences of felony are attached to it by the common law, except in cases where the special nature of the act leads to a different conclusion.

This rule is illustrated by the decisions on the 28 *Hen.* 8. *chap.* 15. which makes piracy, an offence not punishable at common law, felony.

It has been solemnly adjudged, that as this was not a common law offence, it worked no corruption of blood; that accessories to it were not punishable; in short that the statute not being made in imitation or supply of the common law, shall not be construed according to the course of the common law. *Hawkins*, in his *P. C. p.* 152. *c.* 37. speaking of the said act of Hen. 8. making piracy felony, says that " in the exposition of the statute, it has been holden, first, that it does not alter the nature of the offence, so as to make that which was a felony only by the civil law, now become a felony by the common law; for the offence must still be alleged as done upon the sea, and is no way cognisable by the common law, but only by virtue of this statute; which by ordaining that in some respects, it shall have the like trial and punishment, as are used for felony at common law, shall not be carried so far as to make it also agree with it in other particulars which are not mentioned. And from hence it follows, that this offence remains as before, of a special nature, and that it shall not be included in a general pardon of all felonies, which as it was, before this statute, to be expounded of no felonies which are such only by the civil law, shall continue still to have the same construction." " From the same ground also it follows, *that no persons shall, in respect of this statute, be construed to be, or punished as, accessories to piracies* before or after, as they might have been, if it had been made a felony by the statute, whereby all those would incidentally have been made accessories in the like cases, in which they would have been accessories to a felony at common law; and from hence it follows *that accessories to piracy, being neither expressly named in the statute,* nor by construction included in it, *remain as they were before, &c.*"

If therefore I be right in my *postulatum*, that there is no common law of the United States as such, it follows as a necessary consequence, that no persons can be punished for treason, or any other offence under an act of congress, creating such offence, unless they come within the description of the act; that no person can be said to have levied war against the United States, where it had not been levied by himself, but by others; *and that no overt act of others* can, under the statute, *be made his overt act.*

That such was the opinion of the framers of the act of congress, (*Laws of the United States, vol.* 1. *page* 100.) for the punishment of treason and other offences, is manifest.

In sections 10 and 11. of the act, the punishment of accessories *before* and *after* the *fact* is defined; that of the former is death, as in the case of a principal; that of the latter, fine and imprisonment.

If the English rule, concerning accessories to felonies, were thought to obtain, to what purpose was the 10th section enacted? By the 10th section, the person who *advises* the *piracy* is declared to be an accessory and made punishable. If it were implied, why was this provided? In section 16th persons stealing military stores, their *counsellors* aiders and abettors are mentioned; why were they expressly mentioned, if they would have been necessarily implied? In the 10th section some offences are enumerated, the accessories to which, before the fact, are expressly made punishable with death; and in the 11th section the *accessories* to the same crimes, after the fact, are in express terms made punishable with imprisonment not exceeding three years, and with fine not exceeding five hundred dollars; but even in this enumeration, treason is not included. In both sections the offences of murder, robbery or other piracy are mentioned, and in the latter, felony is added. The obvious conclusion resulting from this provision in these sections is, that without it, accessories to those offences neither before nor after, would have been punishable; and that as treason is omitted, accessories to that offence, whether before or after its commission, are not subject to be punished. The 23d section affords an argument still more directly applicable to the present question. It provides that " whoever shall by force set at liberty or rescue any person who shall be found guilty of treason, murder or any other capital crime, or rescue any person convicted of any of the said crimes, going to execution, or during execution, every person so offending, and being thereof convicted shall suffer death."
" And if any person shall by force set at liberty or rescue, any person who before conviction shall stand committed for any of the capital offences aforesaid, or if any person or persons, shall by force set at liberty or rescue any person committed for, or convicted of, any other offence against the United States, every person so offending, shall on conviction, be *fined not exceeding five hundred dollars and imprisoned not exceeding one year.*"
This provision punishes those who rescue persons guilty of

these crimes after conviction, with death, but after commitment and before conviction, with fine and imprisonment only.

Now, according to the gentlemen's arguments, all are principals, as well the mere receivers after as the procurers, or the actual perpetrator of the offence. There is no distinction in the books. The English writers consider persons who rescue or set at liberty traitors, as accessories after the fact; and they are said to be indictable as traitors. Why then was this clause inserted? A receiver of a traitor is as much a principal, according to the doctrine laid down in the English books, as a person aiding before the fact. Will the counsel for the United States contend, that such a receiver is punishable as a traitor, while the person who forces open the doors of the prison, and rescues the principal out of the hands of the marshal, shall be punishable only by a fine of five hundred dollars, and by one year's imprisonment! If so, a man might rescue a traitor before conviction, and conduct him to another who receives him. The receiver who, like lady Lisle, only entertains him but for one night, would be punishable with death, while the rescuer and conductor whose crime has the additional ingredient of force, and that force directly employed in opposing the administration of justice, would be only fined and imprisoned! It is so absurd and contrary to the rules of equal justice, that it is impossible that the legislature could have intended it. It proves that congress were of opinion, that aiders and abettors were not, according to the constitutional definition of treason, traitors and principals. If this were an English statute made with reference to the common law, I might with propriety contend, that it was the intention of the legislature, that when counsellors, aiders and abettors of some offences are named and not those of others, those not mentioned should be considered, as not within the meaning of the act, according to the maxims of law.

If this were not their intention, why did they mention these terms in one and not in the other?

But it will be said, that in high treason, it is unnecessary to mention counsellors, aiders, &c. because in treason there are no accessories, all are principals. Now this argument is founded on a total misapplication of terms. If they can be punished at all, it is as principals; but in *point* of *fact*, there may as well be aiders and abettors in treason as in other offences. Indeed there are many instances to be found in the statute-books, of these very words " *aiders, counsellors* and *abettors*" being used and applied to treason. The statutory treasons between the 25 *Edw. 3.* and 1 *Mary* are collected by Lord Hale, in the 24th chapter of his *Pleas of the Crown, p.* 258. and among others I would refer the court to the 20 *H. 6. chap.* 3. mentioned by him in page 270. 26 *H. 8. chap.* 13. and 27 *H. 8. chap.* 2. in

page 275. 35. *H.* 8. *chap.* 1. in *p.* 280. all of which, and I doubt
not many more, expressly mention *counsellors,* aiders and abettors. If it be not necessary to mention aiders and abettors to
make them punishable, why are they inserted in these statutes?
In page 275 " maliciously to wish, will or desire by word or
writing, or by craft, to imagine, invent, practise or attempt any
bodily harm to the King, Queen, heir apparent &c. to detain
his castles &c." is " enacted to be treason in the offenders,
their *aiders, counsellors, consenters* and abettors." " Counterfeiting the privy seal, privy signet or sign manual is made treason, and the offenders, their counsellors, aiders and abettors, to
suffer as in case of treason &c." The statutes, which are made
with a reference to the present law, mention aiders, counsellors and abettors, in some clauses, and not in others. Is not
the inference fair, that where they are not mentioned, they are
not intended to be subjected to punishment? And when congress took up the doctrine of treason, with reference to the
constitution, and did mention the aiders and abettors in some
cases, but not in others, is not the conclusion equally fair that
they did not intend that they should be involved in the guilt
or punishment of treason, except where they are expressly
mentioned? But a still better reason may be given why congress did not mean to include aiders, counsellors, &c. in the
guilt or punishment of treason. It was prohibited by the constitution of the United States to enlarge the doctrine of the
commission of treason, and that they knew that such a provision
would be void. This brings me to the consideration of the constitution itself. I have before endeavoured to demonstrate
that this instrument is not to be explained by the same nar-
now technical rules that apply to a statute made for altering
some provision of the common law; but that such a construction should be given, as is consistent not only with the letter,
but the spirit in which the great palladium of our liberties was
formed.

The object of the American constitution, was to perpetuate
the liberties of the people of this country. The framers of
that instrument well knew the dreadful punishments inflicted,
and the grievous oppressions produced, by constructive treasons in other countries, as well where the primary object was
the security of the throne as where the public good was the
pretext. Those gentlemen well knew from history, ancient as
well as modern, that, in every age and climate, where the people enjoyed even the semblance of liberty, and where factions
or parties existed, an accusation of treason, or a design to overturn the government, had been occasionally resorted to by
those in power, as the most convenient means of destroying

those individuals whom they had marked out for victims; and that the best mode of insuring a man's conviction, was to hunt him down as dangerous to the state. They knew that mankind are always the same, and that the same passions and vices must exist, though sometimes under different modifications, until the human race itself be extinct. That a repetition of the same scenes, which have deluged other countries with their best blood, might take place here, they well knew; and endeavoured as far as possible to guard against the evil, by a constitutional sanction. They knew that when a state is divided into parties, what horrible cruelties may be committed even in the name and under the assumed authority of a majority of the people, and therefo⁻ endeavoured to prevent them. The events which have since occurred in another country, and the sufferings under Robespierre, shew how well human nature was understood by those who framed our constitution.

The language which they have used for this purpose is plain, simple and perspicuous. There is no occasion to resort to the rules of construction to fix its meaning. It explains itself. Treason is to consist in levying war against the United States, and it must be public or open war: two witnesses must prove, that there has been an overt act. The spirit and object of this constitutional provision are equally clear. The framers of the constitution, with the great volume of human nature before them, knew that perjury could easily be inlisted on the side of oppression; that any man might become the victim of private accusation; that declarations might be proved which were never made; and therefore they meant, as they have said, that no man should be the victim of such secret crimination: but that the punishment of this offence should only be incurred by those whose crimes are plain and apparent; against whom an open deed is proved.

Now let me ask the opposite counsel, what security is afforded by the constitution, to the best or meanest man in this country, if the construction on which they insist be correct? and whether instead of a safeguard to the citizen, they do not reduce it to an unmeaning phrase? According to the construction on which they must insist, or abandon the prosecution, all that is wanted to fix the guilt of treason on any individual, *is*, that an insurrection shall have existed somewhere in the United States, no matter where. Observe, sir, that I am arguing on abstract principles, and not with a particular application. But suppose the government wished to destroy any man: they find him in Georgia; an insurrection happens in New-Hampshire. This will suffice for the purpose, and if this cause go on they will be obliged to contend that less will suffice;

that an insurrection is not necessary; but that even a peaceable assemblage going down the Ohio is sufficient for the purpose. They merely undertake to prove the existence of an insurrection: that a number of people have committed an act of insurrection: the man who is selected to be a victim is dragged from one end of the continent to the other, before a judge who is the creature of the government, appointed at the pleasure of the government, liable to be thrown out of office, if he offend the government: the cause comes on to trial: they prove an insurrection; and when once this insurrection or assemblage can be proved by two witnesses, nothing remains but to connect with it the individual thus marked for destruction; and as this may be done by evidence of his secret acts or even his declarations, he may be seized and hurried by force, from New-Hampshire to Georgia, or to any part of the United States, which his accusers may choose as best fitted for their purpose: it is in vain that he may prove, he was not present when the offence of which he is accused was committed; that he never at any period of his life had been there; that the actors and the scene were alike unknown to him; wretches, who from views of interest or revenge are ready to further the views of his oppressors, will present themselves, and he may be convicted of treason in levying open war against the government, with people whom he never saw, and at a place where he never was. Gentlemen may say, that this only shews, that the citizen may be equally the victim of false accusations of other offences; that it proves nothing, but that the innocent may be condemned on the testimony of perjured witnesses. In no other crime can a man be punished except in the county or district where he committed the act. Let gentlemen mention for what other offence an individual may be tried in a different district from the one in which he did the act which constitutes the essence of the crime; and admitting their principle in its full force, what becomes of the constitutional provision on this subject? where is the constitutional tribunal to try him, " an impartial jury of the state, wherein the offence has been committed?" It is reduced to a mere nullity. The constitution meant something; but according to this construction, it means nothing, and deceives instead of affording any security. It may be objected that treasonable conspiracies might thus go unpunished. To this it is a sufficient answer, that they may be prosecuted and charged, according to the truth of the case. Here I will mention an authority, which shews the propriety and safety of limiting and fixing the definition of treason; and how much the English statute, from which the words of our constitution are taken, has been approved of in that country. Hume's History of England, vol. 2. p. 487.

" One of the most popular laws enacted by any prince was the statute which passed in the 25th year of this reign, and which limited the cases of high treason, before vague and uncertain, to three principal heads: conspiring the death of the king, levying war against him, and adhering to his enemies; and the judges were prohibited, if any other cases should occur, from inflicting the penalty of treason, without an application to parliament. The bounds of treason were indeed so much limited by this statute, which still remains in force without any alteration, that the lawyers were obliged to enlarge them, and to explain " a conspiracy for *levying war* against the king, to be equal to a conspiracy against his life; and this interpretation seemingly forced, has, from the necessity of the case, been tacitly acquiesced in."

But it will be objected, that admitting the full force of this reasoning, it cannot avail us, as the point has been settled by a decision of the supreme court; and that argument must yield to authority.

At the same time that I deny the legislative effect of a decision of the supreme court, I will admit that it is entitled to the highest respect, as evidence of the law; and that the reason which would warrant the court in departing from it, must be strong and apparent; but to entitle it to this respect, the decision must have turned upon the very point in issue: and if the case should ever occur of an anomalous decision of that court, in opposition to known and established rules of law, I have no hesitation in saying, that it ought not to form a rule for this court. A mere *dictum* or an expression thrown out in argument without consideration (or if there were consideration, yet if the point in issue did not turn upon it) ought not to be deemed an authority.

There is however no such decision; the case never has occurred; for until the present instance, there never has been an attempt in the courts of the United States, to convict an individual for treason, who was not actually on the spot, when the act charged in the indictment was committed.

I will admit that in the case of Messrs. Bollman and Swartwout, which was only a question of commitment, decided by the supreme court, there is a *dictum*, which is reported to have fallen from the chief justice in delivering the opinion of the court, that is in opposition to the doctrine I have been contending for; but the decision of the court did not turn on that point: a determination of that question, one way or the other, would have no effect on the judgment: it was therefore extrajudicial. Your honour can set me right if I be mistaken; but I believe the point now relied on by the prosecution, either did not come before the court, or was very slightly touched on by the bar: it was a mere *dictum* of the judges stated arguendo, an *obiter* opinion delivered without argument, and not necessary to have been decided. A decision on the very point in controversy is evidence of the law; but an *obiter* opinion, a mere *dictum* or decision on a point not before the court, is no authority at all. Points of law, not immediately arising on the question, are frequently mentioned by judges, by way of illustration or explanation; and such opinions never have the force of precedent. The question before the supreme court was, who were concerned in the conspiracy, and who were not; but the point now before this court, never came before the supreme court; for as I have already observed, this is the first attempt in this country, to convict a person of treason, who was not present when the act was committed. It is well known, that Vigol and Mitchel, the only persons of the multitude concerned in the western insurrection in 1794, who were convicted and sentenced to die, (but were afterwards pardoned) though the most actively engaged, were mere instruments instigated and persuaded by others; but what was the conduct of the government of the United States on that occasion? Were those who fomented, advised or encouraged the insurrection, but were not actors in it, indicted and prosecuted? No, *actors* and *actors only, were indicted;* and I trust that this attempt, which is as novel as it is dangerous, will never be sanctioned by this court; and if I know my own mind, I feel a better and more powerful motive than professional duty, in endeavouring to prevent the establishment of their doctrine; a most ardent desire to avert from my country, my family and myself, an evil so very pernicious and repugnant to every principle of civil liberty. I would unite with themselves with as much zeal and energy as possible, in opposing it; for if it were to be sanctioned as a confirmed doctrine, it might be justly said that, however perfect in theory, our government was a practical tyranny, at the pleasure of those who have the administration of the government in their hands. It is on these grounds, that I have argued this cause; not solely in defence of my client, but for the sake of the community at large, and of posterity.

If the law be as I have stated, it is not very extraordinary, that the court should in a point not immediately before it, have adopted the *dicta* of writers in England as authority, and have applied them to this country, without full consideration of all the points on which the question turned.

I think, therefore, that it is proved, that under the constitution of the United States, no man can be convicted of treason, who was not present when the overt act charged in the indictment was committed.

Before I proceed further I beg leave to remark, that all my arguments and illustrations are on abstract principles; that I wish to make no particular or individual allusions; and that I do not mean the smallest reflection on the government: nor should I think myself justified to waste the time of the court, in making such observations. I now proceed with my argument.

If, contrary to my firm conviction, I should be mistaken on this point, I contend,

Secondly, That the offence if it be punishable, should be laid in the county and district where the act was done by the accused which renders him guilty. If he be guilty, it is by means of some *act done by himself;* and that *act* must have *locality.* The prosecutors must prove the fact as laid in their indictment. They have pledged themselves to furnish proof in support of the charge therein specified. It being admitted that colonel Burr was not present when the act was done, we contend, that they should at once withdraw their indictment, as it does not contain a specification that can be supported by the evidence. If he have conspired to levy war against the United States, and it be admitted that the war was carried on by others in his absence, his offence can only be punished by a *special indictment charging the facts as they existed.*

To this will be objected the rule of law, that in treason all are principals; and that therefore, in construction of law, the accessory was present aiding and abetting at the same time and place where the overt act was committed. But this objection arises from a misapplication of the rule: aiders and abettors *after* the fact are as much, in construction of law, principals, as those before the fact; yet there is no doubt that they must be tried, not in the county where the war was levied, but where they did the act, which makes them principal traitors by relation. The rule of law is not founded on arbitrary principles, but on maxims of immutable justice and reason. Though it requires, as the best mean of deterring people from the commission of so heinous a crime, that all who are in any manner concerned in it, should be equally punished, yet to prevent oppression, it must be so construed as to be consistent with another sacred rule of law, that the accused must be informed of the precise nature of the charge against him, in order that he may be prepared to defend himself. The accusations, whether in an indictment or information, should specially state the offence, which is intended to be proved against the accused. He cannot otherwise be prepared to defend himself. An offence, different from that which is charged against him, and which alone he can be expected to meet with his defence, is never allowed to be given in evidence. This is the foundation of all the niceties in criminal prosecutions; but this objection is not founded on any critical nicety, but on the broad merits of the case. If the indictment were not to give notice of the precise nature of the accusation, the party accused might be oppressed and destroyed. Does this indictment inform us that it was meant to be proven, that colonel Burr was not present when the *overt act* was committed, but that he was guilty of treason, by being connected with those who perpetrated the overt act? On the contrary, is it not presumable from the charge in this indictment, that colonel Burr himself committed the act, and levied the war against the United States in person? What information does the indictment give of the true nature of the charge meant to be supported? For what purpose did they comply with the formality required by the act of congress of giving him a copy of the indictment, but to inform him, that they meant to prove, that he did the act on Blannerhassett's island in person? It could admit of no other rational construction, than that they intended to prove, that he was there at the time. Presuming this, we could not make this motion till we found by what proof they meant to support the indictment. The accused therefore concludes, that the charge to be supported is, that he in person levied the war against the United States at the place mentioned in the indictment. In order to completely negative the idea of his being charged as an accessory or aider to other people, this indictment is drawn in a special and peculiar manner; not as indictments are generally formed. It charges that he committed the act on Blannerhassett's island, *with divers persons unknown.* Neither Mr. Blannerhassett nor Tyler, nor any other particular person is named, but he is alleged to have done the act with persons *unknown.*

But it will be objected, that if guilty, he must know whether the act is done or not, and be prepared to defend himself; and that if not guilty, no evidence can be given that will fix the crime upon him; and there is no necessity of a specification. But this objection goes directly to prove, that there is no necessity for an indictment at all. The court knew that an accusation might be supported by perjury, and circumstances may create a presumption of guilt, which testimony would explain, and which explanation would evince the innocence of the accused. Besides, if the general doctrine, contended for on the other side, be correct, a man may be guilty of treason in being connected with a conspiracy to levy war, and be really a stranger to the commission of the *overt* act, which makes him a traitor by relation.

It will be said that levying war is always a public act, and therefore there is no difficulty in knowing what is intended to be proved. Two answers may be given to this objection: one is, that granting this to be true, the accused is to be informed of the charge against him, not by public rumours, but by the terms of the accusation itself. The other applies to this particular case only. The general doctrine always has been, that to prove the charge of levying war, it must be shewn that there have been overt acts; and as the charge must correspond with the proofs, the course has always been to state in the indictment, that the accused levied *public* war. In every indictment for treason that I have met with, in the *State Trials* or books of entries, the word "*public*," or an equivalent word is inserted. The words, "public war, did prepare begin and levy," are in the indictment in the following cases: 8 *State Trials*, page 219. in the prosecution against Damaree; in that against Willis, and in that against Purchase, page 220; In 9 *State Trials*, page 543. in the indictment against Townly, the words "did prepare, order, wage and levy a public and cruel war" are used; and it is stated in the report, that *that* form of indictment was made use of against all the rebels who were tried in Surry, except one for a special reason.

The same words are used in the indictment against lord Kilmarnock, page 592. of the same volume, and against lords Cromarty and Balmerino, in page 593. It is also so stated in *Foster's Crown Law*, page 6. In *Tremaine's Pleas of the Crown*, page 2. the indictment for levying war is in the same form, "traitorously did prepare levy and ordain *public war;*" and in this country the indictment against John Fries has the same words, "did ordain, prepare and levy public war against the United States."

In the present instance, gentlemen do not say in the indictment, that there was a public war; they only tell us of an act that may be private or public. They do not pretend to say that there were marching and counter-marching in military array; that they had great guns, &c. drums beating, &c.

In the present, the word *public* is omitted in both counts of the indictment; I do not suppose that it was done studiously. Whether this were done by accident, "*currente calamo*," or to make it more palatable to the grand jury, need not be inquired. Whether this word be not considered as operative or be omitted in any indictment in this country, I do not know, but it is used in all the English precedents. I only use this argument for the purpose of shewing that there is no ground for presuming knowledge of the fact, if indeed such a fact ever existed. On principle, therefore, it is apparent that this indictment does not warrant the introduction of evidence to charge the accused with the acts of others when he was present. Let me ask if a fiction that the accused levied war be admitted, what necessity is there for another fiction, that he was at a place where he was not?

The only argument on common law principles that can justly be urged, would go to prove, that he could not be tried any where.

In another branch of this argument I have had occasion to shew, that although it is laid down in the English books, that all are principals in treason, yet that this rule only applies to the degree of punishment and denomination of the offence; that in the progress of the prosecution, the same rules of law, which apply to the case of accessories in felony, are to be followed with respect to aiders and abettors before the fact in treason; and that this principle has been stated by most of the writers who have stated the general rule. I shall have occasion in another part of my argument to explain this principle more fully.

Now it is clear that at common law, an accessory to a felony which was committed in a different county from the one where the accessorial act was done, was not punishable at all. At common law, the accessory could not be arraigned till the principal were attainted. If the principal had never been indicted at all, had stood mute, had challenged above 35 jurors peremptorily, had claimed the benefit of clergy, had obtained a pardon, or had died before attainder, the accessories, in any of these cases, could not be arraigned. At common law, therefore, if a felony were committed by A, and B had counselled, procured or commanded him to commit it, and A had died, been pardoned or stood mute &c. so that he had not been and could not be convicted, B could not be tried at all. But a statute amended the law in this respect, (See *Hale's P. C.* chapter 57. page 62.) But the constitution of the United States has fixed the place of trial, if indeed it can take place any where.

The 8th article of amendments to the constitution, provides that " in all criminal prosecutions, the party accused shall have a speedy and public trial, by an impartial jury of the state or district where the crime was committed. This was meant to be a substantial provision, securing a trial by the vicinage; and yet according to the construction contended for by the gentlemen on the other side, it is merely illusory, and a man who was born in Virginia and was never out of the limits of the state, may, notwithstanding the constitutional provision in his favour, be hurried off to New-Hampshire, and tried for an offence which he never did commit, and which it is impossible he should have committed there. At all events the rule must be uniform. Now it must be admitted that an aider or abettor after the fact must be tried in the county and district where he committed the offence; and what sufficient reason can be assigned for a different rule in the case of an aider or abettor before the fact?

No precedent can be produced in point on either side; because, except in the case of Sir Nicholas Throgmorton, there is no instance to be found in the whole judicial history of England, (under any of its different forms of government, being sometimes a despotism, sometimes a limited monarchy, sometimes a republic) of an attempt like the present, under any form of indictment; and that case, as far as it is an authority, is directly in our favour. He was indicted for levying war against the queen; and the evidence was a connexion with Sir Thomas Wiatt, who raised an insurrection in Kent, and marched towards London, but did not enter within the jurisdiction of the city, which begins at

Temple-bar. Yet Throgmorton was tried within the jurisdiction of the city, and the lord mayor presided at the trial, and he was acquitted.

It is true that it is laid down in *East*, an elementary writer, who certainly is himself no authority, that there is nothing to remark of difference between principals and accomplices in respect of the indictment; but so far as we can judge from cases in any degree analogous, the rule has been different. In *Tremaine's Pleas of the Crown*, in the case of an indictment against Mary Speke, for aiding the duke of Monmouth and others in the act of levying war against the king, the charge is special. As this was in the 4th year of the reign of James the 2d, and the act is charged as having been committed in the county of Somerset in the west of England, it must have been one of the cases that came before the inhuman Jefferies; and it seems that *even he* deemed it necessary that the accused should at least be apprised of the nature of the charge, by a special indictment charging the facts as they existed.

It may be said, that the accused, in that case, was in the nature of an accessory after the fact; but this cannot be supported, for she was an assister *at* or *during* the fact, which is the same thing as an accessory before the fact. How was she charged? The indictment is, that she, knowing the said James Scott (the duke of Monmouth) to be a false traitor, and that he, with many other false traitors to the number of 4000, had assembled and collected and " had traitorously prepared, levied and raised war, insurrection and rebellion against the king &c. *for the comforting assisting*, *aiding* and *supporting* of the said James Scott &c. *in the war, rebellion* and *insurrection aforesaid*, &c. did cause to be conveyed and carried to the said James Scott, &c. cart loads of bread and of cheese &c." In a case of felony, such an accomplice would be an accessory before the fact. There are in law but two species of accessories, one *before*, the other *after*. A person aiding *at* the time when the act was done has always in construction of law (except where present and deemed a principal) been considered as an accessory before the fact.

In the case of Somerville, 1 *Anderson's Reports*, page 106, although the indictment is not set out at large, the form is particularly described, and it appears to have been settled *on great consideration*, " *that aiders and the other procurers of the treason should be indicted specially for the procurement*." Somerville was procured and persuaded by Edward Arden and his wife, to kill the queen. It was on great consideration determined, that according to law, if all three were indicted for "levying war," that he should be charged with doing the act, and that they should be indicted specially for procuring and aiding him; that each ought to be charged according to the truth of the case: but that a general indictment was sufficient to support the charge of compassing the death of the queen; and on this great consideration they determined that aiders and other procurers of treason should be indicted specially for the procurement.

But if this form of indictment be insisted on as being proper on this occasion, it must be under a general rule applicable to all cases of aiding, in the commission of an overt act of treason: and if in any case, a departure from the rule for the purposes of justice would be proper, it would be such a one as the present; none requires specification more.

Now among the treasons created by act of parliament, which are collected in 1 *Hale's Pleas of the Crown, chap.* 24. *p.* 280. is one created by the 28 *Hen.* 8. *chap.* 18. by which " marrying any of the king's children or reputed children, or his sisters, or aunts of the father's part, or the children of the king's brethren, or sisters, without the king's licence under his great seal, or deflowering of any of them, is enacted to be treason." Now we may suppose a very probable circumstance, that a female accomplice in one of those treasons, for instance one of the maids of honour, should be prosecuted for aiding and abetting the principal traitor, would she be indicted by her name, as a female, with the addition of spinster, for marrying the king's aunt, or deflowering his daughter? or would she be charged specially with *aiding or abetting the male person who did the act?* 33 *Hen.* 8. 1 *Hale* 281. By another act of parliament of the same reign, it is made treason in any woman the king shall intend to marry thinking her to be a true maid, to marry him if she be not so. Now it is a very possible case that the paramour of such a woman (I will suppose her to be one of the maids of honour, and him to be a lord of the bedchamber) should aid her in imposing on the king. She is tried, found guilty and executed. How is he to be charged? would he be indicted by the name of A. B. gentleman, or by his title of lord, for marrying the king, not being an unspotted virgin, or to use the language of the act, a *pure and clean maid?* This may seem to be treating the subject with more levity than I could wish to do; but the argument directly applies: it exposes the fallacy of gentlemen's arguments. It may indeed be said, that in these instances, there would be a physical impossibility in the act, as charged in the indictment, and that therefore in such a case it ought to be charged so as to correspond with the fact; but this is an admission that it may be charged, and if in any case, it surely ought in such a one as the present: for it is as much a physical impossibility that colonel Burr should be at Blannerhassett's island and in Kentucky (places several hundred miles distant) at the same time, as that an individual should be at the same time a man and a woman.

A little attention to principles must satisfy us, that levying war may consist of a great variety of acts; yet it is one entire offence. The expression in the act is "levying war," in the indictment "levying a public war." Now a war may consist of a single act of hostility, or a great variety of acts. If a man were concerned in the rebellion of 1715 and in that of 1745, though there is a complete space of thirty years between them, he might be indicted for both, because they are separate rebellions and insurrections; but if he were concerned in that of 1745 only, he could not be charged with the battles of Preston Pans, Culloden, the taking of Edinburgh, Manchester, Carlisle, &c. in separate indictments in succession: for if so, there might be a thousand or more trials, though there was but one rebellion: it might be divisible *ad infinitum.*

After charging generally that war was levied, every indictment charges certain overt acts, and these overt acts are laid for the information of the party. The prosecutor may lay as many overt acts as he thinks proper and select which he chooses; but they must be all laid at once in the same indictment. They are the charge which, if proved by evidence, supports the indictment. If the charge be for the information of the party, is he not excused if it be not made good? Was it ever heard that a person might be tried over and over again for treason in the same rebellion? Has it ever been pretended, that, when a person came prepared to contest particular facts, other facts were to be proved against him? For example, a person is charged with a succession of facts done at Edinburgh, Falkirk, Preston Pans, Carlisle &c.; he comes prepared to prove an " *alibi;*" but on the trial finds instead of these facts being intended to be proved, that the counsel for the prosecution introduce evidence of facts committed at places totally different from those in the indictment, and not committed by himself, but by others when he was not present; would not this evidence be a surprize upon him? would it be admitted? So in treason for compassing the king's death, is there a single instance in which an overt act, not charged in the indictment, and distinct from that which is charged, has been attempted to be proved on the prisoner? There is not. An overt act not charged may be proved when it tends to prove that which is charged; but then that is never admitted *till after the overt act charged is* proved.

They charge colonel Burr with being at Blannerhassett's island, when he was two or three hundred miles off in Kentucky, and instead of proving it, they offer to prove that the

cessory after the fact, or a receiver of a traitor, be indicted under the constitution? If he cannot, no more can the accomplice before the fact. If a special charge be necessary on an indictment of an accessory after the fact, it is equally necessary to charge the accessory before the fact specially; and then the indictment does not conform to the constitution, which requires that the war should be levied by the accused. *Treason consists in "levying war,"* not *in advising it*, or receiving him who has levied it. If you allege an act as done by others, do you not charge that it is done by the others? In England a special charge, particularly stating the act of procurement or comforting, is proper; but here it is forbidden by the constitution, treason being expressly limited to the act of war, not of advising or receiving. But the spirit and meaning of the constitution are not to be evaded by charging generally what ought to be charged specially. I submit, therefore, whether upon principle or practice, any evidence can be given of the acts of third persons, not named in the indictment, when it is admitted that the accused himself was absent.

Although I trust that some, if not all the points that I have contended for, are decidedly in favour of the accused, there is one more, which, as it rests not only on the plainest principles of reason and justice, but on a concurrence of all the authorities on the subject, is too clear to admit of a doubt; and were the case of less importance, I should have deemed it unnecessary to submit any other to the court. I lay it down as a rule that cannot be controverted, that even if aiders and abettors in treason be considered as principals, yet that their guilt is derivative, and can only be established by legal proof, that the persons whose acts they are answerable for, have committed treason; that the only legal proof is a record of the conviction of those persons; that without such proof, no testimony connecting an aider or abettor with those persons is admissible; and of course if there be no such record the prosecutors fail in their case, and cannot proceed with their testimony.

In order, therefore, to prove the guilt of an aider or abettor, the person from whom his guilt is derived, must be shewn to be guilty by the highest evidence.

But I would not narrow the grounds of my client's defence, nor do I mean to admit that others who are alleged to have been connected with him in the imputed conspiracy have been guilty, when I insist that his guilt, if it exist, is derived from theirs. I deny that any of them are guilty. This is an act of justice not only to him, but to them. Mr. Blannerhassett, Mr. Tyler and Mr. Smith, as individuals, are deservedly respected; but they have been held up throughout the United States and in this court as arch traitors. I mean no reflection on the gentlemen on the other side, but judging them on general principles, from the zeal and perseverance which they have already manifested, they will continue strenuously to contend, that those injurious reports are well founded, and that their guilt is unquestionable. Colonel Burr, therefore, considers it not an act of justice to himself only, but a sacred obligation respecting them, that this charge should be inquired into; and, if not established, that those unfounded calumnies should be refuted. Unless the record of the condemnation of some persons who are proved to be traitors be produced, and the connexion between them and colonel Burr be proved, no other proof is admissible or can be received. That this is the rule in all felonies is beyond all question; the accessory never can be convicted until the principal be found guilty; and a record of the conviction of the principal must be produced on the trial of the accessory. But perhaps it will be observed, by the gentlemen on the other side, that in treason there is no accessory, and all are principals. That rule is general, and applies to accessories *after*, as well as to accessories *before* the fact. I contend that with respect to accessories *after* the fact, it has always been adjudged and considered as settled law, except by chancellor Jefferies, that in order to fix guilt on such accessory, the principal who did the act must be convicted. Lady Lisle's attainder was reversed by act of parliament, because the person whom she had received had not been convicted. She was a lady of rank and fortune, and tried, convicted and executed (as before stated) for entertaining, concealing and comforting John Hicks, knowing him to be a false traitor. It was thought necessary to reverse her attainder by act of parliament. The act calls her trial and condemnation " *an irregular and undue prosecution*," and declares that the " verdict was injuriously extorted by the violence, menaces and other illegal practices of judge Jefferies;" but it particularly mentions, as a principal ground of the reversal, " *that the said John Hicks* (the person whom she had entertained) *was not at the trial of the said Alicia Lisle, attainted or convicted of any such crime.*" Unless it had been thought that the law was settled, that an accessory could not be prosecuted till the principal had been convicted, and that she had been deprived of the benefit of this law by the violence and cruelty of Jefferies, the act of parliament would not have been passed.

In several other prosecutions before Jefferies, the convictions were produced. On the trial of William Ring an accessory after the fact, for receiving and comforting and providing meat, drink and lodging for Joseph Kelloway and Henry Lawrence, who were in the rebellion in the duke of Monmouth's army, the first evidence produced was the record of the conviction of Kelloway and Lawrence, 4 *St. Trials*, 130—134; and on the trial of John Fernley for harbouring and concealing James Burton who had been outlawed for treason, and had been in Monmouth's rebellion, the first evidence produced against him was the record of Burton's outlawry, *ibid. p.* 137. Now as aiders after the fact are as much traitors as those before, the same rule applies to accessories before, with equal force. They stand on precisely the same ground; the guilt of the accused is consequential in both cases. The difference of time does not affect the question, because the act of procurement or advice is never heard of, if the act of treason be not committed; so that the procurer or accessory before is a traitor by relation, as much as a receiver after. In this point of view there is no distinction between them; so that the guilt of the procurer or accessory is a consequence of the act; and if the act be not done he is not guilty.

But it is unnecessary to rely on general reasoning however conclusive; express authorities on the subject may be produced.

Lord Hale in the first volume of his *Pleas of the Crown*, states, that " as to the course of proceeding, it hath been, and *indeed ought to be the course, that those who did actually commit the very fact of treason should be first tried, before those that are principals in the second degree*, because otherwise this inconvenience might follow, viz. that the principals in the second degree might be convicted, and yet the principals in the first degree may be acquitted, which would be absurd." Apply this doctrine to the present case: colonel Burr is charged with being an aider before the fact, to Blannerhassett, who being charged with " having actually committed the very fact," must be first tried. His guilt is derivative; and you must prove that the act is done by the conviction of the principal, before you are let into evidence against the accessory. In confirmation of this doctrine he refers to *Anderson's Reports, p.* 109. Somerville's or Arden's case. Arden and wife, and Somerville were (as before stated) indicted for treason, in compassing the death of the queen; the two former as procuring or advising the act to be done, and the latter as the actor. It was ruled on great consideration as a general principle, " that the jury must first be charged to inquire of the principal offender, and if they found him guilty then to inquire of the receipt; and if the principal be not guilty then to acquit both; that this was the law where the offence charged was ' levying war;' but where it was for compassing the queen's death, that there was no need that he who undertook to do the act should be first tried; for the movers and procurers are guilty of compassing the death, though he that was procured should never assent thereto."

In the *2d volume, p.* 223, the learned author states, that " if A be indicted of high treason, and B be indicted for receiving or comforting him, or procuring or abetting (but not present) here it is true that they are all principals; but inasmuch as B, in case of a felony would have been but accessory, and it is possible that A may be acquitted of the fact, it seems to me that B shall not be put to answer of the *receit* or procurement till A be outlawed, or at least jointly with A and in this case the same jury may be charged with both, and their charge shall be first to inquire, whether A were guilty, and if not, then to acquit both A and B; and if A be found guilty, then that they inquire of B. And in *Somerville's case* (26 *Eliz.*) mentioned before, the inquiry was first of the principal offender, and then of the receiver or procurer, to avoid that inconvenience and aweroust, that might happen in case B were first convict of the procurement and receit, and yet possibly A might be acquitted of the principal fact."

It cannot be contended that by indicting B. as accessory or procurer singly, the prosecutor can evade this rule of law, which is founded on the soundest principles of moral right. He cannot allege that the defendant has waived it, because the indictment has given him no notice that he was to be charged as principal in the second degree; there being no reference to any other individual named in the indictment.

If then Lord Hale be an authority on this point, he is conclusive. He says, that aiders and procurers before the act, and receivers after, never can be guilty, if the principal be innocent. In order to prove that the accessory is guilty, you must have the highest evidence, and that is not conclusive, for he may controvert the guilt of the principal; but the prosecutor is not at liberty to say that he is guilty, without producing the record of his conviction.

But this question also proves, that I was right on a point I have already argued, that the indictment should charge the offence specially, and state that the accused procured the act of treason, which was committed by another, who should be named in the indictment.

The *next* law writer, in point of authority, to lord Hale, and one certainly no otherwise inferior to him, than in his having confined his disquisitions to particular branches of criminal law, is Foster. He may be said to be of equal authority with Hale, for in point of correct judgment and understanding none is superior to him. In his chapter on accomplices, he states with explicit approbation the opinion of Hale, and agrees with him in every essential particular. The whole of the first section, from *p.* 341 to 347, is apposite to the present question; and as his thoughts will not admit abridgment, I will read the whole to the court.

" It is well known, that in the language of the law there are no accessories in high treason, all are principals. Every instance of incitement, aid or protection, which in the case of felony will render a man an accessory before or after the fact, in the case of high treason, whether it be treason at common law or by statute, will make him a principal in treason; unless the case be otherwise provided for by the statute creating the offence, or where the special penning of the act, leadeth to a different construction.

" This rule hath long obtained and will not now be controverted; but I think it a matter of great importance, that the rule be rightly understood; I mean with those limitations which sound sense and common equity require. For cases have frequently happened, where an offender in the final issue of the prosecution may be considered as a principal in treason; and yet, during the intermediate steps towards his conviction, he ought from a principle of natural justice, to be considered *merely as in the nature of an accessory before or after the fact.*

" For instance, A. adviseth B. to counterfeit the king's coin or seals, or indeed to commit any of the offences declared treason by the 25 *Ed.* 3. and furnisheth him with means for that purpose; (that species of treason which in judgment of law, falleth within the clause of compassing the death of the king, queen, or prince always excepted:) If B. in consequence of this advice and encouragement doth the fact, A. is a principal in the treason; for such advice and assistance in the case of felony would have made him an accessory before the fact; and in high treason there are no accessories, all are principals. But if B. forbeareth to commit the fact to which he is incited, A. cannot be a traitor merely on account of this advice and encouragement, though his behaviour hath been highly criminal; for bare advice or incitement, how wicked soever, unless in the cases already excepted, will not bring a man within the statute, where no treason hath been committed in consequence of it. So in the case of assistance or protection supposed to be given to a traitor after the fact, the party knowingly affording such protection, *if the treason hath been in fact committed*, will be a principal in treason for the reasons already mentioned. But if a person lying probably under a suspicion of guilt, conscious of his own innocence, should think it advisable to withdraw, and patiently to wait the issue of things when the storm, which gathereth round him, shall be blown over; the party who received and harboured him, during his retreat, cannot be a traitor for so doing, provided the conduct of his friend shall appear, upon examination, to have been blameless. Lord chief justice Coke, who while he was in the service of the crown, seemeth to have had no bowels in state prosecutions, when he layeth down and applieth the rule I have mentioned, that *all are principals in treason*, plainly goeth upon a supposition, *that the treason, presumed to have been procured, was afterwards in fact committed; or that the party supposed to have been knowingly received and harboured had been actually guilty of high treason.* It would have been absurd to the last degree, to have gone upon any other supposition: for it cannot be said with any sort of propriety, that a person procured an offence to be committed, which in truth never was committed; or that any person knowingly, viz. *with a full knowledge of a treason to have been committed*, (that I take to be the legal sense of the term *knowingly*,) received and harboured the traitor, if such treason never had been committed by him.

" There needeth very little to evince the truth of this observation, more than to give a proper attention to the rule already mentioned, *that every act which in the case of felony, will render a man an accessory, will in the case of treason make him a principal;* especially if we add to it, according to lord Hale, *that nothing short of such an act will.* What circumstance therefore is necessary to render a man an accessory in felony? Plainly this above all others, *that the felony charged upon the principal, hath been in fact committed by him.* For which reason no verdict can pass against the accessory, till the truth of this single fact shall have been legally established either by the conviction of the principal if he continueth amenable to justice; or by judgment of outlawry if he abscondeth or flieth ; unless the accessory chooseth to waive the benefit of the law, and to submit to a trial.

" This rule is founded in good sense and natural justice. The accessory *is* indeed a felon, but guilty of a felony of a different kind from that of the principal. It is, if I may use the expression, a derivative felony connected with and arising out of that of the principal and cannot exist without it. Whether the same equitable rule is by parity of reason to be extended to treasonable actions of a similar nature, I mean to such as are of the derivative kind, and though in the language of the law styled principal treasons, yet partaking of the nature of mere accessorial offences, cometh now to be considered. This is the point of importance I hinted at in the outset of this discourse. For if in prosecutions for treasons of this kind the same rule of equity be observed as in cases of felony, it will become a matter of very small importance to have been learning by what special technical expression we are to describe the offence.

" Lord chief justice Hale spendeth a whole chapter on this point, which he intitleth, " Concerning Principals and Accessories in High Treason." And though in conformity to the established mode of speaking, he calleth every person who can any way be considered as an accomplice in treason *a principal in it;* yet when he cometh to speak of the course and order to be observed in the prosecution of the offenders, he considereth those accomplices whose supposed guilt is connected with and dependeth upon the real guilt of another in the light of mere accessories; and stateth a few cases by way of illustration and proof. A person is committed to prison for high treason, the gaoler voluntarily suffereth him to escape; or a stranger knowing of such commitment breaketh the prison and setteth him at large; or knowingly rescueth him after an arrest and before he is brought to prison. In all these cases the gaoler and the person breaking prison or rescuing, whom he in a passage I shall presently cite, calleth *a kind of accessories*, are principals in treason, if the party imprisoned were really a traitor. If he were not so, it will be no treason in them; and therefore they shall not be arraigned till the principal offender be convict; for if he be acquitted of the principal offence the others shall be discharged.

" I have used the words *knowing* and *knowingly*, because I think that circumstance is a necessary ingredient in the case. It is true it was resolved in Benstead's case cited here by the learned author and at *page* 141. *but I think not with entire approbation of the rule*, that the party breaking prison would have been guilty of treason *though he had not known that traitors were there*. I am by no means satisfied with this opinion. For the single authority upon which this point is said by Hale to have been so ruled, doth by no means warrant it. The book expressly stateth it, *that the party did know that traitors were there*. And Brooke who abridgeth the case is express to the same purpose; *sciant que traitors fueront en ceo*. And Coke citing the same case layeth a great stress on this circumstance, *that the party knew that traitors were there*, and conducted them out of prison. I have upon another occasion taken some notice of this short and imperfect report of Benstead's case, and observed that the prosecution against him appeareth to have been carried on with uncommon expedition, not to say with some degree of precipitancy. And probably the forcing of prison doors, *as many were forced during the tumult*, was given in evidence on his trial, among other outrages of the night, as overt acts of levying war, the species of treason for which he stood indicted.

" The same rule of equity and natural justice the learned judge in another place applieth to the case of felonious escapes and rescues, and addeth, If the principal offender be convicted and hath his clergy, ' I think the gaoler or rescuer shall never be put to answer the escape or rescue, as the accessory where the principal hath his clergy is thereby discharged, for the rescuer and officer are a kind of accessories.' He calleth them a kind of accessories, because there can be no felonious escape or rescue where no felony had been previously committed. But in strict legal propriety they are not accessories to the original felony, for though a man should be committed for many felonies, yet the escape or rescue is considered as one single felony and is so charged.

" With regard to a person knowingly receiving and harbouring a traitor, the learned judge in the place lately cited argueth, that though he is in the eye of the law a principal traitor and shall not be said to be an accessory, *yet thus much he partaketh of an accessory*, his indictment must be special of the receipt and not of the principal treason. If he is indicted by a several indictment, he shall not be tried till the principal be convicted; if in the same indicment with the principal, the jury must be charged to inquire first of the principal offender, and if they find him guilty, then of the receipt; and if the principal be not guilty, then to acquit both. For though in the eye of the law they are both principals in treason, yet in truth he (the receiver) is so far an accessory that he cannot be guilty if the principal be innocent.

" In the case of Mrs. Lisle whose hard fate it was to fall into the hands of perhaps the worst judge that ever disgraced Westminster-Hall, no regard was paid to this doctrine. I would not be thought to mention this case as an authority upon which a doubt can at this day be possibly raised. I do it for the sake of what happened afterwards, which I take to be an authority with me. Her attainder was afterwards reversed in parliament; and the act reciteth among other hardships of her case, *that she was by an irregular and undue prosecution, indicted for entertaining and concealing John Hicks a false traitor knowing him to be such; though the said Hicks was not at the time of the trial attainted or convicted of any such crime.*

" The same learned author in other parts of his work argueth to the purpose for which I have already cited him; and applieth the same rule of equity to the case of a person indicted for contriving, abetting, aiding, or consenting to treason, which happeneth never to have been carried into execution.

" But here we must distinguish, though the learned judge speaking in general terms apposite to his present purpose, doth not. For with regard to every instance of incitement, consent, approbation, or previous abetment in that species of treason which falleth under the branch of the statute touching the compassing of the death of the king, queen, or prince, every such treason is in its own nature, independently of all other circumstances or events, a complete overt act of compassing; though the fact originally in the contemplation of the parties should never be effected nor so much as attempted. *A.* inciteth *B.* to a treason of this kind, *B.* in abhorrence of the crime, and from a just sense of the duty which every man oweth to his king and country, and which every good man in the like circumstance will pay, maketh a discovery; by means whereof *A* is brought to justice. This incitement on the part of *A.* is a complete overt act of treason within this branch of the statute, and hath no sort of connexion with, or necessary dependence upon the future behaviour of *B.* And therefore whatever the learned author hath advanced in general terms touching fruitless ineffectual advice or incitement to treasonable practices, must be understood of such treasons only as do not fall within this branch of the statute."

In *page* 341. he states that an accomplice in treason, though in the final issue he may be considered as a principal, yet, during the intermediate steps towards conviction, he ought to be considered merely as in the nature of an accessory before or after the fact. In *page* 346 he cites lord Hale's opinion with approbation, except that he properly distinguishes between treason, in compassing the death of the king, and every other species of treason; as in the former the treason is complete in the very act of conspiring. Now it will be admitted that a conspiracy to levy war is not in itself an act of treason. Judge Foster then, as well as lord Hale, is a direct authority in favour of my position.

The same doctrine is laid down and illustrated by a modern writer, who certainly is not of himself authority, though he merits the name of an industrious and accurate compiler, and who, from causes that might be conjectured, on all occasions, seems little inclined to relax the severity of the law on the subject of treason.

Mr. East, in his treatise on *Crown Law, chap.* 2. *sec.* 39. *p.* 100. lays down with great clearness the same rule of law, and expressly states, that proof of the treason of the agent can only be established by his conviction. I shall cite what he saith though his words differ but little from Hale and Foster. " But further, with respect to the trial, the general rule, that *all are principals in treason*, must be understood with more limitation. In regard to all acts of approbation, incitement, advice, or procuring towards that species of treason, which in judgment of law falls within the clause of compassing the king's death, or that of the queen or prince, there is no doubt but that the party may be tried before the person who acted upon such incitement; because the bare advising or encouraging to such actions is in itself a complete overt act of compassing; and it is totally immaterial whether the atttempt were ever made or not. The case of Somerville proves no more than this; though the rule is there laid down in general terms, that a person aiding or procuring a treason may be tried before the actor. But with regard to all other treasons within the statute

25 *Edw.* 3. if one advise or encourage another to commit them, or furnish him means for that purpose, in consequence whereof the fact is committed, the adviser will indeed be a principal; for such advice or assistance would have made him an accessory before the fact in felony: but if the other forbore to commit the act thus advised, the adviser could not be a traitor merely on account of his ineffectual advice and encouragement; though his conduct would be highly criminal: for it cannot be said that a person procured an offence which in truth was never committed. In these cases therefore the treason is of a derivative nature, and depends entirely upon the question, whether the agent have or have not been guilty of such treason? *the proof of which can only be legally established by his conviction,* if he continue amenable to justice, or his attainder by outlawry, if he abscond; unless the accessory choose to waive the benefit of the law, and submit to a trial.

" The same rule holds in case of assistance or protection to a traitor after the fact in all cases, or of permitting, or procuring his escape from custody. The party knowingly affording such protection or contributing to such escape, if the treason have been in fact committed, will be a principal traitor; but *the fact of the principal's guilt must first be established,* and notice of it must also appear to have been received by him who may be called the accessory after. For it cannot be said that a person received or succoured a traitor knowingly, that is, with a knowledge of the treason's having been committed, when in truth either no such treason was committed by him, or the receiver was altogether ignorant of it."

It will be observed that he too considers the case of an accomplice before and after the fact, as being governed in this respect, precisely by the same rules.

It need only be remarked, that he considers the case of Somerville (*Anderson* 109) as being at first view against the position, and endeavours to explain it. Now the case of Somerville being an exception from the general rule and so stated, according to the maxim *exceptio probat regulam,* is directly in favour of this doctrine: as the decision in that case proceeded solely on the ground of the indictment being for treason in compassing the death of the king, which being in itself a complete act of treason, was distinguishable from the other species of that offence. The words are " car le procurement est un compassement et imagination del mort le roy quel en soy mesme est treason."

The prosecution is not against us as accessory to a crime committed by another; the indictment informs us, that it is against ourselves not for an accessorial but a principal treason committed by us in person; and we come to defend ourselves against that charge only.

The only doctrine, in any of the books to the contrary, is that of sergeant Hawkins in book the 2d. *chap.* 27. *sect.* 2. *p.* 439, 440. (Leach's edition.) " As to the first particular, in what offences there can be no accessories, but all must be principals, if any way guilty, it seems to have been always an uncontroverted maxim, that there can be no accessories in high treason or trespass. Also it seems to have been always agreed, that whatsoever will make a man an accessory before in felony, will make him a principal in high treason and trespass, as battery, riot, rout, forcible entry and even in forgery and petit larceny. And therefore wherever a man commands another to commit a trespass, who afterwards commits it in pursuance of such command, he seems by necessary consequence to be as guilty of it as if he had done it himself. From whence it follows, that being in judgment of law a principal offender, he may be tried and found guilty before any trial of the person who actually did the fact."

Now it is observable that this is only a general expression of the general rule, that he goes into no detail and does not pretend to argue on the question. The doctrine is admitted to be correct so far as it applies to treason in compassing the death of the king. The only difference, between him and the authorities I have quoted, is that he does not distinguish between this and the other kinds of treason; but he does not enter into the particular question whether derivative guilt can be proved otherwise than by the conviction of the principal offender.

But if he were in direct opposition to them, he does not stand on such high ground as they do; the names of lord Hale and justice Foster are certainly entitled to much higher respect than his. Sergeant Hawkins, though his work is a very valuable institute of criminal law, is not considered a great constitutional lawyer.

He is not only opposed by Hale and Foster, but even his own editor corrects this *dictum* in the later editions. Mr. Leach, his very able and accurate Commentator, has a note on this very passage, in which he corrects the generalty of the expression, and confines it to the case of treason in compassing the death of the king. The words of the note are " this rule requires distinction: in that species of treason touching the death of the king, &c. every accessorial agency is, independently and in its own nature, a complete overt act of compassing, and renders the offender guilty though the fact itself should never be attempted. But in every other species of treason, the accessorial offence is of a derivative kind; some act must be done, to which act the offender must be accessory, and out of which his guilt must spring before he can be converted by this rule of law, into a principal offender. It seems therefore, that though in the event of the prosecution such an offender may be considered as a principal, yet, in his progress towards conviction, *he ought, from a principle of natural justice, to be considered merely as in the nature of an accessory, before or after the fact; and if under such a consideration he were tried, before the person who actually did the fact, the absurdity might follow, that the accessorial agent may be convicted, and the principal, who did the act, and on whose guilt the offence of the accessory must alone depend, may be acquitted.*"

The authorities therefore all correspond; and, supported as they are by the strongest reasons drawn from the rules of common sense and natural justice, place the position I have contended for, beyond the reach of controversy.

But it is objected, that no adjudged case can be produced in support of it; it is a sufficient answer, that there has never been an attempt, except in the case of Lady Lisle, to charge an accessory in treason before the principal. The counsel on the other side must rely on that decision of Jefferies, or they must abandon the prosecution; and even that case is conclusive in our favour, for judge Jefferies's sentence was annulled, and the attainder reversed by act of parliament, expressing strong disapprobation of his conduct.

I cannot quit this point without remarking, that all the authorities go upon the supposition that the indictment must be *special;* a point I already have insisted upon. It is barely possible that an objection will be made, which may be thought to deserve an answer, that " the accomplice may waive the benefit of the law, and submit to a trial;" and that as the accused has done so in the present instance, the objection now comes too late. A reference to the authorities and a moment's consideration will satisfy the court that there can be no force in this objection.

The indictment gives us no information of the nature of the charge; it is against colonel Burr himself, who had no reason to doubt that it was meant to be proved, that he in person committed the overt act of treason in levying war as a principal in the first degree. The charge, that the act was committed by him in conjunction with persons *unknown*, excludes the idea of a derivative treason or a responsibility for the act of any particular individual or set of men.

But if it were *specially* charged, and the persons, whose acts the accused was to answer for, were named in the indictment with every necessary description of time, place and circumstances, the party going to trial according to the course of the court, without a special prayer to be tried before the principal, and an express waiver of his right entered on record, could not be concluded from taking this exception. The words, " *waive the benefit of the law*," mean an *express renunciation of a right*, and none such certainly has been made in the present instance.

But admit that *all* these points are against us, still there must be some legal proof adduced of the guilt of the principal who committed the act, before the prisoner can be made a traitor by relation. Admit, that a person may be generally charged as present, who was absent; that the record of the conviction of the principal is unnecessary; and that they are at liberty to prove the act of the principal by mere parol testimony; yet before colonel Burr can be connected with Blannerhassett, they must prove an overt act to have been committed by Blannerhassett, and of this the court and not the jury must judge; that is, the court must judge, *what* in law constitutes an overt act of treason, though the jury only can decide, whether such an *overt* act have been in truth committed or not. Admitting the correctness of the statement of the only witness whose testimony bears upon this point, *Allbright*, (who is at one time in jest, at another in earnest) yet still there is nothing like the semblance of an act of war. Admitting further, for the sake of argument, that what *he* states amounts to proof of *an overt* act of war, yet still he is a solitary witness; and as the law requires two witnesses to prove the same overt act of war it is impossible to connect us with him. Every inference, that can be rationally drawn from the facts proved by this single witness, may be drawn by the jury; but this cannot supersede the necessity of complying with the constitutional requisition of proving the overt act by two witnesses.

According to the universal doctrine of all authors on this subject, the overt act, which is to be thus proved, must be an act of *public hostility* (not a mere private act) and must be particularly set forth in the indictment. The principle is maintained by writers and confirmed by the form of the indictments.

1 *East's Crown Law, p.* 116. " In every indictment for high treason upon the *stat.* 25 *Ed.* 3. for compassing the death of the king, or for levying war, or adhering to his enemies, the particular species of treason must be charged in the very terms of the statute, being a declaratory law, as the substantial offence, and then *some overt act must be laid*, as the means made use of to effectuate the traitorous purpose." " The *overt acts so laid are in truth the charge to which the prisoner must apply his defence.* And therefore it is in no case sufficient to allege, that the prisoner compassed the king's death, or that he levied war against him, or adhered to his enemies; for upon a charge so general and indefinite, he cannot know what acts he is to defend." In *page*

121, he states, however, that "the whole detail of the evidence need not be set forth." "The rule, prescribed by the statute of William 'that no evidence shall be admitted or given of an *overt act* that is not expressly laid in the indictment,' is in truth no more than the common law itself directs generally. For in no case is a prisoner bound to answer unprepared, for every action of his life, but only to that which is the subject of the indictment against him." The true sense of the clause is, "that no *overt act* amounting to a distinct independent charge, though falling under the same head of treason, shall be admitted in evidence, unless it be expressly laid in the indictment; but an overt act may be given in evidence, though it be not expressly laid or not well laid in the indictment, if it amount to direct proof of any overt act, which is well laid. Thus in the case of Rockwood (*p.* 122) who was indicted for compassing king William's death, two of the overt acts charged were, that he and others met and consulted upon the proper means for way-laying the king, and attacking him in his coach; and also that they agreed to provide forty men for that purpose. Upon this indictment the counsel for the crown were allowed to give in evidence a list of the names of a small party who were to join in the attempt, of which the prisoner was to have the command, with his own name at the head of the list as their commander; for though not charged in the indictment, yet it amounted to a direct proof of the overt acts laid, viz. the meeting and consulting together how to kill the king, and then agreeing to provide forty men for the purpose." The same doctrine is laid down in *p.* 123. but in that page it is stated that "if the overt acts, offered in evidence and not laid in the indictment, be no direct proof of any of the overt acts charged, but merely go to strengthen the evidence or suspicion of some of those *overt acts* by a collateral circumstance, such evidence cannot be admitted notwithstanding the opinion of Lord Hale to the contrary. As in the case of captain Vaughan, before cited." And Foster in *p.* 194, states the same doctrine, that the overt act must be laid in the indictment. "In every indictment for this species of treason, and indeed for levying war, or adhering to the king's enemies, an *overt act* must be alleged and proved. *For the overt act is the charge to which the prisoner must apply his defence*, and if divers overt acts be laid and but one proved, it will be sufficient." The object of charging the overt act is to give the accused full notice to come prepared to answer it.

Here Mr. WICKHAM observed, that as the usual hour of adjournment was now past, he could not finish his argument to-day, but wished to be indulged with permission to resume it to-morrow, which was granted; and the court adjourned.

FRIDAY, AUGUST 21st, 1807.

As soon as the court met, Mr. Wickham observed that he would by no means wish to take up the time of the court unnecessarily; but that it might not be improper briefly to advert to some parts of his arguments yesterday. He then proceeded:—The court will recollect the several points which I endeavoured to establish yesterday. The first was founded on the absence of the accused from the scene of action, at the time of committing the act charged in the indictment; and the second on the necessity of proving the act as laid. The third point was, that the guilt of the accused, if it exist at all, is in its nature only derivative, and cannot be proved without first producing the record of the conviction of the principal.

Hawkins, in his *Pleas of the Crown*, ch. 29. sect. 2. p. 440. as I stated before, is the only authority which says that the accessory may be tried before the principal; and his commentator Leach denies it, in his note subjoined.

The rules of law require, that the prosecutor, before he can convict the accessory, must produce on his trial the record of the conviction of the principal. Foster supposes that the production of that record is sufficient to put the accused on his defence. But he admits that it is no more. Hawkins says that such evidence is only introductory to other testimony, which is necessary to connect him with the principal.

The court will observe that Foster lays down the doctrine with great clearness, that the conviction of the principal is necessary to be produced, in order to put him on his defence; but that the accessory may prove that the principal is innocent, notwithstanding the production of the record of such conviction. In *pages* 364, 365, he says that " The accessory may be brought to justice, notwithstanding the principal has been admitted to his clergy or pardoned; and very proper was this provision. For in the scale of sound sense and substantial justice, the only questions, in which the accessory can have any concern, *in common with the principal*, are, whether the felony were committed, and committed by the principal. These facts the conviction of the principal hath established with certainty, *at least sufficient to put the accessory to his answer*. And therefore in whatever manner the principal may have been treated after his conviction, seemeth to me to be a matter perfectly foreign to the question, whether or when the accessory shall be brought upon his trial." *Sec*. 3. " At a conference among the judges upon the case of M'Daniel and others before reported, a general question was moved how far, and in what cases the accessory may avail himself of the insufficiency of the evidence in point of fact, or of the incompetency of witnesses in point of law, produced against the principal; and in what cases he may be let in to shew, that the facts, charged and proved against the principal, do not in judgment of law amount to felony. There was in that case no occasion to enter far into these questions, since the facts, upon which the point of law then under consideration must necessarily turn, were all found by the special verdict." *p.* 365. " If the principal and accessory are joined in one indictment and tried together, which I conceive to be the most eligible course, where both are answerable, there is no room to doubt whether the accessory may not enter into the full defence of the principal, and avail himself of every matter of fact, and every point of law tending to his acquittal. For the accessory is in this case to be considered as *particeps in lite*, and this sort of defence necessarily and directly tendeth to his own acquittal. When the accessory is brought to his trial, after the conviction of the principal, it is not necessary to enter into a detail of the evidence on which the conviction was founded; nor doth the indictment aver that the principal was in fact guilty. It is sufficient if it reciteth with proper certainty the record of the conviction. This is evidence against the accessory *sufficient to put him upon his defence.* For it is founded on a legal presumption, that every thing in the former proceeding was rightly and properly transacted. *But a presumption of this kind must, I conceive, give way to facts manifestly and clearly proved. As against the accessory, the conviction of the principal will not be conclusive;* it is, as to him, *res inter alios acta.* And therefore if it shall come out in evidence, upon the trial of the accessory, as it sometimes hath, and frequently may, that the offence of which the principal was convicted did not amount to felony in him, or not to that species of felony with which he was charged, the accessory may avail himself of this, and ought to be acquitted." Hawkins, *p.* 456. *b.* 2. *c.* 29. § 47. says, " As to the fourth point, whether the principal and accessory may be both tried by the same inquest, and in what manner they are to be tried. It seems to be settled at this day, that if the principal and accessory appear together and the principal plead the general issue, the accessory shall be put to plead also; and that if he likewise plead the general issue, both may be tried by one inquest; but that the *principal must be first convicted;* and that the jury shall be charged, that if they find the principal not guilty, they shall find the accessory not guilty. But it seems agreed that if the principal plead a plea in bar, or to the writ, the *accessory shall not be driven to answer,* till *such plea be determined."* In the note subjoined, the foregoing authority of Foster, and *Smith's case, O. B.* 1784, *p.* 69. are referred to; and the sentiment repeated that the production of the record of conviction of the principal, is sufficient to put the accessory upon his defence.

So that it is perfectly clear, from all the authorities, that the first step is to produce the record of the conviction of the principal to put the accessory on his defence, though it is not conclusive against him.

I hope to be excused for having taken up the time of the court, so long on this part of the subject. I will now proceed to make some remarks on another point.

If it be possible that I am wrong in this last point, as well as in the several other positions I have endeavoured to support; if an absentee can be convicted on this general form of indictment, and if the record of the conviction of the principal be not necessary, and parol testimony be admissible to prove the acts of the accused, yet still I contend, that before Mr. Burr can be put on his defence, or testimony exhibited to shew his derivative guilt, there must be some evidence to prove to the court, that Blannerhassett, the principal offender, is guilty. If there be no evidence against Blannerhassett, none can be admitted against colonel Burr. Let us suppose, that there was no proof whatever of the guilt of Blannerhassett, would it be competent to them to say that he was guilty, and to connect colonel Burr with him? to say that his guilt was derivative, when there was no original source from which it could be derived? I presume that the gentlemen would give up the point if there were no such proof. It would be the same thing as if there were no evidence at all against the accused, for it would have no relation to the charge exhibited against him.

If there were evidence of a merely friendly meeting, it would be the same as if there were no assemblage. If they were to give evidence that Blannerhassett and some of those with him were in possession of arms, as people in this country usually are, it would not be sufficient of itself, to prove that the meeting was military.

Arms are not necessarily military weapons. Rifles, shot guns and fowling pieces are used commonly by the people of this country in hunting and for domestic purposes; they are generally in the habit of pursuing game. In the upper country every man has a gun; a majority of the people have guns every where, for peaceful purposes. Rifles and shot guns are no more evidence of military weapons than pistols or dirks used for personal defence, or common fowling pieces kept for the amusement of taking game. It is lawful for every man in this country to keep such weapons. In England indeed every man is not qualified to keep a gun; but even to those who have not that privilege the possession of dirks and pistols is not unlawful. Surely their possession at that island, of such arms as every man in this country is legally authorized to keep, and which most people do keep, can be no more evidence of a military project, or an intention to subvert the government, than if they had not been there at all. What is the rule to distinguish in such cases? There must be such evidence of a hostile assemblage proved to the court, as if true in point of fact, would constitute a treasonable assemblage.

But it may be said on the other side, that if the court will undertake to judge in this case, it will invade the province of the jury. Sir, it will not. It is the right of the jury to decide on the *weight* of the evidence. They are to find facts. They may find a special verdict, and if all facts be inferred by them that can be properly inferred from the evidence, and are found by them, the court can decide on their finding. If they do not find facts to that extent, the court is bound to infer whatever may be legally inferred from their finding. The overt act must be particularly set forth in the indictment. It is clear on principle, and supported by a number of authorities, as the case of Deacon and several others, which have been referred to, that after the *overt* act laid is once proved, evidence of other overt acts not laid, may be adduced if they be direct evidence of that which is charged; but it is a preliminary and essential point, that two witnesses must prove the overt act.

The principle for which I am contending is the same in civil cases. If A make a contract with C by B, before A can enforce his contract against C, or give proof of it as made by B, he must prove that B was in fact his agent; and then he can go on and prove the agreement, but not before the agency, without proving which, it would be irrelevant and improper to prove the agreement. The court would require the production of this previous proof of his agency; yet the court does not decide on the weight of such evidence. This principle is further illustrated by the right, which the party possesses, to require a special verdict, and by his right also to demur to the evidence, and draw the case from the jury to the court. But he subjects himself to this condition, that every inference which the jury might draw, the court must draw. I do not mean to say that the jury may wander into the field of conjecture, and that the court may do so also when the facts are thus referred to it; but that of every inference which the jury might draw according to sound reason and law, the court must necessarily judge, and give the party the full benefit of it.

Here I may properly refer to the same authority in *Hawkins p.* 456. in the note of his commentator, where after stating the necessity of producing against the accessory, the record of the conviction of the principal, he adds "but it seems that some additional evidence is necessary for that purpose, in order to apply and connect it with the case of a prisoner indicted as accessory; for a bare unqualified record can only be evidence against those who are parties to it."

I come now to a most important inquiry, what constitutes an overt act of " *levying war;*" which must be proved before the guilt of treason can attach to the principal.

The CHIEF JUSTICE asked him if any adjudged case could be produced, where the court was called upon to decide, and did decide, that the evidence submitted to the jury did or did not amount to proof of the *overt* act.

Mr. HAY said that he never knew the attempt made but once, before judge Patterson, which was unsuccessful.

Mr. WICKHAM. The overt acts must be such as if true, that is in reality committed, constitute treason. I do not say, that the court will undertake entirely to perform what is the province of the jury, and proceed to inquire whether an *overt* act have been proved to have been committed, but that it is the right and duty of the court to instruct the jury, what amounts in law to an *overt* act of levying war &c. The counsel for the United States has undertaken to give a definition to the jury, of an act of treason in " levying war." The position taken by themselves, as stated in a newspaper now in my hand [here he read a passage from it] we mean to controvert. We have a right to oppose gentlemen on the ground taken by themselves. I deny the correctness of his definition. When we differ as to the law, the court must decide between us. The real meaning of his definition is that a mere assemblage of men, without force, but met with treasonable intention, constitutes a complete act of levying war. On this ground the most peaceable meeting, if with treasonable designs, might be said to levy war.

Mr. HAY denied that his definition was accurately stated; he meant to rely on the definition given by the supreme court of the United States, to which he referred. The gentleman did not understand me, said Mr. Hay, as I meant to be understood, and as this must be obvious he ought to have the candour to admit it. The great object of my argument was, to shew that an assemblage of men convened for the purpose of effecting by force, a treasonable object, and which force is meant to be employed before their dispersion, is an overt act of levying war against the United States. I appeal to you and the gentlemen themselves, if this were not the sum and substance of my argument. I took the ground that the force to be employed, was meant to be employed before the separation of the party; because if it were a part of their design to disperse and meet at another time and place, for the purpose of carrying the design into effect, it would be only a conspiracy to levy war, and not an act of levying war itself. It is easy to attempt to bring an argument into ridicule. I have no objection to his doing so; but he is bound to shew the precise words which I did express, and not to impute to me terms which I never used or arguments which I should have disdained to employ.

Here a desultory discussion ensued between the counsel, on this point: when the chief justice observed that he understood *four distinct* propositions to be stated to the court, (which he repeated) every one of which was independent of every other: and the last proposition he considered to be, that if the record of the conviction of him who is alleged to be the principal were not necessary to be produced, parol evidence was admissible; yet *the act itself*, which was charged to have been committed, *must be proved*.

Mr. WICKHAM expressed his regret that he was misunderstood; that as to ridicule, he meant no such thing. He admitted that it was not always, though it was sometimes, the test of truth; and though he might have been justified by the example of others in using it, he had then no such intention; but he insisted that what the gentleman denied was substantially what he contended for. For, said Mr. Wickham, the only objection which he makes to my construction of his definition is this, that I did not state that the purpose was to be effected before the separation of the party; that is, that they must execute it on the spot, which involves *locality*. This is but a small deviation, and can make no essential difference in the offence; but how is it possible to establish by satisfactory evidence, that a number of men intend to act before any separation? But he relies on the decision of the supreme court; and he dignifies the meeting on Blannerhassett's island with the name of an assemblage of men convened to effect a treasonable purpose; and this assemblage *without force*, because convened with an intention to use force thereafter, he says, is sufficient to constitute an act of "levying war," within the true meaning of the decision of the supreme court. Though some parts of the opinion of the supreme court may be expressed too vaguely, yet, if attentively considered throughout, it cannot justify the construction which that gentleman thinks proper to put on it. It may indeed be deemed marvellous, that gentlemen who ought to comprehend it, do not. *Part* of that opinion is stated and relied on; *but not the whole*. When duly and fully considered, it will be found to be what has always been considered to be the law in England. Part of this decision is in these words: " It is not the intention of the court to say, that no individual can be guilty of this crime, who has not appeared in arms against his country: on the contrary, if war be actually levied, that is, if a body of men be actually assembled for the purpose of effecting by force, a treasonable purpose, all those who *perform any part*, however minute, or however remote from the scene of action, and who are actually leagued in the general conspiracy, are to be considered as traitors. But there must be an actual assembling of men, for the treasonable purpose, to constitute a levying of war." It must be evident even to the gentleman on the other side, that to complete the definition of treason to be found in this opinion, the whole doctrine therein stated should be examined; yet it seems as if he thought that we were to look no further than this clause for the definition of treason. If he had looked at the next paragraph, it would have shewn him the contrary: " To complete the crime of levying war against the United States, there must be an actual assemblage of men for the purpose of executing a treasonable design. In the case now before the court, a *design to overturn* the *government* of the United States at New-Orleans, *by force*, would have been unquestionably a design, *which if carried into execution* would have been treason. And the assemblage of a body of men, for the purpose of carrying it into execution, would amount to levying of war against the United States; but no conspiracy for this object, no inlisting of men to effect it, would be an actual levying of war. In conformity with the principles now laid down, have been the decisions heretofore made by the judges of the United States."

" The opinions given by judge Patterson and judge Iredell, in cases before them, imply an actual assembling of men, though they rather designed to remark on the purpose to which the *force* was to be applied, than on the nature of the *force* itself. *Their opinions, however, contemplate the actual employment of force.*" " Judge Chase in the trial of Fries was more explicit. He stated the opinion of the court to be, ' that if a body of people conspire and meditate an insurrection to resist or oppose the execution of any statute of the United States by force, they are only guilty of a high misdemeanor; but if *they proceed to carry such intention into execution by force, that they are guilty of the treason of levying war; and the quantum of the force employed* neither lessens nor increases the crime; whether by one hundred or one thousand persons is wholly immaterial. The *Court are of opinion* (continued judge Chase, on that occasion) *that a combination or conspiracy to levy war against the United States, is not treason, unless combined with an attempt to carry such combination or conspiracy into execution: some actual force or violence must be used in pursuance of such design to levy war*, but it is altogether immaterial whether the *force* used is sufficient to effectuate the object;

any force, connected *with the intention, will constitute the crime of levying war.*'" The opinions of these three judges are stated to be law; and all three declare some *force* to be actually necessary. Is it not very plain from all these parts taken together, that wherever the supreme court speak of any body of men assembled for the *purpose of effecting by force*, a treasonable purpose, they mean that the *force* of which they speak must be actually used in order to make it treason? Is not one part of their opinion to be construed *with* and explained *by* another? In construing it, are gentlemen at liberty to take one part and reject another which qualifies it?

I should think no other argument would be necessary to shew this; but I will refer to your own opinion on the commitment of colonel Burr; you said on that occasion, that " an intention to commit treason is an offence entirely distinct from the actual commission of that crime. *War can only be levied by the employment of actual force; troops must be embodied,* men must be assembled in order to levy war." Again, you stated that, " to constitute this crime, troops must be embodied, men must be actually assembled; and these are facts which cannot remain invisible. Treason may be machinated in secret, but it can be perpetrated only in open day, and in the eye of the world. Testimony of a fact, which in its own nature is so notorious, ought to be unequivocal."

The act of levying war must therefore be an act of force and of public notoriety exhibited before the world. Compare your own opinion with the picture which the gentleman has chosen to draw, and see how dissimilar they are.

We are then told of the opinion and admissions of Fries's counsel on his trial in Pennsylvania; and an eulogium is passed on that counsel (Mr. Lewis) on account of that supposed opinion. The opinion of counsel is no authority however unequivocally expressed. But if we are to refer to the opinion of counsel, let us refer in like manner to that of the counsel for the prosecution. Mr. Rawle is equally as respectable as Mr. Lewis. In *Fries's trial, page* 179. Mr. Rawle conceived himself authorized upon good authority to say, " that levying war did not only consist in open, manifest and avowed rebellion against the government, with a design of overthrowing the constitution; but it may consist in assembling together in numbers *and by actual force*, or by terror, opposing any particular law or laws. There can be no distinction as to the kind or nature of the laws, or the particular object for which the law was passed, since all are alike, the acts of the legislature who are sent by the people at large to express their will."

" Force need not be used to manifest this spirit of rebellion; nor is it necessary that the attempt should have been successful, to constitute the crime. The endeavour by intimidation to do the act, whether it be accomplished or not, amounts to treason, provided the object of those concerned in the transaction is of a general nature, and not applied to a special or private purpose." The attempt to effect the purpose by terror is sufficient. I will refer to the case put by the gentleman himself by way of illustration, that if an assemblage of men were to march unarmed into this town for the purpose of attacking the capitol, and in such immense numbers, as to render all resistance vain and ineffectual, and no resistance were therefore made, their object would be effected by terror and imaginary alarm. Their numbers in that case would supply the want of arms. The only difference is between actual and potential force; and in that case, there would be potential force sufficient to effect their object.

In Fries's case, he came forward with an armed multitude. He employed force as well as terror, to break prisons, to rescue prisoners and to oppose the operation of the laws of his country.

The opinion of Mr. Sitgreaves, the other respectable counsel of the United States, is still more explicit on this subject. In *page* 19. of that trial, he says, that " if the arrangements are made, and the numbers of armed men actually appear, so as to procure the object, which they have in view, by intimidation as well as by actual force, that will constitute the offence." In *page* 20. he says, " It must be war waged against the United States. This is an important distinction. A large assemblage of people may come together, in whatever numbers, however they may be armed or arrayed, or whatever degree of violence they may commit, yet that alone would not constitute treason; the treason must be known; it must be for a public and not a private revenge; it must be avowedly levying war against the United States. If people assemble in this hostile manner, only to gratify revenge, or any other purpose independent of war against the United States, it will only amount to a riot; but if it is an object in which the persons have no particular interest, this constitutes the offence of treason." With respect to the definition of Foster, I will not take up the time of the court by detailing it fully, or repeating what may have been already quoted. Suffice it to say, that he considers it a fixed principle, that there must be actual violence or hostility, and that the overt acts must be public acts. In *page* 211. after mentioning several specific instances of treasonable acts, he adds, that " *all risings, to effect these innovations of a public and gene-*

ral concern by an armed force, are, in construction of law, high treason, within the clause of *levying war;*" and he gives one principal reason, " that they have a direct tendency to dissolve all the bonds of society and to destroy all property and all government too, by numbers and an *armed force.*" And likewise that " insurrections for redressing national grievances," " or the reformation of real or imaginary evils of a *public* nature, and in which the insurgents have no special interest; *risings to effect these ends by force and numbers* are by construction of law, within the clause of *levying war.*" In short, all the English precedents shew, that the overt acts are cases of actual hostility of a public nature.

Vaughan's case in 5 *State Trials page* 37. may be considered as the strongest on this point. He had a commission from the French king, to cruise in the vessel or barge called the *Loyal Clencarty* against the subjects of England. He commanded this vessel under French colours, and met an English ship of superior force and struck his colours without a battle or making any resistance. The court will observe, that in the indictment against Vaughan, there were two counts, one for levying war, and the other for adhering to the king's enemies and aiding and assisting them. Mr. Phipps, the prisoner's counsel objected, that there was no *overt* act of war proved against him, because there was *no act of hostility.* But this objection was overruled, and he was found guilty of adhering to the king's enemies, and aiding and assisting them; and it was determined that *actual war must be proved* under an indictment for *levying war.* The opinion of the chief justice was as follows: " When men form themselves into a body and march rank and file, with weapons offensive and defensive, *this is levying war with open force, if the design be public.*" " When a ship is armed with guns, &c., and doth appear on the coast, watching an opportunity to burn the king's ships in the harbour, and their design known, and one goes to them, and aids and assists them, this is an adhering to the king's enemies. Here are two indictments, one for levying war, and the other for adhering to the king's enemies; but the adhering to the king's enemies is principally insisted on; and *there must be an actual war proved upon the* person indicted in *the one*, yet *not to be proved in the other case.*" The court observed that the prisoner's counsel would make no act to be " *aiding and assisting*," but *fighting*, which was wrong; that they were armed and had surrounded the ship twice, and nothing prevented his making an attack, but the superiority of the ship by which he was taken. They were afraid to proceed on the *count* which charged the levying war, because *public war* and *open hostility* must be proved, to support it; they went therefore on the other, for adhering to, and aiding the king's enemies.

On further consideration, I admit that perhaps the word "*public*" need not be inserted in the indictment. In the English precedents, and also in the first indictment against John Fries, this word *public* is used; but I find that in the subsequent indictment against Fries it is omitted. I should only rely on the general usage being an evidence of the law.

But what did the gentleman say in defining the "*levying of war?*" that there is no necessity for arms, nor the employment of force! that there is no necessity even for *potential force* to effect the intended purpose by terror! that there is no necessity for the act to be public! that an *overt act of treason, may be committed without arms, without force, either actual or potential!* If this were law, there would be no safety. We know, however, that a man may conceive a criminal intention, but that the law does not punish it, unless carried into execution. But the gentleman takes away the "*locus pœnitentiœ.*" Men might be misled from their duty as citizens, and induced to agree to resist the government and levy war, but before they proceeded to action, might *repent*, from prudential or patriotic motives; but according to the doctrine of the gentleman on the other side, they could not retract. The intention once formed, though without reflection, and though soon followed, after deliberation, by sincere repentance, would be as severely punishable, as the actual execution of the treasonable design. A man who had agreed to join in a treasonable project, but repented and never joined the party, would be punishable as highly as the traitors who actually perpetrated the crime. This doctrine can never be correct.

He introduces another point to which I slightly adverted before. After having taken away every inducement to repentance and reformation, he rests the innocence or criminality of the accused on their intention to *separate or not*, before the accomplishment of their purpose. What would the gentleman call separation? Perhaps no two individuals have the same idea on this subject. Such an indefinite, vague, indeterminate idea of what would constitute guilt opens a door to constructive treason, and is dangerous in the extreme. This definition fits no case but this case, and must have been intended to fit it; it is the more alarming, as it may put the safety of any individual in the power of the government; but I hope it will be disclaimed. It has never been heard of before, and I trust in God it never will be heard of in this country again.

I will now make some few observations on the testimony, from which it will be seen that there was no hostility of any kind committed. In the evidence of the first witness, who was examined as to the transactions on the island (Peter Taylor, the gardener) there is not one expression that gives the remotest idea of a treasonable assemblage. He saw a few men and four or five rifles, which were perfectly innocent; but what is more wonderful he saw some bullets run! There is no impropriety in running bullets, if the object be not criminal; the rifles were of no sort of service without the bullets; but they had a little powder! Of what use would their bullets be without powder? The quantity of each was so very limited as to answer no other than innocent purposes. He saw no military array or parade; he saw no improper act, nothing that could be justly construed to be criminal or unlawful in their conduct. He says that he saw Mr. Woodbridge in the night down with Blannerhassett's party at the landing; but Mr. Woodbridge denies it. What does another of their own witnesses, Mr. Love, say? He says they were frightened at the proclamation; but he saw no military parade whatever; nothing like hostility; that they were afraid of the mob who were about to pull down Blannerhassett's house. Has the government a right to pull down houses?

" But they were prepared to defend themselves." Had they not a right to do so? As the witness said, if a man struck him a blow on the face, he had a right to return it. Mr. Woodbridge saw no military *array or hostility*, nothing criminal, turbulent, tumultuous or disorderly in their conduct; he saw nothing more than was peaceful and ordinary and natural on such an occasion.

Here Mr. HAY expressed a hope, that the court would excuse him for interrupting the gentleman. He asked if it were not absurd to argue on one half of the testimony? He declared that they had several other witnesses who would prove the character of the acts on the island; and that the intention of the party was to take possession of New-Orleans; that he never knew a criminal prosecution interrupted in this way; only one half of the evidence commented on, to the court, before the other half was submitted to the jury.

Here a desultory discussion took place. Colonel Burr and his counsel contended, that they had *distinctly* understood that the counsel for the prosecution had gone through or produced all their testimony relative to what was deemed the *overt* act, or the transaction on Blannerhassett's island; that they had called on them to adduce more evidence on that point if they could; that they had answered, that they had only one or two more witnesses, whose evidence was to the same effect as that of the others who had already been examined; and that as they happened to be *then* absent, it was clearly understood they were at liberty to proceed to state their propositions to the court; and Mr. Burr added, that it was his desire that every thing relative to what they called *war*, should be first proved; that he had permitted many things, which were extremely improper, to be brought forward, without objecting to them, as he wished every thing that regarded that point to be proved; that he urged them to prove an overt act, but that it could not be proved. He desired to avail himself of the opportunity of shewing the defect of evidence and the futility of the prosecution; and that it was expressly declared by the counsel for the prosecution, that they had examined all their witnesses, except as before stated.

Mr. HAY insisted, that gentlemen were mistaken in their supposition that there was to be no other evidence; that he had expressly told the court and them, that it was not admitted that there was no other evidence on this subject; that they had no right to say that it was admitted, or to assume as a fact that there was no other evidence; that he *had* other testimony, and wished to prove the connexion between those who were on the island, and those who went down to Cumberland river, and were proceeding down the Mississippi under the command of the accused; that for the purpose of more clearly shewing this connexion, all the testimony bearing upon the subject, should be examined and considered together; that he could not discern what could warrant such an extraordinary motion as this was, to exclude evidence, on a supposition that there was no other testimony on a particular point, in the cause.

CHIEF JUSTICE.—I understood, and it was certainly so expressed, that the testimony relating to the transactions on Blannerhassett's island had been gone through, but that there was other evidence with respect to the intention, to shew the character and nature of the assemblage; and it is contended on the other side that you have no right to introduce such other evidence. I do not conceive the motion to be irregular. So far as it is a personal inconvenience to hear a lengthy discussion, I regret it, for the sake of others, who are affected by it; but the court feels it to be a duty which it must patiently and cheerfully perform. Every legal proposition which is made, the court is bound to listen to, as well as to reflect on and determine according to its best skill and judgment. You mean to connect the transactions on Blannerhassett's island, with evidence of extrinsic circumstances drawn from other sources. But I understood you to state most explicitly, that as far as related to the character of the transactions on Blannerhassett's island, you had examined all your witnesses. I do not undertake to say, that it is proper or improper to admit this other evidence, which is sought to be excluded. The counsel for the defence say, that having completed your evidence as to what happened on the island, you cannot connect that testimony against the accused, with proof of opinions and intentions and such extrinsic circumstances happening out of the district, as you desire to adduce. Their arguments may be very unsound, and if you think so, you have a right to shew it; but to say, that they have no right to advance them, is more than the court can undertake.

Mr. HAY said, that his object was to shew what his judgment deemed the impropriety of the course which gentlemen had adopted; that he had not been distinctly understood; but that as he did not wish to take up the time of the court, he had no objection to their going on with their observations.

Mr. WICKHAM then resumed his argument. The counsel on the other side having proved every circumstance they could, relative to the overt act, it does not appear on the face of it, that what occurred on the island amounted to an act of " *levying war.*" Their declarations, relative to the *quo animo*, are irrelevant, and must be confined to the assemblage itself. An intention to commit treason is not treason itself. In supporting the proposition, that the act of levying war must be proved to have been committed by the principal before the accessory can be affected by it, I am under the necessity of speaking of the testimony; how can I otherwise do it?

Woodbridge saw no improper act, no hostility. Being asked what passed between him and Tyler, he answered, that Tyler declared that he would not oppose the constituted authorities, but that if attacked by a mob he would not yield to it. He had a right, and every man has a right to resist unlawful aggression. In common with every other citizen, he had a right to stand or fall by the laws of his country. As there were no acts, his intentions can only be judged by his words. None can discern what designs a man has in his bosom.

Mr. Dana agrees perfectly with Mr. Woodbridge. He passed over that night in his own boat to the island; he saw nothing hostile or improper. Though the people were in great haste to leave the island, and though most of them were strangers to him, yet they manifested no alarm when he entered the hall where they were.

Mr. Belknap saw precisely the same things, and states the same facts, as Woodbridge and Dana. Yet during all this time, we are told that a most bloody war raged on the island.

But Mr. Poole was employed by the governor of Ohio to apprehend Blannerhassett. But even *his* evidence proves nothing like hostility. He thinks that some of the men had guns. He heard expressions about calling for a boat; that when a boat was called for from the Ohio side, the answer was, what boat? and if the reply were, " *I's boat*," that a boat would be immediately sent off, that otherwise it would not. He thinks the word was " *I's boat*," or something like it, and that it was a watchword or countersign. He was half a mile from them and it was a dark night. He therefore might be deceived in his vision or hearing. Tyler's boats were there. It might be a mere private signal among themselves, which might have been necessary to prevent mistakes, as they were using great dispatch to leave the island, in order to avoid the attack of a mob.

But they have one more witness, *Jacob Allbright*. It is impossible, that this man's testimony can be true. But the testimony of one witness, however correct, is not sufficient to establish the *overt act*. There must be two witnesses for that purpose. But his evidence is contradictory and incredible. He proves one act of hostility against general Tupper, whom they did not choose to examine, though attending here to give his evidence. They would have examined him, if they had believed that he would have confirmed Allbright's evidence. Their not doing it, proves that they thought he would have contradicted Allbright. He says, that Tupper laid his hand on Blannerhassett, in the name of the commonwealth, and that immediately seven or eight muskets were pointed at him. Yet no warrant or authority was shewn by him; and that he had no such authority must be presumed, as he was from Ohio. For against what state was the treason committed? It was treason against Virginia, if it existed at all; Blannerhassett had a right to resist, if Tupper had no warrant; and this evidence of his arresting a man is without the production of any authority whatever; and yet this is called resistance to law. But even if he had a warrant, and had been opposed in attempting to serve it, it would not have been treason; resistance to process is not treason, though a great offence.

But he had sworn before, that those who levelled their guns at Tupper were not in earnest; and he now admits, that he does not know that they were in earnest, as " there was no quarrel among them, and no firing afterwards."

He mentions another circumstance, which, connected with the rest of his evidence, is equally incredible; that he saw at different times a number of guns equal to the whole number of men. He acknowledges that he did not see the men all with arms at once, and that he did not know the men who had guns, nor could he tell the number of guns; how then could this man venture on his oath to say, that he had not seen the same arms at different times, in the hands of different persons? It is obvious from his own statement, that this might have been the case, and therefore no confidence ought to be put in what he says. If this be an *overt act*, any thing that any government chooses to consider as such, may be an *overt* act.

But the counsel on the other side seems to think that the doctrine of treason may be extended, because no danger can be apprehended from it in this free country. This argument may be very sound, if compared with his other argument, that a majority of the people are always right.

In every free country there is more occasion for guarding against factions, than in a despotism. It is an evil in the very nature of free governments, as every thing good in human institutions has its attendant evil. While it is the effect of political freedom, it has ever been the cause of its extinction. We ought to profit by the experience of other nations, and repress that intolerance and party spirit, which progressively but certainly lead to despotism; in producing which, the most dangerous and successful engine has always been the doctrine of constructive treason. In a despotism there are no factions or civil commotions. There are no factions in the camp or army of Bonaparte. But in this, as well as in every other free country, parties struggle for power; the popular endeavouring to crush the unpopular party. Hence the danger of departing from correct principles, which in such a struggle are too often disregarded. I have now gone through every point, which I meant to submit to the consideration of the court. The importance of the question is very great, not only as it concerns my client, but every man in this country. I will only observe to the counsel, that, as I have endeavoured to support they must oppose my arguments, on abstract principles, which must be tested by reason and truth. These principles must be just and true at all times, and in all places, without reference to particular persons or circumstances, and are intimately connected with the public liberty and happiness. If the principles for which I have contended be correct, this prosecution cannot succeed: it appears to my judgment, that if they be disregarded, and the doctrines supported by the gentlemen on the other side prevail, these will be the consequences:

First. If a man can be indicted as being present, for overt acts, committed by others, when he was absent in a different state and district, the constitution of the United States, which was so ably and carefully drawn up, in order to secure and perpetuate the freedom of the people of this country, will be a dead letter. A citizen may be seized by military force, dragged from one end of the continent to the other, tried far from his family and friends, where he is a stranger, at a place where he never was, and among people whom he never saw; nay more,

Secondly. He is to be tried without any notice in the indictment of the real nature of the charge against him, or where the *war* was, which he is accused of levying. The indictment against him states, that he did the act himself, when in truth he was hundreds of miles distant from the scene of action, and the act charged against him was done by others.

Thirdly. The doctrine of the cruel Jefferies is to be applied against him. He is to be tried for an act done by another, without producing a record of the conviction of that other, for whose alleged guilt he is to suffer.

Fourthly. The law of treason, and the rules concerning it, as heretofore universally considered, are totally misunderstood. A new definition of treason is adopted. The levying of war may be *secret*, without arms, without force, without any *overt* act.

All these arguments will apply, not to this case only, but to every case that may happen in any part of the United States. These will be the certain consequences of the doctrines contended for by the gentlemen on the other side, if sanctioned by this court. Will they seriously contend for doctrines, that will expose all the people of this country more to the dangers of constructive treason, to greater oppression and hardships, than the people of any other country have ever been subjected to? Certainly they will not. The records of this trial will be a monument of an attempt to establish principles that must infallibly introduce slavery. The attempt cannot succeed. But while I thus speak of the principles themselves, God forbid that I should make the smallest reference to the conduct of the government, or the motives of the gentlemen on the other side. I disclaim all personal allusions, which must be without reference to the merits at all times, and frequently tend to substitute invective for argument. I believe the government will disclaim all agency in the business, and that if they wish the accused to be convicted, still they only wish him to be convicted *according to law.*

Will gentlemen advance doctrines which the government will disclaim? If indeed it were possible, that they wished to conduct the prosecution on principles that would destroy the liberties of their country, those which they have advocated would certainly produce that dreadful effect; for it is obvious they have a direct tendency to root out and destroy every principle of freedom; but I trust they will never be sanctioned in this country.

END OF FIRST VOLUME.